European Socialists and
the American Promised Land

EUROPEAN SOCIALISTS
AND THE AMERICAN
PROMISED LAND

R. Laurence Moore

New York
OXFORD UNIVERSITY PRESS
1970

To the memory of
ANNETTE HILLIN MOORE
from a grateful husband

ACKNOWLEDGMENTS

In telling the story of socialist recastings of earlier visions of a "brave new world," I have accumulated the unpayable debts owed by all researchers. Professor George Wilson Pierson of Yale University directed this study as a dissertation and read various drafts with care and an uncanny perception. He humbled me (painfully) for unwarranted pride which I took in early versions, but also provided the encouragement necessary to pass through periods of ebbing enthusiasm. For pushing my thoughts beyond what now seem timid limits, for invaluable lessons (not nearly mastered) in graceful prose composition, above all for his own examples of high excellence, I gratefully acknowledge the guidance of my mentor.

Professors Franklin L. Baumer and Firuz Kazemzadeh, both of Yale, scrutinized the manuscript in dissertation form and suggested some broader avenues to my subject. So also did Professor C. Vann Woodward, who in a hundred other ways has put me in his debt.

Simeon Wade brought a fresh and discerning eye to these pages at a crucial stage of revision and pointed out to me dozens of places where the reader might lose his way. Special appreciation is due Professor Eugene D. Genovese of the University of Rochester. A scholar of Marxist proclivities, he read the entire study, suppressed his annoyance at the bias, and supplied me with innumerable friendly and helpful comments. This service to a stranger was generous beyond belief.

I am extremely grateful for the assistance supplied by Mrs. Judy Bockman in preparing the final manuscript. To two colleagues on the Yale history faculty who progressed with me through graduate school—Timothy H. Breen and R. Hal Williams—I owe the general debts which arise from friendship and a daily exchange of ideas. The economic support of my parents is a more calculable obligation, but my greater appreciation is for the unreasoned pride they have taken in a sometimes erratic son.

The major part of this study was researched and written during a year I spent as a Fulbright scholar in the Netherlands. Without the unique holdings of the International Institute of Social History (*Internationaal Instituut voor Sociale Geschiedenis*) in Amsterdam, my work would have taken years. My thanks to the staff members of the Institute for their helpfulness and courtesy are heartfelt.

For what my late wife contributed through her love, endurance, and great gift for life, there can never be adequate recognition.

R. L. M.

CONTENTS

INTRODUCTION

The American Promised Land! Rarely has a concept in modern Europe contained as great an admixture of myth and reality or provoked more tangled responses. It has filled some men with great hope; others it has led into blind alleys of misunderstanding; still others (and the number is not small) it has plunged into deep abysses of bitter disillusionment. Columbus had only to tell Isabella about his blundering discovery, and Europeans began arguing and rearguing the meaning of the New World.

Europeans have too frequently clouded their debate about America with fantastic inventions which prevented realistic appraisals of this country. The Spanish conquistadors who rode off in search of the fabulous cities established a pattern of laxity, and Europeans ever since, forgetting how that trek petered out in the dusty plains above Texas, have not been very careful about getting their facts straight. On the occasions when they turned their attention toward the United States, they usually were motivated by events close to home. More than once a heated dialogue about America was merely a roundabout way for Europeans to talk about local problems when circumstances prohibited free and open discussion. America was important, but not necessarily for its own sake. Because the image of this country had important polemical uses, Europeans called upon it selectively and did not characteristically make accuracy their only, or even their primary, concern.

Yet if few of the participants in this continuing exchange have over the years penetrated (or cared to penetrate) as deeply into American realities as Tocqueville and Bryce, they have never failed in their arguments to reveal a great deal about themselves. After all, the colonization and expansion of the trans-Atlantic republic had serious implications for Europe's future and, for many, raised questions no less important than God's ultimate cosmic scheme. In such disputes, men of the Old World did not choose sides lightheartedly or dispassionately; and while America never dominated the European consciousness, Europeans of all classes gathered fixed ideas about the New World which they were prepared to defend upon a moment's notice.

While specific issues have not stayed the same, the general outline of the debate has been clear from the initial European exploration of this continent. One faction has for various reasons always looked upon the discovery of America as regrettable. From venereal disease and tobacco to Coca-Cola, so these prophets of gloom have insisted, the New World has subjected Europe to a steady flow of debilitating influences. The Comte de Buffon and the Abbé Raynal, two ubiquitous children of the French Enlightenment, set the tone for this side even before the French Revolution. A damper air and a marshier ground on the new continent, they said, had both unbearded and unsexed the native male population. Europeans wandering into the American wilderness might not immediately face similar emasculation, but sturdy adventurers to these shores presumably ran some risk of waking one morning to find milk in their breasts. Rationalist to the core, the Comte and the Abbé were suspicious of the disorder and intellectual carelessness fostered in a primitive setting, and so far as they were concerned Europeans were better off if they stayed home.

Those belonging to the opposing faction have at all times shown equal dedication in picturing the United States as Europe's last and best hope for redemption. They too could trace their ancestry to eighteenth-century Frenchmen. Michel Guillaume Jean de Crèvecœur, a worthy cultivator of a patch of this "garden paradise," saw a new man arising here who would finally realize humanity's grandest dreams. The labors of the American would, in Crèvecœur's words, "one day cause great changes in the world." The Marquis de Condorcet, reflecting the shift in the opinion of many French philosophes after the events of 1776, agreed. "It is not enough," he wrote in his great *Sketch of an Historical Pageant of the Progress of the Human Mind,* "that the rights of men be written in the tomes of philosophers and in the hearts of virtuous men. The weak and the ignorant must be able to read them in the example of a great nation. America has given us that example."

The American Revolution and the association of the United States with radical democracy set the framework for the debate in the nineteenth century. A man's politics usually determined whether he stood with the defenders or the detractors of the United States. The heirs of Burke and Maistre regarded the influence of American egalitarianism on Europe's hierarchical social structure with increasing alarm. In their minds American manners were vulgar, ideals shabby, and politics corrupt beyond imagination. The notion of malleable men and institutions promulgated by New World enthusiasts tempted men to meddle disastrously with the social order and undermined the grounds for decent collective human behavior.

Political liberals and social radicals, on the other hand, generally sided with those turning hopeful eyes to America. To members of the European left the United States enshrined goodness, opportunity, prosperity, and equality and gave men a reason to believe in a better future. They were not uncritical of life here. Slavery badly tarnished America's image before the Civil War, and after emancipation Tammany Hall and Standard Oil arose to keep European liberals uneasy. Nevertheless, these men, who were working to alter the established ways of Europe, found much to admire in American life. American institutions, especially American political institutions, offered important guides for Europe out of its own social disorders. Whatever its flaws, America was the freest and most blessed republic yet in operation.

This neat lineup of European political opinion was disrupted from time to time in the nineteenth century, but only Marxist intrusions after 1880 finally shattered it. For the first time a group of European radicals refused to accept any belief in America's redemptive powers. Indeed, a number of Marxists placed a surprisingly high priority on disassociating themselves from the traditional admiration of the United States shared by other parties of the European left. For if "Americanism" were accepted as a surrogate for militant Marxism, then the Marxists' own special program for world revolution would be a dead letter. Marxist stalwarts might just as well emigrate (as many, so it was sadly noted, did) or join with those working to remodel Europe according to American specifications. If there existed anywhere a bourgeois republic whose free enterprise system did not disrupt social harmony and equality, Marxism had a severe theoretical problem. European liberals knew this, which was one reason their praise for the United States sometimes so clearly outdistanced common sense.

Thus when European Marxists looked at America, they made a great leap across the political spectrum to link hands with members of the European right in insisting that America offered no alternatives to life in Europe. Following the lead of the United States' severest critics, they ridiculed the notions that regeneration might be accomplished by the simple expedient of physical relocation and that European class struggles would terminate with the duplication of American ways. Compared with Marxist attacks on alleged Yankee virtues, the estimates of the many critics who had gone before looked generous.

As this investigation seeks to show, some prominent European Marxists did present their own revised versions of an American Promised Land. But they first specifically repudiated the "old" promise of America which liberals had founded upon the differences between the New World and the Old. The American Canaan of the Marxists was premised instead upon a New World which had grown decadent and corrupt. By entwining the most pointed criticism of American life advanced by European conservatives with their own dialectical process of history, Marxists could visualize a sudden inversion of the American capitalist inferno into a socialist paradise.

Except for Chapter 7 and a brief backward glance in Chapter 1 the study falls within the years from 1880 to 1917. In 1880 European socialism was struggling to make a comeback from the damaging setbacks of the 1870's. That decade had begun with the bloody suppression of the Paris Commune of 1871 and the effective demise of the First International in 1872 with the removal of the headquarters to New York City (a formal death certificate was not issued until 1876). It had ended with Bismarck's declaration in 1878 of his Anti-Socialist Laws which attempted (as it turned out, unsuccessfully) to destroy the strong socialist party fused in 1875 by August Bebel and Wilhelm Liebknecht out of several disparate radicalisms. Almost everywhere in Europe in those years, trade unionists had felt the sting of bourgeois reaction and had suffered under new legislative obstacles or hastily revived old ones. In England, the one country in which both political and economic conditions seemed to favor a strong drive by workers and socialists, the industrial proletariat had shown a puzzling indifference to revolution. All this, combined with the lingering attraction of workers to anarchism and unscientific socialism, had made the 1870's discouraging years for those who championed Marx as the leading prophet of a great world movement.

By 1880 there was reason to believe that the reaction had done its worst. Marx himself, beyond his great work of *Capital* and approaching death, could look with guarded hope on what was happening around him. After many years of relative obscurity he was now eclipsing the reputations of Saint-Simon, Proudhon, Lassalle, Bakunin, and more recently Eugen Dühring. His disciples, though often self-proclaimed and disliked by Marx, spent the 1880's busily establishing Social Democratic parties across Europe. Liebknecht and Bebel in Germany had already indicated in the previous decade how mighty an influence socialism could exert when wedded to labor causes, and aided by such brilliant theorists as Eduard Bernstein and Karl Kautsky they went on in the 1880's to purge their party of remaining Lassallean elements and embarrass the great Bismarck by making a shambles out of his legislation against them. Pablo Iglesias established a Spanish Social Democratic party in 1879. Jules Guesde and Paul Lafargue formed *le Parti ouvrier* in France in 1882. In England, Marxists came to life with the creation of H. M. Hyndman's Social Democratic Federation and, a few years later, the Socialist League of William Morris and Edward Aveling. By 1883 the Russians G. V. Plekhanov and P. B. Axelrod had founded, while in exile, the Group of the Liberation of Labor. A Norwegian Social Democratic party followed in 1887, one in Austria and one in Switzerland in 1888, and one in Sweden in 1889. The progress was exhilarating, and in 1889 European socialists looked optimistically across national frontiers and flexed their collective muscle to launch the Second International.

In 1890, Marxists had not succeeded in eliminating other socialists from the field of radical activity. In Italy, Spain, Belgium, and Holland the situation was confused, and doctrines ranging from anarchism to moderate trade unionism were stronger drawing cards to labor than Marxism. Even in the countries mentioned in the preceding paragraph, most notably England, Marxists had very strong rivals. Revisionism, the doctrine which challenged the fatalistic implications of Marxists' millennial vision and offered a more tempered critique of the internal flaws of capitalism, was not the sudden invention of Eduard Bernstein in 1899. The earlier activities of English Fabians and French *possibilistes* attest to that. But, it is the Marxists who first attract the eye of one who looks back on this period. (In fact, for reasons which will become apparent, Marxist socialists are the principal focus of this study.) Marx was known at least secondhand to everyone, and rhetorical clichés of the Marxist movement infiltrated the European socialist press, whatever the nominal stance of a particular journal. The spirited confidence of the Marxists was infectious, and in the late 1880's and early 1890's they rested comfortably and more or less uncompromisingly in their revolutionary assumptions. They sensed the beginning of a great change, and time had not yet stretched thin their belief that with tomorrow came the deluge. A more cautious and a more practical mood always existed among Marxist leaders, and paradoxically after 1890 it would grow stronger with every success at the ballot box. Marxists talked in more radical ways than they behaved, and their activity tied them more and more to a legal, parliamentary course. Yet, strengthened by the trials of the 1870's and emboldened but not yet mellowed by progress in the 1880's, Marxists in 1890 felt themselves riding easily on the wave of the future. Until 1917 they constituted the majority of the policy makers of the German Social Democratic party which in turn tended to dominate the councils of the Second International.

Marx, who had predicted the new burst of activity set off in the 1880's, was the first to link the improved fortunes of European socialism with developments in the United States. Goaded by the explosive advance of American capitalism after the Civil War, Marx began around 1880 to define a "new" promise for America—a promise which guaranteed a swift end to the impatient waiting of European revolutionaries (Chapter 1). He died in 1883, but through

Engels his enthusiastic interest in the American continent was passed on to his disciples in Europe. Important European Marxists first made sure that they had cut the ground out from under earlier versions of American promise (Chapter 2), and then went on to fill in their own hopes for a socialist America (Chapter 3). Formulations of the latter view, though begun in the 1880's, were most popular in the decade from 1895 to 1905 and drew for inspiration on the American trust phenomenon (Chapter 4). After 1905, Marxist pronouncements about any kind of American Promised Land, whether old or new style, underwent an erratic but steady decline. Events in the United States posed questions which European Marxists found more and more difficult to answer (Chapter 5), and revisionist socialists, especially after 1900, challenged Marxists with second looks at the "old" promise of America (Chapter 6). By 1917 the United States had become a large stumbling block for the many Marxist theorists who still believed in economic determinism, and following the Russian Revolution their hopes for a strong capitalist America changed into fear and disgust. A detailed study of changed socialist attitudes toward the United States in the post-World War I era would entail consideration of the enormously altered political situation in the world as well as the complicated reorientation in Marxist thought. It is not a study I have undertaken. A look at the opinions about America expressed by Lenin and Trotsky, however, suggests some of the new currents and conflicts in European socialist reactions to this country after the formation of the Third International (Chapter 7).

European Marxists who today are watching the simultaneous growth of America's "affluent society" and the Americanization of Europe are the heirs of the disappointment and frustration first felt by their predecessors in the pre-World War I period. But, at the same time, Americans are left to wonder whether the uniqueness of their country, once an unmitigated blessing and an inspiration to rising people everywhere, is now their greatest handicap in trying to capture the imagination of the world.

An author cannot expect to disarm all criticism by giving forewarning of difficulties in his study. Nevertheless, an initial reference to certain troublesome matters is due the reader. In the first place, an inevitable distortion results from selecting material to organize according to a specific theme. When a multitude of European socialist comments about the United States is picked out from here and there and placed together in one volume, the reader is easily misled into thinking that the United States was the overriding intellectual concern of the men and women who comprised the Second International. As indicated earlier, the vision of Europeans, socialist and non-socialist alike, tended to become singularly myopic when directed toward the United States, and the attention of the observers was easily diverted. They explored American perspectives enthusiastically but selectively for brief periods, and then abruptly turned away. If one were to rank countries by the number of times they were referred to in the European socialist press, the United States would fall far down the list. Socialist chroniclers of the American scene passed over events which seemingly should have aroused their liveliest interest. Many of the most important labor disputes, great movements like Populism, and vast social problems like discrimination against black Americans were almost totally ignored. Algie M. Simons, reflecting on the strong nationalistic tendencies of European socialists, lamented that the United States delegates to the 1907 International Socialist Convention in Stuttgart were treated more as guests than as members.* Simons might have added in fairness that the European habit of looking first at what was closest to home was constantly reinforced by the disappointing realities of socialist progress in America.

The American theme was hardly central to the major concerns of the Second International, but it did not, on the other hand, constitute an unimportant footnote. The United States, because of its particular qualities and the uniqueness of the myth surrounding it, formed a significant subject to which many socialist leaders addressed themselves again and again. An impressive number took the trouble to come here. My tracing of the interesting patterns of socialist opinion about the United States is not intended to add worlds to our knowledge of the Second International. It does offer,

---

* Letter of A. M. Simons to Gaylord Wilshire, *Wilshire's Magazine*, XI (Oct. 1907), 3, quoted in Ira Kipnis, *The American Socialist Movement, 1897–1912* (New York, 1952), 244.

I think, some revealing insights into the intellectual habits we have long recognized as characteristic of the men and women who in those days sought to revolutionize the world. Moreover the reader should remember that this is part of a larger story of how Europeans have looked at America, how they have used it and misused it, how they have understood it and misunderstood it. On its most general level, this is simply another tale which seeks to say something about how men have tried to adjust their ideals to the realities of a distressingly non-pliant world.

A related warning must be given about the degree of importance belonging to various stray pieces of Marxist polemics. To carry out this study, I sifted through countless opinions about the United States. Many of these analyses were ambiguous or contradictory; some were obviously disingenuous. How much significance and what kind of significance can one assign to such comments? The same problem besets all studies about foreign attitudes toward the United States. When was the United States merely being used as a convenient but extraneous sounding board to amplify previously held convictions? When, in calling the United States the likely site of the first socialist victory, was a European socialist leader venting a profoundly held conviction, and when was he merely genuflecting to conventional and easily rattled-off wisdom? When, in speaking of troubling dilemmas posed by developments in America, was a European Marxist more than momentarily taking his eyes off problems closer to home? To ask these questions is not to suggest that the bulk of the references appearing in the socialist press are without significance. Quite the contrary. But the researcher must keep in mind his involvement with different kinds of expression, for, depending on the degree of seriousness he judges to be attached to an opinion, he can draw quite distinct conclusions.

Since several scholars who have read this manuscript have suggested that the dilemmas of Marxist thought touched on in this story were easily avoidable, I should say right now that nowhere am I concerned in the text with whether Karl Marx, properly read, furnishes an adequate background for understanding economic developments in the United States. My interests are more concrete. How did Marxists (who, as it is repeated again and again, often in the period from 1880 to 1917 misrepresented Marx to stress economic determinism and never stopped talking, despite their behavior, about the imminence of revolution) and other European socialists manipulate the image of the United States? What questions did they ask, and what developments concerned them? What circumstances at home prompted their interest, and what circumstances quelled it? Why did they give such great coverage to an event like the Haymarket riot and write so little about the I.W.W.? How did they use information garnered on these shores in doctrinal disputes, and what effects, if any, did it have on theoretical and tactical considerations? Asking such questions and frequently paying attention to answers given in the socialist press does not always provide a view of socialist thought at its best and most sophisticated. Even Marx in writing about the United States could be found guilty of the romantic delusions he deplored in soberer moments. (Marxists are not Marx, but Marx and certainly Engels share partial blame for subsequent misunderstanding.) Nevertheless, the rhetoric is revealing about socialist expectations and divisions in the years around the turn of the century. If I sometimes criticize actual Marxist observations about this country, it is not necessarily because I think Marx's theories gave his followers no alternatives for better understanding. But Marxist doctrine, as then usually expressed, did make America a problem for many of the leading theorists of the Second International and offered revisionist socialists an easy line of assault on what, rightly or wrongly, had hardened into Marxist orthodoxy.

Decisions about the scope of research were obviously necessary before this study was ever begun (if for no other reasons than the lack of time, unavailability of material, and unfamiliarity with languages). While the title suggests a survey of all European countries, the work in fact concentrates almost entirely upon Germany, France, and England, and includes a chapter on Russia and occasional references to socialists in Belgium and the Netherlands. Of Italy, Spain, Scandinavia, or the countries of eastern Europe, there is not a word. Something, then, needs to be said about the reasons for the countries included as well as the reasons for the omissions.

Germany, France, and England, I think, would be anyone's first three choices in undertaking a study of this sort. Germany had by far the largest socialist movement in Europe and provided an impressive amount of the intellectual leadership for the Second International. In addition, because of the heavy flow of German immigrants into this country and the German composition of the early American socialist movement, there was a high degree of communication between American and German socialist leaders. In fact, the reader will quickly discern, at least in Chapters 2–5, a preponderance of German illustrations. In part that reflects the genuine interest of many prominent German Marxists, Wilhelm Liebknecht, Karl Kautsky, and August Bebel among them, in the events which took place here. In part, however, it simply reflects the distribution of the material. The German press was far wealthier than that in any other country, and it never stopped rolling. German Marxists said more about America than the French, for example, but then they said more on every question touching on general concerns. When one does any work on the Second International, one is stuck with the great importance of Germany.

France ranked second among the powerful Continental socialist movements, and, though far less tied to the United States by immigration, historical contacts as well as the admiration for American institutions expressed by many French republicans, made the United States an unavoidable subject for France's socialist writers. If the French people were and are more inwardly directed than most, they have nevertheless made some of the most important contributions to the European image of the New World.

The English socialist movement does not receive the attention it does in these pages primarily because of its strength. In fact its strength, especially on its Marxist side, never approached that of the German and French movements, lagged behind that of the Austrian and Italian, and was no more vigorous than that of the Belgian or Dutch. Rather, it was the close cultural ties between England and the United States which give England priority here. English socialists were the most keenly interested of all the national groups in what was going on in this country.

A separate question from whether England, Germany, and France are the most logical choices for inclusion is whether a wide enough net has been cast to justify the study's title. Actually, in the process of combing socialist literature for material about America, one reaches a point of rapidly diminishing returns. Instead of coming across new ideas and insights, one keeps finding increasingly repetitious variations of already familiar themes. Much of the literature, as the reader will soon see, is framed polemically to persuade and encourage. Even the more scholarly socialist material about America tended to pose a very limited set of questions, and the answers, once stated, became standard fare in the socialist press. I have in fact surveyed the literature of Italy, Austria, and the Low Countries as well as the writings of the most important figures in the Second International; and, in my opinion, further perusal of newspapers and archival material in western Europe would not get sufficiently beyond the main outlines of this study to justify the effort. The stereotyped phrases that emerged in socialist discussions about America appear to have crossed national frontiers quite easily. Conceivably eastern Europe would suggest some different national patterns, but a treatment of that area lies beyond my competence.

The terms "socialist" and "Marxist" invariably cause confusion. Except for the various revisionist socialists dealt with in Chapter 6, the major figures in this study considered themselves Marxists. It has not seemed appropriate to this historian to dispute their own evaluations, and I have consistently called them and their journals Marxist. When I use the term "socialist" alone, my reference, while including Marxists, applies as well to a broader spectrum of opinion within the Second International. I have tried to include enough of the basic history of the Second International to make the theme understandable to the general reader.

This study grew out of research I was doing on the American Socialist party. I was struck particularly by the fact that American socialists at the turn of the century, by using a simplified version of the Marxist stage theory of history, had extraordinarily high expectations about their future. Wondering how American socialists could possibly have arrived at such inflated notions, I began researching the extent to which European socialists shared their sanguine hopes. This led to some further questions about how European socialists used America, and more generally how Europeans have always used America. In the final manuscript my research on the movement in the United States was pushed ungraciously and somewhat awkwardly to the end. The issues raised there are important, however; and, since the reader should have no difficulty relating it to the rest, I have let the material stand.

I should finally alert my readers to a few miscellaneous matters concerning quotations in the text. The problem of how much and what to quote is never an easily soluble one. In most cases to put together long strings of quotations saying the same thing seemed needlessly repetitious. Many of the cited quotations could be replaced by a dozen others, and I have used those which best illustrated a point and which came from the most important sources. Voices of significant socialist leaders have always been given first place. In some cases, however, particularly with respect to statements predicting America's emergence as the first socialist commonwealth, I have been more willing to cite repetitive material. In these instances I have tried to find opportunities to use more exhaustively the comments uncovered in my research. For the convenience of the reader I have cited published translations of foreign material when possible; otherwise the translations are my own.

European Socialists and
the American Promised Land

CHAPTER I

MARX AND ENGELS
LOOK TO AMERICA

For Mark and Engels the years between 1848 and 1880 had been bewildering and frustrating. When they had written the *Communist Manifesto,* the red "specter" haunting Europe had seemed certain to sweep away the old order of capitalism within a few years. Thirty-two years later the prospect of a victory for the world proletariat was farther away than ever. In 1880 the socialist party was illegal in Germany. Stirrings of discontent among English trade unionists had as yet failed to turn them into enemies of capitalism; and continental workers, if more restless, were no more daring in their behavior. There were many encouraging signs of progress. The German movement was strong despite Bismarck's best efforts to overpower it. Jules Guesde was just about ready to launch a Marxist party in France, and a middle-class Englishman named H. M. Hyndman was preparing himself to teach scientific socialism to workers across the Channel. But the times were not ripe for an organization to replace the First International which had quietly expired in Philadelphia in 1876. In 1880 Marx had three years to live. He was to die knowing that the influence of many of his enemies, Bakunin, Proudhon, and Lassalle among them, still corrupted the thinking of the working classes on the Continent. Neither he nor Engels (who was to die in 1895), although they both counseled caution on many occasions, ever put aside their belief in the imminence of the socialist revolution. But neither did they explain completely, even to their own satisfaction, the unexpected staying power of European capitalism.

Prior to the rapid growth of the American economy after the

Civil War they had been able to assign part of the blame for the persistence of European capitalism on the New World. For one thing, the very discovery of North America, with the subsequent settlement of the United States and the opening of rich new markets, had greatly stimulated the expansion of capitalism. In addition, the continuing agricultural base of the American economy had given Europe for many years a convenient outlet for its surplus manufactured products and enabled it to avert the normally disastrous effects of capitalist overproduction. As late as 1867, in the first volume of his great work *Capital,* Marx had analyzed the United States both as a colony of Europe and as a pillar of exploitive European class society.[1]

Even worse, from the standpoint of Marx and Engels, pre-Civil War America had exerted an alarming attractive power over proletarian participants in the European class struggle. Lured by the promise of opportunity and independence, European socialists had forsaken the fight at home and sailed across the Atlantic in search of a rural paradise. Moreover, many of Marx's and Engels' allies, who had been forced to immigrate to the New World following the upheavals of 1848, had cast off their radicalism almost as soon as they had disembarked at an American port. Engels had not neglected to caution his friend and co-worker Joseph Weydemeyer upon the latter's sailing for New York in 1851:

> That you are going to America is bad, but I really don't know what other advice to give you if you can't find anything in Switzer-

---

[1] *Capital: A Critique of Political Economy,* translated from the third German edition by Samuel Moore and Edward Aveling, edited by Frederick Engels, revised according to the fourth German edition by Ernest Untermann (New York, 1906), 493. See also Marx's and Engels' preface to the 1882 Russian edition of the *Communist Manifesto.* England especially had benefitted from American trade. In the opinion of Marx and Engels the conservatism of the English worker had rested on his participation in England's relative prosperity resulting from England's trade with America. Before the Civil War, America had not only imported great quantities of English goods, but the southern states had provided England with one of its most essential raw materials—cotton. Marx had referred to slave-grown cotton as one of the two pivots on which English industry rested (New York *Tribune,* Oct. 14, 1861)—a fact which had explained to him the sympathy of the English bourgeoisie for the southern cause.

land. . . . Your greatest handicap, however, will be the fact that the useful Germans who are worth anything are easily Americanized and abandon all hope of returning home; and then there are the special American conditions: the ease with which the surplus population is drained off to the farms, the necessarily rapid and rapidly growing prosperity of the country, which makes bourgeois conditions look like a *beau idéal* to them, and so forth.[2]

Nor had Marx concealed his anger toward Hermann Kriege, a former member of the League of the Just and a German immigrant to the United States, upon Kriege's almost immediate acceptance of "Americanism" as a surrogate for his former socialism. In his new homeland Kriege had come to believe that a sensible homestead act could provide a permanent solution to any American social problem.[3]

For Marx and Engels the promise of purity and innocence associated with America's distance from Europe and its vast unsettled areas had only spelled trouble. At the same time that many other European radicals had looked at the relatively unmarked, pre-Civil War face of America with longing and hope, Marx and Engels had shown complete exasperation. An image of Eden had not attracted their fancy in the slightest; socialist progress everywhere, they knew, was contingent upon America's fall from grace. For so long as America provided Europeans with an alternative to their life at home, European radicals would be tempted to follow one of two equally futile courses: to immigrate or to try to refashion Europe in America's image. Either line of action, Marx and Engels had warned, would ultimately lead nowhere.

Both men in the 1840's had insisted that what then seemed to many a paradise would soon be spoiled by the same social conflicts prevailing in Europe. *Men and Manners in America*, a book (contemporary with Tocqueville's more famous study) by the English visitor to the United States, Thomas Hamilton, provided Marx with evidence of an urban proletariat which already in the mid-

[2] Letter from Engels to Weydemeyer, Aug. 7, 1851, *Letters to Americans, 1848–1895*, ed. by Alexander Trachtenberg (New York, 1953), 25–26.
[3] Peter von Struve, "Zwei bisher unbekannte Aufsätze von Karl Marx aus den vierziger Jahren," *Die Neue Zeit*, Vol. XIV, Part II (1895–96), 4–11.

1840's was springing up along America's eastern seaboard.[4] The American economist Henry Carey had taken the early experience of his country as proof of the ability of capital and labor to coexist harmoniously; Marx had replied contemptuously,

> That bourgeois society in the United States has not yet developed far enough to make the class struggle obvious and comprehensible is most strikingly proved by *H. C. Carey* (of Philadelphia), the only American economist of importance. He attacks *Ricardo,* the most classical representative (interpreter) of the bourgeoisie and the most stoical adversary of the proletariat, as a man whose works are an arsenal for anarchists, socialists, and all the enemies of bourgeois society. He accuses not only him, but Malthus, Mill, Say, Torrens, Wakefield, McCulloch, Senior, Wakley, R. Jones, etc., in short, the economic masterminds of Europe, of tearing society apart and paving the way for civil war by their proof that the economic bases of the different classes must give rise to a necessary and ever-growing antagonism between them. He tries to refute them, not like the fatuous Heinzen, to be sure, by linking the existence of classes to the existence of *political* privileges and *monopolies,* but by attempting to demonstrate that *economic* conditions—rent (landed property), *profit* (capital), and wages (wage labor)—are conditions of cooperation and harmony rather than conditions of struggle and antagonism. All he proves, of course, is that he takes the "undeveloped" social conditions of the United States to be "normal" social conditions.[5]

Engels had further forecast in 1845 America's rapid emergence from a colonial status. Within twenty years, he had written in *The Condition of the Working Class in England in 1844,* American competition in the world market would deliver a fatal blow to English capitalist prosperity and dramatically reverse the former role of America as a prop of European capitalism.[6]

[4] Lewis S. Feuer, "The North American Origin of Marx's Socialism," *Western Political Quarterly,* XVI (March 1963), 53–67. See also Maximilien Rubel, "Notes on Marx's Conception of Democracy," *New Politics,* I (Winter 1962), 78–90.
[5] Marx to Weydemeyer, March 5, 1852, *Letters to Americans,* 44–45.
[6] *The Condition of the Working Class in England,* trans. and ed. by W. O. Henderson and W. H. Chaloner (New York, 1958), 333.

For these reasons the American Civil War had assumed great importance for Marx and Engels. They had both wished the end of slavery and had entertained some fantasies about a labor-based abolition movement—even calling Abraham Lincoln "the single-minded son of the working class"—but this was not the main thing. The war, so their interpretation went, by destroying the considerable power of southern agrarian interests and by clearing the way for the untrammeled growth of northern industry, had made it possible for the United States to enter the "revolutionary phase." The United States could not dampen revolutionary flames in Europe much longer because capitalism had been freed to produce the same lamentable social conditions it had spawned in Europe.[7] The termination of America's colonial status with respect to Europe and the loss of America's power to enervate the revolutionary spirit of European workers would have decisive effects on the European class struggle. European capitalists would soon find themselves in serious straits, and the proletariat would no longer do them the favor of sailing off to America in search of alternatives to oppression and suffering in Europe. Marx had been jubilant and had written in the 1867 preface to *Capital*, "As in the eighteenth century the American War of Independence sounded the tocsin for the European middle class, so in the nineteenth century, the American Civil War sounded it for the European working class."

By 1880 Marx and Engels felt justified in congratulating themselves on the total disappearance of the pre-Civil War America which had been so troubling to their schemes. The American economy, once slaves and slaveholders had been rudely kicked into modernity, had leaped forward with such great energy that Marx and Engels now saw only cause for optimism in the American situation. In the world picture confronting them in 1880, the United States was the one thing which evoked unqualified cheerfulness. It gave them an assurance, soon justified, in the impending resurgence of socialist strength in Europe. For in place of a rural economy,

[7] Marx to Engels, April 23, 1866, *The Civil War in the United States*, ed. by Richard Enmale (New York, 1937), 277. For some illuminating comments about Marx's and Engels' writings on the Civil War, see Eugene D. Genovese, "Marxian Interpretations of the Slave South," in *Towards a New Past: Dissenting Essays in American History*, ed. by Barton Bernstein (New York, 1968).

there was now in the United States a strong and rapidly growing industrial economy. In place of a harmonious social situation, there was now the inception of class struggle. In place of equality, rich and poor were more clearly differentiated than anywhere else in the world. Opportunity and social mobility in the United States, Marx and Engels thought, were as obsolete as the unselfish dedication of Washington or the homespun integrity of Lincoln.

The exasperation which a pre-Civil War America had brought Marx and Engels was now gone, and in its place rose the expectation (fulfilling Engels' prophecy of 1845) that American competition in the world market would precipitate a permanent economic crisis in European capitalist countries. In their 1882 preface to the Russian edition of the *Communist Manifesto,* recalling the earlier time when the United States acted as a "pillar" of European capitalism, Marx and Engels wrote,

> How very different today. Precisely European immigration fitted North America for a gigantic agricultural production, whose competition is shaking the very foundations of European landed property—large and small. At the same time it enabled the United States to exploit its tremendous resources with an energy and on a scale that must shortly break the industrial monopoly of Western Europe, and especially of England, existing up to now.[8]

Matters so stood in 1880 that Marx's and Engels' initial regard for the tremendous growth of the American economy was dictated by the expected impact of American expansion on Europe. These men had long been involved in European affairs, and they did not easily shift their focus. What they looked for was something to activate insurgent sentiment at home. Inevitably, however, the spectacular rise of the American economy forced them to give attention also to the future of the American socialist movement. In 1870 Marx had expected the socialist revolution to come first in England because it was the most advanced of all the bourgeois economies.[9] But Eng-

[8] *Communist Manifesto,* intro. by Harold J. Laski (London, 1948), 107–8.
[9] See, for example, Marx to Siegfried Meyer and August Vogt, April 9, 1870, *Karl Marx and Friedrich Engels Correspondence, 1816–1895: A Selection* (hereafter *Correspondence*), ed. by Dona Torr (New York, 1934), 290, and an interview in the New York *Herald,* Aug. 3, 1871.

land lagged behind in the next decade; and, when an impressed Marx announced in 1879 that "the United States have at present overtaken England in the rapidity of economic progress," he was suggesting a possible new champion for the socialist cause.[10] Once America took the lead away from England in the accumulation and concentration of capital as well—and the day was not far off— the odds would suddenly favor the New World as the site of the first socialist victory. Far away from the battlegrounds where labor and capital had been waging war for half a century, the flag of the cooperative commonwealth would rise.

America has been pictured as a promised land by many different sorts of people, and it is difficult to keep track of them. Sober Puritans and less sober silkworm enthusiasts, recluses camped by a seemingly infinite number of Walden Ponds and gregarious types immersed in the cooperative effort to raise new cities, humanitarian democrats and ruthless entrepreneurs—all these had seen some special virtue in America. In 1880 Marx and Engels were adding their names to the long list of those who had looked with hopeful eyes to the New World. The youthful energy and buoyancy of the United States, so often admired by European visitors to America, had finally gained a usefulness for Marx and Engels. These cliché virtues of American life did not promise a better life for European workers, but they became, in the hands of Marx and Engels, instruments with which to lay low the bourgeoisie. American capitalism had suddenly come to be regarded as a likely spark to ignite socialism's initial victory.

One cannot say with precision when the thought occurred to Marx that the United States might just possibly be the first nation to throw capitalism aside. As early as 1872, when Marx had urged the transfer of the General Council of the First International from London to New York, he had referred to the United States as "becoming the world of the worker, par excellence." [11] The location of the seat of the International in New York, he had said without candor, would be appropriate because the world socialist movement would soon be stronger in the United States than anywhere else.

[10] Marx to N. F. Danielson, April 10, 1879, *Correspondence,* 360.
[11] Rudolf H. Meyer, *Der Emancipationskampf des Vierten Standes,* I (Berlin, 1874), 141-42.

Marx might have believed this, but it had not been important to him at the time. In negotiating for the removal of the General Council, he had been primarily concerned with keeping it safely out of the hands of his enemies in Europe; America's remoteness, not the actual or potential strength of the labor movement in America, had suggested New York to him. By consigning the International to America, Marx had engineered its destruction, and he knew it.

Judging from the contents of his bulky correspondence with various Americans, one would gauge Marx's interest in anything happening in the New World throughout the 1870's as nil. He had written to German-American colleagues, not to ask them what was going on in the United States (although this was a period of considerable labor turmoil), but to get their opinions about the ebb and flow of European developments. To many immigrants who had corresponded with Marx, Europe had still represented home—the place from which they had been forced to leave and the place to which many wanted to return as soon as the socialist revolution began there in earnest.

Marx's sudden burst of interest in the United States at the end of the 1870's, on the other hand, was unquestionably genuine. The ripening of the plants of industrialism growing since the Civil War, as we know from the correspondence of his late life, stimulated his attention in plans for an American harvest. In the latter part of 1880 he asked his friend and confidant Friedrich A. Sorge to send him information about California's economic development, for "nowhere else has the upheaval most shamelessly caused by capitalist centralization taken place with such speed."[12] And in 1881 he criticized Henry George sharply for not having wondered:

> How did it happen that in the United States, where, relatively, that is, compared with civilized Europe, the land was accessible to the great masses of the people and still is to a certain degree (again relatively), capitalist economy and the corresponding enslavement of the working class have developed *more rapidly* and *more shamelessly* than in any other country![13]

[12] Marx to Sorge, Nov. 5, 1880, *Letters to Americans,* 126.
[13] Marx to Sorge, June 20, 1881, *Letters to Americans,* 129.

Moreover, the masses in America, Marx thought, were quicker (because of past privileges) than the masses in Europe to "resent the form of a progress accomplished at their expense"; they also possessed greater political means to make their resentment felt.[14] Marx's arguments in 1872 for the transfer of International headquarters to New York were spurious at the time. But within the decade he found that he might have been right after all and that the "transference of the center of the International to the United States may obtain a very remarkable post festum opportuneness."[15]

Marx's death cut off any further speculation on his part about the chances for a socialist victory in America. He was not to see in his lifetime the rise of either a strong socialist party or a strong socialist-oriented trade union in the United States. In the early 1880's, America's Socialist Labor party, already a weak organization of 1500 members (mostly German), split into warring factions over the issue of anarchism. Several independent workingmen's political parties had earlier made brief appearances on the American scene but had not achieved even moderate success. While bourgeois ideas might have become hollow and self-destructive in America, the American worker had, at least through 1883, clung stubbornly to them.

The legacy of Marx's interest in America passed on to Engels. From the early 1880's until his own death in 1895 Engels kept a watchful eye on occurrences in the United States. In 1888, he even undertook a brief voyage across the Atlantic to see things for himself. Unhappily for Engels the welcome expansion of American capitalism did not immediately have noticeably adverse effects on the old order either in Europe or America. The 1880's, in contrast to the 1870's, did witness an extraordinary burst of socialist activity in Europe. Social Democratic parties which united workers and socialist intellectuals into organizations inspired by Marxist principles came to life in most European countries. Yet the revolution remained as elusive as ever, and Engels discovered that the flowering of American capitalism, despite its prospective healthy effects, burdened him with a new puzzle: in view of America's rapid industrial growth, what

---

[14] Marx to Danielson, April 10, 1879, *Correspondence,* 360.
[15] Heinz Neuman, *Marx and Engels on Revolution in America* (Chicago, 1926), 27.

accounted for the continuing obtuseness of the American laborer? Why could the Yankee wage earner not accept, as did so many of his European brethren, his degraded condition under capitalism as irreversible and turn to socialism? Engels' first tentative answers revealed blithe optimism. The American worker, he wrote, had not been exposed long enough to the abuses of capitalism. European workers had understood and accepted socialism only after long years of experience with capitalist oppression, and Americans could learn about the laws of capitalist development only through the same kind of contact. Moreover, Engels thought, all Anglo-Saxons showed a bent toward practicality at the expense of theory—a tendency which grew especially marked when they were placed in a young, expanding nation like the United States.[16] American workers were naturally suspicious of a complex theoretical system for which objective experience had not yet prepared them.

Engels saw none of these factors as disabling or even troublesome. On the contrary, socialism would sink into the American consciousness far more quickly than it had in the European. An initial fumbling with abstract doctrines, Engels thought, was of negligible significance in view of the dynamic qualities of American life which had in the past moved the United States forward with incredible speed. Americans might not stop to analyze where they were going, but they did succeed in getting there faster than any other people. They had blindly zipped through the capitalist phase of development; they might just as blindly tumble into socialism. Where else in fact (according to Engels' fundamental assumptions) could they go? Capitalism, like everything else in America, had developed too rapidly to become a fixed institution; and the lack of institutional barriers always favored progress. Engels reiterated over and over in his correspondence that, once started, the American socialist movement would move "with an energy and impetuousness compared with which we in Europe shall be mere children."[17]

By the mid-1880's Engels' optimism, if it were to be sustained, needed a measure of objective confirmation. For this reason Engels greeted with great enthusiasm Henry George's 1886 campaign to

---

[16] Engels to Florence Kelley Wischnewetzky, Aug. 13, 1886, *Letters to Americans*, 160.
[17] Engels to Hermann Schlüter, March 30, 1892, *Letters to Americans*, 243.

become mayor of New York City. George was not a socialist, and neither Marx nor Engels ever took him for anything but a petty bourgeois economist. Yet Engels both publicly and and privately urged socialists in America to work for George's election. The theoretical position of the author of *Progress and Poverty* was not so important. George was running on an independent labor ticket, and for the moment nothing else mattered. To Engels the emergence of a third-party labor movement marked the establishment of a strong and genuine class consciousness among American workers. In an 1887 preface for the American edition of *The Condition of the Working Class in England in 1844* he wrote,

> Ten months have elapsed since, at the translator's wish, I wrote the Appendix to this book; and during these ten months, a revolution has been accomplished in American society such as, in any other country, would have taken at least ten years. . . . In European countries, it took the working class years and years before they fully realized the fact that they formed a distinct and, under the existing social conditions, a permanent class of modern society; and it took years again until this class-consciousness led them to form themselves into a distinct political party, independent of, and opposed to, all the old political parties, formed by the various sections of the ruling classes. On the more favored soil of America, where no medieval ruins bar the way, where history begins with the elements of the modern bourgeois society as evolved in the seventeenth century, the working class passed through these two stages of its development within ten months.[18]

The remaining problem of getting the American labor party to adopt proper socialist principles would take care of itself. For Engels it was enough to witness the breaking down of the apathy of the American proletariat; once things were moving, "they will go fast, too, faster than anywhere else, even though on a singular road,

---

[18] *Letters to Americans,* 285–87. This preface was written especially for an American edition of Engels' book translated by Florence Kelley Wischnewetzky. The unduly enthusiastic report of two recent English visitors to America, Eleanor Marx and Edward Aveling, had influenced Engels' optimistic appraisal of American conditions; but he had independently observed signs of labor unrest outside New York City. In eleven states other than New York, workers had organized some type of labor party.

which seems, from the theoretical standpoint, to be an almost insane road." [19]

Engels found it extremely gratifying to see events in the United States vindicating the earlier predictions of Marx and himself, especially in view of the substantial uplift in the Marxist crusade elsewhere in the 1880's. It would not do for America to be left behind in the great sweep of history, and Engels took frank pleasure in announcing the breakdown in American social harmony twenty years after the Civil War. The country which European liberals had pointed to for so long as an exception to Marxist-predicted class antagonism was probably to become the most blazing inferno of all those created by the contradictions of capitalist production. With great satisfaction Engels wrote to Sorge in November 1886,

> In Europe the effect of the American elections in November was tremendous. That England, and America in particular, had no labor movement up to now was the big trump card of the radical republicans everywhere, especially in France. Now these gentlemen have been utterly contradicted; on November 2nd the whole foundation, especially of Mr. Clemenceau's policy, collapsed. "Look at America," was his eternal motto; "where there is a real republic, there is no poverty and no labor movement!" And the same thing is happening to the liberals and "democrats" in Germany and here [England]— where they are also witnessing the beginnings of their own movement. The very fact that the movement is so sharply accentuated as a labor movement and has sprung up so suddenly and forcefully has stunned the people completely. [20]

Engels happily imagined that the sudden progress of the labor movement in the United States would prompt European labor leaders to more vigorous action. Especially in England he detected a trace of jealousy among trade union officials and predicted a competition in socialism between the two great Anglo-Saxon nations: "John Bull doesn't want to be outdone by those other fellows;

[19] Engels to Sorge, Sept. 16, 1886, *Letters to Americans*, 161.
[20] Engels to Sorge, Nov. 29, 1886, *Letters to Americans*, 164.

it is the *only* foreign influence that has any drawing power here." [21]

The George candidacy, as it turned out, did not produce a movement up to Engels' expectations. In 1886 George, the candidate of the United Labor party, had run second in a field of three (the unfortunate third man being Theodore Roosevelt). Before the next election a split developed in the ranks of the party between orthodox socialists and single taxers, and it ceased to be an effective vote-getting mechanism. Engels' hopes for one or two million votes for a workingman's party at the next election proved to be wildly chimerical. Meanwhile the European movement which briefly in 1886 had struck observers as no more, and in many cases less, advanced than the American surged forward and made the Yankee wage earners' bovine qualities more noticeable than ever before. Rather than becoming completely disheartened by this turn of events, Engels merely resigned himself to the erratic nature of American development. In 1887 he wrote,

> History is on the move over there at last, and I must know my Americans badly if they do not astonish us all by the vastness of their movement, but also by the gigantic nature of the mistakes they make, through which they will finally work out their way to clarity. Ahead of everyone else in practice and still in swaddling clothes in theory—that's how they are, nor can it be otherwise. But it is a land without tradition (except for the religious), which has begun with the democratic republic, and a people full of energy as no other. The course of the movement will by no means follow the classic straight line, but travel in tremendous zigzags and seem to be moving backward at times, but that is of much less importance there than with us.[22]

The zigzags could be colossal and bring great defeat on the tail of great success; but even in 1892, when the socialist movement was at a low ebb in America, Engels remained convinced that "the

[21] Engels to Sorge, April 9, 1887, and Engels to Florence Kelley Wischnewetzky, Feb. 22, 1888, *Letters to Americans*, 183 and 197.
[22] Engels to Sorge, Aug. 8, 1887, *Letters to Americans*, 190.

advances always become more powerful, the setbacks less paralyzing." [23]

The disappointing sequel to the encouraging beginning of 1886 did prompt Engels to reassess his earlier views about the reasons behind the slow progress of socialist ideas in the United States. A second look forced him to see other factors at work besides the American workers' relatively recent exposure to capitalism. After all, in the absence of other barriers, twenty years of sharply rising class antagonisms should have pushed American workers toward some permanent alignment with socialism. The apparent progress in that direction indicated by the George campaign had backfired. Rather than an unshakable betrothal, American workers had demonstrated an unwillingness to begin even a mild flirtation with socialism. Engels remained generally (even enthusiastically) optimistic about the prospects for socialism in the United States, but the failure of any concrete progress to materialize remained a problem to vex him the rest of his life.

One source of difficulty which Engels located in the German leadership of the American Socialist Labor party aroused his fury. Engels was instinctively suspicious of all European immigrants to the New World. Perhaps the political situation at home had left them with no choice except to move across the Atlantic. But perhaps (and this often seemed more likely to Engels) their migration was motivated by a simple failure of nerve; many of them in going to the New World, while not deserting the radical socialist cause, evidently preferred an environment where their heroic posture would get them into less trouble. In any case, Engels' estimate of German socialists in America was not high, for with few exceptions, he thought, only the least competent of the German revolutionaries had wound up in the United States. His quarrels with the leaders of America's SLP grew more and more heated and led to a complete break by the end of the 1880's.

A part of the basis for the hostility between Engels and the German socialists in America resulted from personal misunderstandings. Part also resulted from the unfortunate and bitter aftermath of a tour of America undertaken in 1886 at the request of the SLP by two of his good friends, Edward and Eleanor Marx Aveling.

[23] Engels to Schlüter, March 30, 1892, *Letters to Americans,* 242–43.

But Engels blasted the German socialists in America mainly for their refusal to adjust to American conditions. Their tactics, Engels believed, were self-defeating. The arrogance with which the Germans hawked socialist ideas, their old-maidish concern for rigidly pure orthodoxy, their disdain for the theoretical backwardness of the American (and, for that matter, all aspects of American life), singularly ill-equipped them to lead the Anglo-Saxon worker from the shadows of his bourgeois cave. How could Americans become acquainted with socialist ideas when the socialist press in America was almost entirely printed in German? To be effective schoolmasters, the German socialists would have to Americanize themselves and learn to work from within existing trade unions. Marx and Engels both demonstrated considerable flexibility in devising tactics for various countries, and throughout their long lives they showed very little concern about the doctrinal purity of any party other than the German. In many countries, and especially in the United States, where experience had not brought workers to socialism, an insistence on a narrow orthodoxy could serve only to slow advance. In 1894 Engels, who was finally convinced the Socialist Labor party would never learn that lesson, wrote from London,

> The Social-Democratic Federation here shares with your German-American Socialists the distinction of being the only parties that have managed to reduce the Marxian theory of development to a rigid orthodoxy, which the workers are not to reach themselves by their own class feeling, but which they have to gulp down as an article of faith at once and without development. That is why both of them remain mere sects and come, as Hegel says, from nothing through nothing to nothing.[24]

The stubborn practices of the Socialist Labor party did little but reinforce the idea, already strong among American workers, that socialism was an alien ideology unsuited to the climate of the New World.

Aside from the pig-headedness of the German sectarians one special factor endemic to the American environment worked very strongly against an immediate acceptance of socialism. Even before

[24] Engels to Sorge, May 12, 1894, *Letters to Americans,* 263.

the Civil War, Marx and Engels had noted with chagrin the escape-valve qualities of the great western hinterland (again a chagrin contrasting sharply to the attitude of other European social radicals toward the frontier). Workers dissatisfied with their condition in the eastern cities did not rebel—they merely moved. Both Marx and Engels had counted on the rapid rise of American capitalism after the war to nullify this factor, but as late as 1892 Engels was still pointing to the unmanning effect of the American West on proletarian class consciousness. The West did not merely offer the oppressed eastern worker a place to go—a way out and up. Even more damaging to a struggling socialist movement, the large land reserve often turned the laborer into a speculator (or, at least, a potential speculator) and kept his mind running in the same bourgeois circles. Engels wrote,

> Only when the land—the public lands—is completely in the hands of the speculators, and settlement on the land thus becomes more and more difficult or falls victim to gouging—only then, I think, will the time come, with *peaceful* development, for a third party. *Land* is the basis of speculation, and the American speculative mania and speculative opportunity are the chief levers that hold the native-born worker in bondage to the bourgeoisie. Only when there is a generation of native-born workers that cannot expect *anything* from speculation *any more,* will we have a solid foothold in America.[25]

The paradox of a bourgeois-minded proletariat had long bothered Engels in analyzing the English masses. In England and America, he knew, the disturbing phenomenon of workers who admired bankers and industrialists and scorned their own class owed much to the relatively high wage scale prevailing there. Both countries for special historical reasons had been able to maintain a level of prosperity high enough to infect Anglo-Saxon workers with a snobbish sense of superiority (especially toward workers in continental Europe). But in America the cause of a docile proletariat went even beyond the workers' relative well-being and involved their condition of complete innocence. Earlier, Engels had described America's escape from a feudal past as fortunate because, held back

[25] Engels to Sorge, Jan. 6, 1892, *Letters to Americans,* 239.

by few traditions, the United States could move with infinitely greater speed into the future than was possible in Europe. But, as he soon discovered, the one tradition the country did have, the dream of going from rags to riches, from an unpropertied to a propertied condition, had very deep and tangled roots; the main trunk of the tradition might be cut, but the land was still not ready for the growth of new ideas. The lucky escape of Americans from the experience of feudal despotism had its unfortunate side, for it handicapped them for recognizing oppression when it appeared in a more brutal modern form. Ironically, the European worker could perceive more easily the exploitation of the American worker under capitalism than the American himself.

Unhappily for Engels the youth of America did not prove to be a completely unmitigated blessing. Youth was another word for immaturity, and along with it went gullibility and a certain soft-headed wistfulness. As Engels correctly stated in one of his last letters about America before his death, these were also the qualities of old age and senility:

> America is the *youngest,* but also the *oldest* country in the world. Over there you have old-fashioned furniture styles alongside those you have invented all yourselves, cabs in Boston such as I last saw in 1838 in London, and in the mountains stagecoaches dating from the seventeenth century alongside the Pullman cars, and in the same way you keep all the intellectual old clothes discarded in Europe. Anything that is out of date over here can survive in America for one or two generations.[26]

Americans did not have much of a past, but what they had they liked and were loath to discard. Idyllic remembrances defined the uniqueness of their nation, an exceptionality on which many had gambled their future. Industrial production might move ahead with tremendous strides, but the worker at the bottom of the social heap still preferred to identify with independent yeoman farmers rather than exploited, enslaved members of the European proletariat. As Engels noted, it was touch and go whether "the mind of the industrial worker or that of the pioneering farmer gains predominance

[26] Engels to Sorge, Jan. 16, 1895, *Letters to Americans,* 269.

in the average man's head."[27] The American worker had yet to comprehend how the acceptance of his present dismal plight as inevitable under capitalism would move him to the verge of his ultimate emancipation and salvation. This understanding, Engels realized, would come only with several more years of increasing poverty. How many, he was no longer sure.

A few additional factors peculiar to American life, Engels noted, further slowed the otherwise-rushing currents of socialism. The varied makeup of the working-class population was one of them. A cultural barrier separated native-born and immigrant labor, and neither group really got along with the other. This situation was further complicated by additional splintering within the two large groups—the native-born into white and Negro and the foreign-born into almost every nationality conceivable. Engels recognized the talent of American capitalists for playing off these various elements against one another, and on account of this he concluded that labor could not speak with one voice until it could speak in one language.[28]

Finally, American socialists confronted the obstacle of the long-standing tradition of two parties in the United States. Engels was only echoing Bryce when he pointed out that because American political parties were based on the acquisition of power rather than concern for principle, third parties could make headway only with great difficulty. In his 1891 preface to Marx's *The Civil War in France,* Engels wrote,

> There is no country in which "politicians" form a more powerful and distinct section of the nation than in North America. There each of the two great parties which alternately succeed each other in power is itself in turn controlled by people who make a business of politics, who speculate on seats in the legislative assemblies of the Union as well as of the separate States, or who make a living by carrying on agitation for their party and on its victory are rewarded with positions.

Engels' disappointing experience with the United Labor Party in

[27] *Ibid.,* 270.
[28] Engels to Schlüter, March 30, 1892, *Letters to Americans,* 242.

1886 led him to caution his American friends in 1892 that "there is no place yet in America for a *third* party." [29] Before a socialist party could expect to win success at the polls, socialist principles had to make considerably more headway among the masses.

These difficulties belonged—and Engels was adamant on this point—to a changing scene and would disappear within a short time. Events in America had not progressed with the rapidity he had thought possible in 1886 and America's inability to get out of "its hobbledehoy stage" was extremely perplexing.[30] But in pointing to the difficulties of socialist advance in America, Engels was in no way trying to define an exceptional category for the United States or exempt it from the general laws of capitalist development. There were difficulties everywhere, and neither he nor Marx had ever expected exactly the same pattern of development in every country[31] One thing alone was certain in the eccentric American growth pattern: capitalist production and capital accumulation could not go forward in the United States much longer without calling forth the antithesis of the bourgeoisie—a strong proletariat determined to destroy the parasitic capitalist system. This was an essential belief for Engels because if capitalism had somehow found a sanctuary in the New World he had lost his claim of being scientific.

By 1895, then, the attitudes of Marx and Engels toward the United States had undergone an interesting cycle. Before the Civil War they had used the New World to explain their way out of a gnawing theoretical difficulty—the failure of the world socialist revolution to materialize. In 1880, shortly before Marx's death, America's rapid

[29] Engels to Sorge, Jan. 6, 1892, *Letters to Americans,* 239. Both Marx and Engels had thought that workers in certain countries where they had an effective political voice could achieve their goals by peaceful means. In a famous speech in Amsterdam in 1872, Marx had predicted that violence might be avoided in the United States, England, and Holland. (Also see interview in New York *Herald,* Aug. 3, 1871.) Yet Engels' letter to Sorge indicated awareness that peaceful acquisition of power might prove impossible—even in a supposedly democratic country with a broad franchise.

[30] Engels to Sorge, Dec. 31, 1892, *Letters to Americans,* 243.

[31] This explains their insistence on flexible tactics. Lenin made some self-serving but interesting comments on this aspect of Marx's thought (comparing Marx's attitudes toward the proper tactics for the labor movement in America, England, and Germany) in his preface to the Russian translation of *Letters from J. F. Becker, J. Dietzgen, F. Engels, K. Marx and Others to F. A. Sorge and Others.* (Reprinted in *Letters to Americans,* 273–85.)

growth as a capitalist power had completely changed this perspective. Rather than frustrating socialist revolution, America now seemed likely to promote revolutionary activity in Europe. America might even prove to be the site of the first successful revolution. In either case America would become the Socialist Promised Land. By 1895 the perspective had shifted again. The theoretical problem of capitalism's unexpected longevity which had faced Marx and Engels all their lives still remained, but post-Civil War America could no longer help to explain it. On the contrary, the failure of socialism to make significant headway in America despite its rapid capitalist development only added new dimensions to old headaches. Engels did not ever lose all of the enthusiasm with which he and Marx had begun to greet developments in America in 1880. Once America had passed England in the rate of economic growth, the possibility was always open that the future of socialism rested on America. But at least some question had been raised as to whether New World youth and vigor would prove more effective than Old World sophistication and wisdom in the realization of socialist goals. (Or, more darkly, whether any of these things would be to any avail.)

The interest of Marx and Engels in America, of course, should be placed in a larger picture; after all they were not the first European socialists who toyed with the idea of America as potentially a promised land for the cooperative commonwealth. (Nor, as the rest of this study seeks to show, were they the last.) Throughout the nineteenth century, utopian visionaries built colonies in America with the expectation of springing from these small beginnings a new social order. For some of the utopians the attraction of America was a supply of cheap land which made their experiments economically feasible. This was what first brought Robert Owen to America. Once he arrived, however, Owen detected in the United States a spirit of adventure and idealism auguring success for his colony at New Harmony. Novelty was still a possibility in America, as was purity and goodness.

The great Saint-Simon, who took a brief and undramatic part in the Battle of Yorktown, was soundly struck by his two-month encounter with the young nation and recalled later, "I realized that the revolution in America signalled the beginning of a new political era, that this revolution would necessarily bring about major progress in general civilization, and that in a short time it would cause great changes in the social order which then existed in Europe." [32] In 1854 Victor Considérant, a French disciple of Fourier, summed up his hope for America: "When we observe the general march of humanity, we easily perceive that progress, while advancing in Time, displaces itself in Space, and that the focus of social light and impulsion has always proceeded from the East to the West like the Sun." [33] These men saw the same promise in America which attracted political liberals and non-socialist radicals to the New World —its freedom from European influences. On a new continent with a fresh start, men might at last accomplish something commensurate with their best dreams.

Marx and Engels, taking another road to the truths of social science, dismissed the utopians with contempt. The utopians' notion that they could erect a perfect society in their minds and plunk it down in the middle of existing conditions (however virgin those conditions might be) was absurd.[34] Marx and Engels were looking for an entirely different spirit in America than any of the social radicals who had preceded them in Europe. Socialism would not rise from a pristine seed planted in a rural community, but from the decay of an existing social order. What they looked for in America was not purity but corruption, not harmony but chaos, not love but antagonism, not rural seclusion but urban complexity. Engels did seem to speak like some of the utopians when he talked of America's energy and vitality, but it was an energy that led to violence, a vitality that had to tear down before it could build. America would not be a promised land for socialism because it was younger and simpler than Europe. Only as the New World

[32] Quoted in Frank E. Manuel, *The New World of Henri Saint-Simon* (Cambridge, Mass., 1956), 20.
[33] Quoted in Halvdan Koht, *The American Spirit in Europe: A Survey of Transatlantic Influences* (Philadelphia, 1949), 205.
[34] Anyone familiar with much nineteenth-century socialist literature will realize the danger of overdrawing a distinction between Marxist and utopian views of America. The utopian and scientific schools did not always turn out to be as different as Marx and Engels had intended. The moral outrages of a utopian writer were sometimes scarcely distinguishable from the supposedly detached, scientific evaluations of a Marxist. None of this, however, vitiates the main point of the paragraph.

grew old and became more complicated and decadent than Europe could it lead the world toward a better society. Most observers who spoke of the promise of America found that promise in America's differences from Europe. Marx and Engels turned this vision on its head. America could become a promised land to the extent that it became just like Europe—and multiplied its vices. Marx and Engels had no use for American goodness, but they found a use for its evil. As things got worse and worse in the New World, its prospects became better and better.

CHAPTER 2

EUROPEAN MARXISTS
REJECT THE OLD
PROMISE OF AMERICA

In the fall of 1886 the American Socialist Labor party played host to three very important European visitors. At its invitation Dr. Edward Aveling and his consort Eleanor Marx (both from England), and Wilhelm Liebknecht (from Germany) made the long boat trip across the Atlantic to undertake an extended agitation tour through the United States; in New York, Boston, Washington, Pittsburgh, Milwaukee, St. Louis, Minneapolis, Chicago, and Kansas City they addressed enthusiastic rallies of America's socialist fledglings.[1] Although their primary purpose was to raise money for socialist party struggles back home, the three guests took the opportunity of tourists to make personal observations of life in the New World.

European Marxists, who were just beginning in 1886 to join in an old and heated debate about the meaning of America, saw this expedition by their esteemed colleagues as an important opportunity. They had a number of questions about conditions in the New World which had occasionally disturbed them in the past and would cause increasing concern in the future. How did the American worker

---

[1] The Avelings stayed in the New World almost four months, while Liebknecht returned to Germany at the end of three. Their itinerary (the Avelings and Liebknecht had somewhat different schedules) also included stops in New Haven, Springfield, Manchester, Providence, Syracuse, Rochester, Niagara, Detroit, Toledo, Indianapolis, Cincinnati, Philadelphia, and Baltimore. For the best account of the tour, see Chushichi Tsuzuki, *The Life of Eleanor Marx, 1855–1898* (Oxford, 1967), 133–58.

eat and dress? Did he expect, and get, more from life than the European did? Did the American system of government make capitalism a bearable system? Was it true that socialism was weak in America; and, if so, was it an indication of worker comfort or rather the reflection of ignorance, oppression, and indifference? How many years would it take for the proletariat to form a political party based on strict class lines? Marxists in waiting for answers to these questions from their itinerant comrades might somewhere in their inner consciousness have feared honest answers. But this apprehension, if it existed, did not show. In 1886, Marxists were buoyant because of the increase in the number and size of socialist parties and trade unions in Europe, and they fully expected statistics from America to confirm the evidence which they saw at home. Capitalism was a condemned system.

All three of the American travelers were recognized leaders of the European Marxist movement; but, as was often the case among Marxists, accord on fundamental matters of policy and tactics proved an elusive ideal. To judge from the published accounts of their peregrinations, Liebknecht and the Avelings shared some of the same compartments on the trains which bore them across America's mosaicked landscape but none of the same thoughts. The former's *Ein Blick in die Neue Welt* and the latters' *The Working Class Movement in America* seemed to describe different continents, and their allies back in Europe were left to ponder how both books could have been inspired by the same tour across the United States.[2] They also had to choose because the antithetic images in the two reports implied different answers to the questions uppermost in their minds.

America never had a better advocate than Wilhelm Liebknecht. By the time he made his voyage to the United States in 1886, Liebknecht had become an object of veneration among European Marxists. Born in 1825, he could not claim working-class origins, but he had been on the right side in all the great struggles of the century. In 1875, along with August Bebel, his younger friend

---

[2] *Ein Blick in die Neue Welt,* first published in Stuttgart in 1887, consisted mainly of letters and daily sketches written aboard boats and trains. *The Working Class Movement in America,* a more finished work, was not published in book form until 1888, but much of the account appeared earlier in various journals. Edward Aveling also published a collection of articles he had written en route entitled *An American Journey.*

whom he had converted to Marxism, Liebknecht had managed to combine German socialists into one force by mixing in the party platform Marxist scientific formulas with a few Lassallean economic nostrums. Marx never entirely forgave Liebknecht for this compromise (consummated at the celebrated Gotha Congress) with the followers of Lassalle, the romantic bon vivant who ran his socialism and nationalism together and longed for a miserable (Marx supplied the adjective) alliance with Bismarck. But the product of the compromise, the Social Democratic party of Germany, soon silenced the criticism from London. Dodging the steady stream of legal brickbats which Bismarck hurled at it, the party in the mid-1880's was the oldest, strongest, and best organized Marxist union in Europe. Its leadership in international circles was not effectively challenged until World War I.

Liebknecht's detractors, and there were many, knew that both Marx and Engels had time and again entertained doubts about his wisdom and judgment. Well educated, he had a romantic and expansive, rather than critical and precise, mind, and his mastery of the revolutionary conclusions of the doctrines of Marx and Engels was far surer than the details of their economics. In the early 1860's Liebknecht had made the prime goal of his party the winning of fundamental political freedom, and for a few years he had persevered in the petty bourgeois belief that political conditions determined social conditions rather than vice versa. Marx had finally educated him away from this opinion, but the materialism of Marx and Engels never fully erased Liebknecht's earlier stains of idealism.[3]

When Liebknecht had agreed to go to America in 1886, Engels had urged Bebel to accompany him on the trip, for, if the elder mentor went alone, "who knows what might happen?" Later Engels expressed relief in learning of the Avelings' plans to travel along with Liebknecht: "Tussy Aveling will give him a tug from time to time to keep him on the right path."[4] Yet Liebknecht had fol-

[3] Guenther Roth, *The Social Democrats in Imperial Germany: A Study of Workingclass Isolation and National Integration* (Totowa, N.J., 1963), 33.
[4] Letters of Jan. 20(–23) and Aug. 18, 1886, *August Bebel Briefwechsel mit Friedrich Engels*, ed. by Werner Blumenberg (The Hague, 1965). In the first letter Engels had urged Bebel to take "this opportunity to see with your own eyes the most progressive land in the world"; he had recalled how he had

lowed Marx sincerely and for a long time. If Engels could claim to be Marx's Peter, Liebknecht had some claim to being his Paul. Imprisonment in 1848, a long exile from 1849 to 1863, imprisonment again in 1872, untiring and courageous party work, election to the German Reichstag—these things had earned Liebknecht a secure place in the pantheon of socialist heroes. Intellectuals in the party, most notably Karl Kautsky, grumbled about him in private correspondence, but they recognized his influence and could not curtly dismiss his remarks on any subject.

Liebknecht's *Ein Blick in die Neue Welt* made clear the warm regard with which he viewed the American nation. He recalled an earlier episode in his life when he himself had nearly turned his back on the tired old continent of Europe. While still a very young man he and a few of his friends had laid plans to build a socialist community in Wisconsin, and in 1847 Liebknecht had actually started a trip which was to have taken him to America. Only a chance encounter with a Swiss professor on a train from Frankfurt to Mainz had altered his destination to Zurich.[5] Several years later, when another opportunity to emigrate had presented itself, he had chosen to remain in Europe, regarding emigration then (following the 1848 upheavals) as equivalent to desertion. Yet, clearly, the attraction Liebknecht had felt to America in his youth had not dimmed with the years.

Liebknecht's portrait of the United States in 1886 was not altogether uncritical. He did mention the corrupt political life, the excesses of laissez-faire capitalism, and the grim, haggard faces of female and juvenile workers in Manchester, New Hampshire. Yet he did not dwell on these aspects of American life and chose rather to emphasize the advantages of the American worker over his counterpart in Europe. He dismissed accounts of terrible work and wage conditions in the United States as fictive creations of the German junker press and reached his own overgenerous conclusion that "generally the badly paid worker here is better off than our well-paid worker." Wandering through workers' quarters in New

---

always wished to make the trip with Marx. Engels, of course, did make a short trip to the New World before his death, but political involvements and health never permitted Bebel a similar chance.
[5] Liebknecht, *Souvenirs,* trans. into French by J. G. Prod'Homme and Ch. Bertrand (Paris, 1901), 76, 105, 112–18.

York City, he saw happy, healthy children; "in one day," he wrote, "a worker's child eats more meat here than he eats in Germany in three months." [6]

The American people had achieved in 1886 a reputation for conservatism among European progressives, but in Liebknecht's mind their tenacious attachment to past ideals simply reflected the great political and social endowment of the United States. Citizens of the New World had something worth holding to. No remains of a feudal past weighed down the people: "No traditions, no rubbish of handed-down prejudices" robbed them of their sense of participation in a "fresh, pulsating present." The American Constitution provided for a truly free government and guaranteed that "equality in our America is, despite the monied aristocracy, no empty word . . . the Republic with its Stars and Stripes has no second-class citizens; for everyone there is only one class, and that is the first!" While American society had its dark spots, Liebknecht was in essential agreement with earlier European commentators who had looked across the Atlantic and said with Goethe, "Amerika, Du hast es besser als unser Kontinent, das alte." Liebknecht wrote,

> It is not necessary for me to maintain that there prevails in America no materialism and egoism—in the worst sense of the two words. But what I certainly deny is that America in this respect stands behind Europe in any way—or more correctly, stands ahead of it. I know—and no one knows better—the corruption that predominates there in public life, I know the disgraceful frenzy of exploitation by American monopolists and capitalists—but next to these dark sides, which . . . are all to be found equally in our Old World—I find bright sides that I look for vainly in Germany. I find a public spirit, of which we have no understanding, an enthusiasm for justice, freedom, progress, the common good that I have not discovered to any approximate degree in the countries of the Old World.

Liebknecht even went out of his way to compliment the American police force which he found was "not a state institution, but a community business . . . that stands in the service of the public." [7]

[6] *Ein Blick in die Neue Welt,* 102 and 63.
[7] *Ein Blick,* 58, 75, 271, 235.

How different was the report of Marx's sensitive youngest daughter and her knavish partner of a "free marriage." While the impressionable Liebknecht found himself wondering in reading over his travel notes whether their publication might inadvertently encourage immigration to the United States, Dr. Edward Aveling, without a trace of diffidence, summed up his journey through America: "I never disliked England less than during the few weeks wherein I was brought into contact with American manners and institutions." If there were any charms lingering on the American scene, Aveling missed them. In the same working-class sections of New York where Liebknecht had walked and seen smiling faces, Aveling found children whose "faces are quite hard; their voices empty of music; their ways no more the ways of children than an ape's grimaces are human." This "decrepit race of wizened little men and women" was the inevitable product of America's ruthless capitalistic system, and the "mad race for wealth for which all New York seems entered." [8]

Aveling and his wife, along with H. M. Hyndman, William Morris, Harry Quelch, and E. Belfort Bax, were among the principal founders of a Marxist party in England. The movement did not stay united long. At the end of 1884 the Socialist League split away from the older Social Democratic Federation. The Avelings and the poet-visionary Morris led the disenchanted away from the SDF while Quelch and Bax remained with the quarrelsome and obstreperous Hyndman. Personality was as responsible for the breach as doctrine. Hyndman, who had come from the English upper middle classes and had been to Eton, wanted authority even though his intellect would ill support his pretensions. His ego had alienated Marx, another man of considerable pride, shortly after they had met, and when Hyndman in 1881 had published *England for All* without due acknowledgment to *Capital,* from which he had taken all his ideas, any chance he had of gaining the favor of Marx and Engels vanished.

Aveling no more arose from the masses than Hyndman, but at least his tastes were not middle class. He dabbled in the theater, was known after a fashion in London's artistic circles, and looked down upon bourgeois sexual morality with extravagant disdain.

[8] *An American Journey* (New York, *ca.* 1887), 227 and 30–31.

For some reason, perhaps because of his considerable personal charm and undeniable brilliance, Engels and Eleanor Marx liked him and, unfortunately, trusted him. Eleanor Marx was important because of her father, but the energy and devotion she brought to the socialist movement would have made her a significant figure in any case. All three of Marx's daughters were talented, but Eleanor alone in her tortured lifetime revealed touches of greatness. The Socialist League never overcame its rocky start, and it was absorbed by the anarchists in 1890. After that, Hyndman's SDF carried the burden of Marxist agitation in England alone. But for a few years the Avelings labored hard in the league's causes; and, guided by Engels, they did their part in turning English labor toward an independent course in politics.

In recounting their visit to the United States, Aveling and his wife wrote with a single-minded assurance that the European worker had absolutely nothing to envy in the lot of the American worker: "The average condition of the average wage-labourer in America is as bad as it is in England." In many ways the American worker endured even more wretched circumstances than the typical worker endured in Europe. Safety precautions in factories were primitive, the employment of women and children was more common than elsewhere, labor disputes ended more frequently in violence, and factory foremen demanded a work pace which wise owners would have expected neither of slaves nor of donkeys. In addition to these horrors the Avelings found class divisions in America more pronounced than anywhere in Europe:

> At the one end of the scale is the millionaire, openly, remorselessly crushing out all rivals, swallowing up all the feebler folk. At the other end is the helpless, starving proletarian. . . . The real division of society into two classes, the labourer and capitalist, veiled in England and other European countries by the remains of old systems, by artificial classes of royalty, nobility, and so forth, in America stares one in the face.[9]

A farcical dispute which erupted between the Avelings and their American hosts at the conclusion of the visit no doubt reinforced

[9] *The Working Class Movement in America* (London, 1888), 23 and 14.

the distaste of the English visitors, especially Edward Aveling, for life in the New World. The Executive Committee of the American Socialist Labor party charged that Aveling had spent party money with aristocratic abandon while he toured among the American proletariat, and it refused to reimburse Aveling for money which it claimed had gone for flower bouquets, fine wines, theater tickets, and plush hotel suites. The accusations were never settled to anyone's satisfaction. Engels angrily and publicly came to Aveling's defense.[10] Yet Aveling's taste for luxury if obtainable at someone else's expense was already becoming notorious in England, and at his death in 1898 no one would be left to mourn him as anything other than a scoundrel. This was the man, after all, whose amorous inconstancy would drive Eleanor Marx, an incredibly kind and loyal person, to a tragic suicide.[11] Considering his personality traits, the American SLP probably had some grounds for complaint against the visiting Englishman, but the charges did little to incline Aveling and his wife toward a charitable view of their host country. Unquestionably, Aveling's quarrel with America revolved around his inability to find there a style of life commensurate with his epicurean desires even on borrowed funds. Aveling never behaved like a proletarian in his life. But in America he felt like one and cursed a spiritual poverty which owed more to a deformed Puritanism than to a low income.

European Marxists, because of the varying tastes and assumptions of the travelers, suddenly became heirs to two diametrically opposed accounts of the United States. Who was right? Liebknecht's remarks could not be summarily repudiated, but his report obviously conflicted with Marxist ideas about what life should be like in a developed capitalist society. The Avelings were younger and could not

---

[10] Engels' warm feeling for Marx's daughter impelled the defense. In a letter of Feb. 9, 1887, he wrote Florence Kelley Wischnewetzky, "Had he tried to swindle the party, how could he do that during all his tour without his wife being cognizant of it? And in that case the charge includes her too. And then it becomes utterly absurd, in my eyes at least." *Letters to Americans,* 171. For Aveling's answer to the charges, see letter to the *Chicagoer Zeitung,* Engels Archives, International Institute of Social History, Amsterdam.

[11] For an account of the romance by someone who knew the persons involved, see Eduard Bernstein, *My Years of Exile* (London, 1921), 160–67. George Bernard Shaw used the Avelings as the bases for the characters of Dubedat and his wife in *The Doctor's Dilemma.*

match Liebknecht's prestige, but their observations comfortably bore out Marxist expectations.

A dramatic event which rocked America in the spring of 1886, about six months before Liebknecht and the Avelings arrived in America, had actually already decided the question in the Avelings' favor. On a rainy May 4, at the conclusion of a rather unspirited labor rally in a corner of Chicago's Haymarket Square, someone tossed a bomb into a crowd of policemen who were trying to disperse the demonstration and killed seven of them. In a hysterical aftermath to the episode America extracted a senseless revenge.[12] There were scores of arrests and eight anarchists (some with foreign names) were brought before a Chicago court on charges of being co-conspirators and accessories to murder. Historians have not labeled their trial the fairest in America's past. But had the judge conducted the proceedings with impeccable impartiality it would not have mattered: the press had long before decided the verdict. On August 20, seven of the defendants were sentenced to be hanged, and the eighth (who was associated with the Haymarket rally only in the vaguest way) to fifteen years in prison; on November 11, 1887, four of the men (the sentences of two were commuted from death to life imprisonment and one of the condemned took his own life) died on the gallows.

The European Marxist newspapers gave a truly impressive amount of coverage to the events flowing from the Haymarket disturbance. Indeed, no future incident on the American scene was given so much space or remembered so long. The bomb which exploded in Chicago and the treatment of the condemned taught clear lessons to Marxists: the promises of prosperity, opportunity, and equality, long associated with America by many European liberals and radicals, had become fraudulent. Capitalist societies everywhere, no matter how admirable their constitutions and no matter under what favorable conditions they had begun, all wound up in the same sad shape. H. M. Hyndman, the Avelings' erstwhile ally who had been to America several times, wrote that, despite America's lack of an aristocracy, a House of Lords, and an established Church, and its possession of a universal ballot and free education, "all are now driven to admit that the same class struggle is going on under the guise of nominal

---

[12] The standard account is Henry David, *The History of the Haymarket Affair* (New York, 1936).

peace and freedom." [13] James Blackwell, another English Marxist, though a lesser luminary than Hyndman, commented on Haymarket,

> The whole business is so monstrous as to be almost incredible. Even in despotic Germany and enslaved Russia they would hardly venture to hang men for having written articles and made speeches against the existing rule. It was left to the country whose political institutions are the delight of so many of our Radical friends here in England to commit this crime.[14]

In view of traditional liberal images of America circulated in Europe, it is not hard to understand why this particular evidence of social disorder was so welcomed by many European Marxists. Marx and Engels had been troubled by the economic crutch which pre-Civil War America had held out to European capitalism and the steady drain of revolutionary potential away from Europe. While many non-socialist European radicals had been enchanted by the prosperity, opportunity, and equality prevailing in the New World, Marx and Engels had developed a positive antipathy for these old promises of American life. To their way of thinking, the social harmony in pre-Civil War America had been tragically misleading. Workers in Europe had hoped to escape their difficulties merely by moving, while well-meaning but empty-headed reformers had laid down plans for the remodeling of Europe following an American blueprint. All of this effort could lead nowhere, according to Marx and Engels, because as America moved into the capitalist era its society would be violently shattered by social disruptions.

When Marx died, he was certain that the old myth of an American paradise had been sufficiently destroyed by the plain facts of post-Civil War America. However Engels, as well as the rest of Marx's disciples, were surprised and chagrined to discover that many Europeans continued to look to America as if nothing had changed since the 1840's. In the 1880's republicans, democrats, parliamentarians, and other representatives of European liberalism still

[13] *The Chicago Riots and the Class War in the United States* (London, 1886), 1.
[14] "The Anniversary of a Crime," *Justice,* Nov. 10, 1888.

found persuasive the words of the Englishman Ernest Jones, who pictured the United States as transforming men who had been "corrupted, and degraded, and debased" by the European system "into the worthy citizens of the happiest country in the world." [15] Men still depicted the American Canaan in words echoing the merry Norwegian folksong *Oleana*:

> I'm off to Oleana, I'm turning from my doorway,
> No chains for me, I'll say good-by to slavery in Norway.
>   Oh, Oleana!

> They give you land for nothing in jolly Oleana,
> And grain comes leaping from the ground in floods of golden manna.
>   Oh, Oleana!

> The grain it does the threshing, it pours into the sack, Sir,
> And so you take a quiet nap a-stretching on your back, Sir,
>   Oh, Oleana! [16]

Influential European republicans like Georges Clemenceau still predicated the salvation of Europe on the imitation of American institutions. The America of the 1880's was a sordid capitalist power, but workingmen heedlessly sailed from Europe by the thousands every year to seek their fortunes in the New World. The enemies of socialism seized the United States as a handy bludgeon for slaying the prophet Marx. Portrayals of a land flowing with milk and honey served to undermine Marxist expectations about the inevitable triumph of socialism, for in at least one capitalist country a happy breed of men had found it possible to escape the wearisome cycle of poverty and class struggle. European liberals were not as blind to the realities of America's Gilded Age as Marxists imagined nor did most of them mistake America for utopia. All the same they had spun tales about an American Promised Land; and since, to the Marxist, actuality could bear no part of the responsibility, he blamed

---

[15] *Democracy Vindicated: A Lecture Delivered to the Edinburgh Working Men's Institute on Jan. 4, 1867* (Edinburgh, 1867), 14.
[16] Quoted in Halvdan Koht, *The American Spirit in Europe* (Philadelphia, 1949), 76. For an account of the generally favorable reports of the condition of the American worker given by European visitors to America between 1885 and 1910, see Robert W. Smuts, *European Impressions of the American Worker* (New York, 1953).

the liberals for keeping alive the notions about American virtue and
prosperity.

In the mid-1880's a number of influential Marxists decided it was
time to deliver to Nature the corpse which only liberal guile had
denied Her. Leaguing with men on the right side of the European
political spectrum long engaged in similar work, they undertook to
finish off the ailing American Canaan promise by promise. Haymarket, they thought, was perfectly suited to put an end to non-
sensical talk about a New World paradise. European Marxists now
had the words of the Chicago anarchists, some of whom were
native-born Americans, to show how badly the American republic
had faltered as a panacea for the social woes of Europe. If one
could believe the speeches of the condemned Haymarket leaders,
their radicalism was not something which they had carried over on
the boat or had gotten out of a European book; they had turned to
revolutionary activities only after disillusioning contact with American conditions had forced them to choose either socialism or despair.
George Engel, one of those hanged, reported, for example, that his
great hopes for the United States had been crushed when he discovered people "for whom no table is set" who were left to "gather
their daily food from the garbage heaps of the street." [17] According
to Michael Schwab, who was eventually pardoned by Governor
John Altgeld in 1893, the "so-called better paid skilled laborers [in
America] were degrading rapidly into mere automatic parts of
machinery"; and Spies, another who died on the gallows, depicted
the life cycle of the American worker as an endless treadmill of
misery ending "in one of those charitable or reformatory institutes
known as the insane asylum, the penitentiary, or poorhouse." [18] The
propaganda value of these utterances was instantly manifest to
European Marxists who had been watching America, and they were
not remiss in giving the speeches of the Haymarket "martyrs" a
wide European circulation.[19]

[17] *The Chicago Martyrs: Their Speeches in Court* (London, *ca.* 1890), 24.
[18] *Ibid.,* 14. Spies, *Auto-biography: His Speech in Court and General Notes,*
ed. by Nina Van Zandt (Chicago, 1887), 8.
[19] Full editions of the speeches appeared in such diverse places as London,
Glasgow, and Rotterdam. The speeches also appeared in Europe's most widely
circulated socialist periodicals. See, for example, the *Revue socialiste* in the
first issues of 1890 and the Nov. 5, 1886, issue of *Die Sozialdemokrat.*

When Liebknecht after Haymarket innocently rose to report favorably on the American police force and other admirable American institutions, the European Marxists who read his report momentarily stood aghast at the waywardness of their distinguished leader and then swept his book under the carpet. "Tussy" Aveling, as it had turned out, had simply not tugged hard enough to keep her kindly mentor in line. Seeing the mind of one of the founders of the German socialist movement permanently affected by the "American myth" only underlined for Marxists the importance of destroying it. From 1886 on, Marxists in Europe, intermittently but with surprising single-mindedness, pursued the task, so well begun by the Avelings in the aftermath of Haymarket, of showing that any hope of social betterment founded on existing American models was a "pernicious fallacy." [20]

As it turned out, the work of European Marxists was cut out for them. In spite of Haymarket or any other single event which Marxists could point to in the period before 1917, persuading European workers that average conditions in America were as bad as or worse than in Europe was a formidable goal. The American myth, as Marxists admitted, had a certain basis in historical fact, and workers were understandably reluctant to accept their Eden as vanished. As an additional complication, certain factors responsible for the creation of the myth had not entirely disappeared at the close of the nineteenth century. The rapid expansion of the American economy across the vast continent had permitted a degree of social mobility unknown in Europe, and American workers had been too busy scrambling out of their class ever to consider trade union activity a permanent commitment. Moreover, wage statistics at the turn of the century showed the American workers taking home two or three times as much money as their counterparts in Europe. American prosperity, whether fictitious or real, remained a strong influence in Europe.

European Marxists who dealt with the problem tried not to be dismayed by this data and kept up a steady attack on the assumed advantages of the American workers' higher pay check. In the first place, they contended, Americans paid out more for necessities like

[20] *The Commonweal* (official organ of England's Socialist League), Jan. 29, 1887.

rent, clothing, heat, and food. Higher wages reflected only a higher cost of living, not a higher standard of living. And with prices following an upward course in America, small increments in nominal wages could not halt the declining position of the proletariat. It is possible to dip anywhere into European Marxist literature in the period between 1886 and 1917 and find this argument—the only variation would be in the supporting statistics. The Avelings had made high living costs a central point in their study of American conditions.[21] In 1884, two years before the Avelings' visit, Ernest Langkavel, a minor party theorist who can exemplify many others, sought to demonstrate in *Die Neue Zeit* (a journal which under Karl Kautsky's direction became the most important outlet for theoretical Marxism in Europe) that, taking differences in price scale into consideration, the average American worker had a *lower* wage than the European.[22] Two decades later Karl Kautsky made extensive use of American census reports to point up what he believed was a steady and serious decline in the buying power of American wages after 1890.[23] In 1911 Fritz Kummer, another respected German Marxist who wrote frequently for *Die Neue Zeit* and the party newspaper *Vorwärts,* estimated the ratio of the increase of living costs to wage increments in the United States as no lower than 2.5 to 1 and perhaps as high as 4.2 to 1 (for the decade 1900–10). From Kummer's point of view the windy claims of American trade unionists (most disgustingly Samuel Gompers) about great advances in the position of American labor were self-serving cant and bordered on buffoonery. German workers, for all their suffering, were really much better off than workers in America.[24] Americans have normally rejected such statistics smugly; but for the unorganized workers, the Negroes, and the sharecroppers these estimates were accurate enough.

---

[21] In addition to *The Working Class Movement in America,* see Edward and Eleanor Marx Aveling, "Die Lage der Arbeiterklasse in Amerika," *Die Neue Zeit,* V (1887), 241–46 and 307–13.

[22] "Soziale Zustände in Nordamerika," *Die Neue Zeit,* II (1884), 506.

[23] "Der amerikanische Arbeiter," *Die Neue Zeit,* Vol. XXIV, Part I (1905–6), 778.

[24] "Gompers über die Verhältnisse in Europa und Amerika," *Vorwärts,* July 16, 1911. This was a point of view heartily endorsed by European businessmen —it was easier to meet wage demands of workers who were not envious.

European Marxists were not the first to discover poverty in the United States. By the turn of the century it had become obvious to almost anyone who bothered to look at the evidence that America was crowding many of her recent arrivals into urban ghettos and allowing them to live in conditions which could be called livable only as a sardonic euphemism. Marxists added little that was remarkable to existing evidence and overlooked with everyone else the special wrongs done the American Negro. Marxist theory actually handicapped partisans in dealing with Negro problems sensibly, for it seemed to forbid (at least to its duller interpreters) the singling out of any segment of the proletariat as an exceptional case. It is also true that a number of Marxists both in Europe and America shared racist assumptions and were somewhat shy of inflating the concept of brotherhood to fully universal dimensions.

Marxists deserve credit as early publicists of American poverty, for they wrote endless comparisons of squalid urban slums and the palatial residences of America's wealthy elite. Even friendly visitors to America in the late nineteenth century remarked on the demarcation between levels of permanent hunger and conspicuous consumption in a land which had never known a formally organized and fixed class structure. Marxists were unrestrained in drawing what were to them the evident conclusions. To Fritz Kummer, America's "upper four hundred" had built a larger wall between themselves and the people than existed between any of the crowned heads of Europe and their subjects.[25] Social mobility in America no longer existed in 1890, and the road from poverty lay in a state beyond repair. To play the game of American capitalism, a person had to have a stake; and the size of the stake required had become staggeringly large.

Even American workers who lived substantially above the poverty line, Marxists thought, drew little satisfaction from their existence. Marxists, agreeing with many earlier social critics, argued that poverty was partly a state of mind. Even if workers won some improvement in their wages under capitalism (which most Marxists regarded as possible), this could not reverse the inevitable degradation of the proletariat. Marx in his *Wage-Labour and Capital* had given his followers a formula to deal with the situation in America:

25 *Ibid.*

While the worker now satisfies more of his wants, yet the social satisfaction which he enjoys has decreased in comparison with the
increased satisfactions enjoyed by the capitalist and inaccessible to
the worker, and also in comparison with the stage of development
of society. Our needs and satisfactions originate from society; they
are not measured by quantities of objects consumed, but only by a
social yardstick; since they are of a social nature they are also of a
relative nature.[26]

In the end it did not matter much whether American wages were
higher than European wages or not. Nor did it matter whether
American wages were going up or not. American laborers referred
to their own society and to their position vis-à-vis other classes in
their society. Their only concern was whether their share in the
national wealth was keeping up with that of other groups or whether
they were being left in somebody's dust. European Marxists were
normally content to sum up this line of reasoning with a passing
reference to the fortunes of Carnegie and Rockefeller. America's
great fortunes, they believed, cast a gloomy shadow which left the
vast majority of the American people feeling penurious and helpless.

If these various arguments repeated over and over failed to knock
down the belief in "American prosperity," European Marxists had
not exhausted their resources. In references to the exploitation of the
American worker, Marxists reserved what they considered a final
and crushing blow. American laborers might in some cases earn
more, but they had to work far longer hours and at a much faster
pace than laborers in Europe. Nothing became more commonplace
in European Marxist accounts of the United States than the image
of a harried wage slave working himself into an early grave. It
appeared to one English correspondent for H. M. Hyndman's newspaper that laborers in America were treated "as mere profit-making
machines, to be used up as soon as possible." The number of duped
immigrants from Europe guaranteed an endless supply of replace-
ments for every one who broke down.[27] Gustav Eckstein, a party
intellectual whose book reviews and articles regularly appeared in
the Marxist press, put the argument forcefully when he commented,

[26] Quoted in Carl Landauer, *European Socialism,* I (Berkeley, 1959), 176.
[27] H. W. Lee, "The International Outlook," *Justice,* Nov. 28, 1885.

"In America, where the systematic exploitation of labor power has reached the highest and most well-developed forms to date, a worker forty years old is already regarded as an old man. . . . The death rate among the middle-ages has increased there an alarming amount. But what does industry care so long as immigration remained strong enough to plug the created gaps?" [28] The American capitalist system conceded nothing to the worker's need for job security or steady employment. Economic crises regularly threw thousands of men into the street without resources. The progressive mechanization of tasks formerly requiring skilled labor sent production figures soaring, but left many men without a profitable or, worse, a meaningful calling to follow. Progress had required the worker to develop special skills. Now, what was he to do when further progress made those skills obsolete? A laborer's father might remember a time when life had been good in America. But the ongoing development of capitalism had by 1890 effectively killed the last promise of the present course of American life.

In attacking American prosperity, European Marxists, as they knew, were hitting at only one facet of the American myth. America's reputation as "the land of the free" had been as strong a drawing card to the oppressed of Europe as that of the "land of wealth and opportunity"; successfully scotching the latter reputation accomplished little if the other were left to thrive. The former was potentially more damaging to Marxist purposes, for the old American myth had attributed the prosperity of the new continent largely to the widespread dispersal of political liberties. The absence of feudalism or any other institutional barriers to universal political participation, so this interpretation went, had placed wealth within the grasp of anyone who worked for it. Capitalist society in Europe, rather than dying from an incurable disease, had ailments which stemmed from its unwise swallowing of indigestible elements from a remote feudal past. Reform European political institutions according to American standards, as most of the non-Marxist political left was urging in one way or another, and social complaints in Europe would vanish. This argument was a direct challenge to Marxism, and recognizing its power Marxists reserved their severest attacks for America's republican and democratic institutions.

[28] "Löhne und Steuern," *Die Neue Zeit,* Vol. XXXI, Part II (1912–13), 336.

Marxists in Europe from the beginning of their movement had difficulty defining the proper revolutionary attitude toward a democratic republic. Should socialists in Germany, where the bourgeoisie had capitulated to Bismarck and the Prussian Junkers in the 1870's and had failed to establish an effective parliamentary government, make liberalization of political institutions a primary goal, or should they direct all their energies toward economic and social revolution? In 1875 in his *Critique of the Gotha Program,* Marx had made clear his hostility toward all forms of state authority. Any state, whether monarchical or democratic, was an instrument designed to keep society going with no change in form; and, so long as the bourgeoisie retained the exclusive privilege to squat on the economic resources of a country, the nominal form of the state had no perceptible effect on the treatment of the proletariat. To Engels a democratic republic merely had been "the last form of bourgeois society."

If they took such statements literally, Marxists had no business becoming committed to any issue of political reform. Their interest lay not in establishing a parliament which the owning classes would dominate, but in completely overturning the bourgeois state. On the other hand, ever since the upheavals of 1848 Marx and Engels had encouraged the proletariat to aid the bourgeoisie in wresting power from the old feudal aristocracy, for this shift toward greater democracy moved society dialectically into a new stage of history and brought socialism closer to victory. In addition, as European Marxists, beginning in Germany in the 1870's and spreading to almost all the European countries in the 1880's, started tactical maneuvers on the political field, their attachment to free political institutions grew more and more positive. In a country where workers enjoyed the vote, where there were no anti-socialist laws, where elected legislative assemblies had final authority, socialism might come with considerable ease. In 1872 Marx himself had imagined a victory in democratic countries like England and the United States without violence, and Engels had said in the 1890's that the working class could come to power only through the democratic republic.[29] Workers would first gain a majority in political assemblies and then vote in their programs.

29 Vernon L. Lidtke, *The Outlawed Party: Social Democracy in Germany, 1878–1890* (Princeton, 1966), 324.

The election of socialist candidates in significant numbers to parliamentary assemblies in the 1880's bolstered Marxist interest in fighting for political reforms. Marxists tried to keep their eyes pinned on the final achievement of a socialist society, but the psychology of their millennial movement proved to be ambiguous and complex. The revolution did not come as quickly as many had expected, and although their anticipations remained high, Marxists found it essential to balance the vision of a grand, but ever-receding, utopia with attention to immediate problems. By the early 1890's Marxist parties all over Europe included reforms of the capitalist system in their political platforms. In 1891 in Germany, where democratic and parliamentary institutions were extremely weak, Karl Kautsky in a celebrated exposition of the party's newly adopted Marxist platform listed freedom of the press, the right to organize, and the universal ballot as essential conditions prerequisite to the sound development of the proletariat.[30]

Kautsky will appear again and again in these pages. Lenin's unrelenting attacks upon him for his lack of sympathy with the Bolsheviks have dimmed the luster of this former "Pope of socialism" among contemporary Marxists. He has been blamed for the gradual acclimatization of the German party to Eduard Bernstein's revisionist socialism after 1900 as well as for European socialism's unwhimpering capitulation to nationalist feeling during World War I.

These charges are unjustified even in retrospect. As Europe's leading defender of orthodox Marxism, a reputation he had had since the mid-1880's, Kautsky was awkwardly caught in the middle of a doctrinal dispute which arose after the publication of Bernstein's *Evolutionary Socialism* in 1899 and continued until the dissolution of the Second International. Rosa Luxemburg was largely responsible for Kautsky's discomfort. The brilliant young incendiary, deceptively feminine, amassed her considerable intellectual resources and tore into Bernstein. In the process of devastating his compromis-

[30] *The Class Struggle,* trans. by William E. Bohn (Chicago, 1910), 188. The Marxist platform referred to was the Erfurt Program, adopted by the Social Democrats after the repeal of the anti-socialist laws. Marxists did not regard the immediate demands in the program as compromises, for Marx himself had helped Jules Guesde write similar demands in his platform for *Le Parti ouvrier.* In fact they assumed that the Erfurt Program put the Social Democrats on firmer Marxist ground than ever before because Lassallean aspects of the former Gotha Program were wiped away.

ing propositions, she hoped to push Marxists into a new, and decidedly more revolutionary position. Marxists, she thought quite eccentrically, should act as if they believed their speeches about demolishing capitalism.

Kautsky, not seeing very clearly what was happening on his left, entered a repudiation of Bernstein which was no less sharp; but he intended to keep the German party mindful of its growing political power and wished to preserve its respect for the conservative trade unions. This was a temporizing stance to some young party workers, but it had the weight of tradition.

The man in the middle is rarely popular after the battle, and Kautsky was no exception. His occupation of the center appeared less heroic with the election of each new Social Democrat to the Reichstag, for success brings the aura of respectability which is contemptible to the revolutionary mind. But this should blot out neither Kautsky's unrivaled position in the Second International nor the fact that his brand of Marxism, however wrongly it tended to place the master's theories in a straitjacket of economic determinism, was the prevailing one of the times.[31] The books and articles of this theorist, editor, and close friend of Engels were viewed as the clearest expositions of Marxist doctrine available, even after Rosa Luxemburg's challenge. His mind was not original, but he was an incisive thinker, an indefatigable worker, and a skilful systematizer of ideas. When in 1891 he wrote about the importance of freedom of the press and the universal ballot, he was speaking for the orthodox.

Vernon Lidtke, in his study of German Social Democrats during the years of Bismarck's repressive measures against them (1878–90), has very ably described their ambivalence toward participation in a bourgeois parliament. Such activity threatened to corrupt them and seriously tame their fierce revolutionary determination. Still, tactical use of parliamentary institutions offered tremendous opportunities to advance the cause. It was a maddening position to be caught in. They wanted more political freedom and a set of ministers responsible to the Reichstag rather than to the monarch; yet they were scared to death the bourgeoisie would grant liberalizing

---

[31] For a discussion of the Marxist synthesis put together by Engels and Kautsky (aided by Bernstein, Plekhanov, W. Liebknecht, Bebel, Guesde, and Victor Adler), see George Lichtheim, *Marxism: An Historical and Critical Study* (New York, 1965), 234–76.

measures and rob them of one of their most effective rallying cries.

August Bebel, in a famous exchange with Jean Jaurès at the 1904 International Socialist Congress, insisted that Marxists should not get their heads broken "for the sake of a democratic republic." [32] Yet Bebel was, and remained until his death, the German party's leading parliamentarian. Led into the revolutionary fracas by Liebknecht, Bebel had been prepared for radicalism by a childhood of poverty. Strictly speaking, he could not claim a proletarian genealogy, for his father had been a non-commissioned officer in the military. But Bebel usually made the claim anyway. He lacked his teacher's romanticism and fell below Liebknecht in education and intellectual ability. This worked to his advantage in some ways because his narrow interest in doctrine and tactics made him a more reliable Marxist with an unfailing sense of what was necessary. As well known in the circles of the International as Liebknecht, Bebel possessed that mystical faith in the revolution which kept him oblivious of discrepancies between theory and practice. It never occurred to Bebel that his behavior did not conform to his radical creed. Other Marxists whom he inspired with the same faith could both attack and defend republican government in the same speech.

German Social Democrats, when considering the impotence of the Reichstag, sometimes openly envied the Americans (and to a lesser degree the French and the English) for their political freedoms. Franz Mehring, who belonged among the most radical Social Democrats, wrote after a trip to the United States, "Just as one sees in the United States what political freedom cannot accomplish, so one sees what it can truly accomplish and this knowledge we do not wish to see spoiled for us by the selfish cries of Junkers and Philistines." [33] A bourgeois republic alone was no remedy for capitalist injustice, but it provided a far more favorable field for progress than the system under which many workers lived.

Praise of American democratic procedures, however, was not the normal result of Marxist ambivalence. The resolution of Marxists to wipe away all lingering traces of admiration for a bourgeois America was too unwavering. Even while following a course of increasing

---

[32] *Sixième Congrès socialiste international tenu à Amsterdam du 14 au 20 août 1904: Comte-rendu analytique* (Brussels, 1904), 85.
[33] "Eine Fahrt nach Amerika," *Leipziger Volkszeitung,* July 14, 1906.

rapprochement with the institutions of political liberalism (a trend which continued to grow until 1917), they never, on the occasions when their attention was turned in this direction, let up in their efforts to smirch the glorious reputation of the United States. Marxist consciences, queasy about the acceptance of policies formerly deemed bourgeois, no doubt found flailing away at democratic institutions across the ocean cathartic. In any case, America remained Marxists' favorite illustration of the uselessness of democratic political institutions unless accompanied by social equality and social cooperation.

What had the vote accomplished for the American worker? Was his position any better than workers living in a monarchic state? Had American laborers succeeded in passing effective legislation regulating working conditions or controlling the notorious abuses of the trusts? Had their "privileges" enabled them to make the least start toward nationalizing public utilities? The firm No given by Marxists to all these questions pointed to a lesson which any child could master: "The mere possession of the franchise does not . . . protect the workman against the tyranny of capital." [34] August Bebel, in his Amsterdam speech cited earlier, reminded his fellow comrades that nowhere "could workers be treated in a fashion more brutal, more cynical and more vile than in the great bourgeois republic across the ocean which is the ideal of so many people." [35] Several years before Bebel's remark, H. M. Hyndman recalled how "several visits to the United States between 1871 and 1880 convinced me that mere Radical Republicanism had no good effect on the social question." [36] Immediately after Haymarket, the most powerful and most uncompromising of France's Marxist leaders, Jules Guesde, made precisely the same observation about America:

> There we were made to notice universal suffrage; there, the Republic; there all the liberties that have been promised you for years without ever being extended; there, no permanent army and no reli-

[34] J. Sketchley, "Political Reform and Social Revolution," *Justice*, Aug. 30, 1884.
[35] *Sixième Congrès*, 86.
[36] "H. M. Hyndman: An Interview by H. Quelch," *The Comrade*, I (Feb. 1902), 115.

gious budget; there, local autonomy—and there, however, just as in less free and less republican France, the misery in the price of over-work, unemployment, the mechanization of women and children, all the hell, in a word, of the proletariat. In the school of the grand American republic . . . what we have taught our workers is that their servitude was independent of governmental conditions, that it had its source exclusively in the economic order, or more exactly, in the private ownership of the means of production.[37]

Guesde was a narrow sectarian who founded *Le Parti ouvrier* in France in the early 1880's. Exiled for five years for his part in the Paris Commune, Guesde outgrew an adolescent fondness for an-archism and went to see Marx in London in 1880. The encounter changed his life, and he returned to France assured that he now knew the proper rules for radical agitation. He lacked personal charm and almost no one liked him. His energy, honesty, and dis-interestedness, however, compensated for an unexceptional mind; and counseled by Paul Lafargue, Marx's son-in-law and a much better thinker, he maintained his leadership over French Marxists until World War I.

A. Bruckère, one of his followers, shared Guesde's attitude toward the United States. He warned the more sanguine of his countrymen that "the most advanced program of the most radical member of the majority bloc [in France] is an accomplished fact in the United States," and still the class struggle raged on.[38] None of these were casual comments. Each of these men was fighting to prove that his formula alone offered a solution to Europe's problems. For many of them a fight for ideals was equivalent to a fight for life.

If constant reiteration is an indication of strong belief, the argu-ment in the above statements lost none of its force for Marxists in the period from 1886 to 1917. Bourgeois admiration for the American Constitution, Marxists claimed, was based on a number of erroneous assumptions. For one thing, the possession of the franchise did not guarantee, as many had implied, a meaningful choice at elections.

---

[37] "Il n'y a pas d'Atlantique," *Le Socialism au jour le jour* (Paris, 1899), 353. This book contained editorials written between 1884 and 1886 for the *Cri du peuple*.
[38] "Colorado," *Le Socialiste*, Oct. 2–9, 1904.

Marxists enlarged on a theme taken from Bryce to show how the Civil War had ended any real disagreements between the two entrenched American political parties. Both parties by 1900 were equally beholden to the interests of capital (although the Democratic party spoke more for small capitalists); and, as *Vorwärts* editorialized in 1904, the only thing at stake in an American election was the spoils of victory.[39] Put more crudely, the choice of workers in casting their ballots was whether to be cheated by the Republicans or to be robbed by the Democrats. Marxists saw nothing to choose between Cleveland, who broke the Pullman strike, McKinley, under whose regime "the politics of gaining riches in any manner" passed for transcendent morality, and Theodore Roosevelt, "a cunning American politician who . . . on account of his character and mendacity could find no admittance to a club of gentlemen."[40] Moreover men like Bryan or William Randolph Hearst, who professed a sympathy for the cause of labor, were to Marxist commentators either fools or scoundrels or both. Even the Populist party, which a very few European socialists had accorded a brief enthusiasm, was greeted by most European Marxists as a meaningless sideshow. After Henry George, they were skeptical about the economic nostrums which sprang from American soil, and the plucky band of southern and midwestern farmers who tried to dream a better America passed by them scorned or unnoticed.

Judicial safeguards, supposedly guaranteed by the Constitution, had been no more effective than the franchise in protecting American workers against their employers. Judges, Marxists believed, acted as paid agents of the propertied class and limited their activities to the dual task of issuing anti-strike injunctions and nullifying legislation smacking of reform. American legal forms might bear a democratic stamp, but ultimately the application of force against labor was no less brutal than it was in Europe. As one German newspaper noted, "For what one uses the police in Russia and Prussia, the administration of law must tender in the United States."[41] The "fair American trial" of the Chicago anarchists was

[39] "Republikaner und Demokraten," Oct. 16, 1904.
[40] "Der Anschlag gegen McKinley," *Vorwärts*, Sept. 8, 1901; "Roosevelt," *Vorwärts*, May 13, 1910.
[41] "Justizverbrechen in den Vereinigten Staaten," *Vorwärts*, Dec. 14, 1912.

a good measure, according to Marxists, of the impartiality of American courts. "Class justice perpetrated by the representatives and hirelings of capital" was the same everywhere.[42] Future indictments of William Haywood, Charles Moyer, and George Pettibone (illegally extradited from Colorado on charges of murdering the former governor of Idaho) and leaders in a 1912 strike at Lawrence, Massachusetts, gave further evidence of the "justice of an omnipresent state."[43]

In 1906 two leaders of the Western Federation of Miners, William Haywood and Charles Moyer, were charged with plotting the murder of Idaho's former governor, Frank Steunenberg. Although they lived in Colorado, they were taken across the state line without an extradition hearing and held for trial. In 1912, leaders of a bitter strike in Lawrence, Massachusetts, were indicted on the flimsiest of charges. The defendants in these cases were acquitted, but the European press gave both incidents enormous attention. Harassment of two popular American socialist journals, *Wilshire's Magazine* and *The Appeal to Reason,* concluded the Marxist case against the American Constitution and its Bill of Rights. August Bebel delivered the brief summation: "All the liberties and all the rights, though written down on paper, give to the proletariat in reality neither liberty nor justice."[44]

Through the years Marxist pronouncements betrayed occasional lapses into the old view of American promise fostered by other Europeans who were left of center on the political spectrum. The case of Franz Mehring is worth noting. A well-educated man who became a Marxist in 1890, Mehring allied with Rosa Luxemburg, Karl Liebknecht, and Georg Ledebour against Kautsky in the opening years of the twentieth century and through his writing tried to inspire Social Democrats with a new spirit of intransigence. His brilliant editorship of the *Leipziger Volkszeitung* usually made the paper livelier reading than the official party organ *Vorwärts,* but his best efforts could not prevent what he interpreted as an ebbing enthusiasm among co-workers for a revolution.

---

[42] "Aus Anlass eines Gedenktages," *Die Sozialdemokrat,* Oct. 27, 1888.
[43] Karl Liebknecht, *Rechtstaat und Klassenjustiz* (Stuttgart, 1907), 29.
[44] *Septième Congrès socialiste international tenu à Stuttgart du 16 au 24 août 1907: Compte-rendu analytique* (Brussels, 1908), 80.

In 1906 Mehring traveled to the United States and, to his admitted and perhaps unsettling surprise, enjoyed himself. He recalled Wilhelm Liebknecht's maligned account of American life and told his readers that Liebknecht had not been as blind as many colleagues had assumed. Exploitation of the American worker went on just as in Europe, and "the American exploiter is in the end the worst of all." But bright spots in American society had survived the worst excesses of capitalism, and Mehring sensed immediately upon landing in America that he was breathing a much freer atmosphere.[45]

Such comments were distinctly exceptional. Far more typical was the view of Karl Liebknecht who inherited much of his father's romanticism without the accompanying admiration for America. No more than his parent was he a first-rate thinker, but his great courage made him a hero and eventually a martyr of the socialist cause. Ideologically close to Mehring and Rosa Luxemburg, he fought for the general strike and wrote pamphlet after pamphlet against European armament. His *Militarism and Anti-Militarism* of 1907 cost him eighteen months in a German prison, and in 1914 he alone defied his party to vote against war credits in the Reichstag. He helped organize the Spartacus uprising during the war, and in January 1919, he and Rosa Luxemburg were horribly murdered by government soldiers under the new Weimar republic.

In 1910, almost twenty-five years after his father, Karl spent two months touring America. He visited most of the cities his father had seen and took an additional swing out to California. Unlike Mehring, he made no attempt to redeem his father's judgment; the United States of *Ein Blick in die Neue Welt* and the United States he reported on had nothing in common. He recalled in one speech a time (and he was referring to a time long before 1886) when "America was the Savior of the entire world; it was the paradise of all adventurers and banished men; it was the safety valve for Europe which exploded when political or economic tensions grew

---

[45] "Eine Fahrt nach Amerika," *Leipziger Volkszeitung,* July 14, 1906. Mehring reported on his trip further in the following issues of the *Leipziger Volkszeitung*: July 7, July 11, July 26, Aug. 3, and Aug. 4. See, in addition, "Mehring in Amerika," *New Yorker Volkszeitung,* June 8, 1906.

Professor Bruce Garver has also referred me to the extremely favorable comments of the important Czech leader František Soukup. His book *Amerika* recounts impressions of his 1912 visit to the United States.

too powerful. America was the sign of the new world economy."
How different were the prospects which the present reality of
America offered to the oppressed of the world. The United States
had become the "witches' Sabbath of high capital." [46] The freedom
of the American worker was now the "freedom to starve and commit suicide." The famed impartiality of American justice had grown
corrupt, the trusts had spread their tyranny into every corner of the
nation, and the attempt of workers to correct legitimate grievances
had time and again resulted in bloodshed. The younger Liebknecht
asked, "America, you savior of the World, what has become of your
past?" His answer would have upset many generations of American
pioneers: "It has all become as in Europe, only worse, much worse."
No longer was the "dream of Paradise" dreamed in America—
only the "dream of Hell." [47]

Thus, especially after the Haymarket explosion of 1886, a number
of European Marxists, writing frequently in all the major party
organs, gave their time to the task of exposing what they viewed as
spurious claims about a "workers' paradise." Tired of the migration
of European proletarians to the New World and tired of the influence of the United States in seducing European radicals to settle
for bourgeois reform, Marxists looked across the Atlantic and drew
angry caricatures of the society where capitalism had developed
more quickly and with fewer obstacles than in any land in the
world. After 1890 American liberty meant only the entrepreneur's
complete freedom to do anything he wished to make money. If the
absence of feudalism had once worked to the advantage of the
American worker, he now woke up to the disconcerting news that
the want of a tradition of noblesse oblige exposed him all the more
fully to the cruelty and brutality of an impersonal economic system.
The greater privation and greater despair of the American worker
left the European worker without any further cause for envy.

Marxists, just as most Europeans before them, were biased in their
study of America. The United States had been, and was in the late
nineteenth century, a battlefield where Europeans tested their

---

[46] Speech in New York, Oct. 14, 1910, Karl Liebknecht, *Gesammelte Reden
und Schriften,* III (Berlin, 1960), 505.
[47] Speeches of Oct. 14, 1910, and Dec. 2, 1910, *Gesammelte Reden,* III, 509–10
and 513.

ideologies and sharpened their creeds. Anti-democrats and champions of freedom alike struggled to claim the New World for their own, and what they wrote about it formed a literature of propaganda. They assumed facts in advance and prejudged truth. Events arising while the conflict was raging had no effect on one's allegiance.[48]

When Marxists appeared on this battlefield, they did not join the side in the combat normally associated with European social radicals. Their cause and the cause of Europe's reactionary anti-democrats ran curiously together. But Marxists formed no alliances and fought their battles independently. After all, the expected result of their "anti-Americanism" differed sharply from that of European conservatives. Armored with their own assumptions, Marxists shelled all the other armies on the field with American statistics. They did not fight according to the canons of objectivity, but it is doubtful whether they violated scientific standards of detachment any more than other politically committed Europeans who looked to America to prove something to themselves. Marx had once found Hegel on his head and turned him right side up to get at truth. His followers in Europe thought it essential to treat previous images of America similarly in order to show that what had once seemed a new dream was in reality the same old nightmare of Europe. Marxists saw some things in America with great clarity and managed to remind the world (however unwelcome the lesson) of the flaws in the myth of rebirth through physical relocation. To Marxists a rebirth was possible only by standing one's ground and there seeking to erect a better society. What they failed to consider was whether in substituting new myths for old they had succeeded any better than their opponents in leaving a world of fantasy.

[48] *The American Spirit in Europe,* 34.

CHAPTER 3

THE AMERICAN PROMISED LAND
Two New Marxist
Versions, 1880-1905

G<small>AYLORD</small> W<small>ILSHIRE</small>, the wealthy, eccentric, and highly unpredictable American socialist, seldom wrote with great wisdom. Yet he came close to the mark in his estimate of international socialism when he said in 1901, "It seems to be typical of all social revolutionists that national pride always asserts itself, no matter how much patriotism may be decried as mere racial selfishness whenever discussion arises as to which nation is to be the first to throw off the shackles of capitalism." [1] Marxists (at least before events in Russia and the world after 1917 forced Stalin to reconsider many issues) professed not to believe in the possibility of an isolated socialist triumph. A single, friendless cooperative commonwealth could not possibly endure the hostility of surrounding capitalist nations and would survive no longer than the glorious, but brief, Paris Commune. With this in mind Marxists normally spoke of a wave of victories which would carry all countries more or less simultaneously into the new era and warmly renewed every year or so their dedication to international solidarity.

This kind of sentiment was not idle pretense, but it had weaknesses. Wilshire did not have to travel far in England and on the Continent to sense the strength of workers' attachment to a fatherland, the *Communist Manifesto* notwithstanding. European nationalism, expressed not as intellectualized dogma, but merely as a half-

[1] See Wilshire's preface to the American edition of the *Fabian Essays* (New York, 1891), xii.

conscious sense of place and belonging, had deep roots in history, tradition, and language. As World War I was to prove, the majority of the proletariat had never left it far behind, even while marching under the unfurled banner of the Second International. In theory, the victory that workers sought recognized no national frontiers. In fact, the primary tie of European socialists was to a national party organization, and a steady advance on national lines most effectively kindled the pride of party workers and kept alive their hope for a better tomorrow. A breakthrough for socialism had to come first somewhere, and, even if an initial national success were only the signal for world revolution, the eminence which would belong to the country leading the way was worth a spirited competition. Or so it seemed to many comrades who easily reconciled this limited kind of struggle with their other ideas about cooperation and brotherhood.

For much of the nineteenth century, English Marxists, at least on theoretical grounds, had the most reason for optimism. In the years between 1840 and 1880 their country was without a peer in the extent of its capitalist development. And measured by the Marxist dialectic, a nation's movement along the paths of capitalism was a rough indicator of its nearness to the ultimate socialist revolution. Temporary circumstances might slow progress toward socialism in an industrially advanced country while special factors might accelerate the prescribed course of events in one where capitalism was only beginning to make inroads. Marxists (at least when they were careful) avoided the flat statement that the revolution could come only in the country where the capitalist structure was most highly developed. Nevertheless, economic maturity was the critical factor; and, because England's lead in matters of bourgeois production and exploitation had for so long been unchallenged, Marx had described it in 1870 as "for the time being the most important country for the worker's revolution, and moreover the *only* country in which the material conditions for this revolution have developed up to a certain point of maturity." [2]

As Germany and France hastened to shake off the last of their feudal habits and emerged as rival capitalist powers to England, the latter's claim to priority in the revolutionary struggle faded. During

[2] Marx to Meyer and Vogt, April 9, 1870, *Correspondence*, 290.

the 1880's, socialist organizations in England remained relatively weak. The failure of H. M. Hyndman to interest English Labor in his programs was matched only by his sensational bungling of personal relations with Marx and Engels. The latter two men had a hearty contempt for their self-christened disciple and furiously denounced his Social Democratic Federation for its hairsplitting concern with doctrine. The Socialist League, though granted Engels' stamp of approval, could survive the guidance of the superb but highly erratic William Morris only a few years, and this Marxist society gave over its floundering organization to the anarchists in 1890. The Fabian Society was somewhat more successful in the late 1880's than the others in influencing trade union leaders, but Marxists on the Continent had no sympathy for its scholarly pursuits and tactics of class accommodation. In their minds, as long as the working class had to learn socialism from men like George Bernard Shaw and Sidney Webb, the chances of the English movement getting off the ground remained remote.

While English socialists had trouble emerging from obscurity during the 1880's, comrades on the Continent made substantial, in some cases spectacular, gains. The German Social Democratic party successfully got around the heavy restrictions which Bismarck placed on its activity from 1878 to 1890 and grew into a political force which became an ideal for socialist parties all over Europe. Its organization was the most unified, its theorists were the most influential, its relations with the trade unions were the strongest, and (most important) its skill in capturing the electorate had proved the most effective. When Bismarck's anti-socialist laws were cast aside as failures in 1890, it regularly polled more votes than any other party in Germany.[3] As is human, the growth of party pride matched, if not surpassed, the growth of party membership.

Other European socialists studied German successes with measured admiration, but their bows of obeisance were never low and from the German point of view never appropriately humble. Jean

[3] One must bear in mind that Germany before World War I did not have a parliamentary government. The Reichstag had very limited powers. Also, owing to Germany's suffrage structure, the number of representatives the party elected was never commensurate with its vote. In 1893 the Social Democracy obtained for the first time a plurality of the popular vote, but not until 1912 did it become the strongest party in the Reichstag.

Jaurès' stinging rebuke to the arrogance of German comrades at the 1904 International Socialist Congress effectively demonstrated the unwillingness of socialists in neighboring states to linger in Germany's shadow. In fact, almost all of the nations which formed the Second International in 1889 harbored secret suspicions about their own likely preeminence. While French socialists squabbled among themselves and could not count on trade union support to the same degree as the German Social Democrats, while they continued to follow the diverse banners of Guesde, Brousse, Jaurès, and Allemane and never quite wove the fabric of a flag that would have given them a common purpose, the French counted on at least two (though not particularly compatible) advantages over the Germans. First, the country had inherited from the past century a strong tradition of revolution. Second, France's parliament was not powerless like the Reichstag and afforded socialists a machinery which could be used to change economic policy. Either or both of the factors, so claimed the local party presses, could allow France to outstrip her rivals in entering the socialist era. This was an abstract confidence, but victories in local elections and contests for parliamentary deputies were encouraging and gave French desires a plausible basis in fact.

Socialists in less important countries naturally found it more difficult to draw attention to their successes. But everywhere in Europe social ferment drew socialists and labor into a common struggle and raised the expectations of this newly created political force. Comrades in diminutive countries like Belgium and Holland turned their size into an advantage and argued socialism could more easily find a majority in a small country. Voices even from so unlikely a candidate for socialist victory as agrarian Russia offered the village commune (or *mir*) as evidence that socialism was part of the Russian soul. No nation was willing to accept in advance an unquestioned consignment to second place. In the rapidly changing world of the early twentieth century, anything appeared possible.

Given such levels of national feeling, one wonders that European Marxists ever bothered to cast even a condescending glance at what was transpiring in the young republic across the Atlantic. Many of them, as the reader has been cautioned, never did. They ignored, and were consequently ignorant of, the simplest facts about American life. America was too far away to have an appreciable effect on day-to-day activities of European socialists, and it did not seem worth the bother of close study. Daniel De Leon, the quarrelsome leader of America's Socialist Labor party, found this inattention galling. In his mind the Germans were especially guilty, for their vanity completely blocked their view of more significant socialist progress in countries far ahead of Germany in both political and economic development. (De Leon wrote "countries" in the plural, but he was thinking just of the United States.) He went so far as to assert that a certain class of immigrants from Germany tried to hold back the socialist movements in countries where they took refuge "lest—oh, horror!—it outclass the Movement in Germany." [4]

De Leon's considerable bitterness toward the German Social Democrats was, while irrational, understandable. A number of German-American socialists, including Morris Hillquit, Victor Berger, Henry Slobodin, and Hermann Schlüter, had been instrumental in the formation of the Socialist party of America which for all practical purposes had put his own Socialist Labor party out of business. The leading German figures consistently sided with De Leon's rivals, and *Die Neue Zeit,* the official journal of the Social Democrats, brought his name up only when it wished to criticize his tactics. Nevertheless, many socialists in Europe complained, albeit in different terms than De Leon's, of their countrymen's slender knowledge of the events changing the face of America. One can take seriously the remark of Karl Kautsky, who said of European socialist scholarship, "We produce so little about America and yet American conditions are of the greatest importance." [5]

These lamentations are significant, but they somewhat overstate the case. From its origins the United States had enjoyed a special sort of fame in the world's list of nations, and its growth in the late nineteenth century into a major political and economic power added a more ordinary, though no less significant, dimension to its importance. From 1880 on, the danger of European observers forgetting entirely about the United States was greatly lessened. Especially for

[4] De Leon, *Flashlights of the Amsterdam Congress* (New York, 1904), 6 and 41.
[5] Letter of Kautsky to Hermann Schlüter, May 17, 1904, Kautsky Archives, International Institute of Social History, Amsterdam.

Marxists, forces at work in post-Civil War America, even if they rarely forced this country to the center of Marxist consciousness, prevented the situation from ever getting quite as bad as Kautsky or De Leon pretended. Chief among these was the impressively rapid growth of American capitalism. America's rise to industrial supremacy was phenomenal, and by 1890 most European observers regarded the United States as the most highly developed of the capitalist nations. Only a few doubted that its complete preeminence in world markets was inevitable. No Marxist writer, however parochial, could ignore this incredible story of capitalist development. What England had been for so much of the century, the United States was now becoming. And just as England's ascendancy had had certain implications for Marxist theory, so now had America's. No other event of the century, in fact, had more potential importance to the Marxist framework of thought. If socialist knowledge of the United States remained weak (which it did), the cause was not really attributable to a lack of attention; it lay much more in the ingrained habit of Marxists of looking to America with preconceived notions of what had to happen there.

The scholarly Kautsky, who carried on an extensive correspondence with many American socialists, did as much as any man to keep his European confederates apprised of the flow of events in the United States. In the 1890's and early 1900's, reports from America, filed by F. A. Sorge, Hermann Schlüter, Adolf Hepner, Max Beer, Philipp Rappaport, G. A. Hoehn, J. L. Franz, and Julius Vahlteich, took up a great deal of space in *Die Neue Zeit,* which Kautsky edited. In an article he wrote in 1902, Kautsky made it clear why he attached vast importance to such information:

> The United States are today unquestionably the most important and the most interesting of the modern culture lands. Not England, but America shows us our future, in so far as one country can reveal it at all to another, since each has its own peculiar development. In America capitalism is making its greatest progress; it rules there more absolutely and with more ruthlessness than anywhere else. The class struggles are sharpening there to the highest possible degree. And at the same time through the growing competition of America this tendency toward sharpening class struggles is pressed on the

other industrial countries—or rather this tendency which exists everywhere is growing through the pressure of American competition.[6]

Kautsky's reasoning here should seem familiar, for he was rephrasing ideas which Marx and Engels had suggested long before: America's meteor-like rise to economic power might prove to be the factor in international economics which all Marxists had so eagerly awaited, the factor which would topple capitalism and clear the ground for the raising of a new economy. Europeans of many persuasions had for years found reasons to portray America as a promised land. Now, in their own peculiar way, some important European Marxist spokesmen found reasons of their own.

European Marxists had launched a major propaganda attack in the mid-1880's on what they thought was a sentimental, but common, myth about the United States as a land of equality, prosperity, and opportunity. Yet because of the ironical view of progress ensconced in the Marxist dialectic, the same evidence employed in exposing imaginary stories about capitalist America could be turned around and used to confirm the idea of a unique destiny for the trans-Atlantic nation. America's brutally oppressive economic system had changed a vision of paradise into a vision of hell. That much was clear. Everyone could see now how short-sighted had been former bourgeois admiration for the United States. Nevertheless, the very ruthlessness and strength of America's burgeoning economic system made the United States a special country with a vitally important role to play on the world stage. John Winthrop, in embarking on his famous voyage on the *Arabella,* had held out different hopes for the New World than nineteenth-century Marxists, but many of the latter came around to the view that the fulfilment of European dreams awaited developments in the New World. No sooner had Marxists rejected and swept out the back door one image of the American Promised Land, than they were ushering a new version of the American Canaan in through the front.

Kautsky's remarks in his 1902 article, as well as the earlier writings

[6] "Bauernagitation in Amerika," *Die Neue Zeit,* Vol. XX, Part II (1901–2), 453.

of Marx and Engels, direct attention to a basic dualism in European Marxism's revised conception of an American Promised Land. The United States was capable of exciting Marxist interest for two reasons which could be (and usually were) entirely separated from each other. On the one hand, according to Marxists, the class struggle might take a dramatic turn in the New World, produce a swift victory for socialism in the United States, and bring America's happy citizens into the era of the cooperative commonwealth sooner than anywhere else. This view represented a sharp reversal in all expectations prevailing prior to 1880. On the other hand, an older Marxist opinion held that the United States, either through its growing financial competition with Europe or as a result of one of its repeated industrial crises, would provoke the long-delayed revolution in Europe. A prior socialist revolution in the United States was not anticipated or required. Although both possibilities were suggested by the mighty advance of American capitalism and relied for force on images of Yankee bourgeois corruption, the latter conveniently left the initiative for the revolution with the comrades of the Old World whose hands and bodies showed the scars of a class struggle waged over many decades. Marxists who waited impatiently to remake Europe and consequently attached critical importance to American developments were not necessarily prepared to see those same developments giving American socialists any claims to pre-eminence.

America's promise as viewed from Europe had always contained this duality. Europeans looked for the rejuvenation of European men who actually ventured to the New World as well as the converse transforming influence of American power and strength on the men and institutions which remained behind in Europe. Americans, because of their political and social environment, became different from what they had been in Europe, but their changed ways had an influence which stretched back across the Atlantic. Tocqueville and Bryce had managed to keep both things in mind when they wrote about America; but when Marxists set out to strip these two varieties of American promise of their bourgeois sentimentality they sometimes did not see, as had many of their predecessors, rebirth in the Old World and regeneration in the New as opposite sides of the same coin.

When European Marxists looked to America as the site of the first socialist victory, their story, despite the dramatic inversions of the reasons behind the New World's own reinvigoration, had discernibly traditional outlines. At least the transformation of America preceded and prescribed the transformation of Europe. On the other hand, when Marxists linked America's beneficent transforming power to the expansion of its capitalist system, they were sharply revising this pattern. America would not convert Europe by the force of its good example but would serve in a mechanical and terrifying way to destroy the old order of Europe. From this point of view, if America underwent a metamorphosis too soon and switched to socialism, the transforming pressures it exerted on Europe would collapse. The Marxist interpretation of history required that badness precede and give birth to goodness, and European Marxists, at least in the opinion of some, needed American evil for a little while longer.

To Marx and Engels no single factor had seemed better able to explain the unexpected delay in the collapse of capitalism than the ability of European industry to dispose of its overproduced goods in foreign countries. They had credited the opening of new markets in North and South America as well as in the Orient with saving Europe (especially England) from total collapse in the mid-nineteenth century. The deferment had disappointed Marx and Engels, but knowledge of the world's finite size saved them from despair. One day the number of untapped markets in the world would be used up, and the countries which had absorbed European markets would supply their own needs and turn their backs on Europe. Advanced European nations were in an inescapable dilemma because every effort to extend their trade into another part of the world introduced Western techniques there and soon created a competitor. Kautsky summed up succinctly what Marxists anticipated as the denouement of this process when he wrote in 1891, "The moment is drawing near when the markets of the industrial countries can no longer be extended and will begin to contract. But this would mean the bankruptcy of the whole capitalist system." [7]

Of all the developing areas the United States quickly stood out as the most important. Not only by 1880 was this previously important

[7] *The Class Struggle,* 84.

outlet for European surplus goods supplying a large part of its own needs, but American agriculture and industry were competing with Europe for markets around the world. European manufacturers even discovered their own sales at home threatened by an influx of American goods. Cries went up in commercial circles all over Europe (especially in Germany) for high protective tariffs to ward off the "American danger," and Marxists jumped to the conclusion that even the bourgeoisie no longer believed it possible to keep the capitalist system running smoothly for much longer. Every retreat from free competition testified to the bankruptcy of the old order.

Through the 1880's and most of the 1890's Marxists could write about the coming catastrophe of European capitalism with a heedless holiday spirit. When Wilhelm Liebknecht in 1880 predicted the collapse of the Old World's economy because of America's entrance into the European grain market, *Die Sozialdemokrat* declared calmly that "scientific socialism sees in American grain competition one of the best guarantees of its quick success." [8] The world of the nineteenth century would come tumbling down like a house of cards. Engels, although more cautious and soberer than many of his followers about the immediate outlook, wrote enthusiastically to Florence Kelley Wischnewetzky in 1886 on the prospects of America's breaking England's virtual monopoly on the world market. Once industrial countries had lost the luxury of being able to dispose of surplus products at will, gluts in domestic markets would bring the class struggle to its last stage and ensure the workers of a quick control of the reins of power.[9]

August Bebel, as Eduard Bernstein was only too delighted to point out, performed his duties in the Reichstag with a truly bourgeois feeling for give and take, but he was also master of all the incendiary rhetoric of the labor movement.[10] As was true for most Marxists who lived in the world of the Second International, images of flames and destruction revolved in his mind on an independent track. Never far beneath the surface, they were always available when Bebel wished to buttress his belief in the imminence

[8] "Die revolutionäre Kraft des amerikanischen Kornes," Oct. 24, 1880.
[9] Engels to Florence Kelley Wischnewetzky, Feb. 3, 1886, *Letters to Americans,* 149–50.
[10] Bernstein's remark quoted in Max Beer, *Fifty Years of International Socialism* (London, 1935), 131–32.

of revolution. Again and again through the 1880's and 1890's he linked the death of Europe to the rise of the American colossus and its pouring of goods into the already overflowing pool of the world market.[11] Somehow the failure of each successive crisis to materialize never bothered him, and he and his co-workers became adept at shifting the timetable of revolution. What was not permissible, at least to those who reduced Marx's theories to a simpleminded mechanism, was to set the date of capitalism's breakup more than a decade away. For if the achievement of socialism belonged to some remote future era, revolutionists might just as well join the bourgeois reformers and concentrate on rendering capitalist methods of distribution, production, and welfare more equitable. Marx had never said this; but as long as America persevered in its aggressive quest for economic power, his followers saw no reason to search the patriarch's writings for better answers.

Marxists had one problem in picturing the United States as the vehicle to humiliate the owning classes of Europe. The propaganda of economic breakdown, however vivid and useful it was for stirring faith in the nearness of victory, did not leave its intended hearers entirely comfortable. Many trade unionists showed an increasing concern that any impending economic disorders would involve them as well as their enemies. They might take some comfort in the vision of capitalists shortly getting tumbled from power; but, if socialism were to come as a result of the sudden crumbling of the capitalist edifice, the worker was most certainly going to be hit by a few flying bricks. Many workers reasoned correctly that since they stood at the bottom of the social structure the bulk of the rubble would fall on them.

In the 1880's and 1890's Marxists seeking to make the United States into an unwitting avenging angel did not duck the issue. The author of the article in *Die Sozialdemokrat* who heralded American grain competition as the greatest boost to scientific socialism in years conceded that the laborer would be the first to feel the strains of a general economic depression and would be the first to be out of

---

[11] Letter to Engels, Nov. 14, 1882, *August Bebel: Briefwechsel mit Friedrich Engels*, 140–41; *Unsere wirtschaftliche und politische Lage* (Zurich, 1893), 15–16 and 23; Speech of Jan. 22, 1903, *August Bebel: Auswahl aus seinen Reden* (Berlin, 1926), 87–88.

work. But while there was cause to "regret the poverty that it [economic collapse] calls forth," while anyone would be "sorry for the unhappy victims of an overwhelming power," such economic misery would force workers "to grasp on to the only thing that can help them—socialism." [12]

Vorwärts, which became the official daily of the German Social Democracy after the legal ban on activities was lifted in 1890, came to similar conclusions in 1896. Certainly, as a result of America's intrusion into the arena of world capitalism and its anachronistic tariff policies, "the worker will suffer in the most severe degree," but the event would also "promote in Europe the dissolution of the intermediate layer between large capital and the proletariat, deepen class opposition, and accelerate greatly the collapse of the present economic order." [13]

How heroically a worker might respond to these declarations of Marxist science depended largely on his sense of well-being. From the depths of Hell nothing seems bad, but in Purgatory one can imagine worse; and going to Hell with the worthless plutocrats in the world, no matter how this might improve one's chances of admission to Paradise, is an alarming prospect. Trade unionists had normally been far more conservative than Marxist leaders, and certainly by 1900, European workers had won enough benefits through trade union activity to believe that they had a great deal to lose and could not listen to Marxist descriptions of Europe's chaotic collapse with equanimity. For that matter, socialist parties were established well enough in Europe to have developed bureaucratic attachments to the system. A Marxist did not have to become revisionist to see that parliamentary activity was getting him somewhere and that he had as much to lose as anyone in a few weeks of revolutionary struggle.

Pressures from both inside and outside the ranks of the orthodox put Marxists in a dilemma. They did not want to lessen in any way their dedication to the millennium. On the other hand, the fate of Christian churches which had tried to make the notion of temporary suffering for the sake of a higher reward palatable to the working

[12] "Die revolutionäre Kraft des amerikanischen Kornes," Oct. 24, 1880.
[13] "MacKinley's Sieg," Nov. 5, 1896.

man gave timely warning. The pews of the International could also be emptied. Marxists met the situation by giving words in the traditional rhetoric different meanings. In the 1890's revolution had already lost for most Marxists its connotations of violence and turbulent upheaval. At least most of them had ceased to regard attempts to escape violence as equivocation. Also, although they had incautiously continued to suggest the imminence of revolution and had emphasized the suddenness of the transformation from capitalism to socialism, they explored increasingly around the turn of the century the possibility of a bridge to the cooperative commonwealth which would span the chasm of chaos and economic collapse.

These shifts in emphasis impinge on our story in an important way. Against a growing caution among European workers, the aspect of America's image of a Promised Land which has been under scrutiny grew less noticeable in Marxist literature. Deliverance from capitalist oppression would have to come in some other way. Nowhere was the changing attitude more evident than in the arguments which German Social Democrats began to use shortly before 1900 to answer the industrial and agricultural interests in Germany who were demanding higher protective tariffs. European Marxists had long been unwavering proponents of free trade, but at this late date the Social Democrats had evidently forgotten the revolutionary grounds on which Marx and Engels had based their support. Marx had closed his famous 1848 speech on the subject with the fighting peroration:

> The protective system in these days is conservative, while the free trade system works destructively. It breaks up old nationalities and carries antagonism of proletariat and bourgeoisie to the uttermost point. In a word, the free trade system hastens the social revolution. In this revolutionary sense, alone, gentlemen, I am in favor of free trade.[14]

In a similar vein, Engels, after having erroneously predicted that Grover Cleveland's Democratic administration would lead America into the era of free trade, welcomed in 1892 the disruptive effect of

[14] Closing lines of *Free Trade,* a speech delivered before the Democratic Club of Brussels on Jan. 9, 1848.

the fall of the protective tariff in America. The expected crisis signified "the final battle of socialism in England."[15]

Somewhere along the line, as one Junker paper the *Kreuz-Zeitung* happily pointed out, Marxists had shifted the argument.[16] Social Democrats at the end of the century ignored Marx's and Engels' explicit caveat that free trade could in no way better the economic situation of the worker and argued for a lower duty, not because it hastened the demise of the old order but because it gave the worker a fairer share of the spoils of capitalism. Paul Lensch, writing in 1905 in the *Leipziger Volkszeitung,* did not object to protection because it dulled the outlines of the class struggle. Rather, to raise German tariffs would make bread, as meat already was, "a delicacy for the worker's household."[17]

To pursue this contention, German Marxists had to extricate themselves from a self-created inconsistency. Their business-oriented opponents in the tariff controversy maintained that American economic competition threatened to ruin German agriculture and industry—a possibility Marxists themselves had pointed to in the past and an eventuality which they had in erstwhile days sincerely desired. The mood of labor had changed, or at least their true conservatism was now apparent; and Marxists had to reverse ground and portray America as a paper tiger, urging German commercial interests all the while to meet the threat of American competition with more intelligent business methods and new technology.[18]

Social Democrats feared that a tariff war between Germany and the United States would greatly impair the health of Germany's economy, and they now voiced belated concern about the consequences to the worker. *Vorwärts* spoke in 1897 of the desirability of a "better regulated arrangement of our trade connections [between the United States and Germany] based on good will on both sides"

[15] "Die amerikanische Präsidentenwahl," *Vorwärts,* Nov. 16, 1892.
[16] See comment on this in *Vorwärts,* Oct. 29, 1901.
[17] "Ein echter Schippel," Oct. 23, 1905.
[18] See, for example, "Deutschland und die amerikanische Zollpolitik," *Vorwärts,* Aug. 1, 1897; "Die amerikanische Konkurrenz," *Vorwärts,* July 16, 1901; "Der englisch-amerikanische Konkurrenzkampf," *Vorwärts,* Feb. 3, 1901; "Die amerikanische Gefahr," Parts I and II, *Vorwärts,* May 15 and 16, 1902; Der Handelsvertrag mit den Vereinigten Staaten," *Leipziger Volkszeitung,* Oct. 7, 1905; "Ein echter Schippel," *Leipziger Volkszeitung,* Oct. 23, 1905; "Das Handelsabkommen mit Amerika," *Vorwärts,* May 7, 1907.

and said, "We will resist with all our might the outbreak of a tariff war for which the German workers must pay with an increase in the price of their bread, their meat, and their light." [19] For years Marxists had pointed to the shrinking outlets for European products and predicted that the capitalist powers would go down struggling for some remote corner of Africa. In a different context, they not only saw opportunity for accommodation among these nations, they were actively urging cooperation. Karl Kautsky argued in 1903, "As long as the present regime lasts, not only the capitalists, but also the workers, have an interest in trade agreements." [20]

The apparent confusion in goals was best illustrated in an article by J. Karski which appeared in the *Leipziger Volkszeitung* in 1909. Appalled by the idiocy of protective duties in both Germany and the United States, he pointed out that a threatening tariff war between the two countries "would doubtlessly harm both lands very much, especially the workers here and there." Karski proceeded, without any sense of the impropriety of the task, to warn the bourgeoisie of its own folly: "Furthermore, the raising of the protective tariff in the United States would be grist for the mill of the English protectionists; and that is perhaps the most dangerous consequence, for the moment England breaks with the system of free trade and grasps onto protection . . . an era of capitalist struggles will open such as the world has never before seen. Only the capitalists should not forget that in these fights capitalism itself can be blown up." [21] Marxists had the golden opportunity to hasten capitalism's demise by encouraging businessmen to engage in a death struggle on an international scale, but most comrades shied so far away from the effort that they came very close to preaching sermons in entrepreneurial solidarity.

All of this fits into the familiar story of the rightward drift of European socialism in the years before World War I. In the 1880's and 1890's Marxists had usually been careful to employ a less inflam-

[19] "Deutschland und die Vereinigten Staaten," April 11, 1897.
[20] "Die Handelsverträge und der Zolltarif," *Vorwärts,* June 7, 1903.
[21] "Der neue amerikanische Zolltarif," May 8, 1909. Interestingly, one group of very conservative revisionists led by Max Schippel and Ludwig Quessel did urge retaliation to American tariff policies. Their motives, however, were strictly nationalistic, and they were hardly interested in promoting the collapse of the German economy.

matory vocabulary when speaking before legislative assemblies, and after 1900 the mainstream of European Marxism approached more and more, if not the theoretical position of socialist revisionism, certainly its untroubled attachment to tactical parliamentarianism. Electoral gains redirected proletarian interest toward winning peaceful control and brightened the proletariat's chances of legislating socialism without first having to endure an uncomfortable period of violent turmoil. As Carl Landauer summed up European socialism on the eve of World War I, "Everywhere on the European continent and in the United States, socialist theory was dominated by Marxism, but emphasis was laid on the evolutionary rather than the revolutionary traits of Marxist philosophy." [22] By 1914 cooperation between socialist and liberal parties inside and outside of parliaments existed on a scale utterly unpermissible twenty-five years before. Against such a historical perspective the idea of the juggernaut of American capitalism overwhelming Europe had little true relevance.

Marxists were creatures of their habits and traditions, and they still wrote about capitalism coming down with a crash. Orthodox Marxists did not stop to adjust theory to practice (as critics on the right urged) or practice to theory (as critics on the left argued) and tried to go on carrying an intellectual load that soon became impossible to balance. The new century barely slowed down the Marxist custom of pointing to each economic crisis in the New World and announcing the *Götterdämmerung* of world capitalism, although they stood prepared to vote for almost any measure to prevent it. The anticipated crash (and this is the key point) had lost the savage force of the original image; and the Marxists who had predicated a European victory on American competition now expected workers to have sufficient political power in the decisive days ahead to catch the economy on the way down and to build it back up into a socialist state before serious harm had been done. If America still offered some hope for initiating the metamorphosis of Europe, it had to be in a gentler way. For twenty years Marxists had threatened European capitalists with American economic power; the time came when they looked at the menacing face of America and became frightened themselves.

[22] Landauer, *European Socialism,* I (Berkeley, 1959), 482.

If America was not to be part of a violent transformation of Europe, it could perhaps work to change Europe by its own good example. Only before it could do this, America first had to shed its former skin and produce new citizens and new institutions which *this* time would truly merit the world's emulation.

The Marxist writers discussed so far believed that America held the key to the future, but that it unlocked a great future only for Europe. The promise they saw in the New World was reserved strictly for the Europeans who stayed home and was not designed to offer comfort to native-born American workers or the thousands of European laborers who had fled across the Atlantic in search of a better life. Most European Marxists who addressed themselves to the question no doubt appreciated the poetic justice of this view of America's special destiny, for the rewards did not fall to the deserters. Old World revolutionaries never forgave their comrades who, accepting "Americanism" as a substitute for socialism, had left Europe in search of an easy way to Paradise, and the stigma attaching to these apostates threw suspicion even on the unwilling immigrants whose Marxism remained sincere.

The other possible interpretation of the American Promised Land did not occur to Marxists as early as the first, but it also appeared in the 1880's. Perhaps developments in America simply would not allow the European proletariat to assume a preassigned role of leadership, but would hurl the United States into a position where it would transform Europe only after it had transformed itself. No matter how difficult it was to concede priority to America in the coming world revolution, Marxist science as then interpreted strongly suggested the probability of a very early socialist victory in the United States. If capitalism was growing there by such enormous leaps and bounds and if the expansion of capitalism by necessity called forth its antithesis which was socialism, America had an excellent chance of leading the world into its final historical stage. If the American worker really suffered most (as many European Marxists had heard and said), fairness required that he should have the first taste of a life which had left the "wonders" of free enterprise behind. The identical evidence of capitalist oppression and corruption which Marxists had used to ridicule America's bourgeois admirers forced these same tough-minded critics of the "American way" to see a new glimmer of promise. After Haymarket, Marxists writing about this country had almost uniformly depicted the United States as the worst of all possible worlds. A decade later many of them had accepted at least in part the old myth about the regenerative qualities of the American experience and were arguing (faithful to their understanding of the dialectic) that the worst would soon become the best. Out of the raw and unfettered savagery of American capitalism (an image which compares in an interesting way to some earlier visions of the American wilderness) would come the initiative, energy, and imagination to construct a better world. The people who had been most blessed at the inception of their nation would shortly recover their favored position. Their city on the hill would become the commune on the hill.

The history of the United States in the last half of the nineteenth century should have furnished European Marxists with a textbook model of the operation of their theories. The origins of class struggle in Europe were remote by the latter part of the century, and capitalist modes of oppression had been confused with those lingering from the feudal period. The continuing power of the Junker class in Germany as well as the perilous course of the French Republic in the 1890's supplied evidence that the bourgeois revolution in Europe was neither complete nor secure.

Things were more clear-cut in the United States. Feudal vestiges did not confuse understanding of modern social ailments, and the class struggle had only emerged with America's post-Civil War industrial boom. Marxists looked to America for a simple and unmixed confirmation of their thesis about the parallel rising of capitalism and socialism. Although he was to feel differently by the end of the century, Eduard Bernstein in 1890 confidently rested his Marxism (at that time, Orthodox) on evidence from the United States: "We see modern socialism enter and take root in the United States in direct relation to the spreading of capitalism and the appearance of a modern proletariat." [23] The statement was immoderate because Marxian socialism in the United States at the time had the allegiance of only a handful of immigrants who knew

[23] "Herr Sartorius von Waltershausen über den modernen Sozialismus in den Vereinigten Staaten von Amerika," *Die Neue Zeit*, Vol. IX, Part I (1890–91), 73.

neither the language nor the customs of their adopted land, but it was quite ordinary.

Bernstein and others who felt as he did in 1890 were still showing the lingering effects of the enthusiasm generated in 1886 by the Haymarket incident and Henry George's mayoralty race in New York as a labor candidate. In 1886 many observers had found reason to regard the American labor movement as the most advanced in the world, and except for Germany the claim was not without foundation. The strike that was called for May 1 to demand an eight-hour working day had been a unique venture; and although the tradition was not continuous from that year, America had celebrated the labor movements first May Day on this occasion. Few European countries could boast of a political force as successful as the one Henry George had led in New York later the same year. One journal of Marxist opinion in France had declared bluntly four months before Haymarket, "Two labor classes occupy the head of the international movement, the German proletariat and the American proletariat: we must keep abreast of all their activities." [24]

A score of additional comments in the European Marxist press of 1886 revealed the eagerness with which Marxists seized any evidence of movement in the United States. Of course, Marxists made news of progress anywhere in the world; but, agreeing with Engels who had expected a single explosive event to jolt the American worker out of his complacency, many responded with unusual enthusiasm to Haymarket as a second shot heard round the world. The incident became more than an occasion to express outrage at capitalist abuses and expose the emptiness of the American legacy. It was for some, however briefly, a declaration of America's primacy in the revolutionary struggle.

According to Jules Guesde's paper *Le Socialiste,* the die was cast at Haymarket, the breach in the American capitalist fortress was opened: "The social revolution announces itself in the United States . . . and is the tocsin for the social revolution in England, France, Germany, in a word, in all the civilized world." [25] Later on in 1886, Guesde went on to describe the 67,000 votes cast for George in New York as an "entire army" of socialist-minded proletarians

[24] *Le Socialiste,* Jan. 16, 1886.
[25] "Lettre d'Amérique," May 29, 1886.

sprung suddenly from the soil.[26] Guesde's *Parti ouvrier* was only a few years old, and what was happening in America struck him, quite honestly, as being as promising and encouraging as events at home.

The English Marxist James Blackwell, a relatively minor functionary in the Social Democratic Federation, saw things at first-hand. Writing back an article for *Justice* in 1886, he declared, "Organised Socialism is strong in this country. All the material for a Social Revolution lies at hand."[27] Both Edward Aveling, who traveled to the United States in that year, and H. M. Hyndman, who had made several trips to America before 1886, agreed about the implication of Haymarket. Who would have thought before that class warfare was "almost more threatening" in the New than in the Old World or that the United States perhaps stood nearest to the "greatest and most universal revolution, whose end will be the abolition of wage-slavery?"[28] English socialists, if one were to believe a report which Aveling and his wife made before the Socialist League, were not so numerous as their American counterparts, ran behind them a poor second with respect to organization, and were not even in the running when it came to ties with the working class.[29]

Signs in 1886 of a great transition in the attitudes of American labor stirred the attention of normally chauvinistic Germans as well. An article in a September issue of *Die Sozialdemokrat,* while designating America the "classic land of the free middle class," said, "The American labor movement, as the social development of America generally, lays claim increasingly to our interest."[30] Wilhelm Liebknecht, the Avelings' traveling companion in the New World, saw numerous and clear examples of the spirit of laissez-faire giving way before the spirit of cooperation. And he added, "The conquering —not of individualism, but its ugly and generally harmful abuses— will be carried out far more easily and more quickly, in my firm

[26] "Comme en Amérique," *Le Socialisme au jour le jour,* 393–94.
[27] "American Notes," May 15, 1886.
[28] For Hyndman's comments, see his pamphlet *The Chicago Riots and the Class War in the United States* (London, 1886), 8. For those of Aveling, see *An American Journey,* 39–40.
[29] *The Commonweal,* Jan. 29, 1887.
[30] "Von jenseits des Ozeans," Sept. 22, 1886.

opinion, in the New World than in the Old." America was "fated by providence as the land of the future."[31] August Bebel was so impressed by the apparent upward surge in labor militancy that he predicted Henry George would be swung over completely to socialism and would lead the workers to significant triumphs in the next election as the presidential candidate on an independent labor ticket.[32] Marxists in the capitals of Europe stood waiting while America prepared once again to show the world its future.

The sequels to the events in 1886 were a great letdown. George moved right rather than left (even going so far as to say that the Chicago anarchists were justly condemned), and the entire experiment with a third-party labor ticket crumbled. Guesde's trumped-up army vanished, and New York workers scampered back to their accustomed places in the Republican and Democratic parties. European Marxists had to adjust themselves to writing about a socialist movement in America which always was to be but never quite was, about a labor class which struggled fiercely (no one would deny that) but which never became class conscious. They forced a good bit of fantasy into their writings and substituted obstinacy for observation, but their predictions helped sustain a central belief of the Marxist theoretical system, the inevitability of socialism.

Setbacks were not sufficiently discouraging to overwhelm the faithful; and confidence in the potential strength of the American labor movement showed, at least until 1905, no signs of weakening. In fact, if one counted six or seven years on either side of 1900, one would have the years when optimistic statements about the future of American socialism were most numerous. The number of such utterances in this span of years alone would indicate the heightening of expectations, and the statements themselves showed a freshness and vitality which were notably lacking later.

The reasons why European Marxists in these particular years expected great things of the American socialist movement were not entirely, or even mostly, attributable to objective circumstances. Predictions about America were rarely far removed from doctrinal preoccupations, and especially in this period there was a need to respond to revisionist socialists who had accepted the liberals' con-

---

[31] *Ein Blick in die Neue Welt,* 133 and 281.
[32] Bebel to Engels, Nov. 2, 1886, *Briefwechsel mit Engels,* 300.

tention about the American experience refuting Marxist orthodoxy. Extravagant answers were sometimes required. In some exceptional cases high expectations for America grew out of discouragement with progress at home.

Nevertheless there was a restlessness in the American working class, marked by several major strikes in the 1890's and early 1900's, which Marxists could legitimately look upon as encouraging. The socialist vote was growing, native-born Americans were finding their way into the movement, and socialist leaders were gradually resolving splits in their ranks. A convention in Indianapolis in November 1901 gave birth to the new, unified Socialist party which was big enough to house socialists of almost every persuasion. De Leon's choice of aloofness was largely for personal reasons and it was probably just as well. Socialist influence within the American Federation of Labor remained a constant headache for Samuel Gompers, and delegates to the 1902 AFL convention narrowly defeated a socialist-backed resolution advising "the working people to organize their economic and political power to secure for labor the full equivalent of its toil." [33] The defeated proposition sounded no ringing endorsement of Marxism, but members of the International in Europe were content. Any movement of the American workers beyond the stage of complete theoretical backwardness, when seen against the readiness of economic conditions in the United States, was highly auspicious. To push forward to victory, the proletariat in the New World would need little further prodding.

Paul Louis, though not a leading activist in the socialist ranks, was one of the most respected interpreters of Marx in France. His books on economics and history became standard texts for a young man grappling with socialist classics for the first time. Speaking of conditions in the United States, he wrote in *La Guerre économique* in 1900, "No country has shown an equal or even a comparably rapid growth of movements and of progress. In no country have there been produced similar concentrations of capital. If the class struggle possesses, or must possess, a site where a successful revolution is likely first, it is the American territory that one must automatically

[33] Philip S. Foner, *History of the Labor Movement in the United States,* III (New York, 1964), 383.

pick." He continued in a later reference, "On this ground, where capitalism has reached an unequalled point of development, where its ruthless dictates, its corruption and all its fatal defects have burst forth overnight with a blinding crudity, the hour of socialism cannot be far off." [34] These forecasts would have startled a Marxist in 1880, but in 1900 no one bothered to take the slightest exception to what Louis wrote. The possibility of America's starting the revolution before Europe had become a conventional piece of wisdom which one could accept or ignore, but not challenge.

Plastering the label Marxist on Jean Allemane is dangerous, though probably not misleading beyond what normally results from the need to have men pigeonholed. This French socialist leader did not pretend to be a strict proselyte of Marx as did Louis, Guesde, or Lafargue; and, as a rival to Guesde's *Parti ouvrier,* he founded *Le Parti ouvrier socialiste revolutionnaire* in 1890. He quarreled with Marxism largely on the propriety of political action, Allemane being closer to the anarchists on this point; but off and on through most of the 1890's he shared with Guesde a disdain for gradualism, an acceptance of the class struggle, a belief in capitalism's destruction through inherent contradictions, and a faith in socialism's inevitable rise. Marxist assumptions guided all the interpretations of the United States in Allemane's paper *Le Parti ouvrier.* For example, in 1895 a news article reported that the upswing of the competitive system in the United States had called forth the proletarian elements which would overturn it: "The decadence and the end of the capitalist regime in the United States had commenced." Optimism had grown when in 1897 the same paper wrote, "The movement of the proletariat recently has taken on formidable proportions in the United States where the social revolution, favored by mechanization, will perhaps break out before it does in the industrial countries of Europe." In 1899 it recorded a triumphal ten-year increase in the socialist vote in the United States of 3500 per cent. A poll of 82,182, up from 2065, was not threatening America with proletarian control, but *Le Parti ouvrier* assumed a geometric skyrocketing of the

[34] *La Guerre économique* (Paris, 1900), 262, 293. Louis' remarks about America also appeared as an article "La Grandeur des États-Unis," *La Revue socialiste,* XXX (Aug. 1899), 181–99.

vote and imagined that one more election, or possibly two, would give Washington, D. C., to the socialists.[35]

Guesde's newspaper *Le Socialiste* was more careful in its use of evidence from the United States, but its conclusions were not more restrained. Commenting on what was a noteworthy increase in socialist votes in the 1904 American election, it editorialized, "One time launched into socialism, our American friends will perhaps astonish the Old World by the rapidity of their march forward. And it is predicted that they will finish by justifying the socialist theory which says the success of socialism must, all things considered, go hand in hand with capitalist evolution." [36] Charles Rapoport, a fighting young party worker who in a few years would gather fame as one of the founders of the French Communist Party, commented in 1908 (an election year which, in contrast to 1904, proved extremely disappointing to American socialists) in another paper edited by Guesde that the United States would soon make up for the previous slowness of the Anglo-Saxon nations in approaching socialism; there the class struggle would assume "the most sharp and violent forms." [37] These were the convictions of Frenchmen whose ancestors had slightly more than a century ago followed America into another kind of revolution.

Similar comments among English Marxists were widespread, but an additional factor not present in France helps account for their interest in the United States. The only Marxist organization left alive in England by the end of the century was H. M. Hyndman's Social Democratic Federation; its successes, always uneven, were not increasing. If Europeans could sometimes be jealous or contemptuous of America, they could also use it as a place to transfer their own frustrated hopes. English Marxists around 1900 needed just such a terrain. It was far better after all to see your dreams realized in a distant place than to give them up as illusions. Hyndman's assessssments of the United States varied, and a rise in his optimism about American conditions usually concealed an increasing dis-

[35] "Revue socialiste," May 9–10, 1895; "La Disparition de la petite industrie aux États-Unis," Feb. 19–20, 1897; "Le Mouvement politique du prolétariat aux États-Unis," March 11, 1899.
[36] Editorial, Nov. 13–20, 1904.
[37] "Aux États-Unis," *Le Socialisme*, May 17, 1908.

couragement with progress at home. In 1897 he said, "Nowhere, not even in Great Britain, are the economic conditions in the cities more favourable to a rapid advance"; in 1901 he added, "Nearly all of us revolutionary Social-Democrats are drawing our clearest illustration of the approaching and inevitable transformation of capitalism from America"; and in 1904 he said, "There are plenty of signs that just as North America is to-day the most advanced country, economically and socially, so it will be the first in which Socialism will find open and legal expression." [38] Hyndman's colleague John E. Ellam called on fellow Marxists to face the facts of life. England was no longer the most hopeful field of socialist agitation: "The centre of capitalist activity has been shifting across the Atlantic, where those developments, foretold by Marx, are rapidly culminating to the point of social-revolution." [39] For Charles Lawrin in 1906: "the United States of America is directly on the verge of a revolution." [40] The melancholy of English Marxists found some relief in seeing signs of an approaching success in America. Victory there, in a kindred Anglo-Saxon nation, was a cheerful prospect when English workers had stopped, momentarily it was thought, to listen to other prophets.

No such discouragement with his own national movement prompted Karl Kautsky in anything he wrote, but he all the same made frequent allusions to the revolutionary potential of America. For Kautsky the anticipation of an early victory across the ocean was a simple matter of scientific scorekeeping. In a typical statement of 1903 he remarked that "the immensity of the trusts, the crises, unemployment—all these factors which take on already greater dimensions than they do in Europe—could very well indicate that the proletariat on that side of the Atlantic will come to political power sooner than here." [41] A similar and sober respect for

[38] "The International Outlook," *Justice*, May 1, 1897. There were two issues of the paper on this day; this refers to the special May Day issue; Hyndman to H. G. Wilshire, Feb. 13, 1901, quoted in Henry Pelling, *America and the British Left* (London, 1956), 86; "A Socialist Survey of the Time," *Justice*, April 30, 1904.
[39] "The Situation in the United States and Its Lesson for English Socialists," *The Social-Democrat*, VII (Jan. 1903), 19.
[40] "America," *Justice*, April 28, 1906.
[41] "Allerhand Revolutionares," *Die Neue Zeit*, Vol. XXII, Part I (1903–4), 655.

Marxist theory also led Henriette Roland Holst, an energetic Dutch Marxist and close friend of Rosa Luxemburg, to endorse the United States as "the land of the future." On the basis of the 1904 American election returns, she projected a vote of three million for the Socialist party in 1908, or what she thought would be about 20 per cent of the vote.[42]

The most interesting of all these prognostications and certainly the one most widely quoted at the time came from Germany's venerable Marxist leader August Bebel. Bebel had since the days of the First International poured all his enthusiasm and effort into the German movement, and De Leon no doubt had him uppermost in his mind when he accused Germans of blindness with regard to progress in other countries. Nevertheless in an interview granted to Nicholas Klein in Berlin in 1907, Bebel said, "We are waiting for you Americans to do something. You see, your country is far ahead of Germany in industrial development, and, besides, you have compulsory education and a progressive republic—things for which we Germans are fighting." When the interviewer, no doubt surprised by the praise showered on American democracy by the aging Bebel, protested that many democratic institutions in the United States were mere shams Bebel replied, "O, yes; I know all that and more. But despite that, you Americans will be the first to usher in a Socialist republic; you are now in the darkness before dawn; your wonderful development, your revolution in production, will shortly make it necessary to change your titles of ownership and methods of distribution." He told the interviewer that "my one ambition just now is to visit your country and study your trusts." [43]

One might question the accuracy of the reporter in attributing such a flat-footed observation to Bebel or wonder if he was merely being kind to his American questioner. There was at least a tinge of humbug in his expressed desire to tour the United States, for invitations to do so had been declined by him time and again. Health and other commitments had intervened, and Bebel contented himself to pursue his interest in the New World at second hand and from afar. He never tried to qualify his widely circulated

[42] "Socialistische Overwinningen en Tekortkomingen," *De Nieuwe Tijd*, IX (1904), 791–94.
[43] "Bebel Sends Greetings," *Appeal to Reason*, July 13, 1907.

comments, however, and in a second interview with Klein in 1912 he again said that "the United States will shortly declare for public ownership of public utilities, and . . . it will advance so rapidly as to be the first nation to declare a Co-operative Commonwealth." [44]

For Bebel, as for many other Marxists in the few years surrounding the beginning of the twentieth century, the inauguration of the cooperative commonwealth in America seemed the best and most fitting conclusion to the social struggles of the nineteenth century. Most of them equivocated more than Bebel. But whenever the question was raised about the likely site of a socialist victory, answers of leading Marxist intellectuals, which were based primarily on theoretical projections, were rather unanimous in portraying the United States as a plausible candidate. No matter how late had been America's start along the road to revolution, no matter how hostile American labor remained to the name of Marx, a belief in the ability of New World socialists to overtake their comrades in Europe had secured them a place in socialist folklore. Important Marxist leaders foresaw a rebirth and a new order in America and looked for the effects to pass around the world. Here and there in these various carefully shaped phrases, some features of an older version of the American Promised Land were detectable.

Wilhelm Liebknecht, whose puzzling admiration of American life has been discussed previously, had a ready explanation of how such swift and enormous alterations of American society would be possible. No abrupt change in American attitudes was requisite to enshrine cooperative principles there, for socialism, Liebknecht thought, was the logical culmination of sentiments long present in the American people. He spoke of a freedom from the dead hand of the past and a national animation which had led the Americans to build a "powerful community partnership that is and remains the grandest and most perfect form of state which humanity has yet produced— a remarkable memorial to human activity, the hopeful security for the triumph of the highest ideal of state and society." In reference to the Civil War he got even more lost in his eloquence:

> The power which for four years led one and a half million combatants in battle for an idea and for an abstract idea, the abolition

[44] "The Lion of Germany: An Interview with August Bebel," *The Labour Leader*, Nov. 14, 1912.

of slavery, and preserved them in the field, is a higher power than the Almighty Dollar; and it will prevail. Its name is duty, public spirit, republican virtue, justice, freedom, equality, humanity, or whatever one wants to name it.[45]

Those Marxists, who for other reasons wondered how well Liebknecht understood the concept of historical materialism, found fresh ground for doubt in the above comments. Historical materialism by no means meant that some spirit or ideology such as Liebknecht described could not exist or, as was more commonly assumed, could not influence the direction of history. It meant rather that the economic substructure of any society gave the original shape to all ideologies and creeds. What astonished Marxist writers who reviewed Liebknecht's commentaries was his ascription of an altruistic national character to the world's most bourgeois society. Such coexistence over a long period of time, according to the Marxist assumptions of Liebknecht's critics, was simply not possible. Capitalism made men selfish. Scarcity, the fight for existence, the competition for the places in the sun, which were all too few, led all classes to defend their economic interests. Thus, the class struggle. From greed and hunger, capitalists and workers became imbued with spirit, and on them they constructed their ideologies.[46] Under capitalism there was no higher power than the "Almighty Dollar."

European Marxists did recognize the effectiveness of special American circumstances, historical and actual, in pushing change forward with much greater speed than was possible in Europe. Engels had been impressed by American progressiveness and attributed it to the lack of a feudal past. The American people were more adaptable and accustomed to change than the Europeans. No innate respect for the upper classes nor regard for hoary institutions made them afraid to break with the past. Also, as many Marxists noted, the American worker was favored in his struggles to free himself by a better education, a readier access to economic information, and a long experience with participation in political life. These things, as should be clear from the discussion in Chapter 2, consti-

---

[45] *Ein Blick,* 288 and 282.
[46] This did not prevent Marxists from idealizing the workers, but Marxist propaganda and Marxist science were not always in harmony.

tuted no magic formula. But they did enable the American proletariat to understand its mission better and put in its hands the means
to speed up sluggish historical forces. Disgust with American institutions did not completely kill in Marxists the old European respect
for American efficiency and energy.

However—and this cannot be too strongly reemphasized—American capitalism itself promised to bring the New World to the brink
of revolution. This was the dominant theme, although it sometimes
led to a foolish complacency at odds with everything Marx had
stood for. But Marx had introduced the theme, and for his followers
the application was simple. It was the unfolding of capitalism with
its inhumanity, its inequities, and its inevitable crises which pushed
mankind into the socialist era. The very same process with the very
same underlying forces was at work in Europe. What was different
in America was not the process, but the stage of its development.
Other factors might alter the manner in which socialism came or
the time at which it actually came, but between capitalist maturity
and readiness for revolution Marxists drew a rough equation. When
Marxists in Europe looked to the New World at the turn of the
century, they saw a free enterprise system more advanced than in any
other country of the world. Capitalism, they reasoned, had spread
in the United States so quickly and with so little opposition that
socialism could not help but make progress. And looming above all
other phenomena as the factor which would turn progress into a
headlong rush was a new and uniquely American development—
the consolidation of business into the form of the all-powerful trust.

CHAPTER 4

THE AMERICAN TRUST
Welcome Confirmation
of the Marxist Theory, 1900-1905

ACCORDING TO MARXIST WRITERS one of the surest measures by which to judge the progress of capitalism in a particular country was the extent to which the ownership of capital and the means of production had come to reside in a few grasping hands. Whatever laissez-faire economists might maintain, the end product of capitalism was not a free market place, but monopoly. Large industrial plants utilizing scientific methods, new machinery, and mass production techniques gradually replaced scattered production units. Workers suffered under these combines, former owners of property were brutally hurled into the ranks of the dispossessed, and political corruption flourished under the new hegemony of a small, elite, monied aristocracy. This was all in the necessary course of things; and, as far as capitalism was concerned, it was ultimately self-defeating. In the process of the concentration of capital, as Marx wrote,

> [There] grows the revolt of the working class, a class always increasing in numbers, and disciplined, united, organised by the very mechanism of the process of capitalist production itself. The monopoly of capital becomes a fetter upon the mode of production, which has sprung up and flourished along with, and under it. Centralisation of the means of production and socialisation of labour at last reach a point where they become incompatible with their capitalist integument. This integument is burst asunder. The knell of capitalist private property sounds. The expropriators are expropriated.[1]

[1] *Capital*, 836–37.

The appearance of trusts (and later holding companies) on the American scene in the last decades of the nineteenth century came for many European Marxists as the dramatic confirmation of everything Marx had predicted. Never before had capitalist power been so brutal, so naked, or so enormous. By consolidating together under one management a number of enterprises, that were already large, the trust put effective control over the lives of millions of workers into the hands of a shockingly small group of men. In the minds of many critics the American nation no longer had a will or direction apart from what a clique of Rockefellers, Morgans, Carnegies, and Vanderbilts dictated from secret chambers reserved for the most important Captains of Industry.

European entrepreneurs had made some progress toward greater concentration through rings and cartels; but European Marxists considered these devices, when compared to the more formal organization of the trust, primitive and clumsy. The control and management of capital resources in Europe at the turn of the century remained relatively diffuse. Only, many Marxists thought, after the European capitalist followed the lead of his American counterpart and bound his enterprises together in a trust structure, would economic conditions in the Old World fully favor the triumph of socialism. For this reason the reputation of the United States in the era before World War I as "the land of the trust par excellence" gained for the young republic an important place in party literature.

As has been seen, since the mid-1880's various Marxist writers had been giving recurring attention to American phenomena. Initially, their remarks had been primarily directed toward discrediting idyllic visions of life here to show that America constituted no exception to the general laws of capitalist development. The debunking impulse never died in the decades before World War I, but it was joined by a more positive response to America's potential. Marxists came to realize that the old image of the American Promised Land might still retain some meaning within their framework of thought. Yet prior to 1900 many of their hopes for America remained vague and, since unsupported by actual developments, helplessly vulnerable. Then, with the turn of the century, the sudden prominence of the trust added a new and more concrete dimension to their growing attraction to America and brought Marxist interest in the New

World to its peak. The trust seemed to fasten their dreams and theories onto something solid, confirming Marx's economic laws not just for America, but for the entire capitalist world. Many European Marxists who had formerly given scant notice to the United States began with the opening of the new century to take their first close look at the evolution of institutions across the Atlantic in a search for indications of their own future. While the American theme can generally be regarded as a peripheral concern for European Marxists, the American trust was a topic of major interest.

Curiosity about the American trust phenomenon was first awakened in the 1880's. Almost simultaneously with the formation of the Standard Oil trust in 1882, European socialists recognized the trust as having great importance for Marxist theory. Even in the *Fabian Essays,* a landmark socialist tract which challenged many Marxist predilections, William Clarke wrote about the immense industrial concentration inaugurated in the United States by the trust as a powerful stimulus to the growth of socialism.[2] Several years later another Englishman, W. C. Owen, who belonged to the Marxist-oriented Social Democratic Federation, pointed to the potential of the trust in easing the difficult task of socialist agitation. He wrote:

> By the introduction of the "trust" not only is he [the entrepreneur] crushing out, and turning into revolutionists, the whole of the previously conservative middle-class, not only is he rendering clerical work a drug in the market, for the formation of one single trust has been advertised as causing the discharge of 12,000 clerks and salesmen; not only is he manufacturing all this revolutionary human material for us Socialists to use, but he is knocking the old trade unionism out at a single blow.[3]

With such impersonal influences at work comrades had little more to do than sit back and wait for party membership to swell. Such a conclusion was vulgar Marxism, but many partisans found it difficult to reason their way out of the inaction of mechanism. Lenin at

[2] See Clarke's contribution on the "Industrial Basis of Socialism" in the *Essays.*
[3] "The American Storm Cloud," *Justice,* Jan. 28, 1893.

least knew to avoid that temptation lurking in the dialectical theory.

References to American trusts were common enough in the 1890's, but beginning around 1900, European Marxists discovered an extremely compelling reason to justify a greatly quickened interest in these business consolidations. There have been previous opportunities to mention the manner in which doctrinal controversy could direct European socialist attention toward the United States. For example, Marxists in Europe turned to statistics on the income of the American wage earner, not necessarily because they had the slightest curiosity about the New World, but because attacks from their liberal critics forced them to refute the notion of a workers' paradise in the New World. The United States was a category in an ongoing argument. It had become one of the issues in a debate about the future of Europe. The extraordinary flood between 1900 and 1905 of European Marxist literature on the combination of American business was the natural response to the attack on the Marxist system by Eduard Bernstein and can be explained only by reference to the publication of Bernstein's revisions of Marxist economics in the closing years of the nineteenth century.

Bernstein was not the sole inventor of "revisionism." What he said in *Evolutionary Socialism* in 1899 had immediate intellectual roots in Fabianism, in the French *possibiliste* movement guided by Paul Brousse, and in the arguments of his own aristocratic countryman Georg von Vollmar.[4] But the publication of Bernstein's book, coming at the same time that the entrance of French socialist Alexandre Millerand into the bourgeois cabinet of Waldeck-Rousseau had blown up a storm in the Second International, brought into clearer focus a number of previously suppressed issues. In doing so, it considerably sharpened the polemics between two groups of socialists— those who insisted on a strict loyalty to Marx and those who thought that the revolutionary rhetoric derived from the heroic uprisings of 1848 and the brief reign of the Paris Commune in 1871 had grown

---

[4] *Evolutionary Socialism: A Criticism and Affirmation* bears no resemblance to the original German, *Die Voraussetzungen des Sozialismus und die Aufgaben der Sozialdemokratie,* but it is nevertheless the English title that is usually used. Bernstein actually put forward most of his ideas in a series of articles for *Die Neue Zeit* between 1896 and 1898.

stale and irrelevant. Bernstein, unlike the earlier socialists who had challenged Marx, had long held credentials as a distinguished Marxist intellectual; and people listened to his recantation with the attention given an abbot who forswears his religious order.

German revisionism confirmed what many socialists had long suspected was true not only in Germany but generally in Europe.[5] The wages paid to workers did not decline under capitalism nor did the operation of a free market place engender a cycle of increasingly painful economic crises. The middle class proved to be more resilient than Marx had suspected and refused to be crushed out. The ownership of capital was not becoming more concentrated but, if anything, more diffuse through sale of corporate stock. These facts taken together meant that if socialism had to await the economic disinheritance of the vast majority of the population, it would never come. Socialism would have to be the unconscious child of history and worsening economic conditions, and it could triumph only by gradual degrees as man's reason responded to the moral challenge inherent in the idea of socialist community. In revisionism the rhetoric of revolution, violence, and class struggle gave way to the rhetoric of reform, parliamentarianism, and cooperation.

Ironically the rapid sliding of European Marxists into an acceptance of tactics compatible with Bernstein's theoretical considerations only heightened their opposition to revisionism. As Sidney Hook has pointed out with respect to Germany, "the more effectively reformist the Social Democratic Party was, the more important for its members was the ideology of apocalypse and the hope for total solutions."[6] Bernstein's book was all the more embarrassing because Marxists themselves sensed a weakening in their previously unyielding posture toward the capitalist system. They were sorry about their frailties but helpless to correct them; and in a self-conscious attempt to convince themselves (and a growing left wing of Marxists) of their continuing dedication to their historical revolutionary traditions, they attached great importance to a powerful refutation of

---

[5] One will find a fuller treatment of revisionism and related schools of socialism in Chapter 6.

[6] Introduction to Schocken paperback of *Evolutionary Socialism* (New York, 1963), xiv. Also see Julius Braunthal, *History of the International, 1864–1914* (London, 1966), 265.

Bernsteinism and the vindication of Marx's analyses of capitalist economies. In casting about for some convenient symbol to summarize the worst errors of revisionism and to reinforce belief in the inevitability and nearness of socialism, they found nothing more useful than the American trust.

In the Marxists' minds, developments in America proved that the concentration of capital had no intrinsic limits except monopoly. They demonstrated to Marxists that, however strong labor unions might grow, capitalists could build organizations to keep the workers impotent. They showed that to whatever extent wages might increase, employers would always be able to depress the standard of living by raising prices on trust-produced products. Finally, and perhaps most important, they proved to Marxists that the principle of cooperation, which was to be the basis of the future society, was the natural and ineluctable product of the interplay of essentially amoral forces in history. The capitalist himself had been the first to ditch the laissez-faire economic system. He, just like the most rigid Marxist, had been forced to conclude that the economy could not remain based on the chaos of a free market place and had tried in America to eliminate competition. To the Marxist a single point of disagreement separated him from the American trust magnate; but from that point of cleavage, the proper locus of ownership, there opened the great gap between revolution and reaction.

Just like economic depressions and bourgeois parliaments, the trust gave Marxists cause both for hope and for despair. On the insidious side, business consolidation usually brought an immediate worsening in the condition of the worker. Gigantic corporations fostered an odious tyranny and pushed the abuses of capitalist exploitation to new extremes. On the other hand, such brutality stiffened the opposition of the worker to the system and steeled him to his revolutionary task. And, quite apart from the convulsing effect of the trust on the class struggle, the capitalist's increasing rejection of competition and his construction of huge industrial plants smoothed the way for government appropriation of the means of production. The trusts, more than merely reflecting the level of economic development, laid the foundation for an economy of abundance so necessary to a socialist state and provided the means for an easy changeover from capitalism.

An individual Marxist writer might emphasize the role of the trust as an agent of social discord which would impel workers to "seize" control violently, or he might view trustification as the building of a transitional bridge between the old and the new order which would allow workers to "assume" control peacefully. The emphasis varied, but all Marxists agreed that the trust marked the entrance of capitalism into its final stage. Marxists encouraged the proletariat in its efforts to fight price rises, they urged trade unionists to offer an unyielding resistance to the enveloping power of trust magnates, and they supported laws requiring trusts to publicize their methods of operation and their financial position. This much was allowable. Yet whatever new burdens trust control laid upon the worker, Marxists cautioned the workers against joining in the chorus of voices demanding legal dissolution of giant industries.[7] Trust-busting was a reactionary game for the petty bourgeoisie, and party members were not allowed to forget that the emancipation of the worker could come only through accepting the work of consolidation and turning it into revolutionary channels.

Germany was the subject of much Marxist literature in the early twentieth century because of the strength of the socialist movement there. In America, by contrast, a socialist movement was barely alive. But the role of the United States in bringing forth the trust assured the country a status and importance which no increase in the socialist vote could have provided. Economic conditions there told Europeans what was going to develop next in their own countries. Moreover, those European Marxists, who expected America in all likelihood to inaugurate socialism first, usually rested their prediction squarely on the trust. An interviewer of Paul Singer reported the veteran German Marxist as saying, "The concentration of industry in this country [the United States] was bringing it to Socialism more rapidly than Europe could hope to attain to that desired state."[8] Paul Louis, the Frenchman who was so impressed by America's potential to initiate socialism, considered the trust "an admirable ferment for revolution." He asked, "Are not these enor-

---

[7] One might note, for example, the resolutions passed on the trust at meetings of the International at Paris in 1900 and at Amsterdam in 1904.

[8] Richard Kitchelt, "A Chat with Paul Singer," *The Comrade*, I (Aug. 1902), 277.

mous alliances of material forces which the Old World does not know the very expression of the monied aristocracy constituted as a class?" and wondered "what dreadful social war will be unleashed on the other side of the Atlantic on the day when the proletariat will feel itself strongly organized and will retain its part of the wealth that it has produced and accumulated for others?" [9] Similarly, H. M. Hyndman, hinging his most enthusiastic predictions about America on business concentration, wrote, "From the domination of the Trusts to emancipation by Social Democracy is but a short step." [10]

English Marxists looked with familial interest at the practices of American entrepreneurs, for they felt some kinship of Anglo-Saxon blood would quickly lead English businessmen to duplicate the American ways of production. When John E. Ellam wrote that in the United States the great concentration of industry had forced "class antagonism between plutocracy and proletariat" very near the point of revolution, he was already anticipating the effects which the trustification of English industry would have on the sagging fortunes of the Social Democratic Federation. [11]

Members of the SDF insisted on aloofness from any alliance with non-socialist labor organizations; and, since the path they trod was a lonely one, they welcomed any sign that it was leading somewhere. In 1903 Hyndman told doubters, who were preaching compromise, to look across the Atlantic, "to the most industrially developed community of all," for assurance that socialism resulted from the completion of monopoly. To him "the quadrupling of the American Socialist vote in two years" was no accident; it only reflected the declining status of the middle classes and "the disgust of all educated America at the loathsome set of ostentatious slavedrivers who now control North as well as South, West as well as East." [12] And whatever happened in America, it went without saying, would also happen in England.

A year later Hyndman again referred to the rapid progress of socialism in the United States and commented on the educational

[9] *La Guerre économique*, 291 and 262.
[10] "A Socialist Survey of the Time," *Justice*, April 30, 1904.
[11] "The Lack of Economic Knowledge," *The Social Democrat*, VI (Nov. 1902), 330.
[12] "The First of May Celebration," *Justice*, May 2, 1903.

value of the concentration of industry there. The monopoly and tyranny of the industrial trusts in the "great Republic" had forced "all but the wilfully blind" to face "the choice . . . between sacrificing all liberty to the caprices of a knot of worthless plutocrats, or the acceptance of Socialism with its inevitable solution of antagonism." [13] As the economy of England grew more and more like the economy of its former colony, the English proletariat would move as swiftly toward socialism. Indeed, implicit in Hyndman's comments was the notion that the English worker, if he would study the American example and understand the potential ruthlessness of trust domination, could establish socialism before trustification was very far along in England. In any case, reports from America satisfied Hyndman as to the folly of socialists who were urging a retreat from militancy. English workers would soon enough be disillusioned with the newly formed Labour party. When their thirst continued to go unslaked in the fouled pools of opportunism, they would turn finally to the pure springs of Marxism rising from the Social Democratic Federation.

Continental Marxists did not suffer the same isolation from the labor movement as Hyndman did in England, but reports from the United States greatly encouraged them in their efforts to keep Marxist doctrines intact. In America they were learning something of profound importance to their own situation. Marx's French grandson Jean Longuet referred to America in 1902 as "the great social laboratory in which one can follow with certainty the most marked phenomena of modern evolution." [14] Longuet's intellectual career in the socialist party was characterized by a steady movement to the right, but his debt to his illustrious ancestor was clear when he reasoned, "But with the formidable economic development of the republic, the concentration of capital attains under the form of the trust an importance unknown in Europe, and inevitably, socialist ideas find conditions more favorable for propaganda." Longuet's opinion undoubtedly found an audience. The son of Charles Longuet and Marx's daughter Jenny, he wrote dozens of articles about the United States and was certainly more attuned to the situation in the United States than any other French Marxist.

13 "A Socialist Survey of the Time," *Justice*, April 30, 1904.
14 "Aux États-Unis," *La Petite République*, Nov. 5, 1902.

The longest and most influential Marxist commentary on the American trust issued from the pen of another French relative of Marx, Paul Lafargue. In 1903 Lafargue expanded a series of articles which he had written for the Guesdist organ *Le Socialiste* into his small volume *Les Trusts Américains*. Lafargue was the worthiest of Marx's sons-in-law. The other two were good socialists; but Jean Longuet's father, Charles, was entirely undistinguished, and Edward Aveling was, while charming and talented, a rogue. Lafargue possessed admirable qualities of leadership and intellect which made him Guesde's main ally in building the *Parti ouvrier Français*. He vigorously combatted the influence of Bernsteinism in France (especially as it was represented in the person of Jean Jaurès), and, until in his later years when he took a less active role in politics, he was among the most prolific and discerning contributors to Marxist literature. In 1911, alarmed at the prospect of a useless and dreary old age, he and his wife, Laura, poisoned themselves. It was another tragic end to the life of members of Marx's family and a palpable loss to the leadership of the Second International.

Lafargue attached enormous importance to the subject of his investigation. On the flyleaf of his book he had imprinted the Marxist dictum, "The most industrially advanced country shows to those who follow it on the industrial ladder the image of their own future"; and in the preface he wrote, "The American trusts are a new historical phenomenon with such a strong effect on the capitalist world that they relegate to second place all the economic, political, and scientific facts seen in the last forty years." It was no longer possible to assign America a place on the periphery of socialist concern. The United States occupied a central place in the world movement, and European socialists who continued to ignore it stood in peril of being tossed into the dusty and forgotten place history reserved for outmoded theorists.

Lafargue made no secret of the motives behind his research. His bête noire was Bernstein, "the prophet of the bourgeoisie," whom Lafargue accused of falsifying statistics to deny the inevitability of capital concentration "at the moment the American trusts give the world the spectacle of the most formidable concentration of wealth that has ever been seen."[15] Lafargue wrote, "If Karl Marx's ma-

[15] "Les Trusts Américains," *Le Socialiste,* Jan. 18–25, 1903.

terialistic theory of history . . . had need of a new and dazzling confirmation, the trusts would furnish it." [16] Lafargue was not looking to America just for information; Bernstein had forced him to look there for courage. The evidence he found of capital concentration was and still is one of Marxism's most effective challenges.

French Marxists in the first decade of the twentieth century found themselves in approximately the same dilemma as their counterparts in Germany. The French socialist party, finally united in 1905, remained outwardly faithful to Marxist thought, but the movement toward tactical positions urged by Bernstein and other revisionist socialists proved irresistible. The proclamation of orthodoxy became in these circumstances all the more important; and, particularly with the emergence of a militant syndicalist opposition on the left which denigrated parliamentary activity, the Marxist was forced to parade his aversion to Bernstein publicly and minimize the importance of his participation in electoral processes. Lafargue was reciting an answer from the socialist catechism when he wrote in *Les Trusts Américains,*

> The socialist gains in the knowledge of the trust system a new faith in his ideal; he can with redoubled conviction affirm that it will be realized in the near future and that the prayers of the priests, the falsifications of the economists, and the deceptions and repressions of the politicians will not retard one minute the coming of the social crisis, which will offer to the exploited the occasion to overturn by a *coup d'épaule* the capitalist oligarchy.[17]

Here was an answer to renew the zeal of the orthodox during a period of apparent prosperity when calls to revolution sounded more and more like quaint echoes from a bygone era.

The American trust, simply because it added so many digits to the previous limit of corporate wealth, became a standard weapon in the hastily constructed armory built to repel the attacks of revisionists and conservative economists on the Marxist system. In the first five years of the twentieth century, when the revisionist controversy attained its greatest heat, Marxists studded their speeches

[16] *Les Trusts Américains* (Paris, 1903), 12.
[17] Pages 123–24.

with constant references to American business consolidation and counted on their hearers to understand the significance without added explanation. They had considerably more to do than merely point to the New World and utter a triumphant *voilà*, however. Non-Marxist writers also took note of the concentration of industry in the United States and for one reason or another refused to see in this development the same implications which had so delighted Marxists. Defenders of capitalism as well as Bernsteinian socialists found it possible to read in American industrial consolidation meanings other than the unavoidable end of capitalism.

Believers in a traditional laissez-faire model of capitalism were apprehensive about any movement of industrial organization toward monopoly. But this apparent trend in America, they insisted, was neither natural nor necessary. Remove government favors, restore truly competitive conditions, and trusts—since they were the creations of men who had managed to buy up the United States Senate temporarily—would disappear. The arch-laissez-faire economist Pierre Leroy-Beaulieu wrote, "As for the trusts, far from being essential components, the majority of them are rather, in our view, the passing excrescences of American industrial progress. While one is frightened by them in Europe, they are beginning to give already in the land where they were born the proof of their fragility." Unsupported by a protective tariff, trusts would find the difficulties of control too great; and these "megalomaniac conceptions, hatched in minds intoxicated by times of exceptional prosperity," would undergo a certain decline.[18]

An entirely different interpretation from Leroy-Beaulieu's, but one remaining within the framework of the free enterprise system, accepted the trusts as natural growths and proposed to meet the admittedly great dangers which they posed to capitalism by positive government action, either in the form of anti-trust laws or stringent control measures. There was variation in this position as well. Those capitalists who pushed for anti-trust legislation wanted a restoration of a fully competitive economy while those who thought in terms of regulation were more inclined to accept big business as an accomplished fact. While this latter group saw little reason to bemoan the passing of fierce price competition, it remained faithful to a

[18] *Les États-Unis au XXe siècle* (Paris, 1904), xvii.

capitalist credo in rejecting any attempt to remove the gigantic corporations from private hands.

Marxists as a rule did not take the trouble to distinguish carefully these various bourgeois positions. They did regard economists who considered the process of consolidation reversible, either through the elimination of tariffs or anti-trust legislation, slightly more foolish than the rest. High tariffs could admittedly in some instances make the formation of a trust easier. So could any legislative favor from government to business. But to assume that the elimination of these various supports would result in the collapse of America's giant corporations was to overlook the vast advantages of centralized management—the capacity to end the wasteful squandering of resources caused by duplication and divided effort, the ability to make full use of mechanization, and the power to exercise unchallenged control over a huge national market. A brief glance at the figures on industrial productivity in the United States, Marxists thought, should have been enough to silence anyone who longed for the return of production to home workshops and individually owned factories. A respect for efficiency, and not some trickery of bourgeois demonology, had called the trust into existence.

As for those who preached the gospel of regulation, Marxists brusquely referred them to the United States as the classic example of the futility of trying to control institutions which were omnipotent. Trusts declared illegal under the terms of the Sherman Act reorganized as gigantic corporations or holding companies and changed very little in their actual operations. The trust magnates, with their tenacious hold over elected assemblies and judges, allowed only such legislation to pass which could be rendered harmless or turned to their own advantage. Reformers ran in an endless circle of futility. Running faster moved them no closer to a goal; it only returned them more frequently to their starting point. So long as capitalism prevailed, the trust could not be broken up and its disastrous effects could not be averted. By a process of elimination the only solution left was placing the giant corporations under common ownership.

Quite a different challenge to the Marxist interpretation of the trust emerged from the camp of the Bernsteinians. Bernstein agreed with the traditional Marxist view of the trust as a logical product of capitalist society, and like the most orthodox he welcomed it as an important step toward socialism. At that point, agreement ended. Marxists, Bernstein believed, had seriously erred in treating the concentration of wealth and the concentration of industry as the same development. He wrote, "For a long time the opinion has dominated in socialist circles that the accumulation of capital and the concentration of industry go hand in hand, as if to say they were only two parallel running lines representing one and the same development." Bernstein countered this presupposition by pointing out that industrial management might become more centralized at the same time capital ownership was growing more diffuse through the sale of corporate stock. Behind the great American steel trust, he reminded his Marxist opponents, stood some 50,000 stockholders.[19] If ownership of capital made one a capitalist, then Marxist images of steadily thinning capitalist ranks needed serious rethinking.

According to Bernstein and his followers the evolution of the trust might very well have a stabilizing effect upon the system, rather than force a collapse of capitalism as Marxists assumed. By gaining control over a market, the directors of trusts could to some extent forestall overproduction and thus moderate the nature and frequency of economic crises.[20] Moreover, the trust, by adding a note of rationality to the economic system, had even improved the position of the worker and made his life more secure. Eugène Fournière, a prominent French socialist drawn into the theoretical camp of Bernstein, made this point very clearly in 1902. It was not, as he said, that the trusts did not break or crush the worker, but that they crushed him less than had been common before. No evidence offered clearer proof of this than the difference in salaries between workers in the United States and those in Europe. Salaries, statistics indicated, were always lowest in countries where the con-

---

[19] *Die heutige Sozialdemokratie in Theorie und Praxis* (Berlin, 1905), 17 and 21. Bernstein also denied that trustification could ever completely wipe out the small producer. He thought that statistics clearly showed that the small independent manufacturer was holding his own.

[20] For Bernstein's discussion of this point, see Chapter 2 of *Evolutionary Socialism*. Bernstein did not argue, as many of his Marxist critics claimed, that trusts could resolve all the problems of the capitalist system; but he certainly thought that they allowed capitalism to work better.

centration of production had made the least progress. Fournière summed up by saying,

> But where the trust renders the most important service, in a social sense, is in the substitution of association for struggle. True it associates only the capitalists. True, also, it fights against workers and consumers. But it passes beyond the stage of internal struggle in production; it regulates production according to the needs of real consumption; it foresees, moderates, and finally abolishes the crises that anarchical production, ignorant of the needs of the market, causes to burst out every ten years.[21]

This interpretation could not have been more directly at odds with the Marxist belief in socialism as the inevitable product of increasing (or projected) capitalist disorder.

To the first argument, that it was fallacious to equate the trustification of industry with the concentration of capital, Marxists answered that the ownership of stock alone meant nothing. While technically the ownership of a company might be spread among many thousands of people, the actual control of the invested capital lay in fewer hands than ever before. J. Karski responded to Bernstein in the *Leipziger Volkszeitung,* "The magnates of high finance command not only their own capital, they command just as well the capital of the smaller stockholders. . . . The joint stock company is not as Bernstein thinks the means to divide capitalistic profit among a large number of persons, but it is one of the approved means to concentrate possession in a few hands." [22] What Karski said applied to a normal corporation. Concentration of economic power in a trust arrangement (and in the slightly different arrangement of the holding company) was actually far more direct and unchallengeable. Stockholders gave a few men all the outstanding stock of many corporations in trust; and, as a typical agreement read, these trustees were authorized "to hold, control, and manage the said stock and interests for the exclusive use and benefit" of the parties to the agreement. Ownership of capital, so Marxists argued, was meaningless unless control was a concomitant of the ownership. The trust, by

---

[21] "Trusts," *La Petite République,* Dec. 1, 1902.
[22] "Aktiengellschaft und Konzentration," Sept. 5, 1908.

separating the two completely, divested the small capitalist of the last vestige of his nominal voice in meetings of stockholders and assured absolute control over vast sums of money to the board. Concentration of wealth, in the sense Marx spoke of it, could find no higher expression.

The second revisionist contention, that the trust tended to stabilize capitalist economies and improve the situation of the wage earner, posed a slightly more difficult problem for the Marxist. Marxists themselves viewed cooperation as a principle superior to competition; and, insofar as the trust represented a step toward cooperation, they had to concede a certain measure of truth to Bernstein's argument. This concession, as an 1899 article in the German paper *Vorwärts* made clear, did not go very far. Admitting that the first stage of trustification in America had brought a regularization of production and sales which had been conducive to economic stability and somewhat higher wages, the article hastened to add that the second stage only confirmed the Marxist belief in the inability of any economic system based on private ownership to maintain ordered and rational growth.[23] Overproduction and crises continued unabated. The wage earner still lived under the threat of sudden unemployment. His trade unions found themselves powerless to protest either the capricious lowering of wages or the complete loss of jobs on account of mechanization. One Dutch Marxist Joseph Loopuit thought that the U. S. Steel strike and Pennsylvania coal strikes in 1901 showed clearly that trusts held unions completely at their mercy.[24] The trust system did not at all alter capitalist greed. It changed nothing in the basic speculative drive of the entrepreneur to conquer a market quickly and to exploit the consumer and worker in the most efficient way allowable by law (the last qualification being a small handicap). It made him no wiser as to the disastrous consequences of overproduction. Consolidation only gave the capitalist more power to carry out his wild programs and, in so doing, hastened his march into oblivion.

Every business crisis in the United States, however small, provided European Marxists who were alert to the American situation with a chance to lecture their revisionist comrades about how wrong

[23] "Zur Entwickelung der amerikanischen Trusts," June 11, 1899.
[24] "Vakvereenigingen en Trusts," *De Nieuwe Tijd*, VIII (1903), 105-13.

they had been in their estimations of the effects of the trust upon capitalism. Responding to a relatively minor upheaval in one sector of the American economy in 1900, Heinrich Cunow spoke for party intellectuals in *Vorwärts*: "How little trusts protect against changes [in the market] and crises is shown by the American iron industry which is almost fully organized into trusts and in spite of that in the last few months was most violently affected by every report of crisis, by every change of the market." [25] Trustification, in Cunow's mind, only aggravated the seriousness of the crisis, for it was more plausible "that the carteled and trustified industries in case of the outbreak of a crisis are exposed much more strongly to convulsion . . . as a result of the concentration of management and sales . . . than that the trusts are able to form a dam against the danger of crises."

A panic and depression which hit the United States in 1907 produced a similar reaction in the European Marxist press. The brevity of the depression really offered much more objective support to the revisionist contention that capitalists had learned to moderate the severity of economic crises (this was especially true because the maneuvers of a single capitalist, J. P. Morgan, had prevented a much more disastrous panic); but, in the initial euphoria of seeing American business floundering, Marxists gave their imaginations a free rein. Hyndman's paper in November of that year reported the crisis as being the worst since 1857 with potentially devastating effects for capitalism. An editorial commented, "Not all the organisation of all the American Trusts . . . have [sic] been able to avert the inevitable crash due to our present anarchical capitalist system." [26] The aroused French Marxist Charles Rappoport wrote the next month,

"No more crises! No more anarchy in production and distribution!" repeated the theorists of the capitalist class with an air of triumph and conviction: the trust has altered all that. Marx is finished! refuted, not by scholastic arguments which collapse like card houses at the first breath of socialist critique, but by economic facts, the only things that the Marxists respect. . . . The unprecedented crisis

25 "Syndikate, Kartelle, und Trusts," Oct. 7, 1900.
26 "The Crisis in the United States," *Justice*, Nov. 9, 1907.

which has just broken out in the very country of trusts—the United States—is destined to disenchant the apologists of capitalism.[27]

Paul Lafargue also used this "formidable crisis" as a reply to those who scoffed at the conceptions of Marx and Engels by naïvely accepting the belief in the newly acquired ability of capitalists to suppress crises.[28] Lafargue reasoned his way from the evidence of 1907 to the time, which was not far off, when the simultaneous outbreak of crises in Europe and America would "occasion such social perturbations as will enable the International Socialist Party to seize political power and commence the social Revolution, as Marx and Engels thought." In such unguarded exclamations the rhetoric of catastrophe and cataclysm sounded strongly. It always did when Bernstein was the target.

The monopolists in America, Marxists thought, had time and again demonstrated their unwillingness to correlate the tremendous productive capacities of their plants to the demands of the market. The cycle of overproduction, market glut, low prices, and unemployment continued as before. Even had the trust magnate used centralized management intelligently to regulate production, he could not prevent sudden unforseen drops in consumption which left him with overexpanded productive facilities. According to *Vorwärts* a sudden slowdown in railroad building in the United States in 1903 caused the demand curve for iron and steel to drop sharply and produced a crisis in the industry. The crisis obviously had nothing to do with overproduction since inventories were low when it began.[29] Nor could the trust solve the problem of a shortage of circulating capital which Lafargue thought brought about the crisis of 1907.[30] These were problems which would find solution only in the cooperative commonwealth.

During the first five years of the twentieth century, when Rockefeller, Carnegie, Vanderbilt, Harriman, and Morgan were household names around the world, European Marxist interest in the United States rose to its greatest heights. The concentration of capital

[27] "Mouvement international," *Le Socialisme,* Dec. 1, 1907.
[28] "The Gold Crisis in the United States," *Socialist,* March 1908. Lafargue's article is printed here in translation; it appeared first in Jaurès' *L'Humanité.*
[29] "Wirtschaftlicher Wochenbericht," Oct. 2, 1904.
[30] "The Gold Crisis in the United States."

resources in America, according to a number of respected Marxists, demanded close and careful scrutiny—especially in view of the protection it offered against growing attacks on sacrosanct Marxist assumptions. Gradually after 1905 when the disputes over revisionism lessened somewhat in importance and gave way to clashes over new issues, the American trust lost, in part at least, its prominent place in European Marxist literature. Marxists in the Old World continued to seek out evidence to bolster their own particular view of historical development. However, imperfections in their interpretations of the trust became more and more apparent. It was not business consolidation in America, as such, which had damaged their argument. That phenomenon, though never as extensive as some extravagant statements had predicted, was real enough. What had disappointed Marxists was the failure of the trust and labor conflicts to spawn class consciousness in America. When Lenin, Rosa Luxemburg, and Rudolph Hilferding made their own extended analyses of trusts, they rarely referred to America. But they were opening the door for a group of postwar Marxists who treated the "problem of America" in a much different context and conducted their analyses according to premises other than those of Marxist theorists who concern us in this story.

Aside from employing the trust as an arguing point in strictly theoretical discussions, European Marxists had also prior to 1905 (and to a lesser extent afterward) used it in conjunction with their various interpretations of the American Promised Land. (Of course, these two purposes often overlapped because Marxist images of the American Promised Land were themselves used to support theory.) Those who were interested in developments in the New World primarily for their catalytic effects on European revolution had greeted the gigantic mergers of American business with great enthusiasm. Not only did the trust strengthen the competitive position of the United States on the world market and thereby threaten the stability of European economies, it also offered European businesses a model for duplication. When the trustification of industry along American lines had been carried out in Europe, Marxists expected a rapid acceleration of the revolutionary movement in their own countries.

The titanic corporations of America provided even greater support to the second Marxist version of the American Promised Land discussed in Chapter 3. With the trust in the center of attention, the view of the United States as the probable victor in the race for the cooperative commonwealth gathered new exponents. The fact that the trust was so firmly a product of the United States did more than anything else to shake European Marxists out of the habit of seeing in the New World only a pale reflection of their own higher state of development. It did not necessarily make their observations of the United States more sophisticated. They could not take off the blinders fashioned by their rendering of the Marxist dialectic which prevented them from seeing any fundamental differences between the experience in the Old World and the experience in the New World. But it forced them to come to terms squarely with the sobering proposition that the future of socialism around the world depended upon the victories won by the American Socialist party.

Paul Lafargue in his book on American trusts wrote, "Our comrades of the New World . . . are conscious of the historic role which the sudden and phenomenal development of American capitalism imposes on them and in their enthusiasm they announce themselves as the initiators of the revolutionary movement that will transform capitalist society." [31] To many observers the trust appeared to end all argument as to where in the world economic conditions were most favorable to a socialist victory. The American proletariat had not been exposed to Marxist propaganda to the same degree as the European and was called on to begin the revolution even though it lacked a full theoretical understanding of socialism. Capitalist demagogues could more easily lead the movement astray in America than they could in Europe, and the class struggle here would as a result suffer sporadic setbacks. Many European Marxists chose to look beyond these difficulties, however, and they agreed with the *Leipziger Volkszeitung* that because of American companies like Standard Oil, "the decisive struggle will be able to commence there earlier than here." [32]

As late as 1910 Karl Kautsky was still chiding revisionists, who, he thought, were wasting time in trying to refute Marxist economics

[31] *Les Trusts Américains*, 136–37.
[32] "König Petroleum," May 26, 1906.

with evidence drawn from tired old countries like England. He wrote, "For three decades England has fallen economically more and more into the background. . . . Not England, but the United States, is the country that reveals to us our social future under capitalism. Nowhere is the overdue sharpening of class conflict developed more strongly than there." [33] Kautsky still believed in the power of the United States to astonish the world by its sudden conversion to socialism. Kautsky had to believe that, for, so he seemed to fear, to admit any other possibility was to throw the whole Marxist dialectic into serious doubt.

[33] "Finanzkapital und Krisen," *Die Neue Zeit,* Vol. XXIX, Part I (1910–11), 768–69.

CHAPTER 5

"WHY IS THERE NO SOCIALISM
IN THE UNITED STATES?"
A Riddle Ending
in Disillusionment, 1900-1917

THE MOOD of European Marxists during the lifetime of the Second International usually touched euphoria. They had set back the date of revolution dozens of times, they had watched many former stalwarts, who grew tired of waiting to be carried aloft by the irresistible tide of Marxism, be swept away by less resolute political currents, and they had seen Western capitalism continue to expand and impose its worst features on remote lands of the world. In spite of these trials they remained unshaken in their basic belief that socialism was coming and that all of them, excepting the very old, would live to see its triumph. Their doctrine assured them of inevitable victory; so long as socialist ideas were spreading everywhere around them, nothing could dispel their faith. There was not yet strong evidence to suggest the somber future awaiting Marxist ideology in the West. Looking at a world as yet unspoiled by the traumas of two great wars and the disillusioning experiment of the Bolsheviks, they could think that in western Europe and America man and his society were about to be reborn.

The enthusiasm which some European Marxist spokesmen had shown toward the United States as a probable site of an early victory was in many ways a reflection of this general optimism. In their efforts to keep America in the vanguard of nations approaching the revolution (something, in their mind, necessary to satisfy the Marxist dialectic and bolster their belief in the nearness of victory at home), they were willing to overlook a number of facts about actual socialist strength in the United States and pretend that a vast proletarian army was marching forth where, in fact, only the ragtag forces of Jacob S. Coxey limped along. Repeatedly, they credited struggling socialist forces in the United States with a potential for immediate growth far beyond what a disinterested observer could possibly have gathered from watching the American scene.

European Marxist commentators also had sober reveries, and in more composed moments they admitted to uneasy feelings about working-class attitudes in the United States. The ball of socialism, which they had frequently seen beginning to roll, was inert. From 1892 to 1898 the vote cast for Daniel De Leon's Socialist Labor party rose from 20,000 to 80,000—a figure notable only for its disheartening insignificance. For a while the Socialist party of America, launched in 1901 with Eugene Debs as its standard-bearer, promised greater success. For the first time, a socialist party in America mesmerized large numbers of native-born members who swelled the party's 400,000 votes in 1904 to almost 900,000 in the election which put Woodrow Wilson in the White House. Along the way American socialists managed to elect a national congressman and hundreds of state and local officials. In 1910 they broke into headlines across the country by capturing the city government in Milwaukee. Yet, even in their peak year of 1912, American socialists won only 6 per cent of the total national vote. In contrast, the German Social Democrats won almost 20 per cent of the vote in 1890 and quickly became Germany's strongest party at the polls. By the outbreak of World War I, German socialists had 110 representatives in the Reichstag; French socialists had 101 parliamentary representatives; the Austrians had 82; the Belgians, 39; and the Italians, 42.[1] All the European parties boasted leaders who could claim true national importance. Compared with such numerical strength, one lonely comrade sitting in the United States House of Representatives was painfully unimpressive.

Respecting such evidence, the European Marxist press issued frequent warnings during the 1890's not to overestimate the strength of American socialist forces. European Marxists had once allowed

[1] Merle Fainsod, *International Socialism and the World War* (Cambridge, Mass., 1935), 40.

their hopes to be ridiculously inflated by the arousal of American labor in its strikes of 1886 and by Henry George's surprisingly strong showing in the race for mayor of New York City in the same year; the more cautious among them were determined to avoid a repetition of the ensuing sharp letdown. A. P. Hazell admonished English Marxists in 1891 to curb immoderate calculations: "There are really but few Social-Democrats at the present time in the United States who can claim to have sufficient scientific knowledge of Socialism to become teachers." In the same year *Le Parti ouvrier* briefly noted the entrance of the American labor movement into a period of general stagnation "interrupted only by isolated manifestations where the workers' organizations have shown some signs of life."[2] The hauteur of the German party asserted itself in an 1892 article in *Vorwärts* which, after analyzing the behavior of the American proletariat, concluded, "These people stand far behind the outlook of class-conscious German workers and the latter have no cause to treat the American working movement as one that could sustain a serious comparison with the German working movement."[3]

In addition to cautions such as these, in which chauvinism mingled with scientific detachment, European socialists could read numerous articles in their press by European comrades living in America which reported the class-consciousness of the American workers as "still very undeveloped."[4] F. A. Sorge and Hermann Schlüter were two German immigrants to this country who continued to hold the ear of Marxists in Europe.[5] Sorge had come over shortly after the 1848 turbulence, and it was to him Marx had entrusted the First International during its American residence. Schlüter's habitation in the United States dated from the late 1880's, but he had lost no time in

[2] "The Working Class Movement in America," *Justice*, April 11, 1891; and "Le Socialisme aux États-Unis," *Le Parti ouvrier*, Sept. 3-4, 1891.
[3] "Der Jahresbericht," Jan. 8, 1892.
[4] See, for example, Philipp Rappaport, "Ueber die Arbeiterbewegung in Amerika," *Die Neue Zeit*, VII (1889), 63; and G. A. Hoehn, "Auf nach Washington," *Die Neue Zeit*, Vol. XII, Part II (1893-94), 431.
[5] I have examined letters between the two men and Marx, Engels, Wilhelm Liebknecht, Bebel, and Kautsky at the International Institute of Social History in Amsterdam. Most of the originals of the Sorge correspondence are in the New York Public Library. Only a part of the correspondence, of course, deals with the situation in the United States.

immersing himself in American socialist activities. Their reports in the 1890's, given both in correspondence and through regular articles in *Die Neue Zeit,* were uniformly discouraging. No one, they observed, and least of all Daniel De Leon and his small German-speaking party, had yet phrased socialist ideals in a language understandable to men reared among American customs and institutions.

Socialism's failure to make inroads in a highly developed capitalist country, where wage workers accounted for almost a third of the population, enjoyed universal manhood suffrage, and knew none of the legal hindrances to organization encountered in many areas of Europe, had become by the early 1890's a "deeply confusing" puzzle.[6] Marxists had long been perplexed by the failure of Marxist doctrine to sink roots in England and had recognized the non-militance of English workers as a significant indictment of their theory. Paul Lafargue asked in 1891,

> How does it happen that England, the most industrialized and monopolized country in the world, which has completely suppressed the class of peasant proprietors, which possesses an industrial proletariat which is the largest, the most concentrated in cities, and the best organized, and craft unions, that are the most disciplined and most capable of conducting and winning strikes, is the country where there exists no socialist agitation and no political movement of the working class?[7]

By the time Lafargue made this comment, however, things were beginning to move in England. While socialism was proceeding in a totally different direction from the one preferred by continental Marxists, it was winning over influential spokesmen and making an impact on the nation's political life. English labor had at last recognized the need for class political organization. Attention now focused on the United States as the black sheep of the Second International. Here labor still marched to the beat of the drum of one of the two major political parties, and existing trade unions showed little interest in independent political activity. Gaylord Wilshire, noting the transfer of Marxist concern from England to America, wrote in the English newspaper *Justice* in 1893,

[6] "Politische Uebersicht," *Vorwärts,* March 29, 1891.
[7] *Le Socialiste,* Sept. 26, 1891.

One of the disappointments in the life of Karl Marx was the slow development of a conscious Socialist movement in England, the country where the unconscious development, as seen by the centralisation of capital, was so pronounced. America is a still more remarkable paradox in this light than England. For while there has begun to be observable a very decided political movement here on Socialist lines, in America, as yet, there is scarcely any at all, although the centralisation of capital is far greater there than here.[8]

With the attack of socialist revisionism at the end of the century adding fuel to fires already lit by non-socialist critics of Marx, the weakness of the American socialist movement became an increasing embarrassment for Marxists in Europe. Was it possible that the rise of socialism did not go hand in hand with the rise of capitalism? Had the tenet of inevitable advance been squelched by developments in the New World? Were Marxist projections of a quick socialist victory in America mindless fantasies? The Austrian-born Max Beer, one of the most prolific writers produced by the Second International and an important historian of British socialism, worked in New York from 1899 to 1901. He made an exaggerated, but revealing, diagnosis of Marxist malaise when he reported that news from America in 1900, had it been from any other country, would not have been noticed in the more invigorating events elsewhere. But European Marxists always paused over the American scene because "all of us are so deeply convinced of the great importance of an American labor movement."[9] Later in his life Beer recalled the worry aroused at the turn of the century by "the attitude of American Labour [which] appeared to stand out as a living contradiction of the Marxian theory that the concentration of capitalist production, and attendant proletarization of the masses, was necessarily bound to lead to class struggles and to the formation of an independent Labour movement with Socialist aims and ends."[10]

Paul Louis, who with other Marxists had in 1900 seen America leading the way toward socialism, began to voice concern a few

[8] "The Socialist Movement in America," Jan. 7, 1893.
[9] "Am Vorabend der Präsidentenwahl in den Vereinigten Staaten," *Die Neue Zeit*, Vol. XVIII, Part II (1900), 582.
[10] *Fifty Years of International Socialism* (New York, 1935), 109–10.

years later over the meager number of dues-paying members of the American Socialist party (25,000 as of January 1904). The disappointing showing formed a target too easy for conservative writers to hit.[11] And Karl Kautsky struck perhaps an unintended note of pessimism when he wrote in 1902, "The future that America shows us would truly be a very discouraging one if it did not show us a strengthening of the socialist movement." [12] Marxists had been searching for concrete evidence of just such a strengthening for fifteen years and had always failed. They had begun in the late 1880's to invent a "new" promise for America. Any later admission that this promise would never materialize was intolerable; but, without more evidence of socialist progress than existed, Marxists needed an explanation for the continuing discrepancy between theory and actuality in the United States.

For a number of reasons the intellectual challenge to Marxism posed by America during the 1890's was considerably less acute than it was to become in the next decade. In the first place, European Marxists had started to anticipate a strong surge of socialist sentiment in America only in the mid-1880's. Obviously, the failure of a ground swell to materialize was much more troublesome after twenty years of waiting than after five. In addition, in 1890 Marxists recognized many factors in the American past which then seemed able to explain American labor's reluctance to enter socialist ranks. The historical stages of the Marxist dialectic had been truncated in the United States, because (as Louis Hartz has brilliantly discussed in *The Liberal Tradition in America*) America was born free. Europe had never known the absence of an oppressed class; the majority of the population had always faced a life of hopelessness and despair. Feudal society in Europe had been as torn by class antagonisms and struggles as the capitalistic society which grew up on its ruins. Capitalism changed the taskmaster, but little else in the broad outlines of human relationships. A man was born into the class of the privileged or the class of the dispossessed and remained an overseer or a slave. It had taken centuries of such oppression for a class of dispossessed to arise which had grasped the barbarity of all

[11] *L'Avenir du socialisme* (Paris, 1905), 18.
[12] "Bauernagitation in Amerika," *Die Neue Zeit,* Vol. XX, Part II (1901–2), 453.

past social arrangements and had moved toward a definitive break from its chains of slavery. The European urban masses, crowded together into factories and cramped living quarters, had finally appreciated the power of their numbers.

In striking contrast to the European pattern, the pre-capitalist stage in the United States had been an idyllic sort of rural life when most men did enjoy a unique degree of freedom. No one was caught in a proletarian class without hope of seeing himself or his children rise above it. Labor commanded a high price, and an indentured servant could expect to save enough to start a small commercial enterprise on his own or to buy a small farm. Even the Civil War, which pushed the capitalist class to unrivaled dominance in the United States and inaugurated a new era, did not immediately change this happy situation. Wage earners pressed into cities, large factories replaced the small workshop, mechanization brushed aside hand labor, and the division of labor pushed the master craftsman back into the pages of history. But the working man managed to hang on to certain advantages. The very wealth of the country enabled the entrepreneur at one and the same time to exploit labor brutally (that is, to skim off from available labor power greater and greater amounts of surplus value) and yet to pay the wage earner a salary which was high when compared to Europe. Profits grew much faster than wages, but the inequity did not immediately become apparent. Besides, a man unhappy with his wages could escape to the frontier. The safety-valve effect of the American hinterland was noted long before Frederick Jackson Turner made his famous address before the American Historical Association.

By 1890, according to one of the central theories of European Marxism, the position of the American worker had altered radically for the worse. Capitalism had taken its expected toll on human happiness, and America had pushed out into the mainstream of the history of Western civilization. But as Marxists pointed out, old circumstances and old ways of thinking molded by those circumstances did not pass away at the same time. The former, being of a material nature, died instantly; but the latter, partaking of intellect, tottered on into senility. Marx was well aware that ideas, once formulated, took on a life of their own and did not instantly submit to changes in the material or economic environment.

Engels had written about the great advantages enjoyed by the United States as a result of its escape from a feudal past. A freedom from traditional institutions and rigid and static codes of behavior had given the country a dynamism which allowed it to move much faster into the future than Europe. On the other hand, the country had lost something in its virgin birth. Or rather, it had failed to gain a measure of worldly wisdom sufficient to make its people sensitive to the oppression gripping them on every side in the latter part of the century. The American people, and especially the American worker, hardly knew what social or governmental evil was all about; and, when they faced it for the first time, their response, despite their usual resourcefulness, was incredibly naïve.

Perhaps it would have been better, after all, if American workers, like their counterparts in Europe, had had to fight for republican institutions and the right to participate in their country's political life. Some European wage earners, like the Germans, had not yet won the struggle; and the combining of the fight for social justice and fundamental political freedoms had greatly strengthened class consciousness. Karl Kautsky knew this when he wrote in 1904, "Just as the struggle for truth is much higher than the untroubled possession of a truth which another has earlier discovered, so the struggle for freedom is very much superior to the effortless possession of a freedom that others have won before." [13]

Even after a fierce struggle the attainment of a democratic republic had its dangers according to Marxists. It might induce the proletariat to relax and divert party followers from their main task of revolutionizing the social and economic spheres. Paul Louis warned that "no form of the state requires from the proletariat more rigidity, more defiance, more haughty and faithful perseverance to principles." [14] Because Americans enjoyed a democratic republic as their birthright, they were especially gullible to its allurements; they had come to equate it with their economic prosperity and had failed to understand that the two were completely unrelated. Unconscious of the power which trust magnates had gathered unto themselves, the American worker continued to

[13] "Der amerikanische Arbeiter," *Die Neue Zeit,* Vol. XXIV, Part I (1905-6), 751.
[14] *L'Avenir du socialisme,* 129.

invoke the Constitution and the Declaration of Independence as if the mouthing of political slogans could bring back a lost prosperity.

The American workers, Kautsky concluded, because of their relatively innocent past, "let themselves be led by the nose by demagogues and fools more than in any other country." [15] His remark received a great deal of support from Europeans who had lived a long time in the New World. Philipp Rappaport reported from the United States, "The American Constitution is for him [the American worker] the embodiment of all political wisdom, all political freedom; and this arrogance is so haughtily maintained that it is no exaggeration to say that the most down-and-out beggar bears his poverty more easily because it is American poverty." [16] The German-born Adolph Hepner, who had been tried for high treason with Wilhelm Liebknecht and August Bebel in 1872, wrote from St. Louis in 1893, "The great mass of the American proletariat are more patient than Job, more patriotic than the Constitution demands, and let themselves be misused like the zero that is placed next to the one to make a ten, but always remains a zero." [17] The American worker had grown up in a world where it had been possible to make money. He had been infected with bourgeois sensibilities and had become independent, selfish, and egotistic. It would take still a few years to overcome the emasculating effect of habit and the fading dreams of glory.

The crucial question became how long the American worker would be blinded by his innocence. After all, European Marxists had started painting a very gloomy portrait of labor conditions in America even before the Haymarket incident in Chicago. Marxists were not terribly consistent in dating the moment when they thought oppression of the American worker had reached the same levels it had in Europe. Depending on what point of their argument needed bolstering, they freely moved back and forth through the years. If they were emphasizing the brutality of capitalism in a general way, they might pinpoint the time as early as the mid-1870's. If they were

---

[15] "Der amerikanische Arbeiter," 744.
[16] "Ueber die Arbeiterbewegung in Amerika," *Die Neue Zeit,* Vol. VII (1889), 66.
[17] "Die Aussichten des Sozialismus in Amerika," *Die Neue Zeit,* Vol. XII, Part I (1893-94), 646.

trying to explain the slow progress of socialism in America, they found it advantageous to keep the moment as close to the present as possible.[18] Nevertheless, there was a limit as to how near the present they could set the date without appearing sophistical. Too much of their rhetoric since 1885 dealing with the New World had been concentrated on denying the American worker an exceptional position and in describing the wretched circumstances under which he lived. To redeem him as a favored creature, say in 1910, would have posed an outrageous contradiction.

Eleanor and Edward Aveling had reported back as early as 1886 on the unenviable position of the American worker. By 1890 the Marxist press everywhere in Europe had at one time or another joined in rejecting the old paradisiacal image of America and was agreed that, considering everything, the American worker suffered to a greater extent than the average worker in Europe. The various commentaries in the press also generally assumed in 1890 that after a few more years of experience with these new oppressive circumstances the American worker would slough off his docile attitudes. While present-day Marxists still sometimes refer to the American workers' blind submission to the American myths of social mobility and Horatio Algerism, Marxists in 1890 were scarcely ready to concede such sticking power to any myth. In this they were perhaps wiser than some of their contemporary counterparts. Remembrance of happy times could not feed or clothe the worker, and he would soon have to look for new solutions. The Avelings reported after their trip to the New World on the tremendous inroads which socialism was making into the subconscious of the American worker.[19] He was becoming a socialist without knowing it. Yet fifteen years after the Avelings came back from the New World, the American worker was apparently still deluding himself, for his unconscious conversion to socialism had not broken out into any significant overt manifestations.

[18] Marxists might at times find other reasons to move the date very close to the present. The author of "Deutsche Gewerkschaftsführer über die amerikanische Schuhindustrie" (*Vorwärts*, Oct. 15, 1913) gave a very favorable image of the position of the American worker in order to refute German conservatives who insisted wages could be no higher than they were in Germany. The influence of Bernstein's revisionism upon the author was very strong.

[19] *The Working Class Movement in America*, 21–22.

Dozens of times during the 1890's European Marxists detected encouraging signs of movement around the American workers' closed eyes, yet on each occasion the eyelids remained firmly shut. In the first decade of the new century critics of Marx assured one another that it was not the American workers' eyes that were shut, but those of Marx's disciples in Europe. The question was not how much longer American workers could go on kidding themselves, but how much longer Marxists could go on trading in illusions. If the American worker had really been as oppressed as Marxists had thought and if socialism had been making rapid inroads into the subconscious, then the first decade of the new century should have seen the growth of socialism into a major political force. The decade did in fact constitute socialism's finest hour in the United States, and American socialists were exuberant with the growth in their ranks. But measured against European expectations, it was not a terribly exciting performance. August Bebel wrote to Hermann Schlüter in 1910, "The American elections have disappointed us very much. It is without doubt hellishly difficult to work over there, but we had still expected somewhat more." [20] By 1910 this was a rather tired refrain. So was the refrain that the explanation for socialism's failure lay in the American past and not in the present.

Many of the dilemmas confronting European Marxists in explaining developments in America in the first decade of the new century were underlined by the publication in 1906 of Werner Sombart's famous study *Warum gibt es in den Vereinigten Staaten keinen Sozialismus?* [21] Sombart was a distinguished German economist whose commentaries on the capitalistic system had gained him an international reputation. Academic socialists, or *Kathedersozialisten,* for it was in this category Sombart belonged, were generally disliked by German Social Democrats; and through the years, even at this stage of his career when he showed strong debts to Marx, Sombart was bitterly attacked by Marxist writers. Social Democrats had no blanket aversion to intellectuals. Too many of their leaders were

[20] Letter of Jan. 13, 1910, Bebel Archives, International Institute of Social History, Amsterdam.
[21] *Warum gibt es in den Vereinigten Staaten keinen Sozialismus?* (Tübingen, 1906). Sombart's study first appeared in 1905 as a series of articles in the *Archiv für Sozialwissenschaft und Sozialpolitik.*

educated men from middle-class backgrounds, and many like Kautsky aspired to be little else than theorists. Intellectuals, however, who served a detached world of scholarship before the party press could never be more than untrustworthy fellow travelers.

Sombart's book on America won a general audience, but the author stated the central problem in a way which only Marxists could truly appreciate:

> If truly (as I myself have often assumed and argued) modern socialism follows as a necessary reaction to capitalism, then the land of the highest capitalistic development—that is, the United States— must be at the same time the classic land of socialism; its working class must be the bearer of the most radical socialist movement.

Since this was demonstrably not the case, since "this land of our future now has an essentially unsocialist labor class," Sombart asked whether Marxists had to revise their fundamental assumptions. Was it perhaps written in Europe's future that, as capitalism moved to the same heights it had attained in America, labor, rather than continuing to lock horns with capitalism in fearsome combat, would give support to the capitalistic system? [22]

There was much in Sombart's book to reassure European Marxists. In his first chapter he gave a vivid portrait of the ruthlessness of American capitalism and pointed to the vast gulf yawning between the rich and poor. He wrote, "I shall try to show later that in no land of the world—objectively considered—are the workers so exploited by capitalism as in the United States, that the worker in no land of the world so works his fingers to the bone in the sewers of capitalism or drives himself so quickly to death." In the conclusion to his study he assuaged Marxist fears by writing that the social situation in the United States would soon resemble Europe's social situation in all essential respects because the various factors which had worked in the past to retard the growth of socialism were rapidly vanishing. Marxists need not revise their basic assumptions on account of America: within a generation "socialism will in all likelihood come to fullest bloom in the New World." [23]

[22] *Warum*, 24–25 and 35.
[23] *Ibid.*, 130–31 and 141–42.

Sombart's comments comforted European Marxists only momentarily, and when they considered the book as a whole, most rejected it as an unacceptable solution to the problem of America's odd development. Sombart demonstrated a remarkable lack of consistency in his study, partly because he left it incomplete. He spent a whole chapter on describing the cruel oppressions of American capitalism, yet he left unfulfilled his promise to show why workers in America were more ill-treated than elsewhere and based his explanation of the weakness of American socialism on the relative well-being of the American laborer. In 1905 the average laborer in the United States ate better, dressed better, and lived in more comfortable surroundings than his counterpart in Europe. Moreover, he did not know the indignities of a social caste system: "Freedom and equality (not only in a formal-political, but also in a social-material sense) are for him not empty concepts, vague dreams as for the proletariat in Europe, but in good part are realities." Wives of millionaires and wives of wage earners shopped in the same stores, rode in the same streetcar carriages, and walked down the same streets in essentially the same dress. In factories, entrepreneurs, foremen, and workers entertained a mutual respect for one another. Considerations like these led Sombart to say, "On roast beef and apple pie, all socialist utopias have gone to pot." [24]

Some European Marxists saw a modicum of truth in these sections of Sombart's book. Franz Mehring, a left-wing German Marxist, wiser than many of his colleagues, after returning from a trip to the United States in 1906, reminded fellow comrades that "The most powerful bulwark of American capitalism . . . is that, next to the dark sides which are inseparable from capitalism, American life also possesses light sides." [25] The majority refused to be as favorable, for this concession raised difficulties which they were yet neither emotionally nor intellectually equipped to handle. To them, an acceptance of Sombart's idyllic portrait of the position of labor under American capitalism forced a repudiation of the bulk of their comments about the United States published in the past twenty-five years. His comparisons of the American laborer with his European counterpart harked back to Wilhelm Liebknecht's *Ein Blick in die*

[24] *Ibid.,* 127 and 126.
[25] "Eine Fahrt nach Amerika," *Leipziger Volkszeitung,* July 26, 1906.

Neue Welt which they had rejected as misguided in 1887. His statistics too closely bore out what an arch-enemy, the laissez-faire French economist Pierre Leroy-Beaulieu, had written in 1904: "It is well to remark that in the United States, also, in this most modern of all countries, facts completely contradict the various socialist theories about the iron law of wages, the growing pauperization of the proletariat, and the exorbitant profits of capital." [26]

If after fifty years of the operation of the most heartless capitalistic system in the world the American worker still enjoyed a relative degree of prosperity, Marxists had somehow misinterpreted the laws of economic development. True, America had once been a blessed continent; few denied its unsurpassed natural wealth and the softening effect of these riches on the normally brutal first stages of capitalistic oppression. Sombart's book implied, beyond this, that American capitalism had continued to improve the living standard of the worker significantly even into the twentieth century. It was this assertion which European Marxists found difficult to swallow, even though it offered them a convenient explanation for the continuing failure of socialism in the United States. Propping up one Marxist assumption (i.e. socialism could not make progress in America or anywhere else until the oppression of the capitalist system had grown severe) brought little comfort, if the use of that prop knocked down a second basic belief (i.e. the ongoing development of capitalism in a country would result in the rapid and complete degradation of the proletariat). One angry reviewer of Sombart's book wrote of the author's "roast beef and apple pie explanation":

> One must suppose, one must conclude therefrom, that just where capitalism had made the greatest expansion it also provides a quite comfortable life for the workman. The author must, then, not only recognize that herewith all socialistic "utopias" are refuted, but also he must revise his own views held hitherto and grant that capitalism does not necessarily breed the socialistic view among the workers.[27]

Accepting the contradiction of worker prosperity in the world's most developed capitalistic country did not offer Marxists in the Second

[26] *Les États-Unis au XXe siècle,* 205–6.
[27] "Kapitalismus und Sozialismus," *Vorwärts,* Oct. 9, 1906.

International a smooth route of escape from their concern over America's feeble socialist forces. It would merely be capitulating to outmoded interpretations of America's promise which Marxists had firmly rejected.

For these reasons the most important German Marxist reviews of Sombart's book were unfavorable and attacked the author unmercifully for his inconsistencies.[28] The American *International Socialist Review* enthusiastically received and printed Sombart's first chapter, but rejected the rest for containing gross distortions in its depiction of the present situation of the American worker.[29] Significantly, none of these critiques, while pointing out very clearly the incompatibility of Sombart's major thesis with their delineation of Marxist doctrine, managed to put forward an alternative answer to the question which the author had posed in his title. Theories were easily torn down, but not so easily replaced. Marxists found themselves hoist with their own petard. The very fierceness of their attacks on American prosperity made explanations of the weakness of American socialism all the more difficult.

Karl Kautsky read Sombart's study and thought it essential to write a systematic account explaining the failure of socialism in the United States. Because of Kautsky's prominence and the importance he gave this work, the points of his study are worth underlining. Kautsky immediately recognized the inadequacies of "roast beef and apple pie" as a solution. Unlike most Marxists, Kautsky was ready to admit that even in 1905 the American worker enjoyed a somewhat higher standard of living than the worker in Europe. But pointing to a sharp and serious decline in the position of American laborers since 1890, he dismissed any cause for envy as a relic of the distant past. From statistics of the United States Bureau of Labor, Kautsky demonstrated to his satisfaction how the buying power of weekly wages had been dropping since 1896. The rate of unemployment was higher in 1900 than it had been in 1890. More women and

---

[28] In addition to the *Vorwärts* review cited in previous note, see the one in *Die Neue Zeit,* Vol. XXV, Part I (1906–7), 584.

[29] See note in *International Socialist Review,* VII (1906–7), 425. It read in part, "The first chapters of the work reviewed above containing the valuable statistical portions appeared in the *International Socialist Review.* When we came to the nonsense on the condition of the American worker we stopped further publication."

children held down jobs in factories, and rich and poor stared at each other from different worlds. The traditional route of escape to the frontier had been blocked, for while land was still available in the United States, there was little whose fertility had not been exhausted. An extensive, superficial, inexpensive working of the soil no longer produced huge profits; and land fell increasingly into the hands of large capitalists who could afford the machinery required for the new and more intensive methods of farming.

Kautsky's reflections on the American situation appeared as a series of four articles in *Die Neue Zeit* in the latter part of 1905 and the early part of 1906.[30] He sought to explain two aberrancies which Marxists had to probe if they were to counter revisionist attacks and vindicate Marx's laws of historical development. America was part of an old problem which England had first posed: how to render intelligible the weakness of socialism in a nation where capitalism was very highly developed. Since 1905, when a vigorous proletariat reared its head in Russia and almost dealt Tsardom a fatal blow, European Marxists found themselves saddled with a second problem: how to account for a strong revolutionary proletariat in a country where, considering the small inroads of modern capitalism, the existence of a proletariat had not previously been expected. Kautsky tried to explain both anomalies by reference to the international movement of men and capital.

Kautsky outlined the mistakes of economists who, because they had used Marxist models only with reference to the development of single countries, had been misled by the contemporary world situation. The operation of the Marxist dialectic, he claimed, ignored national borders. On account of the growing economic interdependence of nations, what happened in one country could have repercussions anywhere in the world. Thus, while according to the dialectical process of history a preexisting bourgeois class created the conditions necessary to produce a revolutionary proletarian class, these two classes did not have to exist side by side in the same country to interact.

Following up this line of reasoning, Kautsky found a neat

[30] "Der amerikanische Arbeiter," Vol. XXIV, Part I (1905–6), 676–83, 717–27, 740–52, 773–87. Kautsky had, of course, read Sombart's study as it appeared in the *Archiv für Sozialwissenschaft und Sozialpolitik*.

analytical tool to attack the apparent paradox in Russia. Russia had a capitalist class, but it was a foreign one. When the time came for the industrialization of Russia, the monetary resources required had not been available at home: "On the contrary, foreign capital had to be attracted to build railroads, open mines, erect blast furnaces, spinning mills, weaving mills, and sugar factories." [31] The very fact that Russia's incipient proletarian force was exploited by entrepreneurs sitting in Paris and London actually guaranteed a more rapid coalescence of revolutionary fever than in countries with an indigenous capitalist class. In the first place, the failure of a middle class to grow in Russia allowed the government to be far more tyrannical than that of any country in western Europe and exposed the proletariat more directly to the abuse of power. Second, since profits earned in Russia were siphoned off by outside sources, a general impoverishment enveloped the whole country and placed the proletariat in a state of severe economic distress. Finally, the lack of a native bourgeois class left the intellectuals, who in western Europe invariably became the hired lackeys of the propertied classes, free to ally with the proletariat. Kautsky wrote, "Every rank, which in Western Europe is occupied professionally in putting to sleep and leading astray class consciousness, works in Russia untiringly for the most part to explain to the proletariat its class position. Nowhere is the number of theoretically educated socialist agitators greater than in this country of illiterates." [32] Although Russia remained largely an agricultural country, although modern capitalism did not have the impact it had in western Europe, a proletariat did exist. It was strong; it was militant; and it was determined, no matter how premature a socialist revolution might seem, to tear down the old order without further delay.

Since the deft importation of a band of foreign capitalists into Russia tidied up the loose ends of the Marxist dialectic with respect to that country, Kautsky attempted to explain the puzzling situation in America by an analogous reference to the foreign composition of its proletariat. America had a strong and relentless bourgeois class, but it lacked a homegrown proletariat. The native-born American worker had by and large made his escape to the frontier, and his

[31] "Der amerikanische Arbeiter," 679.
[32] Ibid., 683.

place in eastern factories had been taken by recent arrivals in the country. Based on statistics derived from the census of 1900, Kautsky concluded that of those engaged in agriculture in the United States, almost 60 per cent were native-born whites of native-born parents. This same group (which was around 50 per cent of the population) accounted for only 40 per cent of the industrial workers. On the other hand, foreign-born whites, while comprising a mere 10 per cent of the farmers, made up over 30 per cent of the wage earners. Moreover, when foreign-born whites were grouped with Negroes and native-born whites of foreign-born parents, they made up nearly 60 per cent of the industrial labor force.

The strong foreign element in the American proletariat, according to Kautsky, seriously crippled its capacity to act together. The heterogeneity of races and nationalities was a constant source of division. Split by religion, language, and cultural peculiarities, as well as deep-seated national rivalries and jealousies carried across the Atlantic, the proletariat could not achieve the same cohesiveness possible in countries where all its members stemmed from roughly similar backgrounds. The Negro was an additional complication in this picture, for no American worker, whether native- or foreign-born, showed an inclination to clasp hands with him. The American capitalist, recognizing these divisions, had become adept at exploiting them and knew that several boxcars of non-English-speaking workers could smash the effectiveness of a union protest anywhere. The native-born workers, embittered at the apparent backwardness of these spoilers, not only made no attempt to integrate them into their ranks, but deliberately excluded them. Until American laborers learned to say brotherhood in the same tongue and with the same accent, socialism would advance unevenly.

Kautsky's movement of men and capital across national borders clearly did not serve him nearly so well in America as it had in Russia. With Russia he had both elements he needed—a strong bourgeoisie (albeit a foreign one) and a strong proletariat—and he only needed to draw them together in such a way to make the former account for the latter. With America he had only a strong bourgeoisie to work with. The anomaly remained that, even after years of suffering under the highly publicized crimes of the bourgeois class, a class-conscious socialist proletariat had not arisen. There was marked national and cultural diversity within the American labor force; but, as was equally true from Kautsky's own statistics, 70 per cent of the wage-earning class were native-born Americans. Native-born whites of native-born parents made up numerically the largest single element in the labor force. While no one could dispute the existence of deep divisions among American workers, the growth of the trade union movement during the 1890's proved their potential for effective organization. Socialist ideas had plenty of room to make progress before running into cultural obstacles. Kautsky's explanation, for all its borrowed truth, did little to explain why the great majority of native-born American workers remained uninterested in socialism; and this aloofness was what European Marxists found most disturbing in the American situation and most damaging to their own view of the American Promised Land.[33]

If this had been the only drawback to Kautsky's argument, it perhaps would have carried conviction. There was a greater one. By 1905 the explanation had grown old. Since Marx and Engels had first cast their glance in the direction of America, Marxists had remarked on the difficulty of organizing a diversified proletariat. But without the slightest hesitation they had made the additional observation that in view of the brutality of American capitalism the difficulty was temporary and would not prevent the American proletariat from shortly rallying around the banner of international socialism. Just as with the arguments of remembered prosperity and the durability of the American myth of economic opportunity, Marxists found themselves endlessly repeating phrases which they had originally thought would become obsolete within a few years. This was not a difficulty confined to these particular lines of thought. The same quality of déjà vu stamped most of the other explanations used by European Marxists in the first decade of the new century to account for the slow advance of socialist ideas in America. The power of persuasion of any argument, no matter how strong, grew weaker as the years passed.

For example, Marxists after 1900 frequently remarked on the heavily rural orientation of America's economy which had survived

[33] This represents only the core of Kautsky's argument. He does at the conclusion of his series advance some other reasons for the slow progress of socialism in America. These further arguments were not original and are subject to the same criticism as the ideas discussed in the rest of this chapter.

in spite of the fantastic advance of industry in many areas. Large-scale industry, according to some statistics mustered by Franz Mehring in 1906, existed in only ten of the forty-five states and left the United States "still overwhelmingly an agricultural country." [34] A farm mentality seriously interfered with the attempts of labor to publicize socialist ideas across the continent because the strong attachment of the small farmer to the ideology of private property made him a natural enemy of the urban proletariat. Socialism appealed to large but relatively isolated groups. The party might make progress in urban centers, but somehow the achievement was swallowed up in the vastness of the continent. Only a national victory for socialism could really advance the cause, for, so long as the Supreme Court stood ready to interpret the American Constitution as a handbook of laissez-faire economic principles, locally elected socialist officials were helpless to introduce effective reform programs which could transform basic social inequities. Since a national victory awaited the apparently far-off time when states like Iowa and Montana would feel the effects of the class struggle, it was hard to get anyone interested in party work.

The argument was not altogether convincing to Marxists, not least because too literal an acceptance of it would have made a victory in the New World much too remote. European Marxists could not forget that they had judged the American urban proletariat in 1886 to be large enough to start a revolution, and by 1905 American labor had grown rather than diminished in significance. If labor had voted as a unit for its own party, it could have elected just as many congressional representatives as the parties in any European country, and it no doubt would have exercised as great, if not greater, an influence over national political life. Moreover, the experience in Europe had long demonstrated the fallacy of viewing the farming segment of the populace as one great mass of reaction. In countries as diverse as Russia and Germany urban socialists had been able to make valuable allies among rural elements. It is not entirely paradoxical that the Socialist party of America was to run up its greatest vote in the state of Oklahoma.

European Marxists also continued to repeat in the 1900's a theme picked up from Bryce's *American Commonwealth* which empha-

---

[34] "Eine Fahrt nach Amerika," *Leipziger Volkszeitung,* July 26, 1906.

sized the difficulties facing third party movements in America. The Republican and Democratic parties had consolidated political machines in every section of the country. Men adhered to a party in America, not from devotion to principle, but because of a lust for the favors of patronage. Each large party had unlimited funds to purchase votes and, what was worse, to buy off labor leaders who were flirting with radicalism. Samuel Gompers became for European Marxists the symbol of the union boss who, for pay, betrayed his class. His attacks on the Socialist party and his determination to keep the AFL free of class politics were bad. His participation in the National Civic Federation, an organization of businessmen and trade unionists who met together to promote harmony between labor and capital, was unspeakable.

Against entrenched political power, socialist parties had serious difficulty making headway. Isolated socialist victories did not easily consolidate into a national pattern of victory.[35] The enthrallment of the Americans with majority rule made voters reluctant to cast ballots for a party without a reasonable chance of winning and held progress in limbo. Since America lacked a system of proportional representation or a system by which one could mark a second choice on the ballot, a vote cast for a minor party was a vote cast away.

Yet, again, mere reiteration of an old argument, however valid a starting point, became a hackneyed way to evade the more obvious point that workers in America did not vote the socialist ticket because they had not been persuaded socialism offered them a better solution to their problems (or even because they did not think their problems as serious as socialists imagined). European Marxists had the example of German Social Democrats constantly before them. Had they not built a strong party under a political system which on the face of things offered them very little chance of success? The timidity of the labor force in a country where, once organized, it could have enjoyed enormous influence, yet awaited a satisfactory explanation.

[35] The Socialist party of America found that if it did manage to pose a real challenge to the two major parties, as it did in Milwaukee, the two parties were not above joining forces to defeat socialist candidates. The Republicans and Democrats formed just such a fusion ticket in Milwaukee in 1912 and managed to prevent the reelection of a number of socialist candidates who had won in 1910.

Imperialism did offer Marxists a fresh theme to utilize in the 1900's as a reason for the tardiness of the revolution in the United States and everywhere else. It was by no means an entirely new argument. Marxists had long been attributing capitalism's survival in the West to the opening of markets in lesser developed areas of the world. To recall an earlier part of this study, the United States for many years, according to Marxist writers, had served Europe, and especially England, in much the same way as a colonial possession. Slave-produced cotton had provided a cheap source of raw material to keep English mills running; and the American provincials, in turn, had brought the excess of overproduced European goods.

Late nineteenth century imperialism involved more than a search for markets, and after 1900 the competition for actual colonies among the European powers stimulated Marxists to sketch out more systematically the cumulative effects of imperialism, particularly the impact which foreign exploitation had on the domestic labor movement. Distinguished luminaries of the Second International, Karl Kautsky, Rosa Luxemburg, and Lenin among them, wrote extensively on the subject of imperialism and quarreled bitterly over what attitude socialists should take toward the expansionist ventures of their own countries. On one point they all agreed: the proletariat in imperialistic countries was somewhat better off materially than the proletariat in non-imperialistic countries, because capitalists used part of the vast profits derived from abroad to ease the situation of the lower classes at home. Moreover, the money exploited from labor in the Far East could be employed to bribe domestic labor leaders. It was a shabbily calculated design on the part of Western capitalists to defeat socialism; and for several decades it had worked very well, better in some countries than in others.

The significant obstacle preventing an easy application of this line of reasoning to the United States resulted from its lack of colonies. America's merry and ill-conceived excursions abroad in the 1890's made it an imperialist power, but not nearly on the scale of Germany, England, and Holland. In terms of both their absolute size and importance to the economy, the overseas possessions of the United States were not great.

America's own vast hinterland suggested one way out of this

difficulty, for, as it was pointed out, the sparsely settled areas of the west provided the United States with a built-in colony. Developed capitalistic systems, according to Marxists, had to prey on pre-capitalistic societies to survive, but American capitalism, unlike European capitalism, could find such societies within its own continental borders.[36] It already had a great interior market to relieve the pressures of chronic overproduction.

Again this argument had its difficulties. To carry it too far pushed one back into the assertion that American workers did in fact enjoy a prosperous existence (the old bourgeois myth of the American Promised Land again), which was exactly the position from which Marxists wanted to extricate themselves. Furthermore, when European Marxists wrote about imperialism in Europe and America (this remained true until after World War I), they were trying to explain why the revolution had not come twenty years before. Before the Russian Revolution a search for long-range reasons to explain socialism's failure in developed industrial nations did not suggest itself to them. Unlike more sophisticated Marxist economists of our own time (and some of their own time like Rudolph Hilferding who were disassociating Marx from the deterministic assumptions which informed so much of the Marxist thinking discussed in this period) they never accepted the problem as one which could continue for many years into the future. Informed (and fatally prejudiced) by a belief in the immediacy of revolution, their explanations looked backward rather than forward and were intended to account for what had happened rather than what was to come.

Marxists prior to 1917 never dreamed that imperialism might be used to explain the continuance of capitalism for another fifty years. The very reason they wrote about imperialism was to announce the dead end which capitalist evolution had finally reached. Lenin characterized imperialism as the last stage of capitalism to demonstrate that capitalism was in the last of its nine lives and faced imminent extinction. The two greatest imperialist powers, Germany and England, already had large proletarian armies. In the light of this evidence, America's recalcitrance about falling into line became more, not less, of a problem.

[36] Rosa Luxemburg's *The Accumulation of Capital* (trans. by Agnes Schwarz-schild, New Haven, 1951, first published in 1913) is instructive on this point. See especially pages 395–410.

European Marxists, in casting about for reasons to dispel the confusion raised by developments in America, sometimes seized on the very brutality of capitalist institutions. The trusts, after all, had become all powerful in the New World, and it was hard to conceive of any force growing large enough to challenge them. Trust magnates intimidated the American worker with blacklists, lockouts, and court injunctions. Reprisals against workers who tried to shake the establishment by speaking out for socialism followed them all over the country. Profitable employment in their chosen calling was permanently barred to them. Economic oppression of this sort was the prime mover behind socialist agitation, for without it workers would never join together in a revolutionary army. However, to inject another instance of Marxist ambiguity, if oppression went too far it could dull the workers' sensibilities, sap their strength, and reduce them into a listless, aimless class of *Lumpenproletariat*. This apparently was at the bottom of H. M. Hyndman's fears about the English proletariat when he wrote in 1907 that four generations of capitalism, years of bad housing, bad air, and bad food, had taken a heavy toll and left the workers devoid of any aspirations toward revolution.[37] Kautsky had warned as early as 1891, "The more degraded the groups from which the proletariat is recruited, the more difficult it is to elevate the recruits to the point at which they are willing and able to join the ranks of the militant proletariat." [38] Perhaps, some Marxists claimed, the degradation of the American worker explained his irresolution.

This argument did no more than any of the others to help Marxists out of their theoretical difficulties. If anything, it only served to stress the state of confusion at which most of them had arrived in trying to deal with the socialist movement in America. The real emotional appeal of Marxism to the workers lay in the association of heroism with their degraded and lowly position. The thought that they alone, surrounded as they were by all the baseness and drabness which human life had been able to create, were the bearers of a better social order gave them a reason to go on. To suggest that the spark of proletarian heroism had gone out in the New World under the weight of exploitation was hardly a way to bolster spirits.

[37] "Darkness and Dawn of May-Day, 1907," *Justice*, May 4, 1907.
[38] *The Class Struggle*, trans. by William E. Bohn (Chicago, 1910), 213.

Fortunately the revolution of 1905 in Russia came in time to reassure the European proletariat of the survival of courageous will in the worst of circumstances. Most Marxists who thought about the problem preferred to believe that as a result of the heavy degree of capitalist exploitation in America the final revolt would be all the more swift and decisive. In the meantime, while Marxists stood in nervous anticipation, there remained the uncomfortably long wait.

A number of important European Marxists in the five or six years surrounding 1900 named the United States as the probable site of the first socialist victory. In this land where capitalism had advanced without restraint, where justice and legislation had been brutally pressed into the service of the monied elite, the proletariat could not help but be the first to deliver the old system its coup de grâce. The slow progress of socialism in America sent these Marxists scurrying for explanations, but it did not at first dampen their glowing predictions. The initial effect was probably quite the opposite. The more non-socialists and revisionist socialists pointed to America's development as a sufficient refutation of Marx, the more blatantly—perhaps even recklessly—some Marxist writers insisted that America, on the contrary, would shortly furnish the strongest evidence of the validity of Marx's predictions. Marxists writing about the future of America sometimes acted like ladies who protest too much; they kept talking to cover up a feeling of lost virtue. Adversaries had taken unfair advantage of them, but time would vindicate their honor.

Marxists chose to take comfort in Paul Louis' statement: "If it is true that communist ideas have not succeeded at a particular instant in some country in continuing to make progress, that is no cause for discouragement. For one cannot by isolating several months or several years in the life of a people deduce rational or legitimate conclusions." [39] They clung to what they believed was the truth in Charles Rappoport's argument: "The industrial proletariat can be momentarily stopped in its march toward revolutionary socialism. It may be deceived by some interested individuals or by the advantages of a temporary period of economic prosperity, blinded by the more or less apparent liberties of a democratic regime, but sooner or later it will become socialist." [40] Karl Kautsky concluded his own

[39] *L'Avenir du socialisme*, 15.
[40] "Le Mouvement international," *Le Socialiste*, Dec. 21–28, 1902.

articles in which he discussed the obstacles facing the development of socialism in America by saying, "America will perhaps show us earlier than Europe the example of a proletariat that overcomes the political and economic means used by the capitalist class to maintain power and founds a socialist society." [41] A series of setbacks was not alone sufficient to destroy the idea of America as a socialist promised land, and announcements concerning it periodically appeared in the European socialist press.

The passage of years eventually did take a toll and result in a dimming of European Marxist hopes for America. After 1905, as the revisionist controversy died down, as socialists in Europe continued to make impressive gains, and as Marxist attention was drawn increasingly to the growing quarrels between European nations and a possible war, the attention and enthusiasm showered on America grew noticeably less. Orthodox Marxists had matured under the strains of hard political work and were less receptive to images of sudden and dramatic victory. If Marxists wanted to bet on a long shot, the Russian Revolution of 1905 suggested a younger and more flashy entry. The Marxist press was as enthusiastic as ever about the general prospects for world revolution, but time marched on without giving the readers any new reasons to be interested in the United States.

Algie M. Simons reported sadly after the 1907 International Socialist Convention that American delegates were treated more like guests than like members. The other delegates "seemed to act as though we Americans meant well—but we were not 'doing things.'" [42] The Socialist party of America, launched so enthusiastically in 1901, had brought disappointing results. One frequent reporter on American conditions for Die Neue Zeit, Philipp Rappaport, had written shortly after the formation of the party, "It is astonishing what progress socialist ways of thinking have made here in the last few years. . . . The polling of a million socialist votes in the next general election would be no more surprising than the polling of a greater figure." [43] Several years later Rappaport was

[41] "Der amerikanische Arbeiter," 787.
[42] A. M. Simons to Gaylord Wilshire, *Wilshire's Magazine*, XI (Oct. 1907), 3, quoted in Ira Kipnis, *The American Socialist Movement*, 244.
[43] "Verfassungsrecht und Arbeiterschutzgesetzgebung in den Vereinigten Staaten," *Die Neue Zeit*, Vol. XXI, Part II (1902–3), 826.

considerably less sanguine. The party in 1904 had not even polled half a million votes, and Rappaport now feared that comrades in America would have to wait for victory until they could convert the Democratic party to their program.[44] Working within a third party, to this observer, was a hopeless cause.

The editor of *Die Neue Zeit* as a pro forma matter registered his disagreement with Rappaport's latter conclusion and continued to voice confidence in the ability of the American Socialist party to carry the country. The Marxist American Promised Land, though dying, was not dead. To some it had become a habit; to others it still seemed a necessary deduction from Marxist economics. Kautsky and Bebel continued to believe in it. In 1910 *Vorwärts* announced the election of the socialist ticket in Milwaukee saying "the weakness of the socialist movement in America was constantly a hindrance for European socialism." Before long, it now appeared, "socialism will take in the United States the position that corresponds to the development of American capitalism." [45]

English Marxists especially continued to reflect their own disappointments and frustrations by heralding in the American movement the progress they so devoutly wished at home. They saw in the American Socialist party the counterpart of their own organization. The American party, like the Social Democratic Federation, had for many years been a very small sect without much influence among common laborers. Also, like the SDF, it had refused to compromise with non-socialist elements in the labor movement in order to increase its strength. If now, after so many years of struggle, the American party was finally coming to life, could this not possibly presage a similar reward for their own efforts? Every socialist official elected in the Anglo-Saxon republic across the Atlantic could be used as a reproach to moderate socialists in England who insisted on cooperation with the non-doctrinaire Labour party as the only way to power. Tom Quelch, on the basis of victories won by the American party in 1910 and 1911, wrote, "The day is not far distant when the Red Flag will wave over the Capitol at Washington. . . . It is in the United States that I believe the first great decisive battle

[44] "Parteipolitisches aus den Vereinigten Staaten," *Die Neue Zeit,* Vol. XXV, Part I (1906–7), 291–98.
[45] "Die Wahlen in den Vereinigten Staaten," Nov. 10, 1910.

between the working class and the capitalist class will be fought." [46]
When Eugene Debs corralled almost a million votes in 1912, Hyndman seized upon it as a splendid occasion to pontificate:

> Never in my life has there been anything more encouraging in the whole movement than this. For let there be no mistake about the significance of this splendid achievement by our American comrades. We old and much-abused Marxists are justified of our children. All that we have taught, all that we have preached, all that we have striven for, has been accepted and acted upon by the overwhelming majority of our Party over there. [47]

Unfortunately, Hyndman's words were brave words rather than realistic ones, and like most of his words they found a small audience. If Debs' poll in 1912 was the most encouraging news in the world movement for over a generation, then Marxism was in deep trouble. Most Marxists on the Continent preferred to look elsewhere for comfort—especially to progress in their own countries. They liked to see signs of life in the American movement, but few of them reflected any longer a convincing faith in America's ability to lead the way to the cooperative commonwealth.

Declining interest in the prospects of the United States was evidenced as much by the tone as by the quantity of commentary in the Marxist press. After 1905 little that was said about America was new, and much was drawn directly from old copy and reprinted unaltered. Nothing as dramatic as the rise of American capitalism or the consolidation of the trusts appeared to give fresh inspiration, and the old themes were not as interesting. European Marxists had trapped themselves in the rhetoric of the past. They could not repudiate it, but they found it increasingly difficult to defend. All they could do was to go on saying the same things and behave as though the arguments had lost none of their persuasiveness. Explanations offered to account for the slow development of socialism in America grew tiresomely repetitious and revealed considerable confusion and contradiction. There was no way to pretend any longer that progress was up to expectations, and many European Marxists, lacking any

[46] "Socialism in the United States," *Justice*, May 4, 1912.
[47] "Social-Democracy Wins," *Justice*, Jan. 18, 1913.

satisfactory answer to the disappointing results, found it the better part of valor to withdraw their attention from the other side of the Atlantic.

The outbreak of World War I destroyed the Second International. The unity of the International was illusory anyway, as it had never been more than a loose association of autonomous national units. Nevertheless, when nationalism proved to be a stronger force than proletarian solidarity, the crest of optimism on which international leaders had been riding for two and a half decades collapsed. Some comrades of the extreme left wing of the Marxist movement welcomed the armed conflict as the last gasp of a dying and corrupt capitalistic system; it could end only with the establishment of socialism. For most comrades the despair of war was too immediate, and they focused their attention on bringing their nation safely through the holocaust. Rather than working to turn opposition at home into an internal civil war between classes, they joined in bourgeois governments to present a united front to a common external enemy.[48]

Gustav Eckstein, writing in *Die Neue Zeit* in 1914, reacted to the outbreak of war and the fumbling efforts of European socialists to prevent it by saying that the hope of socialism now more than ever before had come to rest in the New World:

> The war, which is now trampling down the fields of Europe and is causing enormous loss in human life and value, will probably transfer the chief weight of economic life from the old to the new world. Because of that . . . the American labor movement will become far more important for the fate of the world proletariat than one could have imagined only a short time ago. This significance is heightened by a special circumstance. The war had violently shaken the proletarian International. . . . After the war . . . the impulse for a new, hopefully even more firmly concluded International can most easily arise from the proletariat of the United States; they seem to be called to fasten together again ties cut by the war. For they

---

[48] The standard account is Merle Fainsod, *International Socialism and the World War*. It should be noted, however, that Fainsod's thesis that doctrinal splits in the International in the first years of the century foreshadowed the splits which took place in socialist ranks when war broke out has been so qualified as to make it almost useless.

unite within themselves members of all the nations which are
fighting today.[49]

Eckstein's comment was wistful. Few Marxists could bring themselves to re-pin great expectations on America. The United States
had been for years a great disappointment for them, and nothing
had happened to convince them of any likely change in the pattern.
When they did turn their attention to the New World during the
war years, they did not look to it as a potential promised land—at
least, not in a socialist sense. The chief concern of European Marxists about America had become whether it would enter the war and,
if so, on whose side. Nationalism, not Marxism, informed these
speculations.

When the guns of war finally quieted, it became apparent how
poor a prophet Eckstein had been. The American Socialist party was
in ruins. The call for a new International emanated, not from the
country whose capitalistic economy was the most advanced, but from
one that was very nearly the least. The course of the Russian Revolution inevitably shifted attention away from the degree of capitalist development as a reliable indication of a nation's readiness for
revolution. Marxists who supported the Bolshevik cause put more
emphasis than heretofore on the will of the proletariat—or, more
correctly, on the will of a small vanguard of the proletariat. They
used the doctrine of imperialism to explain why revolution, in fact,
could sometimes come more quickly in the underdeveloped countries
of the world than in the developed. Their whole timetable for the
revolution in developed nations became vaguer.

The endurance of capitalism in the United States and the continuing antagonism of the American worker to socialist principles
remained problems; and, as the problems became more permanent,
European Marxists became less good-humored in their assessments
of the United States. Before the Russian Revolution, Marxists heaped
abuse on American capitalism, but many saw a great future for the
country. America was not the promised land which European
liberals pictured it to be. But there was little doubt that the favored
position of the continent might produce a socialist commonwealth
capable of arousing the envy and admiration of the entire world.

[49] "Aus Amerikas Arbeiterbewegung," Vol. XXXIII, Part I (1914–15), 120

The postwar history of Europe killed this benign expectation in the breasts of the Marxists who turned toward Bolshevism. It did not happen immediately after the Russian Revolution; but, inevitably, in the gradual poisoning of relations between Soviet Russia and the United States, the latter took on the countenance of an enemy. America had become more than an abstract theoretical problem for the Marxist dialectic; it was an aggressive capitalist power seeking to destroy socialist revolutions wherever they were successful. In that dark role the image of America fostered by so many of its bourgeois admirers in the nineteenth century found its complete antithesis. The American Promised Land was now dead, and this time Marxists offered no revised versions.

CHAPTER 6

REVISIONIST SOCIALISTS TAKE
ANOTHER LOOK AT THE OLD
PROMISE OF AMERICA

EDUARD BERNSTEIN's apostasy was sudden, or so it seemed at the time.[1] A decade of exile in England before he published *Evolutionary Socialism* had exposed him thoroughly to the conciliating doctrines of English socialists; but Engels, who scrutinized his movements in London closely, had only detected a small sign of *Fabian-Schwärmerei* in these years and had attached no importance to it.[2] When Engels died in 1895, his confidence in Bernstein was intact, and he left his literary remains trustingly to Bernstein and August Bebel. The gesture was appropriate. Bernstein's career in the Marxist movement up to that date had given him unassailable credentials to interpret both the letter and the spirit of scientific socialism. Serving the party as theorist, journalist, and editor, the former Jewish bank clerk, born in Berlin just two years after the great liberal awakening of 1848, had joined the Social Democratic movement at the age of twenty-two (in 1872) and worked for it tirelessly and courageously. Yet one year after Engels' death Bernstein started a series of articles in *Die Neue Zeit* which was to make his name synonymous with heresy among orthodox Marxists.

[1] This chapter is about socialists who challenged Marx from the right. Opposition existed on the left as well, but I have not tried to deal with it in a separate chapter. Anarchists and syndicalists, so far as I have been able to determine, did not differ significantly from Marxists in their ideas about America.
[2] Peter Gay, *The Dilemma of Democratic Socialism: Eduard Bernstein's Challenge to Marx* (New York, 1952), 55–56.

Why did Bernstein in the late 1890's decide to disturb the reigning peace in the Second International by affronting the accepted premises of Marxist thought? The answer is that he had intended to consolidate, not divide, the movement. Bernstein had a normal share of vanity, but he was not seeking to begin a great schism. No one was more surprised by the attention his articles and book received nor more concerned about the acrimonious controversy they stirred. Although ordinary virtues are infrequently given credit these days, Bernstein seems to have been inspired by simple intellectual honesty. *Evolutionary Socialism* of 1899 was an attempt to understand a bewildering variety of developments in the capitalist world in the late nineteenth century. Any Marxist who pulled his head out of the sand could see that the cataclysmic disruptions of economic systems and the dramatic polarization of social classes had not taken place to the degree Marx had foretold. And, according to Bernstein, if he did not immediately thereafter push his head into the clouds, he could also see that the parliamentary practices of the Social Democrats bore little resemblance to their revolutionary phrases.

Bernstein wanted to pull socialist theory and practice together again and relate both to the real world. For his labors (although he was very well liked) Marxists branded Bernstein with the title "revisionist," a scornful epithet they have subsequently used to impugn all socialist opponents who they think have capitulated to reformist or opportunist ideas. Bernstein did not appreciate the pejorative content of the label, but he accepted it. Revisionism, in his mind, by reassessing, rearranging, and redefining Marxist principles with a view to contemporary trends, was the only way to preserve the detached, critical spirit of Marxist inquiry.

Anyone who has dealt with the socialist literature of the late nineteenth and early twentieth centuries will recognize the difficulty (though it might appear easy from socialist polemics) of making very clear demarcations between the Marxist and revisionist camps. For one thing, personality clashes and leadership struggles frequently opened wider splits in socialist ranks than divergences in theory and pushed socialists in a direction opposed to their normal intellectual sympathies. Also, since there could be no agreement over a single interpretation of Marx, the ones who understood Marx the least often insisted on their orthodoxy the most. Marxists were perhaps more bound together by a belief in the infallibility of Marx and Engels than by a clear and general consensus over a set of socialist propositions. Those who had read even one volume of *Capital* with comprehension formed a small minority at any Marxist gathering, and they usually paraded their literacy by bickering among themselves.

The term "revisionist" grew to designate an even more amorphous group of thinkers. Though originally applied to Bernstein and his followers in Germany, it opened like an umbrella to cover all the right-wing socialist parties in Europe at the turn of the century. While the leaders of these various parties recognized a convergence of their views on certain assumptions and attitudes and developed ties of loyalty among themselves, they were not all prompted in their deviations by the same impulses which prompted Bernstein in his; and the level of consensus among them was considerably less than among Marxists. Several of their movements, the most famous being the *possibiliste* movement in France and the Fabian movement in England, predated Bernstein's aberrations by a decade or more and arose not so much as a reaction to Marxist orthodoxy, as was the case with Bernstein, as an indifference to it.[3]

In addition, revisionism was a two-headed monster with one head silently contemplating the theoretical fallacies of Marx and the other head vocally urging a moderation of Marxist revolutionary tactics. Sometimes these two heads could sit comfortably on the same shoulders. For example, Bernstein's recommendations for a moderation of socialist tactics followed naturally from his alterations of Marxist theory. But more often the two heads split apart and went off in search of separate bodies. Many European socialists in the early twentieth century found themselves drawn to revisionist tactics, which allowed a full reconciliation with parliamentary methods, put primary emphasis on reforming the capitalist system according to socialist specifications, and opened the door for collaboration with non-proletarian elements in society, but were either totally unconcerned with what Bernstein or anyone else said about

---

[3] In this chapter, I have used the term "revisionism" to cover Fabianism, possibilism, reformism, socialist trade unionism, Bernsteinism, and related right-wing schools. This is a convenience which is appropriate enough for the questions asked by this study; it should not lead the reader to think that in precise historical terms there were no differences between the groups.

the need to modify Marxist theory or expressly rejected that side of the revisionist coin.

The career of the French socialist Jean Jaurès illustrates very well this tendency to straddle the fence separating Marxism from revisionism. Jaurès was one of the towering figures of his era, a brilliant, compassionate, and charismatic man. His tragic assassination in the summer of 1914 made him the symbol of the brotherhood which the Second International wished so desperately to preserve yet fumbled away with the opening guns of World War I. The British labor leader Ramsay MacDonald, in recalling the moral fervor and oratorical skill of Jaurès, said, "Jaurès rejected Marxism because he saw soul everywhere." [4] MacDonald, understandably, was eager to identify Jaurès with his own firmly revisionist stance; but, in truth, Jaurès' rejection of Marxism was a mixed case. When the written debates between Bernstein and Kautsky captured the attention of the European socialist world and forced comrades to take clearly defined positions they would normally have preferred to leave shadowy, Jaurès came down firmly on the side of Kautsky in his defense of Marxist theory. At exactly the same time, in 1899, he defended the acceptance by socialist deputy Alexandre Millerand of a portfolio in the bourgeois cabinet of Waldeck-Rousseau. Such a compromise with the representatives of capitalism constituted according to the guidelines of accepted Marxist tactics the worst form of opportunism.

Jaurès' role in the matter, as well as his continuing determination to tie socialism to a parliamentary course, led most of his contemporaries, despite his firm protests, to link him to the revisionist camp. Did he not in practical matters almost always side with Paul Brousse and the *possibiliste* wing of French socialism against Jules Guesde and Paul Lafargue? While he did, Jaurès considered himself as good a Marxist as any man and insisted that his attempts to moderate socialist tactics only carried to a logical fulfilment trends in the direction of compromise which the most militant Marxists had long accepted. In saying this, Jaurès hit an exposed and tender Marxist nerve, which was the main reason Marxists worked so hard to cast the persuasive Frenchman in the role of an adversary.

Less frequently, a socialist reversed this split by rejecting the

[4] Lord Elton, *The Life of James Ramsay MacDonald* (London, 1939), 79–80.

tactics associated with revisionism and adopting the major part of the theory. In the case of the English socialist E. Belfort Bax, the results were bizarre. Bax was one of the great eccentrics of the European socialist movement, if for no other reason than because he adamantly opposed the suffragette campaign for the emancipation of women. He considered himself a devout Marxist and remained a leading member of Hyndman's Social Democratic Federation. From that vantage point he kept up a heavy attack on the socialists in the British Labour party who worked alongside men who not only did not understand socialism but positively rejected it as a final goal. However, having established his Marxist purity by this theatrical rejection of compromise, Bax saw no harm in throwing out Marx's materialistic interpretation of history. Bax's view of man allowed for the persuasive effect of factors other than those associated with strict economic wants and needs. When the similarity between his own ideas about the moving causes of history and the theoretical portions of Bernstein's works was pointed out to him, Bax accused Bernstein of plagiarism and insisted that a belief in historical materialism was not basic to Marxism. To Kautsky, who was a much more gifted interpreter of Marx, Bax's position was indefensible.

A final difficulty in differentiating Marxism from revisionism arises from the fact that revisionists around the turn of the century were not usually anti-Marx. In most cases they were decidedly pro-Marx; and many, ignoring their critics, continued to characterize themselves as Marxist. The quickest way to put a revisionist writer on the defensive was to accuse him of ignorance of the classic works by Marx and Engels and assail him as a throwback to the empty-headed dreaming of the utopian school of socialism which flourished before the publication of *Capital*. The English Fabians, perhaps the group most snobbishly independent of Marx, had adherents like William Clarke and George Bernard Shaw who showed the effect of having made their way carefully through Marx's writings. By the turn of the century Marx and Engels had become the starting point of everyone who seriously claimed a voice in the Second International. Revisionists filled books and articles with appeals to their authority, and their works often revealed a more sophisticated understanding of Marxist economics than was manifested in books by more venerated Marxist leaders. Some of the latter unfortunately showed a marked propensity to freeze a few superficials of the Marxist scheme into a simpleminded caricature of the original. One is reminded in this respect of Marx's much quoted exclamation to his son-in-law Lafargue shortly before Marx died: "What is very certain is that I am no Marxist!" [5]

As the best approximation of truth, let us regard Marxism and revisionism at the turn of the century as only tendencies (or, perhaps better said, tensions) within the socialist movement and say that the majority of comrades did not swing wholly one way or the other. Like the Belgian socialist leader Émile Vandervelde a socialist might, at one moment, call himself a Marxist and vigorously attack Bernstein and, in the next breath, question Marx's position on materialism and call for an electoral program aimed at a temporizing compromise with the capitalist system rather than its overthrow. However, so long as in calling a man a Marxist we are not misled into thinking him a perfect oracle of the master or in calling him a revisionist we do not imagine we have stripped him of all links with the school of scientific socialism, we may still make some generalizations. We may point to certain traits which joined the Marxist to the world view of the two founders of scientific socialism (even if in some cases Marx and Engels disclaimed their disciples) and certain traits in the revisionist which in terms of the history of ideas put him on a different path altogether.

The following discussion is simplified, but does not distort the theoretical positions which the opposing camps usually took in their journals and newspapers. As has been apparent throughout the book, America did not normally spark original or sophisticated socialist thinking, but was used to buttress conventional—and easily grasped —socialist wisdom. Thus, the United States, although frequently used as a propaganda weapon, was simply ignored in many theoretical studies. I have laid out the differences between Marxists and revisionists in the only way which makes their disagreement about the United States understandable. The European socialists who tended toward revisionism found many reasons to portray the United States in a very different light from the one beamed on it by the more unsmiling adherents of orthodoxy. The selective evidence

[5] Widely cited. See, for example, Eduard Bernstein, *Aus den Jahren meines Exils* (Berlin, 1918), 228.

which they managed to draw from the United States offered in their opinion convincing proof of their own views and a conclusive refutation of those of their opponents. Concurrent with Marxist attacks on capitalist America, revisionists often found it useful to defend certain aspects of the old, glowing version of the American Promised Land associated with the non-Marxist European left.

To begin, revisionists of whatever school, whether Fabians, *possibilistes,* ministerialists, trade unionists, or Bernsteinians, objected to the stress which Marxists laid upon material factors in the historical drama. Most of their deviations can be discussed as flowing from this single shift of accent. All revisionists conceded the necessity of Marx's materialism as an antidote to the vague idealism of Hegel and agreed with Marx's emphasis on basic economic organizations and institutions as among the most vital shaping forces of history. But Marx (or rather his followers like Guesde, Liebknecht, Bebel, and Hyndman), they hastened to add, had gone too far in his desire to clear away the romanticism of the past. Revisionists could not concur with common Marxist assumptions that there were no aspects of human behavior ultimately divorceable from the economic organization of society.[6] Put more simply, revisionists thought it possible to get a man to do something or believe something because it was right and not simply because, as they read the Marxist interpretation, it was in his self-interest.

The human will played a shifty and complicated role in the Marxist world view. Despite revisionist charges, Marxists did not regard men as mere automatons reacting predictably to changes in their economic welfare and playing out unwaveringly and unconsciously a predetermined role in a predestined world order. Marx and Engels were not ready to let the dialectic work itself out unassisted, as the whole of their adult activity demonstrated. Both, on the contrary, allowed a substantial role to conscious human will in affecting the course of history. The proletariat suddenly inflamed by a clear knowledge of its historical mission and armed with proper tactical plans for fomenting the revolution could speed up by years the transformation to a socialist society. Similarly, the bourgeoisie

[6] For a view of how Marxists distorted Marx's view of historical materialism, see Eugene Genovese, "Marxian Interpretations of the Slave South," *Towards a New Past,* ed. by B. J. Bernstein (New York, 1968).

suddenly aroused by the threat to its privileged position and equipped with the oppressive powers of a ruling class could ward off for a discouragingly long time its own final destruction.

But for Marxists in the Second International the broad contours of historical change were clear enough. So long as capitalist societies went forward, there was only one possible end to the story. Socialism would eventually triumph no matter how carelessly the proletariat looked after its interests or how skillfully the bourgeoisie looked after its. Progress depended upon conscious human will, but according to Marxists the particular economic organization of a given society originally determined the motivations of this will, whether they took the form of morality, religion, or simply selfishness. Capitalism divided men into the categories of property owners and dispossessed and, in so doing, determined the firm commitment of the former to private gain and the belief of the latter in common ownership. From such polarization emerged conflict and eventually transformation of the system.

Revisionists, in contrast to this, freed human will from dependence on economic institutions and posited certain rational spurs to human behavior which were universal and present in all historical eras, whether feudal, capitalistic, or socialistic. They did not on this account cease to speak of the inevitability of socialism. For the most part all European socialists in 1900 felt themselves coasting on the wave of the future. Sidney Webb's phrase "the inevitableness of gradualness" was a Fabian invention intended to counter Marxist emphasis on revolution, but it nevertheless echoed the Marxist belief in socialism as a sure thing. What revisionists did do was to alter the whole basis on which Marxists erected the proposition of inevitability. They could not go along with Kautsky, Bebel, and Guesde in believing in the predetermined and unavoidable collapse of capitalism. As they saw it, capitalism had proved its ability to survive economic crises and had even demonstrated a capacity to heal some of its worst abuses. Events had not borne out Marxists' predicted movement of the poor toward more miserable circumstances while a diminishing number of entrepreneurs divided up the profits. Revisionists tended to agree with Ramsay MacDonald, the illegitimate son of a maid servant who learned socialism from J. Keir Hardie and the Fabians and rose to become England's first

Labour prime minister, and regard socialism as "inevitable, not because men are exploited or because the fabric of capitalism must collapse under its own weight, but because men are rational." [7]

Because this point of view stressed the importance of planning and of thoughtful, methodical action, revisionist writers did not envision the end of capitalism coming with the dramatic suddenness imagined by many Marxists. When Marxists wrote about the advent of socialism, they most frequently assumed an abrupt transition. One day there would be no socialism. The next, there would be a flash of light and the cooperative era would begin. Revolution had ceased to imply violence for many Marxists by 1900, and most of them by that time were shying away from images of street fighting and bloodletting and were pinning their hopes on a parliamentary solution. But, if they ceased to emphasize the violent aspects of revolution, they all the more began to speak about the revolutionary point in time when there would be a swift and complete transformation of economic institutions. Socialism was not something which lent itself to minute divisions and introduction by degrees. When the workers won control of the state and abolished almost at a stroke all the obnoxious features of capitalism, one could then, and only then, speak of socialism. Any reforms of the capitalistic system prior to that revolutionary transformation were insignificant.

For this notion of revolution, revisionists substituted the concept of evolution. Admittedly there were great quantitative and qualitative differences between capitalism and socialism, but precisely for this reason the change from one system to the other could not be made overnight. Revisionists likened Marxists who preached revolution to the utopian socialists who believed society could be made or unmade at will. The process of transformation would have to be slow and subtle, and no one in reviewing the course of events would be able to pinpoint a decisive moment when capitalism passed into its opposite. [8]

---

[7] *Socialism and Society* (London, 1906), 126.

[8] Marxists in 1900 could speak so confidently of a brisk clearing of the boards because they never faced the problem of constructing a socialist state. When the Bolsheviks seized power in Russia in 1917 and tried to impose a system of communal ownership on a poorly developed industrial base, Marxists discovered conversion was not so easy. Marxist pens were now directed toward a justification of a transition period of considerable duration. Even with this

Because they resigned themselves to a prolonged death of the old order, revisionists did not look upon reforms wrested from bourgeois governments as unimportant. While almost all Marxists came around to supporting so-called immediate legislative demands to aid the workers until the final goal was won, they gave these measures no weight in their ultimate scale of values. Small gains of this type received a typical offhand dismissal from Paul Lafargue:

> The most profitable and useful economic reforms for workers have a very relative efficacy; thus the weekly repose that the English and American workers have possessed for some centuries and the eight-hour day that the International has put at the head of its list of reforms for over half a century and which is applied in the United States in certain industries have brought no lessening in capitalist exploitation.[9]

To revisionists, legislative enactments, such as the eight-hour day, government ownership of utilities, and public insurance for the worker, were the elements necessary for socialism. None of them alone constituted socialism, but they were socialistic in their implications and together would bring about the desired result. This was a consideration leading Bernstein to his phrase so much reviled by Marxist writers: "To me that which is generally called the ultimate aim of socialism is nothing, but the movement is everything."

Since reforms of the capitalist system mattered—indeed, they were everything—to revisionists, they were willing to go to greater lengths than Marxists to win them. Marxists, at least officially, adopted a position denigrating parliamentary activity as ineffective until socialists gained a clear majority in the government. Election deals were forbidden because they dulled proletarian solidarity and, even when successful, won only sops. Revisionists, to the contrary, allowed a lot of room for legitimate compromise and could not fathom hair-

---

modification Marxists could still point to the October Revolution of 1917 as the decisive moment in time when the old order suffered a mortal blow. The Bolsheviks had not come to agree with revisionists by an admission that socialism had to be introduced by degrees, for according to the Bolsheviks the transformation could begin only with the advent of the workers' state, "the dictatorship of the proletariat."

[9] "Les Réformes et le parti socialiste," *L'Humanité,* Sept. 24, 1908.

splitting that at one time or another led Marxists to refuse to vote for government budgets favorable to their interests, accept one of the vice presidencies in the Reichstag to which their seats entitled them, or to negotiate election deals with other parties to ensure the election of the most progressive candidate if their own candidate was eliminated. Their emphasis on reform also rendered revisionists extremely sympathetic to trade union activity, and they did not make their support contingent on union men embracing socialism.

Such tactics of collaboration dulled the outlines of the class struggle, but an emphasis on class lines was exactly what revisionists wanted to eliminate. While acknowledging the considerable truth in Marx's descriptions of the class struggle under capitalism, they saw nothing to be gained in making the struggle any sharper or in summarily rejecting prospective bourgeois allies who refused to accept completely all the goals of socialism. Since socialism grew on foundations more solid than mere economic deprivation (which was the foundation on which revisionists with considerable justification thought Marxists were building their predictions), revisionists held out considerably more hope than Marxists for the eventual rallying of many property owners to the socialist cause.

To sum up, while both socialist camps differentiated themselves from the earlier utopian socialists by drawing heavily from the Darwinian legacy, neither embraced this legacy entirely, but took from it only what it wanted. While the Marxists dipped in *The Origin of Species* and ladled out the ideas of struggle and of man's development through interaction with his environment, they chose to retain a notion of cataclysmic change derived from an earlier biology and geology. The revisionists understood much better the basic ideas of evolution, which were continuity in development and change by imperceptible degrees, but they refused to see what Darwinism implied about the amorality and blind materialism of historical forces. They retained from the past a bit of Hegelian idealism.[10] From these two starting points in Darwin they were able to go in quite different directions.

The seizure on the gentler side of Darwinian theory by the revisionists divested their socialism of the violent tensions which had

[10] Neither, it might be noted, took from Darwin the idea of an open-ended future where anything was possible.

uneasily coexisted in Marxist thought. Marxism, at least as it was treated by members of the Second International, called on the worker to try to improve his position, yet often suggested that it was impossible. It challenged him to engage in heroic struggles for socialism, yet reminded him that the course of events did not much depend on his efforts. It preached brotherhood, yet insisted the worker remain constantly aware of class divisions. It portrayed for him a brilliant utopian future, yet cautioned him to expect only despair in the present. The vision of progress it gave the worker contained as much terror as hope.

In revisionist thought these contradictions simply disappeared. Revisionism moved into an intellectual framework characterized by a more genial optimism regarding the progress and the processes of mankind. The worker could anticipate better times both in the present and in the future; and, while the responsibility for the victory of socialism rested squarely on his shoulders, it was not a burden demanding unreasonable sacrifice. Revisionism lost something of the heroic dimensions of Marxism, but it was better designed for the temper and institutions of the countries of western Europe. Its ability to achieve tangible successes reduced considerably the viability of revolutionary methods there.

Having briefly discussed the main features of these diverging lines of thought, we may now return to the main flow of our theme and relate the theoretical and tactical differences of Marxists and revisionists to differences in their interpretations of the United States and their respective glimpses of America as a prospective promised land. At the outset it bears emphasizing that revisionist departures from Marxism did not lead right-wing socialists to repudiate abruptly all aspects of Marxist analyses of the United States and endorse all the clichés associated with the old promise of America. Because they saw some light in the dark corners of the decaying order of capitalism, they did not turn from cynical debunkers of the New World republic into uncritical admirers in the manner of some nineteenth-century liberals. Revisionist writers did not for a moment accept the delusion of the American proletariat living in a sort of demi-paradise. Quite the contrary. As vigorously as Marxist writers, they attacked the myth of American prosperity, scoffed at the alleged social equality, described political corruption, and por-

trayed the injustices resulting from the growth of private mo-
nopolies.[11] Regardless of whether they sat at the right or the left
pole of the Second International, European socialists were united by
their disdain for bourgeois traditions and their passionate belief in
the injustice of capitalism. They expected to see the dreadful scars of
human irrationality in any society based on private ownership and
competition.

George Bernard Shaw, the most devastatingly iconoclastic critic
and most brilliantly gifted writer among the English Fabians, was
not untypical among right-wing socialists in maintaining a consistent scorn toward America whenever (and the occasions were rare)
he turned his attention in that direction. When Gaylord Wilshire's
lively socialist publication lost bulk-rate mailing privileges in the
United States, Shaw wrote to Wilshire, "You thought you were in
an advanced country because you were under the star-spangled
banner. And now you have had to cross the frontier to Canada in
order to enjoy the ordinary liberties of monarchical Europe." [12]
Another of the Fabian essayists, William Clarke, practically credited
America's performance in the Gilded Age for his conversion from
liberalism to socialism. With all its initial advantages, he wrote, the
United States had not managed to avoid the social injustices found
in the capitalist nations of the Old World:

> A quarter of a century ago the American Republic was the guiding
> star of advanced English political thought. It is not so now: candour
> compels me to say that. It is not merely a question of machine poli-
> tics, of political corruption, of the omnipotent party boss. . . . Over
> and beyond this is the great fact of the division between rich and
> poor, millionaires at one end, tramps at the other, a growth of
> monopolies unparalleled, crises producing abject poverty just as in
> Europe. These facts proved to men clearly that new institutions

[11] In Chapter 4 it was noted that Bernstein and certain revisionists who followed him argued that the trustification of industry could in some ways improve the situation of the laborer under capitalism. Not all right-wing socialists
agreed. For example, English socialists who cast their lot with the non-Marxist
Independent Labour party agreed with Marxists that private trusts only lowered
wages, pushed up the cost of living, created unemployment with the introduction of machinery, and made strikes exceedingly difficult to win.
[12] "Socialism in a Bad Way," *The Labour Leader*, May 31, 1902.

were of no use along with the old forms of property; that a mere theoretic democracy, unaccompanied by any social changes, was a delusion and a snare.[13]

On the other hand, the relaxation of the rigid framework of Marxist orthodoxy gave revisionists more freedom to interpret American life without respect to preestablished assumptions and enabled them to approach certain phenomena in America in a more equitable frame of mind. Not believing that capitalism brought increasing misery to the workers, revisionist writers saw no compelling reason, as did so many Marxists, to focus entirely on urban and rural poverty in the United States and to cite only those statistics making wages in America appear as depressed as in Europe. Unpersuaded by the tenet that the materialization of socialist agitation had to follow hard and fast on the expansion of capitalist institutions, revisionists had less difficulty than Marxists in explaining why socialist parties remained weak in the United States. And, most important, not accepting the growth of a class-conscious proletariat openly at war with society as the only measure of the sympathy for socialist ideas in a country, they did not experience the same unease as Marxists each time they read election results from the United States. In short, the United States posed far less of a theoretical problem for revisionists than it did for Marxists. Rather than worrying about embarrassing evidence from the New World crushing their intellectual framework, a number of revisionist writers found in the United States a mine of data they could use to attack certain aspects of the Marxist position.

The Scottish trade union leader James Keir Hardie made tours of the United States in 1895, 1908, and 1912. Hardie's name was well-known to American labor because of his proven ability, in glaring contrast to Hyndman's ineptness, to interest British workers in socialism. Born in 1836, he spent a childhood of poverty in a coal-mining village near Glasgow. He breathed in radicalism with the dusty air of his environment, and he was not very old when both mine owners and mine workers knew his name. The former blacklisted him, and the latter made him their leader. In the late 1880's he

[13] "The Fabian Society," *Fabian Essays in Socialism* (Am. ed., reprinted Boston, 1908), xxi, quoted in Pelling, *America and the British Left*, 65.

became a socialist of the non-Marxist variety, a mongrel ideology which in England had been parented by a combination of Fabian tracts and the tough realism of the new unionism. One observer, trying to flatter Hardie, summed up his socialism by saying that it was "questionable whether he has even taken the trouble to read Karl Marx, and were he to do so it is certain that he would be incapable of following, much less of absorbing, its dry, almost mechanical, logic." [14] (Anti-intellectualism did not trouble that observer.) Hardie deserved major credit for moving English labor out of the traditional two party system. In 1892 he became the first independent labor member of Parliament. In 1893 he engineered the formation of the socialist-oriented Independent Labour party. And in the first years of the twentieth century he joined the ILP to the larger, but less doctrinaire, Labour party. British workers in their new political course did not formally declare socialistic goals, but Hardie never on that account considered his leading position in the Labour party inappropriate.

Clearly, from the accounts Hardie wrote of his travels in the New World, he enjoyed himself a great deal in the United States and found Americans a friendly, open, and dynamic people. Though he had the opportunity to meet Americans from all strata of society, Hardie interested himself mainly in uncovering the truth about working conditions in America. It proved a complicated task and each time he took back a mixed picture. Obviously many laborers, especially in western mining areas, lived under horrid conditions. But in other locations, trade unionists were moving toward a standard of living which was just as obviously a comfortable one. What he saw of rising wages and living conditions throughout the United States led him to remark after his visit in 1908, "Capitalism has a power of adaptability for which some of its Socialist opponents do not make sufficient allowance." [15] Hardie intended the comment as a thrust at his Marxist comrades in the International who, he thought, placed too much faith in the coming collapse of capitalism. Socialists, rather than feeding their expectations on the decay of the capitalist system, had to come to terms with a system still on an

[14] "James Keir Hardie, M.P.: A Character Sketch," *The Labour Leader,* Sept. 5, 1903.
[15] "Socialism in America," *The Socialist Review,* III (April 1909), 94.

upward path. A mature capitalist system and social progress, as it turned out, were not as completely antithetical as Marxists had imagined.

Hardie's conclusions about the resiliency of American capitalism found support in the comments of numerous other revisionist-minded socialists. The leading Belgian socialist Émile Vandervelde returned from the United States in 1904 and told a group of collectivists in Paris, "No one seriously disputes that, all in all, American workers have a position very superior to that of the European worker." [16] Apparently, Vandervelde had not been reading the Marxist press with any great care. While Vandervelde went on in his address to recognize the sharpening of class lines in America, most Marxists would have regarded a statement admitting the relatively prosperous existence of American workers at so late a date as too damaging a concession. The same proposition, it will be recalled, formed the exact grounds on which many Marxists had attacked Werner Sombart's famous study of American social conditions.

Vandervelde was not a full convert to revisionism. He liked to retain some claim to Marxist orthodoxy although he often found himself at odds with Marxist writers who refused to bend in the direction of moderation. A more partisan and self-conscious revisionist, such as the German socialist Ludwig Quessel, was willing to go much further in portraying the wage situation of the American worker in a favorable light. Quessel in 1909, in a reply to Karl Kautsky's contention that the buying power of American wages had declined seriously in the past decade, presented statistics which he believed demonstrated the enjoyment by many American working families of an almost "bourgeois standard of living." This observation, it might be noted, was made over twenty years after the Haymarket riot in Chicago. According to Quessel, American prosperity was not an inheritance from the past, but was a by-product of an American capitalism which was still very much alive. Quessel, of course, was trying to drive home a point to his Marxist opponents. He wished to show how vigorous trade union activity could result in tangible and significant benefits for the worker even under capitalism. It could not solve all the problems of unjust distribution, but it was not the labor of Sisyphus which Marxists sometimes

[16] "Impressions d'Amérique," *La Revue socialiste*, XLI (March 1905), 287.

seemed to suggest. Dipping into the inkwell for a trenchant conclusion, Quessel wrote, "The striking success of the American unions has reduced to absurdity the opinion of the vulgar economists that the gains won by trade unions can have only a temporary character." [17] Those socialists who advised the worker to reserve all of his strength and enthusiasm for the day of the revolution were doing him a great disservice.

Aside from wage statistics revisionists drew other evidence from America indicating capitalism's progression along lines other than those of inevitable decline prescribed by Marx. Max Schippel was as partisan a convert to German revisionism as was Quessel. In many ways disturbing to Bernstein he went beyond what the revisionist leader thought appropriate in yielding to bourgeois sensibilities. Most notoriously Schippel's nationalism led him to support middle-class demands for the raising of German tariff levels in response to American competition.[18] However serious this rupture, Schippel was in perfect accord with Bernstein in refusing to accept a view of a doomed capitalism chained to a rocky path of economic crises which ended in destruction. In 1909, after the swift passing of a mild economic crisis which a few indiscreet Marxist journals had once again greeted as the beginning of the end in the United States, Schippel wrote,

> How little the old crisis theories, which have been passed to us all in flesh and blood, correspond—or perhaps better put: how little they have been able to tie together thoroughly and with general validity the unexpectedly many sided motivating forces of present-day economic development—that is demonstrated to us once again best by occurrences in the United States. And it was precisely here we should have seen, as has often been maintained recently, all the crass insupportable elements and contradictions of capitalism pushed to the last and highest possible point.[19]

According to Schippel, Marxists in Europe who expected to see a

[17] "K. Kautsky als Vulgärökonom," *Sozialistische Monatshefte*, Vol. XV, Part 2 (1909), 1105. Also article by Quessel in *Vorwärts*, Oct. 3, 1909.
[18] Schippel, *Amerika und die Handelsvertragspolitik* (Berlin, 1906).
[19] "Der wirtschaftliche Wiederaufschwung in den Vereinigten Staaten," *Sozialistische Monatshefte*, Vol. XV, Part 3 (1909), 1214.

renewed outburst of chaos in the market place with each forward step of capitalism and a momentary surge of anarchical forces overwhelming the economic institutions of the old order would find small profit for attention lavished on the United States. They would do better, if they wished to keep the faith, to pretend that the New World simply was not there.

Revisionists were in an enviable position. They could agree with their Marxist colleagues about the injustice and misery in the United States, yet dispute the assumption that capitalism in the United States pushed workers into more and more desperate straits. They could attack the capitalist system, yet insist it was not as tragically flawed as Marxists suggested. This flexibility in their position allowed them to play the role of farseeing social critics without having to blind themselves to all inconvenient statistics issuing from the United States. Revisionists could make use of both the good and the bad sides of capitalist America while their rivals had to prove the inveterate evil of all the sides.

Moreover, revisionists had Marxists over an additional and particularly uncomfortable barrel with respect to the American situation. If Marxist writers insisted on instructing their revisionist colleagues with portraits of the unrelieved brutality and oppression of the American worker, then revisionists could turn on them with the embarrassing question: "Then why is the Socialist Party in the United States so weak? If what you say about capitalist oppression in America is correct, then the Marxist materialistic interpretation of history which teaches that the callousness of the capitalist overlords must call forth a proletariat united in a dedicated fidelity to socialist ideas is incorrect." Such comments contained perhaps an unfair summation of the Marxist position, but they were not easy to answer. The dilemma was real enough. Once Marxists painted in uncompromising terms the wretched conditions of workers in the New World and rejected as fantasy all the old promises which capitalist America had once seemed to hold forth, they found it difficult to explain why proletarian class consciousness remained so undeveloped.

E. Belfort Bax, whose unorthodox Marxism was mentioned earlier, regarded the imperceptible advance of organized socialism in America and England as confirmation of his wisdom in rejecting historical materialism. Bax accepted totally the usual Marxist descriptions of the great misery in these countries but pushed the implications toward much different conclusions. He wrote,

> The proletariat is larger, and probably greater misery exists in the cities of Britain and America than in most parts of Germany, yet Socialism in Britain and America is as yet struggling with an imperfectly class-conscious working class. Economic conditions, let them press never so hardly [sic], require the fertilising influence of an idea and an enthusiasm before they can give birth to a great movement, let alone a new society.[20]

The relation of this statement to a pure expression of revisionist principles becomes clear when it is compared to one made by the French moderate socialist Gérault-Richard. In *La Petite République,* a newspaper partisan to the views of the most conservative wing of French socialism, Gérault-Richard described McKinley's reelection in 1900 as proof that the advance of socialist forces hinged on a lot more than the stimulus of growling proletarian bellies. He, like Bax, was ready to concede the miserable working conditions in the United States; but the stubborn insistence of the American workers in lining up with one of the two bourgeois parties led Gérault-Richard to exclaim, "How true it is that the social revolution does not at all depend solely on material factors!" [21] America might be the most advanced capitalist nation in the world. Its great mass of people might be more oppressed by its economic system than anywhere in Europe. But without the trace of some generous impulse to inspire the proletariat, some capacity of rationality compelling it to substitute a collective solution for the selfish drive motivating men's social ambitions, socialism would make no progress.

This line of reasoning could be pushed to conclusions even more strikingly at variance with current expressions of Marxism. For example, G. H. Perris, trying to interpret what was going on in America for Hardie's newspaper *The Labour Leader,* decided that economic misery could never aid socialist growth; rather it acted

[20] "The Materialistic Doctrine of History," *Essays in Socialism* (London, 1907), 17.
[21] "Mac-Kinley, président," Nov. 9, 1900.

as a positive hindrance. He wrote, "However it may have been in the revolutionary crises of the last century, a great dislocation of trade and finance does not now help the cause of independent Labour and Socialism, but, so far as public representation goes, severely injures it." [22] What prompted Perris in his reflections was the failure of the party of Eugene Debs to make any headway on the national level after an economic crisis had rocked the country. The 1908 election to which Perris had reference resulted in setbacks for the American Socialist party almost everywhere.

It was only a short step beyond Perris' comment to the remark of his countryman J. Bruce Glasier that "If, as August Bebel believed, America is likely to be the first country to establish the Socialist Commonwealth, it will not be through any catastrophe caused by the goadings of Capitalism, but rather from the ripening of economic opportunities, and the upgrowth of the Commonwealth spirit in the nation." [23] Such a view completely reversed all the values sacred to Marxism and conjured up parts of the old bourgeois myth of the American Promised Land. It was America's goodness which made it special, its liberty, equality, and opportunity. As the editor of *The Labour Leader* from 1904 to 1909 and one of the leading spokesmen for the ILP, Glasier was only carrying to an extreme his party's decision to push the Marxist concept of class warfare to one side. If, Glasier concluded, the road to the future society did not lie in the direction of increasing antagonism between social classes, it could only follow a route of reconciliation and peaceful cooperation. Going far beyond what Karl Kautsky had written in *The Class Struggle* when he cautioned Marxists against putting exclusive faith in poverty as the midwife of socialism, Glasier linked socialist advance to advances in material prosperity. He made the victory for socialism dependent on the sharpening of the moral sensibility of the working class, not its class antagonism. This could only come with the elimination of poverty, for, as Glasier correctly surmised, misery normally does not breed high-mindedness.

Following up this conclusion, Glasier proceeded to point out the errors of Marxists who greeted bloody labor disputes in the United States as evidence of the nearness of a socialist victory. Such disputes,

[22] "Socialism and Reaction," *The Labour Leader,* Nov. 27, 1908.
[23] "The Review Outlook," *The Socialist Review,* XII (July–Sept. 1914), 204.

which Glasier admitted were more violent than those in Europe, were ascribable to the newness and unsettled condition of many parts of the United States and not to the advance of capitalism. Marxists, he maintained, too often forgot about the civilizing components of capitalism. Whatever its shortcomings, it represented progress over the anarchic society of private vengeance which had preceded it and had replaced raw savagery with law, order, Shakespeare, and Bach. Glasier took heart in watching capitalism's taming processes at work in the United States quieting labor quarrels and diminishing the din of controversy in the most turbulent area, the sparsely inhabited western mining states. Glasier believed that a collective society was impossible until men had overcome their brutal instincts and learned to live in a civilized manner. For Marxists to applaud men at war with one another was the greatest folly in Glasier's opinion. Violence and harmony were opposites which even the remarkable fusing power of the Marxist dialectic could not bring together.

Like Glasier, the well-known and prolific French *possibiliste* writer Gustave Rouanet, who over the years showed a great admiration of American life, saw a substantial betterment in the status of the working class as the best hope of socialism. In a review of Carroll D. Wright's *The Industrial Evolution of the United States,* a book that was not uncritical of American industrial society but that showed the material circumstances of the laborer on the rise, Rouanet wrote,

> The superior intellect and morality that the material improvement of living conditions has created in the working class in the two worlds have had the consequence of rendering it more sensible to privation . . . to the conditions of inequality that have not been effaced by putting at its disposal greater quantities of goods.[24]

According to Rouanet the victory of the cooperative commonwealth would be conceivable only when man had become a moral being sympathetic to the suffering of his fellows. Men had great difficulty acting as responsible moral agents when their own sufferings prevented them from thinking much beyond the source of their next meal.

[24] "Review of Carroll Wright's 'L'Évolution industrielle aux États-Unis,'" *La Revue socialiste*, XXXIV (July 1901), 121.

Most revisionist writers in Europe were unwilling to join Glasier and Rouanet completely in the joyous resurrection of old myths and refused to associate the potential role of America in leading the way to socialism with the general prosperity fostered by capitalism, rather than the general misery. Most of them, despite their feeling that Marxists laid inordinate stress on economic discontent as a motivating force behind socialism, did accept suffering as an important factor. Keir Hardie wrote after his 1895 visit to the United States (compare with his comments after his 1908 visit) that the heart and mind of the American people were being prepared for socialism by the growing precariousness of job security, the advance of the trusts, the crushing out of small capitalists, and steadily falling farm prices.[25] The Reverend R. J. Campbell, a well-known exponent of the New Theology as well as milder forms of socialist theory, wrote of the United States, "The country is riper through sheer desperation—yes, that is the right word—for immediate Government regulation of big industries."[26] And Adrien Veber wrote in *La Revue socialiste* in 1894,

> The growing concentration of industrial monopolies, the division of the national wealth by a smaller and smaller number of privileged capitalists, the progressive diminution of salaries at the same time unemployment increases, the increase in the number of local strikes . . . here is a more than sufficient explanation for the extension of genuine socialism.[27]

All such remarks hark back to the original caveat that the common opposition of Marxists and revisionists to capitalism often led them to portray the United States in precisely the same words.

The sentiments which Glasier and Rouanet expressed were important all the same. Socialists sympathetic to revisionism did look forward to a slow and steady passage to socialism without turmoil or commotion—a transformation which would be stimulated not so much by everything wrong with the old order as by the moral at-

[25] "My American Diary," *The Labour Leader,* Sept. 14, 1895.
[26] "With the Socialists in America: Interview with Rev. R. J. Campbell," *The Labour Leader,* Feb. 23, 1912.
[27] "Mouvement social," *La Revue socialiste,* XX (Aug. 1894), 255.

traction of the new order. A few particularities about America's past and present, distinguishing life in the New World from life in the Old, seemed to make America supremely well-suited for such a passage. Unlike Marxists, revisionists did not need to base predictions about America's likely leading role in the prospective victory of socialism on a belief in the growing sameness of America to Europe. Along with many liberal and radical admirers of America the vision of the United States as a promised land, which many of them expressed, rested in large part on the uniqueness of the young republic. Without the ambiguity characteristic of Marxist analyses of republican governments, revisionist writers envied America's possession of political liberties which permitted a direct translation of the will of the proletariat into legislation. However badly such institutions of government might have been corrupted—and the corruption of American political life was recognized—revisionists commenting on life here did not question their value or doubt the overriding importance of achieving them. Bebel's famous remark that a bourgeois republic was not worth the cost of socialists' getting their heads knocked together made no sense to them. Carl Legien, Germany's most powerful trade union leader and a staunch ally of the right-wing members of the Social Democratic party, had political freedom in the forefront of his mind when he told American socialists at their convention in 1912 that Europeans believed "the United States may possibly be or become the first nation of practical Socialism" partly because of the rapid growth and concentration of capitalist institutions and partly as a result of "the privileges and possibilities that are open to the workers of this country."[28]

Jean Jaurès, who carried on a running dispute with Marxists sharing Bebel's view, never missed an opportunity to praise American republican institutions. In his efforts to turn back the tides of reaction in France in the late 1880's and the 1890's, he often held America

[28] *Proceedings: Socialist Convention of 1912,* 59. For a fuller report of Legien's impressions see his *Aus Amerikas Arbeiterbewegung* (Berlin, 1914). The extensive arrangements for Legien's American tour of 1912 appeared very odd to European socialists; on one half of the trip he traveled under the sponsorship of the AFL and on the other half under the auspices of the Socialist party. That a rift between these two organizations made impossible a more unified arrangement brought home to European socialists exactly how weak the movement was in the United States.

up to doubting conservatives as proof of the compatibility of order and stability with free political institutions.[29] Anti-republicans in France feared the right to strike, yet, as Jaurès argued, American workers freely organized strikes without harming state authority. The President of the United States (he had Theodore Roosevelt in mind) had once gone so far as to force management into unwelcome arbitration proceedings. Again, as Jaurès pointed out, while anti-republicans in France viewed the slightest challenge to the prestige of the military as destructive of the social fabric, Americans had managed to do away with a standing army altogether without giving up a position of world leadership. French conservatives feared the extension of free speech to dissident political elements, yet trade unionists in America hurled bitterly derogatory remarks at their country's leaders without embroiling society in general chaos. Jaurès threw the ball solidly back at French conservatives: only through the extension of republican laws in France could violence and disorder be avoided.

John Martin, a member of the English ILP and a party journalist, represented the extreme position to which a revisionist writer might be led in admiration of the American government. Martin, agreeing with Glasier about the desirability of finding a social solution through class accommodation rather than class warfare, believed strongly in the capacity of a democratic government, even one dominated by capitalists, to respond to the will of the people; his proof was the United States. The equality generally prevailing in America had resulted in a government which truly belonged to the electorate. Martin wrote, "There is no ruling class in America convinced of its own superiority and secretly despising the opinions of 'the lower clarr-ses,' because every official has either lived recently among those classes or his family has so lately evolved from among them that a good many relatives still earn their bread with their hands." This description of American society struck Marxists as perniciously designed to mislead; so did Martin's additional comment about Theodore Roosevelt as "the most conspicuous example of a statesman with his ear always to the ground listening for the

[29] As examples, see the parliamentary speeches of Jaurès reported in *La Petite République,* Oct. 27, 1895, May, 21, 1898, Oct. 25, 1902, and in *L'Humanité,* May 12, 1907.

orders of the electorate." [30] If Roosevelt had his ear to the ground, the Marxists believed, it was only in order to detect the least costly and most ambiguously worded piece of reform legislation which, when passed, would temporarily misguide the American workers into thinking Washington had their best interests at heart.

Most revisionists remembered to share with Marxists reservations about bourgeois republican governments. When weighed against the final arrangements of a socialist state, they gave them also a relative value. Martin's comments represented an extreme point of view rather than a typical one among the writers under survey, and most right-wing socialists were much more guarded in their praise of American democracy. Since they wanted, however, a free political society and believed it the basis for any future peaceful progress, they were quite ready to have their heads knocked together to achieve it; and they were not too proud to admit, when it seemed appropriate, their jealousy over American workers' prior and fuller possession. For revisionists the legacies of political liberalism were a positive good. For Marxists the positive attraction was much less marked. Democratic republics were useful, perhaps even necessary, but the vocabulary of political liberals had traditionally served to mislead the working class. As the expected dawn of the cooperative commonwealth drew nearer and nearer, Marxists felt duty-bound to keep socialists constantly alerted to the dissimilarities between socialism and the American Constitution.

Because for revisionists a free society, defined in political terms, was almost as important as a socialist society, defined in economic terms, they were frequently ready to take sides in controversies where Marxists saw nothing to choose. In 1898, when Marxists demanded that followers remain neutral in the Spanish-American War (both sides being equally motivated by greedy imperialistic aims), a number of revisionist commentators expressed open disagreement. The Cuban worker, they felt, as well as workers everywhere, had much to gain in the substitution of American rule for Spanish rule. "Latinus," an editorial writer for *La Petite République,* welcomed the prospects of an American victory, for it would help to throw European royalty off its anachronistic throne. "Another like suc-

[30] "Socialism and Labour in the American Presidential Election," *The Socialist Review,* II (1908–9), 849.

cess," he wrote, "and the monarchical system in Europe will give way to the Republic." [31] No other eventuality could better advance the democratic cause and speed along the ultimate triumph of socialism.

In another article in which Latinus summarized the factors catapulting America into the front ranks of world leadership, he made clear the distance he had traveled from the Marxist camp. He wrote,

> In America one sees surge forth a formidable power, before which all others must sooner or later give way. In spite of the very pronounced corruption of the directing classes, in spite of the monstrous grievances that capitalism has produced, the United States, being a country without traditions, not having to wipe away the faults of past centuries, possessing democratic institutions, the proletariat there enjoying comparatively a more satisfactory economic system, appears to be called to a great future. [32]

While Marxists recognized some of these advantages as helping socialist advance in America (though, as we have seen, they could turn these advantages into disadvantages), their main contention was entirely different: America was called to a great future, not despite "the monstrous grievances" of capitalism, but because they existed in that country in such abundance. To the revisionist bent on a peaceful and smooth transition to socialism, the features of American life long praised by bourgeois enemies of Marx had by no means lost their significance.

The arguments which have been sketched out above carried with them certain corollaries. Of foremost importance, since the American worker possessed the tools of effective political power and since, in the minds of revisionists, socialism was to be achieved in piecemeal legislative fashion, revisionist observers of American life did not automatically view the failures of the American Socialist party as a cause for great discouragement. Unlike many Marxists they did not need to see for reassurance a class-conscious proletariat hurling invective at its capitalist taskmasters. Other evidence of a more modest and low-keyed sort could indicate to them a significant

[31] "Le vieux et nouveau-monde," *La Petite République,* Aug. 15, 1898.
[32] "L'Europe et l'Amérique," *La Petite République,* Oct. 25, 1898.

movement of collectivist sentiment throughout the country. If in bargaining a union won an eight-hour day, revisionists found cause for encouragement. If American reformers pushed through any kind of legislation regulating business, they cheered. Or if the drive for woman suffrage recorded some gain, they issued congratulations all around.

John Martin, whose admiration for American governmental institutions was apparently limitless, again serves to illustrate the extreme degree to which a revisionist socialist might be heartened by various reforms in the United States. On the basis of the significant legislation passed in the Progressive Era, Martin managed to conclude, "Altogether to-day more Socialism probably has been put in effect in the United States than any other country." Martin was extremely generous in his interpretation of what constituted socialism. He put down in his gallery of American socialist enterprises such projects as the Erie Canal, which was open to all without charge, the vast national parks and forests, which Congress set aside to protect natural beauty from waste by private competition, the large irrigation and reclamation projects, which the government undertook on an unheard-of scale, and the Department of Agriculture's free distribution of crop information to farmers. Martin saved his best illustration for last. Free towels and soap were thrown in gratis at every public bath. What greater evidence in a burgher economy could testify to the pervasiveness of socialist influences? When Martin reached the end of his extended survey, his voice was raised to a triumphant shrillness. One could "declare that never in the history of the world was a convention held of greater importance for the progress of Socialism than the first conference of the Governors of the United States of America." [33]

Marxists would have taken Martin's list of American socialist programs and dismissed them as irrelevant. Most revisionists would have stood somewhere between Marxist contempt for American reforms and Martin's clearly premature ecstasy. Few of them could have given much credence to any view making William Howard Taft a sort of socialist folk hero, and probably most would have agreed with Sidney Webb when, after a trip to the United States in

[33] "Socialism in Action in America," *The Socialist Review*, II (1908–9), 693 and 702.

1888, he characterized the United States as a generation behind Europe in its handling of social problems.[34] Nevertheless, the Progressive Era did furnish evidence of some first steps, however small and faltering, being taken toward socialist goals. And Martin was not saying anything offensive to the revisionist mentality by assigning great importance to these beginnings. In addition, the trust, which revisionists thought had displaced or at least discredited the principle of competition in America, prepared the way for the smooth government takeover of business and made the transition to socialism without unpleasantness a certainty. Ramsay MacDonald had this latter fact particularly in mind when he wrote in 1910, "In no country in the world is there so much revolutionary energy stored up, and in none could the process of a sudden and wholesale transference of industry from capitalist into public possession be accomplished with less economic disturbance to the workers and lower middle class."[35]

Such encouraging prognoses could not always prevent revisionists from confronting the problem which had often disturbed Marxist complacency: why had socialism as an organized movement not made more headway in America? The disappointing growth in the vote for the Socialist party might not be cause for despair, but it was surely odd. Most revisionists recognized with a sigh that the American workers regarded the social reforms made under the banner of Progressivism as reforms of the capitalist system and wanted no part of socialism. While revisionists thought it wrong for the working class to separate itself from other elements of society and rigidly refuse all compromises with the property-owning class, they had doubts about the American labor movement and wondered why it was not more alert to the final goals of labor agitation.

Among right-wing socialists, no more than among Marxists, could there be final agreement as to the cause of the undeveloped social conscience of the American worker. To members of England's Independent Labour party it boiled down to a question of the stubbornness of American socialist leaders. Being totally convinced of the irresistible attraction of their cause, they refused to be teachers and

[34] Edward R. Pease, "Webb and the Fabian Society," in *The Webbs and their Work*, ed. by Margaret Cole (London, 1949), 18.
[35] *The Socialist Review*, X (1912), 246.

waited for American workingmen to come to them of their own accord. They refused to make the necessary overtures to American trade unionists who alone could give strength to the cause. One member of the ILP wrote of them in disgust, "They will ban every one who does not socialise the whole world right off the reel. . . . Unless you get every Union to hoist the red flag forthwith, you are to turn your back on them, and go your own isolated way." [36] Other revisionists tended to accept with Werner Sombart the excess of roast beef and apple pie as the cause behind socialism's unsatisfactory performance in the United States. Still others, huffily mindful of Europe's maturity, merely shrugged their shoulders over what they deemed adolescent misbehavior. The United States was not settled (or civilized) enough to permit its citizens the leisurely reflection necessary to construct a more sophisticated society.

What is important is not this disagreement, but the fact that the more a socialist tended toward revisionist thinking the less reason he had to be concerned about the whole matter. That is, the more he pushed Marx's materialistic theories with their mechanistic implications into the background, the less he was troubled by socialist reverses in America. In his opinion, knowing how far a nation had progressed along the road of capitalism was not to know everything, or even the greater part, about the readiness of the country to adopt socialism. Marxists tried to avoid a simplistic formula saying socialism was bound to come first in the country of the highest capitalist development, but it was very easy for them to fall into the pattern of thought which expected socialism to draw one step nearer with every forward step of capitalism. A Marxist could not easily reconcile himself (at least prior to 1917) to the paradox of the bare shadow of a socialist party in the country where capitalism had expanded most aggressively. This anomalous situation might be terribly disappointing to socialists who traveled the paths of revisionism, but it could never pose the same intellectual challenge. They found paradoxes in the American situation much less surprising and much less troublesome. If it was helpful to accept some idea of American goodness associated with the old bourgeois myth, that alternative was always open to them, and this flexibility gave them a decided polemical advantage over their Marxist opponents.

[36] J. H. Harley, "On the Watchtower," *The Labour Leader,* Nov. 18, 1904.

Perhaps a book by H. G. Wells provides the most fitting conclusion to a discussion of the many paths along which revisionism could lead a man in interpreting the United States. Wells' fascination with the pliancy of the future, his passionate concern for man's present suffering, and his glowing vision of a better organization of society pushed him into an alliance with English conservative socialists. The association remained of the loosest sort, for he always was very nondoctrinaire about his socialism. Even his ties to the Fabians, whom he joined in 1903, were not strong, and he criticized them as often as he did Marxists. Most definitions of socialism failed to suit him, and he was drawn to it as much from a preference for order over muddle and as a means of escape from a Philistine Victorian world which had in so many ways institutionalized cruelty, as from an acute analysis of economic problems.

Wells' 1906 book, *The Future in America,* was based upon a trip to the New World which gave the Englishman an opportunity to see many parts of the United States. He confessed that he had been driven by a boyish curiosity to see the continent with his own eyes in order to lay some foundations for predicting America's course in the next thirty years. His subject proved a complicated one, and for every bright spot of hope he saw in the American scene there seemed to be a corresponding dark one. Like Marxist writers he saw "a secular decline in honor, education, public spirit, and confidence, of a secular intensification of corruption, lawlessness, and disorder." He criticized American government in saying, "The plain fact of the case is that Congress, as it is constituted at present, is the feeblest, least accessible, and most inefficient central government of any civilized nation . . . west of Russia." All of this led him to ponder whether America was a "giant childhood or a gigantic futility." [37]

Wells parted company with most socialists, whether Marxist or revisionist, in refusing to view the triumph of socialism in America or anywhere else as inevitable. For him, although prior to World War I he optimistically believed in a general evolution toward utopia, anything was possible in the future. He did see encouraging signs in the American present pointing to an early victory for socialism. "The trend," he wrote, "is altogether away from the

[37] H. G. Wells, *The Future in America: A Search after Realities* (New York, 1906), 255, 244–45, and 251.

anarchistic individualism of the nineteenth century, that much is sure, and towards some constructive scheme which, if not exactly socialism, as socialism is defined, will be, at any rate, closely analogous to socialism." But prophecy could not rest on trends, and the many discouraging signs Wells saw left him far less hopeful. He ruminated, "These people, I say, might do anything. They are the finest people upon earth—the most hopeful. But they are vain and hasty; they are thoughtless, harsh, and undisciplined; in the end, it may be, they will accomplish nothing." [38]

If Wells finally came around to the conclusion that the leadership of the world would ultimately fall upon America, it was not because he saw capitalism crumbling there, but because he recognized an energetic population "caught up by the upward sweep of that great increase in knowledge that is everywhere enlarging the power and scope of human effort, exhilarated by it, and active and hopeful beyond any population the world has ever seen." In this statement Wells clearly identified himself as a revisionist and showed the revisionist debt to earlier non-socialist admirers of America. He agreed with Ramsay MacDonald that the coming of socialism depended on man's rationality. He wrote, "You see, my hero in the confused drama of human life is intelligence; intelligence inspired by constructive passion." The things which would save America from the control of a "tacitly organized and exhausting plutocracy" and from "decline towards violence and social misery" were the "great unprecedented reservoirs" of men and women who could read and write and could understand the social forces at work around them.[39]

Wells did not need evidence of a strong proletarian army to give him faith in America's future. Like J. Bruce Glasier he saw no cause for optimism in bloody labor disputes. Socialism went forward with the development of more civilized virtues, and civilized virtues rested to a large degree on general prosperity. There was poverty in the United States but "no general effect of impoverishment." Wells wrote,

The European reader must dismiss from his mind any conception

[38] *Ibid.,* 250 and 255.
[39] *Ibid.,* 257, 133, 207, and 206.

of the general American population as a mass of people undergoing impoverishment through the enrichment of the few. He must substitute for that figure a mass of people, very busy, roughly prosperous, generally self-satisfied. . . .

He found on his visit a nation intoxicated by the "sheer virtue of its size, its free traditions, and the habit of initiative in its people." It was an intoxication which often led to the excesses of selfish individualism, but it also allowed for a measure of largeness and generosity in the American people unknown in the older European nations.[40]

How far Wells strayed from Marxist paths is most aptly revealed in his choosing for a symbol of America's future hope, not the American proletarian wielding his hammer or sickle, but the ultra-patrician Theodore Roosevelt fighting battles vicariously on the White House lawn. In his interview with the American President, Wells discovered a man who embodied all the good and bad of the character traits he had found in the American people: "In his undisciplined hastiness, his limitations, his prejudices, his unfairness, his frequent errors, just as much as in his force, his sustained courage, his integrity, his open intelligence, he stands for his people and his kind." [41] If America was to precede other nations into the era of socialism, it was men of this type who would provide the country with the necessary energy and drive.

For a revisionist like Wells the puzzle of American behavior went far beyond the stubborn refusal of events to conform to any preconceived expectations about the development of a capitalist society. It went down into the enigma of the entire American character which seemed to contain in equal degrees violence and humanitarianism, bold daring and timid conservatism, optimism and pessimism, egalitarianism and status consciousness, individualism and conformity. Possibly America would lead the world into socialism. Wells finally inclined to that view. Yet to observers in the older countries of Europe some question lingered as to how ready this raw continent with its swaggering populace, with its great vices and its great virtues, really was to assume a role of leadership.

[40] *Ibid.*, 105, 106, and 257.
[41] *Ibid.*, 253.

CHAPTER 7

THE UNITED STATES
IN THE WRITINGS
OF LENIN AND TROTSKY
An Instance of Marxist Ambivalence

WHILE MARXISTS in western Europe continued to scan the horizons of the powerful capitalist nations for signs of the red glow of revolution, Russia was seething.[1] There was considerable irony in these circumstances. In 1900, Russian Marxists worth their salt were, or were soon to be, in exile; and from their gossipy enclaves in London and Geneva they looked back to a homeland totally unready for socialist agitation. Capitalism, with its huge industrial complexes, its urban squalor, its ruthless dehumanization of men, had scarcely touched the vast perimeters of the future Soviet republic. Social history for the broad masses of the Russian people had comprised for many generations a chronicle of unrelieved misery. But the

---

[1] This chapter does not pretend to make an exhaustive study of Russian attitudes toward the United States. Such an attempt would push off into a different era of world socialism and would involve consideration of completely different problems than are of primary concern here. Some comments, however, seem appropriate regarding Lenin and Trotsky, not only because of their overwhelming importance in bringing about and shaping the course of the Russian Revolution, but also because both men were deeply influenced by years of exile in western Europe and contact with leaders of the Second International. A study of their feelings toward America takes us beyond our nominal stopping point, but it serves both to emphasize certain ideas long evident in the Marxist view of the United States and to introduce new themes that became prominent in Cold War diplomacy many years later. To pursue the latter beyond the suggestions made here would require another book.

166

chronicle had been the collaborative effort of reactionary Tsars, overstuffed landlords, and a horde of avaricious bureaucrats. Capitalist overlords had added only a few pages toward the end which, when weighed against the rest, added little more than footnotes. Yet an uprising of the masses in 1905 followed in just slightly more than a decade by the epochal 1917 revolution alerted a startled world to the fact that conscious human will and the dedicated and militant leadership of a small minority of radicals were as important in producing the socialist revolution as impersonal economic forces. The October Revolution of the Bolsheviks did not follow classical Marxist lines, but it momentarily aroused the spirits of Marx's disciples everywhere.

Bolshevik aggressiveness and boldness undeniably opened a gap between Marxist theory (stressing the economic readiness of a country for revolution) and practical realities (forcing socialist revolutionaries to seize upon any favorable moment regardless of economic conditions) which has never been closed. Indeed, with socialist ranks today growing fastest in the underdeveloped countries of the world, it has grown wider. Bolshevik leaders had certainly not wanted or expected it to happen that way. The two principal masterminds behind the overthrow of the Provisional Government, V. I. Lenin and Leon Trotsky, would have hesitated, perhaps fatally, in those crucial days of late autumn had they realized that they were propelling Russia, with its primitive economic structures, into a lengthy career as an isolated socialist state. Lenin until only a short time before the revolution had carried on an acrimonious quarrel with the descendants of Russian Populist socialists. These romantic terrorists, whose most famous deed had been the assassination of Alexander II in 1881, wanted to build Russian socialism directly on existing rural communal structures and bypass a capitalist stage altogether. Surprisingly, Marx had in one letter to a Russian revolutionary leader accepted, although with qualifications, the Populist contention. This letter raised some eyebrows, but Marxists never took it very seriously before 1917. Lenin, being fully aware of the fundamentally unsocialist character of the peasant commune, was no exception. Warning against the folly of a premature establishment of a socialist regime, Lenin argued that Russia would first have to get beyond the present agricultural base of its economy and pass through the prolonged stage of capitalism characteristic of growth in the West. Trotsky, though his doctrine of "permanent revolution" indicated an early unconcern with most accepted versions of the Marxist dialectic, nevertheless based his hopes for a successful revolution in Russia on the anticipated collapse of the capitalist powers of Europe.[2] Both men in their sudden willingness to commit Russia to the daring program of 1917 counted on friendly socialist powers in the West shortly coming to the assistance of the underdeveloped Russian economy. In their opinion Germany's old government could not survive the war; and, once a new revolutionary regime had proclaimed the principles of Marx (which to their minds was the only logical alternative to the old system), other European countries would dismantle their capitalistic structures and quickly join in toasts to the Bolshevik heroes. In retrospect this notion appears absurdly fanciful; but, given the turmoil and uncertainty of those bitter war years, the vision was not entirely unworthy of the usually uncompromising realism of the two Bolshevik leaders. In any case, it gave them the courage to take a step which they might otherwise never have taken.

When Western capitalism failed to follow the expected sequence of decline and fall, Bolshevik leaders found themselves in an awkward quandary. Understandably proud of their domestic victory and contemptuous of the capitalist powers which continued to rule the West, they were nonetheless uneasy about the future. Rather than ushering in Russia's Golden Age, 1917 introduced years of civil war, foreign intervention, famine, and general misery. Verbally committed to a program of full socialism, Soviet leaders faced the task of creating an economy of abundance out of nothing. And for

---

[2] A discussion of Lenin's position on the question of Russia's readiness for revolution both before and after 1917 is available in a number of sources. A good general presentation is Alfred G. Meyer's *Leninism* (Cambridge, Mass., 1957). For the differences between Lenin's and Trotsky's views in the days before the revolution and a discussion of Trotsky's theory of permanent revolution, see the first volume of Isaac Deutscher's controversial, apologetic, but superb biography of Trotsky, *The Prophet Armed* (London, 1954). The best biographical treatment of Lenin is Adam B. Ulam, *Lenin and the Bolsheviks: The Intellectual and Political History of the Triumph of Communism in Russia* (London, 1965). The last is brilliant and provides a needed balance to Deutscher.

a moment, a brief one, they hoped to accomplish it employing the managerial skills of workers and peasants.

The establishment of a society based on socialist cooperation had before this time been premised on the takeover of the vast productive powers built up by capitalism. Socialist theorists had concentrated their energies on exploring ways of correcting inequalities in distribution in highly developed economic systems and had never imagined that the dynamics of socialism could alone move a country from feudal backwardness into the advanced industrial age. Capitalism, whatever its injustices and cruelties, was a historically progressive force which laid the foundation on which socialism was to be erected. Marxists hated capitalists for their crimes against the worker, but admired their efficiency and coveted the empire they had built. Because there was very little, besides land, to take over in Russia in 1917, Bolshevik leaders could not help but mingle feelings of longing and envy with their habitual sentiments of animosity whenever they turned toward the capitalistic nations of the West. The country which quite logically was to evoke the most pronounced forms of both responses was the United States, the most industrially advanced of all the Western nations.

The post-revolutionary Bolsheviks were certainly not the first European Marxists to entertain ambivalent feelings toward the United States. European Marxists, like Europeans of every other political persuasion, remained at least partially captive to the old idea positing the unique potentialities for man's mind and spirit in the remote and privileged environment of the New World. Things presently impossible in Europe might come true first in the United States. Marxist attacks upon the corruption of American politics, their portrayals of the brutalities of its economic system, all their efforts to redress the myth of a workers' paradise across the Atlantic, did not completely erase a respect for the energy and progressiveness of American life. To European Marxists and liberals alike, America arose before them as the land of the future. Their disagreements stemmed from their respective analyses of America's present.

Lenin and Trotsky were exposed to the positive and negative facets of all traditional European assessments of the United States, whether Marxist, non-Marxist, liberal, or conservative. Russian intellectuals had traditionally taken a great interest in America. The American scholars David Hecht and Max Laserson have made important studies of pre-Soviet Russian attitudes toward the United States, and there is no need to duplicate their work.[3] It is sufficient to recall the considerable admiration of the United States found among Russian radicals and non-Marxist socialists throughout the nineteenth century. Alexander Radishchev, Alexander Herzen, and Nicholas Chernyshevski, among others, treated the energetic, youthful American federal republic as an object of emulation for the Russian people. In his book *The Soviet Image of the United States* Frederick Barghoorn has written, "In the now dim days before the communist revolution America represented to Russians more than to any other people a promised land. Particularly to Russian liberals, and also to most Russian radicals, the United States symbolized human dignity, the pioneer virtues, and dazzling material progress."[4]

A more negative view of contemporary America was formed in the late nineteenth century by Russian Marxists who, along with everyone else in the Second International, kept American institutions under steady attack. Peter Lavrov (Lavrov moved away from Marxist socialism, but its influence in molding his opinions about the United States was extremely important), Paul Axelrod, and George Plekhanov all argued the familiar Marxist brief about the complete uselessness of American political liberties in bringing workers a better standard of life. Plekhanov wrote, "You see that even in the United States, the freest of all countries, the yoke of capital continues to press down upon the working class. The men of labor, by whose hands all social wealth is created, remain in poverty while their exploiters enjoy all the good things of life."[5]

Just as those in western Europe, Russian Marxists in their hostility to "republican federal America" were, as Max Laserson has indicated, drawing on the traditional attitudes of reactionary conservatives.[6] It

---

[3] Max M. Laserson, *The American Impact on Russia—Diplomatic and Ideological—1784–1917* (New York, 1950); David Hecht, *Russian Radicals Look to America, 1825–1894* (Cambridge, Mass., 1947).
[4] Frederick C. Barghoorn, *The Soviet Image of the United States: A Study in Distortion* (New York, 1950), 3.
[5] Quoted by David Hecht, "Plekhanov and American Socialism," *The Russian Review,* Vol. IX (April 1950), 115.
[6] *The American Impact on Russia,* 141.

was not the only example of such an unholy alliance. Conservatives and Marxists in the 1880's and 1890's had sometimes fought together for socializing programs opposed by laissez-faire liberals. A common cause was not, however, indicative of common motives. Supporters of autocratic Tsarism had never liked America and had brushed aside pressures for reform as more foolishness from the New World. Marxists joined the conservatives in attempting to dispel the American myth for quite different reasons. While, like the conservatives, their propaganda about America was aimed at killing the spirit of liberal political reform, their ultimate intent was to clear the path for a thoroughgoing social revolution.

The inheritance of this deeply mixed group of attitudes toward the United States freed Lenin and Trotsky and other Bolsheviks from the burden of having to think very hard or very originally about the American situation. Depending on what circumstances forced them to take cognizance of America, they could choose from a variety of phrases and slogans which had long been second nature to them. When they wished to spew forth venom about the United States, as they often did following the Russian Revolution and the American support (albeit reluctant) of Allied intervention in the ensuing Civil War, they had a large vocabulary already created for them. If, instead, they wanted to pay tribute to American inventiveness and efficiency, which was frequently their wont, a tradition of praise for such qualities also lay at hand. Nevertheless, Lenin and Trotsky adapted traditional attitudes toward America to their own particular uses and their own singular view of historical events. Like almost all Europeans, whether socialist or non-socialist, who wrote about the United States, they used the overseas republic as a political football and saw there only those elements which fitted a pattern of preconceived ideas.

Lenin, particularly, for all his wide-ranging interests, was a profound Russian nationalist; and anything he tried to learn about other countries was directed unhesitatingly and without any playful digression toward understanding the trials of his own nation. What can one say about a man who spent a year in London and saw, besides the books in the British museum, only the city's parks? [7] Marx alone came close to this unenviable record; but Marx, unlike

[7] Ulam, 170–76.

the more parochial Russian, took the time to meet some Englishmen. Lenin's universe was intensely self-contained, and only a few kinds of impressions slipped through the outer screening devices of his mind. Compared to this selective process, the Atlantic posed a very small barrier to understanding America.

Lenin developed his first sustained interest in the United States as a result of the theoretical and practical problems raised by the Russian Revolution of 1905. On Sunday, January 22, 1905, Father Gapon, a deranged priest who liked fame almost as much as gambling and drinking, led a peaceful procession of workers before the Winter's Palace to lay before the Tsar a "humble" supplication for reform. The Tsar's police answered with gunfire, killing around 1000 workers, and by a senseless act of bloodletting awakened a Russian proletariat which no one before had even noticed. Strikes and agrarian riots followed, the first Soviet of workers' deputies was convened in St. Petersburg, and Nicholas II reluctantly agreed to reforms and an elected legislature. It all came to very little, and Russian liberals, let alone Marxists, were bitterly disappointed with the results. From 1905 until the early part of 1907, however, the old regime trembled; and Marxist pens scribbled furiously to keep on top of events.

Following the first upheavals, Lenin tried desperately to define a program for his party which, while not conflicting with Marxist theory, would allow the Bolsheviks to seize the initiative in shaping the next phase of Russian development. At the time Lenin was in perfect agreement with most of his fellow Marxists (not Trotsky it should be remembered) in accepting as axiomatic Russia's total unreadiness for socialism. The next stage of growth should properly result in Russia's bourgeoisification and conversion to capitalism. This necessitated the overthrow of the Tsar and the introduction of laissez-faire economic principles.

Lenin conceded nothing else to the received orthodoxy. For Lenin the bourgeoisification of Russia did not require, as it had required in western Europe, the acceptance by the proletariat of the political dominance of the middle classes. Lenin could not go as far as Trotsky in dismissing the stage theory of history as an outmoded curiosity, but he could obviously not stomach the prospect of working with the bourgeoisie. Marxists both in Lenin's Bolshevik party

and the rival Menshevik faction were puzzled by this completely
un-Marxist prejudice, but Lenin was in a bigger hurry than most
of them realized. Russia needed a capitalist revolution. Very well, it
would have one—but without the middle class directing it. The
Russian bourgeoisie, in Lenin's mind, were vacillating, weak, and
inept, and incapable of wresting from the Tsar even a system which
ostensibly benefited them. The opportunities opened up by the outbreak of violence in 1905 should not be lost, and to Lenin a combined
force of proletarians and peasants could best guide Russia through
its capitalist stage. He was in the same mind as he would be in
April 1917, when he would demand "all power to the Soviets" while
interdicting any talk of immediate socialization.[8]

This reworking of normative Marxism indicates the extent to
which Lenin emphasized conscious will and leadership in bringing
about the ultimate goal of socialism. Lenin was anxious to speed
Russia through its capitalist phase as quickly as possible, and he was
determined to leave nothing to fate or chance. In his mind the transformation of Russia after 1905 into a capitalist economy could follow
one of two possible paths which he labeled the Prussian and the
American ways.[9] The former would lead Russia over a tortuously
long path of gradual change, and the latter would introduce capitalism in Russia overnight. The former would be the course pursued
if the premier, Stolypin, and the liberal Kadet party were allowed
to direct the destiny of Russia. The latter would result if Bolsheviks
were successful in obtaining, as Lenin demanded, a Revolutionary
Dictatorship of the Proletariat and Peasantry.

Specifically, in discussing the American versus the Prussian way,
Lenin was speaking about the capitalization of Russian agriculture
and addressing himself critically to a set of land reforms proposed
by Stolypin in 1907. His discussion sought to balance several considerations. The most immediate was to find a way to turn aside

---

[8] Ulam, 333.
[9] Lenin discussed these alternative paths of development in numerous articles.
See, for example, "The Strength and Weakness of the Russian Revolution,"
*The Agrarian Programme of the Social-Democracy in the First Russian Rev-
olution, 1905–07,* and *The Agrarian Question in Russia Towards the Close of
the Nineteenth Century.* These writings from the years 1907 and 1908 have
been translated and can be found in Vols. XII–XV of Lenin's *Collected Works*
(Moscow, 1960–66).

moderate constitutionalism and keep the revolutionary cauldron boiling with a fiery appeal to Russia's peasantry. Lenin's various programs over the years to woo the Russian peasant provide a study in obfuscation and broken pledges unto itself, but in 1907 he considered the support of the countryside the sine qua non of any revolutionary drive. On a more long range basis, Lenin deemed the question of land reform crucial to the future economic development of Russia. The pattern of change set in the agricultural sector would determine the pattern of Russia's industrial and political metamorphosis for years. The proposal which Lenin credited to Stolypin, the vast resettlement of small peasants on land in Siberia, would according to Lenin leave the feudal structure of Russian society intact and not eradicate sufficiently the vestiges of serfdom which had survived in Russian life despite Alexander II's celebrated Manifesto of Liberation in 1861. Stolypin's proposals in Lenin's view would not break up the latifundia, the large gentry estates; and, as a result, Lenin foresaw the great Russian landlords consolidating into a class comparable to the Prussian Junkers—a class conscious of privilege, anti-egalitarian, ultra-conservative, disdainful of business and industry, and, worst of all, a class politically powerful far beyond the warrant of its numbers. The awed peasants would continue to bow and scrape before them and would make no attempt to escape the undynamic, secure paternalistic rural environment so long as it provided them with a minimal subsistence.

Lenin summed up what he expected from Stolypin's program:

> Once the latifundia are retained, this inevitably means also the retention of the bonded peasant, of métayage, of the renting of small plots by the year, the cultivation of the "squire's" land with the implements of the peasants, i.e., the retention of the most backward farming methods and of all that Asiatic barbarism which is called patriarchal rural life.[10]

The Prussian way, Lenin admitted, would over a long period of time produce the desired goal of capitalistically managed farms and release the majority of the Russian people from their bondage to the

[10] *The Agrarian Question in Russia Towards the Close of the Nineteenth Century, Collected Works,* Vol. XV, 139.

land for work in industrial centers; but the creation of a politically dominant Junker class would not generate the kind of precipitate energy required to remake society quickly.

The only correct way to modernize Russia, according to Lenin, was to eliminate medieval survivals at a stroke—to nationalize land, to abolish the latifundia, and to distribute land to the one "who really wants, and is *able,* to cultivate it according to the requirements of modern farming in general and of the world market in particular." [11] This plan, as Lenin well knew before Menshevik voices challenged him, departed from traditional Marxism, not only in promising the peasant privately managed parcels of land, but also in breaking up already consolidated holdings. Had not Marxists consistently characterized any type of trustbusting as reactionary? But Lenin was ready to go to any lengths to accelerate the process of capitalization in Russia. His scheme, he insisted, however unconventional, would most directly set Russia out along the American way in developing its economic resources. It alone would allow Russia to make the sharp break with the past and tradition which had spurred the economy of the United States to such spectacular success.

The key to America's rapid capitalist development, according to Lenin, lay in the completely unchecked operation of the principle of competition. No feudal barriers dampened the individualistic spirit of self-advancement. Land was cheap in America from the early days of settlement, and the Homestead Law of 1862 guaranteed the accessibility of the western domain to small settlers. Caste privilege and a social structure reminiscent of European feudalism had flourished for many generations in the South; but Americans, in contrast with the Russian's halfhearted attempts to eliminate serfdom, had rooted out those anachronisms in a fierce and bloody war.[12] From the end of the Civil War capitalism boomed. After the crushing of the political and economic power of the slaveholder no significant institutions remained in America to succor the idle, the incompetent, and the unprogressive. Those who built their small homestead stake into a booming, gigantic commercial enterprise

[11] *Ibid.,* 139.
[12] A closer look at the position of the Negro and poor white in the postwar South might have led Lenin to modify his position on the effectiveness of the American Civil War in clearing away the rubbish of the past.

were those who remained abreast of modern farming techniques, those who skimped, saved, invested, and reinvested to build up their capital resources. This same entrepreneurial zeal nurtured the huge industrial plants which appeared and multiplied so rapidly in the United States in the late nineteenth century.

Lenin summed up the alternative consequences of Russia's adoption of the American or Prussian way:

> One alternative is evolution of the Prussian type—the serf-owning landlord becomes a Junker; the landlords' power in the state is consolidated for a decade; monarchy; "military despotism, embellished in parliamentary forms" instead of democracy; the greatest inequality among the rural and non-rural population. The second alternative is evolution of the American type—the abolition of landlord farming; the peasant becomes a free farmer; popular government; the bourgeois-democratic political system; the greatest equality among the rural population as the starting point of, and a condition for, free capitalism.[13]

It was not Lenin's intention in such passages to act as an apologist for America's Gilded Age. The abuses of any capitalist system were axiomatic to a Marxist writer, and Lenin did not need to remind his followers at every turn of the special opportunities for those abuses to flourish in the United States. What was important to him was not that the American experience revealed life under capitalism as happy (which it most certainly did not), but that it offered encouragement about Russia's passage through its next necessary stage of development. Lenin's Marxism resigned him to a period when middle-class attitudes would be extolled; but fortunately, and the American example reassured him, it would be brief.

Here was America's special promise confined within the narrowest possible limits. America just before its Civil War was a nation of small farmers. By 1900 it was the most highly developed capitalist nation in the world, fully primed for a socialist revolution. There was no reason why Russia could not rush through historical stages at the same speed, indeed even faster, because Russia could draw on

[13] "The Strength and Weakness of the Russian Revolution," *Collected Works,* XII, 356.

advanced Western technology unknown to America's first capitalists. Lenin wanted a program which would permit the present generation of Russian Marxists to see and enjoy a socialist state. Insofar as the materialistic, profit-seeking American way brought his goal nearer, he was prepared to see Russia adopt it without amendment.

These considerations about American and Prussian ways occupied Lenin's interest for several years and then dropped out of his writings. So it was with all the theoretical designs of this incredibly active man. His interests changed abruptly with the altered context of events. By 1909 the progressive movement in Russia had ground to a halt; and Lenin, once again in exile, remembered 1905 as a lost opportunity, a cause not to be mourned any longer. Policy decisions in Russia indicated clearly that Russia was not going to pursue the American way, and Lenin's tracts from 1907 and 1908 ceased to be relevant.

When he found himself in another revolution in 1917, Lenin, digging out his earlier writings, might have looked again for guidance in New World patterns. He did not, at least not in the same way. Throughout the early tumultuous months of 1917 Lenin was not exactly sure what economic structure Russia should adopt. Capitalism in Russia was about where it was in 1905; and, if socialism had been wrong then, it was wrong now. But by the time Lenin seized power from the Provisional Government in October, he was fully committed to the immediate introduction of socialism. Marx's clear outlines of economic development were blurred by historical pressures and Bolshevik impatience. As a result discussion about the necessity of any kind of capitalist stage for Russia, whether according to Prussian or American specifications, was pushed into the background and kept there until the New Economic Policy of 1921. For the time being the new Russian leaders raised the banner of War Communism and launched experiment after experiment in worker-controlled factories and peasant communes. Completion of the system would have to await aid from the West; but, in the first flush of enthusiasm supported by the prospects of victories all over Europe, there seemed every reason to press forward.

When revolutionary expectations in the West failed to materialize, Bolshevik leaders faced a traumatic reassessment of their situation. As a reflection of their disappointment over the failure of revolutionists to rise in Europe and the United States, Bolshevik leaders stepped up in intensity their usual verbal attacks on the capitalist nations, especially the United States. This was not simply because of a continuing aversion to capitalism but also because the capitalist powers, choosing to regard the Bolsheviks as outlaws, made their willingness to do anything to overthrow the new Russian leaders painfully clear. Particularly, this last fact made the most powerful nation in the West seem potentially the most dangerous. Bolshevism, like any political system and particularly any unstable political system, thrives by stirring up among the people a certain amount of nationalistic paranoia. The case of Allied intervention in Russian affairs during 1918 and 1919 made this task very easy for the Bolsheviks. The United States and the other Allied powers showed themselves through their actions to be implacable enemies of the new government in Russia and, by implication, enemies of the principle of self-determination for Russia. Lenin did not forget the "handful of arrogant multimillionaires" in the United States who tried to strangle the Russian Socialist Republic in 1918.[14] In the early 1920's, when the United States continued to refuse an extension of official recognition to the Bolsheviks, Trotsky wrote, "There is no enemy of Bolshevism more principled and more savage than American capitalism." [15] World history had become for Trotsky a struggle between two great forces—Leninism and American imperialism: one of them was bound to sweep the world. Already the two countries had settled into their respective illusions about the imminent collapse of the other's government, and neither expected the establishment of normal and harmonious diplomatic relations until the leadership of the other had changed.

In addition to these portrayals of America as an aggressive enemy Lenin and Trotsky loudly echoed earlier Marxist condemnations of bourgeois democratic institutions in the United States. In a speech of 1919 Lenin said,

---

[14] "Letter to American Workers," *Collected Works,* Vol. XXVIII, 63.
[15] *Europe and America* (Colombo, 1951), 33. This is a pamphlet containing two speeches that Trotsky delivered in 1924 and 1926. Professor Firuz Kazemzadeh has kindly pointed out to me that a more accurate rendering of the Russian text would be, "There is no enemy of Bolshevism more sworn and more opposed to it in principle than American capitalism."

One of the most democratic republics in the world is the United States of America, yet nowhere (and those who have been there since 1905 probably know it) is the power of capital, the power of a handful of multimillionaires over the whole of society, so crude and so openly corrupt as in America. . . . You say your state is free, whereas in reality, as long as there is private property, your state, even if it is a democratic republic, is nothing but a machine used by the capitalists to suppress the workers, and the freer the state, the more clearly is this expressed.[16]

In his famous speech of the preceding year at the Michelson factory, celebrated because afterward a distraught Russian woman fired two bullets into Lenin and almost prematurely gave the Soviets a great martyr, he declared, "Take America, the freest and most civilized country. There you have a democratic republic. But what do we find? The brazen rule of a handful, not even of millionaires, but multimillionaires, while the people are in slavery and servitude." [17] Trotsky in his *Terrorism and Communism* of 1922 interpreted the experience in the United States as a clear demonstration of the uselessness of liberties like freedom of the press in easing the exploitation of labor by a ruling capitalist class.[18] Such comments are scarcely distinguishable from countless others which had filled the Marxist press in western Europe in the several decades before the Russian Revolution.

There is one interesting and important difference between these remarks of the Bolshevik leaders and the earlier comments of more moderate Marxist thinkers. The direction which the Bolshevik revolution took alienated Russian leaders, not only from the ruling bourgeois powers of the Western nations, but also from many of their former comrades in the Second International. As the difficulties of cementing the gains of the revolution forced the Soviet leaders to change the concept of the dictatorship of the proletariat from an idea of a broad-based, worker-led democracy into a justification for

[16] "A Lecture Delivered at the Sverdlov University, July 11, 1919," *Collected Works,* Vol. XXIX, 485–87.
[17] "Speech at a Meeting at the former Michelson Works, August 30, 1918," *Collected Works,* Vol. XXVIII, 90.
[18] Quoted in *The Basic Writings of Trotsky,* ed. by Irving Howe (New York, 1963), 149.

a narrow one-party rule, enraged criticism arose among the ranks of comrades whom Lenin had once regarded as staunch allies. The ruthless and bloody suppression of political opposition brought out-cries of indignation from important Marxists like Karl Kautsky, and even from hard-shelled, uncompromising, left-wing revolutionaries like Rosa Luxemburg. Expressions of disbelief, to the beleaguered Bolsheviks, were exasperating and hypocritical; they deserved a sharp answer. When the victorious heroes of the revolution picked up the theme of the counterfeit nature of American political liberties, they were not now primarily speaking to liberal admirers of the United States who had formerly been the target of Marxist rhetoric of this sort; they were rather rebuking their Marxist critics in Europe. The sudden defense of free expression by the latter only indicated to the Bolsheviks how far their Western colleagues had stumbled down the paths of revisionism.

Actually, the defense was not as extemporaneous as the Bolsheviks imagined. While Marxists had been unimpressed observers of exist-ing democratic republics (using the United States as the prime exam-ple of republican corruption), they had never expected a future socialist state to stifle critical thinking and institute methods of political oppression scarcely distinguishable from the Tsars'. The final goal of socialist society was, according to Marx and Engels, the total elimination of the state. Some Marxists had anticipated, relying on Marx's controversial *Critique of the Gotha Program,* a transi-tional state, bridging the period between capitalism and full social-ism, based on a dictatorship of the proletariat. This undefined con-cept implied for them the necessary dominance of the proletariat for a short time over the dispossessed capitalists; and, since Marxists expected proletarians to form the vast majority of the population by the day of the revolution, the proposed dictatorship did not seriously conflict with their desire for a completely open society. What the Bolsheviks were making of the concept did. Summary executions by the Cheka, the tightening control over dissent, and the exaltation of a single party bothered consciences in Europe. According to the Kautskian old guard, free expression and political liberties were not bad per se; they had merely become corrupted and useless in the context of capitalism. The Bolsheviks had forgotten this, and as a result Marxists could never again find places in one International.

Bolshevik methods of repression were justifiably condemned, but the Soviet leaders did have a problem. Confronted with the Russian masses who did not prove to be as heroic and farsighted as their leaders had originally hoped, Bolsheviks had no choice if they wished to retain power except to put aside idealistic and romantic ideas about the proletariat's capacity to choose wisely among alternatives. The example of the United States helped convince them that in breaking with the traditional liberal assumptions which had heretofore found a place in all European radical programs, including their own, they were leaving nothing of importance behind.

This was one side of the coin. The other bore a different imprint. Despite the decadence and corruption characteristic of Western societies, despite the inevitable day of judgment awaiting capitalism, Lenin and Trotsky were quickly forced to seek some sort of rapprochement with the governments whose destruction they awaited. Their efforts invariably enticed them into open admiration of what they hated. A socialist Russia was going to have to live with bourgeois republics like the United States for a few more years. How long was uncertain, but as early as the latter half of 1918 Lenin's *Letter to American Workers* made it clear that Bolsheviks did not consider their final goals so proximate as had once been the case:

> We know that help from you will probably not come soon, comrade American workers, for the revolution is developing in different countries in different forms and at different tempos (and it cannot be otherwise). We know that although the European proletarian revolution has been maturing very rapidly lately, it may, after all, not flare up within the next few weeks.[19]

Imperialistic ventures had apparently given the capitalist powers an extra few years to survive. This had not been Lenin's expectation when he wrote his treatise on *Imperialism* in 1914, for then he had sought to show how capitalism's entrance into a final phase of development made the revolution possible at any moment. The "superprofits" derived from the exploitation of workers in foreign countries had unfortunately proved very effective in bribing the upper levels of the working class and had deprived the proletariat in

[19] "Letter to American Workers," 74–75.

the mother country of its most capable leaders. This had led to the anomalous situation, noted by Lenin in 1918, that for the time being revolutions could start more easily in the lesser developed countries (like Russia):

> Today we see a different combination of international socialist forces. We say that it is easier for the movement to start in the countries that are not among those exploiting countries which have opportunities for easy plunder and are able to bribe the upper sections of their workers.[20]

America's emergence after World War I as the leading economic power in the world had dealt a sharp blow to previous Marxist hopes for an early socialist victory in America, and would probably enable the United States to hold out a long time as the last bastion of capitalism. This was Trotsky's conclusion in the mid-1920's. The war had enabled the United States to make Europe its economic vassal. Its ultimate goal was to put "capitalist Europe on rations"; America would furnish the aid necessary to allow Europe to rise again, but "within limits set in advance." It would regulate the activities of European financiers and industrialists to its own advantage and would tell them what to produce and how much. (Trotsky's remarks here were an uncanny foreshadowing of Marxist attitudes toward the Marshall Plan.) By giving up its economic self-sufficiency, America tied its economic fortunes to very unstable areas of the world; and the parasitic nature of its imperialistic ventures worked to stimulate the very socialist revolution it hoped to keep down. In those senses America's strength was its Achilles' heel. But in 1926 Trotsky did not foresee the defeat of American capitalism until a unified Europe stood in "revolutionary collaboration" with the socialist nations of Asia, an eventuality which no one any longer thought lay just around the corner.[21]

[20] "Speech at Third All-Russia Congress of Soviets of Workers', Soldiers' and Peasants' Deputies, Jan. 11, 1918," *Collected Works,* Vol. XXVI, 471–72. See also his 1920 Preface to the French and German editions of *Imperialism.*

[21] *Europe and America,* 16 and 71. Communist disappointment with the failure of an important socialist movement to develop in America led some Russian and American comrades to accept the so-called doctrine of American exceptionalism—a theory which postulated that American capitalism had not

Russia's leaders had no choice but to adjust to this unpleasant reality. Their task became to use the time between the revolution in their own country and the delayed one in the West to take all they could get from Western capitalism without sacrificing the ultimate goals of communism. This left much to be done in the interim, and the ambivalent feelings toward capitalist progressiveness, never absent from Marxist writing, appeared in more striking relief than ever before. In somewhat the same spirit that Lenin had written about the advantages of the American way in the first decade of the century, Lenin and Trotsky, in plotting the course of the new order in Russia, turned to the West for the valuable lessons it could still teach them. They looked upon the period of the early 1920's as a sort of orchestral prelude before the curtain opened on a stage creaking under the drama of world revolution. So long as the auditorium was darkened, there was no harm in doing a little surreptitious handholding with the powers of capitalism. The fair damsel of the West had her treasures to bestow, and Russia's task was to get at them without entering any entangling agreements leading to marriage.

When Lenin in 1921 led Russia back into the semi-bourgeois paths of the New Economic Policy, when he strove actively to open trade channels with the West, when he sought to attract American business to develop certain areas in the Soviet Union, he stirred heated opposition among the more uncompromising Bolsheviks.[22] But there was nothing incongruous about Lenin's actions. Machines, organization, and technology had always fascinated Lenin. When he had written favorably about the American Way in 1907 and 1908, these had been in the forefront of his mind. According to his best biographer, Lenin's enthusiasm for War Communism was no better at any time than lukewarm, and he never hesitated to reinstate bour-

---

yet entered a period of decline. Orthodoxy quickly labeled the doctrine as heresy, but its brief vogue is indicative of the state of confusion in which the American situation had landed many Marxist thinkers. For a discussion of the theory, see Theodore Draper's *American Communism and Soviet Russia: The Formative Years* (New York, 1960), Chapter XII.

[22] For a discussion of Lenin's efforts to open up contacts with the United States, see Ulam, 483–86; Louis Fischer, *The Life of Lenin* (New York, 1964), 557; George Kennan, *Russia and the West under Lenin and Stalin* (Boston, 1960), especially Chapters XIII and XIV.

geois managers, calling them "specialists," into their old positions.[23] He did not like them, for their attitudes were still antediluvian; but because they were effective, Lenin pampered them, paid them more, and let them order the workers around just as before. The laborer in the factory had cause to wonder whether anything but the labels had changed.

In 1920, when an American adventurer Washington B. Vanderlip, Jr., offered to rent and develop an eastern chunk of Russia, Lenin was delighted for the opportunity it would give to observe how American capitalists did things. (He also hoped that Vanderlip's activities there might provoke a war between the United States and Japan.) By such patient learning, he thought, Russia could make up for its slighting of a capitalist stage of economic development. Unfortunately, Warren G. Harding heard of the deal and was not delighted, and Russia was deprived of Vanderlip's dubious services.

"To have Bolshevism shod in the American way": that was how Trotsky in 1924 summed up the task facing the Russian people. "We must get shod technologically with American nails." [24] Again in a 1925 essay he used statistics drawn from the United States to remind his Russian readers of the still great strength and effectiveness of capitalist methods of production. It might be true, he said, that "the lion is stronger than the dog"; but it was equally true that "an old dog may be stronger than the lion's cub." [25] And the old dog, despite its proverbial conservatism, might still know a few old tricks which the young cub would do well to learn.

Several years earlier, in 1920, Trotsky went so far as to acknowledge the lessons which Russia could learn from Frederick Winslow Taylor, the American economist whose principles of scientific management represented some sort of culminating point in the Yankee drive for industrial efficiency.[26] To Marxists, Taylor's methods of eliminating wasted motions had usually connoted labor exploitation carried to its most coldly, scientifically calculated extreme. But in Trotsky's businesslike opinion Taylor's methods, once lifted out of the system of private ownership, could boost enormously the pro-

[23] Ulam, 467.
[24] *Europe and America,* 35.
[25] From 1925 work *Whither Russia?* Quoted in *The Age of Permanent Revolution: A Trotsky Anthology,* ed. by Isaac Deutscher (New York, 1964), 133.
[26] *The Prophet Armed,* 499.

ductivity of Russian industry without harmful side effects. He was not bothered by the possibility, which Daniel Bell and others would point to later, that a worker's feeling of alienation arose, not from institutions of private property, but from the actual work process of large-scale industry, with its emphasis on production, the division of labor, and the use of machine technology.[27] For him the American way, properly adapted to Russian conditions and Bolshevik ideals, offered the best chance to put Russia on its feet. It provided the fastest means of speeding Russia through the process of industrial and agricultural consolidation which alone would make possible the raising of the roof on the grand, but half-completed, edifice of Russian communism.

At all times these concessions to American skill, and especially to the knack for getting things done quickly, were weighed down by harsher judgments of the American system. Nevertheless it is worth recalling, as Frederick Barghoorn pointed out, that Russian respect for American methods allowed a moderate amount of unofficial contact and a considerable amount of good feeling to pass between the countries. Barghoorn wrote, "After the October revolution America was cast in the negative role of the greatest capitalist power. But the United States continued after 1917 to be regarded as a model of technological progress. Moreover, a surprising degree of good will toward America persisted even under the Bolsheviks, especially among Soviet citizens who did not belong to the new ruling party."[28] The labors in the early 1920's of Herbert Hoover's American Relief Administration to bring greatly needed assistance to famine-stricken Russia left behind a strong measure of gratitude among the Russian people which reached up into government and party circles.[29]

Bolshevik leaders already regarded capitalist America at this early date as an implacable enemy, but they did not yet portray the United States as the repository of all reactionary and unenlightened ideas.

[27] Bell, *The End of Ideology* (Glencoe, Ill., 1960), 364–68. Also see Bell, "The Debate on Alienation," in *Revisionism: Essays on the History of Marxist Ideas,* ed. by Louis Labedz (New York, 1962), 210–11.
[28] *The Soviet Image of the United States,* 3.
[29] See discussion in Foster Rhea Dulles, *The Road to Teheran: The Study of Russia and America, 1781–1943* (Princeton, 1945), 172–73. I am also indebted to Professor Firuz Kazemzadeh for information on this point.

That was to happen at a later time when the enthusiasm and optimism of the early years of the Revolution had become less spontaneous and confidence was formalized in the doctrine of "socialism in one country." The longer capitalism lingered in the twentieth century and the longer the Russian people had to endure hardships and deprivations in building socialism, the more Soviet leaders had to work to convince their followers of the unenviable lot of workers in other nations and the less they were willing to talk about the progressiveness of any other style of life. Russia had to catch up with America and the West, but it had to be via the Russian way with Russian techniques and Russian inventions. During the Cold War in the early 1950's this obsession reached the point where all innovations borrowed from the West had to be ascribed to Russian discoverers. Innovation and capitalism were, according to this tenet of Soviet "revisionism," incompatible; and, if history did not support that assumption, it was bad history and needed to be rewritten. As the Soviet Union and America emerged after World War II as chief rivals in a struggle to win the allegiance of the underdeveloped nations, efforts to picture the historical role of the United States in the worst possible light gathered momentum. This again necessitated throwing out old history, and Soviet scholars started to recast the period after 1917 as a titanic struggle between the good represented by Russia and the evil embodied by the United States.[30] Reading too much of the implacably hostile rhetoric of the Cold War back into the attitudes of Lenin and Trotsky in the first few years after the Russian Revolution distorts their points of view and suggests too strongly the fatalistic assumption that Soviet and American relations could have gone in no other direction than one of increasing sourness and suspicion.

Lenin's overtures in the early 1920's to the United States, as everybody recognized, were neither candid nor honest. Lenin's official foreign policy shamelessly tried to play the capitalist powers off against one another, while the Comintern, the unofficial instrument of Bolshevik foreign policy, worked to overthrow the very

---

[30] As an example of historical revision in the case of America's role in the intervention of 1918 and 1919, see George F. Kennan, "Soviet Historiography and America's Role in the Intervention," *American Historical Review*, Vol. LXV (Jan. 1960), 302–22.

capitalist regimes with which the Soviet Union expressed a wish to trade. Yet, the responses of the United States during these very hard years for Russia, especially in view of America's great position of strength, were not terribly farsighted. If the United States had cashed in on Russian admiration for American efficiency and accepted the invitation to open official contacts, a basis might just have been laid which in time would have improved Soviet-American relations. Friendship between the two countries was out of the question, but peaceful coexistence, had it been gropingly approached in the beginning, might have long before now settled onto firm and secure foundations.

Lenin did not live to see in what direction his successor carried the October Revolution. Trotsky was less fortunate. Within a decade Stalin had snatched from Trotsky's brow his laurels as hero of the Revolution and had sent him out of Russia with curses as Bolshevism's worst enemy. From various posts of exile Trotsky watched Stalin's sure and brutal hands pounding out a future for Russia on an anvil which is still stained with the blood of the victims who fell under the hammer. On August 21, 1940, he himself died at the hands of an assassin, utterly disenchanted with what he thought had become a tragic parody of a workers' state in Russia. It had been twenty-three years since he and Lenin had committed Russia to a socialist future. Instead of Europe having followed Russia down revolutionary paths and brought it much-needed assistance, Germany was preparing to enter a period of reaction which would darken the whole continent. In such a world, Trotsky thought, it was perhaps unavoidable that the Russian Revolution should go off the track and land in the Stalinist purges of the 1930's.

Trotsky never considered the October Revolution a mistake. With proper leadership, he maintained until the end, the outcome could have been favorable. But, as his disappointment mounted in the closing years of his life, he could not help reflecting that things would have gone easily for socialists everywhere if America had preceded the other nations into the communist era. In his autobiography of 1930, Trotsky recalled the few months he had spent in New York just before the first uprisings occurred in Russia in 1917. For him it was too short a visit to penetrate all the complexities of American life. He wrote, "I was leaving for Europe, with the feeling of a man who has had only a peep into the foundry in which the fate of man is to be forged. My only consolation was the thought that I might return. Even now I have not given up that hope." [31]

The political climate in the United States never permitted Trotsky to make a return trip. In his late life, however, it more than ever appeared to him that man's fate would be forged there. Trotsky's ideas and his criticisms of Stalin found the greatest audience in communist circles in the United States. By 1938 the strongest section of Trotsky's abortive Fourth International was in New York, and his correspondence with American communists grew to tremendous proportions. This activity led him to reverse his opinion of the mid-1920's when he had viewed America as probably the last bastion of capitalism and had looked for the defeat of American capitalism only after a revolution had triumphed all over Europe. In the 1930's Europe was lost to the Nazis. If communism had any prospects for success in the immediate future, those prospects lay in the United States.

Trotsky considered conditions favorable in America for a quick communist advance. The Great Depression which had flattened the American economy made all earlier pronouncements about the stability of American capitalism look ridiculous. Trotsky regarded the floundering efforts of the New Deal to correct the situation as proof of the total bankruptcy of any bourgeois formula. None of them could cope with the problems caused by the concentration of wealth. Declarations about America similar to those made by Marxists at the turn of the century crept into his writing. America had come "closest to that ideal type of capitalism" depicted by Marx and was logically the country most vulnerable to socialist propaganda. In 1940 he wrote,

> Now dawns the new epoch of an independent class movement of the proletariat and at the same time of—genuine Marxism. In this, too, America will in a few jumps catch up with Europe and outdistance it. Progressive technique and a progressive social structure will pave their own way in the sphere of doctrine. The best theoreticians of Marxism will appear on American soil.[32]

[31] *My Life: The Rise and Fall of a Dictator* (London, 1930), 239.
[32] *The Living Thoughts of Karl Marx* (London, 1940), 37 and 38.

A Soviet America, because it would have progressed through the capitalist stage anticipated by Marx, could avoid all the mistakes of the underdeveloped nations, who because of imperialist oppression had been violently, chaotically, and prematurely hurled into the era of socialist revolution. The advanced technology and productive capacities of the United States would make possible the elimination of poverty and discontent. A Bolshevik America would know none of the problems of trying to govern a nation whose people suffered from severe privation, and the undemocratic and oppressive bureaucracy strangling Russia would be unknown. "Within a century," he wrote, "out of your melting pot of races there will come a new breed of men—the first worthy of the name of Man." [33]

This late attempt by Trotsky to cast America again in the role of a socialist promised land differed from comparable Marxist propaganda of the turn of the century in one significant respect. In 1900, enthusiasm was running high. Capitalism seemed to have reached the end of its rope. According to the prognostications of European socialists, the breakthrough might very well come first in the United States, but they were equally optimistic about prospects in their own countries. Trotsky's portrayal of the American Promised Land betrayed no hint of innocent cheerfulness. He was disillusioned with all that had happened in Europe and in his own Russia. Now he turned his eyes to the United States where fulfilment might yet come, but his pronouncements belied any real optimism and had the desperate ring of a man calling on a last hope.

Setbacks joggled but did not destroy Trotsky's confidence in the world revolution. It would come. There was, as he noted in the decade before his death, great promise in the social turbulence stirring the underdeveloped areas of the world. But Stalin had frightened him. At the end of his life he found it necessary to return to the original emphasis of the Marxist dialectic: the forces making for socialism grew from the oppressions of a developed capitalist system. And until revolutionary aspirations throughout the world were supported by a victory in one of the developed capitalist nations in the West, socialist governments might continue to find their policies

---

[33] *If America Should Go Communist* (New York, 1957), 21. An article first printed in *Liberty* magazine in 1935.

pushed into the terrifying excesses which characterized the Stalinist regime of the 1930's.

It is somewhat anticlimactic to say after having come through so many European socialist interpretations of the United States, Marxist, revisionist, and Bolshevik, that, on the whole, they fail to add up to a very penetrating critique of American life. Revisionists were more flexible in their analyses of America than Marxists and were more alert to the complexities of the United States; but none of their notes on the New World approached the caliber of Tocqueville or Bryce or even first-rate political and social commentary. In some significant respects European socialists did make a searching and important social critique. They focused attention on the poverty and suffering of many Americans (except the Negro) when almost everyone else blinked at the evidence of urban putrescence. They tried to recapture America from the mythmakers and turn it over to the social realists and they argued effectively that the "American Way" did not necessarily provide a solution to the social problems of Europe. For these efforts they may be thanked. But one cannot pass by basic failures of observation in these socialist works which rendered even their valuable parts suspect. European socialist views of the United States remained superficial, prejudiced, and polemical, and were often perversely ill-informed.

The fault cannot altogether be assigned to the Atlantic Ocean, for there was considerable movement across that barrier. Curiosity drove many European socialists over the ocean for visits to the New World. Wilhelm and Karl Liebknecht, Beatrice and Sidney Webb, H. M. Hyndman, Émile Vandervelde, Ramsay MacDonald, Keir Hardie, Edward and Eleanor Aveling, Carl Legien, Franz Mehring, H. G. Wells, Parvus, Trotsky, Max Beer, even Engels himself, made the journey at least once. From the slum tenements and Fifth Avenue mansions of New York City to the black mill towns of New England, from the bustling urban sprawl of Chicago and Detroit to the dilapidated mining camps of Colorado, they made their way across the continent speaking to labor rallies and gathering countless impressions to take back to Europe. Their gaze was not perfunctory. They chatted with miners, judges, and politicians, ate at elegant restaurants, rubbed shoulders with America's elite, and took in the tourist sights from Niagara Falls to Pike's Peak.

Traffic went in the other direction as well. Many American socialist leaders, F. A. Sorge, Hermann Schlüter, John Spargo, Victor Berger, and Morris Hillquit among them, were immigrants who traveled back to Europe to visit family and friends and to attend various conventions of the International. Native-born socialists like Gaylord Wilshire, whose name adorns one of America's most glamorous boulevards, and George Herron, who became one of America's many expatriates following the scandal of his unconventional marriage with the daughter of wealthy socialist benefactress Carrie Rand, also were familiar presences on the European scene. These men wrote articles frequently on American conditions for European socialist journals. F. A. Sorge, in fact, who had been Marx's most trusted confidant in the New World, was a contributing editor of *Die Neue Zeit* during the 1890's and wrote dozens of reports from the United States before his health failed at the turn of the century.

Nonetheless, distance did make a difference. European socialists made serious claims to internationalism, but they were like people everywhere in concentrating their attention hardest on what was closest to home. German socialists were not well informed about the situation in France. Why should their vision improve when they had to look all the way to America? Interest in the United States flared when there was some dramatic event to report. The Haymarket riot, the Pullman strike, the first socialist victories in Milwaukee, the 1912 trial of the McNamara brothers in Los Angeles, all drew enormous attention. In the interim periods, when these events failed to lead anywhere, interest flagged; and other situations, such as the plight of the Negro or the rise of the IWW, went largely unnoticed. Attention even among the most interested observers was sporadic.

None of the American socialist leaders proved able to capture the imagination of the rank and file in the International as had the elder Liebknecht, Bebel, Plekhanov, Jaurès, or Adler. The most charismatic among them, Eugene Debs, had more the qualities of a jovial hail-fellow-well-met, or an itinerant preacher who carried his booze next to his Bible, than a strong leader who could change the face of the world.

As has been indicated again and again, all socialist discussions of the United States became entangled in a web of party polemics. This immediately reduced the premium on objectivity and consistency. The range of questions asked about America by European socialists was decidedly limited. They read haphazardly, and what they read they used selectively. Bryce they knew, but not Tocqueville. Most were content to take information at second hand, and none of them made a critical use of evidence. They grabbed onto whatever fit. Kautsky employed census reports, and they all showed a fascination with figures. But the attitude which they brought to this material determined the conclusions, not the data itself.

A few, Wells certainly and also the elder Liebknecht, tried to see America as something other than statistical ammunition. However, most turned to America to draw a lesson or drive home a point. If they portrayed America as a promised land, it was usually not because they had any real desire to see American socialists triumph first, but because this expectation fitted easiest with their theoretical assumptions or else gave hope to a failing movement at home. America has often served as a wish-fulfilment device for Europeans disappointed in their own domestic schemes. Infrequently did European socialists look at the New World with a real anticipation of discovery. They had deduced the laws of society from studying Europe (or from reading Marx); and, when they watched capitalism at work in America, they were seeking confirmation of what they thought they already knew.

This kind of attitude stifled quests for the uniqueness of the American nation and people. European Marxists especially were always looking to American society as if it were on the verge of a great change—a change which would bring life there closer to the patterns prevailing in Europe. Any differences in the two societies they pronounced to be temporary. The America emerging from their portraits was an abstraction, the model of a society as it was to be after a few more years of capitalist development. Other European observers proved more acute and recognized that, whatever might be wrong with society in the New World, it was Europe which would become more like America, not vice versa.

Some Marxist criticism, it should be said, grew wiser after it grew mature enough to face squarely the collapse of the Second International, the totalitarian course of the Bolshevik revolution under Stalin, the unrevolutionary dimensions of the proletarian mind, and the absurdly delayed revolution in the advanced capitalist areas of the world. Once Marxists tired of treating American capitalism as a thing of fleeting duration, once they moved away from the economic determinism implied by Marxism, and endeavored to use class theory in a more dynamic way, they found in Marx's writings some bases for more sophisticated analysis.

In the period before World War I, however, Marxists looking at America wrote themselves into a deep intellectual hole, and none of them seemed to know how to get out. Their opinions in this earlier era are very easy to take apart, and it has not been the primary purpose of this essay to castigate Marxists for astonishing naïveté in order to indulge a fierce anti-Marxist bias. Neither was the study dictated by a sadistic refusal to let people's errors die with them nor an antiquarian belief that all utterances more than fifty years old have an intrinsic importance. If European socialists did not go very deep in their comments about America, if they often missed reality altogether, if they repeated certain pronouncements with deadening frequency over twenty years with scarcely a change in their punctuation, if they drew some of their most perceptive remarks directly from the pages of Bryce, these critiques remain extremely interesting documents for what they reveal about the authors. European observations about America have usually told us far more about the situation in Europe than about the situation in America. European socialists could not get away from the thought that in the New World they might be looking at their future, and, depending on what they saw and their particular stance along the socialist spectrum, the visions could delight or horrify them.

In tracing their preoccupation with the United States, it is possible to see at work many of the problems and conflicts which worried and divided European socialists in the era before 1917 when the brightest prospects for the cooperative commonwealth still seemed to lie somewhere west of Russia. One can also discern the genesis of many enigmas which were to persist even after socialism had evidently found a champion. Marxists, even today, have never forgiven America for its recalcitrance, but they have never either completely given up on it. Most contemporary Marxists, in contrast to what

Trotsky had written, would not welcome the establishment of socialism in America because a great nation had at last established its right to lead. They would hail it because a wealthy and arrogant nation had finally been humbled and made to behave like the rest of the world. Such uncharitable feelings have been the result of fifty years of impatient waiting.

CHAPTER 8

AMERICAN SOCIALISTS
The Long Wait for Dawn

CONSIDERING how meager have been the triumphs of organized socialism in the United States, the inordinate fear it has generated here is nearly inexplicable. Flamboyant defenders of the American Way have consistently behaved as if they shared with the now aging representatives of American communism an inability to dismiss Marx's gloomy forecast for their cherished capitalism as errant nonsense. If today discussion of the possibility of a classical Marxist revolution in America (Negro revolutionists are talking about something else altogether) is neither widespread nor fashionable, it is well to recall times when respectable American opinion gave serious attention to the possible triumph of socialism in the New World.

At no period was the possibility of a Marxist victory in the United States more extensively entertained among the American bourgeoisie (despite the hysterical days under Attorney General Palmer and under Senator McCarthy and the more logical era of the Great Depression) than in the first decade of the twentieth century—not surprisingly the same period European Marxists looked with their greatest hopes across the Atlantic. The American middle class during the Progressive Era had little direct acquaintance with the writings of Marx, but they had read or heard enough from European sources to understand something about the doctrine of class struggle. They knew that the growth of the American economy in the late nineteenth century marked their country as an object of special interest for Marxists, and they uneasily watched amid the labor violence which had been flaring sporadically since the mid-1870's the transformation of many cherished American values into excuses for crassness, greed, and callousness. Many reformers came to believe with the distinguished economist Richard Ely that without a systematic attack on the ills of society, violence in America would shortly make European class struggles look like recess time in a day nursery.[1] Even the Republican stalwart Marcus Alonzo Hanna dropped an admonishing hint to the smug guardians of bourgeois values. The fight of the future, said Hanna at a Lincoln's Day Banquet in 1901, would be between socialism and Republicanism unless business leaders accorded organized labor a genuine respect.[2]

The vote tallied by American socialists in the period between 1900 and 1912 was never very great. Membership in the Socialist party showed a heavy turnover and centers of socialist strength constantly shifted. A promising electoral machine put together by socialists in Massachusetts during the 1890's fell apart before the new century ever began. (The Massachusetts victories were products of the Socialist Labor party and the Social Democratic party. The more important Socialist party, which is the primary concern of this chapter, was not organized until 1901.) American statesmen nevertheless sprinkled their speeches with references to "the rising tide of socialism," and popular and scholarly magazines opened their pages to serious discussion of the steady growth of the political force led by Eugene Debs. In 1906 the respected *Yale Review* used a featured editorial to warn about the dangers of European ideologies. Sombart's expectations of a full-blown class struggle in the United States, it said, were quite conceivable without immediate and far-reaching reforms in the structure of capitalism.[3] The political economist Robert F. Hoxie concluded after a substantial analysis of the socialist vote in the fall elections of 1911, "We are at last face to face with a vigorous and effective Socialist movement—a movement which is nation-wide, which is laying the foundation for a permanent structure by building from the bottom of the political

---

[1] See Richard Ely, *Recent American Socialism* (Baltimore, 1885), and *Socialism: An Examination of Its Nature, Its Strength and Its Weakness, with Suggestions for Social Reform* (New York, 1894).
[2] Socialists usually quoted Hanna as if he regarded this dramatic rise of socialism as an absolute certainty. Actually, Hanna had little doubt that the spirit of cooperation in America would prevent European socialism from gaining a firm hold in the United States. Socialism posed a challenge to the established order, but it was one which could be met.
[3] "Socialism in the United States," XV (May 1906), 1–7.

system, which is recruiting its main strength in the important civic and industrial centers, and which is growing at a rapidly accelerating rate." [4] J. N. Larned capped this sort of speculation by flatly telling his readers in 1911 in a lead article of the influential *Atlantic Monthly* "to prepare for socialism." The movement was ready to break into "avalanches and floods." [5] The Socialist party in 1912, having elected over a thousand officials across the nation, including two congressmen and mayors in such diverse urban areas as Milwaukee, Berkeley, Butte, Flint, and Jackson, had gained a respectable third-party status. By assuming an increase in party growth in its second decade similar to that enjoyed in its first, sober imaginations forgot themselves and carved out a great future for American socialists.

If such speculation was possible in journals not habitually given to heralding the Marxist dialectic, it is easy to guess what beautiful dreams American socialists could construct from the same evidence. As long as their vote was rising, no one could really prove to members of the American Socialist party that the march to the cooperative commonwealth was not inexorable. They might not presently enjoy successes comparable to those of their counterparts in Europe, but the absolute certitude of eventually standing in the spotlight of world attention made up for present insignificance. This faith held together the American socialist movement for over a decade. It gave the party life and vibrancy. Its cocksureness easily meshed with other Americanisms—the Puritan mission to found a city on a hill, the millennial vision of the backwoods revivalists, the belief that nothing was impossible in this new land, the deep-seated commitment to change and progress—and sank the roots of the Marxist movement into native soil for the first time. When the underpinnings of the conviction were knocked out by the drastic interruption in the party's growth after 1912, something went out of the heart of American Marxism. There was never a true recovery.

American Marxists were more than ready to agree with their

---

[4] "The Socialist Party in the November Elections," *The Journal of Political Economy*, XX (March 1912), 213.
[5] "Prepare for Socialism," *Atlantic Monthly*, CVII (May 1911), 577–80. These cited articles are representative of a vast number of others which appeared in important American journals in the first decade and a half of the new century.

counterparts in Europe who regarded the United States as the likely site of the first socialist victory. What had seemed a possibility for many European Marxists in 1900 became a dead certainty for American comrades. The capitalist playground of the United States would shortly become a socialist paradise. Gaylord Wilshire as early as 1891 had said in answer to the nationalistic pride of his European comrades, "I, as an American Socialist, put forth my patriotic plea in favor of my own country's prospects of being the first to inaugurate the era of industrial emancipation." In his opinion four men, Gould, Astor, Vanderbilt, and Rockefeller, had virtual control over the country. Given this "concentration and crystallization of capital," the United States "should naturally and logically be the first to strike for economic freedom." [6]

Wilshire stands out as one of the oddest characters in a movement where eccentricity was entirely normal. It was not simply that he attended Harvard, that he put together a sizable fortune out of mining, banking, and real estate interests, or that he laid out and left his name on a famous Los Angeles boulevard. Other American socialists, including J. A. Wayland, J. G. Phelps Stokes, and William English Walling, managed to produce personal fortunes from the corrupt capitalist system.[7] But Wilshire, by any standards, stepped over the bounds of socialist propriety when he tried through the pages of his colorful magazine to interest dedicated party workers in schemes designed to bring fantastic returns on capital investment. His efforts to peddle stock in a worthless gold-mining venture at Bishop Creek, Colorado, were notorious in party circles. Wilshire

---

[6] Preface to the American edition of the *Fabian Essays,* xiii and xiv.

[7] The observant Mr. Dooley was led by the wealth of some American socialists to make the following comment: " 'Tis far diff'rent now. No cellars f'r th' Brotherhood iv Man, but Mrs. Vanderhankerbilk give a musical soree f'r th' ladies iv th' Female Billyonaires Arbeiter Verein at her iligant Fifth Avnoo mansion yisterdah afthernoon. Th' futmen were dhressed in th' costume iv th' Fr-rinch Rivolution, an' tea was served in imitation bombs. Th' meetin' was addhressed be th' well-known Socialist leader, J. Clarence Lumley, heir to th' Lumley millyons. This well-known prolytariat said he had become a Socialist through studyin' his father. He cud not believe that a system was right which allowed such a man to accumylate three hundherd millyon dollars. . . . Th' ladies prisint cud appreciate how foolish th' captains iv industhree are, because they were marrid to thim an' knew what they looked like in th' mornin'." Finley Peter Dunne, *Dissertations by Mr. Dooley* (New York, 1906), 266–67.

heard the criticism, but it did not alter his behavior. He continued to exploit the capitalist system and work for its downfall with equal enthusiasm. In his buoyancy, his garrulousness, and his frankness he was a genuine American booster. If socialism were the order of the day, then, by God, America would have it first! There were to be no compromises, only a summary dismissal of the former power structure and a direct inauguration of the workers' state. Boldness and ruthless dedication to necessary change constituted in Wilshire's mind the American Way.

Wilshire spoke from the left wing of the American socialist movement. Other Americans of the same revolutionary stance invariably shared his overcredulous belief in the ability of the United States to reach socialism before Europe. George Herron, a respected party intellectual who espoused an interesting muddle of Christian socialism and militant Marxism, told an applauding Socialist convention in 1904,

> I have no doubt, although this is not the place for prophecy, but what the great international or world catastrophe—if it is to be a catastrophe—of the capitalist system will be precipitated here in America. I have no doubt but what, in the spread of the commonwealth of labor around the world, that the sun of that Co-operative Commonwealth will rise here on the American continent, and in this republic.[8]

Two years previously, Ernest Untermann, one of the few American comrades who had taken the trouble to read the entirety of Marx's *Capital,* wrote that "all indications point to the probability that American Socialism will be the champion who will batter down the walls of capitalism." [9] In 1903 Mary Simonds Johnston listed the difficulties facing socialism in America, the unavailability of many socialist classics in English, the earlier tactical blunders of sectarian leaders like Daniel De Leon, and the still-large farming population in the United States. In her opinion, in spite of all these obstacles,

[8] *Proceedings: Socialist National Convention of 1904,* 219.
[9] "On the March," *International Socialist Review,* III (Aug. 1902), 119. Untermann is usually remembered for his fanatic defenses of white supremacy. Racism, as Untermann proves and contrary to what has sometimes been written, was not the exclusive property of the party's right wing.

the American socialist movement would likely outstrip the movement in Europe and would spread "with amazing rapidity" in the
next industrial crisis.[10] Julius Wayland's widely circulated newspaper *The Appeal to Reason* was ready on the basis of the 1904
election returns to pinpoint the probable date for a socialist victory
in 1908.[11]

Members of the party's right wing, though more prudent in their
estimates of when a total victory might be achieved and more concerned with short steps than vast leaps in the approach to the cooperative commonwealth, were just as ready during the course of
the party's first optimistic decade to bet on the ability of American
muscle and aggressiveness to crowd European socialists into the
back seat. The widely read Danish-American socialist Laurence
Gronlund, who died in 1901, just before the fortunes of American
socialism began to pick up, came to believe as early as Wilshire in
America's likely priority over Europe in launching socialism and
lost no time in announcing his discovery to European comrades.[12]
His first book, *The Co-operative Commonwealth,* owed a very
strong debt to Marx, but by the time he wrote *The New Economy*
in 1898 he had completely repudiated the idea of class struggle.
In his new non-Marxist frame of mind it was the very absence of
class feeling in the United States, along with economic self-sufficiency and political democracy, which made the country readier than
Europe to accept socialism. Here were the echoes of an old refrain
which Marxists had flatly refused to sing: America would succeed
where Europe failed because America was morally superior to
Europe. The social evils brought by the trusts would weigh on the
conscience of the American people and lead them quickly to remake
their society.[13]

[10] "The Rise of Socialism in America," *Wilshire's Magazine,* VII (Oct. 15,
1903), 595–603.
[11] "Shall We Have a Socialist Victory in 1908?" *Appeal to Reason,* Jan. 16,
1904, and the election editorial, Nov. 19, 1904. Wayland boasted that he kept
this most popular of all socialist newspapers, printed in the unlikely spot of
Girard, Kansas, free from the controversies which divided comrades in the
American Socialist party; but the language of the editorials and the willingness
of the editor to imagine victory at so proximate a date reflected a close affinity
with the party's left wing.
[12] See his letter to the *Revue socialiste,* XVI (Aug. 1892), 244–48.
[13] *The New Economy: A Peaceable Solution of the Social Problem* (Chicago,
1898), 52.

Morris Hillquit, the German-born Jewish lawyer who directed the socialist struggle in New York City, was also reflecting sentiment on the more conservative side of American socialism when he wrote Karl Kautsky in 1908, "In a very few years the world will be surprised at the advance of socialism in this country," and when he told Jean Longuet in a 1913 interview, "I firmly believe that the first and decisive blows directed at the capitalist society will come on our side of the Atlantic."[14] Even Victor Berger, the unquestioned leader of the Socialist party's right wing who put together in Milwaukee the party's only sustained alliance between socialism and labor, boasted to an English interviewer in 1911 that no country was so ripe for a transition to socialism as the United States. In Berger's analysis the economic interdependence of European countries forced them to wait upon one another. Germany had to put off socialism until France had gotten around to it, and neither could move successfully without recalcitrant England following along. By contrast, the United States was "the only country which can establish a Socialist commonwealth without regard to other countries." Given the corruption of its capitalist system and the extent of its capital concentration, America could not help but lead the way.[15]

Upton Sinclair, the well-known muckraker and novelist (some would also say crank), made perhaps the most giddy proclamation for the party (Sinclair could not properly be identified with any faction of the party—his mixture of right- and left-wing formulas was uniquely his own) when he foresaw in his 1907 work *The Industrial Republic* the socialist era in the United States beginning with the election of William Randolph Hearst on the Democratic ticket in 1912. After a total collapse of business as capitalists one after another threw in the towel, a socialist state could be fully achieved by 1913.[16] Sinclair had made clear in an earlier essay his belief that victory would come first in the United States and only then (in descending order of priority) in Australia, Germany,

[14] Letter from Hillquit to Kautsky, Nov. 17, 1908, Kautsky Archives, International Institute of Social History, Amsterdam; and "La Croissance du socialisme aux États-Unis," *L'Humanité*, Oct. 4, 1913.
[15] "Interview with Victor Berger," *The Labour Leader*, April 28, 1911.
[16] *The Industrial Republic: A Study of the America of Ten Years Hence* (New York, 1907), 201–14.

France, Japan, Spain, Russia, and England.[17] (The last, it might be noted, he listed as a backward nation.) Now he ventured to fix the date; and, in so doing, he claimed "to speak, not as a dreamer nor as a child, but as a scientist and a prophet."[18] Few members of the American Socialist party followed Sinclair's vision to the point of seeing Hearst as the champion of their cause. No ticket other than a socialist ticket, according to conventional party wisdom, could inaugurate a true victory for the workers. But Sinclair's book constituted a typical and vivid expression of an era when American socialists could afford brave dreams.

The hardy confidence revealed in these comments was to a large degree a reflection of the generally uncompromising and pugnacious nature of the American Socialist party from 1901 to 1912—especially at the national level. The American party had its right and left wings, but the radical leanings of both ends of the spectrum, when compared to their equivalents in Europe, were impressive. As Henry Pelling has pointed out, an Englishman like John Spargo, who belonged in his native country to Hyndman's revolutionary Social Democratic Federation, might find, upon removal to the American context, himself siding with "conservative opportunists" in party debates.[19] Unfortunately, some of the general histories of the American Socialist party which have traced the rightward drift in party policy between 1901 and 1912 have tended to obscure this fact. Ira Kipnis in his pioneer study was so eager to dispute the party's wisdom in refusing to embrace the Industrial Workers of the World and in recalling Wobblie leader William Haywood from the National Executive Committee in 1913 that he characterized the party in 1912 as a small bourgeois sect, just to the left of the Progressives, completely shorn of Marxism, militancy, or radicalism. Although he recognized some shortcomings in the attitudes of members of the left wing, Kipnis attributed the party's subsequent decline primarily to the left wing's loss of control over party policy.[20]

[17] *Our Bourgeois Literature: The Reason and the Remedy* (Chicago, 1904), 6–7.
[18] *The Industrial Republic,* xiv.
[19] "The Rise and Decline of Socialism in Milwaukee," *Bulletin of the International Institute of Social History,* X (1955), 91.
[20] *The American Socialist Movement, 1897–1912* (New York, 1952), *passim,* but see especially pages 425–29.

David Shannon's standard account of party history and especially James Weinstein's more recent description of the American socialist tradition from 1912 to 1925 have given us a much better understanding of the surprisingly intransigent posture of the party both before and after 1912.[21] There was an undeniable movement to more conservative policies which generally characterized all parties belonging to the Second International. Leaders like Victor Berger, who emphasized the need to "compromise" and take "one step, two steps or six steps at a time," and John Spargo, who denied that socialism was the inevitable result solely of the ongoing development of capitalism, gained increasing influence within the party.[22] Many of the victories the party won in the first twelve years of the century had no relation to theoretical socialism and resulted from the relatively tame Progressive impulse to throw the bums out of city hall. Walter Lippmann worked briefly for the socialist mayor of Schenectady, and found, to his dismay, that socialist water commissioners behaved like Republican water commissioners. Yet significantly the American party, almost alone among the parties of the Second International, remembered the solidarity pledges supposedly linking the proletariat in all countries and resisted the national patriotic appeals which drove the world into the first of the terrible large-scale wars of this century. The anti-war stand cost the American socialist cause dearly, both in terms of leadership and nativeborn adherents, but the party stood firm in its view of the war as the by-product of shameless capitalist crimes.

Most leaders of conservative factions in the American Socialist party (the rank and file was a different story) remained impervious to the homegrown non-Marxist theories of Edward Bellamy and Laurence Gronlund or even to those of Continental revisionists like Eduard Bernstein. One leader of the American right wing wrote that, while Bernstein's critique of Marx "stirred up a sensation in Europe" and won an instant following, Bernstein remained "almost unknown in American intellectual circles so that an English trans-

---

[21] Shannon, *The Socialist Party of America* (New York, 1955); Weinstein, *The Decline of Socialism in America, 1912–1925* (New York, 1967).
[22] See, for example, articles by Berger in the *Social Democratic Herald:* "Reform or Revolution Once More," Dec. 7, 1901; "No Impossibilism for Us," Aug. 11, 1906. Also an editorial by Spargo, *The Comrade,* II (Feb. 1903) 108.

lation appeared first in 1911." [23] Robert Hunter, who moved from a career as a muckraker alarmed about poverty in America's cities to join with conservative socialist leaders, learned about Bernstein's policies at first hand while touring Europe in 1907 and rejected them as dangerous. The German Social Democratic party, he concluded, would "be destroyed if revisionist tactics should prevail." [24] And Victor Berger, who was frequently called the American Bernstein because of his insistence on framing municipal programs with broad electoral appeal (hence, the epithet "sewer socialist"), remained, as he always claimed, much closer to Bebel and Kautsky than to any of the German revisionists. He did not accept Bernstein's corrections of Marxist beliefs in the increasing severity of economic crises within the capitalist system and the steadily widening gulf between social classes. Although many of Berger's policies smacked of "opportunism," he warned his fellow comrades in 1903 that "we should soon sink in the slough of political 'reform' and be devoured by the politicians if we followed Bernstein." [25] Berger's followers formed, as G. D. H. Cole has written, a right wing "of a peculiar kind" who "insisted that the bourgeois progressives must come to them and accept the Socialist label." [26] The class struggle never became passé for right-wing socialists in America; and, while they might not have been terribly sophisticated Marxists (how many of Marx's disciples were?) and did not always draw their revolutionary formulas from the economic theories of *Das Kapital*,

---

[23] I. M. Rubinow, "Marxens Prophezeiungen im Lichte der modernen Statistik," *Archiv für die Geschichte des Sozialismus und der Arbeiterbewegung,* VI (Leipzig, 1916), 131.

[24] "First Impressions of Socialism Abroad," *International Socialist Review,* VII (April 1907), 586.

[25] "The German Social Democratic Congress," *Social Democratic Herald,* Sept. 26, 1903. Kautsky backed up Berger's disclaimer of being the American Bernstein in "Die Civic Federation," *Die Neue Zeit,* Vol. XXVIII, Part I (1909–10), 133. Furthermore, Bernstein's correspondence at the International Institute of Social History in Amsterdam would indicate that the German revisionist leader had no significant contacts with American comrades.

[26] *The Second International,* Part II (London, 1956), p. 806. (This is Volume III of Cole's *A History of Socialist Thought.*) Cole went on to say that Berger and his followers were quite ready to accept the "revisionist" label; but even that, as has been noted, was not true. Also see the following Berger articles in the *Social Democratic Herald*: "After the Big Battle," April 16, 1904; and "Suggestions for the Coming National Convention," April 23, 1904.

their refusal to identify with many of the European revisionist tendencies has sometimes been too lightly dismissed as hypocrisy.

European Marxists were impressed and quickly conceded the radical cast of the American Socialist party. They observed with astonishment the wrangles of American socialists in their first few conventions over the wisdom of including immediate demands in their political platform. In Europe the issue had been decided long ago against the "impossibilists." The last important attempt in the German party to eliminate immediate demands from the party program passed with the defeat of the anti-parliamentary *Jungen* faction in the early 1890's. No one by 1900 regarded the Erfurt Program, which the Social Democrats had proudly adopted when the Anti-Socialist Laws were lifted, as any less Marxist because it was embellished with a long list of entreaties for reforms under capitalism. The Marxist party of Jules Guesde in neighboring France had included a *programme minimum* in its platform since the 1880's. The first had been drafted in the London study of the great patriarch himself.

American impossibilists also lost the main issue in the 1901 Unity Convention, but they remained a vocal element within the party. British socialists in the Labour party, who gave Bernstein lessons in moderation and kept Marxist heads shaking in dismay, felt a kinship with very few of the American socialist leaders. From their point of view, the insistence by the latter on strict socialist independence thwarted in advance the attempts to win over American labor.[27] Sometimes British socialists had a good word to say about Berger, for he now and then appeared receptive to the idea of an American labor party based on an English model. But they considered Hillquit, who sided with Berger on most issues, foolishly sectarian because of his equivocation on the labor-party question. By their lights they were right. To the French socialist Jean Longuet, the attitude of American comrades in 1906 indicated that the "modern socialism of Marx" had made itself more profoundly felt "in

[27] J. R. Clymes, "The Situation in America," *The Labour Leader*, Dec. 24, 1909; "The Socialist Vote in America," *The Labour Leader*, Jan. 8, 1909; "On the Watchtower," *The Labour Leader*, Nov. 1904; "Editorial," *Socialist Review*, II (Nov. 1908), 728.

the new and already vast American socialist movement" than in any other country, except Russia.[28]

Since Kipnis has used 1912 as a date to mark the capitulation of the American party to reformism, a word should be added about the events of that year. Significantly one prominent member of the left wing who was ever alert to the dangers of opportunism, Eugene Debs, interpreted the 1912 party convention quite differently than Kipnis. Debs wrote,

> The spirit of the convention was perfectly revolutionary. There was never any danger of getting off the main track or of following after any of the many gods of opportunism. A very great majority of the delegates were red-blooded, clear-eyed, straight-out and uncompromising. The last thing they thought of, if they thought of it at all, was trimming or trading, or setting traps to catch votes.[29]

The convention, as had all previous conventions, avoided hurling direct insults at the American Federation of Labor. It shied away from approval of the Industrial Workers of the World, which, though once lovingly welcomed by many American Marxists, had incurred disfavor by moving away from political action to preach the more nebulous doctrines of syndicalism and direct action. The convention went on record, however, in support of the principle of industrial unionism; and few delegates to the convention doubted the superiority of the organizational principles of the IWW to those of the AFL. If the delegates refused to sever all connections with the AFL, it was merely because American socialists still hoped to convert this important labor organization to their cause—a process which did not imply compromise.[30]

Even the recall of Haywood from the National Executive Committee in 1913 did not grow simply from a timid wish to appease bourgeois sensibilities (though undoubtedly that was part of the story). Since the days of the First International, Marxists had been sensitive to the common equation drawn between themselves and

[28] "Un grand roman socialiste: La *Jungle,*" *La Revue socialiste,* XLIV (Dec. 1906), 704–5.
[29] "This is Our Year," *International Socialist Review,* XIII (July 1912), 17.
[30] For more on this point and the continuing firm attitudes of many in the party, see Weinstein.

anarchists. The Second International expelled members who did not believe in political activity. Haywood's positions toward doctrines inextricably linked in the public mind to the anarchist movement, such as direct action and the rejection of political agitation, were confused and usually misreported. The evidence of his flirtation with them, however, was incontestable and strong enough to stir legitimate Marxist concern. Few Marxists in Europe rose to protest the American party's treatment of Haywood, and even the radical *Leipziger Volkszeitung* supported the American party in setting its face against syndicalism and sabotage.[31] If political expediency alone prompted the party in censuring Haywood, it was a stupid move because it cost the party both votes and members. Political expediency in this case, as in all cases, called for polite compromise. The Germans kept their party big enough to house people as far apart as Carl Legien and Eduard Bernstein at one extreme, and Rosa Luxemburg and Karl Liebknecht, at the other. American socialists, had they been less stubborn, might well have profited from the example.

Naturally enough the farther left one moved along the spectrum of the American Socialist party, the stronger was the assurance in the nearness of a conclusive socialist victory in the United States. This misplaced confidence was more than once interwoven with political ineptitude, as the career of Daniel De Leon ably illustrates. Absolutely convinced that socialism would triumph in the United States before any other nation, De Leon and his followers in the Socialist Labor party engaged in an almost perverse attempt to cut themselves off from the American electorate. Anyone who so much as breathed in his propaganda more than the revolutionary phrase "complete overthrow of the capitalist system" became suspect in their eyes as a bourgeois reformer. Some relaxation of socialist dogmas might be acceptable in countries where feudal conditions had not disappeared. Thus De Leon, with a great show of condescension and feigned magnanimity, excused aberrations in the actions of the German Social Democratic party: "The path of 'Reform' that

[31] Note there were really two issues here. A number of left-wing European Marxists approved of Americans' writing provisions in their constitution barring membership to those who objected to political action and preached sabotage, but objected to the use of these clauses against Haywood.

it treads is imperative. No fault may be found with it for having abandoned that of 'Revolution.' " (He, of course, did find fault in the obstinate refusal of German leaders to admit the passing of leadership within the International from Germany to the United States.) But tactics of compromise were totally unacceptable when the bourgeois revolution was complete and a country stood only a few years or even months away from the socialist revolution.[32]

Aided by such reasoning De Leon could turn his party's consistently dismal showing at the polls into a positive virtue. Lack of electoral success was proof that the party had guarded sufficient revolutionary militancy to lead the American proletariat on the day when it would suddenly become entranced with the image of socialism. On that day, conversions would be made wholesale, and the party would have more than the votes it needed to transform America. Besides (in a more cynical vein), if the tactics of De Leon won him few victories, the victories of his enemies (i.e. the leaders of the Socialist party) were rarely spectacular. Until he could fill his paper with information about his own party's successes, news about the setbacks of his rivals made gratifying reading. The outbreak of war in Europe and the failure of the International to do anything about it gave Arnold Petersen, the National Secretary of the SLP after De Leon's death, a chance to lecture comrades everywhere on their blindness to De Leon's wisdom. What happened in Europe in 1914 was the International's reward for dismissing the SLP in America as too doctrinaire.[33] There was something sadistic in the party's negativism. But the SLP still goes on as a fierce little sect, no longer with the same confidence in a swift victory, but with a firm faith in the errant ways of everyone outside the party.

Distinct echoes of the De Leonite mentality were present in the demands of the impossibilists who played so important a role at the founding convention of the Socialist party in 1901 and at its next convention in 1904. (This was true in spite of the fact that the Socialist party came into being largely as a reaction to De Leon's policies and personality.) The group, led by such significant figures

[32] "Here and There," *Weekly People,* Jan. 9, 1904.
[33] Letter from Arnold Petersen to Affiliated Parties of the International Socialist Bureau, Dec. 12, 1914, Robert Grimm Archives, International Institute of Social History, Amsterdam.

as A. M. Simons, George D. Herron, Ernest Untermann, and Gaylord Wilshire, urged the party to take as uncompromising a stand as possible on the revolutionary goals of socialism. The most extreme among them, agreeing with De Leon about the nearness of victory in America and the advanced state of American capitalism, could not see the necessity of any planks in the party platform other than the demand for pure and simple socialism. American socialists, they said, were called by destiny "to stand upon a platform more distinctly revolutionary than had ever been adopted by any previous socialist party." [34] George Herron summed up their expectations:

> There has never come to Socialism so plain an opportunity as that now offered by the American political situation. . . . A united and harmonious socialistic movement may now make clear to all the people the lines of conflict between capitalism and Socialism; between despotism and liberty. The lines of conflict may be made so definite that *NO Party of Compromise* or tinkering can enter the political field. Now is the time of Socialist salvation, if we are great enough to respond to the greatness of our opportunity.[35]

American socialists did write into the party program of 1901 and into all subsequent programs immediate demands calling for reforms of the capitalist system until the arrival of socialism, but members of the party left concurred in Ernest Untermann's opinion that these superfluous planks had "more educational value than political significance." Convinced of the capacity of American socialists to "shortly outdistance the proletarian movement of all other countries," they took pride in bragging about their party's willingness to take more radical positions than parties in Europe.[36] In 1901, so A. M. Simons said, there was "not a Socialist Party in Europe which stands upon anywhere near as 'narrow class-conscious and revolutionary' a position as does the new Socialist Party." [37]

[34] A. M. Simons, "A New Milestone for American Socialism," *International Socialist Review*, II (Sept 1901), 233.

[35] "The Curtain Is Rung Up," *The Challenge*, Feb. 6, 1901. (Original name of *Wilshire's Magazine*.)

[36] Ernest Untermann, "Socialism Abroad," *International Socialist Review*, II (Sept. 1901), 220.

[37] "The Socialist Movement in America," *The Social Democrat*, V (Dec. 15, 1901), 365.

None put more emphasis on the class struggle and less emphasis on the winning of palliative reforms. When a party referendum recalled Victor Berger from the National Executive Committee in 1905 for supporting a non-socialist candidate in a local election where socialists had no candidate of their own, an editorial in the *International Socialist Review* conceded, "There is probably no Socialist Party in Europe in which a man would be censured for doing what Comrade Berger has just done." [38] Strategy in European party circles was circumscribed by less advanced economic conditions and offered no guide for the United States. The domination of capitalism and the division of classes in Europe were not so pronounced as in the United States where the victory of socialism "in the near future seems as certain as fate." [39] These enthusiastic American socialists in the first few years of their party's existence accepted the European Marxist version of the American Promised Land completely; disappointment with actual party growth had not yet begun to prompt misgivings.

A strong streak of fatalism, in some cases interlaced with a trace of irresponsibility, went into the formation of left-wing attitudes. Gaylord Wilshire went along with the introduction of immediate demands in the party platform because "I feel that we are too far advanced economically for anyone of them to be put into effect without really starting the social revolution, and I think that having the demands in our platform attracts a good many half-baked people to us that we might as well have with us as not." [40] He contrasted this situation to circumstances in Europe where "all the demands that form a part of our program could be granted by any European government, and it would have little or no immediate economic or political effect toward bringing on a social revolution." [41] Wilshire cared very little about the impact of immediate demands on a particular election. Elections meant next to nothing to him, for in his opinion the crisis of capitalism would come long before American workers gained political power.[42] Socialism would triumph not

[38] "The Wisconsin Situation," VI (July 1905), 52.
[39] "The Socialist Party," *The Worker*, Oct. 27, 1906.
[40] "Economic Development and Socialist Tactics," *International Socialist Review*, III (July 1902), 32.
[41] *Ibid.*, 30.
[42] "Kautsky: Is He Sound?" *Wilshire's Magazine*, May 1903, 6–7. See also "Shaw's 'Super-Man,'" *Wilshire Editorials* (New York, 1906), 144.

when the proletariat won a national election, but simply when the capitalist system fell in exhaustion.

Charles Kerr, the publisher of the *International Socialist Review* who fired A. M. Simons as editor when Simons' revolutionary ardor cooled, was operating on the same intellectual wave length as Wilshire when he wrote in 1908, "Industry is rapidly evolving to the point where the final grapple between laborer and capitalist is near. We can do little to hasten or delay this; what we can do is to think, talk and write clearly, and organize the workers who know what they want into a machine for getting it." [43] So also was Robin Ernest Dunbar when he wrote in 1909, "Revolutions do not come through politics or politicians; they come through the operation of economic law to which politicians are the first to yield. . . . To think that by electing a Socialist President, we can hasten the dawn of the Co-operative Commonwealth is to imagine that we can veer the wind around by sheering the weather vane." [44]

The extreme left wing of the party, in expressing such sentiments, never abandoned a belief in the necessity of political agitation. The Socialist party, after all, was a political party. But the true purpose of agitation was education; and when it involved compromise, as most excursions into practical politics do, it became useless, and even dangerous, to the purposes of socialism. Not surprisingly, some of the most famous agitators for the socialist cause, men like Wilshire, Kerr, Wayland, and Jack London, took little interest in formal party work or the building of local political machines. They confined their activities to spreading the word and operated under the casual assumption that if workers were educated, the details of organization would take care of themselves.

In no person was this detachment from the give and take of daily political life more notoriously embodied than in the person of Eugene Debs. In every election between 1900 and 1912 he headed the party's national ticket. (In 1900 it was actually the Social Democratic ticket.) Aside from Jack London and Upton Sinclair, he was the only member of the party who was well-known nationally, and the only one who was nationally loved. No other man traveled more

[43] "What Shall Our Platform Be?" *International Socialist Review*, VIII (April 1908), 623.
[44] "A Conflict Among Leaders," *International Socialist Review*, X (Aug. 1909), 151.

miles or made more speeches in behalf of socialism nor remained more a stranger to party work. He stayed away from conventions and refused service on national committees. Temperamentally he was not suited for the infighting of party activity. Debs was an instinctive socialist, tutored but not begat by Marx, and the impassioned rhetoric of class struggle could not disguise what he owed to Christian expressions of universal benevolence (which is not to deny Debs' atheism). He spoke the words for which he will be best remembered when he was sentenced to prison in 1918 for violation of the Espionage Act: "While there is a lower class I am in it; while there is a criminal element, I am of it; while there is a soul in prison, I am not free." In the 1890's Debs helped to draw up plans for an extremely un-Marxist utopian community to be founded in the West. He wrote, "Give me 10,000 men, aye 10,000 in a western state with access to the sources of production, and we will change the economic conditions, and we will convince the people of that state, win their hearts and their intelligence."[45] Although soon convinced of the futility of utopian enterprises, Debs never ceased to believe that socialism would come, not by trying frantically to drive workers into a political party with the same techniques employed by capitalist politicians, but by holding up true socialist ideas and waiting for workers to gather around the banner. The wait would not be a long one. Socialism had long ago made the only important alliance—the alliance with the forces of evolution: "the votes will come rapidly enough from now on without seeking them."[46]

Indifference to building a political base of power for the Socialist party, so characteristic of the left wing of the party, drove the primary wedge between it and the party's right wing. Right-wing socialists, Berger among them, usually agreed on theoretical matters with the party left. As far as they were concerned, capitalism's advance in America made socialism inevitable. But, more suspicious

---

[45] From a speech at the convention of 1898 of the Social Democracy, quoted in Howard H. Quint, *The Forging of American Socialism: Origins of the Modern Movement* (Columbia, S. C., 1953), 313.
[46] Debs, "Danger Ahead," *International Socialist Review*, XI (Jan. 1911), 415. For further evidence of Debs' optimism, see "What this Election Means," *The Worker*, Nov. 20, 1904, and "The Issue," *Debs: His Life, Writings and Speeches* (Girard, Kansas, 1908), 488.

of fate than the party left, they vigorously combatted the tendency of this point of view to result in inattention to party work. Not being as sanguine about the nearness of socialist victory, they were far more concerned about holding together party loyalty during what might prove to be a fairly long period of capitalist decline. Berger's newspaper, *The Social Democratic Herald,* made a cautious prediction in 1901 (intended as a warning against overconfidence) that "within thirty years the people of the United States will have committed themselves definitely to industrial reorganization on the lines of Socialism." [47] This was a far cry from the pronouncement of a man like Wilshire who called himself in 1902 a "five year man, with the possibility of three." He said, "If I had to be in 'the hundred year, step at a time, take-what-you-can-get' class, you would find me automobiling my life away at Newport with Reggie Vanderbilt instead of editing this magazine." [48]

To more conservative members of the party, Wilshire could afford his attractive illusions because, when one was shattered, he always had the money to buy others. Factory workers were less lucky and did not have the pleasant alternative of hobnobbing with millionaire sportsmen if socialism failed of a quick victory. They needed tangible signs of progress if they were to be expected to continue to give their votes to the party. This was why the right wing considered elections so important. Elected officials and passage of party-backed ameliorative reforms were the only evidences of progress sufficient to hold workers' allegiance until complete socialist victory was possible. As seen from the right, "the Dream of Debs" would remain just a dream unless the party moved away from unrealistic expectations of an overnight victory and settled down to the business of gathering provisions for an extended siege.

These differences were real enough, but it is easy to emphasize the wedge between the right and the left wings of the party too strongly. The left wing, for all its insistence on the relative insignificance of elections, shared with the right wing jubilation over all victories won at the polls. Even when such victories rested a bit too obviously on non-socialist support, even if they counted little

[47] "What We Anticipate," Dec. 21, 1901. One can find similar warnings against expecting too quick a victory in many subsequent editorials.
[48] "A Psychological Problem," *Wilshire Editorials,* 232–33.

toward the victory yet to be won, the party left could not help but rejoice. The right wing, for all its prudence, had to concede something to the truth of H. L. Slobodin's opinion that "it would be folly verging on insanity to organize political parties and make an issue of an object to be achieved, say, five hundred years from now." [49] The right wing's successes at the polls (and nearly all socialist successes at the polls were engineered by the party's right) were never so great as to alone keep the enthusiasm of the workers at a high pitch. The election of a socialist congressman or mayor or water commissioner might be portrayed as a big event in the capitalist wasteland of America, but it was not going to make much difference in the economic situation of the worker. Right-wing socialists, to keep alive their own dedication, had to share something of the faith expressed in *The Appeal to Reason* in 1902: "Socialism is coming. It's coming like a prairie fire and nothing can stop it . . . you can feel it in the air. You can see it in the papers. You can taste it in the price of beef . . . the next few years will give this nation to the Socialist Party." [50] All factions of the party, whatever the differences in their timetable, believed in America's coming day as the promised land of socialism.

In sad truth all American socialists in the period between 1900 and 1912 allowed their thoughts to drift into the realm of fantasy. An editorial in *The Worker* in 1902 said, "The Socialist is never discouraged nor weak-hearted in times of trouble and of slow progress such as we have often had in the past; nor is he carried off his feet with enthusiasm in the time of greatest success." [51] It is difficult to conceive of a more dishonest assessment. Nothing was more unwelcome to American socialists swirling in their initial intoxicated expectations than realistic appraisals of their situation. They concealed disappointment at every setback and did their best to turn every seeming defeat into a victory. When the vote in the national election of 1908 failed to show a very large increase over 1904, they agonized and rationalized and finally decided that many of the votes cast for them in 1904 had not been true socialist votes while

[49] "What Is the Issue?" *The Comrade*, III (Nov. 1903), 26.
[50] "Attention Battalion," *Appeal to Reason*, May 3, 1902. See Berger's article "The 'New' State Issue," *Social Democratic Herald*, May 16, 1903.
[51] "Election Hopes and Fears," Nov. 2, 1902.

all those of 1908 represented the voice of dedicated party members.[52] Therefore they celebrated in 1908 just as they had in 1904 when no meddler had been around to tell them about their large gains resting on the fleeting support of disgruntled Democrats and Republicans. If they had a legitimate cause for optimism, socialist excitement spilled over into six-inch headlines in the socialist press. The casting of nearly a million votes for Debs in 1912 signified to many the party's arrival as a truly significant political force. The *National Rip-Saw* wrote, "It takes no prophet to forsee [sic] that the election of 1916 will be the last possible time that any of the capitalist parties can hope for success, and it will not by any means be wonderful if the Socialists capture the country four years from now."[53] Kate Richards O'Hare, the remarkably strong-tempered product of poverty in Kansas, settled down in her armchair to recall how a million votes once seemed the rosiest of dreams: "It was the far-off goal towards which we ever turned our eyes—a goal that sometimes seemed to be but a will-o-the-wisp [sic], ever fading, yet ever luring us on over the rough and rock strewn path of Socialist agitation." Now that dream had been realized; and it was "good to be alive, better to be a Socialist, and to feel yourself a part of the great, resistless movement that slowly but surely opens the eyes of the economically blind, and quickens the ears of the politically deaf."[54]

The members of the left wing of the American Socialist party were always on the lookout for some dramatic confirmation of their belief that American capitalism stood weak-kneed at the steps of the gallows. Debs' race in 1912 furnished their evidence. Those on the right wanted with equal longing a sign that the party had at last become a stable political force and would go on electing officials until the day when the "International" sounded at the inaugural ball of an American president. Debs' vote also provided their sign.

After raising American socialists up so high, history quickly cast them down again. By the time the votes for the Socialist party in

[52] As Kipnis pointed out (see 213), socialists of both right and left wings expected the vote in 1908 to rise to a figure somewhere between one and a half and two million. The actual vote was only 421,000, an increase of 13,000 over the 1904 vote.
[53] "A Million Socialist Votes Means that Capitalism Is Doomed in America," Dec. 1912.
[54] "Coming Out of the Night," *National Rip-Saw*, Dec. 1912.

1912 were tabulated, the fortunes of the party were already on the decline. There is perhaps too strong a tendency among historians to seize on symbolic events, but the death of Julius A. Wayland is a tempting one. Wayland had for years been involved in the socialist movement. Attracted to it after making a considerable sum of money in real estate and business, he settled in Girard, Kansas, to edit the colorful *Appeal to Reason*, the only socialist paper in America ever to achieve mass circulation. The paper consistently reflected the intense optimism which all socialists felt in those first years of the new century. As Wayland saw things, the speed with which Americans had carved an industrial civilization in the wilderness would enable the establishment of the cooperative commonwealth within the first decade of the new century. On Sunday, November 10, 1912, not one week after the triumphant election of 1912, Wayland was found dead at his home. He had aimed an automatic revolver into his mouth and shot himself. Depression over the death of a beloved wife and an upcoming trial on federal charges were perhaps sufficient reasons for the suicide. But he expressed another in the note he left behind: "The struggle under the competitive system is not worth the effort; let it pass." [55]

The heart which went out of Wayland's fight to overthrow the capitalist system drained in fairly rapid order from the movement as a whole. To Wayland the large vote cast for Debs was good, but it was not good enough. In 1901, when American socialists launched their new party, even the more cautious among them expected to replace the Democrats as the second major political force in the country by 1912. Now 1912 had come and gone. The Democrats had just elected a President; and their own party, while growing, was still no better than a minor third party.

James Weinstein has argued in several articles and an important book that, contrary to the findings of Shannon, Kipnis, and Daniel Bell, the Socialist party of America did not undergo a serious decline after 1912 and remained a strong force through World War I.[56] Membership in the party fell off precipitously after 1912. The national vote for the party was lowered in 1916 by over 300,000 from

[55] "Story of the Tragedy," *Appeal to Reason,* Nov. 23, 1912.
[56] "The Socialist Party: Its Roots and Strength, 1912–1919," *Studies on the Left,* I (Winter 1960), 5–27; *The Decline of Socialism in America, 1912–1925.*

the previous national election, and its percentage of the tally was cut in half. Cognizant of these facts and more, Weinstein still refused to regard 1912 as a watershed date in American socialist history and reacted especially vigorously to Daniel Bell's characterization of everything following the apogee of Debs' popularity as a "trailing penumbra."

The Socialist party did not collapse after 1912, and Weinstein performed a valuable service in showing how in many areas (though not in all), despite an undistinguished standard bearer in 1916, the party organization from 1913 to 1918 remained as viable as in any peak year. Socialists were not for the most part maladjusted Progressives of middle-class origin who took Woodrow Wilson for their Savior. But in his efforts to revive a native socialist tradition which he feels has been denied the youth of America by both liberal historians and latter-day Marxists, Weinstein covered over a point which escaped no contemporary observer, whether inside or outside of the party. The inability of the party to continue growing, its fatal impotence in consolidating gains anywhere, and the calamitous declension on the most perceptible levels of observation struck party leaders hard and left a very broad intellectual watershed. What had been disappointed were expectations, and expectations could only have been replaced by dramatic achievements which were not forthcoming. The party made some spectacular and brief gains in Oklahoma, but few at this late date were satisfied with gains in Oklahoma, even if they had stuck. The press remained numerically healthy. Debs managed to breathe some life into the monthly *National Rip-Saw*. Berger founded an important daily in Milwaukee, and a group of intellectuals newly attracted to the party launched *The Masses*. The latter was a lively and justly famous journal, but its appeal was largely lost on the working class. Old standbys like *The International Socialist Review* and *The Appeal to Reason* more accurately reflected what was happening. Neither was more than a shadow of its former self. The vote of 1916, seen from almost any perspective, was a sharp blow. Members of the party found it difficult any longer to imagine an invincible movement toward their goal. And as that myth faded, the old optimism which cheered the party through its first years vanished forever.

In two years, 1917 and 1918, socialist opposition to our entry into

World War I sent sparks flying again. Support for the party's anti-conscription campaign raised hopes of recouping losses of the past five years. The party won electoral victories in a number of areas and gained sympathetic admiration for the courage of the many partisans who were jailed and beaten for their views. But for several reasons these successes did not indicate in any way a revival which could be meaningful for the future of American socialism. Everywhere the Great War severed the continuity of national socialist traditions. Former cleavages dividing right and left in the Second International meant next to nothing when it became a question of rallying behind the nation. In Europe, Ramsay MacDonald and Eduard Bernstein made serious and protracted criticisms of their countries' policies, while Jules Guesde and H. M. Hyndman outdid each other in jingoistic hyperbole. In America socialist opinion was similarly confused. Hillquit and Berger united with Debs in unyielding opposition to the war, while Ernest Untermann, Jack London, Frank Bohn, William English Walling, Henry Slobodin, and George Herron (all left wingers) leagued with John Spargo, A. M. Simons, Robert Hunter, Allen Benson, and Charles Edward Russell and submitted, along with widely publicized denunciations of American socialist leadership, their resignations to the party.

Because of its anti-war (many said Pro-German) stand, the party was bereft of most of its intellectuals. It also lost most of the native-born rank and file. When the war was over, foreigners again dominated the American socialist movement just as they had twenty years before. The gains which the party did make during 1917 and 1918 often had little to do with the economic issue of socialism. Men might vote for the party because they opposed the war or because they were Anglophobes, and not because they cared much about the cooperative commonwealth. Some like John Reed (who did care about the cooperative commonwealth) had endorsed Woodrow Wilson in 1916 for his stand on peace, and many, had Bryan continued to oppose Wilson's policies, would have given the old Populist their support when America declared war. For about the only time in their history American socialists could champion more than a single great cause, and they made the most of it. To speak under these conditions, however, of a revival in socialist feeling or a continuous socialist tradition is misleading. Many men took a brave stand over the war issue. But they were not the same men who had filled party ranks in 1912; it was not the old stand; and it left the party, once the war was over, with nothing to build on.

The United States government for all practical purposes outlawed the Socialist party during the war. Only where Bismarck had failed, Wilson was more successful. The iron master of Germany had found a great mass of bedrock support for the Social Democrats which he could not crush. Nothing like that existed in America. Weinstein has accused liberal historians of trying to cover up a lively American socialist tradition. This is not true. They have simply not tried to stretch it much beyond 1912. If one does not confuse pacifism or radicalism with socialism and if one excepts the refreshing amalgam of intellectuals and proletarians who frequented the Mabel Dodge salon, it is hard to see how they are wrong.

Not all socialists responded to the failure to win the cooperative commonwealth in 1912 as did Wayland. But they all reacted, some even sooner. The successes of the party had never been great enough to support the enthusiasm which had gone into its founding. If they had been, losses in any particular year would not have been so serious and the party might have weathered ebbs and flows in its strength. As it was, disenchantment was evident in several important figures even before the post-1912 decline.

Jack London's interest in socialism has always posed a problem. He expressed an uncompromising antagonism toward the capitalist system, but no man's character was ever more corrupted by it. From the time he became a socialist until his resignation from the party in 1916, he identified with a militant left-wing revolutionary position which was determined to bring the old order down at whatever costs. Yet Austin Lewis, a former mentor of his in socialist doctrine, remarked that London always "stood with one foot in social democracy and the other in the philosophical teachings from which have sprung Fascism." [57] In his almost psychotic attachment to physical toughness, his unrestrainable craving for the marks of bourgeois success, and his undisguised contempt for the spineless masses, parts of London's personality were profoundly at odds with the strong

[57] Quoted in Richard O'Connor, *Jack London: A Biography* (Boston, 1964), 384.

humanitarian bias in both European and American socialism. He may have intended *Martin Eden* as an indictment of individualism, as he so stoutly maintained; but the failure of his message to get through clearly even to his most careful readers indicated London's inability to subdue an ambiguity in his feelings toward the ideal of communal living. London was a revolutionary because he was obsessed with the image of the strong man who would master his environment (violently if necessary) and create some form out of the brutal chaos which made up the world. Small wonder that Lenin read Jack London on his deathbed.

London gave American socialists a terrifying vision of their future with the publication of *The Iron Heel* in 1907. The quick victory they expected in the United States was, according to this surprising account, to be drowned for the immediate future in a sea of blood. The American capitalists, alerted to the impending challenge of socialism, would meet proletarian force with overwhelming power. They would buy off large sections of the labor force with direct bribes, muzzle the press and other channels of free thought, ruin those within their own class sympathetic to labor, and drive socialist leaders into underground hiding. Between 1912 and 1932 there would be several abortive uprisings among the masses, but they would be ruthlessly crushed by the proto-Fascist regime of the Iron Heel. In 1902 London had predicted that America would be the first country to establish socialism.[58] By the time he wrote his tale of Ernest Everhard five years later, he had put off the triumph of the cooperative commonwealth by several hundred years.[59] America might still be the first to achieve socialism, but the victory was well beyond the caring of the present generation of American socialists. Their struggles were to usher in a period of reaction and subjugation such as the world had never before known.

London took his theme from W. J. Ghent's *Our Benevolent Feudalism* (published in 1902), a book which foresaw capitalists responding to proletarian challenges by the establishment of an iron-fisted dictatorship. In this version of the future, Marx was shown to have been correct in describing the corruption of the capitalist

[58] "Wanted: A New Law of Development," *International Socialist Review*, III (Aug. 1902), 74.
[59] *The Iron Heel* (New York, 1907).

system and the rise of a strong proletarian mass bent on the destruction of capitalism, but he had seriously underestimated the power and effectiveness of the capitalist response. In a vast land like the United States, where profits were enormous, capitalists found it easy to keep workers in line with meaningless social reforms. A few yearly legislative sops effectively took the eyes of the proletariat off the behind-the-scenes machinations through which the capitalists tightened their stranglehold on the nation. Such palliative measures cost the capitalists little, but cost the proletariat its soul. It was a good bargain; and in the few cases where benevolence failed to keep the worker content with his place under industrial feudalism, naked force would end any protest.

George Herron, who in 1901 had located the rapidly dawning sun of world socialism in the United States, also caught some of Ghent's grim vision. In an interview with a French socialist newspaper in 1910 he summed up his fears for the United States with an attack upon Theodore Roosevelt, whom he called "the single most deadly and menacing force on the contemporary political scene." [60] In contrast to his earlier cheerful predictions, Herron now regarded America as absolutely the last country where socialism had a chance. Callous individualism, moral and intellectual servitude, and shameful hypocrisy had sunk their roots too deeply. He wrote, "All the nations are approaching a similar crisis. We are approaching one of those epochs where the world returns to the principle of brutal force, where civilization decomposes into its primitive elements, where the tyrant appears as the unique Savior. Mr. Roosevelt is the man of this epoch." Roosevelt would return to America and be reelected President. War with Japan would follow for the possession of China's markets. Glutted markets, crises, universal strikes, the paralysis of industry would come next. Then America would turn, not, as Marxists thought, to socialism, but to the proclamation of Roosevelt's dictatorship. Herron's vision was gloomier than London's, for he could not point with any confidence to a better time beyond the next dismal historical era. It lacked even the quality of heroic revolt put down. America had failed to meet the expectations of Herron's Christian soul, and in the best revivalistic tradition he

[60] "Théodore Roosevelt jugé par un Américain," *La Petite République,* May 6, 1910.

called down God's wrath upon his nation, leaving the finality of the judgment an inscrutable question.

The effects of disillusionment did not have to take such an extreme form to be noticeable. Especially after 1912 they manifested themselves in more subtle fashions. Several former prominent members of the party's left wing reacted to their loss of confidence by moving right. A. M. Simons, who had begun his career in the party as an enthusiastic impossibilist, confessed in a letter to Karl Kautsky only a year after the 1912 election that "the movement here is in a somewhat discouraging condition." [61] In the same year he planted himself firmly in the camp of Victor Berger by enlisting on the staff of the *Milwaukee Leader*. Several more years of frustration with the party's futile efforts to win over the American people swept him out of the movement altogether. The letdown for a man who had begun with high expectations was especially hard.

The Appeal to Reason took a shamelessly conservative swing. A new editor reacted to the election of 1916 with the admission that socialist propaganda and tactics had been wrong for the last twenty years. American socialists had borrowed from Europe too many stock revolutionary phrases unsuitable for the American temperament. He urged the party to play down its portrayal of the end of the capitalist system and to concentrate its power in pushing for one legislative enactment at a time. The initial campaign, he thought, should be for nationalization of the railroads.[62] Such a demand, to the original editor of *The Appeal,* would have represented the most boring kind of bourgeois reform. Frank Bohn, at one time semi-syndicalist in his attitudes, also responded to the calamity of 1916 with an appeal to retreat from former heroic positions. Overnight his ideal became the British Labour party, and he started telling his fellow comrades what British socialists had been saying to them for years: "The socialist party, as a small religious sect, will always fail." [63]

While members of the left wing did not usually beat such a hasty

[61] Letter from Simons to Kautsky, Sept. 1, 1913, Kautsky Archives, International Institute of Social History, Amsterdam.
[62] "A Criticism and a Confession," Feb. 3, 1917, and "Socialize Now: Railroads First," Feb. 10, 1917.
[63] "The Future of Socialism in America," *International Socialist Review*, XVII (Feb. 1917), 482.

retreat from their former intransigence as a result of the party's dimming electoral fortunes, they could not hold their former enthusiasm intact. In 1914 Ernest Untermann moved up by fifty years his estimate of the date when socialist voters would gain a majority in the United States.[64] Debs surveyed the losses of the party in 1916 and called on its members to sit down and assess its weaknesses realistically. Blaming the drift toward opportunism for the party's recent failures, he demanded a renewal of an uncompromisingly independent spirit. One great difference separated this appeal from the former pronouncements made by members of the left wing. Gone was the hope of quick victory which had earlier supported their argument. Gone was the belief that any sacrifice of militant ideals was wrong because capitalism was living on borrowed time, eking out an unglamorous existence for a last few hysterical days. According to Debs' analysis in 1916, the very fault with what he labeled right-wing tactics was their efforts to move things along too swiftly. Impressed by party electoral gains and eager for a decisive victory, right-wing leaders had hurriedly thrown up political organizations on totally inadequate foundations. The party's showing in 1916 was the result of this haste. Debs wrote of the left wing: "We may build more slowly and we may not catch so many votes by building on a secure foundation, but *in the long run,* we shall save time and money and bitter disappointment by building up a working-class party on a working-class foundation." [65] John Macy, who also blasted Hillquit and Berger for their tactics of moderation, reflected sadly, "The worker has a long road of endurance still to travel before he is ripe for revolution." [66]

The time for sober reflection and the setting aside of boyish enthusiasm was no doubt long overdue; but unfortunately for the party a little sober reflection led many socialists to conclude, as it had Wayland, that the game was not worth the candle. One longtime militant, Henry Slobodin, managed to hang on to his optimism and assert that socialism was coming very soon: "Without that convic-

---

[64] For Untermann's revised timetable, see F. W. Van Valkenburgh, "Our Onward March," *The New York Evening Call,* Nov. 9, 1914.
[65] "The Socialist Party and Its Future," *National Rip-Saw,* Sept. 1916. (Italics added.) See also "The Decline of the Socialist Vote," *National Rip-Saw,* Jan. 1917.
[66] John Macy, *Socialism in America* (New York, 1916), 106.

tion I see no sense in being a Socialist. If Socialism is to come a thousand years from now, how do we know that it will come at all? At any rate, why bother?" [67] Unknowingly, Slobodin had hit exactly upon the cause of the declining fortunes of the American party. Members found belief in a swift victory in America untenable and ceased to care.

Some of the optimism of the party flared again in 1917 and 1918 during the high point of the party's anti-war campaign. Frank Eastwood was led to announce in the *National Rip-Saw* that finally "the harvest is at hand." Those who had waited so long and so patiently for results would not have to wait much longer: "The splendid courage, which has survived every seeming set-back, is about to reap a reward unmistakable in character and magnitude. A thousand signs and symptoms are now reinforced with records of positive gain." [68] Debs recovered his former exuberance when he declared that "the predictions made by Socialists twenty years ago in regard to the collapse of capitalism are being fulfilled. . . . Beyond the war the gates of opportunity open wide for The International Socialist movement, whose historic mission it is to proclaim peace and good will among men and to lead the nations of the earth into the new and entrancing Republic of the World." [69] This hope came to nothing. The party at the end of the war was back where it had started from at the turn of the century, but this time its prospects were much less favorable. The ground was prepared for a new and permanent split in the ranks of American Marxists. American Communists in the 1920's and 30's liked to talk about the nearness of the revolution in the United States, but their mood was not the inheritance of the native tradition which prevailed from 1900 to 1912. Their attention was on the Soviet Union, and when they spoke of the rapidly approaching revolution they were gabbling in a foreign tongue.

Even before the soldiers came home from the battlefields of World War I and before the Bolsheviks began their harrowing experiment in Russia, Marxists both in Europe and America discovered their

---

[67] "The State of the Socialist Party," *International Socialist Review*, XVII (March 1917), 541.
[68] The Harvest Is at Hand," Nov. 1917.
[69] "We Must Not Waver," *National Rip-Saw*, April 1918.

version of the American Promised Land to be as mythical as any which had preceded it. Many non-socialist observers had long been entranced by the lovely face of a new American continent; it had suggested to them a promise beyond all previous dreams. Although, according to Marxists in the late nineteenth century, American capitalism had completely disfigured the lovely face of the continent, in their own odd way they had continued to see concealed in the new hideous visage some hint of paradise. American and European socialists had gone about portraying its abominable features with scarcely concealed joy, for somewhere underneath, they had been sure, still lay a beautiful countenance.

Times changed. As the outlines of the face remained hard and cold, Marxists grew less certain about its coming transfiguration. When the pockmarks only became deeper and more horrid, the dreams of socialists crumbled and their enthusiasm waned. The idea of a special American promise or a special American destiny proved an empty illusion. Paradise was no nearer in the New World than anywhere else. America returned to the role it had played for Marx and Engels in the days before the Civil War, a spoiler of socialist revolutions, suggesting after 1917 only a longer and more tortured sojourn for the world in a bourgeois hell.

SOURCES CONSULTED

The greatest frustration involved in a study of this type results from the lack of guidelines to direct or limit the research. One must look everywhere, for illuminating remarks about the United States can appear anywhere and in any kind of European socialist literature. Unfortunately, the titles of books and articles are not always very helpful. After spending long, barren days of research tracking down promising references which lead nowhere, one can happen upon dozens of useful citations in works which on their face would seemingly have yielded nothing. To aid the reader in evaluating the use of sources, I have broken down material into categories and have made brief comments about the general value of each grouping in filling in the outlines of the study.

MANUSCRIPTS AND ARCHIVAL MATERIAL

Unpublished material provided a relatively unimportant source of information. Except for the discovery of correspondence between American and European socialists, the time consumed in searching letters for scattered references to the United States did not produce results commensurate with the efforts. Only infrequently did unpublished material furnish insights which pushed research off in a new direction. Enough of the private papers and correspondence of major socialist leaders has now been published so that on the subject of the United States archival research produced few surprises.

However, working a full year as a Fulbright student at the International Institute of Social History in Amsterdam (International Instituut Voor Sociale Geschiedenis) did give me ample opportunity to use its rich archives. Indexes to the major manuscript collections made it easy to locate correspondence between American and European socialist leaders. The German immigrants F. A. Sorge and Hermann Schlüter carried on an extensive correspondence with many German socialists, including Marx, Engels, Bebel, Wilhelm Liebknecht, and Kautsky. The Institute has plans in conjunction with the New York Public Library to publish correspondence both to and from Sorge. (Of course, not all of the letters refer to the situation in the United States.) The publication will be a great aid to scholarship as Sorge's hand is well-nigh unreadable. There were also at the Institute in Amsterdam scattered letters between German socialist leaders and prominent American socialists like Eugene Debs, Victor Berger, Morris Hillquit, Louis Boudin, Daniel De Leon, Henry Demarest Lloyd, Upton Sinclair, and A. M. Simons. Most of it proved unimportant for the purposes of this study, either dealing with the situation in Europe, bargaining about details of publication, or sending congratulations for one achievement or another.

The correspondence of the German socialists did point up their strong and genuine interest in the United States. Articles and statistics about America often accompanied the letters sent from the American side. Interestingly, neither Eduard Bernstein nor Jules Guesde, whose papers are at the Institute, had any significant correspondence with Americans. The absence in the case of Bernstein might be explained by the general lack of interest in German revisionism among American socialist leaders; but the failure of links to develop between American socialists and Guesde, who exhibited on occasion a keen interest in the United States, is strange. The fact that Guesde evidently neither had nor sought first-hand sources of information perhaps indicates again the general casualness shown by European socialists in getting at the truth about the American situation (a tendency present among all European observers of America). Marxists and non-Marxists nourished myths for their own particular purposes.

PUBLISHED PAPERS AND CORRESPONDENCE

Several of the volumes of published correspondence of Marx and

Engels were of central importance in writing Chapter 1. The other volumes listed below were less crucial, but provided valuable background information and cleared up a number of points of detail.

August Bebel: Briefwechsel mit Friedrich Engels. Edited by Werner Blumenberg. The Hague, 1965.
Briefe und Auszüge aus Briefen von Joh. Phil. Becker, Jos. Dietzgen, Friedrich Engels, Karl Marx u. A. an F. A. Sorge und Andere. Stuttgart, 1906.
Karl Marx and Friedrich Engels: Correspondence, 1846-1895. A Selection with Commentary and Notes. New York, 1934.
Karl Marx and Frederick Engels: Letters to Americans, 1848-1895. A Selection. Edited by Alexander Trachtenberg. New York, 1953.
Wilhelm Liebknecht: Briefwechsel mit Karl Marx und Friedrich Engels. Edited by Georg Eckert. The Hague, 1963.

NEWSPAPERS AND JOURNALS

The various periodicals of the socialist parties of Europe furnished the single most important storehouse of information. In them, all the key figures of European socialism at one time or another directed their attention to the United States. In them also appeared numerous articles by American socialists about conditions in their country. The International Institute of Social History in Amsterdam has preserved files of many important journals and newspapers representing all shades of European socialist opinion. Many American socialist periodicals were available to me at the Yale University Library, the New York Public Library, the Tamiment Institute of New York University, and the Harvard University Library. Below I have listed the periodicals I examined, pointed out briefly their nature and point of view, and indicated the dates of the issues consulted. If the file was not reasonably complete, the dates are enclosed in parentheses. I have not attempted to make a separate listing of articles about the United States found in these sources.

Appeal to Reason. 1895-1917. The most popular American socialist newspaper. Edited at first by J. A. Wayland and Fred Warren, this weekly proclaimed neutrality in party struggles, but tended toward the left wing. Later under the editorship of E. Haldeman-Julius it took a sharp swing to the right.

Archiv für Sozialwissenschaft und Sozialpolitik. 1904–1920. Edited by Werner Sombart, Max Weber, and Edgar Jaffé, this was a scholarly journal independent of any particular social philosophy. Articles by European socialists did appear in it, and references to the United States were useful.

L'Avenir social. 1896–1906. The monthly journal of the *Parti ouvrier belge.* Published in Brussels.

Chicago Daily Socialist. 1906–1912. A. M. Simons became the editor of this moderate-to-conservative American socialist newspaper.

The Comrade. 1901–1905. Edited by John Spargo, the English immigrant who allied with right-wing forces in the American Socialist party.

Fabian News (1890's). A publication of the Fabian party in England, this journal often printed reports on discussions about the United States.

L'Homme libre. June–August 1888. Organ of the Blanquist socialist forces in France.

L'Humanité. 1904–1914. Founded by Jean Jaurès, this was the newspaper of moderate socialists in France. Many articles about the United States by Jean Longuet appeared in the issues.

International Socialist Review. 1900–1917. The most theoretical of the American socialist journals. The monthly, originally edited by A. M. Simons, accepted articles from all segments of the party until 1909 when its editorial policy took a sharp swing left.

Justice. 1884–1890, (1891–1903), 1904–1917. The weekly organ of H. M. Hyndman's Social Democratic Federation. Always critical of the Fabians, the Independent Labour party, and the English Labour party.

The Labour Leader. 1891–1914. Founded by Scottish labor leader Keir Hardie, this weekly newspaper became the official organ of the English ILP in 1904. Many contributions in the early years were Marxist in orientation, but it generally conformed to the predominantly revisionist tone of English socialism.

Leipziger Volkszeitung. (1894–1905), 1905–1917. The most radical of the dailies of the German Social Democratic Party. For a time the favorite outlet for Rosa Luxemburg.

The National Rip-Saw. 1912–1918. (Changed name to *Social Revolution* in March 1917, and to *The Social Builder* in May 1918.) This radical American socialist newspaper, appearing monthly, tried to breathe life into a dying movement. From 1914, edited by Eugene Debs.

Neue Rheinische Zeitung. June 1, 1848–May 19, 1849. Famous short-lived newspaper edited by Karl Marx.

Die Neue Welt. 1876–1887. A popular, illustrated German socialist journal edited by Wilhelm Liebknecht. As one would expect in a journal edited by Liebknecht, criticism of the United States was muted.

Die Neue Zeit. 1883–1917. The most important of the European journals dedicated to discussions of theoretical socialism. Edited by Karl Kautsky, most of its contributions were Marxist in orientation. The United States received a great deal of coverage in issues throughout the years.

The New York Evening Call. 1908–1917. (Title changed to *New York Call* on June 29, 1909.) A daily whose editorial policy reflected the moderate position on the opinion scale of the American Socialist party.

Die Nieuwe Tijd. Edited by Henriette Roland Holst, F. Van der Goes, H. Gorter, Herm. Heijermans, and J. Saks, this journal was the official monthly of the Social Democrats of Holland.

Le Parti ouvrier. 1888–1899, (1900–1914). Became the organ of the French socialist party led by Jean Allemane, a party which split off from the conservative *possibiliste* movement in 1890.

Le Parti socialiste. (1892–1894). A weekly organ of the French Blanquist forces.

The People. Weekly 1891–1900. Daily and weekly editions 1900–1914 entitled *Daily People* and *Weekly People.* This was the most radical of all the American socialist newspapers. It belonged to Daniel De Leon and his small Socialist Labor party.

La Petite République. 1892–1906. In the beginning this French newspaper encouraged contributions from socialists of all shades of opinion. It quickly became the journal of the conservative socialists who supported Alexandre Millerand.

Le Proletaire. (1882–1893). A newspaper belonging to the *possibiliste* wing of French socialism.

La Revue socialiste. 1885–1908. This journal, founded by Benoît Malon, was one of the most respected on the Continent. It professed to accept articles by all brands of socialists, but most of the contributors belonged in the revisionist camp. All of its editors came from the *possibiliste* wing of French socialism.

The Social Democrat. 1897–1911. One of the few English socialist journals reflecting a Marxist point of view.

Social Democratic Herald. 1898–1913. This well-known American socialist newspaper printed in Milwaukee expressed the conservative position of Victor Berger.

Le Socialisme. 1907–1913. Jules Guesde was the editor of this French Marxist newspaper.

Socialist. (1904–1906), 1907–1909. Founded in Edinburgh, this journal became the organ of the Socialist Labour party, an English Marxist sect that stood to the left even of Hyndman's SDF.

The Socialist Review. 1908–1918. This was the official monthly (later quarterly) journal of England's Independent Labour party. It was edited by Ramsay MacDonald until March 1912, and then by J. Bruce Glasier.

The Socialist Standard. (1904–1916). The official organ of the Socialist party of Great Britain, a left-wing sect that broke away from Hyndman's SDF.

Le Socialiste. 1885–1913. Edited by Jules Guesde and Paul Lafargue (among others), this French newspaper was solidly in the Marxist camp.

Der Sozialdemokrat. 1879–1890. This weekly publication, edited by Bernstein from 1881, sustained the German Social Democrats during the years when their party was outlawed. It was printed in Zürich and London and smuggled into Germany. The editor at this early time was still an adherent of Marxism.

Sozialistische Monatshefte. 1898–1915. This important German journal was the most important theoretical outlet for German socialists of the revisionist stamp.

Vorwärts. 1891–1917. This daily newspaper became the official organ of German Social Democrats after their party became legal again.

Wilshire's Magazine. 1900–1915. (Published under various titles.) Edited by Gaylord Wilshire, this magazine espoused an eccentric, but generally left-wing point of view.

The Worker. 1901–1908. (Changed name to *New York Socialist* in April, 1908.) A weekly newspaper reflecting the moderate stance of most New York socialists.

PROCEEDINGS AND REPORTS

Proceedings of various socialist conventions and reports of several labor groups provided some extremely good material. America frequently turned up in such sources as a point of controversy, and ensuing discussions or speeches exposed the question in the mind of European labor leaders as to whether the "American Way" offered any solution to the social ills of Europe.

The First International: Minutes of the Hague Congress of 1872 with Related Documents. Edited and translated by Hans Gerth. Madison, Wisconsin, 1958.

Mosely Industrial Commission. *Reports of the Delegates.* London, 1903. A report of English trade union leaders after a visit to the United States (October to December 1902) which caused some consternation in Marxist circles. The leaders found that American workers were much better off than their counterparts in Europe and were not overworked.

Social Democratic Party and Socialist Labor Party. *Proceedings of the Unity Convention of 1901.* Indianapolis, 1901.

Socialiste International. *Cinquième Congrès socialiste international tenu à Paris du 23 au 27 september 1900: Comte-rendu analytique.* Paris, 1901.

——. *Sixième Congrès socialiste international tenu à Amsterdam du 14 au 20 août 1904: Comte-rendu analytique.* Brussels, 1904.

——. *Septième Congrès socialiste international tenu à Stuttgart du 16 au 24 août 1907: Comte-rendu analytique.* Brussels, 1908.

——. *Huitième Congrès socialiste international tenu à Copenhague du 28 août au 3 septembre 1910: Comte-rendu analytique.* Ghent, 1911.

Socialist Party of America. *Proceedings of National Convention of 1904.* Chicago, 1904.

——. *Proceedings of National Convention of 1908.* Chicago, 1908.

——. *Proceedings of National Congress of 1910.* Chicago, 1910.

——. *Proceedings of National Convention of 1912.* Chicago, 1912.

Rapports de la délégation ouvrière à l'exposition de Chicago en 1893. Edited by Camille Krantz. Paris, 1894. A report of French trade union leaders following a visit to the United States which Marxists found very useful in refuting the notion of a workers' paradise in America.

Report of the Delegates of the Social Democratic Party to the International Socialist Congress. Paris, 1900.

Report of the Socialist Labor Party to the International Congress held in Stuttgart, August 18–25, 1907.

Report of the Socialist Party to the International Socialist and Trades Union Congress, Amsterdam, 1904.

Report of the Socialist Party of the United States to the International Socialist Congress at Copenhagen, 1910.

BOOKS, MEMOIRS, PAMPHLETS, COLLECTED WORKS, AND SPEECHES

These various primary sources, taken together, furnished the majority of the information for this study. Many of the titles of the listed works indicate their direct relation to the central topics under investigation. Many were written by European socialists; a few, European socialists used as sources of information about the United States. Still other socialist works in the list were not concerned centrally with the United States but contained valuable references to developments in this country.

Aschrott, P. F. *Die amerikanischen Trusts.* Tübingen, 1889. A work by a non-socialist, but one of the first European studies of the American trust. Widely noted by socialist writers.

Aveling, Edward. *An American Journey.* New York, *ca.* 1887.

——, and Aveling, Eleanor Marx. *The Chicago Anarchists.* n. p., n. d. A pamphlet reprinted from *Today,* Nov., 1887.

——. *The Working Class Movement in America.* London, 1891.

Bax, E. Belfort. *Essays in Socialism.* London, 1907.

Bebel, August. *Aus meinem Leben.* Three volumes. Stuttgart, 1910–1914.

——. *Auswahl aus seinen Reden.* Introduction by Kurt Kersten. Berlin, 1926.

———. *Nicht stehendes Heer sondern Volkswehr.* Stuttgart, 1898.

———. "Die Sozialdemokratie und das allgemeine Stimmrecht." Berlin, 1895.

———. "Unsere wirtschaftliche und politische Lage." Zürich, 1893.

Beer, Max. *Fifty Years of International Socialism.* London, 1935.

Berger, Victor L. *The Voice and Pen of Victor L. Berger: Congressional Speeches and Editorials.* Milwaukee, 1929.

Bernstein, Eduard. *Die Arbeiterbewegung.* Frankfurt, 1910.

———. *Evolutionary Socialism: A Criticism and Affirmation.* Introduction by Sidney Hook. New York, 1961.

———. *My Years of Exile: Reminiscences of a Socialist.* Translated by Bernard Miall. London, 1921.

Bryce, James. *The American Commonwealth.* Two volumes. New York, 1923. European socialists learned a great deal from Bryce, although Marxists violently opposed his general tone of praise and his conclusion that socialism would never make much headway in the United States.

———. *The Predictions of Hamilton and de Tocqueville.* Baltimore, 1887.

Chevalier, Michel. *Lettres sur L'Amérique du Nord.* Brussels, 1844. A work Marxists blamed for the creation of a myth about the United States.

The Chicago Martyrs: Their Speeches in Court. Glasgow, n. d. Many editions of these speeches appeared in many places.

Debs, Eugene Victor. *Debs: His Life, Writings and Speeches.* Girard, Kansas, 1908.

———, *et al.* " 'Practical' Socialism. Is There Any Such Thing?" *The Saturday Evening Post,* CLXXXI (May 8, 1909), 8–9, 55. Short statements by American socialist leaders. Usually cited as evidence of the rightward drift of party attitudes.

De Leon, Daniel. *Flashlights of the Amsterdam Congress.* New York, 1904.

Deutscher, Isaac, ed. *The Age of Permanent Revolution: A Trotsky Anthology.* New York, 1964.

Ely, Richard T. *The Labor Movement in America.* New York, 1905. An important American economist sympathetic to labor whose works European socialists used selectively.

———. *Recent American Socialism.* Baltimore, 1885.

Engels, Friedrich. *Anti-Dühring: Herr Eugen Dühring's Revolution in Science.* Moscow, 1959.

——. *The Condition of the Working-Class in England in 1844.* With 1892 Preface by Engels. Translated by Florence Kelley Wischnewetzky. London, 1892.

——. "The Labor Movement in America." *The Communist,* VII (June 1928), 346–54. Originally published as a preface to the American edition of *The Condition of the Working-Class in England in 1844* (New York, 1887), translated by Florence Kelley Wischnewetzky. It was also published in 1887 in New York as a pamphlet entitled *The Labor Movement in America (The George Movement—The Knights of Labor—The Socialists).*

——. *Socialism: Utopian and Scientific.* Introduction by Engels. Translated by Edward Aveling. New York, 1892.

Ghent, W. J. *Our Benevolent Feudalism.* New York, 1902.

Ghio, Paul. *L'Anarchisme aux États-Unis.* Paris, 1903.

Gilman, Nicholas Paine. *Socialism and the American Spirit.* New York, 1893.

Gronlund, Laurence. *The Co-operative Commonwealth: An Exposition of Modern Socialism.* London, 1891.

——. *The New Economy: A Peaceable Solution of the Social Problem.* Chicago, 1898.

Guesde, Jules. *Le Socialisme au jour le jour.* Paris, 1899.

Halle, Ernst von. *Trusts or Industrial Combinations and Coalitions in the United States.* New York, 1899.

Hamilton, Thomas. *Men and Manners in America.* Two volumes. Philadelphia, 1833. An early English view of the United States with an influence on Marx.

Herr, Erich. *Der Zusammenbruch der Wirtschaftsfreiheit und der Seig des Staatssozialismus in den Vereinigten Staaten von Amerika.* Jena, 1906. An unorthodox account which makes Theodore Roosevelt the high priest of State Socialism.

Hillquit, Morris. *History of Socialism in the United States.* New York, 1903.

——. *Recent Progress of the Socialist and Labor Movements in the United States: Report of Morris Hillquit to the International Socialist Congress at Stuttgart.* Chicago, 1907.

Hoehn, G. A. *New America.* St. Louis, 1896.

Howe, Irving, ed. *The Basic Writings of Trotsky*. New York, 1963.

Hughan, Jessie Wallace. *American Socialism of the Present Day.* Introduction by John Spargo. New York, 1911.

Hyndman, Henry M. *The Chicago Riots and the Class War in the United States.* London, 1886.

———. *Further Reminiscences.* London, 1912.

Jaurès, Jean. "Bernstein et l'évolution de la méthode socialiste." Paris, 1900.

———. *Studies in Socialism.* Translated by Mildred Minturn. London, 1906.

Kautsky, Karl. *The Class Struggle.* Translated by William E. Bohn. Chicago, 1910.

———. *The Road to Power.* Translated by A. M. Simons. Chicago, 1909.

Kerby, W. J. *Le Socialisme aux États-Unis.* Brussels, 1897.

Laboulaye, Edouard. *Paris en Amérique.* Paris, 1863. Laboulaye's praise of the United States was bitterly resented by European Marxists.

Lafargue, Paul. *Les Trusts américains: Leur action économique sociale, politique.* Paris, 1903.

Legien, Carl. *Aus Amerikas Arbeiterbewegung.* Berlin, 1914.

Lenin, V. I. *Collected Works.* Thirty-two volumes. Moscow, 1960–66.

Leroy-Beaulieu, Pierre. *Les États-Unis au XXᵉ siècle.* Paris, 1904. A laudatory, non-socialist view of America that came under Marxist attack.

Levasseur, Émile. *L'Ouvrier américain.* Two volumes. Paris, 1898. A favorable scholarly account of working conditions in the United States which received a great deal of attention from European socialists.

Lewis, Austin. *The Rise of the American Proletarian.* Chicago, 1910.

Liebknecht, Karl. *Gesammelte Reden und Schriften.* Berlin, 1958—.

Liebknecht, Wilhelm. *Ein Blick in die Neue Welt.* Stuttgart, 1887.

———. *Hochverrath und Revolution.* Berlin, 1892.

———. *Souvenirs.* Translated into French by J.-G. Prod'Homme and Ch.-A. Bertrand. Paris, 1901.

London, Jack. *The Iron Heel.* New York, 1907.

Longuet, Jean. *Le Mouvement socialiste international*. Vol. IV, *Encyclopédie socialiste, syndicale et coopérative de l'Internationale Ouvrière*. Edited by Jean Lorris. Paris, 1913.

Louis, Paul. *L'Avenir du socialisme*. Paris, 1905.

———. *La Guerre économique*. Paris, 1900.

Luxemburg, Rosa. *The Accumulation of Capital*. Translated by Agnes Schwarzschild. New Haven, 1951.

MacDonald, J. Ramsay. *Socialism and Society*. London, 1906.

———. *The Socialist Movement*. New York, 1911.

Macy, John. *Socialism in America*. New York, 1916.

Marx, Karl. *Capital: A Critique of Political Economy*. Translated from third German edition by Samuel Moore and Edward Aveling. Edited by Frederick Engels. Revised according to fourth German edition by Ernest Untermann. New York, 1906.

———. *The Class Struggles in France, 1848–1850*. Introduction by Friedrich Engels. New York, 1924.

———. *A Contribution to the Critique of Political Economy*. Translated by N. I. Stone. Chicago, 1904.

———. *A Critique of the Gotha Programme*. New York, 1938.

———. *The Eighteenth Brumaire of Louis Bonaparte*. Translated by Daniel De Leon. Chicago, 1913.

———. "Free Trade. A Speech Delivered before the Democratic Club of Brussels, Belgium, Jan. 9, 1848." Translated by Florence Kelley Wischnewetzky. Preface by Friedrich Engels. Boston, 1888.

———. *Revolution and Counter Revolution: Or Germany in 1848*. Edited by Eleanor Marx Aveling. Chicago, 1912.

———. *Value, Price, and Profit: Addressed to Working Men*. Edited by Eleanor Marx Aveling. Chicago, 1913.

———. *Wage-Labor and Capital*. Preface by Friedrich Engels. Translated by Harriet E. Lothrop. New York, 1902.

———, and Engels, Friedrich. *The American Journalism of Marx and Engels: A Selection from the New York Daily Tribune*. Edited by Henry M. Christman. New York, 1966.

———. *The Civil War in the Uinted States*. Edited by Richard Enmale. New York, 1937.

———. *Communist Manifesto*. Introduction and notes by D. Ryazanoff. London, 1930.

———. *The German Ideology,* Parts I and III. Edited with an Introduction by R. Pascal. New York, 1939.

———. *The Russian Menace to Europe.* Edited by Paul W. Blackstock and Bert F. Hoselitz. Glencoe, Ill., 1952.

Meyer, Rudolf H. *Der Emancipationskampf des Vierten Standes.* Two volumes. Berlin, 1874–75.

Rousiers, Paul de. *Les Industries monopolisées (Trusts) aux États-Unis.* Paris, 1898. A well-known European work on the subject of industrial consolidation by a Liberal.

———. *La Vie américaine: Ranches, fermes et usines.* Paris, 1899.

Sagot, François. *Le Communisme au nouveau monde.* Paris, 1900.

Schippel, Max. *Amerika und die Handelsvertragspolitik.* Berlin, 1906.

———. *Grundzüge der Handelspolitik.* Berlin, 1902.

———. *Hochkonjunktur und Wirtschaftskrisis.* Berlin, 1908.

Schlüter, Hermann. *Die Anfänge der deutschen Arbeiterbewegung in Amerika.* Stuttgart, 1907.

Semler, Heinrich. *Geschichte des Socialismus und Communismus in Nord Amerika.* Leipzig, 1888.

Shaw, George Bernard, *et al. Fabian Essays in Socialism.* Preface to American edition by Gaylord Wilshire. New York, 1891.

Sinclair, Upton. *The Autobiography of Upton Sinclair.* New York, 1962.

———. *The Industrial Republic: A Study of the America of Ten Years Hence.* New York, 1907.

———. *Our Bourgeois Literature: The Reason and the Remedy.* Chicago, *ca.* 1904.

Sombart, Werner. *Socialism and the Social Movement in the Nineteenth Century.* New York, 1898.

———. *Warum gibt es in den Vereinigten Staaten keinen Sozialismus?* Tübingen, 1906.

Spies, August. *Auto-biography: His Speech in Court and General Notes.* Edited by Nina Van Zandt. Chicago, 1887.

Stead, W. T. *Chicago To-day or the Labour War in America.* London, 1894.

Trotsky, Leon. *Europe and America.* Translated by John G. Wright. Colombo, 1951.

———. *If America Should Go Communist.* New York, 1957. Reprint of a piece that first appeared in *Liberty Magazine,* March 23, 1935.

——. *The Living Thoughts of Karl Marx.* London, 1940.

——. *Marxism in the United States.* Introduction by Albert Gates. New York, 1947.

——. *My Life: The Rise and Fall of a Dictator.* London, 1930.

——. *The Strategy of the World Revolution.* Translated by Max Shachtman. New York, 1930.

Vandervelde, Émile. *Collectivism and Industrial Evolution.* Chicago, 1904.

——. *Impressions d'Amérique.* Ghent, 1909.

Vigouroux, Louis. *La Concentration des forces ouvrières dans l'Amérique du Nord.* Paris, 1899.

Walteshausen, August Sartorius von. *Der moderne Socialismus in den Vereinigten Staaten von Amerika.* Berlin, 1890.

Webb, Sidney, and Webb, Beatrice. *The Decay of Capitalist Civilization.* New York, 1923.

Wells, H. G. *The Future in America: A Search after Realities.* New York, 1906.

Wilshire, Gaylord. *Wilshire Editorials.* New York, 1906.

Wright, Carroll D. *L'Evolution industrielle des États-Unis.* Preface by E. Lavasseur. Translated into French by F. Lepelletier. Paris, 1901. This book by the United States Commissioner of Labor was well known to European socialists. The statistics of the United States Bureau of Labor as well as census reports were extensively used by the more careful European socialist students of America.

SECONDARY WORKS

Most of the works listed on subjects related to my own have been discussed in the text. The bulk of the books in this category are standard works on the history of European and American socialism and require no critical comment beyond what is found elsewhere on a few specific studies.

Barghoorn, Frederick C. *The Soviet Image of the United States: A Study in Distortion.* New York, 1950.

Baron, Samuel H. *Plekhanov: The Father of Russian Marxism*. Stanford, Calif., 1963.

Bedford, Henry F. *Socialism and the Workers in Massachusetts, 1886–1912*. Amherst, Mass., 1966.

Bell, Daniel. *Marxian Socialism in the United States*. Princeton, 1967.

Bernstein, Samuel. *The First International in America*. New York, 1962.

Braunthal, Julius. *History of the International, 1864–1914*. Translated by Henry Collins and Kenneth Mitchell. London, 1966.

Browder, Earl. *Marx and America: A Study of the Doctrine of Impoverishment*. New York, 1958.

Carr, E. H. *Karl Marx*. London, 1934.

Charnay, Maurice. *Les Allemanistes*. Paris, 1912.

Cole, G. D. H. *A History of Socialist Thought*. Five volumes. London, 1953–1960.

Collins, Henry, and Abramsky, Chimen. *Karl Marx and the British Labour Movement: Years of the First International*. London, 1965.

Cowden, Morton H. "Early Marxist Views on British Labor, 1837–1917." *Western Political Quarterly*, XVI (March 1963), 34–52.

David, Henry. *The History of the Haymarket Affair*. New York, 1936.

Deutscher, Isaac. *The Prophet Armed: Trotsky, 1879–1921*. London, 1954.

———. *The Prophet Outcast: Trotsky, 1929–1940*. London, 1963.

———. *The Prophet Unarmed: Trotsky, 1921–1929*. London, 1959.

———. *Stalin: A Political Biography*. London, 1966.

Draper, Theodore. *American Communism and Soviet Russia: The Formative Period*. New York, 1960.

———. *The Roots of American Communism*. New York, 1957.

Dulles, Foster Rhea. *The Road to Teheran: The Story of Russia and America, 1781–1943*. Princeton, 1945.

Egbert, Donald Drew, and Persons, Stow, eds. *Socialism and American Life*. Two volumes. Princeton, 1952.

Fainsod, Merle. *International Socialism and the World War*. Cambridge, Mass., 1935.

Feuer, Lewis S. "The North American Origin of Marx's Socialism." *The Western Political Quarterly,* XVI (March 1963), 53–67.

Fine, Sidney. "Is May Day American in Origin?" *The Historian,* XVI (Spring 1954), 121–34.

Fischer, Louis. *The Life of Lenin.* New York, 1964.

Foner, Philip. *History of the Labor Movement in the United States.* Four volumes. New York, 1947–1967.

Gavett, Thomas W. *Development of the Labor Movement in Milwaukee.* Madison, Wis., 1965.

Gay, Peter. *The Dilemma of Democratic Socialism: Eduard Bernstein's Challenge to Marx.* New York, 1952.

Genovese, Eugene D. "Marxian Interpretations of the Slave South." *Towards a New Past: Dissenting Essays in American History.* Barton J. Bernstein, ed. New York, 1968.

Ginger, Ray. *The Bending Cross: A Biography of Eugene Victor Debs.* New Brunswick, 1949.

Glaser, William A. "Algie Martin Simons and Marxism in America." *Mississippi Valley Historical Review,* XLI (Dec. 1954), 419–34.

Goldberg, Harvey. *The Life of Jean Jaurès.* Madison, Wis., 1962.

Harris, David. *Socialist Origins in the United States: American Forerunners of Marx, 1817–1832.* Assen, 1966.

Hecht, David. "Plekhanov and American Socialism." *Russian Review,* IX (April 1950), 112–23.

———. *Russian Radicals Look to America, 1825–1894.* Cambridge, Mass., 1947.

Herreshoff, David. *American Disciples of Marx: From the Age of Jackson to the Progressive Era.* Detroit, 1967.

Joll, James. *The Second International, 1889–1914.* London, 1955.

Kamman, William F. *Socialism in German American Literature.* Philadelphia, 1917.

Keep, J. L. H. *The Rise of Social Democracy in Russia.* Oxford, 1963.

Kennan, George F. *Russia and the West Under Lenin and Stalin.* Boston, 1961.

———. *Soviet American Relations, 1917–1920.* Two volumes (*Russia Leaves the War, The Decision To Intervene*). Princeton, 1956–58.

———. "Soviet Historiography and America's Role in the Intervention." *American Historical Review,* LXV (Jan. 1960), 302–22.

Kipnis, Ira. *The American Socialist Movement, 1897–1912.* New York, 1952.

Koht, Halvdan. *The American Spirit in Europe: A Survey of Transatlantic Influences.* Philadelphia, 1949.

Kolko, Gabriel. "The Decline of American Radicalism in the Twentieth Century." *Studies on the Left,* VI (Sept.–Oct. 1966), 9–26.

Labedz, Leopold, ed. *Revisionism: Essays on the History of Marxist Ideas.* London, 1962.

Landauer, Carl. *European Socialism: A History of Ideas and Movements from the Industrial Revolution to Hitler's Seizure of Power.* In collaboration with Elizabeth Kridly Vakenier and Hilde Stein Landauer. Two volumes. Berkeley, 1959.

Landy, Avrom. "Engels on the American Labor Movement." *The Communist,* VII (May 1928), 307–13.

———. "Marx, Engels and America: Attitudes toward America in the Early Period." *The Communist,* VI (July–Aug. 1927), 295–309.

Laserson, Max M. *The American Impact on Russia: Diplomatic and Ideological, 1784–1917.* New York, 1950.

Lichtheim, George. *Marxism: An Historical and Critical Study.* New York, 1965.

Lidtke, Vernon L. *The Outlawed Party: Social Democracy in Germany, 1878–1890.* Princeton, 1966.

Lillibridge, G. D. *Beacon of Freedom: The Impact of American Democracy upon Great Britain, 1830–1870.* Philadelphia, 1954.

MacNaught, Kenneth. "American Progressives and the Great Society." *Journal of American History,* LIII (Dec. 1966), 504–20.

Meyer, Alfred G. *Leninism.* Cambridge, Mass., 1957.

———. *Marxism: The Unity of Theory and Practice.* Cambridge, Mass., 1964.

Mins, Leonard E. "Unpublished Letters of Marx and Engels to Americans." *Science and Society,* II (Spring and Summer 1938), 218–31 and 348–75.

Morais, Herbert M. "Marx and Engels on America." *A Centenary of Marxism.* Edited by Samuel Bernstein and the editors of *Science and Society.* New York, 1948.

Morgan, Roger. *The German Social Democrats and the First International, 1864–1872.* Cambridge, Eng., 1965.

Muzik, Edward J. "Victor L. Berger: A Biography." Unpublished Ph.D. dissertation, Northwestern University, 1960.

Nettl, J. P. *Rosa Luxemburg.* Two volumes. London, 1966.

Neuman, Heinz. *Marx and Engels on Revolution in America.* Chicago, 1926.

Noland, Aaron. *The Founding of the French Socialist Party, 1893–1905.* Cambridge, Mass., 1956.

Noyes, John Humphrey. *History of American Socialisms.* Philadelphia, 1870.

O'Connor, Richard. *Jack London: A Biography.* Boston, 1964.

Obermann, Karl. *Joseph Weydemeyer: Pioneer of American Socialism.* New York, 1947.

Page, Stanley W. *Lenin and the World Revolution.* New York, 1959.

Payne, Robert. *The Life and Death of Lenin.* New York, 1964.

Pelling, Henry. *America and the British Left: From Bright to Bevan.* London, 1956.

Quint, Howard H. *The Forging of American Socialism: Origins of the Modern Movement.* Columbia, S. C., 1953.

Rossiter, Clinton. *Marxism: The View from America.* New York, 1960.

Roth, Guenther. *The Social Democrats in Imperial Germany: A Study of Working-Class Isolation and National Integration.* Totawa, N. J., 1963.

Rubel, Maximilien, "Notes on Marx's Conception of Democracy." *New Politics,* I (Winter 1962), 78–90.

Schlesinger, Rudolf. *Marx: His Time and Ours.* London, 1950.

Schorske, Carl E. *German Social Democracy, 1905–1917: The Development of the Great Schism.* Cambridge, Mass., 1955.

Shannon, David A. *The Socialist Party of America.* New York, 1955.

Shub, David. *Lenin: A Biography.* London, 1966.

Skard, Sigmund. *The American Myth and the European Mind: American Studies in Europe, 1776–1960.* Philadelphia, 1961.

Smuts, Robert W. *European Impressions of the American Worker.* New York, 1953.

Struik, Dirk J. "Frederick Engels in New England." *New England Quarterly,* XXII (June 1949), 240–43.

Tsuzuki, Chüshichi. *H. M. Hyndman and British Socialism.* Edited by Henry Pelling. Oxford, 1961.

———. *The Life of Eleanor Marx, 1855–1898.* Oxford, 1967.
Ulam, Adam B. *Lenin and the Bolsheviks: The Intellectual and Political History of the Triumph of Communism in Russia.* London, 1965.
Weinstein, James. *The Decline of Socialism in America, 1912–1925.* New York, 1967.
———. "The Socialist Party: Its Roots and Strength, 1912–1919." *Studies on the Left,* I (Winter 1960), 5–27.
Willard, Claude. *Les Guesdistes.* Paris, 1965.
Wittke, Carl. *Refugees of Revolution: The German Forty-eighters in America.* Philadelphia, 1952.
———. *The Utopian Communist: A Biography of Wilhelm Weitling, Nineteenth-century Reformer.* Baton Rouge, La., 1950.
Wolfe, Bertram. *Marx and America.* New York, 1934.

INDEX

THE MAN OF ONLY YESTERDAY

A  BOOK

FREDERICK LEWIS ALLEN

THE MAN OF ONLY YESTERDAY

Frederick Lewis Allen

FORMER EDITOR OF *HARPER'S MAGAZINE*,

AUTHOR, AND INTERPRETER OF HIS TIMES

DARWIN PAYNE

Foreword by Russell Lynes

HARPER & ROW, PUBLISHERS

New York, Evanston, San Francisco, London

To my mother and father

FIRST EDITION

Designed by Patricia Dunbar

Library of Congress Cataloging in Publication Data
Payne, Darwin.
   The man of only yesterday.
   (A Cass Canfield book)
   Includes bibliographical references and index.
   1. Allen, Frederick Lewis, 1890-1954. I. Title.
PN4874.A38P3   070.4′092′4[B]   74-1847
ISBN 0-06-013296-5

75 76 77 78 79 10 9 8 7 6 5 4 3 2 1

Contents

Foreword

How agreeable to sit down with Frederick Lewis Allen for a few hours, to hear him speak again in the pages of this biography, to reminisce, to reveal himself, to reiterate opinions familiar to his old friends in his lively, amused and optic phrases. The sound and sense and quality are here without frills or furbelows—an unusual man measured and intact.

When I first met him in the early thirties Allen was forty-two (I was half that), and he and Agnes Rogers had just married. He was the Associate Editor of *Harper's Magazine* (which meant that he was second in command), and he was newly and justly famous as the author of *Only Yesterday*, though no one seemed more surprised by fame than he or accepted it more diffidently. He was both a modest and a moderate man and nothing turned his head. He took many matters seriously, but no one ever suggested that one of the things he took too seriously was himself. ("It is all very well to be serious," he said of his magazine, "but there is no excuse for being solemn.") His perceptions were filtered through an unerring sense of the ridiculous, and nothing was more ridiculous in his eyes than pompousness.

He never, I think, quite believed in the eminence of his reputation as an editor and as the inventor of a new manner of writing contemporary history. He never lost his sense of surprise when an honor or a promotion came his way. "Imagine me being a vice-president!" he said when Harper & Brothers, of which his magazine was then a part, made him one.

I had the pleasure of facing him in the office for five or six years; our desks were back to back. He rarely worked at his. He preferred to sit at a drop-leaf maple table, and he was never more at home than with his pencil poised over someone else's manuscript. It was not that he took pleasure in imposing his will on another writer's work; it was, rather, the pleasure of lifting a clod from the page to reveal a nugget that the writer did not realize he had buried there. Allen was not only modest and moderate, he was also methodical. He worked on a manuscript with the same precision that he worked on a watercolor, a medium that does not lend itself to second chances. He liked things tidy and without ambiguities. Beneath his seemingly casual prose is a precision of thought and organization and intent which belies its effortless surface. He frequently said of a manuscript which he found dense or over-academic, "I'm afraid his research is showing." His own extensive research became so integral a part of the easy flow of his style that it never for a moment showed. He managed with his editorial pencil to endow the writing of others with much of the same quality without, by some miracle, changing its personality or distressing its author.

Allen was an exemplar of the tradition of editor-as-gentleman, not its last, to be sure, but a representative of a tradition that does not persist with energy today. He would have been appalled at what is called "the new journalism" in which fact is embellished and beclouded and often falsified by fantasy and the first person singular blots the printed page like a plague of black ants. It took a great deal to provoke him into editorial assault on a personality ("Never," he said to his staff, "impute motives!"), but occasionally he was provoked, as the reader will find he was in the cases of Admiral King and General MacArthur, who were hiding behind what Allen rightly decried as unnecessary and self-seeking wartime censorship. Indeed, neither the admiral nor the general was behaving in a manner Allen considered worthy of a gentleman. His concept of a gentleman was in no sense stuffy. He was assuredly no prig and, though his background might have given him permission, he was the antithesis of a social snob. On one occasion the distinguished British author, Rebecca West, made a careless error in an article that caused the threat of a libel suit. The matter was resolved at considerable cost in legal fees and cables between *Harper's* lawyers and the English newspaper to which a statement was misattributed and which regarded itself with justification to be the injured party. Allen thought it best not to tell Dame Rebecca how the matter was resolved. "It would only distress her," he said, "and the matter is settled."

Like anyone else, Allen, as his biographer has demonstrated in this extremely just appraisal, was not without his blind spots. He was not much interested in the fine arts, except as they illuminated the social context in which they were made. He rarely went to a museum or a gallery or a concert or to the "serious" theater. (The music he most enjoyed was Sousa marches and Viennese waltzes.) He intensely disliked posturing, and it seemed to him that much art and performance was just that, though he was a passionate admirer of craftsmanship and professionalism wherever he encountered them. His preferences were for nonfiction—for biography and history and, as Mr. Payne points out, for economic theory, though he found it hard going. "You know," he said one day while he was doing the research for his last book, *The Big Change*, "I'd much rather read books than magazines. I'm a book reader at heart." Yet no one had a sharper eye for the quality of a magazine piece than he nor was more fertile in producing ideas for articles or discovering the germ of an important idea in a disorganized or inarticulate manuscript. He read little fiction for his own pleasure, though his judgment about short stories for the magazine and his ability to spot a promising new talent were acute if not infallible (no editor's is), and his attitude toward writers of fiction was always respectful as it was, indeed, toward all professional artists, whether he liked their work or not.

Allen was most certainly not one of those writers who contend, "I don't know what I think till I see what I say." When he sat down to his red portable typewriter it was more performance than rehearsal; he had the score of his work clearly in his head. With two fingers he would tap out five thousand words in a day when he was ready to perform, and though he whittled and polished, editing himself as he would edit others, the structure, the pace, the tone, the illumination were there in the first draft. He enjoyed the process of precise planning both at work and in relaxation. When he and Mrs. Allen gave a party, he liked to predict to the last bottle of each kind of liquor and the last bottle of soda exactly how much his guests would consume, and then be delightedly amused by the accuracy of his prediction.

Allen played with the same concentration with which he worked, and he cared more about the process, whether it was cowboy pool or paddle tennis or a paper-and-pencil game than about the results except, perhaps, when he played at being a watercolorist, in which he took the justified pride of a very skillful amateur.

His own well-ordered regimen did not make him a stickler for other editors' schedules at the magazine so long as what was needed got done and on time. He was only grudgingly tolerant of those who failed to meet their deadlines or keep their commitments, though he was always generous to those whose excuses were founded in some genuine personal disaster, however minor. On the rare occasions when he would lose his temper at one of his colleagues for a thoughtless blunder or a solecism or a piece of sloppy copy, he would be around a few minutes later embarrassed and apologizing for his little outburst. His concern for those who worked with and for him erred, if it erred at all, on the side of generosity and compassion. He shared his good fortunes with his colleagues and his employees. When, for example, his salary was raised at *Harper's*, he in turn gave the maids who served in his house an equivalent raise in wages. When a friend was in financial difficulty, he opened his purse. It was said of him, moreover, "He would never consent to a business decision that did not satisfy fully his own personal standards. Whatever engaged his attention—a human dilemma, a literary decision, a business problem—was always weighed not only by his precise and analytical mind but by his calm, unflustered fairness, his sense of the ridiculous and the fallible, the warmth and depth of his compassion."

Mr. Payne, with admirable perception and justice and without the blinders of sentiment has given us a biography in which the often subtle and continuously interesting chips of Frederick Lewis Allen and his times are let to fall where they may. It is a delight to read about such a man—not a paragon or a little tin god, but an editor and author who left an indelible mark on the journalism, the historical writing, and the literature of his day and who in his modesty would have been the last to think he would ever be the subject of such a biography.

—Russell Lynes

1

THE BEGINNINGS

Frederick Lewis Allen's best-selling histories imprinted upon the minds of millions of Americans a captivating and indelible image of their own yesterdays. His engaging style of writing made the past enjoyable as well as informative not only for Americans but for readers of his books in Great Britain, Italy, Japan, and the Soviet Union. His assessment of the 1920s became a point of departure for later historians, and his history of that period, *Only Yesterday*, has been declared a "classic."[1]* Allen, however, considered history to be no more than a secondary interest. He wrote his books by squeezing time out of evenings, weekends, vacations, and occasional leaves of absence from his full-time work.

First and foremost, Allen was an editor. For thirty-one years, twelve of them as editor in chief, he was employed by *Harper's Magazine*, where he dealt with many of America's foremost writers and confronted the nation's most critical problems. His life provides other vistas, too, for seeing the first half of the twentieth century in Amer-

---

* Notes to the chapter begin on p. 283.

ica. He was Allen the Harvard man, writer and editor for the *Lampoon*; Allen the pioneer publicist, shaping public opinion for the government during World War I and later establishing Harvard's first publicity office; Allen the humorist whose sketches appeared consistently in the nation's leading magazines; Allen the collaborator who teamed with Agnes Rogers Allen in producing pictorial history books and television scripts; Allen the man of affairs, two-term Harvard overseer, trustee of the Ford Foundation, and director of the Foreign Policy Association; Allen the family man who overcame personal tragedy; and Allen the disciplined child of Puritan New England who inherited a high sense of purpose.

In many ways Frederick Lewis Allen represents a bridge between the elitist, genteel tradition of nineteenth-century society and the casual, mobile scene that had developed at mid-twentieth century. He found himself no less at home in the modern society of the 1950s than he did in the closely knit cultural and social center of Boston at the turn of the century.

John P. Marquand said of his fictitious proper Bostonian George Apley, whose life was a study in failure to bridge the gulf, that he possessed the "undeviating discipline of background." Allen felt the discipline of a background that was similar in many respects. Although he could not claim membership in a "first family" of Boston, his Massachusetts ancestry traced back to several passengers on the *Mayflower*. His father was a well-known Episcopal minister in Boston; his mother's family held an esteemed position in Philadelphia society. He was reared from crib to manhood on Boston's Marlborough Street (one street over from Apley's Beacon Street). He enjoyed the finest schooling that New England could offer: preparatory work at Groton (where Apley dutifully sent his own son) and two degrees from Harvard. Moreover, Allen achieved what Apley so fervently wished for his son, the honor of being elected a Harvard overseer.

Allen did not, however, share the sense of privileged station felt by Marquand's famous prototype. Apley's disciplined background pointed him inward toward responsibility to the family tradition and guardianship of the family fortune. The Allens had no great family fortune, and the discipline young Allen received from his solicitous father, who was preoccupied with ministering to the downtrodden, was intended to expand his mind and sense of morality. Allen became a democrat in both the general and political sense: he believed in the ultimate wisdom of the common man and he scorned pretensions to class superiority. Allen's relatively advantaged position in life did instill in him a certain noblesse oblige: to attract and inform in a responsible and palatable manner those who might make the effort to be informed.

Allen's ideas, except for a lack of interest in organized labor, fit smoothly into Progressive, New Deal, and postwar liberal positions. The year of his death, 1954, however, marked the beginning of a new era in American life for which Allen and opinion-molders of like mind had not envisioned or prepared the public. The toppling that year of the separate but equal doctrine of racial segregation cast loose indirectly but surely social upheavals that had stirred uneasily but quietly for years. In common with other liberals, Allen believed firmly in equal opportunity and in racial integration as a principle, yet, the general problem of black-white relations and the subservient role of ethnic minorities were not subjects which received a great deal of his attention. The situation, happily, seemed to be improving. The transition that Allen represents, then, is only from the Victorian age to the America of pre-1954. He, along with many others, would have been unprepared for the dramatic and far-reaching developments in race relations just around the corner in the 1960s.

In another perspective Allen may be seen as a representative of the communications revolution of the first half of this century, which united members of a sprawling, diverse continent into a nation with common thoughts, habits, appearances, ideals, and customs. As the mass culture that had emerged by the 1950s displaced the older more elitist culture, there seemed to be a downgrading of the intellectual discipline which Allen, and, in his own way, Apley, had undergone. Values appeared to be tugged downward toward a common denominator as the communications revolution encompassed wider and wider audiences, finally seeking those wider audiences as an end in themselves.

In his career Allen represented both the older values and the new forces. He sought to interpret important events accurately and incisively, but also provocatively. He knew that growing numbers of educated people could appreciate high-quality magazines and books, but he realized that to attract them he must make the material not just significant but inviting. While upholding *Harper's* standards, he worried about its perpetual borderline financial status and he cast side glances tinged with some envy at *Reader's Digest, Time, Life,* and *Look* (often he himself wrote for such popular periodicals).

Forever optimistic about man's potential, Allen believed firmly that the leveling changes which had broadened the base of the culture were of the utmost overall benefit. His life and works stimulated and enlightened the steadily growing numbers of the American middle class.

The young Frederick Lewis Allen no doubt felt intimately a part of the American past as he listened to his parents and grandparents recount family stories. His father boasted of an ancestry in Massachusetts since 1620; his mother traced her family name to a romantic episode in Philadelphia at the time of the American Revolution. Since these early days, both families had been blessed by distinction and good character, and in many instances, more than ordinary prosperity.

Allen's family claimed as ancestors seven of the Pilgrims who arrived at Plymouth harbor aboard the *Mayflower* in the winter of 1620.[2] Their religious convictions were perpetuated through the years in the Allen family: Frederick Lewis Allen's great-grandfather, grandfather, and father all achieved recognition as church leaders.

Otis Allen, his great-grandfather, was a Mansfield, Massachusetts, farmer whose church activities included service as a deacon, choir leader, and Sunday school superintendent. Allen's grandfather, Frederick Deane Allen, left the farm as a boy of fifteen in 1821, and eventually formed Allen, Lane & Company, a wool merchandising business in Boston. When he died in 1894, twenty-one of his fellow dry-goods merchants closed their business doors during the hour of his funeral. Like his father, Frederick Deane Allen was a deacon in the church and a Sunday school superintendent. An exacting parent, he was handy with the rod. His wife, Mary Richmond Baylies of Taunton, provided an antidote to her husband's severe standards with her sprightly conversation and enthusiastic social work.

Frederick Baylies Allen, the father of Frederick Lewis Allen, acquired traits from both his stern father and his livelier mother: his own personality combined a certain stoicism with piety, humor, and an intense interest in the practical problems of man. Born November 5, 1840, he grew to manhood in the Beacon Hill area and attended the Boston Public Latin School. He spent his first two college years at Harvard, but when his younger brother Francis entered college, both were enrolled at Amherst. Frederick's allegiances remained with Harvard, although he was graduated from Amherst, and in 1909, on the petition of his former classmates, he was awarded a Harvard bachelor's degree.[3]

The strong religious leanings of the family pulled Frederick Baylies Allen toward the ministry despite a pronounced literary bent. He prepared for a ministerial career in the family's Congregational faith at Andover Theological Seminary. During the 1865 spring vacation of his final year at Andover, Allen went to the Civil War battlefields in Virginia to work for six weeks with the Christian Commission, an organization which distributed religious tracts and provided a limited amount of relief to soldiers. The experience had a lasting effect on him. As he saw wounded and dying soldiers, he concluded that physical hunger and thirst and pain deserved preferential attention; the message of the Gospel, as designated by the Bible, was subordinate to human needs.

In 1867 Allen married Louisa Ripley Vose, the daughter of Judge Henry Vose of Boston, and the next year he became pastor of the Congregational Church in Canandaigua in western New York state. There he became friends with Horace Bushnell, the great Congregational theologian whose work created a nineteenth-century link to a more socially concerned and liberal theology; Charles Dudley Warner, Mark Twain's collaborator on *The Gilded Age* and next-door neighbor at Brook Farm; and the Reverend Joseph H. Twitchell, the Congregational minister whom Twain met and befriended on his "innocents abroad" trip to Europe and the Holy Land. (Allen later told his children that he had turned down an invitation to accompany Twain on that journey.[4]) On a camping trip with Bushnell, Warner, and Twitchell in the Adirondacks, the group's guide commemorated a terrific rainfall by naming a peak near Mount Marcy, Allen Mountain.[5]

One week after the Allens' third daughter was born in November 1871, Louisa Allen died. Allen was left with sole responsibility for rearing his infant daughter, Louisa Ripley, and two toddlers, Josephine Francis and Rebecca Gorham.[6] He remained at his Canandaigua pastorate for more than a year before he returned to Boston to live with his parents: they, and especially his strong-willed sister, Josephine, could help him with the children.[7] Wise though this decision may have been for his daughters, it proved nearly disastrous for Allen's career. He could find no pastoral position for the next six years.

He finally resumed his ministerial career as an Episcopalian instead of as a Congregationalist because the magnetism of Phillips Brooks of Trinity Church had attracted him to the Episcopal faith in 1879. Soon becoming assistant rector, Allen assumed authority over a number of social projects. One of his initial accomplishments was the founding of Trinity House, a facility designed to assist and to encourage poor women who lived near Trinity Church.

In the summer of 1883 Allen met Alberta Hildegarde Lewis of Philadelphia. They married the following year. The young bride, reared as a Baptist, blended easily into her husband's Boston household, which included stepchildren, sister-in-law, and father-in-law.

Allen's energy and success at Trinity Church led to an appointment in 1888 to take charge of the Episcopal Church's small and struggling mission in Boston. He converted the mission into a far-reaching welfare agency, and by his guidance and money-raising efforts expanded its program into a wide network of social endeavors. Not until 1914, at the age of seventy-four, did he resign as superintendent.

One Boston organization which gained widespread publicity in the 1920s for its censorship efforts owed its inception to Allen, who

6

called a number of leading citizens together in 1878 to found the New England Watch and Ward Society. Allen remained the organization's guiding spirit throughout his life, first as recording secretary and then as president from 1909 until 1925. After his death, the society's long-time paid secretary, J. Frank Chase, caused a national uproar by effecting bans on a number of prominent literary works.

Allen's concern for humanity seemed boundless. For twenty years he served as president of the Robert Gould Shaw House, a settlement house for Negroes that was named for the popular young Bostonian killed in the Civil War while commanding an all-black company of Union soldiers. On Easter Sundays from 1899 to 1919 Allen visited the Concord Reformatory, where he preached to the convicts in the morning and gave blackboard talks in the afternoons, often illustrated by his own impromptu sketches.

In spare moments the vigorous clergyman was an omnivorous reader of almost everything but fiction. His skills as an artist were of professional quality, and on occasion he held exhibitions and sold paintings to raise money for the City Mission or other worthwhile causes.[8] The mature Allen was a dignified man with white hair, long sideburns, moustache, and pince-nez. His zest for the outdoors remained constant throughout life, and he provided a busy and dedicated pattern of living for his only son.

Through his mother, Alberta Hildegarde Lewis, Frederick Lewis Allen's family history included an unusual episode of the American Revolution. A Hessian soldier who came to America as a British mercenary, Johann Andreas Philipp Ludwig of Crailsheim, duchy of Württemberg, gave the family its name. While serving in America with his unit, Ludwig became seriously ill. A German-American family in Philadelphia named Klingemann took pity on the young officer and nursed him to health. One of the Klingemann daughters, Anna Maria, paid particular attention to the patient, and the two grew to love each other in storybook fashion. Ludwig remained in America after the Revolution, forsaking the promise of a government post and the Ludwig family tradition of public service in Germany.

He married Anna Maria, started a new life in the country he so recently had opposed on the battlefield, Americanized his name to Lewis, and began work as a clerk in the Philadelphia city government.[9]

Johann Lewis' son, John, brought wealth and social status to the family through his spectacular success in the China trade. His Philadelphia company had at one time thirteen ships which sailed to China for tea, silk, and other items to sell in the United States.

John's son and Johann Lewis' grandson, Albert, became a banker and married Anne Cornelia Larcombe. The couple's first daughter, Alberta, married Frederick Baylies Allen.

Alberta and Frederick Allen had two children: Hildegarde was born on July 1, 1885, and Frederick Lewis Allen was born on July 5, 1890, when his father was forty-nine.

Four years before their son arrived, the Allen family had moved into a spacious house in Boston's prestigious Back Bay district. Then in its prime, the Back Bay area was home for authors Oliver Wendell Holmes and William Dean Howells; architects H. H. Richardson and William Morris Hunt; the famous families of Lawrence, Adams, Ames, Forbes, Thayer, and Gardner; and churchman Reverend Phillips Brooks. Back Bay contained the very finest churches and houses, and is said to be "still the handsomest and most consistent example of American architecture of the second half of the nineteenth century now existing in the United States."[10]

The Allen house at 132 Marlborough Street was a large, red-brick structure designed by architect John Farrington and built in 1871. Within the neighborhood's overall grandeur, Bostonians themselves noted fine socioeconomic gradations: the old rich lived on Beacon Street, the old poor on Marlborough, the new rich on Commonwealth, and the new poor on Newbury.[11] Henry James, returning to Boston and the United States in 1904 after a long residence in England, was intrigued by an enigmatic quality reflected by Marlborough Street.[12]

The progress made by Frederick—or "Fritz," as his parents soon nicknamed their blond-haired infant—was recorded in loving detail by his mother in a baby journal.[13] Each childhood illness, the emergence of each baby tooth was recorded. A full-time nurse helped provide Allen's mother the time for the many observations in the journal.

A cultivated family such as the Allens naturally had high hopes for the rapid mental progress of their only son. But Fritz was painfully slow in learning to talk. When he was twenty-five months old his mother apologized in the baby journal for her increasingly infrequent entries: her son's mental progress was "so slow that there does not seem much need of a frequent record." His usual discourse was a "hoarse growl," and Alberta Allen said she often felt compelled to explain to astonished passers-by that "he is not an idiot!" But the child was affectionate, more so than older sister Hildegarde ever had been, and his brown eyes and "big laughing mouth full of very white teeth" made him most endearing. The father sketched loving portraits of his infant son. Soon, the boy's progress also began to please his parents. Two months before his birthday his mother noted that her son's sentences were increasing in length and complexity, and he was able to "express ideas, inferences, as well as facts."

Shortly before Fritz's fourth birthday he became intrigued by his cousin, Greta, and decided to become a girl himself. "Girls have more fun," he explained, and those who referred to him as a boy received a quick correction. He even abandoned his much-loved engines and cars in favor of paper dolls because "girls don't care for engines." Alberta wrote, "We are curious to see how long this fancy will last."

Three months later the child developed a passion for clocks, and by his fourth birthday he could tell time. At five and a half his obsession was calendars, then he turned to maps. His mother observed:

He is rather timid and shy, gentle and very affectionate and does not look strong, although he is sick very little. He is very docile and obedient, and a few clear words of explanation of any command which is displeasing to him always bring from him an Oh! of understanding & acquiescence. He is now five years & five months old.

The despair that Frederick Lewis Allen's father had known during his six years without a permanent job had disappeared by the time

9

Fritz arrived. There were servants in the commodious home on Marlborough Street. When Allen was three his father purchased a fifty-nine-acre summer place at Holderness, New Hampshire, on the southern shore of Squam Lake, and a nine-room cottage was constructed there in 1894.

One summer at Squam Lake, Fritz had the romantic notion that he wanted to spend the night on water. His mother cheerfully bundled cushions and blankets into a rowboat and the two of them spent the moonlit night happily afloat. When Fritz was eight, the family toured Europe for four months, and in 1910 they repeated the experience. Some sketchbooks filled with skillfully executed drawings rendered by young Allen provide a rough itinerary for the 1910 tour: Sardinia, Capri, Rome, Florence, and Innsbruck.[14]

The family frequently visited relatives in Philadelphia. As a twelve-year-old Fritz went with his mother's parents to the Frankford church, which his great-great-great-grandfather helped to found, and heard a "corking" sermon by a Mr. Saird who waved his fists around while preaching. "It was funny to hear him," Fritz wrote to his father. The youngster also enjoyed a Mummers' parade and drew for his father a diagram of the escalator he had seen at Gimbel's store.[15]

The Allen home in Boston rang out with lively discussion and debates despite its rather formal furnishings. Dinner-table conversation followed a rigid formula wherein each family member related his experiences of the day. The senior Allen, who enlivened his talk with humor, served as a constant arbiter, and when one point of view seemed to dominate any discussion he would balance it with an opposite position. "Yes, but on the other hand," was his standard interjection into a hot argument.

The Reverend Mr. Allen stressed physical fitness as well as intellectual nimbleness, and when he learned to play golf at the age of sixty he introduced his eleven-year-old son to the game. For years afterward the two played together when possible, and when apart they corresponded in great detail about their games.

When Frederick was twelve, his parents determined to transfer him from the Volkmann day school to perhaps the most exclusive boys' boarding school in the nation, Groton. Headmaster A. L. V. Volkmann expressed disappointment at losing his charge: "He is a splendid fellow and a bright scholar and he will do well wherever he goes."[16]

2

GROTON AND HARVARD

Groton imprinted an indelible stamp on its students, and it was designed to do so. It was one means by which Boston's social elite perpetuated their aristocratic way of life. Merely to attend Groton marked one as belonging to an elevated station. On the school's board of directors were such notable persons as the Reverend Phillips Brooks; William Lawrence, the Episcopal bishop of Massachusetts; and J. Pierpont Morgan, the great financier. In the years to come Groton's alumni would make a remarkable record in public affairs as well as in financial and cultural circles. Franklin Delano Roosevelt was graduated from the school four years before Allen entered. Kermit Roosevelt, son of the then President, Theodore Roosevelt, was a classmate of Allen's. Allen never escaped, forgot, or forgave the powerful forces Groton exerted upon him as an impressionable boy.

The individual who shaped Groton from its formation in 1884 until his retirement in 1941 was the Reverend Endicott Peabody, named for his ancestor, John Endicott, governor of the Massachusetts Bay Colony during its earliest years. Peabody, known as "the Rector," conceived the school and nurtured its development by the power of his intimidating personality, which had left an indelible impression on students long after their school years. In 1934 in his second year in the Presidency, Franklin D. Roosevelt commented, "As long as I live, the influence of Dr. and Mrs. Peabody means and will mean more to me than that of any other people next to my father and mother."[1] The Reverend Mr. and Mrs. Peabody found time, incredibly, to say good night and to shake hands with every boy in the school before bed each evening.

Allen never overcame his awe of Peabody. Thirty years after he had left Groton and earned a national reputation as a historian and magazine editor, Allen and his wife happened upon the Peabodys in Bermuda. Eager to display proper social amenities, Allen invited them to the home of their close friends and hosts, the William Zuills. As they all sat down for refreshments, a cup of hot tea was passed toward Mrs. Peabody via Allen. Rattled at his close proximity to the Rector and his wife, Allen, in his nervousness, drank down the tea himself in one huge gulp and scorched his mouth severely.[2]

Peabody intended for Groton to emulate the rugged atmosphere of England's best public schools, an idea no doubt springing from his own five years at Cheltenham. The curriculum followed a traditional, classical pattern. During Allen's first year (he entered in 1903 in the second form, or year, rather than the first), his courses and those of his fellow classmates were Latin, English, sacred studies, Greek, mathematics, history, and science.

Throughout his five years at Groton, Allen ranked high academically. His form usually numbered about twenty-five students, and he invariably stood second, third, or fourth, and sometimes first. His letters home, of which there were many, detailed the keen competition he entered into with his classmates for academic honors.

The students lived in Spartan dormitories and developed their own rigid code of ethics and protocol. Newcomers faced a trial period before acceptance. Cass Canfield, who entered Groton several years after Allen, was knocked flat on his back with a blow to the nose merely because he was a new boy.[3] George Biddle, who graduated in 1904, the year after Allen entered, recalled thirty-five years later that offenders of the student "code" would find themselves jerked up by some of the biggest boys and rushed to the lavatories where the hapless, upended student was placed under a spigot. The water was turned on full force directly into the offender's mouth. The effect was very much like drowning, and after a stopwatch had ticked off the required ten seconds the hazers jerked the boy, "coughing, choking, retching," to his feet. Even the Rector's own son suffered "pumping" because his "tone" had been found offensive. Theodore Roosevelt's son Teddy had the ignoble distinction of being pumped twice consecutively merely because older fourth form students elected him as "most typical" of the unpopular second form and thus deserving of the pumping.[4]

Biddle described the foregoing "pumping" practice in *Harper's* when Frederick Lewis Allen was associate editor. Neither man thought highly of the Groton system, unlike so many others who retained such fidelity to the institution that they enrolled their own sons at birth. Biddle, who usually headed his form in scholarship, felt that Groton stifled the creative impulse, inculcated a snobbish instinct, and offered an outdated education that ignored recent developments.

Allen agreed, although he acknowledged the value of the academic discipline. Years later he sometimes commented wryly that students who did not distinguish themselves at Groton had to succeed later in life just to prove to the school that they could. He unfairly included himself in this category despite his excellent record. Somehow, through its rigorous standards the school made many students feel inadequate.

As soon as he arrived at Groton, Allen started playing intramural football (required of all students) and he was placed in the choir. "There has been no hazing at all so far and I don't think there will be. The boys all seem better morally than at Volkmanns, and the teachers are very nice," said Allen in the first of many regular letters home.[5]

Outside speakers often came to Groton, and one morning Fred heard the Rector announce that the Reverend Frederick B. Allen of Boston would preach the next Sunday. Writing his sister Hildegarde about the coming event, Fred added a postscript, "Caution father to remember to call me 'Fred' and not 'Fritz' next Sunday." The following spring another visiting minister made a vivid impression on Fred. "He told about the awful corruption all over the country because men loved money more than honour, and he told how we must stand up against all evil of this kind, especially gambling. It was a splendid sermon."[6]

Other occasional speakers also made a considerable impact on the impressionable students. In the spring of 1905 Jacob Riis, the muckraking New York City journalist, lectured and presented stereopticon views of the tenements. "He's a corker! and he's [an] awfully funny old Duchy—but he's a peach."[7]

President Theodore Roosevelt, who had been asked by Peabody to become a master when he founded the school, visited Groton at least twice, once for the twentieth anniversary in 1904 and again in 1907. Allen, a reporter for the *Weekly Groton* at the time of the 1907 visit, paid close attention to the President's oratorical style and provided his mother a vivid description:

The first thing I noticed was his voice. It is very weak, and when he makes a joke, or gets off some particularly apt word, it rises to a squeaky falsetto. He'd say, I don't want you to be *"NICE BOYS"*—the last two words in a falsetto, with a grin on his face. And all through he had that remarkable tenseness, and terseness—he spoke as though he were so angry to get his words out, at first—snarling, in a sort of nasal way, over each word. I saw he was no orator, but what he said was remarkably good and to the point—his point being that we were to get into the fight. He's wonderful—he said "I entered the National Guard, so that, if there should be some shooting, I wouldn't have to hire anybody to do my shooting for me."[8]

Afterwards, Roosevelt's son Kermit introduced Fred to his father.

Always in his studies Allen sensed his father peering over his shoulder. Chastised once for what his father considered too little attention to reading, Allen fired back a heated letter defending himself and listing what he had read in the past two months: Milton's "L'Allegro," "Il Penseroso," *Comus*, and "Lycidas"; Coleridge's

15

"Rhyme of the Ancient Mariner"; Lowell's "Vision of Sir Launfal"; Addison and Steele's *DeCoverly Papers*; and Morse's life of John Adams. He presently was reading the second volume of a work on Montcalm and Wolfe, Macaulay's essay on Addison, and Irving's life of Goldsmith. "No! I read very little!" he concluded sarcastically. Two weeks later he wrote his mother, "I read Evangeline today, from beginning to end. Isn't it beautiful?" He also reported that two of his stories had a good chance of being published in the *Weekly Groton*.[9]

Allen became a sportswriter for the school paper in the fall of 1906. He could be seen walking along the sidelines at football games, pad and pencil in hand. The following fall he became "athletic editor." By now, however, his passion for sports was being equaled if not surpassed by his interest in literature and writing. His avowed aim was to win the English essay prize, and he did. (Later, he credited a Groton English teacher, Walter S. Hinchman, with inspiring him to be a writer.)[10]

When Allen was sixteen his prose appeared for the first time in a book, *Holderness: An Account of the Beginnings of a New Hampshire Town*, written principally by a friend of Allen's father, George Hodges.[11] Young Allen's contribution consisted of a fifteen-page appendix entitled "Walks and Drives in the Neighborhood of Holderness," in which he gave a minutely detailed and straightforward geographical description of the area. Allen had spent many happy summers at Holderness, and his love of nature was manifest in his accounts of the various peaks, walks, and views in the area. The publisher sent proofs to him at Groton, and Fred asked a former newspaperman in the area to show him proofreading symbols. "I have quite a reputation as an author here now, which is foolish," Allen wrote to his mother.[12]

He also composed poetry. One poem, about the hermit thrush, was published in the school paper over Allen's protest that the "slushy effusions in verse spoil the interest of the paper." Another poem about a thunderstorm was scheduled for the next issue. "Didn't know I was a poet, did you?" he wrote home.[13]

Peabody stressed athletics as an integral part of a young man's education at Groton, and Allen participated not only in football, but in track and field, baseball, in an English game imported by the Rector called "fives," and golf. His eagerness to excel at football resulted in a broken collarbone, and fifteen-year-old Allen described in a letter to his father the procedure which led to his injury:

Wednesday I have to begin tackling the dummy in the gym. . . . Now I weigh less than 95 stripped (about 102 clothed ordinarily) and will thus be the lightest fellow to do it. I probably won't be able to bring down the big stuffed man, which as you probably know, is hung from the ceiling and is so arranged that only a tremendous smash will bring it down. I shall have to dive hard as fury if I hope to phase it. (Don't worry—the floor is covered with mattress.)[14]

Less than two weeks later the Rector sent a succinct note: "My Dear Mr. Allen: In 'tackling the dummy' yesterday Fred fell upon his shoulder, and a fracture of his collarbone resulted. There was no displacement whatever. Endicott Peabody."[15]

Less taxing but also enjoyable for Allen was his participation in the school choir. The choir often sang at events in the area, even at funerals. Allen also became a fervent drummer and believed he possessed a natural talent for the drums. *"Drumming is more sport than almost anything* I know of!" he wrote home.[16]

He performed honorably at debating, although he confessed to his sister that he made an "awful mistake" in one contest. "My hopes, which, however, were very small, were dashed. Just think of it! I said, 'sten teps' instead of 'ten steps.' "[17] The age's concern for reform and Allen's own sense of social responsibility were evident in one debating topic: "Resolved—that the municipal misrule is on account of the indifference of the better class rather than on account of foreign immigration." Allen's team sought to prove that misrule resulted from the indifference of the better class, and Fred wrote home requesting pamphlets, editorials, statistics, and anything else that might bolster his argument.[18]

A year later Allen defended Theodore Roosevelt for discharging three companies of black soldiers for their failure to pinpoint the soldiers guilty of killing a white citizen in Brownsville, Texas. Kermit, the President's son, assisted Allen's team, and even wrote to his father's administration in Washington for information about the affair. Upon winning the debate, Allen wrote home with the odd mixture of glee and modesty that forever characterized him, "Shake your little sonny by the hand—he was supposed (dead secret this) to have made the best speech."[19]

He credited his parents with making him work and thereby avoiding the carelessness and laziness evident in the "very rich boys" who did not know how to study properly. His father's reminders to study were gentle enough, as is indicated by the one Fred received at the beginning of his fourth form year. "I hope this will be a good year, your best yet at Groton. If you are faithful you have the ability to take a high stand in your classes and we hope you will acquit yourself with credit." More frequently, Fred and his father exchanged golf scores.[20]

All Groton students received black marks for misbehavior from time to time. When Fred accidentally spilled his pudding at the dinner table as a second form student, he was punished by being placed at the first form table, "rather a degradation, but . . . not very bad," he concluded. One week he received seven black marks. Three or four marks a week was the usual allowance, and Fred quickly wrote to his father with the details. Four of the marks had come at one stroke for talking, and "it was merely because when Brown gave a crazy little snort of a sneeze, I said, 'Oh, Brown, sneeze out like a man!' "[21]

Perhaps Allen's unfavorable recollections of Groton stemmed from an episode of hazing which he underwent at the hands of a few students during the spring of his fifth form year. His letters to his parents convey the misery he felt, and for the first time he expressed his longing to come home. He yearned to catch the mumps or pinkeye, and he begged his mother to come and visit for as long as possible.[22] For the remainder of that spring a touch of melancholy evidenced itself in his letters, but he never explained the cause of the hazing. The following year he referred once again to the trouble. Mentioning his work in the library with students he did not like, he supposed that there would be "a lot of rough-housing, which I *hate*, and most of it on me." He told his mother he felt the "old feelings" emerging "on a small scale" but that he would attempt to drown them, if possible, with hard work.[23]

This was the time when Allen was becoming more serious in his studies, and beginning to publish material in the school paper, including some poetry. Frank Freidel has commented that intellectual brilliance could be "something less than an asset for a young Grotonian" since it might lead to a conspicuousness that was best avoided at all costs.[24] Given the intense and open competition that Allen entered for top class honors, this statement seems extreme. But, perhaps, in a given circumstance, efforts toward intellectual distinction did create a certain amount of disfavor among the students. Allen's growing interest in writing and his decision not to participate in football because of injuries might represent a source of the troubled relations. Of course, the events could be passed off as a normal part of almost any boy's experience at a boarding school.

Despite Allen's expressed disillusionment with the Groton experience, his letters were largely filled with the happy moods of an increasingly probing youth seeking to explore all avenues of life, from the scholarly to the athletic. His correspondence reveals the development of a superb writing style full of wit and precise detail. Allen also developed the strong work habits that would later serve him well. When the 1908 graduation exercises were held, Allen won top honors in three categories: first prize for reading, the English essay prize, and the award for best work in English. In short, the boy at Groton does not seem at all foreign to the man that Allen became. When he entered Harvard, as so many Groton graduates traditionally did, he was well equipped for the success he enjoyed there.

There never was a *decision* that Fred Allen would enter Harvard; it simply always was understood. His father's love for the college and his keen desire that his son receive the best education, the proximity of Harvard to home and friends, and the well-traveled route there from Groton preordained a Harvard education.

As a Harvard freshman Allen was approaching his full growth

at six feet. Very slender, he had blond, somewhat curly hair and hazel eyes. He acquired a room at Randolph House, a private dormitory which represented a distinct financial and social contrast to the less attractive Harvard-owned housing in the Yard. Allen's third-floor room at Randolph cost three hundred thirty dollars for the term, and the room directly beneath him was taken by the Rector's son, Malcolm Peabody. Allen seemed properly at home in prestigious Randolph by virtue of his family connections and his Groton background, yet he was mindful of the financial burden to his parents. The room cost fifty dollars less than another he had investigated, he noted with pleasure. "I thank God that I'm not making you poor, as you were afraid I was going to by my expensive living at college," he wrote to his mother. "I know you are stinting yourselves somewhat now,—but I mean that my college education will cost you not a cent more, perhaps less. Trust me!"[25]

When Allen stepped into the Yard, Harvard was nearing the culmination of one exciting era under Charles W. Eliot and on the verge of beginning a new one. The changes that Eliot had wrought meant that students like Allen had full freedom in selecting the courses they wished to study.[26] During Eliot's forty-year presidency he had done more than revolutionize the curriculum. He had enabled the university to become a famous center for learning which offered a broad range of graduate as well as undergraduate courses taught by eminent professors.

Eliot had transformed the college curriculum not only at Harvard but throughout the land through his conviction that a young man of eighteen or nineteen knew better than anyone else what he needed for a proper education. As Samuel Eliot Morison observed, Eliot upset an idea that had been constant since the Age of Pericles: that an educated man was one who knew certain things.[27] In November 1908, in Allen's first months as a freshman, Eliot announced his resignation, effective at the end of the school year.

When the Boston-dominated Harvard Corporation elected a new president, they chose a scion of the famous Lowell family, Abbott Lawrence Lowell, a government professor who had become a faculty member in mid-career after a successful law practice. Lowell believed Eliot's elective system was overly permissive. Recent findings indicating a surprising laxness in academic self-discipline already had caused some tightening of the schedule.[28] Now Lowell began plans for a system of "concentration and distribution" of courses. This system required students to choose a major field of study and to concentrate some course work there. Lowell also sought, as William James described it, to make "intellectual prowess a distinction in the undergraduate world of opinion."[29]

As Lowell tightened the curriculum, he also democratized social life at the school. Realizing the schism between the private dormitories and the Yard housing, and seeking at the same time to further convert Harvard into a truly national rather than regional university, he had new dormitories constructed and required all freshmen to live in them.[30]

Change of another kind also pervaded the campus. John Reed, an energetic student of the class of 1910 who would gain distinction as a radical, called it "the manifestation of the modern spirit."

> There was talk of the world, and daring thought, and intellectual insurgency. . . . Students themselves criticized the faculty for not educating them, attacked the sacred institution of intercollegiate athletics, sneered at undergraduate clubs so holy that no one dared mention their names.[31]

The campus ferment was an extension of the national mood: discussions raged on reforming the Congress, corruption in politics, conserving natural resources, muckraking, trust-busting, and tariff inequities. Political organizations and discussion groups such as Walter Lippmann's (also of the class of 1910) Socialist Club sprang up to study and talk about modern social and economic theories. Allen came to know Lippmann, and also Reed, whom he described in 1919 to his mother as "not dependable" and preferring the "picturesque to the veracious." But Allen himself did not become a part of political groups or movements; his interests primarily were literary.[32]

Adding to the excitement of the day was a burst of interest in social activities, particularly dancing, the proliferation of automobiles, and increased amounts of drinking. As Samuel Eliot Morison sums up, "Never was College so exciting, or drunks so drunken, or the generous feelings of ardent youth so exalted, as in those last golden years before World War I."[33]

After his freshman year Allen moved into Hampden Hall, a private dormitory overlooking the Harvard Yard. Here he began a delightful two-year association with a congenial group of suite-mates. Sharing the third-floor set of rooms with Allen were Charles M. Storey, a Bostonian who later became senior partner in the law firm of Peabody, Brown, Rowley & Storey; Philip H. Suter and John W. Suter, Jr., Groton graduates and the children of a Massachusetts Episcopal minister; Norman Sturgis, also a Groton alumnus whose father was president of Colorado College; and Robert H. Bolling and Henry Knox Hardon, both from New York. The suite's living room, equipped with a fireplace and piano, served as the focal point for the group's spirited conversations and singing. Freddie, as Allen came to be known now, taught himself to play the piano, and he provided accompaniment for singing sessions.[34]

Off-campus the students enjoyed the operettas and operas performed frequently in the area. Such entertainment was surprisingly cheap. As Charles M. Storey recalls, "You could take the trolley to Boston, dine at Louis with cocktails and Asti Spumanti, take in a show with drinks between the acts and still have enough for breakfast left out of a $5 bill." Allen himself was careful to drink in moderation. He desisted the moment he began to feel the liquor's effect, explaining that he had had an uncle who died from overconsumption. Storey determined to get Freddie drunk at least once as a matter of education, but he never succeeded.[35]

Allen and his friends participated extensively in the social life of Cambridge and Boston, attending dances during winter months as often as once a week. In the spring and fall, weekend house parties included many female friends, but relationships were strictly proper; even kissing was deemed inappropriate.

All the young men had about the same amount of money to spend.

Storey perhaps had slightly more than the others; his father allowed him twelve hundred dollars to pay for everything during the nine-month academic year.[36]

At the end of his sophomore year Allen won a position on the *Lampoon*. As a result, he became intimate friends with an extraordinary set of writers and artists, particularly humorist Robert C. Benchley.[37] Besides Benchley, staff members included cartoonist Gluyas Williams, Bob Hallowell, and John Reed. Allen eventually followed Williams, who had succeeded Reed, as ibis of the *Lampoon*.[38] "That kind of writing was contagious," Allen later reflected about the *Lampoon* style.[39] It also was highly beneficial, for Allen learned techniques that catapulted him directly from campus humor to national magazines.

Benchley was even then an irrepressible wit. On one occasion some of the *Lampoon* crowd, including Allen, were about to board a trolley car when Benchley proposed that he feign serious injury. Pretending that Benchley had a broken leg, the group gingerly carried him onto the trolley and provided consolation while he winced and gasped in mock pain. Passengers crowded around solicitously, offering to help. Finally, at their destination, the youths solemnly carried Benchley off and exploded in laughter as the trolley departed.[40]

Another time Benchley suggested that a number of students inspect a major construction site at Harvard Square, and when the others expressed doubt at being admitted, Benchley assured them that he would take care of everything. Just before they reached the site he scribbled something on a piece of paper. Benchley showed it to the guard, who waved the youths through at once. Inside, Allen asked Benchley what he had written on the paper, and Benchley proudly displayed the message: "Please pass these nice boys." He had signed it with the name of a prominent local politician.[41]

Besides working on the *Lampoon*, Allen was an editor of the Harvard *Advocate*, a monthly publication designed for more serious writing. He also published eight short stories, three poems, a review, and an essay in the *Advocate*.[42]

As he plunged more deeply into extracurricular literary activities

23

and squeezed his curriculum into three rather than four years, Allen's grades dropped. As a freshman he made As and Bs. During his final year of study he made all Cs. He took only one course in history and acknowledged later that he "had no taste for it." While he completed all his undergraduate requirements for a degree in English in three years, Allen's A.B. was not awarded until 1912 with the rest of his class.[43]

His teachers included some of Harvard's most famous professors: Bliss Perry, who taught the English novel, and philosophy professors George Santayana, Hugo Münsterberg, and Ralph Barton Perry. Another professor, Charles T. Copeland, attracted a devoted undergraduate following through his English composition classes. "Copey," as he was known, carried on his instruction outside the classroom as much as inside it. For almost forty years he kept open house every Wednesday evening to discuss with his students a broad range of subjects. In Copeland's class with Allen were Walter Lippmann and John Reed. In another English section Allen's classmates included Benchley, Conrad Aiken, and Harold Stearns.[44]

After two years in Hampden Hall the happy circle of suite-mates largely went separate ways. Allen and Storey stayed together and moved to the top floor rear of Thayer Hall in the Harvard Yard. Storey was impressed with his roommate's facility with words. One night before a test in Perry's English novel class, Storey hurriedly lectured Allen on the assigned book, Hardy's *The Return of the Native*. The next day Allen, who had not read the novel, earned an A on the exam. Storey got a B.[45]

During what normally would have been his senior year, Allen gained admittance as a graduate English student in the Modern Languages Division and began work on a master's degree. Although he was ibis on the *Lampoon* and involved in other writing activities as well, by the end of the year he completed the requirements for the degree. He did not receive his A.M., however, until the following year, 1913. As a graduate student Allen's transcript showed six As and one B+.[46]

While his grades may not have been especially distinguished as an undergraduate, Allen did complete the requirements in three years and gained extracurricular distinction as well. In 1912 his poem "Tripoli" won for him the Lloyd McKim Garrison Prize of one hundred dollars and a silver medal.[47] That same year he provided the lyrics for a two-act musical comedy, *Below Zero*.

Despite his active social life and his Groton background, Allen did not become a member of the blue-blooded Porcellian Club, the ultimate in Harvard society, or even the other so-called final clubs reserved for the elite few. None of his Hampden Hall friends made a final club either. "The threshold was out of our reach," Storey recalls. "Naturally he [Allen] would have liked to have been asked and undoubtedly would have accepted, but it was a dream so far as he was concerned."[48] Allen was elected, however, to the Institute of 1770, the basic society from which smaller clubs chose their members, and this indicated that he was at least "in society," according to Cleveland Amory's definition.[49] He also became a member of the Hasty Pudding Club, which took only a small number from each class. (A fellow member in the Hasty Pudding Club was another Boston youth of the class of 1912, Joseph P. Kennedy, somewhat of an outsider at the still socially-conscious Harvard because of his Irish ancestry.)

When he received his undergraduate degree Allen still had not been certain what he wanted to do. Three possibilities seemed potentially rewarding: teaching, editing, and writing. Being an educator seemed more immediately realizable, and he secured a position teaching freshman composition and assisting Bliss Perry in his comparative literature course.

As a teacher of composition Allen was a stern stylistic disciplinarian. He slashed out ruthlessly all traces of verbosity and floweriness from the writing styles of his students, aiming for simple words and short sentences. Years later one student recalled that Allen reproved him by pointing out that his writing style was "pedantic, lugubrious, uninspiring, verbose, [and] long-winded." To cure the problem Allen assigned the student a book entitled *The Man Who Was Good*, written entirely in one-syllable words and sentences of no more than four or five words. "The shock was almost more than I could stand but I think it did somewhat improve my own use of the English language." Allen was not generous when grading papers: final grade reports for three of his classes with a total enrollment of eighty-five reveal only four As.[50]

Meanwhile, as he taught by day Allen wrote by night and thought more and more of a career in either writing or editing.

3

THE MAGAZINE APPRENTICESHIP

Perhaps the problem of choosing a career was already solved, for Allen realized that he might combine writing and editing. He had been well prepared to take advantage of any opportunity: he had a disciplined mind, sound work habits, healthy family ties, and a well-developed moral sense. There was no youthful rebellion in him, nor had there ever been. He was a serious youth, though his stock-in-trade as a writer was humor. No backslapping life-of-the-party, he exhibited instead a more incisive, dry wit. He was a polished writer, though he had undertaken no serious subjects.

It was understandable that the magazine industry should attract a literary-minded young man such as Allen, for magazines still rode high on the crest of a spectacular burst of energy. The revolution that created the modern magazine had begun late in the nineteenth century, especially in 1892 and 1893 when editors S. S. McClure and Frank A. Munsey dramatically dropped the prices of their magazines to fifteen cents and ten cents respectively and began appealing to a large new audience. So successful was the formula that other editors soon followed, realizing that profits would come from the high volume of advertising which a large circulation attracted. A magazine priced for the masses was necessarily timely, newsworthy, and a closer reflection of modern life itself—in effect, it competed with the newspapers for audiences.[1]

The growth of industry, the development of national marketing techniques requiring national advertising, and technological improvements within the printing industry provided the vehicle for the revolutionary changes in the magazine industry. Meanwhile, a much greater audience for magazines was being created because of the increased enrollment in public high schools and state universities and because of the lyceum movement, added leisure, and economic improvements which permitted a large segment of the middle class to pursue knowledge for its own sake.[2]

It is not difficult to imagine the stresses this new era thrust upon more genteel "literary" publications such as *Harper's*, *Scribner's*, and the *Century*. They struggled painfully to maintain their positions in this fierce new publishing scene, and those that failed to adapt died.

The urbane and striking Frank Crowninshield, an editor on one of those "literary" magazines, the *Century*, detected in the *Lampoon* Allen's talent for humor. He thought he saw a prospective contributor to the *Century's* popular humor column, "In a Lighter Vein," and he invited the Harvard teaching assistant to come to New York City for talk at the *Century* office. Allen responded readily, bringing with him six manuscripts.[3]

The young writer did not disappoint Crowninshield when he stood before him in person, and the New York editor determined to help him. Crowninshield selected the two best manuscripts and returned later the other four by mail with a flattering note, "If anybody can make a career out of humor, you ought to."[4] Crowninshield inexplicably forwarded one of the manuscripts to his friend Thomas L. Masson, editor of the humor magazine *Life*. Masson agreed that Allen might be a "find," and he asked Crowninshield to tell the twenty-two-year-old aspiring writer-editor to send him "everything he writes, good & bad." He advised that Allen should "let himself loose," and believed that a regular magazine job at this stage would be the worst thing for his writing ambitions. He hoped Allen was poor so the need for money would spur him into writing more.[5]

Crowninshield forwarded Masson's letter to Allen, commenting, "Praise from him is worth having."[6] The exchange of letters which ensued between the fledgling and Crowninshield reached a crescendo in the next few years as Allen developed as a *Century* contributor. Crowninshield showed no restraint in praising his protégé's abilities.

One of the most intriguing editors and characters in American magazine history, Crowninshield was the son of an American expatriate painter. He already had been associated with the *Bookman*, *Metropolitan*, and *Munsey's* magazines. Eventually, as long-time editor of *Vanity Fair* Crowninshield brought a sophisticated touch that not only reflected but pioneered the culture of the magazine's 1914–1936 heyday.

During his lifetime Crowninshield befriended such disparate individuals as William Dean Howells and Tallulah Bankhead; he was an organizer of the famous 1913 New York Armory art show; in 1929 he helped to found New York's Museum of Modern Art; he pioneered in presenting in *Vanity Fair* and thus in popularizing in America the art of Picasso, Van Gogh, Gauguin, Braque, and Modigliani; he relished the offbeat, the absurd, and the outrageous; he gained fame for his celebrated and pungent tongue; and despite his feel for the avant-garde, Crowninshield possessed an air of having sprung from a previous age. Clare Boothe once described Crowninshield, who sometimes could be seen on Broadway in opera hat and cape, as having an odd combination of Rabelaisean wit and Victorian language.[7] One brief example of Crowninshield's particular flair may be seen in a note he once sent the young Tallulah Bankhead: "You have been the unseen sugar in my very dark coffee; the little threads of red that run through the dull gray pattern of a Persian rug, the figure of Pierrot amid a company of tragic muses."[8]

There is no trace of Crowninshield's striking personality and wit in his correspondence with Allen; in fact, he displays the image of a rather ordinary editor eager to please a talented young writer from Harvard. Crowninshield agreed with his friend Masson that Allen

29

should resist his urge to gain immediate employment on a magazine, and advised him to "strive hard to be an author. Write a lot of stuff. . . ." Then, Crowninshield said, Allen would be in a position to "make some editorial arrangement with one of the magazines you have been writing for."[9]

Before Crowninshield got around to printing Allen's sketches in the *Century*, the young writer placed three unsigned articles in London's *Punch* between March and July of 1913.[10] The first, "Forced Cards," dealt with the frustrations of an individual who could not master card games. (It was a familiar subject for Allen— he never mastered cards despite his life-long penchant for games.) In the second piece, "The Optimist," he described a young man's fears of going to the dentist and he proposed that the "heroism of the dentist chair" be substituted for the heroism of the battlefield. "The Creative Gift" parodied a playwright's advice that characters be created who would work out their own salvations.

Crowninshield shortly published one of the manuscripts Allen had left in his office on his first visit. "Going Up: Or, the Peril of Exposure After Bathing," which appeared in the "In a Lighter Vein" humor column, followed a formula that Allen often would capitalize on: an innocent and naïve individual caught haplessly in an awkward social situation. In "Going Up" a very proper professor, having entered his summer cottage in a wet bathing suit, sought to hide in the dumbwaiter from some haughty and unexpected guests, only to be hauled up accidentally into full view.[11] The effort earned fifteen dollars for Allen, and Crowninshield reminded him to "please remember that we want to see *everything* [he underscored the word three times] that you do." Shortly thereafter Crowninshield was conscience-stricken by the paucity of the fifteen dollars, apologized for it and promised to make it up in later fees.[12]

Two other sketches followed quickly. "Sleeping Outdoors" described a city-bred man's insomnia during a visit to the summer place of friends because he couldn't control the mosquito netting around his bunk. "A Night of the Bath" concerned a guest who mistakenly entered the wrong house during a summer visit. True to his word, Crowninshield increased Allen's payment for this sketch to fifty dollars.[13] It was easy money for Allen; he had written the article in 1911 as an undergraduate for the Harvard *Advocate*.[14]

Allen by no means intended to limit himself to a career in humor. He offered a short story to Crowninshield, only to receive a scolding. "Tack this up in your mind: What people are wanting and reading and buying is a story. They are not buying style or scenery or dialogue or rambles or preambles. They are buying the *story*."[15]

Probably this advice was aimed at Allen's story, "Who Shall Ascend into the Hill of the Lord?" If Crowninshield thought the plot too weak, the Boston editor of the *Atlantic Monthly*, Ellery Sedgwick, liked it and bought it.[16] The story was set on the observation platform on the Jungfrau peak high in the Alps, easily accessible by a newly constructed cog railroad, and it involved a debate between an English clergyman, proud of his mountain-climbing abilities, and an American tourist. The clergyman was contemptuous of the desecration of the beautiful scene by unappreciative tourists. The American visitor, who had an awkward limp, defended the railway. A few years earlier, while attempting to climb that very peak to gain the dramatic view now before them, he had fallen, fracturing his hip. Crippled by the accident, he had waited three years for the cog railroad's completion so that at last he could reach the pinnacle.[17]

Slight as the story was, as soon as it appeared a woman in Switzerland sought permission to translate it into German for European publication. The flattered Allen assented, of course, and the translated version appeared in a Sunday supplement, *Basler Nachicten*, the following spring.[18]

Meanwhile, Allen chafed to begin his double career as editor and writer. Bolstered by his *Atlantic* story and mindful of Crowninshield's advice that he should establish a reputation before seeking an editorial position, he decided that the appropriate moment had come. The school term soon would end, and Allen longed to escape his freshman English classes. He called on Sedgwick at the *Atlantic* offices in Boston to inquire about a job. None was available. Within days, however, circumstances changed at the magazine, and Sedgwick optimistically mentioned a "remote possibility" which had arisen; he would like to discuss it with Allen in person.[19]

Allen also had repeated to Crowninshield his hope for a magazine position. Crowninshield assured him that if he would come to New York he would help him. "I wish to goodness I were starting a magazine of my own," Crowninshield wrote, "and you would be the assistant editor."[20] Within the month Crowninshield was to be granted his wish. Condé Nast had asked him what he thought of his new publication, *Dress and Vanity Fair*. Crowninshield had observed that there was "no magazine which covers the things people talk about at parties—the arts, sports, humor, and so forth."[21] Nast hired Crowninshield to take over his magazine and to remedy that void, and just as he had promised, Crowninshield sought Allen as his assistant editor.

He needed him right away: he was to assume command of *Vanity Fair* (as it was renamed) in January. Allen, however, had teaching commitments until June, and there remained the *Atlantic* possibility. Crowninshield offered Allen twenty-five dollars a week and assured him that he could supplement his income by writing articles for *Vanity Fair* and other magazines, but Allen resisted.[22]

He cast aside *Vanity Fair* when Sedgwick's "remote possibility" at the *Atlantic* materialized into a February offer to become an assistant editor at the conclusion of the school year. He accepted the twenty-dollar-a-week offer, although it was less than Crowninshield promised. The *Atlantic* offered prestige and none of the risk involved with a new publication; it meant Allen could remain in Boston, where he still lived with his parents. Sedgwick maintained a measure of reserve: "You will have a fair opportunity . . . and if you learn to make yourself really useful, your value will in due course be recognized."[23]

Allen's decision was "frightfully disappointing" to Crowninshield. "I long to see you & talk it over," Crowninshield wrote. "Still, I accept your version as probably best for you." He warned Allen against growing too serious on the *Atlantic* and losing "that wonderful gift of humor of yours."[24] Allen kept writing for Crowninshield and soon earned fifty-five dollars for a piece on opera-going.[25]

As the school year ended, Douglas Z. Doty, editor of the *Century*, told Allen that his publishing company had a "keen desire" for him to write a humorous book—perhaps an expanded version of his "A Night of the Bath," which, Doty believed, "surely [is] one of the funniest things that ever appeared in a magazine." The offer undoubtedly appealed to Allen, but closing out his academic duties and preparing for a new job left little time. Doty did not forget, however. Ten months later he reminded Allen of the request, this time suggesting a collection of humorous stories.[26]

The *Atlantic Monthly* which Allen joined in August 1914, despite its prestigious background under Lowell, Fields, Howells, and other literary lights, now bore the unmistakable stamp of Ellery Sedgwick, owner and editor. The magazine had been operating under the wing of the Houghton Mifflin Company when Sedgwick purchased it in 1908 for fifty thousand dollars. Under the publishing company the once-robust magazine had dwindled in circulation to an anemic 25,000 and had an annual deficit of five thousand dollars.[27] Slowly and surely Sedgwick revived it. He was convinced that the *Atlantic* had been too "dilettantish"; it devoted excessive attention to literature and art and not enough to the affairs of life itself. Now Sedgwick sought essays that dealt intelligently and provocatively with problems of the day. He turned to scientists, professors, professionals, and experts who could write with authority on pertinent issues. Twenty years after assuming the editorship, Sedgwick had increased the circulation from 25,000 to 137,000 and had reclaimed a status the magazine continues to enjoy today. In doing so he also provided a new formula for quality magazines to survive the competition of the more popular periodicals.

Sedgwick was a "strong" editor, and Allen studied him with admiration. A vigorous man in his mid-forties, Sedgwick believed that a magazine "must be dominated by one man, a man of multifarious interests, bubbling over with ideas," and of course Sedgwick considered himself that man.[28] Years later Allen recalled:

The principal thing I got from Sedgwick was the idea that you didn't basically imagine the reading public and try to give them what they would want. You edit to please *yourself*, making allowances for your own eccentricities, and then you are likely to interest other people. He applied that on a very personal basis.[29]

33

Sedgwick also taught him that an editor cannot rely solely on free-lance material that comes unannounced to the office, important though it may be. An editor also must choose certain topics and then find authors to write about them.

"Sedgwick was very strong for human interest," Allen said. "If he found a good writer who was deaf and wanted to write on some political subject, he might say, 'That's fine—but I wish you would write on what it's like to be deaf—and how to deal with deaf people.' A demon on that sort of thing."[30] Sedgwick was a Groton alumnus who also had gone on to Harvard, and the *Atlantic* undoubtedly was a comfortable and rewarding place to Allen.

While he edited manuscripts by day, he wrote his own at night, and the demands Allen made upon himself soon surfaced physiologically. One evening after a day's work at the office he settled down to write and found his right hand mysteriously useless, a frightening situation that continued for weeks. He desperately resorted to scribbling with his left hand, but with awful results. In May 1915, he went to a Boston physician, Dr. Douglas Graham, for help. Graham began a program of therapeutic massaging which gradually released the young editor from his nightly agonies and in two months cured him. Although the ordeal seemed very serious at the time, for years afterward Allen laughed with his family and friends about his strange illness; he particularly enjoyed the doctor's published report of Allen's job as entailing "long periods of writing, pausing at times to think."[31] Allen continued throughout his life to edit by day and write by night, but the symptoms never returned.

As might be expected, the Crowninshield-Allen paths diverged. When Allen submitted a humorous sketch on dancing and photography to *Vanity Fair*, Crowninshield offered fifty-five dollars for it, but wanted to reduce it to seventeen hundred words. "Like a link of sausage," he advised, "it could have a few links removed from it without your knowing the difference, unless you happened to be the author of it." Allen looked at Crowninshield's edited version and declared it unsatisfactory. "It seems to fall quite flat," he said, and consequently he decided that "it can't be materially cut." He instructed Crowninshield to print the original version with only "slight alterations" or to return it so he could publish it elsewhere.[32] The article, "Terpsichore: The Present Rage for Rhythmic Dancing and Blurred Art," appeared in the March 1915 edition of *Vanity Fair*.[33] It was twenty-three hundred words long, Allen's specified length. He had declared his literary independence.

Allen accepted his secondary role under Sedgwick with equanimity, viewing it as a valuable training period under a master craftsman. All apprenticeships must end, however, and as Allen performed the normal editing duties of revising manuscripts, corresponding with authors, laying out pages, and proofreading he surely began to feel restricted under the vigorous Sedgwick.

Furthermore, while the *Atlantic* remained proudly in Boston, it remained there almost alone. More than twenty years had passed since William Dean Howells, now writing the "Editor's Easy Chair" column for *Harper's*, had forsaken Boston for New York and, as often was said, singlehandedly transferred with him the nation's literary center. Allen was eager to make the same two-hundred-mile trip to Manhattan Island.

The *Century* needed a managing editor, and in December 1915 editor Douglas Doty offered Allen, now twenty-five, the position at fifty dollars a week.[34] The magazine had outshone the *Atlantic* for many years, but now was struggling to maintain a satisfactory format, and Allen saw a challenge. He accepted the offer; as managing editor there should be greater opportunity to initiate his own ideas. Allen tendered his resignation to the understanding Sedgwick, said goodbye to his parents, friends, and lifelong home, and moved to New York to join the throng of talented artists and writers who were seeking an artistic and literary mecca.

The *Century* could boast of its noteworthy past largely because of Richard Watson Gilder. Gilder had become editor in 1881 when the publication's name was changed from *Scribner's* (not to be confused with the *Scribner's* of later years) to the *Century*. Until his death twenty-eight years later in 1909, Gilder had made the magazine a giant in prestige and advertising, prospering even amidst the onslaught of ten-cent magazines. The publication of Civil War memoirs in the magazine and in Century books had brought popularity and more than a million dollars in profit.[35] But Gilder's death in 1909 left the magazine leaderless, and during the next twelve years the editorship passed in desperation to five different hands.

Allen's chief function was to serve as right-hand man to one of those editors, Doty, who was editor from 1915 to 1917. The Century Company had decided to emulate the *Atlantic* and switch to a less literary and more journalistic format, and Allen, having served under the master of this genre, seemed an ideal candidate for managing editor.

Doty evidently was miscast as editor despite good credentials. He was a Columbia University graduate (1897) and a former newspaperman, and he had been active on Broadway as a dramatist and producer. He was a genial if not especially talented editor, and Allen described him to his father to be "as much friendlier than E.S. [Ellery Sedgwick] as he is less able editorially." Allen was gratified at Doty's readiness to accept his ideas. There were more responsibilities in the position than he had expected, a pleasing development. "The only hitch is that the make-up, covers, etc., are all in the hands of a touchy art editor with whom I cannot monkey."[36] Like his father, Allen was a skilled amateur artist, and he relished the idea of planning the magazine's art.

Allen's functions at the *Century* were basically those he had performed at the *Atlantic*, but he had greater final authority. He was the "executive officer" charged with coordinating all departmental work; he was responsible for seeing that deadlines were met; he was the magazine's point of contact in dealing with the printer, artists, and casual callers; and he was Doty's chief helpmate in editorial duties.[37] He worked in a large room with three or four others, had his own stenographer, and told his father that he wrote "lots of letters on one thing or another."[38]

The young editor lived about a mile from the office in a rooming house on Fifth Avenue with Richard Connell (who later wrote a famous short story, "The Most Dangerous Game in the World").

Concerned about the possibility of burglars, the two conceived and rehearsed a speech designed to win the sympathy of any larcenous intruder. "Young man," it went, "we are but two poor people here." One late evening Connell lost his key and scrambled up the fire escape so he wouldn't bother his roommate. Allen awoke to see a darkened form climbing through the window. He sat up in bed, sleepy and terrified, but possessed of enough wit to begin the rehearsed speech. At least he *thought* he was making the speech. He was so scared that his carefully prepared address was completely unintelligible. Connell, as frightened by this apparition as Allen, finally managed to say, "It's only me, Freddie."[39]

During Allen's tenure as managing editor, there appeared to be little change in the *Century*. The magazine continued to publish ample amounts of light verse and short stories. Some of the fiction was distinguished, but the nonfiction included a large sampling of rather vacuous articles. In keeping with the earlier decision to tie the *Century* more closely to current events, there were numerous articles about the war. The *Century* even stationed in Europe its own writer-illustrator, Walter Hale, to follow the Allied forces. The magazine's generous use of photographs and art work was one of its particular distinctions. During Allen's one and a half years at the magazine, some of the nation's best novelists appeared in its pages, including Theodore Dreiser, Willa Cather, and William Dean Howells.

Doty helped to alleviate Allen's loneliness in New York by joining him for lunch and occasionally having him to his apartment. There also were connections at the Harvard Club for Allen, and he made a point of getting to know and lunching with other young journalists and writers.[40]

Six months after his arrival in New York, Allen had become well enough known to be invited to join a new club for writers and artists, the Coffee House. "I think I'm very lucky," Allen told his father. Membership was limited to less than two hundred, and some notable members included George Arliss, Frank Crowninshield, Finley Peter Dunne, Charles Dana Gibson, Fritz Kreisler, John

Quinn, and Arthur Woods. Allen remained cautious about pushing himself onto the company of such individuals—even after he had paid his ten-dollar initiation fee and annual dues of twenty-five dollars, he still waited for someone to invite him before venturing there.[41] Soon his shyness wore off, and for years he remained particularly proud of his association with the Coffee House and came to play a significant role in its affairs.

This period in Allen's life included at least one serious courtship. In 1914 at a dance in Andover, Massachusetts, he met Marion Cleveland, a Columbia Teachers College student and daughter of the former president, Grover Cleveland. The two immediately found that they enjoyed many of the same things. Allen presented Marion with a book of Victorian verse, they read poetry together, and they frequently went out to dinner and the theater. In 1917 Allen proposed marriage, but there was another man in Miss Cleveland's life, her future husband. She rejected Allen amicably.[42]

Allen continued to write for the *Century* as well as to help edit it, and at least two casual humor pieces indicate his cynicism toward business mores, an attitude which became one of the dominant themes of the intellectual revolt of the 1920s. In a sketch entitled "Small Talk," he portrayed a Wall Street importer as a pompous individual whose hauteur was so intimidating that Allen felt witless to make even small conversation with him while on a chance stroll downtown. In a free verse poem, "Ode to Professor James Harvey Robinson," he satirized men who go to college to make advantageous business contacts instead of to learn.[43]

Allen's seriousness about his own business, magazines, was revealed in a lengthy letter he wrote to the *New Republic*. He argued that magazines, no less than books and plays, merited regular criticism. He complained that "it has not been the custom to take American periodical literature seriously." He urged the critical journals to undertake assessments of magazines as part of their function and duty. "The magazines command an enormous audience. They have great potential power. They are capable of development which shall make them characteristic of the best things in American life."[44]

38

At this time, President Woodrow Wilson was growing increasingly alarmed over events in Europe, especially Germany's unrestricted submarine warfare. On April 2, 1917, he went before Congress and obtained the war declaration that, after long agonizing, he felt to be vital. Until now Allen's attention had been directed only tangentially toward the foreign situation. The occasional *Century* articles about the war treated it as a foreign concern remote from the interests of the United States. But Wilson's idealistic call to arms stirred not only Congress but Allen's own sense of responsibility to his country. He turned to his former employer, Sedgwick, for advice. Should he volunteer for government service or should he remain at the *Century?*

Sedgwick refused to recommend any course of action save one: deliberation. "One thing I feel very sure of, and that is that it is idle to attempt to move quickly," he counseled. Furthermore, if Allen would only wait the dilemma likely would be solved for him. Sedgwick, who in the *Atlantic* had urged early U.S. entry into the war, predicted "sweeping regulations" that would "save many of us the trouble of thinking." He pointed out the obvious fact that if Allen chose government service he would be most helpful as a publicist. But Sedgwick himself did not care to volunteer his services "just at present." He apologized for such a "lame letter," but added that "I believe we shall all see so much more clearly ten days from now."[45]

But Allen was eager, and within three weeks of Wilson's war message he wrote for the *Nation* his first serious essay, "The American Tradition and the War."[46] Democratic America did not possess a nature that easily adapted to war, Allen wrote. "We are undisciplined, careless of law, too ready to disrespect authority and upset orders." He wholeheartedly agreed with Wilson's stated reasons for going to war, however, and he predicted that the lackadaisical American way of life would give way to efficiency, organization, planning, and discipline. "Socialism will take tremendous strides forward," and inevitably the "drill sergeant" would wield authority. The danger, Allen advised, was that the nation might forget its free and open heritage. "It would be an evil day for America if we threw overboard liberty to make room for efficiency."

America's traditional tolerance would be needed in the months to come, he believed. Allen, as did President Wilson, envisioned awful results from the emotionalism to be engendered by battle.

Hatred will spring up quickly when American blood has been shed. . . . Sensationalism will spread the German spy scare. . . . Reprisals against loyal Americans of German birth will be advocated, and, one fears, frequently affected. . . . If there is a censorship, it will be stupidly managed, and to its aid in making people bigoted will come the censorship of fear: newspapers and magazines dare not advocate the unpopular cause at a time when passions run high.[47]

Finally, following Wilson's admonitions, Allen warned against the temptation of sharing in the spoils of victory. He urged that the nation make up its mind at this early stage to seek no territorial gain or indemnity.

The article reflected fairness, moderation, and liberality. While correctly predicting the inevitable internal dangers war would bring, Allen chose optimistically to believe that emotionalism and authoritarianism could be contained. He eventually saw reason to fear that he was wrong.

4

WARTIME PUBLICIST

Sedgwick's prediction that a short delay should give Allen his answer as to how to satisfy his patriotic impulses proved valid. Boston, accustomed since the Revolution to leading public opinion in times of war, determined to do so in this conflict, too. Early in May Boston's Committee on Public Safety, chaired by retired Admiral Francis Tiffany Bowles, called together area writers and editors to discuss mobilizing the literary forces of New England to further the war effort through their writing talents.[1] Those present took the name of the Writers' Committee for Patriotic Service, and they charged Sedgwick with finding a good man to direct their press bureau.

Sedgwick wanted Allen, and he wired his former assistant that the position needed a man of his "capacity and experience." The salary was two thousand dollars a year, six hundred dollars less than the *Century* paid, but Allen immediately accepted the offer and submitted his letter of resignation to the magazine.[2]

"We Are All Publicists Now," headlined the *Nation* that year.[3] The word "publicist" had become so widespread and popular that the magazine protested the term was losing all meaning. Being a publicist might have seemed by 1917 the most modern and wisest thing to do, but it was not really a new practice. Boston's own Sam Adams, through the famous committees of correspondence, had been a notable pioneer in the endeavor of shaping public opinion toward revolt against the British; Andrew Jackson's "kitchen cabinet," composed mostly of former newspapermen, had functioned primarily as a public relations brain trust; and Phineas T. Barnum had developed a flamboyant style of press agentry later in the nineteenth century. Not until the turn of the century, however, did anything resembling the modern publicity practice begin when Ivy Lee started his pioneering career. The muckraking period generated a broad publicity effort by railroads, public utilities, and other large corporations to influence mass opinion in their behalf. The rapid spread of publicity practice through all segments of society made it seem quite natural for Allen to drop so suddenly his cherished career in magazines for such a position.[4]

Allen's task as director of the press bureau was to secure articles and verse, preferably on specific subjects of timely importance, and to submit them to newspapers and magazines for publication. The material, it was hoped, would "lay before the people of New England . . . the information and expert advice which will arouse and direct their patriotism and help them to serve their country usefully."[5] The committee encouraged articles which would show need for effective action in such areas as shipbuilding, labor, economical food consumption, and the general economy.

Despite high intentions, illustrious backers, and the initial ballyhoo and enthusiasm, the project failed to match expectations. First, there was the awkward situation of spending Boston tax money for a regional, even national publicity effort, and Allen found this a growing embarrassment.[6] Also, the expected contributions from writers rarely materialized, and the 336 newspapers on the mailing list seldom used the submitted articles. Allen himself suffered criticism from the *Christian Science Monitor* for impropriety because a release suggested that if prohibition measures were omitted from an important food bill it might win immediate passage in Congress. Allen also risked censure in a lengthy release signed by himself (as a letter to the editor) which virtually equated excessive criticism of the government with "giving aid and comfort to the enemy."[7]

Allen stayed on the job less than two months. Dissatisfactions about the entire effort culminated when Admiral Bowles requested ten thousand dollars from the city council to supplement the Committee on Public Safety's seventy-thousand-dollar budget. The economy-minded council demanded an itemized account of expenditures to date. Bowles complied, and won the hearty commendation of Mayor James M. Curley, but the submitted material included the resignation of Frederick L. Allen. In a report to the Writers' War Committee Allen had said, "It is my conviction that our work is now on a hopeless basis."[8] As a result of Allen's complete pessimism, the committee voted unanimously to disband. The action was important news, and Allen gave inquisitive reporters frank appraisals as to why he thought the publicity effort had failed.[9]

Before resigning Allen had gone to the nation's capital to inquire into a proposed merger of the Boston's writers' committee with other similar organizations for a national effort under federal direction. The idea had been conceived by the Council of National Defense to supplement George Creel's newly formed Committee on Public Information, which despite its eventual success in influencing public opinion, already was the target of many critics. Several factors indicated to the administration a need for a second major publicity undertaking in Washington, and Allen summarized them for the Writers' War Committee: Creel had no system for enlisting local organizations in his Committee work and thus lacked the means for intimate contact with the people; his publicity program was handicapped by the fact that it was strictly official and that the government was responsible for every word; Creel was "not a big enough man" to handle the vast administrative duties; and, finally, Creel already was discredited by "recent blunders" and the newspapers were prepared "to make him a scapegoat for censorship."[10] Another reason, perhaps unrealized by Allen, was that the spontaneous mobilization of organizations such as his own in Boston pressured the federal government to take action of its own lest the tail seem to be wagging the dog.[11] The Council decided to form an umbrella organization which would coordinate, assist, and advise efforts of state and local agencies.

The first person to assume the mammoth burden of such a far-flung endeavor had resigned abruptly in August, and the head of the Council's Section on Cooperation with States, George F. Porter, turned to the man he had met from Boston. Allen hurriedly traveled to the capital upon Porter's call and accepted at once the offer to fill the vacated position. The kind recommendation which Ellery Sedgwick mailed to Porter arrived after Allen was at his new desk.[12]

The Council of National Defense had been organized in 1916 when the possibility of American involvement in the war could not be ignored. Originally, it had consisted of the Secretaries of War, Navy, Commerce, Agriculture, Labor, and Interior, but soon President Wilson named seven prominent citizens to an Advisory Commission. This commission became the chief executive branch for the Council. Among its members were financier Bernard Baruch, soon to emerge as head of the powerful offspring of the Council, the War Industries Board; Samuel Gompers of the American Federation of Labor; Daniel Willard, president of the Baltimore & Ohio Railway; and Julius Rosenwald, president of Sears, Roebuck & Company. The Council's charge was to recommend measures for the effective use of national resources. Out of the Council eventually sprang not only the War Industries Board but other important temporary agencies which organized the home front for war.

At the Council's request all states which had not already done so formed their own councils of defense, which in turn formed county and city councils. Allen's job was in the Section on Cooperation with States (later States Council Section), a department of the Council of National Defense. The section was charged with directing the official state councils, informing them of activities in the national Council, exchanging ideas and experiences among the various councils, standardizing the overall work of the states, and acting as a relay for the various suggestions arising from the state levels. These duties basically represented a communications function. Judge Louis Brandeis labeled the state councils as forty-eight laboratories in which exciting experiments in war government were being conducted.[13]

On the first day of work Allen's section chief, Porter, loaded him with masses of material for digestion, after which Allen was to submit a written proposal for a publicity program. Within the week Allen complied. He proposed expediting publication and dissemination of pamphlets that the states wanted. Allen himself felt the states needed "an exhaustive report on the doings of German spies and agents in the country." He suggested the compilation of "some kind of atrocity bank," taking care not to sow "the seeds of a lasting hatred and looking like an adventure in yellow journalism." He also proposed locating appropriate material for magazine and newspaper publication, regular publication of bulletins and circulars for the various councils, a speaking campaign, and several other schemes. His proposals were only the bare beginnings of the ambitious work yet to be undertaken by Allen and his section.[14]

Allen carefully avoided poaching on Creel's Committee on Public Information. The distinction between the two agencies may be seen in Allen's definition of the prime functions of his office: to make connections between the Committee on Public Information and the state councils and to see that the councils were available to the Committee on Public Information as a medium of distribution, and to generate publicity only through the state councils themselves or when done under the authority of another federal department.[15]

With all the zest of an inspired idealist, Allen was delighted to be part of the frenzied activity to "make the world safe for democracy." The effort to mobilize an entire nation transformed Washington into a center of fast actions and instant decisions by an army of civilians whose zeal matched that of the New Dealers in the 1930s. Allen thrived in such a heady atmosphere. He ended his first written report home with a hasty scrawl, "I must to my labors. I shall send another bulletin from the front shortly." Such excitement needed to be shared, and Allen tried to talk Robert Benchley into coming to Washington. "Wouldn't it be fun if he could?" he exclaimed in a letter home.[16] Benchley subsequently received an appointment to the Aircraft Production Board. There was no time for resumption of their Harvard high jinks, however.

One of the most exciting things about Washington was the opportunity for Allen to meet important officials very different from Boston and New York literati. Less than three weeks after arriving in Washington he attended a stimulating dinner party at the bachelor quarters of the section chief, Porter. The guests included Felix Frankfurter, the "brilliant young Jew" who had left Harvard Law School to be an adviser to Secretary of War Newton D. Baker, Arthur Willert, formerly Washington correspondent of the *London Times* and now attached to the British mission, and Julian Mason, a Chicago newspaper editor. The conversation sparkled; topics ranged from Lloyd George to the labor situation in America to the personnel of the American army in France.

Frankfurter, always clever—a bit too clever and versatile and inquisitive —was on his high horse; Willert, a modest, alert, distinguished and completely charming young Englishman, kept up his end; the rest of us played very second fiddles.

It was, as Allen summed up, a "feast of reason and flow of inside information."[17]

During the days Allen associated with people like Creel, and in his letters home he gave fascinating descriptions of them. Creel, Allen said, was "strongly entrenched and has the President behind him, although most of the departments dislike him; and we must work through him." Fortunately for Allen, Creel hoped to make full use of the state organizations in his own publicity efforts, and this meant expanded responsibilities and opportunities for Allen.

Creel is certainly unique. Rather short—not at all impressive looking— a shock of black hair brushed straight back without a part—a coarse-featured, full-lipped, sensuous fighting face—a fine set of lower teeth that show when he gets talking excitedly and the corners of his mouth draw down his large lower lip—a tendency in conversation to plunge along and generalize and not answer explicitly—altogether, a hard-working, hard-fighting man who is doing his best against the obstacles of an

46

unbusiness-like force (his own fault, by the way) and a general unpopularity; an unsatisfactory man to plan with, because you can't pin him down, because his life is a series of rushes hither and thither and of interruptions; but a man who is accomplishing more than he is given credit for, because in most of it he never appears and cannot publicly come out as a leader. . . . As he said today, "I'll be an old man when I get through with this job!"[18]

Indeed, Creel suffered severe criticism throughout the war for his alleged heavy-handed censorship, and the foremost history of his war efforts contends he was "one of the most disliked and traduced members of the national government while the war was in progress."[19]

Part of the excitement of Washington was its chaotic activity. Planning the great war effort led to confusion, experimentation, and tenuousness. New agencies were created and shut down overnight. The mammoth influx of dedicated private citizens created mountains of paperwork and a critical shortage of office space. Orders flooded the Government Printing Office and caused agonizing delays for bulletins, pamphlets, and other publications deemed of utmost urgency. "The town is full of girls, girls, girls," Allen observed; yet, "every office is clamoring for assistants and stenographers—particularly the latter; and meanwhile men work till eleven or twelve at night." As Allen went through the new Exports Administrative Board offices he saw "roomfuls of stenographers packed almost elbow to elbow . . . and roomfuls of clerks sorting papers . . . filed cards [that] have to be stacked in piles on the floor." One official told Allen, "I'm looking for 15 stenographers. We've got to have them at once."[20]

The hastily recruited and inexpert stenographic forces could not keep up with the volume of work. Sometimes it took twenty-four hours to send a telegram which was utterly useless by the time of its arrival.

Washington's hot summers sapped vitality: in the Quartermaster Department alone a number of employees passed out from the heat in the summer of 1917. Shirt-sleeves and soft collars were standard office fare, but even so, Allen wrote, a person got as wet as if he had been in a telephone booth.[21]

The city's beautiful trees compensated for the heat, though, and

Allen took long walks through streets where at any moment one could "suddenly . . . get the scent of flowers and growing things." His room, shared by Russell Kettell, was just across the street from Rock Creek Park, and sometimes for fun they scrambled up and down embankments and through the trees and bushes and into the zoo. Occasionally, there was time for golf with people like Christian Herter of the State Department, who, afterwards over dinner at the Chevy Chase clubhouse, told Allen "things that I must never, never repeat about what goes on in the State Department."[22] Allen, just twenty-seven years old, could not but be fascinated with such an existence.

After one high-level confidential meeting he confessed to a sense of awe. "Well, the men there were . . . pretty big and imposing, and all were a good bit older than I, and I felt like an interloping office-boy."[23]

Four months after he had formulated his publicity program, Allen had made substantial progress toward fulfilling it. Of the pamphlets he recommended to the state councils, he had received and processed orders for three hundred thousand of them. Along with Porter, Allen had been instrumental in creating a speaking division for the Committee on Public Information under the direction of Arthur E. Bestor. (A year later the speaking division merged with the "Four-Minute Men" speakers' group.) Allen had obtained Creel's consent to a plan by which the Committee on Public Information would pay the costs for a series of posters to be prepared under his supervision for distribution through the state councils. He had hired a writer to prepare news articles giving up-to-the-minute reports on the nation's war preparations, with an accounting of what the government was getting for its money.

Allen's daily routine included handling all correspondence from the state councils that pertained to publicity or to the Committee on Public Information, editing bulletins and circulars, and supervising printing arrangements with the Government Printing Office. He handled the bulk of the correspondence, did long-range planning, and wrote some of the printed materials. His assistant, Horace Davis

("He's old enough to be my father"[24]), edited bulletins and information circulars, and was in charge of posters and a publicity campaign for the Shipping Board. Another assistant attended to matters concerning the speaking division.[25]

No compunction evidently was felt about one endeavor which today would raise a question of ethics. This was the planting of articles promoting government activities without identifying the authors as government officials. Allen arranged for articles in the *Century* and the *Outlook* on one trip to New York, and they soon appeared under his name without note of his official capacity. The *Century* article explained in flattering terms the work of the state councils of defense, and the *Outlook* piece expressed the importance of the shipyards to the war effort.[26]

Naturally, Allen was curious about the condition of his old magazine, the *Century*, and he inquired about it while in New York. His conclusion, expressed privately, was that it was "going to the dogs." Douglas Doty had left the magazine to become the editor of Hearst's *Cosmopolitan*; the staff members were disgruntled; a "weak sister" had been named managing editor; and the whole shop was "shot to pieces." The publisher implored Allen to return immediately as managing editor, but there was to be no editor in chief, and that, to Allen, meant that the managing editor would actually be "editor-in-chief-with-his-hands-tied."[27]

The saddest part of the government's widespread efforts to mobilize the public mind was its role in promoting indirectly the hysteria directed against "suspicious persons." Committee on Public Information posters alleged that "German agents are everywhere" and encouraged citizens to report names of suspected spies before they could put a bomb in a factory.[28] Allen's article in the *Century* praising the efforts of state councils of defense included an uncritical passage on how officials of two states dealt with suspicious persons. Iowa's Council chairman asked suspected persons point-blank if they were for the United States or Germany; in Missouri a series of cards served as official warnings to those under suspicion.[29] Inevitably, measures such as these led to sterner unofficial measures. Vigilante

49

committees arose whose actions have been embarrassing to recollect ever since, and Allen, to his credit, realized that they should be curbed. He drafted a stern bulletin of reproach in July 1918 and expressed great pride when the message was distributed nationally.[30] State councils were urged strongly to "stop lynchings and tar-and-feathering of supposedly disloyal people." Vigilantism should be stopped by "the full weight of public opinion." No matter what purpose such actions had, they "embarrass the Government and weaken the fighting power of the country." The Council of National Defense charged each state council with seeing to it that these disorders ceased. The entire experience undoubtedly emphasized for Allen a concern for protection of individual civil liberties, and throughout the remainder of his life he always stressed the safeguarding of individual rights.

A more involved undertaking in the summer of 1918 was a campaign to alleviate a national shortage of nurses. The idea was to create a Student Nurse Reserve of twenty-five thousand women in order to free for European service the present force of nurses. Allen prepared releases and informational bulletins, blocked out instructions for state council chairmen, and supervised the publicity campaign. He then moved on to other projects: a program for "the very critical" work of the Conservation Division of the Fuel Administration (which, in addition to its more obvious work, sought to conserve resources by such measures as lowering women's boots and shortening their skirts, and encouraging the sale of pipe tobacco in paper containers instead of tin), a bulletin to educate the public on the need for vocational training and rehabilitation of crippled soldiers, and a project to encourage community singing throughout the nation.[31]

Perhaps the most intriguing was the attempt by the Council to organize community singing to bolster the nation's martial spirits. "We could make the Liberty Chorus movement one of the biggest things in the country," Allen exclaimed. "It needs field men, missionaries, wise and on fire with their zeal for the creation of a singing nation!"[32] The *Outlook* said the movement meant that for the first time in its history the United States government had given official recognition to the art of music, labeling it "an important milestone in the progress of American music culture."[33] The Council, with Allen evidently playing the key role, recommended that all states create "Liberty Choruses." "The simplest songs sung in unison" were to be selected; the choruses should sing at all patriotic mass meetings, all Christmas celebrations, all national holiday festivities, and members of the chorus should scatter through the audience to prompt everyone to sing; the state musical directors were to cooperate with the Four-Minute Men in their patriotic educational endeavors.[34] Tunes such as "America," "Keep the Home Fires Burning," and "The Long, Long Trail" rang out as the "liberty sings" met with marked success.

Occasionally, Allen escaped wartime Washington for Council business in other parts of the country. In August 1918, he traveled by train to Florida for briefing sessions with prohibitionist Governor Sidney J. Catts and the executive committee of the state council. As always, he kept his mother informed by lengthy letters as to his activities, and on the return train trip he wrote:

—And still pinewoods and cornfields fly past—only now the sand is pink-white. Goldenrod in the fields, and shabby frame houses, and pines and maples, and always the posts snapping by the window, and the cantering tune of the wheels going on and on, and the couplings between the cars creaking and groaning and squeaking, and the straw hats on the pegs overhead nodding solemnly as the train lurches.

Then, closing, he apologized for the passage. "When I get to writing description, it's a sign that I'm nearly run out."[35]

Allen was disappointed at what he found in Florida. "Lots of them didn't know what a State Council was! They were like children, who had to be told what to do," Allen wrote. Governor Catts was an "old fathead of a politician" who throughout the day-long session exhibited no understanding of the council's functions. Allen's own initial nervousness soon wore off, and when his turn to speak came he "wasn't a bit scared when that old shuffling windbag of a Governor, peering at his program, shouted: 'We will now immediately have the address of Honorable Frank K. Allen of the Council of National Defense, Washington, D.C.!' " Allen fared little better in local newspaper reports; he was called Francis L. Allen and Fred K. Allen.[36] In a confidential report to his superiors Allen called Catts a weak and silly figure who looked more like a genial, florid farmer than a governor.[37]

The National Council was not without its own problems. After five months on the job Allen began to carp privately about excessive red tape, lack of initiative and indecision by his superiors on the Council, and of internal bickering.[38] After a year he decided that much of the trouble resulted from a lack of good men on the Council.

Then, in June 1918, a minor cause célèbre erupted and hit the front page of the *New York Times*. Secretary of War Newton D. Baker cracked down on the chief field director for the State Councils Section, Dr. James A. B. Scherer, because Scherer called the Hearst papers, frequently attacked for their allegedly pro-German leanings, "treasonable and pernicious." Scherer announced that the Secretary had suspended his Constitutional right to free speech by ordering him to refrain from such comments, and he resigned in protest.[39] Baker acknowledged only that he had instructed all War Department officials not to attack the newspapers.

Allen had come to admire Scherer, as had most of the State Council staff, and the resignation created some consternation in the office. "He is a great man and a great loss," Allen wrote home. He explained that Scherer had decided deliberately to bring the Hearst issue to a boiling point. Despite sympathy for Scherer's cause, Allen and his office colleagues believed Baker to be correct in reprimanding him. Allen did not tell Scherer that he disagreed with his actions, but he expressed to him his genuine sorrow over the turn of events.[40]

The Allen gift for phrasemaking was such that when a Presidential proclamation was felt necessary about some aspect of Council work, it was Allen, at least on two occasions, who wrote the President's material. In July 1918, he participated in a ploy designed to prevent duplication of the Council's work by other government bodies. To call attention to the Council's abilities to undertake many kinds of work, an exchange of letters was devised between Secretary Baker, who was chairman of the Council, and President Wilson. Allen wrote both letters, a three-page summary for Baker of the Council's accomplishments, including a reminder for other agencies to use its services, and a one-page reply for President Wilson, complimenting the "notable record" of the council system.[41]

The entire correspondence was approved word for word as Allen wrote it; yet he never conferred directly with the President and evidently not with Baker either. The Council printed the exchange and sent copies to every council in the nation, with a request that the correspondence be released to newspapers.[42]

Two months later Allen wrote another letter for the President which was widely reproduced. In this letter, addressed to Secretary of the Interior Franklin K. Lane, President Wilson endorsed the recent reorganization of the State Councils Section and the Women's Committee of the Council into a single Field Division as "sound in principle" and serving the "interests of efficiency."[43]

While Allen did not meet personally with the President, he admired him greatly from afar. On a July 4, 1918 outing to Mount Vernon to hear the President speak to a group of foreign representatives who had accompanied him and Mrs. Wilson on a boat ride down the Potomac, Allen easily could see the President in a white duck suit, as well as Secretary of State Robert Lansing, British Ambassador Lord Reading, and George Creel, who was "hustling about telling people where to go and making arrangements in general."[44]

That night Allen described the event in a lengthy letter to his sister Hildegarde in Boston:

The President made no pretense to be *speaking* his piece; he was quite clearly *reading* it,—a clause at a time. He did not trouble to raise his voice: he was speaking for the foreign diplomats, for publication, for cable transmission,—not to the throng before him. There was nothing of the orator in his manner, nothing impassioned; he was urbane, clear, distinct, almost smiling. One would nearly think he were reading to a class in government a piece of nice reasoning on the difference between a league of nations and a court of nations. There was the vestige of the sort of twinkle in the eye which a lecturer often has, and which means: "You and I are intelligent gentle folk, who enjoy distinctions and concise statement, and I'm quite sure you're following me closely."

Shep [Whitney Shepardson, who worked with the Shipping Board] at my side was muttering, "Look at that ass, Creel, reading the manuscript over his shoulder!—What cheek!" Was this, could this be a historic occasion, I kept thinking? With this perspiring crowd so little awed, and that distinguished looking man with the gray hair and the eyeglasses so little moved. . . . Suddenly the President stepped back, bowing and smiling; there was a thunder of handclapping; the crowd began to dissolve—until arrested by [John] MacCormack's voice singing the Star-Spangled Banner. The queerest thing of all, perhaps, was that voice, which everybody could hear, which everybody felt the brilliant beauty and thrill of, held the audience motionless as no part of the President's speech had.[45]

Allen stopped attending events with male friends that summer and began courting Dorothy Penrose Cobb.

5

NEW HORIZONS

Allen loved people and parties, and he enjoyed the company of young women. But at age twenty-eight he remained single. His first few months in Washington so deprived him of the social companionship of the opposite sex that when he and his roommate, Russell Kettell, took a young lady to lunch at the Shoreham Hotel Allen wrote, "I had been so long without the privilege of watching a girl eat ice-cream opposite me that it quite set me up for the week."[1]

In the summer of 1918 Allen met slender, blue-eyed Dorothy Penrose Cobb, a 1915 Vassar College graduate who had come to Washington in March to work in the Intelligence Bureau of the War Department. Dorothy was engaged to a man from Illinois when Allen met her. She found Allen so captivating that she broke her engagement even before a new relationship developed.[2]

The first mention of Dorothy came in a letter Allen wrote to his father on July 25, 1918, when he said he had hired a Victoria, "or as one might say, a Bernard M. Barouche," for a drive about town with his pretty brunette companion. "It is a pleasing form of sport for sultry afternoons." Allen casually mentioned another bit of news to his father. A new copy of *Who's Who* had just arrived with one Frederick Lewis Allen, not yet thirty, appearing in it for the first time. "I say!" Allen exclaimed.[3]

Once the romance began, Allen switched the central subject of his letters from his work to Dorothy. At first his letters were coolly analytical about his own feelings. She was true and sweet and charming, made him feel utterly at home when with her, and had character and ideals. Yet, Allen confided to his mother that he seemed to be in the position of a man feeling his pulse and saying, "She's all I could want a wife to be, but I'm still only one degree above normal. Why doesn't she bowl me over?" While Allen observed that she was not as "radical" as he, he felt confident that he could convert her "because she loves her fellow-men."[4]

Dorothy was the daughter of the Reverend and Mrs. Henry Evartson Cobb of New York City. Her father was a distinguished churchman. He served as pastor of the West End Collegiate Church in New York City and soon would become senior minister of the Dutch Reformed Church in America.[5] Allen told his father that "On dit qu'il est un corker."[6] Dorothy's mother, the former Elizabeth Colgate Penrose of Philadelphia, was a cousin of U.S. Senator Boies Penrose, a powerful Republican. Her grandfather was the Philadelphia judge Clement Biddle Penrose.

However coolly Allen assessed his own pulse regarding Dorothy Cobb, he confessed that when they were together their companionship was sheer joy. "The way our minds jump together is an endless delight," he said. He expressed confidence that she would win over his mother in "about half a minute." On a Saturday morning in September 1918, Allen proposed marriage and Dorothy accepted. Forty-five minutes after the engagement Allen dashed off a note to tell his mother, "We're absurdly happy."[7]

Less than three weeks after the engagement Allen determined to give up Washington for active military duty. Perhaps his romance with Dorothy inspired a new sense of masculinity, or maybe the reorganization of the Council of National Defense, which had left him uncertain as to his exact status, prompted it. On October 1, 1918, the new plan, which Allen had praised so highly for the President, became effective. It represented an amalgamation of Allen's own State Section and the Women's Committee into a single office called the Field Division. The goal was to avoid the duplication arising from the heretofore separate offices for men and women. Grosvenor B. Clarkson, formerly secretary to the Council (Allen frequently had criticized him privately to his parents as either an "ass" or a "consummate ass"), became director.[8] The work of the Field Division now was divided into six sections, and Allen was to direct the Speaker's Section, supervising the organization of speaking engagements and associated activities throughout the country.[9]

Dorothy wrote to Allen's parents of the possibility of military service on the same day that her future husband did. She wondered whether the reorganization would not restrict Fred's work on the Council and justify the move. Allen said that although well placed by the reorganization, now he could be spared and "the time has come to go."[10]

He had decided that he should enter Chemical Warfare Service ("in charge of gas, gas masks, their use, etc."), mandatorily as a private. After ten weeks of training he would earn his commission, perhaps at a rank even higher than second lieutenant. Chemical Warfare seemed appropriate because the need for commissioned officers appeared greatest there, and Allen also knew several high-ranking officers in the branch. He had declined an outright commission as an officer in the Military Morale Section because he would have remained in Washington and simply shed civilian clothing for army khakis.[11]

At the moment Allen pondered entry into the army, events in Europe were pointing toward the war's culmination. It seemed odd for a young man to select this moment to enter active service, and Allen's ever alert father pointed this out in a special delivery letter to his son. He urged delay not only in his plans to enter the army, but for the wedding as well.

"I appreciate ever so much the affectionate thoughtfulness of your inquiries," Allen replied, "but I am frank to say I do not see the wisdom of delaying either my entrance into the army or my marriage." While it was understandable that the action might appear to be impetuous, such was not the case, he assured his father. He had resolved to enter the army as early as June, but his associates at the Council had persuaded him to delay his enlistment. Furthermore, he reasoned that "the diplomatic interchanges" should not influence his plans, and the army still needed officers. A delay in wedding plans did not seem logical either. Officers earned from a second lieutenant's eighteen hundred dollars yearly pay to a captain's twenty-five hundred dollars, and upon returning to civilian life Allen expected to earn between three thousand dollars and four thousand dollars annually.[12]

The situation for Allen soon changed, however. Clarkson, former secretary to the Council, was named director of the new and important Field Division. Earlier, Clarkson had consented to Allen's plan to quit the Council for the army. Now, however, he wanted him to become his assistant. Allen protested that at least two men in the Council were better qualified, but Clarkson explained that he needed an *alter ego* to handle a considerable portion of his work. He thought Allen would prove more useful to his country in this capacity than in the army, and he believed that the war would be over in a month anyway. The new prospect seemed alluring. Yet, much agonizing thought already had gone into the decision to enter military service. Determined to weigh and assess the changed situation anew, Allen and his fiancée talked it through in detail. Allen also confided in a few associates about the offer and was especially eager to see if they would begrudge his advancement over them. After two or three days of deliberation, Allen decided to forget the army and accept the proffered position.[13] The wedding, six weeks away, would be on schedule.

Ironically, Allen never had liked Clarkson, shrewd as he felt Clarkson was politically. Being his assistant would require "tact and self-restraint and strategy."[14] After four days in his new position, though, he reported, "I get on admirably with Clarkson so far, and I think we are going to get things done." Clarkson, he found, followed his advice to "an astonishing degree." His influence, exerted largely through his handling of incoming mail, filled him with delight. Allen arranged to have all of Clarkson's mail come to his own desk, and he passed on only those items needing Clarkson's personal attention. He went over these letters with his superior, making recommendations which Clarkson generally followed. "I have my hand right on the wheel," Allen wrote.[15]

During his first week he devised a plan to expand the division's field staff. Clarkson approved, but he informed Allen that Secretary of the Interior Franklin K. Lane thought otherwise and he would have to be convinced personally. Allen had not met the Secretary, and Clarkson provided him with a letter of introduction, recommended that he remind Lane that he was the man who had drafted the letter for the President's signature which the Secretary previously had praised ("Tell that young man he knows how to write a good letter," Allen quoted Lane as having said at the time) and made an appointment for his assistant to place his proposal directly before the Secretary.[16]

"I got away with it in the finest style," Allen later related. He met Lane in his "stunning great office" in the new Interior Building, accepted Lane's compliments on what Allen termed his Presidential "forgeries," and the two of them discussed generally the problems of utilizing effectively a full staff. Allen found Lane to be "an amenable old cuss—probably too amenable." Lane gave up his own "wild ideas" for Allen's proposal. "Jove, but Dorothy and I were proud—we went out and played golf on the strength of it. Ferdy persuading a member of the Cabinet to change his mind!"[17]

Allen's next assignment concerned one of the possibilities that had lured him into accepting the new job—that of preparing a full report on how the State Council system could assist in demobilization, or, as Allen termed it, "reconstruction." While he realized that the approaching peace diminished the importance of the Council itself, he believed the Council to be the best possible place for jumping to the Reconstruction Commission which was expected to be appointed soon by the President. "And that will be the most interesting place to be for the next few months."[18]

Meanwhile, however, Clarkson was named director of the entire

Council of National Defense, and Allen became the assistant director. It represented a rather astonishing climb in rank since Allen had arrived in Washington the previous year.

Other important events rapidly occurred in early November. President Wilson's appeal to the nation to elect a Democratic Congress in the 1918 November election backfired and the Republicans claimed a majority in the House and important victories in the Senate. The "false armistice" was announced to wild and premature celebrations, followed in four days by the actual cease-fire. The Council's plans for a smooth conversion to peacetime were jeopardized by the general sense of relief that the war crisis had ended and a normal, peacetime society would develop overnight.

A loyal Democrat and Wilson admirer, Allen was "fearfully disappointed" at the 1918 election results. He had disapproved, however, of Wilson's public assertion that unless the voters returned Democratic majorities to the House and Senate, world leaders would interpret it as a repudiation of his leadership.

"I think," Allen wrote to his mother, "the verdict of the country most unfortunate, most blind—to think of not voting confidence in a man whose diplomacy has so gloriously triumphed!—and there is no getting around the fact that a divided government is a weak and bad government."[19]

The fact that the President could represent one political party and the Congressional majority lie in another party seemed to Allen one of the worst faults of the Constitution. Such a situation, he felt, would lead to the two branches of government fighting and nullifying one another, both scrambling for praise and dodging blame.

A few days before the Armistice, Allen continued to envision for the Council a massive undertaking in coordinating an orderly conversion to a peacetime economy. Allen and his colleagues had worked up their reconstruction proposals, but they could not act without the President's initiative. Even Secretary of War Baker dared not move until the President indicated a desire for action.[20]

By November 19 prospects for a well-planned demobilization looked even more remote, and consequently work on the Council now was "dull and discouraging." The plans drawn up by Allen and fellow worker Elliott Smith had shown how state councils could assist in a demobilization program, but the Council's directors apparently frowned on the continued use of the state agencies.[21] Allen was disgusted with the "utter disregard" for national planning.[22]

Perhaps more immediate for him, though, were personal concerns —such as finding a peacetime job to support a wife in proper fashion. He sent inquiries to his former bosses, Sedgwick at the *Atlantic* and Shuster at the *Century*, and one to former classmate Bob Hallowell at the liberal magazine which his friend Walter Lippmann had helped to found, the *New Republic*.[23]

Sandwiched between the Washington work, Fred and Dorothy had visited each other's relatives and laboriously drawn up wedding plans. Because of war conditions they had preferred a simple home ceremony. But Dr. Cobb's parishioners began a gentle howl, and to satisfy them the afternoon ceremony was performed on November 29 at Dr. Cobb's West End Collegiate Church. Allen's father joined Dorothy's father in officiating. The war effort had spread many of Allen's choices for attendants to the far sides of the earth, but he did manage to get Robert Benchley as his best man.

The "ministerial children," as Dorothy labeled themselves, honeymooned leisurely at the rambling Winter Inn at Buck Hill Falls, Pennsylvania. Dorothy devoted much time to writing letters and 360 notes of thanks for wedding gifts, and Allen worked on a freelance article about current politics. Together they read aloud from the newly published *Education of Henry Adams*, in which many of the New England landmarks and people familiar to Allen were so incisively described.[24] The honeymooners also braved the frigid December air to play golf, and after a sleet storm they went coasting on the same golf links. "We are as contented and chummy and used to each other as if we had been married for months," Fred wrote to his mother, adding that he was so proud and happy about Dorothy that he thanked his stars about six times a day.[25]

Back in Washington after Christmas, the couple found a suitable apartment on M Street. The war crisis was over, the pell-mell pace had disappeared (although the crisis over the League cast somber undertones), and the Allens settled down to enjoy what they knew were to be their last months in the capital.

Any well-reasoned demobilization now appeared totally out of the question because of the late date, and Allen expressed delight that the "fiasco" would not be on his or Elliott Smith's hands. The two of them had proposed any number of possibilities, and their consciences were clear. Even though the nation's attention had not yet been riveted to the situation, Allen felt sure that "fiasco" was the proper word because the demobilization, especially industrial demobilization, had been "disastrously haphazard." He predicted that within one or two months more complaints would arise and the Administration's record in the matter would become one of its liabilities.[26]

Allen had not expected to remain in Washington much longer, but he was asked once more to utilize his writing talents. The assignment was to undertake a historical report on the experiences of the Council. It would amount to a full-sized book, and in preparing it he would have free access to the Council's files and minutes. "The report will attempt to be absolutely fair, and will probably be kept confidential (though you shall have a copy), for it will drag out a good many skeletons for an airing," Allen told his father.[27]

The Allens, now living a more leisurely life, studied the political scene about them and raged together as hopes for the League of Nations dimmed. Through the courtesy of Dorothy's influential relative, Senator Boies Penrose, passes for admission to the Senate gallery were readily available. "He would turn cold if he knew what a Bolshevik was getting in on his signature," Allen said. As he observed firsthand the Senate battle which held the nation's attention, Allen concluded that the League's opponents were filled with bigotry and narrowness.[28] Among that group opposing Wilson was Cousin Boies, now in the waning days of a powerful political career in which he identified himself with corporate interests. During his heyday the hefty, outspoken Philadelphian had controlled Pennsylvania politics so tightly and performed so effectively as a kingmaker for the national Republican party that one of his biographers has called him "the last of the great bosses—in many ways the greatest of them."[29] To Dorothy, though, he was "disreputable," and the Allens and Penrose did not meet socially.[30]

While Allen daily reported to the office, Dorothy reported almost as faithfully to the Senate. She soon could identify the Senators on sight, and what events she missed firsthand she soaked up from the pages of the *New York Times*. Allen envied Dorothy's chance to see history being made while he sat at a desk recording it.[31]

Even though the government pay was modest, the couple hired a part-time maid and cook. She prepared the evening meal daily for five dollars a week, and freed Dorothy for her Senate vigil.[32]

As Allen's history of the Council grew in size, his days on the Council correspondingly decreased in number. Nothing had come of his job inquiries to the *Century*, *Atlantic*, or *New Republic*, and in December Allen had rejected an offer from the Treasury Department to undertake the organization of savings societies throughout the nation. By March he was entertaining two further possibilities, both literary. Douglas Doty, his former editor at the *Century* who now was an editor for Harper & Brothers, wanted Allen to move to North Dakota for three to four months and write a book on the Non-Partisan League's aggressive activities there. Allen insisted upon a thousand-dollar guarantee. As he expected, the guarantee could not be arranged and he did not attempt the project. The second possibility appeared more likely: a position as an editorial writer for the *New York Evening Post*. Allen had visited the newspaper's offices in New York and was led to believe that he could step into an opening expected to materialize at about the time he would leave Washington. "I want that position and opportunity," Allen wrote to his mother.[33]

Frank Crowninshield at *Vanity Fair* made another pitch for Allen's talents, too, by offering him the position of managing editor. Once again, Allen declined the opportunity to work on the magazine. Dorothy told her parents-in-law that they would have been "horrified and disappointed" if their son had accepted the position, saying,

"It's the influence of that dreadful New York creature he married."[34] Later that month Robert Benchley became *Vanity Fair*'s managing editor.[35] As soon as Benchley took the job Allen sent him a satirical piece on possible candidates for the presidency in 1920. He included in mock seriousness Douglas Fairbanks, Tyrus R. Cobb, and Al Jolson.[36]

Allen's proximity to the seats of power in wartime Washington and his journalistic skills naturally made him want to write about serious subjects. As a secondary member of the administration he was in no position to write honestly and critically of what he observed about him, but another avenue lay open—anonymous articles.

In June 1918, the *Outlook* published an outspoken, two-part anonymous contribution under the general title, "The Administration: An Appraisal."[37] An editor's note identified the author only as being a person "in a position of responsibility in one of the branches of the Government's service." That man was Allen.

The central theme of the two-part series was the stated need for unifying the various bureaus and departments into a single effective administrative machine. The first installment contained sharply etched portraits of some important personalities in the war government.[38]

Food administrator Herbert Hoover was marked by "his fearlessness, his openness of mind, his unusual personal magnetism, and his astonishing imaginative grasp of his great problem [that] impress every man who has the fortune to come into contact with him." Director General of the Railroads William McAdoo's "greatest weakness would seem to be a tendency to play a lone hand." Secretary of State Robert Lansing's "mediocrity happily does not matter, since for all practical purposes the President is his own very admirable Secretary of State."

Although War Industries Board Chairman Bernard Baruch lacked administrative experience, he had shown "shrewdness and imagination," and it appeared as if he were capable of doing everything necessary to give the War Industries Board the character of a Munitions Department. George Creel of the Committee on Public Information was "clearly not up to his job." He possessed courage, honesty, and living faith in democracy, but those alone were not sufficient qualifications for the direction of national publicity "when they are coupled with administrative inexperience, unconscious partisanship, lack of tact and discretion, and a hot-tempered impulsiveness bordering on petulance."

One of the major obstacles in Washington, according to Allen, was excessive red tape. As a primary example he cited the regulation which had been so personally frustrating: the requirement that government printing be done only at the Government Printing Office, with the result that material related to the war effort often was delayed days or weeks.

Allen pointed to a dire need for a "brain" to coordinate the vast, complex body of the government. He proposed a planning board similar to the British War Cabinet, which determined overall war priorities and policies. One of the reasons President Wilson had been reluctant to appoint such a body, Allen believed, was a fear that he might lose control of policy if a war cabinet took hold.

The President's scholarly bent, Allen felt, made him more comfortable with written communications than with the give-and-take of a round-table discussion. Although Allen definitely considered himself to be a Wilson supporter throughout his life, his personal ideas as to how the government best could function lay to the political left of the President—that is, toward greater centralization of government authority in the name of efficiency.

Allen's identity as author of the articles evidently remained a well-kept secret. Less than a year after they appeared, and with the war over, the magazine persuaded him to write another anonymous piece dissecting the President himself. Allen willingly complied and the article, "President Wilson: A Political and Personal Interpretation," appeared in the April 23, 1919 issue of *Outlook*.[39]

In this article Allen sought primarily to interpret Wilson rather than to criticize him. The key to understanding the President's actions, he pointed out, lay in his view of the American system of government, especially as found in Wilson's book, *Congressional*

Government, written when he was not yet thirty. Basically, Wilson felt that the system of government checks and balances inspired by Montesquieu and integrated into the United States Constitution was in the process of breaking down. Division of authority led to a failure in leadership, and Wilson determined to provide that leadership from the executive branch. On a more personal basis, Allen reported his previous observation that Wilson preferred printed materials to men to help him analyze a situation, and this accounted for his failure to maintain cordial relations with Congress. The third major key toward understanding the President lay, according to Allen, in his "remarkable publicity sense." The prime example of this could be seen in the President's European visit when he talked not so much to the foreign political heads as to the masses who ultimately controlled the statesman. Allen predicted a turbulent final two years for the remaining presidential term because Wilson's ideas on executive leadership would be challenged by the opposition party now in control of the Congress. But, less presciently, Allen also foresaw American acceptance of the League of Nations because Wilson would be smart enough to make the issue a national one rather than a partisan one.[40]

The editor's note described the anonymous author of the article as "an American of exceptional education and training, who is familiar with the political history of the United States, and who has had some experience with the present Administration."[41] Allen proudly told his mother that when she read this she would throw out her chest and declare, "I riz him."[42] Allen, however, still needed a job.

6

RETURN TO HARVARD

Government propaganda efforts during World War I dwarfed by comparison anything previously undertaken in the field of shaping public opinion. The scale and success of the operation gave a new and broader impetus to the practice of publicity. As a result, the postwar era saw public relations spread throughout virtually all of society, especially in business but touching even such noncommercial endeavors as education.

A few institutions of higher learning had recognized since the turn of the century the value of seeking in a formal way to shape public opinion. Harvard was certainly among the first to recognize the need. In the fall of 1900 the university, under President Charles W. Eliot, contracted the nation's first and only publicity firm to handle the university's relations with the news media. The pioneer agency, called the Publicity Bureau, was hired at a retainer of two hundred dollars a month. The agreement, surely the first of its kind between agency and client, set a pattern of charging for public relations work that still is used by firms today. When in 1902 President Eliot stopped paying the retainer, the agency continued to provide service free of charge because it wanted the prestige of having such a respected institution as a client. In 1906 expenses became prohibitive for the gratis service, however, and the firm dropped Harvard. Except for a brief period in 1910 when the company again listed Harvard as a client, the university had since been without professional publicity assistance.[1]

President Eliot had been very conscious of the value of publicity. President Lowell, who succeeded Eliot in 1909, was skeptical of it, and while other colleges and universities established their own publicity offices, Lowell resisted. As early as 1904 the University of Wisconsin had set up an organized press bureau, and by 1917 enough colleges had followed the example that the Association of American College News Bureaus was founded.[2]

Under pressure to create a full-time publicity office at Harvard, Lowell called in the respected Boston editor Ellery Sedgwick for advice. After their discussion in March 1919, Sedgwick returned to his *Atlantic* desk with a prime candidate for the task already in mind: Fred Allen.

Sedgwick wrote to him that afternoon. Would it be worth Harvard's time, he wondered, to speak to Allen about the position? "I myself think there is a chance here, not only for a reasonable living, but for marked usefulness," Sedgwick advised. "It would be the duty of the man who is selected both to prevent misconceptions and to arouse interest in the University and its problems."[3] The position necessarily would entail a close association with President Lowell, as well as confidential relations with all the University authorities.

Two days later Sedgwick wrote in greater detail and with even higher optimism over the job's potential. He seemed worried that Allen might think the position inconsequential. He emphasized the job's complete respectability and importance. "Don't think of a 'publicity man,' half patronized, half shunned by professors," he said, "but rather as an exponent of a great modern force which is recognized as essential to the University's life." Furthermore, he assured Allen that the job would not remove him from the path of subsequent magazine opportunity.[4]

The prospect immediately intrigued both Allen and Dorothy. "The Boston affair is thrilling," Dorothy wrote her mother-in-law, "and I hope [it] will materialize, so that you may have us to keep a watchful eye on in our gambols with the wild tribes of Cambridge. You know I have always wanted to marry a Boston man and live in Cambridge!" Earlier, Allen had rejected a Harvard offer to become editor of the alumni magazine, but that was because the position seemed so "stale" to him. This one appeared different, and President Lowell soon invited him to Cambridge to discuss it.[5]

The interview with Lowell proved satisfactory to both men. Allen accepted the appointment at three thousand dollars per year beginning September 1, 1919, but the job description was "Secretary to the Corporation" rather than publicity director or some other more accurate title. Allen explained that the designation, "of course, is by way of camouflage."[6] Lowell disliked publicity himself, and the inaccurate title undoubtedly was his attempt to conceal what he considered to be the suspect endeavor of generating publicity.

Lowell's desire to avoid calling attention to the position no doubt was satisfied; the new office attracted almost no notice. The various histories of Harvard also fail to mention the school's entry into the publicity field.

Allen, however, was elated. "You can tell anybody. Shriek it from the housetops, bellow it in the cellar. And put in your thanksgivings a word or two of praise for E. Sedgwick, who brought it about," he wrote his parents.[7]

Allen's unfinished work at the Council, consisting now solely of the history, still remained. "The sheer physical labor bores me to death sometimes; but the work has its interesting aspects, and D[orothy] says the chapters make sprightly reading." The stretches of boredom saw frequent relief through outdoor activities, especially golf, and by entertaining friends at their apartment.[8]

Early in May, Allen completed the history. His first book-length work went into the government's files to languish. Years later, Allen's own family did not know that the manuscript existed.[9] Allen seldom discussed his experiences in the capital in later years, and he mentioned only casually his duties with the Council. However, his intimate participation and observance of government during the war years heightened his interest in public affairs, and it provided him with a solid foundation for later articles and books, especially during the next world war.

When Allen began his Harvard job on September 1, 1919, President Lowell had been in office for ten important and creative years. Allen had left the campus in the summer of 1914, months before the opening of the new freshman dormitories intended to democratize beginning students. Lowell also had sought to make intellectual ability rather than social distinction the mark of the "best" students. He instituted "concentration and distribution" for undergraduates, a plan known elsewhere as majoring and minoring in subjects. A new tutorial system prepared students for another Lowell innovation: the general examination before graduation. Another new program designed to enhance the prestige of scholarship was the honors system, whereby undergraduates could obtain honors at graduation by undertaking extra work.[10]

Lowell also had acquired a reputation as a thorough supporter of academic freedom. It began when he steadfastly refused to dismiss a German philosophy professor, Hugo Münsterberg, one of Allen's former professors, for calmly presenting Germany's side before U.S. entry into the war. The school had marched unhesitatingly to war, however, along with the rest of the excited nation. Harvard's R.O.T.C. was expanded early by importing several disabled French officers to teach new methods of warfare; special provisions were made for students and faculty who enrolled in officers' training schools; the chemistry department produced masks and poison gas; and other departments lent their various specialties to the cause as well.[11]

With the war over, a new set of problems soon confronted the school, many of which gained national headlines. They presented severe challenges for Allen as the man now in charge of putting the school's best profile before the public.

Nine days after he arrived at his new desk the Boston police force

70

went out on strike. The university responded by urging Harvard men to volunteer as officers. Posters were printed and displayed at conspicuous points around the campus, and student volunteers were not penalized for missing classes. Some two hundred and fifty students and faculty members answered the call.[12]

One crisis begat another: Harold J. Laski, a brilliant young English political science instructor on temporary appointment, found occasion to praise the striking police officers, an unpopular position. Immediately he was denounced as a traitor and Bolshevik, and Lowell heard strident demands from alumni that Laski, then a little-known faculty member, be dismissed. The Board of Overseers appeared determined to force the issue until Lowell let it be known that if the overseers asked for Laski's dismissal they would get his own resignation instead.[13]

Headlines concerning such matters were not the kind of publicity Harvard had intended to occupy Allen's time, and he did keep otherwise busy. Public notice of the school jumped considerably once the new office was established. The *New York Times* indexes for the years preceding and during Allen's four-year tenure reveal that at least in that publication news stories about the school significantly increased.

The publicity director's role was, insofar as the public was concerned, an invisible one. He served as middleman between the press and the school, and advised Lowell and other Harvard officials on pertinent matters. Sometimes, however, he became highly visible in noncritical affairs. When an official of the U.S. Public Health Service contended that studies revealed a sort of "race suicide" among college graduates because they were bearing fewer children, Allen gained headlines by disputing the assertion. He showed on the contrary an increase in children for married Harvard graduates.[14]

Some of the news about Harvard, like the Laski affair, was entirely unwanted. Several issues fostered widespread newspaper coverage and surely provided Allen with the severest tests of his public relations skills in accommodating the press.

The first resembled in a way the Laski case. Professor Zechariah

Chafee of the law school generated an uprising of influential Harvard alumni when he severely criticized the government's role in prosecuting persons accused of violating the Espionage Act. Professor Lowell staunchly defended Chafee in the face of a determined Overseers' investigation, and an alumni committee finally voted 6–5 not to censure Chafee.[15]

Lowell's ill-conceived recommendation of a quota to limit the proportion of Jews in the Harvard student body created a public relations crisis. Since 1900 the proportion of Jews at Harvard had increased from 7 percent to more than 21 percent. Lowell became convinced that if the increases continued, Harvard would lose its character as a supposed democratic, national university which drew from all classes.[16]

The president's intentions were honest, and, in his own mind at least, based on logic without prejudice to the Jews. But such a proposal naturally brought down a torrent of national criticism upon him and the University, and the Board of Overseers ended the controversy by rejecting Lowell's plan.

Public wrath again descended upon the school a year later when Lowell told a black Harvard alumnus, Roscoe Conkling Bruce, that his son could not live in the freshman dormitory because of his color. Unfavorable headlines once again erupted, and once more, the Board of Overseers rescued the beleaguered institution by voting to admit the black student and further to open all Harvard housing to all students regardless of color. All these diversions from Allen's more routine day-by-day duties undoubtedly distressed school officials because of the "bad" publicity generated, but they made the job all the more interesting and challenging for Allen.

Allen came to know one Harvard undergraduate who later would be his rival as editor of the *Atlantic Monthly*. He was Edward Weeks, who as a student was the part-time campus correspondent for the *Boston Evening Transcript*.[17] In a 1950 speech on the campus, Weeks reminisced humorously about his recollections of Allen at Harvard.

Allen's office, he recalled, was situated in the "cellar" of University

Hall beside the college furnace. His task was "almost impossible" because of President Lowell's dislike of newspaper reporters. "The policy was to keep Fred Allen down there in the coal bin until a catastrophe occurred and only then was he allowed to speak." On these occasions Allen had two choices: a blanket denial of everything or a statement that no comment would be forthcoming. He handed out mimeographed copies of "dull speeches" which were delivered by visiting dignitaries; he provided reporters with advance copies of the President's Report; and each June on commencement morning he delivered the citations of the honorary degrees and a list of donors of more than ten thousand dollars. "That was about all," Weeks claimed. Meanwhile, Weeks said he and other bored reporters "tried to create as many catastrophes as possible." After each contrived catastrophe Allen would "emerge from his coal bin looking worried, and distribute to us one or the other of the statements that I have mentioned."[18] Weeks mailed Allen a copy of his speech with a note saying he hoped his remarks did not offend him.

Allen undoubtedly was perturbed, if only slightly, despite denying it. "No offense at all," he responded cheerfully, "though I think I was able to function from time to time a little more constructively in those days than you made out despite the noteworthy coolness of President Lowell."[19]

He recalled how his office reacted under pressure when an explosion in the basement of the Jefferson Physical Laboratory killed two men and injured several students. Within fifteen minutes Allen had the correct names of all victims and explanations as to how the accident occurred. His office acted as the information station for newsmen who sought details about the tragedy.[20]

Allen considered carefully the implications of his business, and he sought to define the role of this new breed, the college publicity man, in a 1922 article in *School and Society*.[21] It was one of the earliest, if not the first, attempts to deal with the responsibilities of publicity in higher education. Since both private and public educational institutions served and depended on the public, it was, he said, "the plain duty of our educational institutions to let the public know what they are about." He defined the limits of university publicity in ethical terms that surely pleased the austere Lowell. College publicity officers should promote not merely the school but the cause of education as well. Allen lamented the "cult of the athlete" which so completely overshadowed intellectual distinction. Rather than advertising college athletics, the publicist should report campus research in fields such as chemistry, physics, and astronomy, thus promoting more general understanding of the "real function and value of institutions of learning."

Harvard's entry into the publicity field lent added respectability to the activity, and many other schools soon followed. As Harvard's first publicity officer, Allen established a basic pattern for the office. Lowell's attitude almost surely made Allen's position more difficult. As Louis M. Lyons has observed, Lowell administered America's greatest university for twenty-five years in a period marked by "the most tremendous development of publicity the world has yet seen without once yielding to a newspaper interview."[22]

Both Allens, though, enjoyed life among relatives and friends in Cambridge. The couple made frequent visits to the Allen home place across the river in Boston, and they had many outings with friends. Dorothy became involved in a discussion group, the Saturday Morning Club, and the French Club. Allen tramped the woods and the Charles River basin while bird-watching, and he frequently jogged around the cinder track at Soldiers' Field. The Allens lived in a second-floor apartment on Sparks Street in Cambridge, and during these years both of their children were born: Elizabeth Penrose on April 13, 1921, and Oliver Ellsworth on June 29, 1922. Even with this suddenly enlarged family, Allen found time to expand his free-lance writing.

During the war he had given up humorous sketches, but when *Harper's* in 1919 initiated a new monthly humor column, "The Lion's Mouth," Allen revived his touch and for some ten years he was probably the column's most prolific contributor. In establishing "The Lion's Mouth," *Harper's* editors lamented the tendency of the democratic age to flatten the nation into "one dreary level of equality and uniformity," and they dedicated the new column to those "who mentally squirm and refuse to lie flat in the wake left by this steamroller—to those who, like the Venetians of old, are mentally astir and have something of courage, or truth, or beauty, to declare."[23]

Such a column seemed to be a perfect outlet for Allen's brand of humor, and one can see in his many contributions the wry detachment he felt as he watched the mood of the 1920s take shape. Already he viewed with disdain the glorification of business that was to dominate popular thought. In "The Glass-Topped Desk," he described the typical furnishings of a business office—furnishings invariably designed to impress rather than to function. After his elaborate, tongue-in-cheek description, Allen concluded, "Will you be impressed? Probably about as much as I am impressed by the average executive whom I see and the things I read about him."[24]

In another sketch, "The Goon and His Style," Allen expressed his conviction that writing should be lively and readable. He categorized persons with heavy, impenetrable writing styles as goons. Some "goons" were George Washington, Disraeli, James Fenimore Cooper, G. A. Henty, and Warren G. Harding. Those with a light touch were "jiggers," and their numbers included Abraham Lincoln, Lloyd George, and Lytton Strachey. Allen believed that young writers frequently achieved goonishness by trying to overimpress, forgetting that they must communicate with ordinary people. This conviction was central to everything Allen ever wrote. The sketch also provided a platform for one of the Allens' endless parlor games in which individuals were weighed and judged to be either goons or jiggers.[25] (Allen, naturally, was a jigger.)

Other subjects at which Allen poked fun during these years included his own favorite pastime of bird-watching, "newspaperese," secret ambitions, ill-mannered theatergoers, summer vacations, swappers' exchanges, familiar quotations, and rearing children.

For his more serious considerations Allen turned to magazines other than *Harper's*. He published in Sedgwick's *Atlantic* his thoughts on "Newspapers and the Truth," examining the factors and influences which made objective reporting so difficult. War-inspired improvements in methods of swaying the public mind made the problem of newspaper conduct more important than ever, and Allen stressed the need for reporting uncolored by personal opinions. The press's responsibilities to the public required constant improvement within the profession, Allen felt, and he suggested education, better working conditions, and a code of ethics as necessary steps.[26]

He stopped writing after 1920 for the magazine which had been so receptive to his early efforts, the *Century*. His last piece there, "Politics Up to Date," echoed the growing disillusionment with politics which soon would be a trademark of the decade. In it Allen created an imaginary scene in which a young politician visited a political veteran for advice. The seasoned politician shamelessly told the idealistic younger man to disregard the issues and concentrate on such appealing words as "Americanism."[27]

Allen breezily entered a contest held by the Old Corner Book Store for the best poem on reading books. Among the 694 entries he captured first place with:

> "What makes you talk so sprightly?
> What makes your wit so rare?
> Your knowledge sits you lightly:
> I like your savoir faire.
> You're erudite; you're breezy!
> All listen when you speak.
> How is it done?" "That's easy—
> I Read a Book a Week."[28]

By the spring of 1922 Allen had become restless as publicity officer, and he turned once more toward New York. "I began to realize that an administrative job in a university, while pretty exciting at thirty [he was thirty-two], would not be very good at fifty—especially when it was a job which I myself was convinced ought not to be expanded."[29]

The *Century*, still declining from its once prestigious position, wanted Allen again, and he went to New York to inquire. The job would have been as right-hand man and associate editor to editor in chief Glenn Frank, a relative newcomer to magazine work.[30] It distinctly appealed to Allen; the situation offered a challenge. Only the year before, Frank, upon assuming the editorship, had thoroughly reshuffled the magazine's format to arouse it from its doldrums. He changed the cover, raised the newsstand price from thirty-five to fifty cents, and tried to enliven the contents.[31] When Allen appeared in the office, friends cornered him and whispered that he simply *must* come back. He was willing to do so at a certain price. He told Frank that he would expect a starting salary of seventy-five hundred dollars. Frank could offer only five thousand dollars, and he would have to confer with the firm's president, W. Morgan Shuster, about paying more.

Allen returned to Cambridge and waited. Finally, the telegram came: "Five thousand is limit now. Will consider increase as business improves. Write whether interested and when you could come." Allen conferred with Dorothy and Sedgwick, then declined. While five thousand dollars would have represented an increase in pay, he figured higher living costs in New York City actually would lessen his economic status.[32]

The New York visit did boost his ego in another way. While there he dined with a Harvard alumni committee, the Committee on Policy in Publicity, charged with overseeing Allen's own publicity office. The group highly commended Allen on his work, and he confided in them his plans to leave Harvard. Afterwards, the *Evening Post* editor, Edwin Francis Gay, pulled Allen aside and told him to be certain to double-check with him before accepting an offer.[33]

The committee agreed with Allen's own feelings that the publicity director's job was not deemed sufficiently important by his colleagues. Less than two months later the committee recommended that Allen's status be elevated to that of an academic professor. "Want Publicity Professor," read the *New York Times* headline. "The university does not want a mere press agent," the committee was quoted as saying. "It wants a man of faculty rank, whose title expresses a relationship of confidence and authority close to the central authority of the university."[34]

The committee went even further—it advocated relaxation of

Harvard's bias against news coverage of its hallowed ceremonies. Harvard policy prohibited news cameras in the Yard on Commencement Day, and photographers, according to the committee, had frequently been assaulted in the streets during the academic procession to Sanders Theatre. The report further urged relaxation of restrictions on the press at other solemn occasions such as the dedication of buildings. Finally, it extolled the virtues of the motion picture camera.

But the recommendations did not deter Allen from his determination to leave, and he continued to look for a new position. Dorothy was in no hurry to leave Cambridge, and she felt somewhat relieved when it became apparent that no satisfactory job would arise in time for them to leave at the end of the 1922 spring semester.

Less than a year later, though, Allen found what he wanted, a job at Harper & Brothers as a "literary adviser." It would allow him to work part-time with book publishing and part-time with the firm's magazine, *Harper's*. Sedgwick again had been the key to finding the position, but this was the last time that his services would be needed in such a way.[35]

7

A CAREER AT *HARPER'S*

At Harper & Brothers Allen found home at last. Since college, he had idealized a career that would combine both editing and writing, and at thirty-three his wish was fulfilled.

Six years had passed since he had departed the publishing center of New York City. On Allen's return in 1923 it was a city of nearly six million people, some six thousand of whom were editors, authors, or reporters. Since about 1900 the city had achieved unchallenged preeminence in publishing. Altogether some forty thousand people were engaged in printing and publishing, and every day the mails brought in manuscripts from hopeful writers from all across the land.[1]

The Harper & Brothers enterprise did not believe it was sharing fully in the general prosperity of the 1920s. Neither side of the publishing venture was flourishing when Allen joined the firm. Back in 1891 J. Pierpont Morgan had rescued the company from bankruptcy when the Harper family encountered financial difficulties, and when Allen joined the House of Harper in 1923 vice presidents Thomas B. Wells and Henry Hoyns were only then freeing it from a $1,230,000 indebtedness to the Morgan firm by selling certain properties. Wells and Hoyns also were manipulating to have the Morgan man, C. T. Brainard, removed as president. In May 1924, the indebtedness to Morgan cleared, Brainard resigned and Douglas Parmentier of the New York Trust Company replaced him.[2] That same year Cass Canfield[3] became manager of the London office, and in the following year Eugene F. Saxton was named book editor. Allen, then, was joining the house just as it was stabilizing its foundation for future decades. The Harper's book list had had a dearth of best-sellers since World War I; the magazine was in a more serious slump. Optimism prevailed, however. A new six-story, red-brick building was going up at 49 East Thirty-third Street.

The Harper & Brothers imprint on American books dated back to the firm's founding in 1817, and *Harper's Magazine* had almost as lengthy a history. The Harper brothers began in 1850 to issue *Harper's New Monthly Magazine,* not with grand visions of a forceful voice, but as Fletcher Harper later said, "as a tender to our business."[4] Its early emphasis clearly lay in the fiction of English authors, cheap and easily obtainable because of the lack of international copyright laws. The new publication rapidly surpassed the modest original hopes by attracting a starting circulation of 50,000. It became the first important general interest magazine to attain a national circulation. In 1869 Henry Alden Mills was named editor, a position he did not relinquish until 1919 when Wells replaced him. During Mills' remarkable tenure the magazine developed further into an outstanding journal whose only competitors in quality were the *Century, Scribner's,* and the more regionally identified *Atlantic Monthly,* which had blossomed under Sedgwick's guidance and created a more relevant content than that of its competitors.

Harper's, along with the *Century* and *Scribner's,* still labored under an older editing approach. It was, in Allen's own terms, quaintly remote from modern complexities and the more immediate appeal of the recently emerged mass magazines. As Allen later described it, *Harper's* was edited for "ladies and gentlemen of either means or intellectual interests, or preferably both."[5] The pages were heavy with articles about travel, European affairs, and manners; sentimental fiction; and light verse. Its reputation remained high, but circulation was dropping.

With the notable exception of the *Atlantic, Harper's* historic competitors in the quality magazine field also were faring poorly. The changes that Glenn Frank had instituted at the *Century* in 1921 failed to reverse that magazine's steady demise. Frank resigned in 1925; four years later the magazine converted from a monthly to a quarterly; and in 1930 it went out of business. *Scribner's*, likewise, already was in a gradual tailspin that had begun about 1912. Except for brief flurries in the late 1920s and in the mid-1930s, the magazine continued its fall until it collapsed in 1939.[6]

The 1920s nevertheless saw the spectacular birth of several magazines that became the publishing success stories of the mid-twentieth century. The most meteoric, if short-lived, episode began when H. L. Mencken and George Jean Nathan, in January 1924, put out the first issue of the *American Mercury,* a magazine that was to set the intellectual tone of despair and cynicism of the twenties. A slower start, but one destined to become the greatest success of all, was made in 1922 when DeWitt and Lila Wallace began very modestly to publish the *Reader's Digest.* Early in 1923 another great publishing venture, *Time,* brainchild of Yale graduates Henry R. Luce and Briton Hadden, had developed its own new formula for compact journalism. In 1925 the *New Yorker* started in Manhattan under the firm if eccentric hand of Harold Ross. Despite problems for many magazines, then, the period was marked with unusual successes, too.

Harper & Brothers moved to 49 East Thirty-third Street in July 1923, opening its doors just in time to greet the new employee from Boston, Frederick L. Allen. On the evening of his second day at work, the unexpected news came of President Warren G. Harding's death while returning by rail from his trip to the West and Alaska. Only the day before, on Allen's first day at work, the newspapers prematurely had reported the President's crisis over. Allen had not expected much from Harding as a President, and he had been pleasantly surprised by the competence of his administration, although the scandals within the administration were not yet fully known. Allen could not help being amazed at the public confidence expressed in Coolidge as Harding's successor, but he hoped that he, like Harding, would be a pleasant surprise in office.[7]

At Harper & Brothers, Allen found himself situated in the literary or trade-book department in a big room on the top floor which held desks for the department head, William H. Briggs, two other editorial assistants besides himself, and three clerical people. This office force had responsibility only for selecting and editing books for publication and nothing to do with merchandising them.[8] The department worked closely with the magazine, also located on the sixth floor, and magazine editor Thomas B. Wells, a vice president of the firm as well, remained "in constant touch" with the literary department.[9] Wells was a deep-voiced, bald-headed, and commanding individual. "I feel as responsible to him as to Briggs," Allen wrote to his father.[10] The work day began between 9 and 9:30 A.M. and ended between 5 and 5:30 P.M. Frequently, Allen took manuscripts home to read in the evening. His office hours were filled with editorial duties as varied as editing the popular Gamaliel Bradford's biographical studies in *Bare Souls,* reading proof on Anne Ritchie's *Thackeray and His Daughter,* and selecting a title for a two-volume collection of Woodrow Wilson's early papers.[11] He also had occasion to meet authors and suggest ideas for books, secure illustrations for articles, edit manuscripts, write the "Personal and Otherwise" column in *Harper's Magazine,* and take charge of the 1924 *Harper's* Short Story contest, which was so successful that it brought in 10,370 entries.[12]

Allen found editor Wells, a man noted for his frankness, "delightful and tremendously able." In August 1924, he reported the magazine circulation to be "picking up very nicely," and he was beginning to think *Harper's* had "the edge" over the *Atlantic* in quality. Furthermore, his first year's anniversary at the publishing house brought him a yearly pay raise from six thousand dollars to sixty-five hundred dollars.[13]

Wells was less pleased than Allen with the quality of the magazine, and he planned and executed in 1925, the magazine's seventy-fifth anniversary year, a revolutionary change in direction that was to raise dramatically *Harper's* fortunes and save it from the death that awaited the *Century* and *Scribner's*. The conversion took place in the September 1925 issue, dressed for the first time in a bright orange cover. The interior pages were stripped of the old illustrations and photographs, and the typography had been streamlined. A new grade of softer paper replaced the slick and heavy pages of old, and the only illustration remaining was a frontispiece, an American painting to be selected each month and reproduced in color to lead the issue.

Much more significantly, Wells overhauled the content of the articles. He reduced the magazine's fiction and severely curtailed its light verse. The intellectual content took a measurable step upwards in quality. The plan now was to discuss the central issues of importance to American society. It was the same idea Ellery Sedgwick formulated a decade earlier to rejuvenate the *Atlantic*.

As Wells explained, the magazine was to be aimed at the "intelligent minority," to the "thinking, cultured reader who seeks both entertainment and an enlarged and broadened point of view."[14] Henry Alden Mills had pointed *Harper's* toward "respectable and well-to-do gentle folk of nice tastes." Wells de-emphasized the appeal toward upper-class readers and aimed toward readers who might not be genteel but "who combined brains and taste with a concern over public affairs."[15] An adventure story by Zane Grey had led the August issue; the September issue contained provocative articles by Harry Emerson Fosdick, Bertrand Russell, Oswald Garrison Villard, and Rebecca West.

Public response to the new approach was overwhelming. In August the circulation had been about 83,000; the December issue sold 125,00 copies, placing the magazine in close proximity to the *Atlantic's* 140,000 to 150,000 readers. Newsstand sales doubled, and nine months later the magazine had turned the financial corner as well: it again was a profit-maker after years of losses.[16]

As the decade progressed, Allen played an increasingly larger role in editing the magazine, and he gradually shed entirely his duties in book publishing. Wells frequently was away, and the editorial duties were left entirely to Lee F. Hartman, the associate editor, and Allen, who now carried the title of assistant editor.[17] Allen dealt firsthand with many contributors, such as Owen Wister, whom he found to be "a bilious old bird, even if he can write."[18]

In November 1927 Harvard once again approached Allen about returning to his old job, expanded to include editorship of the *Alumni Bulletin*. The salary was to be seventy-five hundred dollars, and President Lowell was said to be particularly interested in bringing Allen back. Allen's answer, after a week's deliberation, was no. His work at the magazine seemed "too interesting and important" to give up.[19]

In June of 1926 the Allens moved into a newly constructed house on Old Army Road in Scarsdale. To help finance it Allen had redoubled his free-lance writing to supplement a bank account which two years earlier had totaled fourteen hundred dollars.[20] One of the articles, "The House Terrible," dealt appropriately with his own hectic experiences in building a house.[21]

Automobiles represented an important part of any suburbanite's life. Just before the carpenters and painters completed the attractive house, the Allens purchased a "new and powerful Ford" which, as Allen phrased it, strained at the leash in the garage. "We now look quite respectable when we go Fording," he wrote his mother.[22]

Allen's love of exercise was evidenced in a happy association with a compatible circle of friends who dubbed themselves "The Old Army Athletes." Along with two other members of the group, Fessenden S. Blanchard and James Cogswell, Allen helped invent paddle tennis. On weekends he luxuriated in the clean, country air of Scarsdale. Each spring he pursued bird-watching, carefully listing each species when he sighted it for the first time.

Allen's old pal, Robert Benchley, and his wife Gertrude also lived in Scarsdale. Benchley had just expanded his humor from the printed page to the night club stage, and one evening in January 1924 the Allens went to the Music Box Revue to see him perform his soon-to-be famous monologue, "The Treasurer's Report." To Allen, Benchley's performance "rambled around and was utterly incoherent and . . . ridiculously reminiscent of many and many a speech." His own silent laughter made his stomach sore, but Allen feared the act came across to the rest of the audience as a rather mild feature in a predominantly raucous review. "But it was so perfect a performance that I was proud to know Bob."[23]

Benchley and Robert E. Sherwood, another former Harvard *Lampoon* staff member, also provided Allen a supplementary source of income. As editors of the humor magazine *Life,* the two purchased picture ideas from him at fifteen to twenty dollars each. During one week in 1924 Allen earned fifty dollars for his suggestions. "They say subjects for pictures are the hardest things to get, as the artists don't have funny ideas," he explained to his father.[24]

In the summer of 1927 Allen took leave from his duties at the magazine and went to Europe with Dorothy. The children stayed with Dr. and Mrs. Cobb while their parents leisurely toured England and France. The Allens returned to New York, which now really seemed like home, and continued giving parties enlivened by parlor games. In 1928 Allen was admitted to the exclusive club for men of letters, The Century Association, which had been founded in 1847 by one hundred men interested in literature and the arts. The Century Club became one of Allen's favorite places for relaxation, and he developed over the years into one of the organization's best players of "cowboy pool," a combination of pool and billiards.

All was not play, however. During the twenties Allen's voluminous outpouring of free-lance writing increased. His humor continued to appear primarily in "The Lion's Mouth." He generally described life's foibles, but a note of optimism, of delight in the day-to-day life about him, undergirded all that he wrote. For subjects he continued to find in his own life experiences that were familiar to almost anyone. He reported on the progress of his one-year-old son, happily concluding with the exaggeration that there was no need for society to be unduly distressed at the cynical younger generation because his cheerful tot seemed to be filling the need for an atmosphere of hope.[25] In "Jack and Jill," he analyzed in a pseudo-scientific fashion the varying behavior patterns of both his children and concluded that, politically speaking, boys are radicals and girls are conservatives.[26] Packing for vacation, antique-buying, husband-wife relations, etiquette books, and budgets all made lively sketches. He wrote humorous pieces on psychological testing, the atom, passport photographs, Mah-Jongg, cynicism, the income tax, high fashion, snobbery, poetry, department stores, speculation in stocks, politics, preaching, and dieting.

He ridiculed the flowery poetry of spring, appropriate for England perhaps but totally wrong for Westchester County, and he offered his own more accurate stylings in "Ode to April":

> The slush it has melted
> But the mud is still here.
> Hail, April, thou messiest
> Month of the year.[27]

His humor techniques had not changed materially, but the subject matter was broader. In "A Little Lecture on the Atom," he gave a mock treatise on the atom's qualities, especially its minuteness. "If a thousand atoms were clustered together they would still be invisible, although if you listened very intently you might hear the little fellows breathing."[28]

At the end of the decade Allen stopped writing the sort of broad humor that was becoming outmoded by the more subtle, sophisticated wit of the New Yorker. Allen himself was on the verge of making the transition in style as his last magazine appearances as a humorist came in the New Yorker in 1929 and 1930.

Many of Allen's friends and associates—writers, artists, and intellectuals in particular—were now in a state not inclined to joking. Allen later would describe the twenties as a period marked first of all by its mood of disillusionment. The mood had been brought about, it was generally acknowledged, by the emotional letdown following the failure to achieve the high purpose which Americans like Allen had carried so fervently into the war effort. A counterfeeling, which contrasted sharply with the intellectual wringing of hands, was the blind overriding sense of faith in the virtues and evergrowing possibilities of a business civilization.

Allen did not share fully in either of these two moods. He struck a middle course, finding fault through his humor with both the cynics and the boosters. He reserved his satire for boosterism; he attacked the mood of despair through both humor and serious arguments. Primarily, he faulted H. L. Mencken, Sinclair Lewis, and their followers because he believed them to be little more than hypocrites who exhibited an unwarranted callousness toward the common man.

In "The New Tories," the name Allen gave to the followers of Mencken, he described most cynics as simply latching on to a fad to appear intellectually fashionable. Mencken himself was clearly a Tory. While laborers toiled in the mills in economic slavery, and while diplomats swapped concessions and brewed new and hideous wars, "these new Tories sit exquisitely and sip their cocktails and fiddle the new jazz, and snap their fingers at the welfare of the common man, and think they're the heralds of a new age!"[29]

Allen's most concentrated attack came in two 1927 articles in the *Independent,* where much of his serious work of the period was published. His "These Disillusioned Highbrows" condemned the exaggerated notions of Mencken and Lewis, who were "bent upon persuading us how vulgar, depraved, and uncivilized we are. . . . It is a fantastic picture . . . of a nation whose business men are boors, whose clergymen are hypocrites engaged in illicit amours, whose leading citizens are inflated bigots, and whose country people are pious morons." He thought Mencken wielded an unfortunate and "extraordinary influence" upon the writing styles of young authors and made them view American life as a stereotype. Close investigation, Allen believed, would reveal the average American to be "rather a good fellow, after all." Those who waxed vindictive about intolerance "might practice a little more tolerance themselves . . . with this average American."

The reason for the current cynical vogue, Allen felt, lay in the extremes to which the opposite forces had gone. The "boosters," "superpatriots," "hundred per centers," and "moral sentimentalists" had insured an opposite reaction because of their own overstatement. "One suspects the pendulum of reaction has swung about far enough.

It is almost time that the debunkers were themselves debunked," Allen said cautiously. He predicted that the very success of the "highbrows" would be their undoing. "Their public will tire of seeing itself butchered to make a highbrow holiday. The books of the nineteen-twenties will gather dust on our shelves, and once in a while we shall pull them down and smile at them and say, 'whew! How they all lit into the old United States in those days.' "[30]

Some of the ideas for the attack against Mencken and his followers had been provided by Allen's mother. Allen notified her happily when he learned that the *Independent* was to display the piece prominently.[31] Perhaps the Allens entertained a special animosity toward Mencken, who had attempted by being arrested in 1926 to bring public ridicule upon the Watch and Ward Society in Boston for banning an issue of the *American Mercury*. Allen's father had died in 1925, but his important role over the years in the Society could not be forgotten.

In "There, There, Little Highbrow, Don't Cry!," Allen contended that a cult of "professional knockers" had arisen, and that a professional knocker was almost as tiresome as a professional booster. In "Sour Grapes," he attacked the disenchanted from another direction by satirizing the intellectual writers, artists, journalists, scientists, and other professionals who pretended to have forsaken wealth in order to pursue "Higher Things." He portrayed them basically as types who did not possess the necessary skills to achieve wealth even if they tried.[32]

In a trio of articles during the mid-1920s Allen examined several problems of higher education, particularly the growing tendency of alumni to urge their wishes on their alma maters. Such outside meddling, he felt, eventually could lead to a "rule of ignorance" because alumni knowledge of the school's endeavors inevitably was shallow and uninformed.[33] President Lowell at Harvard congratulated Allen on the article, saying he had "hit the nail exactly on the head, and with great skill."[34]

Allen charged in "The Fetish of the PhD" that the doctorate did not provide the best training for teaching. The typical doctoral program did its best to cramp the mind, stifle the imagination, and dry up human understanding. He advised aspiring professors, faced with the necessity of obtaining the doctorate, to recognize it only as a necessary evil and to resist its narrowing tendencies.[35]

"Suburban Nightmare" sounded an early cry against the encroachment of pleasant suburbs by urbanization. Developers were spoiling the rural atmosphere of areas such as Allen's own Scarsdale by cutting down trees and building homes, apartments, and stores in the name of "improvement." To escape this syndrome commuters continued to move farther and farther out, only to see the same cycle repeated and to make the hours spent en route to Manhattan totally unreasonable. While the problem had reached New York first, Allen foresaw that the same trend would soon confront other American cities. The only solution he could offer was to return to a society with smaller spheres of business influence. Perhaps by that time, he wrote, we would be advertising our smallness rather than our bigness with signs such as, "Watch Vermont Dwindle."[36]

The communications media continued to bear Allen's scrutiny. In "Public Opinion," he created a realistic fable about how the news media, for the sake of a story, sensationalized into a state-wide crisis a minister's casual aside in a Sunday sermon that the state's blue laws should be enforced.[37] He spoofed the claims of self-improvement advertising in "Success! ! !" The worst aspect of such advertising, he wrote, was its indirect aim of making the average person feel so incompetent in his social and business life that he would seek an overnight transformation.[38]

During these years Allen made his first efforts at writing book-length material. Among the Allens' Scarsdale friends were Mr. and Mrs. Paul Revere Reynolds. Mrs. Reynolds asked Allen to write a brief biography of her husband, a literary agent, for the Reynolds family. The principal condition was that Reynolds himself would not know about it until completed. Allen agreed, and in a burst of energy completed the initial draft in the month of April 1927.

Reynolds certainly was worthy of such treatment, for when he died at the age of eighty in 1944 he had been a literary agent for fifty-two years and had handled some of the best writing produced in America, including works by Stephen Crane, Jack London, Edith Wharton, and Frank Norris. Unfortunately, Allen did not have primary research materials, and the biography was no more than a lengthy "sketch," as the work's subtitle acknowledged. Since it was written without the subject's knowledge, it could hardly be a full treatment in 105 pages. It bore, however, the Allen trademark of a skillfully written, interesting piece of work. Not until Reynolds' death seventeen years later did the family have the manuscript privately printed.[39]

Another idea for a biography soon was broached. Allen's mother asked her son to undertake a "memoir" of his father, who had died at eighty-four two years earlier. It was a total work of love. In the 102-page memoir, published in 1929, he portrayed his father as a "liberal through and through" who hated hypocrisy and had a passion for fairness. Written as a straight narrative of his father's career, Allen ended the book with an introspective note in which he pondered the fact that he somehow had never felt the urge to rebel from his parents. In recent years, Allen noted, there had been a tendency, especially among those reared in clerical households, to be repelled by the "bleak and unlovely aspects of puritanical Protestantism," to be disillusioned by the frequent hypocrisy of many self-professed Christians, and "to break bitterly and contemptuously away from their parents' religious beliefs and ethical principles." Allen said he, who had differed on many fundamental points with his father, often wondered why he had never been rebellious. It must have been, he concluded, because of his father's unimpeachable character, total sense of fairness, and attempts to understand all sides of every issue, and the resulting atmosphere which pervaded the lively household. "My father was a gentleman; and a good citizen; and a follower of Christ. Perhaps that explains why he was sometimes called 'the most beloved man in Boston.'"[40]

When Allen first met Dorothy in Washington he described himself as a radical. That was an overstatement, made probably as a half-jest. In 1925 Groton alumnus George W. Martin wrote to Endicott

Peabody that the school's graduates traditionally were solid pillars of the state who sold bonds, got rich, played polo, and always supported the status quo. "Now come these rotten reds like Freddy Allen and me who vulgarly pillory all the most sacred cows of the Victorian Age."[41] The point was that Allen, expected because of his background to be one kind of man, turned out to be another sort. The 1924 presidential election offered an opportunity for Allen to define himself politically, and when he did, the "radical" stamp clearly did not fit. The Democratic party offered the wealthy Wall Street lawyer from West Virginia, John W. Davis. Davis had good liberal credentials, although since his tenure as Wilson's solicitor general he had been counsel for J. P. Morgan and Company and several large corporations. Calvin Coolidge's conservatism was well known, and the Democratic Allen certainly would not jump the party for him. A third choice, however, offered a distinctive alternative for alienated intellectuals, radicals, liberals, and reformers: Robert La Follette and the Progressive party. Allen chose the middle-of-the-road Davis. La Follette, after all, had been pacifistic during the recent war and no friend of Wilsonian wartime idealism.

The Democratic convention was held in New York City, and work at *Harper's* was punctuated daily by the sound of marching brass bands passing outside. Allen wrote to his father that he supported with enthusiasm Davis' nomination despite his Wall Street connections. New York's Al Smith would have been his first choice, but Allen figured 1924 was too early for a Smith victory. Another politician had impressed him greatly at the convention. The dramatic "happy warrior" nominating speech for Smith, delivered by Groton graduate Franklin Delano Roosevelt, was excellent in Allen's estimation.[42]

Probably the greatest issue of the decade was the worldwide protest by liberals and radicals over the scheduled execution of Nicola Sacco and Bartolomeo Vanzetti for the 1920 payroll robbery and murder in Braintree, Massachusetts. In the rough division between left and right, the liberal-radical-intellectual wing charged that the two aliens had been convicted unfairly because of their political views. Allen did not join in this protest. He watched the spectacle carefully, though, and somewhat critically. Three days after the radicals' execution in 1927, Allen wrote to his mother that he "never knew of a case where I personally had so many friends and acquaintances involved either as participants or picketers."[43]

Allen wished himself that the sentence had been commuted, and he believed the Massachusetts laws should be amended to prevent the original judge from also hearing the appeal. But, he said, there seemed to be no other proper course but to accept the Lowell investigative committee's report that the trial had been in order. "They know more about the evidence than the rest of us, and if they are biased, why then anyone would be and we might as well give up going to college (as Dorothy says)." The whole business, he felt, had been a "catastrophe."[44]

TRAGEDY—AND TRIUMPH

Ample justification existed for Allen's own reluctance to see gloom around every corner. He enjoyed a happy family life which included two alert children, held a prestigious and rewarding job as an editor, and sold his articles about as quickly as he could write them.

In the fall of 1928, however, seven-year-old "Sniggle-fitz," as Allen nicknamed his daughter Elizabeth, fell ill with what was considered at first to be simply a childhood fever. The disease was diagnosed as spinal meningitis, and surgery revealed a badly infected mastoid bone. Dorothy, realizing the truth, told her mother, "I think it's fatal." Two days later a second operation was performed on the other mastoid. "I'm all full of holes," Elizabeth cheerfully said. "I guess they'll have to fill me up with cement."[1] The child's condition worsened, on November 10 she was semiconscious, and the next night Elizabeth died. When Dorothy and Allen soon observed their tenth wedding anniversary, Allen wore a black necktie and black armband and Dorothy a dress of deep mourning.[2]

Dorothy's parents in the next months pressured her and Allen to go to church, believing it would ease their grief. The advice only irritated them, but Dr. Cobb and Dorothy became involved in long discussions about religion. Emily Cobb Holmes, Dorothy's sister, remembers that Dorothy, who had been president of the Christian Association at Vassar, now lost her faith in God.[3]

Two weeks after Elizabeth's death Emily, a frequent guest, visited the Allens, and in an effort to relieve their grief they drove to a resort house at Westhampton, Long Island, for relaxation and a change of scenery. But the hotel was deserted, the day was rainy and cold, and relief could not be found.[4] The following summer the Allens, Dr. and Mrs. Cobb, and Emily went to Switzerland to see about medical treatment for Dorothy's bouts with rheumatism and to Paris to have portraits painted of Oliver and Elizabeth (the latter from a snapshot) by a well-known children's artist, Bradford Johnson.

Oliver was flourishing. He was beginning to excel in his violin lessons, and he provided many moments of humor for his saddened parents.

Allen and Dorothy soon resumed their entertaining, often with unusual parties such as a scrub baseball game in their orchard. And Allen's bird-watching was not forgotten.[5]

In the fall of 1929 an event far less personal than the death of his daughter exerted a profound influence upon Allen's career. The orgy of speculation on Wall Street, buttressed by the widespread and unwavering popular faith in continued business expansion, ended in a panic-filled crash. The great debacle, coming within a year of the loss of Elizabeth, brought an abrupt change to Allen's writing career, and he abandoned humor for a more serious but still witty contemplation of society.

The crash not only shattered the era's seemingly eternal popular optimism, it seemed to Allen almost at once to indicate much more: the end of a unique period of American life and the beginning of another. The idea that the crash had broader implications than just economic ones had come to him suddenly as an inspiration one day over lunch with Walter Lippmann and Charles Merz, both of whom listened approvingly while Allen verbally worked out his thought.[6] At home he could not drop the idea, and he organized his impressions on paper. The result was his article in the February 5, 1930 issue of *Outlook and Independent*, "The End of an Era," and even after writing this piece Allen could not drop the ideas it expressed.[7] He was convinced it deserved fuller, book-length treatment.

It did not occur to him that he should write the book himself; he was too busy with all sorts of satisfying activities. Besides a busy social life in Scarsdale, Allen had begun an association with the internationally minded P.E.N. Club, designed to bring about co-operation and mutual understanding among the writers of the world. *Harper's* editor Thomas Wells was in Europe from early November to mid-February, leaving Hartman and Allen with the magazine. In short, Allen had no time to write a book, and books were not his forte anyway—or so he felt.

Convinced that someone should write the book, he suggested to his friend Charles Merz that he should do it. Merz himself had no time for it, though, and he asked Allen why he did not write it. Shortly after Wells returned from Europe, Allen mentioned the idea to him in the washroom. Wells saw potential in it, and he told Allen, "I think you better write that book."[8] Allen remained reluctant.

Then spring came, lending a special verve to his life. "Every morning is a joy," he wrote to his mother. "The apple-trees came out in full blossom yesterday and my favorite warblers are appearing one by one. . . . Today the sky is clear blue, the clouds puffy white, the wind west, every tiny leaflet green, and the temperature 70°." The entire family was "flourishing." Dorothy had just played one of her best golf games ever, Oliver was in "top-notch" condition, and the Scarsdale homesite was "incredibly lovely" in this burst of spring. After these rhapsodic lines to his mother, Allen announced that he had "decided to do that book."[9]

He went about the project in a highly organized fashion. First, he acquired all the World Almanacs for the years to be covered.[10] Then, he obtained a 12- by 18-inch pad and drew up his own calendar for the period. He listed key events in brief phrases under the appropriate dates so that at a glance he had an overall grasp in sequence of what he considered to be the central developments of the years.[11] He revised his original synopsis and by early May he was ready to begin the first chapter. He worked diligently through the summer of 1930 and was well into the book when a second terrible tragedy struck.

Elizabeth's death had made the Allen family eager for another child, and Oliver said he was going to pray every night for a sister.[12] Dorothy had been told that she had a "tipped uterus," and a friend recommended her to a doctor who determined to correct the situation through surgery, thinking it would enhance the likelihood of conception. Eager, perhaps too eager, to try anything for another baby, Dorothy had the operation in October 1930. Something apparently went wrong during surgery, and the next day she felt very ill and her face was tinged with a yellow cast. Within days she fell unconscious, and she died while her husband and father, who was praying aloud for her recovery, stood by her bedside.[13] She was buried next to Elizabeth at the Sleepy Hollow Cemetery in Tarrytown, New York.

"I feel as though I had been cut in two," Allen told Emily.[14] Now forty, Allen was in a position reminiscent of that of his father years before, when his wife had died from complications following the birth of their third daughter. Allen's father eventually had returned to Boston so his family could help rear the girls. Allen arrived at a similar conclusion regarding the upbringing of Oliver. Within two weeks Dorothy's parents moved from New York City to the home in Scarsdale to help provide a family atmosphere for the child.[15] They remained there for nearly a year. Although Mrs. Cobb, a dominating personality, proved to be extremely vexatious for Allen, he regarded Dr. Cobb with unbounded admiration and love. Dr. Cobb, rather old-fashioned in a most pleasing way in his ideas of virtue and morality, radiated to all, children as well as adults, a friendly and honest glow. "He was a giant of a man, in body and in mind," Allen summed him up.[16]

Two weeks after Dorothy's death Mrs. Cobb insisted that young Oliver should attend church that day. Allen did not approve of the local churches, undoubtedly because they were too literal in interpreting the Bible, and as a compromise he kept Oliver home to give him a lesson about the Sermon on the Mount, all the while feeling "utterly inadequate and lonely and lost."[17]

Young Oliver, at the age of eight, also felt lost. "Daddy," he said, "when Elizabeth died I got over it right away, but I don't get over this."[18] A great-aunt visiting in the Scarsdale house saw a poignant reminder of the impact upon Oliver of his mother's death. Oliver, who was not aware that she was watching, went into his father's room and opened Dorothy's bottom bureau drawer. He took out of it her fur neckpiece, placed it around his neck and smoothed and smoothed it, caressing it as he stood in front of the bureau. Then he carefully replaced it, shut the drawer, and quietly left the room.[19]

Writing proved therapeutic for Allen. He lost little time in returning to his book, which he planned to call *Only Yesterday*. Before Dorothy's death he had completed his initial draft of the first five chapters. Three weeks after her death he had completed another chapter, and he wrote with machinelike precision until the book was finished in the summer of 1931.[20]

Not only did Allen devote his evenings to the book, but he arranged at the office during the last six months to take off one day a week for writing. Busy as he stayed with the book, friends were able to engage him on occasion for dinner or conversation in an effort to assuage his mourning. He spent a long golfing weekend with his friend, the Rev. John Suter, at the Chevy Chase Club where Allen had played during World War I days, and he returned from Washington on his first airplane flight—a bumpy, unsettling two-hour ride.[21]

By March of 1931 he had found a tonic for his fatigue from grief and overwork: Agnes Rogers Hyde, who worked in promotion at *Harper's* and who already had written articles for the magazine. The association appeared rather casual for a long while, and by June, Allen still referred to the attractive divorcée in his letters as "Mrs. Hyde."[22] But they quietly saw more and more of one another.

In May, Thomas Wells decided to retire at the age of fifty-six. He explained that the magazine now was firmly on its feet, a prosperous future seemed assured, and he deserved a rest. Lee Foster Hartman moved up to the editorship, and Allen's title was changed from assistant editor to associate editor. "Not that it makes much difference," he commented privately, but he acknowledged that the recognition was nice.[23] Wells had been absent so often from his job that being number two man was nothing new for Allen. His duties and responsibilities remained basically the same despite the new title. Hartman was an unassuming, easygoing editor who agreed with Wells on magazine policy and continued to guide the publication with high ideals through the Depression.

The effects of the Depression had not yet adversely influenced the magazine's circulation, though it already was affecting advertising. Circulation now was 120,947, a dramatic increase since the new format of 1925. By now the *Atlantic* was its only real competitor.[24] Although readership remained high in 1931, within three years circulation would plummet by 30,000. Advertising revenues had fallen, and this was more immediately critical. In November 1931 an across-the-board salary cut of 10 percent was instituted for all employees of Harper & Brothers as an economy move.[25]

On the first anniversary of Dorothy's death Allen wrote to his mother:

> The first year is over: I am well and confident; and as I told Kate and Andrew [Butler] last night, if I were asked whether I would choose to live this last year over again, I'm not sure that I wouldn't say yes. It has been full of pain and difficulty, but also of happiness at being able to surmount them; and when I look back I don't feel that I am much to be pitied. The really cruel thing is that Dorothy has been robbed of life: that's what I can't forgive.
>
> I find life extraordinarily interesting even when it's difficult. As I look forward to this next year I have the publication of my book to engross me; and the prospect of responsible and rewarding work on the magazine, which is going very well editorially and winning praise although the fearful drop in advertising revenue as a result of panicky general conditions has removed its profit and driven it (temporarily, I hope) into the red; and the problem to tackle of working out a basis of living while the Cobbs are away; and the chance of a real holiday abroad or elsewhere; and the assurances of the aid and support of a fine group of friends; and the expectation of beginning (at Christmas or thereabouts) to begin writing for the magazines once more. There may be worries and tribulations and weaknesses to meet, but I remember that Charlie Storey said last year—"If you can go through this, you can go through anything."[26]

In October Allen's completed manuscript was submitted to the Book-of-the-Month Club for consideration. The judges voted unanimously to select *Only Yesterday: An Informal History of the Nineteen-Twenties* as their November choice.[27] Allen called it "colossal good fortune": aside from the guaranteed sales of 45,000 copies from the club itself, the selection assured the book of additional publicity and sales. "How Dorothy would have been pleased!" he commented.[28] He had dedicated the book to "the memory of D.P.A."

December 1 was the official publication date for *Only Yesterday*, and by then four printings, including copies for the Book-of-the-Month Club, had been made, totaling 52,550 copies.[29] The day after publication the *New York Times* treated Allen's criticism of Hoover for his inaction in the face of depression as a news story in itself. No reviews were yet in, but Allen now had cast aside his natural reserve and expressed confidence that critics would be enthusiastic. In fact, he added, "I shouldn't be a bit surprised if it got into the best-seller lists."[30]

In the Harper offices he kept a sharp eye on the mail from the various book stores and exulted over every big order. Thirteen days after publication, *Only Yesterday* was a best-seller. The sole concern was being able to print enough books to keep up with the heavy pre-Christmas demand. Less than two weeks after publication more than 10,000 copies of the book had sold (not including book club sales), and Allen predicted that total sales eventually would reach 25,000 to 30,000 with his present $9,000 profits likely to reach $20,000. "I have to remind myself that to have a best-seller is after all a break of luck: it may never happen again."[31] Allen was absurdly wrong on both counts. The book has sold to the present far more than a million copies, and virtually every book Allen was to write was destined to reach the best-seller lists.

The successful author was besieged with requests for personal appearances on radio and attendance at endless autograph parties. He realized that the more he appeared the heavier the demands would be. "I've got to learn the art of the tactful refusal," he wrote to his mother, or even of the white lie. "It's all very well to say,

'I'm saving that evening to work at the library,' and 'I can't go because I want to stay at home and put Oliver to bed,' but some people are hurt if you say that sort of thing—better to call it an engagement, I guess."[32]

Allen, exhilarated by his book's high sales, could not, of course, foresee that *Only Yesterday* would prove so enduring, eventually selling more than a million copies and continuing to influence to the present day professional historians and their students.[33] The prevailing image of the post-World War I period for millions of Americans may be traced directly to *Only Yesterday* or indirectly through its host of imitative efforts. Allen never anticipated becoming a "historian" of such influence. He labeled himself a "retrospective journalist," and once, in a self-deprecating mood, a "pseudo-historian."[34] At Harvard he had taken just one history course and declared that he had "no taste for the subject."[35] In *Only Yesterday's* Preface, Allen modestly claimed that he had woven postwar events into a pattern "which at least masquerades as history."[36] The book's remarkable sense of detachment was combined with a breezy, personal writing style in which Allen often directly addressed his readers. As one historian has commented, "Merely to list the titles and subheadings of *Only Yesterday* is to summarize an impression of the period that has long dominated history textbooks, not to mention television and movie screenplays."[37]

The book often is remembered as a social history which emphasized the trivial or picturesque. Allen had in mind something more ambitious. "I have attempted to bring together the innumerable threads of the story so as to reveal the fundamental trends in our national life and national thought during the nineteen-twenties," he declared in the Preface to the book's first edition. His deliberate emphasis was upon "the changing state of the public mind and upon the sometimes trivial happenings with which it was occupied."[38] As such it was as much intellectual as social history. Above all it sought significance in things unusual and in popular thought, an approach not then common among historians. As so often is the case, "trivial happenings" designed to illustrate broader trends sometimes overshadowed the book's serious purposes.

Allen's basic unifying idea was that the period represented a unique era, bounded on one side by the Armistice and on the other by the Great Crash. He interpreted the major themes within this chronological framework as being influenced to an overriding degree by the trauma of war manifesting itself in such diverse areas as the Red scare, the revolution in morals, and even the Big Bull Market itself.

The crusade to curb suspected Reds and radicals represented an inability of the American people to shift out of wartime psychology. Allen made popular a name which was destined forever to identify the era, "Red scare." Much the same explanation accounted for the rise and decline of the Ku Klux Klan. The wartime mandate for hatred toward the enemy shifted rather easily for some to such "unAmericans" as Negroes, Jews, and Catholics. The martial state of mind was held responsible for the adoption of Prohibition because alcohol had been seen as hurting the nation's fighting efficiency. Similarly, the war's end caused Prohibition leaders to lose their positions of importance. With this moral mandate suddenly evaporated, the widespread disregard of Prohibition laws in the 1920s naturally followed and helped precipitate the revolution in manners and morals. Allen also saw Prohibition as immediately occasioning the much ballyhooed outburst of crime in the 1920s, especially in the Chicago area.[39]

Even the "Coolidge prosperity" that most Americans enjoyed was attributed by Allen to a considerable degree to the war. Combat impoverished the European nations and allowed Americans to emerge as "economic masters" of the world. Wartime restrictions also jolted the American businessman who came out of the war with his "fighting blood" up. "He wanted to get back to business and enjoy his profits."[40]

A high point of the book was Allen's rather complete delineation of Warren G. Harding's administration. Allen undoubtedly did as much as anyone to propagate the belief that the Republican bosses met in a "smoke-filled room" in Chicago's Hotel Blackstone and "concluded to put Harding over."[41] He described Harding in what has become the classical picture: a friendly man burdened with a weak intellect, a poor judge of character, and yet a man who *looked* every inch the President. As for the Harding administration, he no longer felt "pleasantly surprised" as he once had. The regime "was responsible in its short two years and five months for more concentrated robbery and rascality than any other in the whole history of the Federal government."[42]

One of the most distinctive images was the "revolution in manners and morals." Allen saw many factors as being responsible: Prohibition, the automobile, Freud, the growing independence of women, confession and sex magazines, and movies. But "first of all was the state of mind brought about by the war and its conclusion." The two million soldiers who left for the perils of the European front infected a whole nation with an "eat-drink-and-be-merry-for-tomorrow-we-die spirit." The emotional stimulus of the war made citizens crave speed, excitement, and passion.[43]

Allen had predicted in 1917 that military necessity would dictate "proper" beliefs and social behavior in the name of patriotism and efficiency.[44] He had been right, and he believed these narrow standards of behavior had helped bring about the intellectual revolt. Middle-class efforts to regulate personal conduct, combined with the failure of the Treaty, had been instrumental in bringing about the revolt by the intellectuals. Sinclair Lewis' *Main Street* and *Babbitt* initially had created a rallying point. Then followed a deeper and more provocative leadership from the Baltimore sage, H. L. Mencken. Allen did not criticize the disillusioned highbrows as he had done in his magazine articles some five years earlier; in fact, he so clearly defined their grievances that he appeared almost wholly sympathetic. While the intellectuals were few, their sense of disillusionment, Allen stressed, came to affect the thought of the entire nation and to underlie the entire decade. Consequently, the heroic figure of Charles Lindbergh was adopted late in the decade as an overnight idol by a "spiritually starved" nation which subconsciously had been anxious for someone like him.[45]

Similarly, Allen explained, the near-blind faith in business was a substitute for the lost faith in political leadership. The climactic rush to speculate in the Big Bull Market replaced the shattered dream of Wilsonian idealism, the spread of political cynicism, the decay of religious certainty, and the debunking of love. In the Big Bull Market Americans found a new dream to spin.[46]

The failure of the market thus meant the culmination of a cycle in mass thinking, introduced a new set of economic conditions, ended the apotheosis of business, and ushered in an age demanding "new adjustments, new ideas, new habits of thought, and a new order of values." American life began turning to different channels. There were many signs of the emerging age: longer skirts, longer hair, more feminine clothing, and a gradual return to formality. All this and more signaled if not an end to the revolution in manners and morals, at least an armistice.[47]

The intellectual revolt, too, had exhausted itself, and the Fundamentalists and Modernists were wearying of battle on the religious front. What Allen termed "the noble art of ballyhoo" had lost its vigor, although he believed the nation remained susceptible to fads. One continuing theme, apathy toward politics, remained. But an exception developed: the nation was less satisfied with a laissez-faire policy for business. "There was a general sense that something had gone wrong with individualistic capitalism and must be set right." The historical drift toward collectivism, interrupted during the 1920s, would be "haltingly resumed once more," Allen correctly predicted. "The United States of 1931 was a different place from the United States of the Post-war Decade; there was no denying that. An old order was giving place to new."[48]

Allen's neat cataloguing of the era, accomplished while Hoover still was President and when the darkest hours of the Depression had not yet emerged, was remarkably perceptive. No one had tied the events together in such a meaningful and detached way, reviewers acknowledged.

The occasional comments that Allen included a disproportionate amount of the decade's glitter represented the only recurring criticism of *Only Yesterday*. Evidently, this distressed him to some degree. In a Preface to the 1946 edition, he explained that for purposes of readability he had illustrated certain of the decade's trends with "rather extreme, though authentic, examples of odd or excited behavior." He urged the reader not to be misled; in "my humble opinion people in the nineteen-twenties were on the average just about as normal and reasonable as they are today."[49]

Aside from newspapers, Allen used very few original sources for *Only Yesterday*. He eschewed footnotes, and his bibliography was a scant three and a half pages. Probably his heaviest single debt was to the famous sociological study of American habits by Robert S. Lynd and Helen Merrell Lynd in *Middletown*, which had been published only at the decade's end.[50]

As for his particularly lively mode of writing recent history, Allen acknowledged in the Preface his debt to Mark Sullivan. In his multivolume series, *Our Times*, Sullivan personalized history by following an average American through the first quarter century to show how events affected his life and ultimate destiny. Sullivan theorized, too, that accomplishments in such neglected areas as "engineering and medicine are fully as important as any political events."[51] Similarly, in his own first chapter, Allen related the changes in daily life between 1919 and the end of the decade for a typical "Mr. and Mrs. Smith." The result was a historical record of daily life that average readers could enjoy and readily absorb.

Allen capitalized upon *Only Yesterday* by accepting offers which inevitably detracted from his more serious initial interpretations. A Hollywood film studio bought the rights to the book for five thousand dollars.[52] In 1933 Universal Pictures Corporation released the full-length movie *Only Yesterday*, directed by John M. Stahl and starring Broadway actress Margaret Sullavan.[53] The film, a maudlin account of an army officer who seduced a woman in Virginia and could not forget her, had nothing to do with the contents of Allen's book.[54]

More than a decade later Time, Inc. commissioned Allen at twenty-five hundred dollars to write a script for a film documentary of the decade, *The Golden Twenties*. Allen not only wrote the script, he also served as narrator for the section on customs and manners. The other narrators were Robert Q. Lewis, Red Barber, and Allen Prescott. The film, a March of Time production, was released in 1950 through RKO.[55]

Despite popularizations such as these, which inevitably were identified with and in some ways detracted from *Only Yesterday*, the book continues to win wide acceptance by historians as a valuable study of a popular period. It does have certain deficiences one would expect from a history written at the tail end of the very period it covers. The most overriding change in historical judgment has been the growing repudiation of the idea that the twenties represent a distinct decade which stood alone. Allen's portrayal has been supplanted by a belief that the era was tied to the preceding age much more closely than he and many historians who followed him suspected. It is, perhaps, understandable that a "pseudo-historian" such as Allen would neglect to point out strands of continuity to the prewar era.

What Allen did so well was to organize and to establish a sense of coherence out of myriad events and details. He exhibited boldness in interpretation and exceptional ability as a phrasemaker.

Some people close to him hold that his informal style in writing history remains his most influential bequest to American letters. Cass Canfield, his publisher and superior at Harper & Brothers, Russell Lynes, his protégé on the magazine, and his own son, Oliver Allen, all point to Allen's informal style as his most lasting contribution.[56] The alternative would be that Allen's historical assessments, particularly in *Only Yesterday*, are more important. Both contributions have been lasting: his ideas about the meaning of the post-World War I era have been accepted by several generations; his polished and witty style of writing popular history set a pattern that continues to this day. Surely neither contribution would have been so enduring without the other.

Throughout his life Allen frequently would be reminded of the impact of *Only Yesterday*. Sinclair Lewis wrote him in 1936, "I'm reading 'Only Yesterday' a second—really a 2 1/2th—time. What a revealing summary—a grand gold-mine for authors to pilfer from!"[57]

9

A SENSE OF MISSION

The Great Crash of 1929 shocked almost beyond belief the people who lived in the richest nation in history. In 1931, the year of *Only Yesterday*'s publication, the worst was yet to come. Economic barometers continued to plummet: unemployment in 1929 had reached just 3.2 percent of the work force, in 1931 the figure was 15.9 percent. Already the Depression had assumed worldwide proportions, and there was a run on the United States' gold supply. By the end of 1932 more than one out of five commercial banks had failed. For those fortunate enough to hold their jobs, salaries of many were being reduced. Panhandlers and beggars might accost a man four or five times in a ten-block walk in the Park Avenue area of Manhattan. Rude shelters assembled from packing boxes and scrap iron were housing men and sometimes families in "Hoovervilles" on the outskirts of town. Among the eight million unemployed an army of drifters had taken to the roads and rails, looking for work or trying to forget. Some wealthier citizens had lost their fortunes, and many had been forced to reduce their standards of living.

Frederick Lewis Allen's situation contrasted markedly with the difficulties of many in the nation. For much of 1932 *Only Yesterday* ranked first on the best-seller nonfiction lists. Allen happily assumed more and more responsibility on *Harper's*, and his romance with Agnes Rogers Hyde was filled with quiet dinners, fun-filled picnics on the beach, automobile rides through the countryside, games with Oliver, and even a roller-coaster ride.

Agnes had come to New York City from her native Hagerstown to pursue a stage career after graduating in 1916 from Vassar. After some theatrical appearances, including a 1916–1917 road show engagement with Stuart Walker's Portmanteau Theatre and performances in a Greenwich Village theater, she left the stage. She worked for *Vogue* magazine, the Foreign Exchange Division of the Federal Reserve Bank during World War I, and then for the J. Walter Thompson advertising agency before joining *Harper's* in 1925 as promotion manager. She had been married in 1923, divorced in 1930, and at thirty-nine was three years younger than Allen. Her quick wit and zest for life helped both Allen and Oliver overcome their lingering sadness. In the summer of 1932, Agnes and Allen became engaged.

Allen's mother, in Europe that summer and unacquainted with Agnes, expressed parental uneasiness about the forthcoming marriage. Allen calmed her with glowing details about his future bride, and he also sought to inform Dorothy's father confidentially of the impending marriage. Dr. Cobb, however, suspecting the nature of the news, declined to hear it. Mrs. Cobb had specifically requested information about the rumored romance, and he preferred to tell his wife honestly that he knew nothing than withhold information from her.[1] The Cobbs no longer were sharing the Scarsdale house, and Allen had taken an apartment in the city for the summer.

Oliver's reaction to the engagement, when Allen told him at summer camp, was an unqualified "Hot-diggety!"[2]

Meanwhile, Allen's new prominence as an author kept him busy and prospering. He declined, after deliberation, to write a monthly column interpreting current events for the *Ladies' Home Journal*, but earned one thousand dollars from the magazine for an article on the effects of the Depression, a sum four times greater than *Harper's* paid its contributors. He appeared on radio station WJZ to give a 13 1/2-minute solo presentation of *Only Yesterday*, and was fascinated to find entirely different demands upon his writing skills in preparing a piece for the exactitudes of the clock. An expected call to Hollywood as consultant for the movie, *Only Yesterday*, failed to materialize, probably because Universal Pictures decided to use only the book's well-known title and not its contents.[3] Allen hardly had time for that, anyway.

In midsummer he computed his probable income for the Depression year, including his *Harper's* salary and royalties, at a handsome thirty-three thousand dollars. The federal government, he sadly figured, would take about four thousand dollars of this for tax purposes. While so many Americans floundered in the stock market, Allen profited even there. In May he purchased American Tobacco stock. In August he announced plans to sell it at a handsome profit: the value of each share had increased twenty dollars.[4]

On September 29, 1932, Fred and Agnes were married in a quiet ceremony in Agnes' apartment on East Sixty-fifth Street. The Rev. Merrill F. Clarke of New Canaan, Connecticut, performed the ceremony before the immediate families and a few close friends. Afterwards, the couple went to Bermuda, a long-time favorite vacationing spot for Agnes. On their return they moved into the Scarsdale home, retaining Agnes' French maid, Anna Clos-Nargassans, and her husband Jean in their employ. Their faithful service freed Allen entirely from domestic duties and assured him of the time he needed for free-lance writing in the years to come.[5]

Allen's central thoughts never wandered far from the economic catastrophe which had struck so many. In the spring of 1933, while the lame-duck Hoover sat in the White House, the crisis found still new depths as bank after bank failed and state governments, in desperation, began declaring bank holidays. On the eve of Franklin Delano Roosevelt's March inauguration, the financial system reached a state of virtual collapse, and after his last, long, crisis-filled night in the White House, Hoover declared, "We are at the end of our string. There is nothing more we can do."[6] Then he got ready for the inauguration to let the incoming President try his hand.

While the new President formulated his own tentative efforts at combatting the Depression, Allen decided that he, too, should be acting—by writing. Two years earlier in *Only Yesterday*, he wrote about a general sense that something had gone wrong with individualistic capitalism. He determined now to write a book explaining how the nation had arrived at an economic system that could be so vulnerable. Once understood, the American people might be able to take remedial steps to cure the system. Allen was convinced that the "economic thread" had become a rope "to which almost everything else in our lives appears to be attached."[7]

He had never pretended to understand economics, and thus the task appeared especially formidable. He embarked upon a broad reading program to prepare himself. After one Sunday morning in late March he exclaimed, "Whew!—I wonder if I'll ever learn enough to begin that book!" By the time he was ready to write in the fall, he still felt uncertain about explaining economic history. "Again I vacillate between feeling I'm the one person who can do this right and feeling that there's so much to learn that I can never, never be more than feebly superficial. We'll see."[8]

Headquarters for research was the New York Public Library, which he could reach by a short stroll from his office or from Grand Central Station. He read secondary histories, biographies, autobiographies, commercial papers such as the *Commercial and Financial Chronicle*, magazine articles, and government reports and documents. He waded diligently into the three volumes of testimony before the 1912–1913 Pujo Committee, which was to determine whether a "money trust" existed ("extraordinarily interesting").[9] He talked with individuals such as the Associated Press's Wall Street reporter about the Morgan firm and its power. Before he began writing, he summed up rather provocatively his central theme:

No class or group in the community is wise enough or public-spirited enough to be entrusted for long with vast power. Sooner or later the rulers become drunk with their own golden opportunities. By and large, those who have held power in Wall Street have been as able a public-spirited group as could be found. But the lust for gain is unsleeping and endlessly inventive. Sharpers are constantly gaining a place in the group. Even the best of the Wall Street group are constantly working out new tricks for money-making, for evading the intent of the law, for skimming the cream off business operations—until these new tricks become established practices which "everybody" engages in as a matter of course. Whenever business is good the golden opportunities become too golden, till the business structure crashes. Then comes a period of revolt by the rest of the community in self-defense: by consumers, by labor, by farmers, by the general public. Reforms are put through, the insiders are curbed. Gradually, they find ways to circumvent the laws intended to curb them, and the process is gone through again. This time they will probably not be humbled for long.

The book may be considered the story of this financial power and its successive victories and defeats since America became an imperial nation without an interior frontier. It may also be considered a study in the process of centralization of control, an inevitable, fatalistic process, which has now got to the point where the only place to which control can be moved from Wall Street is to Washington. (Marx was partly right.) It will be, incidentally, a study of the social group which managed this control in Wall Street—both the aristocrats and the stream of *nouveau riches*.[10]

Meanwhile, Allen paid careful attention to the news of the day, for today's headlines would be the concluding pages of his book.

As Roosevelt experimented and probed to revive the stricken economy, Allen felt much sympathy for him. Their mutual Groton and Harvard backgrounds had stamped them as belonging to a certain class, yet both were in effect rebels to the overriding ideas of that class. Their sympathies lay with the working classes instead of with those of privilege. The excitement of New Deal intellectuals who flocked to Washington reminded Allen of the not-so-distant days when he, too, had worked in the capital.

On at least two occasions Allen had opportunity to examine Roosevelt at close hand. The first had come before the inauguration at a Harvard Club dinner in New York on January 18, 1933, honoring Abbott Lawrence Lowell, who now was resigning from the Harvard presidency. Just as Allen had described very carefully President Theodore Roosevelt on one of his visits to Groton, so did he pay particular attention to one of the guests at the dinner, Franklin Roosevelt:

It is surprising to see how crippled he is—one forgets it when one reads the papers. He came in on the arm of an aide or bodyguard, using a stick and walking very slowly, and although it was a stand-up reception he at once sat down in a big chair. . . . When it came time for him to speak two men came up from behind and helped him up, and he leaned on the back of his chair while speaking; when he finished, they helped him into his chair again. He made an agreeable though not remarkable speech, and he certainly has an attractive personality (just a shade too attractive, if anything). He did one thing which struck me as being in the most perfect taste. Of course it was Lowell's party; well, when the guests of honor came in and filed up to the head table and stood there, there was steady applause from the enormous crowd, yet Roosevelt never once looked at the crowd—he simply looked at Lowell from time to time, thus recognizing him as the person that the applause was for.[11]

Allen had met the President-elect before, probably in Washington when Roosevelt was assistant secretary of the Navy, but Roosevelt obviously did not remember, and upon shaking hands afterwards Allen did not remind him.

The favorable impression was repeated upon Allen nearly two years later when he, Pearl Buck, and Hervey Allen, visited the President in the White House as representatives of a committee formed to give two hundred books to the White House Library. The President was sitting at a big desk, and before the trio was halfway across the room he "made formality impossible by calling out—'Well, you see I've already had the books put out'—and so he had; they had been unpacked and laid out on a big table at the side of the room." The visitors chatted with the President about the books and plans for setting aside a room in the White House as a library, then autographed their own books before leaving. "The President was of course cordial, easy, attractive, as advertised: an extremely likeable person." But Allen still felt that his charm might be to his detriment. "He so completely adjusts himself to people and circumstances as to give his policies a rubbery aspect; but one does not feel it when with him. There is no feeling of being seduced . . . he is simply a thoroughly attractive and engaging man."[12]

Less than three weeks after Roosevelt's inauguration in March 1933, he had taken bold action with his declaration of a national bank holiday, the passage of the Emergency Banking Act and of the seemingly contradictory Economy Act which *reduced* government spending, and astonishing proposals for the national planning of agriculture. The Allens had five hundred dollars of their own money frozen in one closed bank, but did not really mind. "What I most like about this Administration is its attitude—of restoring prosperity from the bottom up rather than from the top down. That's the right program—but it will take nerve, and time, *and* luck!"[13]

Allen felt certain within a month of the inauguration that the nation's financial center was to be transferred from New York to Washington, and that "this, too, will be the story of an era that will be ended."[14] It was a point he would emphasize in the book for which he now was preparing.

"Don't you find the progress of the Roosevelt administration pretty thrilling?" he asked his mother. The administration, he said, was hoping to complete as much financial reform as possible during the grace period. Personally, Allen hoped that all banking ultimately would be put under Federal Reserve control. "They're moving rapidly toward at least a temporary governmental control, a temporary socialism. The Back Bay won't like that, or Wall Street. Yet I think it inevitable and salutary with the right people to run it."[15]

Within two weeks Allen visited at length with the new Secretary of Agriculture, Henry A. Wallace, whose ideas for crop allotments Allen had declared to be a "wild experiment." Wallace had come to New York for a dinner with a dozen or so writers, evidently a move to win the approval of influential opinion-makers. Allen found Wallace "a nice unassuming young fellow, a little shaggy but highly intelligent." He resembled the sort of college professor one found at

Chocorua or Jaffrey, New Hampshire: "A quiet, unexcited man with a sense of humor and no bumptiousness at all; quite ready to look difficulties in the face. We bombarded him with questions about the farm plan, and I got the impression that there were no difficulties that he hadn't thought of." It was frightening, in a sense, for Allen to see that the man administering the "complex and novel and dangerous (economically)" farm plan was rather ordinary in person. He seemed, though, to have a level head, knowledge, and "no crazy illusions," and Allen favored the farm plan, only one of many in the Roosevelt scheme which he considered to be revolutionary or entering uncharted territory.[16]

By October 1933 Allen was ready to begin his book. He very meticulously arranged for a relaxed work schedule at the magazine. He proposed to take off every Wednesday from October 1, 1933 to August 1, 1934, and twenty other days when time permitted. He suggested a reduction in pay of $100 a month for the ten-month period, a substantial cut in Allen's $495 monthly salary as associate editor. Writing the book required more than the ten months he had scheduled, however; the last chapter was not completed until June 1935.[17]

The central figure for his study had to be J. Pierpont Morgan. It was not the first time that Morgan had stimulated Allen's interest. The great financier had served as a director of the Groton School while Allen was a student there. In the spring of 1907 young Allen, then sixteen, had written to his father that one of his best friends was Thornton "Buster" Brown, a nephew of Pierpont Morgan. Nearly a year later Allen portrayed a court lady in a school play, and he reported to his father, "I have been fitted to a stunning dress—one of Mrs. Pierpont Morgan's!" Mrs. Morgan had sent the black and white silk dress to Groton for use as a stage property.[18]

As an adult, Allen retained little sympathy for Morgan, but he wanted to be fair in his book, and he called upon the Morgan firm. Morgan officials agreed to look over the manuscript in progress with regard to accuracy. In early May 1934 Allen met with Thomas W. Lamont, who had become a partner in the firm in 1911, Junius S.

Morgan, nephew to the elder Morgan, and Martin Egan, another member of the firm, to hear their opinions on the first four chapters. Lamont led the discussion by "criticizing, questioning facts, objecting to adjectives, etc." It all remained very cordial, as Allen shortly thereafter described it, although the officials were less than enthusiastic about "the color of the thing."[19]

He selected a title in November 1934, when "the Wall Street book" became *The Lords of Creation*. Before releasing the completed manuscript to Harper & Brothers, he paid another visit to the Morgan firm to hear another critique of the entire book. Afterwards, Allen spent his last working hours going over their memos, "correcting here, toning down there, strengthening elsewhere (in places where I felt I was right but needed more ammunition to show I wasn't just talking)." His friend Stuart Chase, *New Republic* columnist and author John T. Flynn, and Max Lowenthal, a writer whose expertise lay in international affairs, also studied the manuscript and made recommendations. Allen now felt that he had had criticism from "both sides."[20]

The Book-of-the-Month Club examined the volume before publication but opted for an Ellen Glasgow novel instead. Allen learned that *Lords* came fairly close, however, being probably among the top four contenders.[21]

Reviewers found much to like about the book. John Chamberlain's *New York Times* review praised the book as cutting considerably deeper than *Only Yesterday*, and he thought it "eminently fair" as well.[22] The book did cut deeper than *Only Yesterday*. Stockwatering, pyramiding, the intricacies of trusts and holding companies, and other paper transactions were not as colorful as the revolt in morals and Prohibition.

In the book Allen had managed to be sympathetic when dealing with corporate personalities on an individual basis, yet condemnatory of their actions as a group. He traced chronologically the events beginning at the turn of the century which consolidated economic powers among a few on Wall Street and resulted in the faulty foundation made so evident by the 1929 collapse. The chief personalities of the period, beginning with J. P. Morgan and his maneuverings to create U.S. Steel in 1900, were portrayed in full flesh: Morgan, Schwab, Carnegie, Harriman, Rockefeller, H. H. Rogers, Jacob Schiff, Samuel Insull, the Van Sweringen brothers, both Roosevelts, Hoover, and many others.

Of the turn-of-the-century leaders, Allen concluded that their adventures and exploits contained the "thrill of conflict, of immense tasks boldly accomplished and emergencies boldly met, of a continent subdued to the needs of industry." Yet, the "truly heroic note" was missing. Allen saw the dollar as omnipresent and its smell pervading every episode. Everything else was an accessory after the fact.[23]

The capitalists were not deliberate plunderers; they simply acted according to the dictates of a system which they did not question: the doctrine of anything for a profit. The free market theory no longer was valid; the unwarranted urge for profits did not coincide with the public interest; it perverted "selling into an effort to unload goods by hook or crook."[24] Allen approved the Roosevelt design, moderate though it was, because the President, unlike Hoover, thought first of the less fortunate; also, Roosevelt had recognized for the first time the need for ending laissez-faire government policies toward the economy. But Allen observed that the New Deal had failed to bring every bank in the nation under a single system; it did not outlaw holding-company banking; it placed no limitation on pyramiding except in public utilities; and it did not require federal incorporation for large corporations. As time went by, Roosevelt seemed less the "brilliant and decisive leader" and "more the political opportunist" he had been as governor of New York and as presidential candidate.[25]

Allen's "bones" told him that *Lords* would not sell very briskly. Within a fortnight he learned that he was right—the book was off to a slow start. At least part of the reason, he felt, could be attributed to the slowness of the reviews. Yet, he could not complain about their tone once they appeared. Allen figured that sales might not even reach 10,000, which would mean that a planned summer trip to Europe would have to be financed by more writing.[26] He was not far from wrong about the sales: until it went out of print in 1943, *Lords* sold 12,800 copies in nine printings.[27]

The ultimate absurdity became clear in January 1936, when it was obvious that his two years of diligent labor on *Lords* would not earn him as much money as had his effortless purchase of airplane stocks the previous summer. "There's a bit of irony for you—a commentary of the rewards which go to hard work and merit in our system," he wrote to Hildegarde. The stocks had been purchased in an instant with sixty-three hundred dollars, and within a few months the paper profits amounted to forty-four hundred dollars. The book achieved good sales and won handsome reviews, and yet after it sold 9,000 copies, Allen's profits amounted to only twenty-four hundred dollars —before he deducted his expenses.[28]

The cult of the individual—the felt need for freedom for the school-age child and adult alike—had been a central intellectual theme of the twenties. It stemmed from a popular though not accurate reading of both Freud and Dewey. Now, the Depression brought a new idea to radicals and liberals: the individual should be subjugated for the collective good. Allen had never joined in the individualistic emphasis of the twenties; the new mood suited him better. He had been a collectivist during the war; had been critical of the Menckenesque fulminations against the masses; and now in the thirties he resumed with greater emphasis the idea that centralized authority, preferably short of out-and-out socialism, was necessary at this crucial stage. The leftist hopes for leadership from the working class were never shared by Allen. Marxism was incompatible with his nature.

What he was, and what he remained in varying degrees throughout his life, could not be more closely defined than as a left-of-center New Deal Democrat. The tenuousness of even this categorization is evident in a 1935 letter to his sister, Hildegarde. "I'm afraid I'm one of those darned liberals, indignantly protesting against the established order and wanting justice for the underdog—and ready, if the underdog got in power, to shift around and protest on the other side."[29] Back of this attitude seemed to be the passion for fairness his father displayed at the dinner table. It was as if he were mindful of the phrase his father constantly interjected, "But on the other hand . . ."

At this stage the administration did not seem to need criticism from Allen. The Roosevelt administration was in effect the underdog itself, along with the common man, and thus was in opposition to the established power structure. Eventually, when Roosevelt appeared determined to exercise authority in the Supreme Court controversy, Allen's support for him faltered. Meanwhile, in the growing number of speeches Allen was making, as well as in his private letters, he marshaled all the support he could for the New Deal.

The general mood of the American nation, the apathy which prevented it from moving decisively to combat the ills of the economic system, distressed Allen. "I am convinced that this country very gravely needs a rebirth—no, a birth—of a broader public spirit, and wish to heaven I could do something to bring it to birth," he wrote in January 1936. Even Al Smith, whom Allen had admired, seemed to have lost any sense of public spirit, and, in fact, Allen distrusted him "because he is now so thick with the DuPonts and their like, whose idea of freedom appears to me to be irresponsible."[30]

When he spoke at a church in 1935 to a group whom he felt certain to be anti-New Deal, he emphasized the plight of the jobless, whom he numbered at twelve million.[31] These unemployed, he stressed, represented the heart of the problem and it was imperative to return them to economic citizenship. "Anybody who talks of balancing the budget without realizing that to pay the relief bill is the very least that we can do for these neighbors of ours, is romancing."[32]

Allen's views were expressed most directly in a six-page draft for a speech he gave during Roosevelt's first term. He made notes for it on Furness Bermuda Line stationery, perhaps for a shipboard talk aboard the *Queen of Bermuda* en route to vacation. The audience was "on the whole a conservative group of people," and he told them that some form of collectivism not only was inevitable but salutary as well.[33]

The central point which Allen sought to impress upon his listeners was that the day of rugged economic individualism in America, the heyday of independent business, was over—"whether we like it or not." The times called for central controls and, indeed, such a trend had been evident throughout the twentieth century. If businessmen used the NRA codes for "chiseling" or sought to dismantle New Deal legislation before the farmers had recovered or the unemployed had found security, then they could expect even more interference from Washington, or there would be bitterness and bloodshed. "I do not mean a Communist revolt. . . . I mean a revolt by hitherto conservative Iowa farmers, a revolt of conservative Am[erican] working men & small business men who have no use for Moscow but have decided to take their fortunes into their own hands."

Inevitably, a collectivist system would emerge. It might be operated by John W. Davis as a "fascist state-directed capitalism—or by a Huey Long or a man like Mayor Thompson of Chicago—as a political racket—or by out-and-out socialists." Whatever form it took, though, centralization was necessary, or else worse trouble for the nation lay ahead. "Of that I am convinced," he said. No control, however, would last long which did not rehabilitate the dispossessed.

Finally, Allen told the audience that he was highly skeptical of the nation's ability to operate a socialistic system without long practice. Yet, some degree of socialism was essential. "I had rather see it more radical than less; for if it is less, the dispossessed will be left out unless there is a great change of heart." And if they were to be left out: "Look out for trouble."[34]

The speech, given probably in 1934 or early 1935, amounted to Allen's most provocative comments on the Depression. It was as radical as he would ever feel about the American economic system.

Before the end of Roosevelt's first term the Supreme Court made epochal decisions to invalidate both the National Recovery Act and the Agricultural Adjustment Act. Allen had predicted dire consequences if the NRA should fail, but by now it already was in disarray and he was not greatly concerned after all. The decisions did not seem catastrophic; they were mainly irritants.[35]

In 1936 Allen and Agnes, who was a Democratic committeewoman, both enthusiastically supported Roosevelt's reelection. Allen predicted that the President would win by a considerable margin of some 350 electoral votes. He confessed, however, to a degree of unsettlement about it because so many people felt the election would be close. In his own Scarsdale voting district, where among their many friends the Allens professed to know only two other Democratic families, he estimated that five-sixths of the vote would be Republican, "as usual."[36]

He seemed to be apologizing for his vote when he wrote to his elder half-sister Bessie on election day. "Agnes and I are going over to the schoolhouse in a moment to cast our votes for Roosevelt. Does that seem strange to you?" They were voting for Roosevelt, he explained, because the President had the immense advantage of realizing that the fortunes of all segments of society were inseparable, farmer and merchant, rich and poor, East and West. "Some of the medicines he has given it [the economic system] seem to me to have been good, some bad, but at least the patient has been under treatment and is making out pretty well, all things considered."[37]

Roosevelt's massive triumph gave him courage to attempt to circumvent the Supreme Court's strikes against the AAA and NRA. He proposed to Congress his "Plan for the Reorganization of the Judicial Branch of the Government," which instantly became known as the "court-packing plan." Renewed cries of "dictator" immediately sounded, and Allen himself joined many Roosevelt partisans who could not side with the President in this plan. It became the first instance in which Allen, and many others, seriously opposed the President. It was the wrong way, he felt, to attempt a desirable goal. While he favored a "straightforward" amendment, Allen considered this proposal to be "slippery and cowardly and a bad precedent-setter."[38] Others agreed and the plan failed. For the first time, Roosevelt lost control of the Congress.

In late 1937 Allen once again frowned when administration spokesmen began a series of harsh attacks on big business for alleged monopolistic selfishness. The vitriol, he felt, went too far. The administration was partly right, he acknowledged, "but the savageness of the attacks won't help, and anyhow the Administration aided the monopoly process through the NRA and is not in a position to talk. I'm disgusted at both sides in this controversy!"[39]

Americans understandably kept their attention riveted on their own domestic scene during the 1930s. The enormousness of their own problems was reason enough, but also there was the determination not to become embroiled again in a European conflict. Since the debate over the League had ended, a series of revisionist histories had questioned the motives and wisdom of U.S. entry into the First World War. In January 1937 a poll conducted by the American Institute of Public Opinion showed that about 70 percent of those interviewed believed U.S. involvement in the war had been a mistake.[40] For those who cared to contemplate it, however, the world situation in the thirties was indeed perilous. Manchuria fell to Japan; the blustering Nazis assumed power; a Mussolini-led Italy stormed Ethiopia; Hitler directed the reoccupation of the Rhineland; Japan invaded China; the Spanish Civil War raged; and Czechoslovakia suffered dismemberment at Munich. All this did not go unnoticed, certainly not in the pages of *Harper's*, where article after article explored the implications of these events. But it was as if they were being recognized merely as important internationally, not for reasons of American self-interest. These foreign entanglements seemed inimical to the best interests of solving America's own problems, and Allen felt no different from most others about it.

He began, however, in 1935 to take personal note of the situation in Germany. "The temper of Germany under Hitler is a constant provocation, and there is certainly plenty of dynamite lying about in Europe," Allen wrote Hildegarde.[41]

10

PIONEERING THE PICTURE BOOKS

In the spring of 1933, at the same time he had begun doing research for *The Lords of Creation,* Allen and Agnes started work on a joint project in a spirit of fun. The inspiration came from the Allens' friend Cass Canfield, president of Harper & Brothers. Canfield had noticed in Germany the publication of several photographic books, including one which contained photographs of royal family groups going back to 1870. It dawned on him that while the art of photography had developed even before the American Civil War, the technical ability to reproduce halftone photographs had not been achieved until the latter part of the nineteenth century. Canfield suggested to the Allens that they might compile a fascinating pictorial history from photographs taken prior to 1900.[1] A more recent technical development also made the book seem more practical than before: the offset printing process permitted excellent reproduction of photographs on soft, lightweight paper rather than the heavy, slick stock formerly required. A lengthy picture book need not weigh several pounds anymore.

Agnes bore the initial brunt of the job. She collected scores of photographs from the principal photographic services. On visits to the U.S. Signal Corps in Washington she collected numerous Civil War photographs, among them the great work of Mathew Brady. Examining and sorting them was, as Allen reported to his mother, "an entertaining thing—the subjects range from political to the Klondike, the San Francisco fire, Vanderbilt Cup races, Dewey parades, Newport tennis in the 90's, stage and early motion picture views, etc." Originally, the Allens planned to begin with 1890, but they found so many earlier pictures that they decided to let it go back "as far as the camera will take it": 1860.[2]

On the last day of March they submitted a sampling of seventy photographs to Canfield and Harper's editor in chief, Eugene Saxton. By May 1 the photographs virtually had been chosen and attention now focused on the captions—Allen's job. Agnes, totally without experience in art display, served as picture editor. She arranged their sequence, determined sizes, cropped them to eliminate wasted space and improve composition, and occasionally mortised them by cutting out sections. She showed an unusual amount of boldness in choosing to enlarge or "blow up" photographs for dramatic effect rather than electing to include a greater number of small ones. Assisted by Allen, she sought to make as many two-page spreads as possible into units of similar or contrasting subject matter.

While the Allens did not consider their project to be a very serious one, they were aware that it represented at least a novelty. In May they were alarmed to hear of another photographic book being prepared for another publisher. Harper & Brothers determined to rush the Allen project in an effort to be first, although there was also the consideration of withholding publication until November to take better advantage of the Christmas trade.[3]

The rumored picture book did materialize, and it was published first. Laurence Stallings' photographic study, *The First World War: A Photographic History*, in its stark effect, amounted to an antiwar statement.[4] Stallings' book differed from *The American Procession* in its more specific and much more recent subject matter; its captions were no more than brief, headline-like phrases. The Allens, in contrast, were integrating text with photographs, and their more distant

122

subject matter ranged over the entire landscape of American life since 1860.

The completed Allen volume, published in October, contained 275 photographs accompanied by conversational captions totaling 20,000 words.[5] Eight photographs adorning the cover hinted at the content's lively nature: Abraham Lincoln in repose; Union soldiers surrounding a cannon; a female tennis player of the 1880s complete with bustle; a street scene of smart-looking, horse-drawn hansom cabs; a *Police Gazette* burlesque queen; the starting line of an early automobile race with John Jacob Astor as one of the drivers; a fashionable couple at the horse races; and Ty Cobb, the baseball immortal, in his batting follow-through.

Photographs followed only a rough chronology—politicians and actresses and tragedy and scenes of daily life were intermingled. One caption, nevertheless, served invariably to introduce the next photograph and caption. As the authors explained, they wanted to make as full a historical record as possible, "an experiment in the presentation of American social history," but they had decided also to include less significant photographs that seemed "especially striking, or hilarious, or stirring to the memory."[6]

One historian credits the Allens with having "launched the era of the lavishly-illustrated historical spectacular."[7] However, he cites the later 1947 production, *I Remember Distinctly*, as being responsible.[8] *The American Procession* deserves primary credit, but coming in the Depression it did not inspire at once the host of immediate imitators that followed *I Remember Distinctly* after World War II. Certain photographic books did precede *The American Procession*, but they did not approach its contemporary format or contain its human appeal or match the reduced price now possible in such works.[9]

Reviewers generally agreed that the book had real merit. William Rose Benét in the *Saturday Review* commented that the Allen and Stallings photographic books seemed to indicate an approaching fad of relating history through photographs. Benét even believed that the Allen book should be "infinitely suggestive" to fiction writers of a wealth of native material hardly touched. The *Mississippi Valley Historical Review* acknowledged the book's dual endeavor of entertaining the reader as well as having "a serious historical objective." As social history the reviewer found it "spotty," but he conceded its value as an experiment in presenting American social history.[10]

The book sold well from the beginning. Advance sales were estimated at 3,000, and the firm ordered a second printing before the book was published.[11] By the time *The American Procession* went out of print in 1947, 22,500 copies had been sold.[12] In April 1934, Allen jubilantly exclaimed over the book's $7,200 profits. "Isn't that really extraordinary for an experiment like that!"[13]

The book's unexpected success led the Allens directly into a second similar venture the next year. *Metropolis: An American City in Photographs* portrayed one day in the life of a huge city (New York) from dawn to midnight as seen primarily through the eyes of a man from "Middletown."[14]

The Allens hired Agnes' cousin, Edward M. Weyer, Jr., a young archaeologist-anthropologist-explorer, as their photographer and sent him throughout the city to portray the metropolis from its suburbs to its central core, from work to play, and from suburban cottage to dingy tenements. To gather impressions for his commentary Allen arose long before dawn one day to watch the city make its transformation from serenity to frenzy.

Parts of the metropolis that generally went unseen were depicted by the Allen team. When a man picked up a telephone the reader was carried via photographs to the inside of the telephone exchange to show what was happening there. When he washed his hands a series of pictures took the reader through a system of pipes to the reservoirs where the water was stored.

Most of the office photographs were taken inside the Harper & Brothers building. The Allens persuaded friends to pose for many of the pictures, including Russell Lynes, then a fresh Yale graduate working in a noneditorial capacity at *Harper's*, and Lloyd Wescott (novelist Glenway's brother).[15] Allen and Agnes themselves posed anonymously for certain photographs.[16]

Allen felt *Metropolis* to be a finer work than *The American Procession*, but it failed to match *Procession* in sales. Reviewers were more lavish with praise, and the *New York Times* devoted the book review section's entire front page to *Metropolis* in what Allen called a "simply swell review." The book did earn best-seller rankings for New York City, and the exercise put modest profits of seven hundred dollars in the Allens' pockets.[17]

After *Metropolis* the Allens forsook picture books for more than a decade. By the time they returned to the format, others had entered the field, notably Erskine Caldwell and Margaret Bourke-White with their pictorial-essay documentaries on the starkness of the Depression era, *You Have Seen Their Faces* (1937) and *Say, Is This the U.S.A.* (1941); and James Agee's and Walker Evans' *Let Us Now Praise Famous Men* (1941).

Aside from their joint writing efforts, Agnes, as well as Allen, stayed busy during the 1930s with her own literary efforts: she wrote *Flight* in 1935, *Why Not Enjoy Life* in 1937, *Abraham Lincoln: A Pictorial Biography* in 1939, and numerous articles. She continued to work part-time at *Harper's* until she joined the *Literary Digest* as feature editor shortly before its collapse. The couple's common professional lives complemented a marriage that proved satisfying and enduring.

While their immediate plans had been to leave Scarsdale for New York after marriage, they enjoyed suburban life. Agnes' bubbling personality, as evident in one social setting as another, provided a happy complement to Allen's own fun-loving nature. She was a good mixer with people of all sorts (an inheritance from her father, who combined a strong feeling of noblesse oblige with a genuine liking for the human race), and she taught Allen how to talk naturally to ordinary people outside his own social milieu with whom he already empathized. On the eve of his third wedding anniversary Allen wrote Hildegarde that he planned a happy celebration for "three absolutely soul-satisfying years. I am certainly a lucky fellow —and, I may add proudly, a good picker. It has been a delicious time, and it gets better and better."[18]

125

Even yard work seemed pleasurable. "Spring is coming with a rush," Allen wrote his mother after rolling the lawn with Oliver's assistance on May 1, 1933. "Cherry blossoms out, yellow warblers hopping about in the budding apple-branches, and a haze of green all through our spindly little woods." That evening Allen and Agnes settled down to more "very good fun"—making up the pages on *The American Procession*. Later, they went up to Oliver's room to say good-night, and since five minutes remained before his bedtime, the three of them entered into a vigorous session of gymnastics, making a human pyramid: "Me kneeling on the floor, Agnes kneeling on my back, and Oliver standing on hers—a rather hysterical performance."[19]

A week later they lowered the Plymouth convertible top and drove to Hook Mountain on the west bank of the Hudson River for a picnic. "Just Agnes and Oliver and myself . . . leaving the car by the roadside and climbing to the hill-top, where we ate sandwiches and looked down on the patchwork quilt—done in emerald green and other spring tones—of the countryside below by the river." Afterwards they stopped by the house of friends to sing gospel hymns until it was time to listen to one of Roosevelt's fireside chats on the radio. On these automobile jaunts the trio invariably sang their repertoire of musical rounds such as "Three Blind Mice" and "Frere Jacques."[20]

Occasionally, they enjoyed musical evenings at home, using the violin, piano, snare drum, and phonograph simultaneously. "Stars and Stripes Forever" was particularly enjoyable. "When we do that with Oliver he's just our age," Allen commented. Oliver was more than competent on the violin, Agnes played the piano, and Allen alternated between the piano and snare drums, the latter a Christmas present from Agnes.[21]

Sports, too, were fun for all. Allen joined Oliver frequently for baseball and football, and the entire family attended sports events.

Oliver often was invited into Manhattan for weekends with the Allens' French couple, the Clos-Nargassans, where he mingled happily with the city's French colony, including waiters, bartenders, chefs, and hairdressers. As a result, Oliver became well known in many of the city's restaurants.[22]

During the 1933–1935 school years Oliver attended Repton; from 1935 to 1936 he went to Harvey; and he completed his preparatory work at Deerfield. ("We're inclined to think he doesn't get enough competition or incentive at the public school," Allen told his mother upon deciding to send Oliver to Repton.)[23] Oliver's first day at Repton, an unhappy one, made Allen recall his own distress at Groton and filled him with sympathy for his eleven-year-old son. When the Allens came home from work that first day they found Oliver in tears. "He had hated it. We were dismayed and unhappy (how I realized what you must have gone through when I hated Groton!)," Allen wrote his mother.[24] After a long discussion Allen and Agnes learned that the unhappiness had arisen because a brusque physical education teacher made Oliver uneasy as he attempted a new sport, soccer. The next day, though, was better, and on Friday school was "swell." Two years later Oliver was transferred to the Harvey School at Hawthorne because of a minor scandal at Repton—the trustees dismissed the headmaster because of a drinking problem.[25]

Allen's mother, who had been so close to him, died in 1934. He had written to her at least weekly throughout his adult life, and she was both a sounding board for his thoughts and an inspirational source of ideas. Several months after his mother's death Allen told his sister Hildegarde that while she missed their mother in person, he missed her "as a sort of point of reference, a criterion, an appreciator, of good standards."[26] In his last letter to her before her death, Allen included a brief postscript of appreciation. "Talk about things said that one remembers with gratitude and delight: I'll never forget what you said on Sunday about my having been a joy to you! That was a great reward."[27]

With his own mother's death Allen felt a greater sense of responsibility toward Hildegarde, who had never married. He filled his letters to her with information about the magazine, his own writing, his personal life, his ideas on the state of national and international affairs, and advice of all sorts.

127

Agnes' mother, Letitia Cunningham Rogers, was a semi-invalid of high spirits who lived the last ten years of her life with the Allens. Though often bedridden, her humor never faltered and she was good company. "Rogie," as she affectionately was called, at seventy-six weighed her age and she was attractive to the day of her death. Between her and her son-in-law there was an immediate and lasting attachment. Allen referred to her as an "ornament of the house."[28]

The Allens enjoyed a wide circle of friends and acquaintances, and they frequently exchanged visits with friends such as Herbert Feis and his wife. Feis was economic adviser to the State Department, and his wife had been born Ruth Stanley-Brown, a close friend of Agnes' from boarding school and the granddaughter of President James Garfield. At one party in the Feis house, Allen enjoyed hearing Feis lecture to Adolph Ochs about the editorials in the New York Times.[29]

Friends who visited the Allens for weekends filled with tennis, singing, parlor games, picnics, and conversation also included Cass Canfield and his wife, Russell and Mildred Lynes, Mr. and Mrs. Charles W. MacMullen, and Lloyd Wescott. When the Franklin Fields came in May 1934, Allen and Fields played three sets of tennis on Saturday afternoon; two other couples came over for dinner; all of them performed songs and dances until after 1 A.M. (Agnes imitated a high school teacher doing an Egyptian dance at a spring festival, and Allen did a drum solo and an imitation of the announcer at the 125th Street railroad station); and Sunday afternoon there was more tennis.[30]

Doing well financially during the Depression enabled the Allens to help less fortunate friends. By the spring of 1933 Allen had saved twenty thousand dollars from the royalties of Only Yesterday, and in 1935 he and Hildegarde each inherited from their mother just over forty thousand dollars in securities.[31] Allen made wise investments in the depressed stock market, and a special account of about five thousand dollars was set up from profits to help friends in financial need. If borrowers could repay the money they were to do so. If they could not, that was perfectly understandable and part of the fund's *raison d'être*. Twenty or so families availed themselves of the fund during the Depression. Others gratefully told the Allens that just knowing the money was available boosted their spirits. As Agnes recalled years later, the project "made us feel very rich."[32]

When the Civil War in Spain broke out in the summer of 1936, fourteen-year-old Oliver happened to be there with friends, and he saw some of the initial hostilities. Upon his return to Scarsdale, reporters from four local newspapers interviewed him as the first person to return to Westchester County from "war-torn Spain."[33]

Oliver's development seemed to parallel that of Allen's own at a similar age. At the Repton School's field day in June 1935, Oliver won second place in the eighty-yard dash and the top English Prize for the entire school. When end-of-the-year reports were released at Harvey in 1936, Oliver ranked ninth among ninety-two students and received flattering comments from the teachers. Perhaps best of all, however, was the fine relationship which continued between Oliver and Agnes. "The way he dotes on Agnes!—Easy for me to understand, for I do too," Allen commented after they had delivered Oliver to his new boarding school, Deerfield.[34]

With Oliver gone to boarding school, in the fall of 1936 the Allens took an automobile trip to Tennessee. They could not resist eating lunch at the very drugstore in Dayton where the "crime" of teaching evolution had been plotted. Norris Dam, part of the Tennessee Valley Authority project, impressed Allen as "magnificent and beautiful" and a valuable public service.[35]

A shorter daily trip, commuting to Manhattan, could be tolerated while Oliver was growing up and needed space for playing. Now that he was away at school the old desire to move to New York re-emerged, and the Allens began looking for a place. In January 1937 they found a brownstone with which, Allen said, they fell in love. The house, on East Thirty-fifth Street in the Murray Hill section, was only three or four minutes away from the Harper office. Just fourteen feet wide, it contained five floors. The house needed new plumbing but almost nothing else, and the couple resolved to pay as much as $30,000 for it.[36]

They could well afford the brownstone. The Allens' income in 1936 amounted to more than $34,000; just $2,500 went to state and federal taxes and they donated nearly $2,000 to charity.[37] In February the Allens purchased the house for $27,676. They sold their Scarsdale house and moved to Manhattan in September. The Allens flourished in their new residence, which was outfitted elegantly with traditional furnishings. It was pretty on the outside as well, with a garden, flagstones, a border of ivy, and two trees in the back. Agnes complained that she had been born too late, that she should have been the mistress of a great Whig house. Through the years in Manhattan the Allens never looked back with longing toward suburban life.[38]

One evening the Allens attended a dinner party given by Eugene Saxton of Harper & Brothers. Guests included the J. B. Priestleys, Cass Canfield, Martha Foley, and Sinclair Lewis. Agnes made such a hit with Sinclair Lewis that he invited the couple to his penthouse the following Monday evening. Soon it was "Agnes" and "Fred" and "Red." Allen later recalled:

He was most amiable and enthusiastic and rather amusing—a likeable fellow; but he was on the wagon, and I've heard he can be less engaging when drinking. Queer-looking: tall, rangy, red-faced, homely (but more friendly-looking than his pictures—except that his face is a queer shiny scarred-looking red, exactly as if he's been burned). . . . We didn't see D. Thompson; his wife; she'd gone to bed.[39]

During the next couple of years the Allens visited Lewis often, but they never saw Dorothy Thompson. Lewis at this time was in decline, professionally as well as maritally, but the Allens enjoyed his company. He displayed an "eager interest" in everything and, contrary to his reputation, a particular willingness to listen to others. "He never dominated the conversation or seemed to try to show off. And the talk was always lively and good. I had heard accounts of his having ugly moods, but on those occasions we saw nothing of this whatever," Allen recalled years later.[40]

11

IMPROVING THE MAGAZINE

Allen had been so busy with other matters that by 1935 he was feeling guilty over neglect of *Harper's*. "I haven't done my real duty by it for a long time," he wrote his sister.[1] It was a rare mention of the magazine in his letters, which at this point were filled instead with details about his personal life, his writing, and events related to the Depression.

He had even been tempted in 1934 by an offer to return to Harvard, evidently to take over his old job with enlarged responsibilities. James B. Conant, a Boston son of long but nonaristocratic lineage and a friend of Allen's, had succeeded Lowell as president the year before.[2] His selection by the Corporation was unexpected, and on hearing the news Allen exclaimed, "Jim Conant! I'm surprised. But I think he'll be a good one."[3] Conant's offer to return was tempting, and Allen gave it short consideration. He worried Hartman and Canfield by notifying them of the offer, and even after he had decided definitely against it, he kept quiet about it as a matter of strategy. There were too many other interesting goals pending to make such a major change. "The first job is to finish this book [*The*

Lords of Creation]. The next one is to get back into full-time editing for a while."[4] Perhaps a year later, he felt, the time might be appropriate for the change.

The Depression by now had taken its expected toll on the magazine. *Harper's* wavered between profits and losses, and the circulation gains which had brought it even with the *Atlantic* at the end of the twenties had fallen from 121,000 in 1930 to 102,000 by 1939; by the latter date it trailed the *Atlantic* by 6,000 in circulation.[5]

Harper's contents changed only subtly, following the same path Thomas Wells laid in 1925. The Depression and the political decisions regarding it received great attention, naturally, but an emphasis persisted on European matters that in retrospect seems exaggerated. Similarly, in literary articles as much space was devoted to European authors as to American writers, though the Americans enjoyed more space than in the previous decade. The deluge of articles on women, so evident in the 1920s, slowed to something less than a trickle during the thirties.

Some of the magazine's regular writers seemed to be plagued with tired blood. The two monthly columns, "Editor's Easy Chair" and "Among the New Books," were handled in desultory fashion by Edward S. Martin, who would be eighty in 1936, and Harry Hansen, who had been book critic since 1923. Hartman, who had been named editor in 1931 after working on the magazine since 1908, was easygoing and generally happy with the magazine's editorial direction. George Leighton, a plainspoken editor who had joined the magazine in 1932, was, like Allen, a frequent contributor of articles.[6] Completing the editorial staff was assistant editor Virginia Watson, author of several novels.

Allen was not satisfied with the magazine, and by July of 1935 he was seeking ways to improve it. He hoped to expand the humor column, "The Lion's Mouth," by including more serious short essays and sketches. He also wanted another writer to take over the "Editor's Easy Chair" column from Martin. "He's so old that we regretfully admit the department is getting weaker and weaker," Allen told Hildegarde.[7] Martin's successor, Bernard DeVoto, was evidently not Allen's first choice.[8] "I'm not at all sure about DeVoto,"

Allen confessed, "but the department will at least have more vitamins than under Martin, the old dear; he was becoming almost unreadable; and DeVoto has excellent qualities."[9] DeVoto had been contributing articles to *Harper's* since 1927.

His initial "Easy Chair" column (it coincided with a title change from "Editor's Easy Chair" to "Easy Chair") in November 1935 began a long and rewarding relationship between him and *Harper's*, for DeVoto proved to be a popular member of the family. His occasional visits to the New York office from his Cambridge home always enlivened the editorial day, and he frequently attended the Tuesday morning staff meetings. He pursued controversy in his columns, being a zealous defender of civil rights, a vociferous spokesman for conservation of the public lands of the West, and an early advocate of intervention in World War II. He was a fierce, uncompromising, traditional nationalist and quick to debate.

The magazine could be no stronger than its authors, and well-known writers were the mainstays of *Harper's* during the 1930s. By far the most prolific was Elmer Davis, a former Rhodes Scholar, who contributed essays on almost anything that intrigued him—foreign affairs, American politics, religion, history, cats, and many other subjects, and he also wrote fiction.[10] Nathaniel Peffer specialized in international affairs, particularly those concerning the Orient, where he had lived for several years as a journalist and as a Guggenheim Fellow. George W. Gray, Texas-born and a Harvard graduate, was a free-lance writer whose specialty lay in popularizing science. Stuart Chase, John R. Tunis, Harold Laski, John Gunther, and Gerald W. Johnson were other authors whose work appeared in the magazine on an average of once a year or more.

As Allen saw some of his own ideas bear fruit he declared the work to be "great fun." Advertising, of course, was down, and by the end of November in 1935 there had been a slight revenue loss for the year, but the editorial program seemed to him to be "stiffening up."[11] A frequent criticism from readers was that they did not like the magazine's fiction. Staff members thus were heartened when the O. Henry Fiction Awards contest for 1935 saw first and second places go to *Harper's* stories: to Kay Boyle and to Dorothy Thomas.

In 1930, 1933, 1935, 1938, and 1939, *Harper's* stories won first places. The prize *Harper's* contributor in fiction soon became William Faulkner, whose first *Harper's* story, "The Hound," appeared in August 1931. Faulkner remained a frequent *Harper's* contributor, along with writers such as Paul Horgan, G. K. Chesterton, Marjorie Kinnan Rawlings, C. C. Dobie, Wilbur Daniel Steele, and John Steinbeck.

The two broad themes of the thirties, the Depression and the European crisis, provided constant material for articles. European affairs always had received a disproportionate share of space in *Harper's,* and the tense decade justified continued coverage. Having no editorial page, the magazine took no position regarding the obligation of the United States. But in May 1939, the editors assumed that the nation would be forced to take a definite stand, and a special issue was produced in September examining the general theme of the United States in the world of 1939. The issue coincided by chance with the outbreak of war. Seven separate articles examined the theme, and in the lead article, "Giddy Minds and Foreign Affairs," Charles A. Beard argued that America should stress domestic improvements rather than becoming entangled in the European maelstrom.[12] (C. Hartley Grattan, the revisionist historian who had questioned U.S. entry into World War I in *Why We Fought,* also wrote for *Harper's.*[13] He had called for noninvolvement earlier that year in "No More Excursions!"[14]) From this point on, the editors' attention and consequently the magazine's content focused more on the perilous international situation and less on the Depression.

The Depression, of course, was the second great topic for articles during the thirties. Again, there was no editorial position, but authors such as John T. Flynn, George Soule, Reinhold Niebuhr, Stuart Chase, Elmer Davis, and C. Hartley Grattan stressed the need for government action and voiced the activist-oriented arguments which *Harper's* felt most needed expression.

Allen was captivated by the manuscript of John Gunther's *Inside Europe,* ran three chapters in the magazine, and conveyed to the

Harper & Brothers book salesman his view of its great sales possibilities. When *Inside Europe* became a best-seller Allen was pleased that he had recognized its merits and not only pushed it but edited sections for the magazine. The manuscript had not come in unsolicited, however. Cass Canfield had twisted Gunther's arm to make him agree to write the book.[15]

Allen also edited Marquis Childs' contribution, "They Hate Roosevelt," which examined the growing bitterness among the upper classes toward the President. The original manuscript seemed lacking in some way, and Allen took it home and devoted a Saturday to revising it. He added several paragraphs, amended others, inserted a quotation from Dickens, and then suggested another rewrite by Childs. The article appeared in May, and the Democratic National Committee, pointing toward the 1936 presidential campaign, found it so effective for their cause that they purchased 100,000 reprints for distribution.[16]

One article Allen commissioned in 1936 created a sensation because of its unusually critical portrayal of Massachusetts Governor James M. Curley. Boston newspaperman James Dineen had regaled Allen in conversation with Curley anecdotes, and Allen arranged for Dineen to write a profile of the governor which was so provocative that sales in Boston more than quadrupled.[17] Curley, who was called an "Irish Mussolini" in the article, threatened to sue for libel if the magazine was distributed. Hartman naturally refused to yield. For a while Allen feared that Hildegarde might be singled out for reprisal in Boston because of his own position on the magazine.[18] Eventually the furor subsided without legal action.

In the fall of 1937, Allen drew up a list of proposals for changes in the magazine's format.[19] He had no misgivings regarding the magazine's overall approach, but he made specific recommendations indicating that he differed with Hartman's reluctance to change the editorial format. Generally, Allen favored greater flexibility in length and content of articles, including the right to print long poems when merited. (A more or less standard *Harper's* article length had evolved over the years as five thousand words.) The magazine should be opened to subjects such as sports ("which we now consider not quite respectable") and to firsthand narratives. It might seem like a lowering of standards, he said, but actually they would be raised because there would be more catholicity, variety, and unexpectedness. The magazine paid contributors two hundred and fifty dollars per article, which Allen believed to be generally sufficient, but he urged that "trusted performers" be paid more.[20] He wanted mild-tempered book reviewer Harry Hansen to be dropped for "somebody who will speak out." Hansen was foremost a *daily* reviewer of books. His *Harper's* reviews were rewritten largely from his newspaper columns in the *New York World.* Allen called the department low in readership as well as "dull, half-hearted, timid, colorless, unimportant." For Hansen's replacement he recommended John Chamberlain, then reviewing for *Scribner's,* or he suggested transplanting DeVoto from the "Easy Chair" to book reviewer.

The "Easy Chair," Allen felt, should be eliminated despite its long tradition. It was "an unsatisfactory department which is not fish, flesh, or fowl and has a title of antique flavor which suggests idle and relaxed chat: too old-gentlemanly, too sedate, too unexcited." Eliminating the "Easy Chair" would add four pages to the regular text, and Allen hoped that the space could be used to expand the "Lion's Mouth."

Allen also wanted an editorial department which could go to press last and provide more immediacy to the magazine. While *Harper's* long-time contributor Elmer Davis might seem the logical author of such a column, Allen preferred that the editors themselves write it, "thus making it a real editorial department." He believed that he and assistant editor Leighton could handle the job.

Perhaps most important to Allen was his proposal that both he and Leighton be given more free time in return for writing articles for the magazine. Allen aimed for two and a half months off for "travel, for outside writing, and for general education" on the condition that he write four articles a year without extra pay.

Finally, he recommended a new cover. "But maybe that can wait," he concluded.[21]

Seven months later Allen again talked to Hartman about the need for change. He indicated now the existence of a degree of tension on the staff. Part of the difficulty evidently stemmed not only from the magazine's direction but from the conflict of personalities and ideas between Allen and Leighton. They were different types of men, though they had in common Harvard educations. Leighton was outspoken, acerbic, and generally skeptical by nature. He favored giving editors more autonomy in assigning and preparing articles. Allen and Leighton both wanted fuller discussions of magazine policy so that they might work more agreeably and with a clearer understanding of purpose. They agreed on removal of Hansen as literary editor, fewer routine essays and more "brand-new fact-material and unsparing analysis," up-to-date articles in the arts, where the magazine currently was very weak, entertaining and exciting personal narratives of all sorts, more variety in length and subject matter, "more popular stuff—entertaining stuff which can be consumed without effort; *but never ordinary or slick empty stuff,*" an end to commissioning or encouraging articles from old-line "important" writers who lacked electricity or who were too filled with self-importance to be told to rewrite, and avoidance of all routine, habit-following procedures. "We should both like it understood as soon as possible whether we are to make major changes in 1938 or not," Allen said.[22]

After these two confrontations with Hartman the pressure bore results, and alterations gradually came about. In October 1938, a new cover, the first since 1925, adorned the magazine. The familiar burnt orange was discarded for "cocoa-brown," which thereafter alternated monthly with three other colors. Minor changes in the design also were made. Inside, a new columnist, E. B. White, a skillful and perceptive writer whose elegant prose enhanced the *New Yorker,* assumed a monthly department entitled "One Man's Meat."[23] There, White's pungent, personal observations about his seemingly prosaic, day-to-day existence on a Maine farm, won a wide following. Space was made for White by eliminating "The Lion's Mouth," but by then the *New Yorker* had so captured the market for humor and satire that the column was hardly missed.

The October issue also held, as Allen had requested, space for lengthy poetry. The issue's lead piece was a selection of eight poems by Edna St. Vincent Millay, signifying a new status for poetry which heretofore had been relegated to filler material.

Two months later Hansen was dropped as book critic in favor of John Chamberlain, Allen's choice. The column's title changed from "Among the New Books" to simply "The New Books," and its type-face was enlarged to match that of the rest of the magazine. Hansen had attempted to comment on as many new books as possible; Chamberlain was to choose only the books he considered significant. An assistant, Katherine Gauss, would briefly characterize other important books.

As tensions in Europe heightened, as efforts continued to combat the persistent Depression, and as modern communication seemed to shrink the world into a smaller but intensely feuding family, editing *Harper's* seemed much more complicated than in pre-World War I days. The complicated age inspired Allen to a bit of casual poetry entitled "An Editor's Complaint, 1938," in which he lamented (undoubtedly for his own amusement, since the poem was not intended for publication), the passing of more leisurely times:

I

Time was when the world was larger
Time was, when life was slow;
When a man had a chance to learn with half a glance
The things he was supposed to know—

There wasn't much to follow in the papers
You could take them or leave them be;
And they didn't cause a flurry of unreasonable worry.
Why no, you said, this can't touch *me*.

Events were a film in slow motion.
And China was half a world away
If you gave the news a look or two and read a current book or two
Enough; you could call it a day.

Time was, when editors dallied
With art and letters, unabashed;

And their gentle readers thanked 'em to remain within the sanctum,
If a pin fell there, it crashed.

II

Now the tempo is accelerated. Telegraphs and telephone
And five-star final extras and the radio and such—
Need I give you all the reasons?—We don't live by years and seasons
No, we live from hour to hour, and the morning's news is sour
Long before it is digested; there's too much, too much, too much.

Now the world is so much littler that a speech by Adolf Hitler
Gives us apopplexy [sic] instantly, four thousand miles away;
If the Japanese get pranksy and bombard the river Yangtse
We go wild before the pilot hears he hit the ship Panay.
If a speech by Dr. Goebbels compliments the Spanish rebels,
If a Fascist and a Nazi utter words that sound too fratzi
If a U boat at Gibraltar saw a ship and tried to halt her
It's a crisis! It's terrific! And it happens every day.

And at home the scene is changing with a speed that's so deranging
If you miss your morning paper what you know is full of gaps,
In the evening what was ranklin' our indomitable Franklin
Was the economic royalists, this morning it's the Japs;
If we don't have seven cruisers there'll be war and we'll be losers;
But by 3 P M our quarterback has overlooked the slaughter back
In China; now the crisis is the current trend in prices—
What, you hadn't heard the latest? You were sound asleep, perhaps.

. . . .

IV

It's impossible.
It can't be done.
If you want any time
To have any fun.

And that's why you see a poor editor standing here.
Looking as if any moment now he's breathed his last.
He can't take it. There are too many things happening—
And my God! They happen so fast.[24]

139

12

FREE-LANCING IN THE THIRTIES

A disciplined man, Allen, while engaged in a responsible editorial job and an active social life, still maintained a constant production of free-lance magazine articles. Having dropped humor sketches, he wrote on a myriad of topics. Popular culture continued to fascinate him, and he found meaning in American life through examining subjects which normally did not seem significant: from best-seller lists to record-breaking in sports to offbeat American personalities.

Frequently, the articles appeared in *Harper's*, although his position there did not mean automatic acceptance. Other pieces were published primarily in the *Saturday Review of Literature* and *Scribner's*, and less often in such magazines as the *Ladies' Home Journal* and the *American*.

His interest in sports, and particularly in track, provided impetus for examining the perplexing question of why athletic records continued to be broken through the years by men who, after all, maintained largely the same physique from one era to the next. The explanation, he figured, lay not in evolutionary advances but in better equipment, wider participation by more finely trained athletes, and improved competition which sparked emotions and resulted in greater performances.[1]

In "Best-Sellers: 1900–1935," Allen came to an optimistic conclusion about the American reading public. A study of best-seller lists indicated to him that since 1900 reading tastes had shown "a marked gain in substance." This pointed to increased intellectual maturity of the average person. The reason, he felt, was the broadening nature of mass communications.[2]

His conclusion pointed him toward a more encompassing interpretation at the end of the thirties. In "Our Widening American Culture," Allen argued that beneath the usual ominous news of the day Americans were experiencing a cultural flowering. He pointed to the popularity of the Toscanini and Walter Damrosch symphony programs on radio, improved reading habits indicated by best-seller lists, increased education, interest in photography, sleekly designed automobiles, gaily colored kitchens, and even beauty within department store window displays. He declared, "We Americans are a distinctly more mature people, a more culturally enlightened people, than we were a generation ago; and we appear to be better off for the participation of the millions in cultural things that were once considered chiefly the affair of the few."[3]

Allen wrote also on such subjects as Horatio Alger, Jr., Elbert Hubbard, the influenza epidemic of 1918, the Ku Klux Klan, the dance craze of the World War I era, Bermuda, the campaign of 1936, persons who pose as well-known authors, and one day in history.

In October 1938 Allen composed a memorandum to Canfield and Hartman:

I have long planned that in due course I should write a companion volume to *Only Yesterday* covering the nineteen-thirties, and have been more or less casually collecting material. Now I think the time has come for me to begin work. The natural stopping-point for such a volume might be the end of the year 1939—which is only a bit more than a year away—or it might be the election of 1940—about two years away—or it might be some as yet unpredictable event, such as the outbreak of a big war. At any rate, I think I had better get going on *Another Yesterday* as soon as possible.[4]

He asked to take off a total of four months in 1939 without pay, no period being longer than two months. He pointed out that he had not pushed on previous requests for released time because of office needs, and that he had had no holidays longer than three weeks in more than three years. "I don't want to give the impression that I am tired of working for Harper's Magazine and want to edge out. On the contrary, I should hate to leave," he wrote, a statement which certainly did not rule out that possibility. He simply wanted a more flexible arrangement so that he would not be confronted once more with squeezing a book out of half of his evenings and all his weekends.[5] Canfield and Hartman agreed to his proposal, and Allen immediately began preparatory work for his successor to *Only Yesterday*.

Actually, he had been casually collecting material for the sequel ever since *Only Yesterday*. When a newspaper or magazine article or editorial had caught his eye, he circled it with a pen and stacked it with others in a huge pile. Much of this he now found unusable: the best material turned out to be that which was taken for granted at the time but later was difficult to date, like the emergence of pinball machines. He collected a thick folder of anti-New Deal arguments but found nothing that he could use. The best examples of the spirit of the criticism, he found, was the casual gossip one heard at the dinner table, or the anti-Roosevelt jokes overheard on commuter trains. He kept a notebook in which he devoted one page to each month's major events. Perhaps more useful for this purpose, however, were the annual *World Almanacs* which chronologized events. *Variety* yearbooks gave him lists of hit songs, radio program ratings, movies, and other entertainment news. Also, there were far more books and documents describing the period than there had been for the twenties.[6]

Just as he relied heavily on the Lynds' *Middletown* for reporting social changes in *Only Yesterday*, Allen fully utilized their next volume, *Middletown in Transition*, for his review of the thirties.[7] He also turned once again to Charles and Mary Beard, this time to their *America in Midpassage*.[8]

142

The actual writing of the book, thanks to time off from *Harper's,* occurred at three locations: New York, Bermuda, and Tyringham, Massachusetts.[9] The Bermuda stint, lasting about two months, was spent in the spring of 1939 at the rambling house of the Allens' friends, the William Zuills. There, Allen averaged four to five hours a day on the manuscript. He filled the remainder of the time with swimming, lying on the beach, playing tennis, and having lunch or tea with various people. That summer in Tyringham, where the Allens rented a house, the schedule was much the same.

There was a dilemma in finding a logical stopping place for *Since Yesterday.* Allen determined early in 1939 to conclude arbitrarily with September 3, 1939, the ten-year anniversary of the book's starting point. "And when it [September 3] came, I was more surprised than the rest of the world to find Neville Chamberlain declaring war," he told H. Allen Smith, then a reporter for the *New York World-Telegram.*[10] In a feature article Smith described Allen as a "tall, tweedy New Englander with a coolidgeate manner about him." Allen confessed to Smith that the book was not as sprightly as *Only Yesterday* since its chief concerns were economics and politics.

Completed in November 1939, the book was subtitled *The Nineteen-Thirties in America, Sept. 3, 1929–Sept. 3, 1939.* The dedication was for Agnes' mother: "To Letitia Cunningham Rogers, who has a wise head and a warm heart."

Even before publication on February 9, 1940, signs became evident of an assured popular success. As early as October 1939, Metro-Goldwyn-Mayer obtained Allen's permission to read galley proofs.[11] Nothing came of this nibble, but advance sales were seventy-five hundred copies and a multitude of reviews were assured.

Allen never suffered the agony of reading bad reviews, for *Since Yesterday* received favorable critiques and wide popularity. *Life,* inspired by the book, devoted a thirteen-page photographic spread to people and events of the thirties and challenged readers in a game of trivia to identify them.[12] *Harper's* excerpted segments from *Since Yesterday* for three consecutive issues.

With *The Lords of Creation* behind him, Allen had felt more confident about handling the theme which held the book together, economic depression. He was less optimistic about the Roosevelt administration than he had been in *Lords*. It looked as if the New Deal were through—there were no new cards in the Roosevelt deck. Allen declared that "work relief was becoming every day more clearly a tragic makeshift, demoralizing . . . to many if not most of those unfortunate enough to be dependent upon it." For six and a half years the Roosevelt administration had experimented and palliated, merely keeping disaster at bay at a cost of $20 billion.[13] But there were numerous positive aspects of the New Deal, and Allen carefully balanced the ledger throughout the book.

Why had the economy continued stagnant? Allen's fullest and first answer to his own rhetorical question lay in "one of the most significant economic developments of the nineteen-thirties: the increased importance of the great corporations."[14] The general trend toward centralization, seen most directly in the swelling size of the federal government, was taking place in business, too. The great corporations, unlike smaller businesses, weathered the Depression, and throughout the decade they generally were making whatever money was made in business. New investments did not flourish because competition was stifled by a few monoliths such as General Motors, American Telephone, Standard Oil of New Jersey, U. S. Steel, duPont, and General Electric. These six giant corporations, according to a study Allen quoted, earned 24 percent of all corporate profits in 1935.[15]

Only a tiny minority of the millions of shareholders receiving dividends got enough to be potentially important in investment, and they were in no mood to gamble.

Allen's lively chronology of social change in *Only Yesterday* had been a primary reason for its success; in *Since Yesterday* the study of popular attitudes and preoccupations carried an important but secondary role. The book's first chapter re-created everyday life on September 3, 1929; the next four chapters dealt with economics; and not until Chapter 6 did Allen treat changing manners, morals, and customs. Here, he was at his liveliest. The Depression seemed to be the root of many new habits, just as he believed war had influenced those of the twenties. Marriage rates dropped, premarital sex increased, and yet marriage and the family gained in respectability as an institution because the uncertainty of the times made home life seem attractive as a firm anchor.[16]

He saw emerging a "pattern of relaxation" which was evidenced by the widespread adoption of the five-day work week; the boom and democratization of participant sports such as softball, bicycling, and skiing; a spread to all classes of bridge playing; and a growing number of gambling devices such as slot machines, pinball machines, punchboards, and drawing for prizes.[17]

Since Yesterday dealt in considerable depth with the Depression and politics; it scanned popular culture with much insight and interesting detail; and it barely mentioned developments in fine arts, education, science, and philosophy. Unlike *Only Yesterday,* in which Allen purposely avoided foreign affairs, he could not refrain in *Since Yesterday* from occasional passages about ominous events in Europe. The book ended on the outbreak of war, which meant "an era ended for America and another one began."[18] Once again Allen had isolated a decade in history and characterized it as a unique one.

Since Yesterday did not match *Only Yesterday* in sales, but it did earn high rankings on best-seller lists and Allen found himself again feted and promoted. "It's kind of fun to be prominent again," he confessed to Hildegarde. One perquisite was an appearance on NBC's highly popular radio show "Information Please," which had been started in 1938 during a flowering on the airwaves of quiz and contest shows. The prospect made Allen shiver with feigned terror. "Listen and pray for me, please!" he advised Hildegarde, acknowledging that the show surely would help *Since Yesterday's* sales "unless I make a jackass of myself, which I won't. Allee samee, I'll be glad when it's over."[19] Allen appeared on March 5, 1940, for a fee of one hundred and fifty dollars. He was the only guest among the show's regulars: Franklin P. Adams, the *New York Post* columnist, Oscar Levant, the quick-witted composer and pianist, John Kieran, *New York Times* sports columnist, and Clifton Fadiman, master of ceremonies. Allen survived, though he mused that Agnes could do much better than he. Later, when he learned that the estimated audience had been twelve million, he contracted a case of "retrospective jitters."[20]

As a historian Allen's reputation has suffered because he appeared to see history in neat units of time with too little appreciation of antecedents. However, he did develop and enunciate a wider frame of historical reference which interpreted broadly the whole of the American experience. He related it in 1938 in a commencement address, "In a Time of Apprehension," at Bennington College in Vermont, where a year earlier he had become a trustee.[21]

Allen described the Depression as symptomatic of the conclusion of a great boom in American development which began about 1800 and ended approximately with World War I. (His ideas roughly foreshadowed those of Walter Prescott Webb, who wrote of a four-hundred-year land boom.) Allen apologized for the brashness of his bold strokes, and, as he frequently did, he warned the audience of his amateur status as a historian. "I trust that as a non-union historian— or I might say an historian whose amateur standing is unquestioned—I may be forgiven for rushing in where even the best-equipped scholars of history might fear to tread." But he felt compelled to record his conviction that for approximately the last twenty-five years civilization had been entering a new phase, and that unless the differences of old and new were realized "we shall not understand the nature of the predicament in which this country, and indeed the whole world, finds itself in the year 1938."[22]

The old phase covered roughly the nineteenth century and the first fourteen years of the twentieth century. "In it were established the habits of thinking, the expectations, and the folklore by which our American community is still largely ruled."

It had been a time of incredible expansion in industrialization, mechanization, and urbanization; an increasing population; a moving out into vacant spaces throughout the world as well as in the American West; and a rapid depletion of the earth's natural resources. The American economic system, capitalism, works best when expanding; once expansion stops, the system falters badly, Allen explained.

Furthermore, the period was marked by increasingly rapid communication, by an explosion in scientific knowledge, and by advances in political democracy.

This period of immense change brought stresses and conflicts, Allen believed. The rise of industrialism required millions of people to work at routine, specialized jobs. Although they became economic serfs, they retained political freedom, and quite naturally they insisted, "often bitterly," that the state (in whose management they had some say) should intervene in economic affairs (where they had very little say). "The idea slowly gained ground that the political state should in time become the supreme arbiter in *all* the affairs of the people."[23] In short, Allen had explained how Jeffersonian liberal beliefs favoring independent freeholders and minimal government were transformed into the modern liberalism that *advocated* big government.

Allen saw other conflicts as well: in imperialism (it was self-defeating and also caused rivalries); in the depletion of coveted resources such as coal, oil, iron, soil, and forests; and in the economic system's growing complexity, which diminished the individual's independence and made democratic governments more unwieldy. At the same time nationalism, which placed greater demands on governments, was becoming a mighty force.

The period could not be charted precisely ("for history does not fall into exact compartments"), but Allen felt that it lasted until about 1914 when it cracked under tensions that had been growing. "That day is long since ended now—though many of us persist in the habits of thought which set it up." The chance for easy expansion was gone—population growth had stalled and the best open spaces were preempted. As natural resources grew more scarce the processes of mining had become more expensive. The colonial systems of Britain, France, Italy, and Japan appeared to cost more than they were worth. All the familiar aids to expansion, thus, were gone or dissipated and now, "either we must work out new methods of expansion, or we must learn to live somehow without expansion, in a static economy."[24]

An intellectual superman, Allen believed, might rationally and calmly devise a solution to these problems. But mankind did not respond in such fashion:

Man is a creature of habit; and when the system that was good enough for father does not work he is likely to become frightened and angry. He wants to wrap himself about his possessions, if he has any; if he thinks he hasn't his fair share, he wants to grab his neighbor's. He wants to find a villain to blame for what has gone wrong, and smash that villain. Or he wants to run away to some safe island, or to run back to the haven of his happy boyhood. Or, in his fright and bewilderment, he turns to old superstitions and incantations to bring back what has been lost.[25]

Allen's conclusion summed up his basic philosophy and goal as a communicator:

I trust I am not so foolish as to imagine that the American people will ever turn completely rational. But I think it is reasonable to say that the more men and women there are in this country who are willing to accept the fact that the problems which beset America today are not the problems of the nineteenth century, that we cannot go back, that this is a new situation that we are in; and the more people there are who are willing to work at seeking the facts of this new situation, examining them with all the disinterestedness of which they are capable, and who will not start marching or cheering or hating until they have come to reasonable conclusions from these facts—the more of these people there are, the easier it will be to keep the ship of state steady through good weather and bad.[26]

He had not presented ideas of such scope in any of his histories. The continuing irritant of the Depression had set Allen's mind to pondering on such a scale, and the historical perspective he had developed seemed even to explain a new crisis that was approaching.

13

THE EDITORSHIP

The emerging 1940s saw a restless, uncertain America. The Depression apparently had become a never-ending burden. Abroad, the "phony war" provided only a short lull for pondering the meaning of the European conflict, and few sure answers seemed to exist. The very fate of democracy seemed in balance. What might happen if both Britain and France fell before the German war machine? Which was safer, to ignore the European conflagration and concentrate on shoring up America's own pressing internal deficiencies or to face the Fascist menace directly by joining forces with Britain and France and stamping out the fire before it raged out of control? The debate, in all its various shadings, reverberated among the nation's intellectual leaders. Few if any people thought that America had any business entangling itself in European affairs, but Fascist triumph after triumph gradually was eroding that once-staunch conviction. In April 1940 German forces surprised neutral Denmark and Norway with a decisive swoop, and the debate's overtones darkened.

Allen carried his radio to work to catch the news accounts of the invasions—irritating Virginia Watson, who seemed to feel that a radio at work was "vulgar." Allen wrote to Hildegarde in April about the events, concluding that Hitler would make no advance on the Western front. But in May the Nazis cut through powerless Belgium and Holland, turning suddenly and shockingly upon France itself. The French, to the extreme consternation of the democratic world, could not hold their defenses. The new development, obviously perilous because certainly France had been expected to thwart the German juggernaut, caused many Americans to make an agonizing reassessment of the situation. Allen at this point remained an isolationist, but less adamant about it than people like Charles A. Beard, Oswald Garrison Villard, and John T. Flynn, who steadfastly maintained their convictions.

Allen, writing to his sister, no doubt spoke for millions as he painfully followed bulletins and speculated on the developments in France:

I suppose we have all been under the same pall this past week—buying newspapers, listening to the radio, and watching with gathering horror the débâcle in Europe. Today [May 19] the news seems a shade less ugly, but it will be almost a miracle, it seems to me, if the Germans now within a hundred miles of Paris are turned back; one looks forward through ugly vistas of imagined defeat for the Allies—France defeated, either by the capture of Paris or by separating her armies from those of the British; the British isles bombed, their docks and airports and factories smashed; the Germans maybe roaring down through Switzerland (I expected this on Friday, was really surprised when it didn't happen.); Mussolini climbing aboard the bandwagon; maybe the British fleet being surrendered or fleeing to Canada; the Empire broken up; and Hitler becoming the advancing boss of half the world, and a threat of rising proportions to the United States. Maybe it won't happen—but I have a dismal feeling that all the optimists' prophecies have been set at naught so far; why should this process not go on? By this time I fear that the question of American participation or isolation may be becoming academic—in the sense that it would be too late to intervene now (except in the limited way in which we are now aiding the Allies); and also that it is being borne in upon us that if we got into Europe we wouldn't be able to get out again without inviting fresh disaster. There would be little use in going in to shore up a system that would fall to pieces the minute we let go. The trouble is that the Germans, damn their eyes, have put into action an intelligence and imagination and energy that their enemies just do not seem to possess. Well, the tide may turn—but I have only a despairing half-hope of it.[1]

Allen still was not ready for the United States to enter the fray; yet, Agnes had favored intervention for some time despite his reluctance, and she tugged him in that direction.

Paris, where former *Harper's* editor Thomas B. Wells still lived in retirement, fell in mid-June, and by July the French nation was conquered. The eyes of the world turned to England—would she, too, surrender? The resolve and courage from Winston Churchill's dramatic proclamations, the radio broadcasts from London catching the spirit of Londoners singing "Pack Up Your Troubles" while jammed in air-raid shelters, and the desperate nature of it all convinced Allen. That summer he quietly entered the interventionist camp.

Other liberals, not so quietly, converted, too. Bruce Bliven and his *New Republic* editors publicly confessed their error. The *Nation* also became a convert, as did people like Lewis Mumford, Archibald MacLeish, Waldo Frank, and Reinhold Niebuhr. Oswald Garrison Villard, after a career of forty-six and a half years on the *Nation*, resigned in June to protest its editorial change of heart. Later that year John T. Flynn left the *New Republic* for the same reason.[2]

Allen did not take to the public forum to announce his conversion. His reflections largely occurred within his own mind, in conversations with family and friends, and in a letter to his Congressman, William T. Pheiffer, in January 1941. He was seeking to persuade the Republican Congressman to vote for the lend-lease bill proposed by President Roosevelt. "If it seems unneutral to do this, I can only add that in the world of 1941 there is no such thing as real neutrality: every nation is engaged in trying to affect the course of world affairs to its own advantage. And, after all, the lend-lease bill is a long way from sending soldiers to Europe or Africa."[3]

By April Greece had fallen, and Allen believed much worse was yet to come. The United States "ought to go in, lest England fall and the Hitler scourge run like an epidemic almost everywhere." He saw little chance that Hitler could be defeated, but certainly U.S. forces could weaken the German push, lend moral support to wavering nations, save Latin America, and perhaps inspire conquered peoples to rebel against their Nazi lords. "Better now than later, say I; so many peoples have been too late! (I still waver, doubt, inwardly rebel, but I think the moral effect at least would be immense.)" What dismayed Allen perhaps most was the "business-as-usual, easygoing spirit" he found throughout government and industry.[4]

Harper's feelings about the war, implied in its contents, seemed to parallel Allen's own thoughts. Through the thirties the magazine had followed events in Europe quite closely. In 1937 the number of articles devoted to the foreign situation increased considerably, and, coincidental with the outbreak of war, the September 1939 issue contained seven articles examining the American situation in the world. Isolationists such as Charles A. Beard, C. Hartley Grattan, John T. Flynn, and Oswald Garrison Villard prominently expressed their views in Harper's pages, and by the end of 1939 it appeared that the magazine might be isolationist as a matter of editorial policy. The editors now felt obliged to record their impartiality on the "controversial and much debated question."[5] But the following month, two more articles lent further weight to the appearance of sympathy toward the isolationist viewpoint.[6]

In 1940, concurrent with the shifting tide of public opinion, the magazine's articles began to reflect more sympathy for intervention. The special September 1940 foreign affairs issue announced definitely a new mood. Seven related articles were brought together under the general heading, "The American Emergency." In one of the articles Allen himself drew on his World War I administrative experiences and urged effective planning for defense and a willingness to grant sweeping powers to Washington for the crisis.[7] Articles in following months carried a new tone of urgency.

In September 1941 the magazine announced a one thousand-dollar contest for the "best authentic account of first-hand war experience, or war observation" received between August 20, 1941, and July 1, 1942. The incident could have occurred "any place in which the influence of this war has extended," including the United States.[8]

The momentous times seemed to call for a re-examination of the American character, and Allen determined to do just that in his next book. In the spring he began outlining the project, a study of "the American people, how they live, and what are the ideas, codes, and incentives that rule them." It would be a sociological snapshot, and Allen intended it to be like V. L. Parrington's *Main Currents in American Thought* except that following his own customary pattern, he would concentrate on the thought of the average American instead of the intellectual leaders. As part of his research he intended to travel some to sample firsthand the varying thoughts and habits of Americans in separate regions.

To put the idea in a nutshell, this is to be an attempt to do for American sociology what my *Yesterday* books tried to do for recent American history: to reduce the customs and ideas of the American people to informal and understandable terms, avoiding the academic and constantly using material that the Ph.D.'s don't touch or at the best use stodgily.[9]

By summer he had compiled a basic reading list for background information: Parrington, Harriet Martineau, the Federalist Papers, de Tocqueville, Frances Trollope, Dickens' *American Notes*, the Beards, the Lynds, G. K. Chesterton, George Jean Nathan, Charles Van Doren, Van Wyck Brooks, Henry Ford, the Hays Committee rules for the movies, Herbert Satterlee's biography of J. Pierpont Morgan, and Foster Rhea Dulles' *America Learns to Play*.[10]

Finding time for research was more difficult than ever, for Allen's outside activities continued to expand. In 1940, he experienced a great personal thrill: election as an overseer to Harvard. It was a position which the finest families in Boston had considered an ultimate honor.

His magazine duties pressed harder. He stepped in frequently for Hartman, who suffered from a heart condition. In fact, he sometimes felt that he was running the magazine as much as Hartman. Allen handled DeVoto's copy each month for "The Easy Chair" and, as always, dealt with many of the magazine's authors and would-be authors.

The magazine now was showing a profit; earnings for 1939 exceeded those of 1938 in spite of advertising difficulties. Steamship and European travel advertising, always important, had disappeared because of the war.[11] Circulation remained low during 1939, but in 1940 better than 8,500 new readers had brought the figure up to 109,787.[12]

A new kind of duty befell Allen in the fall of 1940. For the first time in American history, men were being conscripted into military service during peacetime. Draft boards, 125,000 of them, were created to register all men between the ages of eighteen and thirty-five. An opportunity to join this significant effort arose in September. Mayor Fiorello LaGuardia appointed Allen to Local Draft Board No. 51. His experiences at sorting out thousands of individual cards and handling other complex and perplexing new duties resulted in a first-person, anonymous account for *Harper's*: "I'm on a Draft Board," written under the staff pseudonym of George R. Clark.[13] The job was more demanding than Allen had anticipated, but, as he told Hildegarde, "I'm glad to be putting in 10 hours a week on the draft board; it makes me feel able to hold my head up, at least part way!"[14]

Allen's reputation as an astute observer of contemporary affairs earned him a radio offer to do a three-to-five-times-a-week, fifteen-minute evening commentary on one of the networks. Tempting though it was, he declined to give up his *Harper's* job "for any gamble like that"—to do it right would require a full-time effort. Ordinarily, he confessed, he would have been in a fever of excitement over the offer, but the grave world events of the week (the German assault on France in the spring of 1940) made it seem "terribly unimportant." At any rate, "it was a feather in my cap to be considered."[15]

The Allens continued to enjoy the company of interesting and important people. They visited mutual friends and attended the opera with the energetic district attorney of New York City, Thomas E. Dewey, who proved to be no favorite of Allen's. Thomas W. Lamont, the J. P. Morgan and Co. chief, had the Allens to dinner. Lamont, who had looked over *The Lords of Creation* in manuscript form for Allen, now was a "white-haired amiable grandfatherly figure" whom the Allens secretly referred to as "Twinkle and Fuzz."[16]

The *Harper's* editors received a rather unusual protest in the fall of 1940 from a writer who had established himself in the thirties as a significant interpreter of the American scene. James T. Farrell, a Marxist sympathizer and author of the notable *Studs Lonigan*, had attempted unsuccessfully for years to be published in *Harper's*. Convinced that a conspiracy of sorts existed between *Harper's* and other magazines to silence him, he sent Allen an irate, two-page letter. He included a volume of his collected short works, pointing out that *Harper's* had rejected many of these same stories over the past ten years. A comparison between these rejected pieces with *Harper's* own fiction should prove that editorial prejudice against him did exist, he said. It was true, Farrell acknowledged, that publication of some of his material would destroy the magazine's goodwill with certain groups: the Stalinists and sometimes members of the Catholic Church as well. "However, on the whole, I have not seriously ever destroyed the circulation of a magazine, and on occasions, my writings have helped build up circulation."[17]

The protest caused genuine concern. Allen appended a note to the letter and passed it around: "We may be wrong. . . . We all might take a look & do a bit of heart-searching." George Leighton responded with a one-page memorandum saying Farrell's letter was "not to be casually dismissed." "Farrell is an artist and by performance has proved it. The three Lonigan books are solid as a rock."[18]

Allen took special care in answering Farrell, assuring him that certainly no conscious effort existed to ban him, that all the rejections had been isolated ones, and that perhaps they had been ill-advised. Allen acknowledged a general trend in magazines to rely more on staff-written articles, thereby diminishing free-lance writers' opportunities. Also, *Harper's* now published less fiction because the quality seemed to have deteriorated and because so many new problems cried out for nonfictional treatment.

It seems ridiculous, though, that a series of decisions unrelated to each other should have had the effect of keeping you out of Harper's all this time. I wonder if you will give us another chance: if you will let us see—again, if we have seen them before—whatever unpublished stories you have on hand, and give us a chance for reconsideration?[19]

Whether or not Farrell complied is uncertain; at any rate none of his stories appeared in *Harper's*.

He need not have felt totally isolated in his rejections, for declining the works of famous authors was practically a daily occurrence at the magazine. Within the next year, 1941, the list of rejected authors would grow to include, as a mere sampling, Max Eastman, Nelson Algren, Vladimir Nabokov, and Ruth Benedict. (Eventually, Farrell would have some consolation, for a year after Allen resigned as editor, C. Hartley Grattan wrote for *Harper's* an appreciation and analysis of Farrell.[20])

Late in September 1941 Allen sat down after breakfast to peruse his *New York Times*. Opposite the editorial page a headline announced Lee Hartman's death. "Incredible to have learned about it first through the newspaper!" he recounted to Hildegarde. It was all the more surprising because Hartman had put in a full day's work the previous day, looking unwell but seeming otherwise to be completely himself. A story for *Harper's* had overlapped slightly onto another page, and a short poem was needed to fill the remaining space. Hartman had said jokingly, "I don't want an 8-line poem or a 12-line poem or a 16-line poem; I want a 24-line poem!" The next day the staff cut the story to remove the overlap and used the full page for Hartman's obituary, which Allen wrote.[21]

Hartman, in his quiet manner, devoted practically his whole life to *Harper's* until his death at sixty-one. Although he had joined the firm in 1904, in Elmer Davis' words, "very likely most readers of the Magazine never knew his name." An editor's note, almost certainly written by Allen, said, "It was the institution which counted with him, not his own leadership in it."[22] Hartman had followed carefully the path already set for the magazine; and he considered no change which seemed to him to dilute in any degree the dignity or distinction of the institution. Hartman insisted on high standards from contributors, and once he accepted a writer's work he did not edit the text, instead, he returned it to the author for revision. Bernard DeVoto said he had never known Hartman to yield to any threat over controversial stands made in *Harper's* pages.[23] He had kept the pages open to all viewpoints, though shunning dogma and crusade, and the overall position of the publication had been one of liberalism.

Allen certainly was expected to succeed Hartman. "Nothing has been decided, but I assume that I'll slide into the Editorship and am already busy with plans for gradual changes," he told Hildegarde six days after Hartman's death.[24] DeVoto concluded instantly that Allen automatically had the job, and as a matter of protocol he submitted, prematurely, his resignation to the "new editor," to be accepted or rejected as Allen saw fit.[25]

The magazine staff was thin in numbers and experience. George Leighton was away on leave of absence and assistant editor John Kouwenhoven was new and inexperienced.[26]

The official confirmation that Allen would become the sixth editor in the magazine's ninety-one-year history came on October 7, nearly two weeks after Hartman's death, and after two sessions between Allen and Harper & Brothers officials. Henry Hoyns, chairman of the board, and Cass Canfield, president, jointly made the announcement.

Although, in effect, Allen had frequently been editor in Hartman's absence, and was better known than his superior, his "second career" as a best-selling historian caused some concern that he might not give the magazine full attention. Kouwenhoven had the impression that Harper management unsuccessfully sought Allen's permission to give up book writing after being named editor. Canfield acknowledges management concern, but remembers no suggestion that Allen write no more books.[27] At any rate, Allen's projected volume on "The

Americans" lay forgotten forever. "The book-writing has to be dropped for the moment—but I don't intend to let it go permanently," he wrote.[28]

Actually, Harper & Brothers management had greater expectation for editorial change than Allen realized. He wrote to Hildegarde a week after his appointment that the firm expected him "to launch a new and ambitious program for the Magazine: a bewildering sensation after having spent years working with a man who regarded innovations with indifference if not with hostility."[29]

His new role actually meant little change in daily routine. The real difference lay in the enlarged authority and sense of responsibility. One of Allen's first objectives was to relieve the staff shortage, so Agnes returned to work part-time on the magazine.[30]

Allen's appointment to the editorship brought him much more attention than he expected. He received ninety-six telegrams and letters of congratulations, newspaper and magazine reporters interviewed him, and a *Time* photographer snapped his picture.[31] The photograph depicted a smiling, amiable-looking, though dignified man with a receding hairline, wearing a tweed suit and a plaid tie. The friendly *Time* article described Allen as being "virtually raised on famed U.S. monthlies" and quoted him as saying he saw no reason why *Harper's* circulation should not be anywhere from 15,000 to 300,000, "depending on how interesting it is."[32] The *New York Times* editorially greeted him, also stressing his many years on quality magazines and praising his three books on American history as being founded on careful study and marked by fairness, tolerance, and wit.[33]

Ellery Sedgwick, who had retired from the *Atlantic* in 1938, wrote, "You have been more patient than men of quality usually are and I rejoice that you've reached your goal. I hope you will go galloping away." Allen, in a kind response, credited Sedgwick with providing every start he ever had in editorial work that amounted to anything. "I feel very much your disciple."[34]

DeVoto wished Allen well and hoped he got enough satisfaction out of the job to "balance the sleepless nights." Dorothy's sister,

Emily Cobb Holmes (Mrs. Leonard Holmes), penned a simple but telling congratulatory note, "But Freddie—How perfect! How natural! How just!"[35]

In the December issue Allen related his goals to the magazine's readers. He would seek more variety, more flexibility, and keener human interest. But the changes would be in method only; the main objectives required "no change whatever."

> Overtones may be somewhat different; but the keynote, we trust, will be unaltered. We shall continue to try to report upon, and interpret, events and trends in this country and the world—not the day-to-day news stories but the long term developments (so vital to our future) which the news reporters do not bring into focus.[36]

Allen was now working until 6 P.M. most evenings. "I am enjoying a lot the chance to drive ahead and do things and plan for future features, and it's fun to realize the subtle enhancement of prestige which has come about," he wrote. Although he already had achieved a reputation aside from the magazine, now he and Agnes felt more comfortable inviting important writers to their house. "We had John Dos Passos in for a drink Thursday evening (he's just back from England) and the next day we had Frank Adams, who stayed for two and a half hours and regaled us with tales of Information Please."[37] Allen soon persuaded Adams to put his stories in writing for an article in *Harper's*.

The new editorial responsibilities were stimulating, not relaxing, and one Saturday in November Allen and Agnes drove to isolated Jones Beach for some relief of tension. They walked on the sand— "such grand space, such a majestic sea, such a change from New York City"—played miniature golf, and had lunch on the beach. Allen resolved to return to his watercolors that winter.[38]

On this eve of Pearl Harbor the American magazine scene bore an entirely different face from the one Allen had encountered eighteen years earlier when he first came to *Harper's*. Glamour publications like *Life*, *Time*, *Reader's Digest*, and *New Yorker* had been established with great success. *Harper's* and the *Atlantic* alone stood preeminent as friendly rivals for the intellectual leadership among monthly publications after *Scribner's* folded in 1939. The *Century*, Allen's one-time base, had given up the battle quietly in 1930. The *American Mercury*, only a painful reminder of what it had been in the twenties, had tied its fortunes to an ephemeral intellectual mood that ended with the Depression. Gone, too, were *Outlook*, *Forum*, *Literary Digest*, and *Independent*, and the humor publications *Life* and *Judge*. *Harper's*, as well as the *Atlantic*, could feel very much alone in a jungle of uncertainties.

Twenty-six publications boasted circulations of better than a million in 1940, and magazine advertising also was climbing; a gain of 6 percent in the field was made for the first six months of 1941 as compared to the same period a year earlier.[39] Advertising rates were determined by circulation, and *Harper's* and the *Atlantic* consequently could hardly hope for substantial profits or for a comfortable operating budget. One result of this relative penury was their total inability to compete in payments to authors. *Harper's* standard fee for an article or short story was $250; even a magazine like *Cosmopolitan* paid an average of $2,500 and up to $5,000 for a single short story.[40] *Harper's* and the *Atlantic* attracted the best authors only because of their prestige and the perquisites that often came as a result of appearing in their pages.

Allen had to maintain *Harper's* integrity and prestige, and he faced certain peril if he failed to divine consistently the correct editorial stance. Finding a formula and staying with it was not enough; one had to be flexible enough to adjust to the ever-changing times without alienating faithful readers. Allen had to resist the temptation to appeal to the broader and more profitable audiences of the rapidly growing mass circulation magazines. His sense of responsibility to the nation as a whole was enormous: for now only two monthly general magazines remained that could provide a platform for the kind of penetrating discussion which seemed critical at this moment in history.

14

WAR COMES TO THE NATION
AND TO *HARPER'S*

Pearl Harbor ended the agonizing argument over American responsibilities and self-interest in a turbulent world. Americans would never
forget what they were doing when they learned the news, and Allen
recorded in full his own actions on that Sunday and on the following
days in a letter to Hildegarde. He asked her to save the long letter
because "some day I might write another book—who knows?"[1]

On that December day Allen and Agnes were enjoying a leisurely
Sunday. Allen completed a watercolor before lunch, then took a
short walk along the East River. Upon his return he and Agnes were
sitting downstairs when John Kouwenhoven called on the telephone,
said he had just heard the news, and wanted to be with someone.
Could he come for supper? "What news?" Allen asked. Later, he
wrote:

Well, from that moment we were practically glued to the radio the
rest of the afternoon, switching from station to station and getting it in
bits—news, comment, etc. The news was intensely exciting but at first
the raid didn't sound so very bad: damage done, a cloud of smoke rising
from Pearl Harbor, the story of the private flyer who got in the way of

the Japs and had machine-gun bullets shot through the wings of his plane, etc.: and our first reactions were that this meant war of course, and that it had been mad of the Japanese to lose all chances of making the Administration appear to be "interfering" in the Orient by this slapping the American face.[2]

Commentators on the radio discussed the probable swiftness and severity of the American response; there were direct radio reports from Honolulu and Manila: " 'Go ahead, Manila' and then a rather staticky voice."[3]

That evening Allen made a talk as scheduled at the Coffee House, the private club for artists and writers of which he was a member, and for some reason "there was absurdly little talk of the event." Back at home, Allen returned to his radio to devour every detail of the news, and next day he carried the radio to work to hear the President's address to Congress. Some thirty office workers crowded around to hear the broadcast and stood silent and awed at the news that the attack amounted to "the greatest naval defeat in American history."[4]

The war meant a nearly total revamping of the magazine's next issue.

When I had left on Friday we had had a brilliant February number coming into being; everything had been coming in on time; we had brilliant names and subjects and all was well. On Monday, what a contrast! In came the William H. Chamberlin article that I had been corresponding with him about—an analysis of American opinion on the war, with the elements and emotions and motives that pulled us each way: it was a good article, but killed as dead as the dodo overnight. In came Stanley High with the final revise of his article on the American Protestants and the War: likewise dead, as he and I agreed, or at least necessitating complete rewriting which it was too late to undertake. I had sent Andy [E. B.] White to Washington to look round for a week and record his observations in a special article; he had gone, and returned to Maine, and was writing his piece; he called up on the long distance to say it was a goner—couldn't even be rewritten because it was all about the flavor of the place before the shooting began; and besides, he had the grippe and was in bed. He would try to write One Man's Meat as usual: that was all he could do. Then one or two other articles got delayed: Vincent Sheean, for instance, didn't produce his expected revise (he now says it will be in tomorrow morning, days late). There was only one good thing to face in this purely journalistic catastrophe: the fact that an article on the great value of long-range bombing, which I had sent to the War Department for advice on its soundness, arrived with the W.D.'s blessing—and now was transparently borne out by the latest news; by Wednesday I was arranging for the author to come in and add a few paragraphs to it about the Hawaiian bombing and the sinking of the two great British ships. Well, we'll come out all right: it'll still be a good number; but nothing like the one we had planned.[5]

In the next few days the Allens shared the city's nervousness about enemy air attack. They listened closely to make certain that fire sirens were not air-raid alarms, purchased extra flashlights and batteries, and kept the house lights at a minimum. Once, on going out, they even filled the bathtub with water—to be used for fighting fire resulting from air attack, as mistakenly advised by New York City's Board for Civilian Protection (it was soon realized that at the sound of sirens everyone would rush to fill his bathtub and the strain would cause water pressure to fall at the critical moment it was needed).

Mayor LaGuardia predicted flatly that New York City would be attacked. Roosevelt, though, sounded reassuring over the radio. On the Tuesday after Pearl Harbor his confident tone, used to such psychological advantage early in the New Deal, contrasted remarkably with a radio address on the same day by Winston Churchill, who, to Allen, sounded "sadly inadequate, either ill or drunk— fumbling and tentative."[6]

Allen could not be certain what the war would mean to *Harper's*. "I suppose we face an opportunity there; but I only wish I had a clear idea of how to discharge it. To keep from being troublesome and still to maintain our freedom and avoid innocuousness will not be easy," he wrote.[7] He hated to think of Oliver's future.

What the war would do was to shape the general direction of *Harper's* and impose a set of conditions on it. Other considerations paled; the nation's survival as a democracy loomed foremost, dictating the basic editorial intent of the publication as well as the tone and subject of unsolicited contributions. Fiction continued to decline in quality as current events became preeminent, Allen noted, and many contributors would disappear into the ranks of khaki. Wartime restrictions would bring a paper shortage, and adjustments to satisfy the war-imposed restrictions had to be made. A not unpleasant result of war would be a boost in circulation and an increase in profits. Yet, because of paper shortages, circulation would have to be held down. Censorship, though voluntary in name, presented an ethical dilemma: what and how much criticism of government actions should be encouraged or allowed in this time of crisis?

Since *Harper's* had no editorial page, any "stance" on war issues would come strictly through editorial judgments as to what sort of articles to accept, emphasize, or reject. The nearest the magazine came to having an editorial page was "The Easy Chair," in which the author, Bernard DeVoto, maintained independence while remaining open to suggested topics and judicious editing by the New York office. Two days after Pearl Harbor DeVoto suggested to Allen a wartime direction for his column that helped answer the question of how *Harper's* could be both effective and independent in wartime. DeVoto wanted to devote his column to a record and comment on civilian life and problems. He would concern himself with the intellectual and emotional problems which he anticipated would arise. "I should expect to criticize freely and vigorously any dangers I might see developing, but in the main I should try to interpret what I see going on round me, on behalf of people who look to *Harper's* for such interpretation."[8]

Allen agreed to DeVoto's proposal and added his own ideas to it. He asked DeVoto to deal for the present, as DeVoto had suggested, only with war-related topics in a detached manner. He urged him to crack down on boastfulness, illusions, wishful thinking, stupid censorship, stupid objections to necessary censorship, small-minded carping at war restrictions and sacrifices, slackening of effort, undemocratic and shortsighted practices generally, and fomenting of unimportant divisions among Americans. Further, he hoped that DeVoto would "stand ready to attack any tendency to defend our territor[y] and then lie down on the bigger job of smashing the enemy; for I dare say that if the conflict should be long, the isolationist mind, rising up again, might balk at seeing the job through."[9] Allen's desire to fight the war to total completion was reminiscent of what he had said about the Depression—that it must not be considered defeated until wide-scale unemployment ended.

DeVoto had advocated U.S. entry into the war as early as November 1939.[10] After Pearl Harbor he told Allen that he resented the isolationists and wondered if it would be appropriate to say so in the column.[11]

In asking Allen's permission he surely had in mind an exchange the previous spring. Then, DeVoto had sought in his column to attack the isolationist Charles A. Lindbergh where it would hurt him most—as an aviation expert. DeVoto wrote that "scores of men in the government and out of it, in the military services and out of them, perhaps hundreds, have far more complete information, far more experience, far better training, far more intelligence." Allen would not permit the statement. He told DeVoto that as far as he knew most air experts regarded Lindbergh's expertise quite highly. "I am wondering on what basis you aim that particular blow at him," Allen asked. DeVoto defended his position but told Allen to remove the offensive sentences if he desired. Allen did, substituting, "His [Lindbergh's] training has been in commerical aviation, and his knowledge of military flying and military strategy is open to question."[12]

Now that war finally had come, *Harper's* joined the rest of the nation in its intense dedication to the all-important effort. The magazine promised to engage in

continuous examination and interpretation of the war. Bearing in mind that the national unity is soundest when it is the unforced unity of men and women of diverse minds and opinions, unmuzzled and proud of it, we shall hold our columns open to such criticisms as we believe may in the long run aid in the victorious conduct of the war; and always we shall try to provide illumination and encouragement. In short, we shall seek to do all that a free magazine can do in a free community toward winning the battle for freedom.[13]

The February issue had been more or less thrown together in desperation; the March issue revealed more considered opinion of what sort of articles the new situation demanded. Seven of the twelve nonfiction articles related to the war. The same pace would continue. Six weeks after Pearl Harbor Allen saw that the war would demand so much space that he dropped the highly popular series of travel articles, "Sightseeing."[14]

War was a topical phenomenon, and the kind of information most Americans sought came in immediate battle reports over the radio, in the daily newspapers, or, at the latest, in the news weeklies. *Harper's*, as a monthly publication, sought to provide perspective on broad military and naval strategy and on the problems of organization, production, financing, civilian defense, and social adjustments to the war; portraits of people in the war; and analyses of situations in foreign countries. It would be no simple job, Allen knew, for expert writers on such matters were scarce, censorship loomed, and fast-moving events could upset the best planned articles. "A magazine which can bring to bear lively civilian brains on surveying the path ahead and informing a thoughtful public has a real job cut out for it," he said.[15]

Harper's had to stimulate as well as to educate even to hold its own more thoughtful audience, and Allen refused to believe that accounts of battles, sure to be outdated, could not be used if vividly written. He sought out John Gunther, a *Harper's* contributor for more than a decade, but Gunther refused, and Allen engaged Fletcher Pratt, author of many books on military subjects, military adviser to *Time,* and writer of a syndicated daily military column.[16] The basic plan was to report fully and with perspective about particular naval battles or campaigns after censorship was lifted. By including details previously withheld for security reasons the accounts could be explicit, comprehensive, and dramatic. Negotiations for Pratt to obtain the official reports were conducted successfully with

Lt. Comdr. Victor F. Blakeslee, who was in charge of the magazine section of the Naval Office of Public Relations.[17] The series, entitled "Americans in Battle," was to begin with a dramatic account of the Java Sea campaign. The project, however, soon was plagued by difficulties in gaining federal clearance for publication.

Two agencies had been established to deal with the flow of news and information, the Office of Censorship and the Office of War Information. The two had separate and opposite functions—censorship and dissemination—which in World War I had been combined under George Creel's office. President Roosevelt established the Office of Censorship on December 18, 1941, naming Byron Price, executive news director of the Associated Press, to head it, and charging him with obtaining the "voluntary" cooperation of the news media in handling war news. In January, Price compiled a list of 105 subjects, later increased to more than 300, and asked editors to print nothing on these subjects except "when authorized by appropriate authority." The subjects included such diverse things as the weather, damage to military objects, movements of the President, the progress of war production, and the location of minefields, archives, and art treasures.[18] The Office of Censorship also exercised control over all information exported outside the nation's boundaries, including such materials as letters, newspapers, magazines, cable transmissions, and radio broadcasts.

Six months after Price's censorship function was established, President Roosevelt, already under pressure to loosen the lid clamped over military news, named Elmer Davis to head the newly created Office of War Information. Davis' function was a positive one: to assemble and release war news for public enlightenment. The appointment of such a widely known and respected journalist was greeted with loud hosannahs, especially, no doubt, at *Harper's*, where Davis had been the publication's most frequent contributor.

Complying with the government's guidelines, Allen submitted Pratt's account of the disastrous 1942 Java Sea campaign to the appropriate authority—in this case, the navy. The result was a series of delays and bickerings which filled Allen with consternation. By the time the extensive critiques of various officers, placed helter-skelter in margins and between lines, had been completed and the article approved, the magazine was four days behind schedule. The delay, Allen wrote to Hildegarde, nearly gave him heart failure.[19]

Problems did not end here. Pratt's second article was to deal with Admiral Halsey's raids on the Marshall and Gilbert islands on January 31 and February 1, 1942, an episode which would be nine months old by publication. This time, instead of being given official battle reports, Pratt received only summaries containing nothing beyond information released in the original communiqués. Upon seeking more data, Pratt learned that the new restrictions had come directly from the highest naval source—Commander in Chief Ernest King's office.

This was all Allen could endure of the "voluntary" censorship regulations, and he wrote a heated letter of protest to Elmer Davis, expressing his opinion that King apparently never wanted the full story of U.S. naval engagements revealed. He pointed out that others, too, had been restive about navy censorship (as indeed they had) and that King's office was "not yet persuaded that the public wants the truth at the earliest possible moment."[20] There was little Davis could do, though he was to fight throughout the war against the military's tendency to conceal unnecessarily.

Despite the troubles, Pratt's series on naval engagements continued through the war. They numbered more than twenty pieces in all and gave *Harper's* readers a comprehensive, vivid picture of the navy at war.

Allen eventually had his own brand of revenge against Admiral King. Davis, in his capacity as OWI director, arranged for a group of influential editors, including Allen, to meet in 1944 with the military leaders directing the war, Gen. George C. Marshall, Gen. Henry H. Arnold, and Admiral King. Allen wrote character sketches of the three for the magazine, and the extreme degree of veneration then accorded such military authorities was hinted at slyly: "Going the cat two or three better, an editor (in this case *Harper's*) may look on a Marshall, an Arnold, *and* a King—and write about them."[21]

The extent of the military trio's national renown was indicated by Allen's omission throughout his article of their first names; they were simply "General Marshall," "General Arnold," and "Admiral King." Allen appeared genuinely to like Marshall and Arnold. But his description of King was caustic.

King, Allen wrote, talked indifferently and told the editors nothing they did not already know. Allen believed King clearly considered spending time with the editors a nuisance. "One felt that he had been persuaded, as a matter of obscure duty, to speak to a group of people whom he saw no compelling reason for informing." He was "not a skilled expositor."[22]

Admiral King acknowledged by mail Allen's description of him. "It is always interesting and valuable to see ourselves as others see us. Please be assured that the article has been evaluated as you intended."[23]

Allen turned to John Dos Passos for a domestic counterpart to Pratt's narrative of Americans at war on the high seas. Dos Passos already had completed *Three Soldiers, Manhattan Transfer,* and the *U.S.A.* trilogy, and he appeared to be at the crest of his career as a novelist. When Allen entertained the author at his house shortly after becoming editor in chief of *Harper's,* Allen seemed somewhat awed. Now he suggested to "Dos" that he wander over the U.S.A. and portray Americans at work in the war industries. Dos Passos agreed at least to undertake two articles for five hundred dollars each plus a five-hundred-dollar guarantee on traveling expenses. Both parties then would decide whether or not the series should continue. To supplement Dos Passos' earnings above the modest *Harper's* fee, Allen went to the "Santa Claus of Pleasantville," DeWitt Wallace, to see if *Reader's Digest* might reprint the series. Wallace agreed to pay seven hundred and fifty dollars for the first article and then to decide on the remaining pieces after they appeared.[24] The series was called "The People at War," and Dos Passos began his travels for it in November 1942, heading first for the neighboring shipbuilding industries in Provincetown.

While others stood in awe of famous authors, Allen was noted for his willingness to edit manuscripts and make suggestions for improvement. On the eve of Dos Passos' departure for the American series, Allen sent him a two-page letter outlining particular aspects he hoped Dos Passos would observe.

We have heard a great deal about loafing on the job, indifference and low morale generally in manufacturing plants, and especially in shipyards, where it seems to be particularly difficult to check up on what workers are doing. I have heard stories of men playing cards except when the inspector was due to come around when they were galvanized into apparent activity. . . . It would be interesting to know whether one gets the sense that the workers are working hard. . . .

I should also like to know whether in those areas one hears them talking about the war. Do they appear to follow news? Are radio broadcasts listened to? What is the tone of the men?

It also might be interesting to watch for attitudes on rationing, taxes, and other privations of war.

And it might be interesting to see whether new patterns of recreation and everyday life are forming—such as the pinball and juke box patterns of the past few years.[25]

Allen expressed concern as well about the reluctance with which aliens, Negroes, and women were being hired. The employment of Negroes, he told Dos Passos, was a "very touchy business" which most managements preferred dodging for fear of trouble in the plant. He noted that employing women seemed to depend upon rearranging jobs that did not require great physical strength. All of his observations, though, were no more than that, and he instructed Dos Passos not to pay any attention to them "unless by chance it might sharpen your eyes and ears."[26]

From New England Dos Passos went to Detroit, then headed South and across to Texas before winding up the six-part series in the nation's capital. The articles appeared from March through October of 1943. Through all of them ran a taut line of tension— labor against management, suspicions between Negroes and whites, rural folk displaced to hostile urban environments, and soldiers versus civilians. There were few "facts" and no names; instead, Dos Passos used his familiar fiction technique of vivid cameo character portrayals and extended dialogue. He talked to workers, foremen, managers, farmers, lower-echelon government officials, soldiers, bartenders, and bus drivers, and from their lips he caught the nervous, wartime American on the home front.

Another aspect of the war, one Allen considered to be most important of all, was the need for early postwar planning. He had been vitally concerned during World War I with the subject, and was disappointed greatly when the plans which he helped to draw up had been ignored. He reasoned that after present hostilities ceased "perhaps a very long period" would exist in which an urgent need would be required of American resources for policing, food, reconstruction, and participation in Allied councils for setting up long-range national systems. He wrote to Cass Canfield, now in Washington as assistant to Milo Perkins on the Board of Economic Warfare, that the magazine was seeking articles for a "carefully planned-out series" to promote a proper plan. Allen feared that an old impulse which had been so disastrous after World War I already was emerging: an impatience to be done with the business.

The minute military victory is accomplished, a great many people will resent going without plenty of food and other comforts to feed people in Europe and Asia. . . . Manufacturers will want to reconvert to civilian goods as soon as possible, in a race to get in first, and will resent our having to send machine tools, and so forth, elsewhere. And of course there will be all the normal desire to return to peacetime ways once the desperate military urgency is past.[27]

Harper's articles should make postwar planning look advantageous to the United States and not simply a "missionary effort." He believed that presenting such information helped fulfill an urgent national need, and he sought potential authors to remind Americans of postwar questions that would demand wise consideration. Hiram Motherwell, C. Hartley Grattan, Peter F. Drucker, William Henry Chamberlin, Stuart Chase, John Fischer, and Benjamin Asken were among those who contributed articles on this question.

Allen's World War I memories reinforced his fear that civil liberties again might be abused. He jumped at the chance in the war's first months to accept an article on the subject proposed by William Henry Chamberlin, and expounded at length to Chamberlin his own ideas about wartime dangers. The greatest potential for abuse, in his opinion, lay not in the Department of Justice or Post Office, where so many World War I irregularities had originated, but in the navy and army and in local war organizations and mobs. The army now held, if it chose to exercise it, virtual martial-law control over large parts of the country along the seaboards. "It would be very easy for an ignorant or intolerant army officer to interpret these powers in such a way as to displace and put out of business men with unorthodox opinions on the ground that they endangered military operations," he said. All statements heretofore had indicated that such powers would be very tolerantly exercised, but the authority was there and Allen knew it could fall into the hands of "zealous generals who view the Civil Liberties Union or the Farm Security Administration about as they'd view the Nazi Bund, and have no training in the tradition of civil liberties."[28]

Allen's own experience on a draft board made him realize that if passions ran high a man might be drafted for his opinions. Similarly, a gasoline rationing board could restrict a businessman's gasoline for his opinions. "This danger runs through the whole business of economic regimentation for war," he told Chamberlin.[29]

Midway through the war Allen realized that his fears were unfounded. With the notable exception of the roundup of more than 100,000 Americans of Japanese descent into "relocation centers," this war would not generate the emotional excesses of World War I.[30] This time, Allen explained in 1943, "having heard again and again how men could be seduced by war slogans, they were inevitably on guard in their inner minds. . . . Yes, this war had to be waged. But they didn't want to be victims of 'hysteria.' They felt uncomfortable about flag-waving. They preferred to be matter-of-fact about the job ahead."[31]

While Allen felt certain by May of 1943 that the tide of battle had shifted to favor the Allies and that there would be no abuse of civil rights, frictions within the nation had become tense, and angry voices were rising. In Washington, Congress and the Executive battled; so did Democrats and Republicans. Another source of friction, Allen wrote in a *Harper's* article, lay in the status of Negroes.

Ever since before Pearl Harbor many Negroes had been angry at the discrimination against them in the Army and Navy, and above all in the war industries; to them their position as steerage passengers on a ship of state headed for democracy for all people seemed cruelly ironic.[32]

Negro uneasiness scared many Southern whites; wild rumors occasionally swept through towns about black uprisings; and open race warfare seemed just beneath the surface. Another touchy situation was labor's resentment of government efforts to freeze wages while prices kept creeping up.

Gasoline was doled out on the basis of rationing stamps, an irritation for a people whose pattern of life had been set by the automobile. Rationing coupons were also required to purchase the limited supplies of food and clothing. Selective Service was summoning married men now, and more and more women donned overalls to work in factories.

Yet Allen found cause for optimism, for although the nation had failed to learn about teamwork the morale of the armed forces remained resilient and the national fiber remained strong. If domestic life seemed to proceed at a relaxed pace, it was like a two-miler running calmly during the first mile, with plenty of breath left in his lungs. "The ordeal ahead will be gravely demanding, but we will meet it," Allen concluded.[33]

In late 1943 Allen was able to see the war firsthand, courtesy of the British Ministry of Information, which paid round-trip transportation costs to England for a number of American editors. Allen spent most of his time in London. He described in his notebook a spectacular air raid he witnessed on his second night there. As enemy airplanes droned above, British searchlights pricked the skies and converged till they

glowed golden in the light of ten or a dozen . . . and then the guns would go off—one very near us—and I would see little flashes of light below the plane—little spangles momentarily flashing; all the spangles seemed *too low,* and the planes swam along at the convergence of all those beams of light, and the guns went on smashing. And a few minutes later—after other lights had picked it up and the ones before us had been snapped off—the sky was just a moonlit sky again, with the Dipper and the North Star gleaming.[34]

All the bothersome wartime regulations at home suddenly took on a meaning which Americans had been unable to comprehend. "The war *is here,* not in the USA: that explains volumes."[35]

15

WARTIME RED TAPE

Allen returned to the United States and *Harper's* to face the continuing intervention of the government in his editorial work. Editing a magazine in wartime meant much more than tailoring the contents to the particular needs of the time, and also more than submitting certain articles to authorities for clearance.

A woman in the Office of War Information's magazine section wrote to Allen, "It is necessary that I familiarize myself with what you are doing in order to be of use to you in making suggestions for the future. Thank you in advance for letting me know on what date I can expect to receive your current issue."[1]

Allen responded wearily. Was she absolutely certain of this need? Already he was turning in advance proofs to another department of the Office of War Information, three advance copies of the magazine to the Coordinator of Information, two sets of advance proofs to the censorship office, and another set of advance proofs to the Coordinator of Inter-American Affairs. "Simultaneously, we are threatened with a ten per cent paper cut," he lamented.[2] The winner of this red tape skirmish is not known, but it demonstrates the manner in which the federal government became intertwined in editorial affairs.

Besides requesting copies of *Harper's*, the OWI's magazine section also prepared propaganda to send to *Harper's* and other publications, following its ordained duty "to increase understanding of the war effort." One such plainspoken offering, entitled "Key to Understanding the Menace of Japan," justified the Asian war on ideological grounds. It explained that the nations fought not because of the "single act of treachery" at Pearl Harbor, but "because Japan has her own totalitarian ideology which, if allowed to exist, will never permit a free and peaceful world." The Japanese way of life was completely opposed to democratic ideals and principles; Japan's plan for world domination was based on the belief that her people were descendants of gods and a race superior to all others ("In carrying out this plan, Japan follows the Axis line: complete domination and economic control; brutality and total disregard for the moral, cultural and national fibre of conquered people, and creation of a master and a slave class"); Japan's control of a vast pool of slave labor and raw materials would threaten free trade and enterprise ("Her 'industrial habits' are not democratic, but based on the medieval serf and owner system.").[3] It was not the type of persuasion favored by *Harper's*.

Sometimes the magazine sought favors from the government. In August 1942 Allen asked Roosevelt's press secretary, Stephen Early, for "the run of the White House for two or three days" so he could write an article on the President's day-to-day routine. Early responded quickly and negatively. Wartime restrictions against visitors prohibited it, and, besides, no favoritism could be shown any one publication.[4]

The government's drives to stimulate war bond sales enlisted magazines as well as film celebrities. When a Hearst promotion manager conceived the idea that every magazine in the nation display on its cover the American flag to show patriotism (and to make the public magazine-conscious) ninety-five million magazines bore the flag's image on their July 1942 covers. Many also carried the sanctioned patriotic slogan "United We Stand." Magazines as disparate as *Harper's, Vogue, Ranch Romances, The Feed Bag, Steel, Screen-*

land (where the flag competed with Veronica Lake for attention), and *Detective* displayed Old Glory. The *National Geographic* changed its cover for the first time in its fifty-four-year-history; *Reader's Digest* transplanted its index from the front to the back cover for the first time.[5] *Harper's*, with considerable misgivings, complied only after extensive office debate.[6]

One reader soon requested Allen to display the flag on *Harper's* cover again and to explain its significance. Allen, skeptical of patriotic excess, replied that he had not been "too keen" on putting the flag on the cover in the first place but he had gone along with the majority. It seemed better, he thought, to let the magazine's content "suggest what is our idea of America and the duties, obligations, and privileges of American citizenship."[7] A year later a general repetition of the flag display on covers was attempted, including this time a slogan urging the purchase of war bonds. Compliance with the suggestion was scattered.

Allen did propose one patriotic gesture to Postmaster General Frank C. Walker during the first months of the war. He recalled that during World War I *Harper's* and other magazines carried notations stating that if a one-cent stamp were affixed, the issue would be delivered to soldiers on the front. If any such plans now were being considered, *Harper's* would eagerly participate.[8] But the program was not repeated.

The Office of Censorship deemed certain *Harper's* passages too great a security risk for overseas distribution and officials snipped out offending phrases or pages. DeVoto once referred to Boston as a "highly inflammable" city, and Allen, anticipating the censors' thoughts, crossed out the word "highly." The small adjustment did not suffice; the passage was censored, along with one which alluded to the damage a plane-load of incendiaries could wreak on Boston. Allen reassured DeVoto that such "blasphemies" did not disturb him at all. "We proceed on the assumption that we are editing the Magazine for an American audience and that an American audience ought to be told this sort of thing." Besides, he said, no more than 1,000 to 2,000 issues of the magazine were being exported.[9]

An article by C. Lester Walker citing deficiencies in the city of

177

Buffalo's civil defense program aroused considerable attention. Buffalo's industries caused it to be one of the American cities considered most likely to be the target of enemy attack. Before the magazine won clearance for export, the two pages concerning Buffalo's inadequacies were cut out. The article itself received front-page headlines in the *Buffalo Courier Express*, and Mayor Joseph P. Kelly, cited as the official responsible for the city's defense inadequacies, said he would ask the Federal Bureau of Investigation, the New York State War Council, and Governor Herbert Lehman of New York to investigate the origins of the article. Kelly, who forwarded a copy to President Roosevelt for possible action, complained that it was "one of the most scurrilous attacks upon the City of Buffalo that could be published at this time." Roosevelt responded calmly to Mayor Kelly and advised him that often the best way to meet such criticism was "to ignore it and continue to saw wood."[10] Allen told Walker not to worry about the censored pages or the mayor's fury. "The defense of Buffalo will be the better for it."[11] The request for an investigation evidently went unheeded.

Allen's worst fears about censorship abuses came to a head when the army refused to clear an article about General Douglas MacArthur, who was being touted for a presidential nomination. A full-page summary by "The Editors" of the incident, "MacArthur and the Censorship," alerted the readers as to what had happened. *Newsweek*, describing the editorial note, said the "usually tempered language of Harper's Magazine was almost violent." According to *Harper's*, the Office of Censorship refused on entirely improper grounds to approve the article—not because it contained military information of value to the enemy, but because in the Office of Censorship's own words, it contained criticism of the General, which "undermines the confidence of this country, Australia, and particularly the troops in that theatre, in their commander and his strategic and tactical plans." Furthermore, "such a result would be of great value to the Axis and damaging to General MacArthur's very difficult campaign in the Southwest Pacific."[12]

Harper's editors protested that the article definitely had not contained information vital to the enemy and that the situation appeared all the more grave because of the current move to draft MacArthur for a presidential nomination:

No candidate for the Presidency, tacit or otherwise, should stand hidden behind a veil of censorship.

One may write what one pleases about the other candidates; about General MacArthur no opinions based on recent direct observation may apparently be given publicity unless they are flattering.

The situation is intolerable in a free country. . . .

Let the public stand warned. The accounts of this candidate which have been appearing are incomplete, biased by censorship, and therefore politically unreliable.[13]

The article had been prepared by British war correspondent Walter Lucas of the *London Daily Express* and *Christian Science Monitor*. The MacArthur "boomlet" for the Republican presidential nomination had been inspired by the *Chicago Tribune* and the Hearst press. Secretary of War Henry L. Stimson publicly acknowledged vetoing the article. "I read the article, and it was my judgment that [it] would be harmful to the operation of our troops in the Pacific area."[14]

Harper's adamant stand undoubtedly precipitated a resolution of sorts within days. On April 30 MacArthur formally withdrew from consideration for the nomination: "I do not covet it, nor would I accept it."[15] The proposed profile never saw print.

Defense needs brought about a curtailment of the pulp products essential to newspapers, magazines, and books. On the last day of 1942 the War Production Board ordered a 10 percent reduction of publishers' paper use because of manpower and electric-power shortages at the mills, transportation difficulties, and the increasing need for paper generated by the armed services.

The reduction came at a time when *Harper's* circulation was booming and its paper requirements therefore rising. Newsstand sales for 1942 had amounted to some 20,000 issues per month, about 25 percent over the previous year. The figure, Allen said, surpassed *Atlantic* on the newsstands by 70 percent.[16] (November sales had been even higher because Walter Winchell declared on his radio show that Quincy Howe's article, "Twelve Things the War Will Do to America," should not be missed. The result was a virtual sellout, 80 percent higher than the preceding December.[17]) By 1943 newsstand sales roughly were doubling the 1941 figures.[18] Because of the restrictions on paper, Harper's could not capitalize on the growing demand for the magazine, and circulation gains would have to be delayed until after the war. The paper shortage hurt other magazines as well. Hearst magazines even announced that no new subscriptions would be accepted. The standard 112-page Harper's issue had to be reduced to 104 pages, but a plan was devised so that the total contents would not be reduced. Allen simply reduced the margins of white space and made the columns wider. The net result was sixty to seventy more words per page than before the cutback. However, in June, facing the prospect of still another paper cut, the 104 pages were reduced further to 96 pages.[19] The new reduction called for a 24 percent decrease in paper use based on 1942 requirements, which had been met partially by the previous 10 percent reduction. Even Christmas cards for 1944 were cut by 40 percent.[20]

While the war tended to pump the circulation primer, though to little avail, its immediate effect upon advertising for Harper's was the opposite. In 1942 the magazine lost almost all of its travel advertising because wartime conditions curtailed leisurely traveling. Fall publication dates for many books had been postponed, causing book advertisements, always a staple for Harper's, to decrease.

Harper's problems with advertising generally were typical of national magazines during the first year of war. Advertising revenues overall dropped two percent from the previous year, with the weekly news magazines being prosperous and notable exceptions. But in 1943 an advertising boom started that carried Harper's with it. The year saw an all-time high in national magazine advertising, and 1944 was even better as advertising revenue increased by 18 percent over 1943. Even higher levels would have been possible had it not been for the paper shortage.[21] What caused the jump was the desire of companies to keep their names before the public through institutional advertising which invariably carried a patriotic theme. The desire was easy to fulfill because of generally high wartime business profits. "Money-making is not the final test but helps," Allen wrote to his sister.[22] By August it appeared that 1943 would be the best year for the magazine since he had joined it in 1923, with the possible exception of 1928 or 1929. In June 1944 Allen raised DeVoto's two hundred-fifty-dollar monthly payment for the "Easy Chair" to three hundred dollars because the magazine had fared so well and DeVoto had been so good.[23] In 1944 Harper & Brothers earned just over a million dollars, but more than $800,000 of it had to go for federal taxes. In March 1945 Allen wrote to Oliver, now in the army, that he had stopped keeping up with newsstand sales because the magazine was selling out regularly. The entire House of Harper prospered: sales were so good during the first two months of 1945 that $250,000 profits already had been earned. The demand for books and the magazine made the firm "frantic," though, because of problems in getting enough paper.[24]

Despite the magazine's prosperity, or perhaps as a result of it, the promotion office persuaded Allen to undertake a task he was very reluctant to do. He agreed to ask a number of influential people for endorsements of the magazine. He told Clifton Fadiman that he was writing with an embarrassing request that Fadiman should feel at liberty to throw out the window. After his tortured explanation, Allen concluded, "If you have made a rule against doing this sort of thing or for any other reason you don't want to—hell, you may hate the Magazine or just be bored to death!—throw this letter in the waste basket and forget that it has been written and don't hold it against me."[25]

High profits or not, Allen could not help feeling that he was engaged in a desperate struggle to maintain the magazine's high standards. He was convinced that the war brought a deterioration of quality in fiction, and also there were censorship problems and what he considered an inadequate budget. Through "hard scrambling," however, he felt the magazine was doing a good job.[26]

Luckily, the military did not call any of his editors to duty, and at least for the early part of the war the staff remained intact. The four of them—Allen, Leighton, Kouwenhoven, and Virginia Watson —were heavily taxed merely to read the one thousand manuscripts that came monthly through the mails.[27] Agnes, now with the OWI, no longer helped as a reader.

In the spring of 1942 Allen named Leighton associate editor and announced his intention to make other changes. He vowed to have at least two short stories per issue, determined to be more hospitable to longer poems rather than use poetry merely as filler, and decided to accept short articles of no more than half a magazine page in length, which would replace poetry as filler material. He arranged for artist and typographer Oscar Ogg to design new layouts for the title pages. The various new decorations, which appeared for the first time in the November 1942 issue, included characteristic American symbols such as the eagle, bison, salmon, and steamboat.[28]

Free-lance writers continued to provide the bulk of the magazine's material, as Allen constantly reaffirmed frustrated would-be contributors who complained that Harper's played favorites and did not consider manuscripts from unknown authors on their merits. New authors did provide a substantial portion of the magazine's contents each month. In 1940 nearly half the articles were written by first-time contributors, although most of them involved some degree of negotiation and planning between the author and editors.[29] The magazine accepted about one poem out of every hundred submitted.[30]

In the spring of 1944, Leighton, quite amicably despite his tempestuous nature, told Allen that their constant disagreements were debilitating and that after thirteen years on the magazine, he was quitting. The resignation evidently was prompted when Leighton learned that Allen and Canfield had agreed privately that he would not become editor upon Allen's eventual retirement, whenever that might be. Leighton's departure was inevitable because of the constant clashes between the two. Leighton wanted to use the magazine as a muckraking vehicle, and Allen would have none of that.[31]

Allen suggested that Leighton take twenty-four hours to reconsider; the next day he accepted his associate editor's resignation.[32] Leighton's departure was both a relief and a problem for Allen's inexperienced staff. Allen and Virginia Watson remained as the only editors with more than three years' experience.

Allen soon took care of the gaps on the staff. Katherine Gauss Jackson, who had been assisting John Chamberlain in reviewing books, became an assistant editor, as did Mary Burnet. Russell Lynes, who had worked at Harper & Brothers for four years after his 1932 graduation from Yale, now joined the magazine as an assistant editor. Canfield had spotted a likely comer in Washington's government circles, an Oklahoma native and ex-newspaper reporter, John Fischer.[33] Allen hired him to be contributing editor from Washington. Grattan, who had been appearing in the magazine since 1935, also became a contributing editor. Kouwenhoven, with three years' experience, became associate editor. Lynes and Kouwenhoven were strongest in the arts, Fischer's expertise lay mainly in economics and international affairs, and Grattan had achieved a reputation as a literary critic, historian, and analyst of current events as well.

Before Leighton left, he was involved in a debate with the Coca-Cola Company over the casual usage in the November 1943 issue of the phrase, "the pause that refreshes." Hunter Bell, advertising manager for Coca-Cola, wrote a caustic letter to Allen, protesting the use of the phrase:

The Coca-Cola Company has for many years used the phrase . . . in the advertising of its product. We recognize of course that there can be no copyright for such a line. Nonetheless, we feel that a magazine of such standing as Harper's would not consciously set out to dilute one of the present advertising themes of a Company like the Coca-Cola Company.

We feel quite certain therefore that this editorial usage of "The Pause That Refreshes" was inadvertent, and we are calling it to your attention simply in the hope that you will prevent its recurrence in the future.[34]

The letter surely brought a round of laughter at *Harper's*, and perhaps because of his bombastic temperament, Leighton was selected to respond in Allen's absence. He wrote:

Now, come. I can't believe that you were serious when you wrote your letter. Every man, woman, and child in this country knows that the phrase "The pause that refreshes" belongs to Coca-Cola. The idea of anybody putting the snatch on this phrase is ludicrous. It would be on a par with trying to sell the Brooklyn Bridge to the yokel.[35]

Such a personality would be missed.

16

DEALING WITH CONTRIBUTORS

The magazine remained top-heavy with war-related articles, and that was how Allen wanted it. He had announced in the conflict's first months that the publication's foremost duty would be to give "all possible information on the imperative problems of the war on all fronts."[1] Nevertheless, he contended that he and the editors did their best to get variety into the magazine, and while the majority of *Harper's* contents related to the subject Allen deemed of "central and overwhelming importance," the remainder did cover a wide range of subjects.[2] The usual goal, Allen said, was to print several good articles each year on some important issues in education, several on developments in scientific or medical research, several on the state of the arts or literature, some on political, economic, business, and social topics, and several on religious subjects.[3]

The low quality of fiction, as Allen analyzed it, could be attributed to the urgency of other matters: the Depression during the 1930s and now the war. Readers had become interested in facts. Perhaps, Allen reflected in late 1942 to Wallace Stegner, the "scarcity" of good fiction might be the result of subconscious inclinations of "article-minded editors." But he knew that he and other *Harper's* editors had a keen desire to publish first-rate fiction. Often, their task had been reduced to determining the "least bad story" they could accept for a particular issue.

The pickings [have] seemed so poor that we were astonished to discover that earnest critics like the O. Henry judges consistently regarded some of our stories as among the best that were being written—which led us to suspect that it wasn't ourselves so much as the story writers who were at fault.[4]

Harper's stories had won many O. Henry top awards. But now the magazine frequently contained only one short story per issue, and the December 1942 issue had no fiction at all. Allen claimed in November 1942 that the magazine had not received a story in more than two months that the editors felt was worth publishing. A key reason, he thought, was "that the themes which in former times absorbed the story writer himself now have come to look to him like pretty small potatoes beside the events of the day." He believed the turning point had come with the Depression and the accompanying idea that an individual's personal fortunes depended so greatly on public events that public issues became more vital to him than private ones. The war had intensified that feeling, and the situation would not change until peace came, Allen believed. Yet, the development was not totally unfortunate, since a clear grasp of facts during a crisis seemed essential. Afterwards, though, he expected a reaction:

The relations of man with man, as individuals, and of man with woman, and of parent with child, and of the family with his own soul and with his God, are of undying concern to mankind; and the day will come when they will seem more vital to us than the actions of politicians, economists, industrialists, and generals.[5]

Allen had always revised contributors' copy with aplomb. In the 1920s, reading an article submitted by H. G. Wells, Allen had snorted and declared that "this isn't what he meant to say." So he took the piece and "ran it through his typewriter" while his colleagues watched in horror. When Wells eventually saw the changes, he declared, "Yes, that's exactly what I had in mind."[6] Despite his readiness to edit copy, Allen was terrified over the prospect of dealing for the first time with William Faulkner. He was determined to make a change on a Faulkner short story, already accepted, because several characters in the story happened to have the same name. Allen told Faulkner that this was unnecessarily confusing and damaging to the story, and he suggested different names as an easy solution. Faulkner readily agreed; name them anything you like, he said.[7] John Kouwenhoven recalls that Faulkner was pleased when Allen punctuated and corrected grammar in his stories—because nobody else would take the trouble or perhaps dared.[8]

Faulkner had a long association with *Harper's*, dating back to 1931. By 1940 his stories had appeared in the magazine on ten occasions, and his "Barn Burning" in June 1939 won the O. Henry Memorial Award as the best short story to appear that year in an American magazine. But after 1940 Faulkner was not published in *Harper's* until the centennial edition in 1950, and the reason largely was Allen. The Southern writer's complex style, rich though it was, always proved perplexing to Allen, who insisted upon certain standards of clarity.

In 1942 he rejected five Faulkner stories, although he was painfully aware that he was declining the work of a master. In February he found "Knight's Gambit" too full of obscurity and complexity, although Allen admitted it brimmed with "electricity." In March he rejected "Snow." In July he declined "My Grandmother Millard" and told Faulkner's agent, Harold Ober, "Faulkner's stories always seem to me to be a sort of battle between obscurity and electricity, and I'm afraid that in this case the obscurity has won out." In August he refused another Faulkner submission:

Parts of the story are grand . . . but I don't think that the ending, which he has so carefully muffled that you hardly know it happens, is effective enough to make up for all the work that the reader has to do up to that point, and I don't believe that revision would do the trick, and I think we had better say no with a groan that can be heard all the way from here to 49th Street.

"Shall Not Perish," Faulkner's moving sequel to "Two Soldiers" which concerned a small boy's reaction to news of his older brother's death in the war, was declined in September. "I have read the Faulkner one two or three times and still feel that it doesn't quite pan out. I am very sorry, because he is an author we want very much to have in *Harper's* again."[9]

In 1944 assistant editor Katherine Gauss Jackson had to tell Malcolm Cowley that despite her own wishes, nobody else at *Harper's* favored Cowley's suggestion that he write a piece about Faulkner. "The idea . . . gets nowhere."[10]

A number of prominent writers did publish short fiction in *Harper's* during the war years. Among them were Eudora Welty, Pearl Buck, Rebecca West, and John P. Marquand. But perhaps more revealing is a listing of notable fiction writers who contributed solely nonfiction to the magazine: John Dos Passos, Richard Wright, Paul Horgan, Jessamyn West, and Wallace Stegner.

Marquand wrote both fiction and nonfiction. Allen sent the novelist of manners to the South Pacific in the spring of 1945 as a special correspondent. Marquand witnessed the fierce battle for Iwo Jima and wrote an article describing it. He paid his own expenses, but collected four hundred dollars instead of the normal two hundred and fifty dollars for the piece.[11]

Glenway Wescott, a writer who had flashed brilliantly during the 1920s, found himself struggling in the forties. He had sold to *Harper's* two reminiscences about France and was trying to finish a novel. Recovering from illness and feeling discouraged, he received a series of letters from Allen, who said his main idea was to get Wescott going on something with full enthusiasm. "Don't pay any attention to yourself when you find yourself thinking that you have 'no trace of talent or of sense of the importance of what I can do.' This is nonsense. You are right in the top rank and ought to know it." He told Wescott that he did his best work when he did it "hot," seldom pausing for revision. "I'd like to station a copy-boy at your shoulder to take the pages to me as they come off the typewriter!"[12]

One week in July 1943, Allen took to bed with a summer cold

and a copy of Alfred Kazin's newly published analysis of modern American literature, *On Native Grounds*. Intrigued by it, Allen wrote a three-page letter to Kazin with his own observations, comments, and questions. Primarily, he was interested in Kazin's long discussion of the "formalists," a name Kazin gave to John Crowe Ransom, Allen Tate, R. P. Blackmur, and Yvor Winters. The categorization troubled Allen because as editor of a magazine which at least pretended to be a literary medium, he confessed that he had not been aware of any movement by that name and that although he certainly knew of Tate and Ransom as individuals, he had not heard of Winters. The question perplexing Allen was whether or not he and the other *Harper's* editors had been derelict in keeping up with literary trends or whether literary people perhaps were withdrawing purposely and forming private cliques. Maybe, Allen ventured, this very thought had perplexed Kazin, too, and that was why he devoted so much space to a topic "that could hardly be of leading importance." Allen said he had encountered some faculty members and students at Bennington who seemed to have divorced the literary art completely from life.

I'd once been naively thunderstruck to hear one of them refer casually to the magazines of the day as commercial and hostile to art, and to discover that he meant *all* the magazines except the little literary sheets and maybe the book columns of the *Nation*—and I'd vaguely realized that there must be lots of occupants of this (to me) ivory tower; but no matter how hard I tried to be humble-minded, I couldn't believe that the movement could amount to much and be quite invisible to me at *Harper's*. . . . Are we such old fogies or so obviously wrapped up in affairs that there's a tacit conspiracy to leave us alone—or have the people who are interested in literature as such dwindled to a little group whose conspiracy is to lock themselves into a closed room and have no traffic with anybody at all?

I really ought to sign this letter ANXIOUS, for it's an odd feeling to be the editor of a magazine that's too difficult and too painstakingly honest to have a big circulation and yet is apparently regarded by the people who are really interested in literary matters as the brutal incarnation of Mammon![13]

189

Allen's letter indicated doubts about his literary judgments now that his chief interest had been channeled toward public affairs, and he suggested that they have lunch together for a discussion. However, they did not.

Part of the daily experience was declining the works of established authors. It was a challenge to write rejection letters that would not alienate them from offering further work for consideration. Vladimir Nabokov, then unknown, greatly impressed Allen and the other editors in late 1941 with a story called "Mademoiselle O." But the editors rejected it because they already had accepted a similar one from another author. Nevertheless, Allen told Nabokov, who had begun writing in English only in 1939 and had come to the U.S. the following year, that "Mademoiselle O" had made a "tremendous hit" at the office. "It's a wonderfully alive and unusual piece of writing . . . I earnestly hope you will give us another chance and let us see another story soon."[14] But not until 1951 did *Harper's* have an opportunity again to publish Nabokov, who turned instead to the *Atlantic*.

Edna Ferber received an Allen rejection that was written in more or less typical fashion to a person of prestige:

Under the circumstances we think we ought to say "no". . . . I am fully conscious of what we are missing and I say it with the more regret because we have been so intolerably slow. And because, incidentally, it seems to me somehow absurd for Harper's to be missing a chance to get Edna Ferber in its pages.[15]

The difficulty of the graceful rejection was illustrated by an office joke in which Allen devised a mock letter to be signed by one of the other editors. It read, "Mr. Allen is in his office crying because we won't let him publish your piece."[16]

Wallace Stegner mailed Allen a portion of "a long novel called The Big Rock Candy Mountain," and had it rejected with the comment that it was a "remarkably good chapter" and "extremely well written," but it remained an episode rather than a story. Allen thought the work so fine that he wondered whether Stegner could not be more valuable to the magazine than he had been heretofore as a writer of nonfiction.[17]

Other rejections included Max Eastman on Isadora Duncan, John T. Flynn on Frederick Jackson Turner's frontier thesis, a short story by Nelson Algren, a proposal by James Thomas Flexner for a piece on how to write biography, Ella Winter (Lincoln Steffens' widow) on what Steffens would think of current events, and even an offering by the First Lady, Eleanor Roosevelt, on world cooperation. (Later, Allen enjoyed telling rejected authors not to feel too disheartened —*Harper's* had even spurned Mrs. Roosevelt.) However, unlike the kind words that so often accompanied the rejections of celebrated individuals, Allen had harsh words for Mrs. Roosevelt's proffered piece. He told her agent, Jasper Spock of New York City:

I will confess that we are all a little embarrassed by Mrs. Roosevelt on the subject of world co-operation. She is a wonderful woman, but it would be doing her no service to print this rather empty little piece, and any value that her name might have for us would be weakened for those who read it. Thanks just the same.[18]

In the twenties Allen had excoriated H.L. Mencken for what he considered to be his baneful influence on American thought and letters. Now, with Mencken largely a forgotten figure, Allen pursued him as a contributor. In February 1943, he proposed that Mencken write about current trends in the American language, which, influenced particularly by *Time* magazine, seemed to be deteriorating.

I am thinking of the educational jargon that has been rampant during the past few years and which is now creeping into general use, such as the word "evaluate"; of the strange influence of the Luce boys on journalistic style in general, and of the tendency that they and other journalists have developed of leaving out the "the" wherever possible, as if they were writing telegrams.[19]

Mencken certainly had an enormous amount of material relative to the subject, but before attempting the article, he told Allen, he must sort out and index his material. He added, "It seems to me that the *Time* boys have done more damage to the American language than the brethren of *Variety*. In the *Variety* dialect there is at least something picturesque and amusing, whereas the *Time* jargon is simply stupid." Mencken hoped that Leighton and Allen could join him soon and "sit down for a palaver."[20]

More than a year later Allen queried Mencken again.

We hunger and thirst after you as a contributor, and we wonder whether, by now, your researchers may not have provided you with a theme—such as what is happening to the American language now—or whether perhaps there is not some part of your book which would be magazineable as it stands. Please think of me as the impersonation of animated eagerness!"[21]

Mencken, ever garrulous, told Allen that he wanted to talk about it in person in New York. The articles, when completed, went not to *Harper's* but to the *New Yorker*, where they appeared in 1948 and 1949.

E. B. White appeared monthly in *Harper's*; he had been writing the column "One Man's Meat" since 1938. White, or "Andy" as his friends called him, was a particular favorite of Allen's, and it was a shock when he abruptly wrote to Allen in 1943 that he was quitting. "This must seem rather odd and sudden to you, but the truth is I have had great difficulty all along, writing essays of this sort, as they do not seem to come naturally to me and I have to go through the devil to get them written." Several times, White said, he had mailed Allen a "department" which did not satisfy his own standard and which he sent only to fulfill a promise. "So the only thing left for me is to quit."[22]

Allen could not accept the announcement easily. He implored White in a three-page letter to change his mind. It would be a blow not only to the magazine but to American writing, Allen told him. Perhaps a sort of "war-weariness" had struck White as it seemed to have hit so many. Perhaps he was overburdened with duties on his salt-water farm in Maine, and an every-other-month basis could be instituted, or maybe after a hiatus of several months he would be ready to resume the column. *Harper's* was paying White three hundred dollars per column, and that could be increased, too, Allen said. As for White's complaint that the monthly piece was difficult to write and the results not pleasing, Allen wrote:

That's one of the almost-unbelievable paradoxes of the writer's art. For the result not only seems easy and spontaneous—which is another sign that a smooth style is the product of sweat—but is, I believe, your own most apt contribution to the writing of our time. . . . If you were to drop this difficult monthly discipline entirely (unless you were dropping it for some more ambitious writing program) you would be abandoning, I truly believe, your biggest and most fitting and most enduring contribution, seen in the long perspective of American letters.[23]

White countered, "The desire is very strong in me to rid myself of any writing commitment. . . . I want to write when and if I feel like it."[24] Allen eventually offered White five hundred dollars per column, twice the amount then given DeVoto, but White remained firm.[25] For the next year he endured periodic reminders from Allen about how *Harper's* readers continued to clamor for his return.

A year later, realizing that White was not coming back, Allen arranged for a kind of sequel to "One's Man Meat." The column, "Another Man's Poison," rotated monthly as a year's experiment among Franklin P. Adams, Rebecca West, Thomas Hornsby Ferril, and George W. Martin. Allen explained to the authors that he envisioned the column as one in which readers bombarded with facts would get instead "personal reactions, whether whimsical or meditative or otherwise."[26] The column lasted just one year.

Bernard DeVoto, who alienated many but won a wide and devoted readership, continued to display a knack for sensing touchy issues and pricking the American conscience about them. In his "Easy Chair" columns he attacked the literary men who had debased solid American traditions; he hailed the frontier as the well of democracy; he fought to preserve western lands; he worried about the state of education; he crusaded for civil rights and against censorship; and he talked about the New Deal, the war, and any issue that caught his roving eye.

In his crusade against censorship he even emulated Mencken in Boston by purchasing in 1944 a copy of Lillian Smith's banned book,

Strange Fruit, for a court test. The book dealt with a love affair between a white man and a Negro woman. The organization which Allen's father had founded years before, the Watch and Ward Society, had been instrumental in effecting the ban. When DeVoto in his column compared Boston unfavorably to the South, where *Strange Fruit* could be read safely, he somehow prompted widespread protest from Southerners, including promises of physical attack and threats by some Southern preparatory schools to withdraw their advertising from the magazine. The attacks, which DeVoto considered illogical since he had intended no insult to the South, caused him now to write a genuine blast on the South's stubborn clinging to myths and historical provincialism.[27] "Benny," as DeVoto was called, went so far as to assail a member of *Harper's* own family, Grattan, for his assessment in the magazine of the literary scene.[28] In short, DeVoto did not confine himself to war-related domestic topics as he had intended, but provided a lively column that dealt with many of society's most provocative situations.

A potential author whom Allen courted in an effort to create what he felt to be needed controversy was former Republican presidential candidate Wendell Willkie. Willkie's book *One World* was nearing publication, and Allen perhaps anticipated the massive popularity which it soon would receive. Allen believed that the State Department needed the sort of shakeup that a stiff article by a respected internationalist such as Willkie might accomplish. The State Department appeared to Allen to be a "rather ramshackle collection of individuals" pulling aimlessly in different directions and being unrealistically frightened at the prospect of cooperating with the Soviet Union. State, Allen felt, was manned primarily by "nice fellows, with nice connections and nice incomes," who thought the Soviets represented a menace to their own comfortable status. As a result, the United States occasionally appeared all too eager to cooperate with Fascist sympathizers such as Peyrouton of France. The fears of Communism which led to such embraces, Allen pointed out, "play indirectly into the hands of the Communist elements in Europe by giving a damaging impression that the United States does not care whether a man is a Fascist or not." The matter appeared definitely not to be a question of New Dealers versus anti-New Dealers, or of radicals versus conservatives. All the issues, Allen told Willkie, should be discussed in *Harper's*, preferably by someone who could not be dismissed as a journalist looking for copy.[29] Willkie evidently had considered the idea in a telephone conversation with Allen, but he now pleaded lack of time to do it.

Beneath the American campaign to win the war lay a strain of racial tension often overlooked as a precursor to the explosive decade of the 1960s. Race riots, notably the 1943 Detroit riot in which twenty-five blacks and nine whites were killed, punctuated the domestic scene. Blacks found hypocrisy in being asked to give their lives to save a society which did not permit them to sit in the same dining rooms with whites. The discrepancy became more apparent as Negro citizens began to share in wartime prosperity but encountered resentment as they pursued new avenues opened by additional income. Many whites could not tolerate the participation of black men in the industrial processes. John Dos Passos caught the anxiety in his *Harper's* article on wartime Washington, describing the "moment of painful tension when a car or bus crosses the line into Virginia and the colored people have to move into the back seats."[30] *Harper's* provided a forum for a series of searching articles about black-white relations. Earl Brown, dissecting the Detroit riot, placed blame upon apathetic public officials and called for substantial corrective actions to make Negroes full citizens.[31] Two months later a former white newspaper reporter dramatically confessed in *Harper's* how he and friends nearly precipitated a race riot in New Orleans through their callous and premeditated provocation of a hapless Negro.[32] Other articles included a forecast of a Negro return to the Republican party because of the nation's failure to alleviate discrimination, a scholarly analysis of the myths upon which racism was based, and an article highly critical of segregation in the many facets of American society.[33]

Probably the most controversial article to appear in *Harper's* during the war was Richard Rovere's scathing profile in 1944 on presidential hopeful Thomas E. Dewey, governor of New York. Rovere portrayed Dewey as a man graced with style but lacking substance:

It is unlikely . . . that any other man in American life today is as devastatingly simple in character and motivation as Tom Dewey. . . . It is no secret that Dewey does not get along well with people. . . . He is incapable of letting down his hair, even for a photograph. . . . Mental vigor he assuredly has, but within narrow limits. . . . Like a third-rate Congressman, he has said only what will keep him out of trouble with the voters.[34]

Public outcry from Dewey supporters was immediate and loud. Many readers cancelled their subscriptions with abusive letters. Herbert Hoover was not amused by Rovere's statement that Dewey, if elected, would rely chiefly on Hoover for advice on foreign affairs. (Rovere described the former President as a "hard-bitten mercantile nationalist who before Pearl Harbor took the American First point of view."[35])

At a small dinner party, arranged by Oswald Garrison Villard for people who had shared his own attitude toward the war, Hoover castigated Allen. The former President and Allen were sitting diagonally opposite at the table when someone mentioned the Rovere profile of Dewey. The comment struck a spark in Hoover, and he launched into a tirade against Allen for publishing a "mean, dastardly, inaccurate article on Dewey."[36] Allen was so flustered and disturbed by the vehemence of the assault that he could hardly respond.

The next day, Allen challenged Hoover by a letter to cite any inaccuracies in the article. Hoover replied from his Waldorf Towers living quarters, "I do not think any man can diagnose and answer a smear. That it neither expresses my social, economic nor international views would be obvious to any accurate student. Likewise, as to Mr. Dewey."[37]

Gerald W. Johnson wrote from Baltimore to call the article the best anywhere in six months. "I think *Life* had already defeated Dewey by photographing him sitting on three telephone directories; but if that didn't finish him, this will." The Democrats agreed; the Democratic National Committee ordered five thousand reprints for distribution. So pleased was Allen over the article that he arranged with Rovere to write four more pieces during 1944 at double the standard payment.[38]

While Allen sought a well-rounded core of material—fiction, education, scientific, sociological, literary, economic, and so on—to supplement the dominant articles on war, he confined his own writing to the question of war. Generally, his pieces were syntheses of recent events or trends: reviews of the war effort, a progress report on Selective Service, notes on his visit to England, short profiles of the top U.S. military officers, and effects of the U.S. military outpost on Allen's favorite vacation spot, Bermuda.

Another article, "Who's Getting the Money?," required more penetrating research.[39] In a similar piece, "The Lesson of 1917," Allen had said that no aspect of the first war's effort had brought more shame to the American people than the "egregious profits" made by many companies out of war orders.[40] He now determined to learn, before it became merely history, who was earning the profits in the present war. Perhaps it would not be too late to correct inequities. His research pointed him toward a much more optimistic interpretation of the American economy than he previously had held. Allen determined that the bulk of the "fabulous" increase in war income was going not to big corporations but to middle-class wage earners, and he was greatly heartened. This contrasted directly with the economic situation he had described during the 1930s. Since Allen never had been known as a friend of big business, his findings appeared particularly striking. Later, he would see this spread of economic gains into the middle class as the key to properly understanding the first half of the twentieth century.

17

ALLEN ON THE HOME FRONT

The Allen family inevitably became involved in the domestic war effort: Allen was profoundly occupied as an editor; his wife joined the Council for Democracy and Office of War Information; and his son became a soldier.

In 1941 Agnes began working part-time in the *Harper's* office and also volunteered to work at a new organization, the Council for Democracy. Headed by Raymond Gram Swing, the Council was chiefly a propaganda agency which prepared pamphlets on critical problems of the day, seeking to enhance and protect the democratic way of life. After several months of donating her services, Agnes finally became a paid staff member of the New York-based organization.[1] In 1942 she joined the Office of War Information, where she contributed writing and administrative skills throughout the war. She first worked as an outpost supervisor, one of several women who saw to it that the needs of the overseas offices were filled. Later, she became assistant division chief in the News and Feature Bureau in the overseas branch. The work was demanding, and Agnes consistently worked a six-day, sixty-hour week.

Oliver, now at Harvard, became ibis, then president, of the *Lampoon*. He apparently intended to follow his father into editorial work, but the Allens had not known for certain until Oliver was selected one of several dozen "most normal" youths in his class and subjected to a case study funded by the W. T. Grant Foundation. When the case worker visited Oliver's parents, the Allens told her that they did not know what their son intended to do in life. "I do," replied the interviewer. "He said that you and Mr. Allen have such a good time that he wants to go into publishing."[2] When Oliver graduated at mid-term in 1943, however, he entered the army as a private.

Allen's load of extracurricular activities continued: occasional speeches and radio appearances, continued free-lance writing, meetings of the Foreign Policy Association, and, beginning in October 1942, visits to Boston as a Harvard overseer. He declined, pleading lack of time, to contribute to editor Robert E. Spiller's monumental *Literary History of the United States*.[3]

In the summer of 1942 Allen again appeared on "Information Please." This time the entire affair simply was dull. "Sure, we were getting the answers, but why should anyone want to *listen*? That was the way it struck me." Afterwards, he and Agnes joined Franklin P. Adams, Clifton Fadiman, John Kieran, and the show's director and owner, Dan Golenpaul, for a drink, enjoying themselves thoroughly. Allen sat next to Kieran, the sports columnist, and found him "entrancing." Kieran, surprisingly, delighted him by joining in an "absurdly" long discussion on ornithology. "He knows birds much better than I do," Allen wrote Hildegarde.[4] He later admitted to Thomas Hornsby Ferril that he had spent the last minutes before the show's broadcast "diligently cramming as if for a college examination."[5]

Three months later Allen read over the Columbia Broadcasting System's radio network a short biographical sketch he prepared on Woodrow Wilson for the U.S. Treasury Department. The sketch was printed in the Treasury Department's *There Were Giants in the Land: Twenty-eight Historic Americans as seen by Twenty-eight Contemporary Americans*.[6]

In the summer of 1943 Dorothy's father, Dr. Cobb, died at the age of eighty. Allen and Agnes attended the large funeral at the Church of St. Nicholas. "I felt no sense of tragedy about the ending of that splendid life—just a feeling of tenderness at all he had meant to me," Allen told Hildegarde.[7]

As the election of 1944 approached, the first wartime election since 1864, Allen made his first political speech at Bennington College, where he was ending his term as a trustee. He admitted having voted for Willkie in 1940, and he confessed to holding a number of objections to President Roosevelt: his indecisiveness, his tendency to play the part of the "Great White Father" who knows best, and his failure to produce further ideas for the New Deal.[8] Allen believed now that Roosevelt's domestic policies were on the verge of stifling the "adventurous, inventive, enterprising people who would like to build a better mousetrap." Members of the administration were bound by an ideological straitjacket. "They have fallen into a way of translating their recollection that they are liberals into just an automatic habit of deciding things in favor of Labor—even when the Labor men happen to be wrong—and of hazing business men—even when the business men happen to be right."[9]

Nevertheless, Allen felt, Dewey lacked presidential qualities. He was "a personally bumptious man, cocksure, capable of making enemies of many who will have to work with him." His eye had been so cautiously upon the presidency that for years his speeches had been masterpieces of "sonorous ambiguity."

Dewey also lacked alternatives to the New Deal, and the "free enterprise" advocates who surrounded him frightened Allen. Their kind of free enterprise meant subsidies for favored industries, hamstringing creative government institutions such as the TVA, and turning government regulation of business into "an easy-going farce." What the "fat boys" around Dewey wanted, in short, was an economy controlled by them and their friends, *not* free enterprise.[10]

The Republican charge that Roosevelt had failed to prepare the nation for war was absurd and ignorant, Allen felt, for Roosevelt had been consistently ahead of public opinion (including Allen himself) in foreign affairs, and it had been Republicans in Congress who fought hardest against war preparations. Allen cited five positive points in Roosevelt's behalf: "remarkably successful" overall American war planning, war production acknowledged to have been a miracle, less profiteering than expected and manageable inflation, no major invasions of civil liberties with the exception of the West Coast Japanese-Americans, and an established wartime unity within the nation.

No matter what the election's outcome, however, Allen would not view it with alarm. "You know the foundations of the Republic *won't* rock if the wrong man is elected," he told his audience. But Roosevelt's remarkable successes certainly justified his re-election, Allen felt.[11]

The question of postwar planning which so concerned Allen became more than academic after the June 1944 invasion of Normandy. The immediate need for ravaged Europe was food. But within the United States, some uncertainty existed as to whether or not it would be able to feed even itself after the war, much less Europe's hungry millions. Allen saw firsthand evidence of the complexities involved when he attended a debate in Washington at the request of the Writers' War Board, of which he was a member.[12] Some ten other writers also were invited, and about fifteen government officials from relevant agencies attended as the food experts.[13]

A fundamental disagreement immediately arose, as Allan Green later described, between the "let-them-have-food-if-they-can-pay-for-it and the we've-got-to-save-lives-regardless groups." Allen labeled the two camps as the "business isolationists" and the "idealists."[14]

Was there sufficient food to feed Europe, and, if so, when would it be available? How long must rationing continue in the U.S.? Just how critical was the food shortage in Europe? What would be the after-effect in the U.S. of an overproduction spurt in behalf of Europe?

"I suppose we had the ten or so best equipped people in the country at the dinner, and listened to them all, and though I inclined, in the end, to the [Clifton] Fadiman point of view [that the U.S. must feed Europe], it was certainly not a one-sided discussion," Allen said.[15]

Another postwar project which Allen followed intently was the new movement to form an international organization of the world's nations. He had witnessed in dismay the futile struggle for U.S. entry into the League of Nations. Now, public opinion soundly supported U.S. participation in a United Nations organization, and the Senate declared its positive attitude in an 85 to 5 vote. In April 1945 a conference of fifty nations convened in San Francisco to draft a charter for the new organization. Allen, before leaving as the *Harper's* correspondent, was briefed at his own home by Undersecretary of State Sumner Welles. The State Department arranged hotel accommodations for Allen and other newsmen, and he mingled with correspondents from all over the world.

President Roosevelt had intended to open personally the San Francisco convention until he was stricken fatally with a cerebral hemorrhage at Warm Springs, Georgia. Now, his successor, Harry S. Truman, decided to address the delegates by radio rather than in person. Allen recorded his impressions of the speech. "Truman's voice sounds a little hoarse—and no oratorical ring. . . . [His] speech runs on, uninspiringly, tritely—why so long?—prosily, with clichés—(You hear paper rustle as those with script turn the pages)."[16]

Unfortunately, the San Francisco visit turned into an ordeal as had Allen's 1943 visit to England. He became ill, and was confined to his hotel room bed for the latter part of his stay with what was later diagnosed as lobar pneumonia.

While delegates laid grandiose plans for a peaceful postwar era, the war continued. The United States home front was feeling acutely the pinch of rationing. Three weeks before he traveled to San Francisco, Allen sent Oliver, now a master sergeant with Eighth Army Headquarters in New Guinea, a detailed letter recounting wartime life on the domestic scene. He intended the letter not only for Oliver's enjoyment, but as a "memory-jogger" to himself for his own files.

The anomaly of growing shortages when the end of the war was in sight, Allen believed, could be explained by military overzealousness. Military officials, he wrote,

have got the chance to order what they think they need without being stopped by civilian officials in the WPB [War Production Board] or elsewhere—and have been buying full tilt. When the war in Europe failed to end last fall, according to plan, and when on top of that the breakthrough took place in Belgium, they found they needed a lot more stuff. They also felt—many of the brass hats—that civilians were taking it too easy and a few acute shortages wouldn't hurt them, and probably the civilians would lie down on the job after the Germans were licked, and so they'd better order on a majestic scale. I echo their sentiments about civilian morale—people, too many people at least, do tend to expect to live much as usual; but needless shortages don't help morale, and some sorts of shortages can have a damaging effect on the war effort. For example, a shortage of steel for railroad repairs can be bad; a shortage of shoes and gloves for war workers can be bad for production.[17]

On a more prosaic level, the cigarette situation continued vexatious. Allen told Oliver of a 100-yard queue he had seen only the day before at a cigar store at Fifth Avenue and Forty-second Street which had received a shipment of cigarettes. As a favored customer Allen was able to obtain a package of Philip Morris every morning at the Ten Park bookshop. Twice a week or so Anna, the maid, foraged among grocery stores and drugstores to obtain more. The liquor situation was nearly normal except for higher prices caused by taxes. More critical items such as shirts were becoming scarcer than ever, and food shortages were worse, too.

The housing problem remained critical, and the automobile situation was growing desperate because of the difficulty in replacing tires and worn-out parts. Detroit had stopped making cars in 1942, and now the average age of automobiles was between seven and eight years.

Allen was somewhat embarrassed at detailing in such length to a soldier problems of civilian life, and he asked Oliver to explain if he showed the letter to anyone that this stuff about shortages is not grousing but recording a situation which, if in some respects it is bad, is not bad because of the discomfort it causes people who have too little opportunity to sacrifice, but bad simply because it causes production troubles and economic pressures which we have so far been providentially—and through good planning—able to avoid.[18]

Oliver soon would leave New Guinea for Morotai, where he served as Order of Battle officer for the 93rd Negro Division. By war's end he had become a first lieutenant.

One Saturday morning in the last days of the war the Allens heard what sounded like distant thunder. Allen switched on the radio to hear the 10 A.M. news and learned that the noise had been an airplane striking the Empire State Building. From their bedroom window the Allens could see only to the sixtieth floor, which appeared eerily serene. Even after they rushed to the fog-capped building they had to circle to the skyscraper's south side before they saw smoke pouring from windows high above. Soon the mist turned to hard rain and they went home. They later learned that a B-25 Mitchell bomber carrying three men had struck the obscured building at the seventy-eighth and seventy-ninth floors, killing thirteen persons. Had it not occurred on a Saturday, when only fifteen hundred instead of fifteen thousand persons were inside, many, many more would have died.

"The strange thing is that we who had so often imagined a plane hitting a skyscraper had imagined it bouncing off—not realizing that it would plow right through the screen of the wall," Allen wrote Hildegarde. The plane's fuselage had penetrated the building and the wings smashed to fragments. A week later people still were craning their necks upward to stare, but the holes in the building were obscured by scaffolding and there was little to see.[19]

Within two weeks of the crash, American B-29 bombers had dropped two atomic bombs on Hiroshima and Nagasaki. Japan surrendered quickly, and the war was over.

But the long-awaited conclusion did not signify a return to the remembered peaceful ways at all, as Bernard DeVoto wrote in the "Easy Chair." "We are not the same people, this is not the same nation or the same world."[20]

18

POSTWAR TENSIONS

"We've been having a lovely Christmas season," Allen wrote to Hildegarde on Christmas Day in 1945.

Last night we croaked "Adeste Fideles" in Rogie's room, and Jean [the manservant] did a solo of "Minuit Crétien (Chrétien?); and I read aloud the Cratchit Christmas Eve; and then Agnes and I went to a 10.30 pm carol service at the Church of the Ascension, getting back home well after midnight. This gray morning we've been opening presents, and as I write this King George, on the radio, is haltingly greeting the British Empah.

Again, Merry Christmas to you—and now especially a Happy New Year.[1]

The American nation enjoyed a Yuletide of peace and homecoming in 1945. For the first time since 1938 the world was without war. Christmas shopping was extravagant, the end to gasoline rationing led to new hustle and bustle, and military uniforms were disappearing. Yet, as Bernard DeVoto said, the nation could never be the same as it was before the war. Beneath the obvious manifestations of a happy peace, new concerns of perhaps even greater import than before had arisen. As *Time* noted, not even Santa Claus was "able to drive the bomb from topmost place in the U.S. mind."[2]

By late 1945 the Soviet Union appeared to be a new, or rather a renewed, menace to the American nation. As postwar difficulties between Western allies and the Russians became more exacerbated the American public gradually was convinced that they now were involved in a new and deadly war over the minds of peoples—a "cold war." America had undergone a series of extreme shocks for years now; the Depression, the excesses of Hitler, and wars in both Europe and the Pacific had been survived. To emerge victorious from these great hazards only to be confronted with a new and even greater threat caused an undue emotional strain on American minds. The resulting era of doubt and suspicion divided Americans in an unusual way—according to the degree and nature of concern expressed against what was generally termed a "communist conspiracy" intent on overthrowing the American form of government. Like many "liberals," Allen believed that international subversion actually was less menacing than the exaggerated fears of it which caused damaging inquiries into a person's political beliefs.

Fifty-five years old at war's end, Allen seemed slightly reserved when a person first met him. Closer association revealed a witty, warm, and modest man. One of his personal goals always was to remain free of intellectual snobbery. He and Agnes were ardent fans of such ostensibly "lower class" entertainment as the roller derby. They loved track and field, and to test their powers of observation they frequently attended schoolboy track meets to see if they could spot future star athletes. Allen continued to play tennis, although not matching his rigorous several-times-a-week schedule of the 1930s.

At times friends seriously urged him to have a showing of his watercolor landscapes, but he resisted even when Boston's Museum of Fine Arts inquired. He described himself to the Museum's W. G. Constable as one who liked painting "literal pictures of things that . . . are beautiful or attractive" with results "something like Winslow Homer on an off day."[3] Most people would consider him "pretty old-timey" in his art, he was certain. He especially enjoyed painting on vacations in Bermuda, his and Agnes' favorite site for reviving spirits and strength.

The Allens enjoyed friendships with younger friends such as the Russell Lyneses and the Eric Larrabees.[4] When Larrabee, a classmate of Oliver's at Harvard, first met Allen socially he got the immediate impression that the well-known historian-editor was something of a "lightweight" intellectually. But soon he realized that Allen, after a heavy diet of such talk at the office, avoided discussions of politics and international affairs on social occasions. More frequently word games or charades enlivened small gatherings of friends. Agnes excelled at these games, and once when she handily defeated Allen, he remarked in comic exasperation, "Agnes, if I had your brains and my character, I could do anything."[5]

Agnes devised one unusual game that caused *Life* magazine to cover an Allen party. In this game Agnes selected a reproduction of a painting and described it verbally while Allen attempted to sketch it from her description. Tom Prideaux of *Life* once attended an Allen party at which all the guests attempted the stunt, and he arranged for a *Life* photographer to record such a gathering. *Life* called it a new kind of pictorial parlor game which was bedeviling and beguiling New York party-goers. The two-page spread, showing guests attempting to sketch Boucher's *Toilet of Venus,* included a photograph taken over Agnes' shoulder as she described the painting. Those present included the Russell Lyneses, cartoonist Robert Osborn, painter Henry Schnakenberg, and actress Nina Foch.[6]

Another parlor game paid off in an unexpected way. The Allens had taken to a game which was devised one weekend at Fire Island by two of Agnes' friends at *Reader's Digest,* Carol Lynn Gilmer and Vera Lawrence. It involved the guessing of clichés. Word of the game reached an American Broadcasting Company official, who suggested the idea to Walter Kiernan as a radio quiz show. Kiernan invited the Allens, Gilmer, and Lawrence to his apartment to demonstrate the game. He liked what he saw, and a recorded session at the ABC offices also proved successful. Beginning in May 1950, the game was played on the ABC radio network's "Cliché Club" each Wednes-

207

day evening during the summer. It featured Agnes as a regular panelist and Allen as an occasional participant. Kiernan was master of ceremonies.[7]

Allen, proud of Agnes' quick wit, announced that she had summarized a precept destined to live forever because of its eternal verity: "Almost anything is easier to get into than out of." He called it "Agnes Allen's Law." Allen continued to play the piano by ear, usually his favorite waltzes. Sometimes a Strauss waltz would affect him so much that tears would flow, Agnes recalls.[8]

At the office Allen kept hidden in a grandfather clock a bottle of Scotch for rare and special occasions. On the morning of Truman's election in 1948 he strode into the office to find his editors already celebrating with the Scotch. Without pause or change of expression, Allen commented solemnly and with an inward wink at the indulgence, "I was under the impression that this was a non-partisan magazine."[9]

Always self-disciplined, Allen did not require the threat of a deadline to force him to work. His books and articles, all achieved as part-time endeavor, could not have been written without careful scheduling of work on evenings and weekends. Neither his nor Agnes' pace slackened after the war. He wrote Hildegarde in 1948 that sometimes they felt they were "daft" to follow such tight schedules.

I keep telling myself that I want to write, but don't want to do another book while carrying most of the responsibility for the magazine and taking only occasional days off. But at other times we realize that we are really very lucky indeed to have more to do than we can do, and all of it what we are proud to do.[10]

Agnes maintained a formidable writing pace of her own. Following the two joint picture-book efforts with Allen as well as her own books in the thirties, she had written *Vassar Women* (1940), *From Man to Machine* (1941), and *Women Are Here to Stay* (1949). She stayed with the Office of War Information until the organization disbanded after the postwar transitional period. In 1947 she joined the staff of *Reader's Digest,* where she helped set up the Condensed Book Club operation.

Oliver, emerging from the army after the war, was ready to take up a career in magazine work himself. He began in 1946 on the clipping desk at *Newsweek*, then joined *Life* in 1947 and moved to the magazine's bureau in Los Angeles. In 1948 he married Deborah Hutchison, a Smith College graduate, and before the year was over, they returned to New York, where he became a writer for *Life*. Deborah soon began to work for a trade magazine, *Interiors*. The "Allen cartel," her father-in-law joked, was "dominating and controlling" the field of journalism.[11]

Between them, Allen and Agnes had considerable expertise in wartime government publicity, for one or the other had served the endeavor in both wars. The matter of what business, if any, the government had in dispensing propaganda during peacetime was open to question now, but President Truman felt it to be an "integral part" of conducting foreign affairs. He named a former advertising executive, William B. Benton, as an assistant secretary of state charged with organizing the government's peacetime information program.

Allen, determined to examine the question of a postwar information service, arranged a Washington interview with Benton in October 1945. He expressed his skepticism of any large-scale government program that might slant or interfere with the free gathering of news and become a nationalistic propaganda mill.[12] Before Benton could present his plan to Congress, Allen published his own article recommending a "modest" information service which would emphasize presidential messages and official statements, backgrounding the news, and establishing American libraries in foreign nations. He also suggested placing an experienced newsman as an attaché in every U.S. embassy or legation.[13]

Benton's proposal to Congress in January 1946 also called for a modest program which would deal with "information" rather than "propaganda." Congress slashed the information program (called the Office of International Information and Cultural Affairs) much further than Benton had envisioned, and not until 1948 when a Congressional delegation visited Europe and saw evidence of a massive

Soviet propaganda program did the United States begin to expand its publicity efforts.[14]

Allen felt uncertain about what policies should be followed in United States-Soviet frictions. Most other Americans similarly were unsure about such issues as the military role in atomic power in the Cold War. A bill by Democratic Senator Brien McMahon of Connecticut would have established exclusive civilian control over atomic energy. Republican Senator Arthur H. Vandenberg of Michigan countered with an amendment that would direct the proposed civilian commission to consult with a military board in determining atomic energy policies, which could be appealed finally to the President. When the Senate Special Committee on Atomic Energy supported the Vandenberg amendment, many of the nation's liberals voiced their objections. Allen was among the protestors; he expressed "grave doubts" about the amendment. He added sarcastically to Senator James M. Mead of New York that his information was "*not* from Communist sources!" The Vandenberg amendment was tantamount to giving the military a veto, Allen said, and "that is a pretty slender safeguard of our sound tradition putting military policy under civilian supervision."[15]

The debate ended in August 1946 when a compromise was reached. President Truman signed the Atomic Energy Act of 1946, creating a five-man civilian Atomic Energy Commission with complete control over research and development of fissionable materials and having a military liaison committee for consultation on military matters.

When the war had ended, the Writers' War Board dropped "War" from its title and continued as a private agency. The Board's attention, under president Rex Stout, turned to such causes as world cooperation and racial understanding, and Allen became a member of the advisory board. Other members included Clifton Fadiman, Franklin P. Adams, Paul Gallico, Oscar Hammerstein II, Margaret Leech, John P. Marquand, Christopher LaFarge, Henry Pringle, and William L. Shirer. In 1946 the Board foolishly sought to organize a boycott against the *Chicago Tribune*'s Sunday literary supplement because of the newspaper's editorial stance of being, as the Writers'

Board termed it, "anti-British, anti-Russian, anti-UNO [UN], anti-everything the world needs and hopes for."[16] The Board mailed a letter on March 1, 1946, urging the nation's writers to persuade their publishers not to advertise in the supplement. Listed on the letter-head as the advisory board were the names of some eighty well-known writers, including Allen. Allen, however, knew nothing of the letter until John T. Flynn called his attention to it.

Flynn asked Allen if he actually endorsed a letter which com-mitted the Writers' Board to an organized boycott of an American newspaper simply because it disagreed with the administration's foreign policy. "Is it not strange that writers, of all people, should set up an organization to punish by economic sanctions those who do not agree with them?" Unless Allen and other writers whose names were used as sponsors were among the first to disassociate them-selves from its purpose the incident would stand as a stain upon every one of them, Flynn contended.[17]

Allen agreed, and although he disliked the *Tribune* and its edi-torial positions, he immediately sent Rex Stout his resignation:

As one who has long deplored interference by advertisers with an edi-torial freedom and who has fancied that he did this out of conviction and not just because it sometimes suited him to say things which some advertisers might not like, I dislike being associated with any effort to bring advertising pressure against anybody.[18]

Besides, he said, he had assumed that the Board's work ended when the war did.[19]

Allen was more enthusiastic about his participation in another organization, the Foreign Policy Association, a nonprofit educational body which promoted an understanding of foreign affairs through its publications and discussions. The prestigious Association had been formed in 1918 to support establishment of an international organiza-tion to promote peace. Its initial membership included such people as Charles A. and Mary Beard, John Dewey, Judge Felix Frank-furter, Judge Learned Hand, William E. Hocking, and Ida M. Tarbell.[20] Allen became a director of the Association, and at the end of World War II he headed a self-study committee for re-evaluation which recommended that the organization continue to be objective and impartial rather than a pressure group.[21]

During the postwar years many Americans particularly feared the possibility of Red espionage, and the result was sweeping investigations into the loyalty of federal employees. Allen consistently minimized the domestic threat, and he expressed great alarm at the damage caused by those who exaggerated the Communist menace at home. He likened the investigations to the abuses of the Red scare which had followed the First World War, and he attributed them to the same emotional causes.[22]

While Allen believed that the Communists represented only a negligible domestic threat, he early acknowledged that the international confrontation between the United States and the Soviet Union had sinister implications. As early as 1946, when Communist guerrillas began fighting the established order in Greece, Allen found Russian behavior "dismaying." If war represented the extension of politics into the battlefield, the Soviets were "certainly engaging in politics in a warlike spirit," he wrote. The Soviet leaders appeared to operate as a prosecuting attorney in an adversary relationship; they represented their own propaganda without regard to opposite views. "But there seems no great hope right now that they will do anything to keep this from being two worlds rather than one, and that is certainly a deeply discouraging outcome of this war."[23]

Allen feared that so much attention would be devoted to the Communists that nothing would be done to discourage the return of Hitlerism in Germany.[24] The only realistic approach, he felt, was to be "tough in counter-bargaining"; to be too conciliatory would simply appease the Russians.[25]

While Allen privately expressed these concerns, a man with whom he had been impressed in 1933, now Secretary of Commerce Henry A. Wallace, was taking a controversial opposite view. In a Madison Square Garden speech on September 12, 1946, Wallace strongly protested any "get tough" approach to Russia. "The tougher we get, the tougher the Russians will get," he said. Less than a week later the newspapers printed a copy of a letter Wallace had written to

President Truman in which he said he was deeply troubled by people who thought the nation had no choice but "to arm to the teeth." An arms race would lead, as always, he believed, to war.[26] The next month Truman requested and received Wallace's resignation.

By the time Wallace campaigned for President in 1948 at the head of the Progressive party, Allen was convinced that he had become a tool of the Communists, whose intent it was "to acquire whatever power they could in American organizations for the sake (whether they fully realize it or not) of aiding Moscow at the appropriate moment." While Allen believed that the United States often had been stupid and overstubborn, and had weakened its position by catering to reactionaries, he also was convinced that the Soviet Union bore the blame for nine-tenths of the world tension because of its brutal disrespect for international agreements. "And to serve the Soviet cause wholeheartedly while sailing under the false colors of humane liberalism, as do some at least of Wallace's communist supporters, seems to me contemptible." Allen acknowledged that many had entered the Communist ranks out of noble motives, but "today they find themselves apologists for brutality and aggression."[27]

Thrusts from the radical left were parried by Allen in such manner; yet, his bigger burden was in defending himself and *Harper's* from accusers on the right who charged him and the magazine with being soft on Communism. He answered one complaining reader by saying that to check criticism for fear it might give aid and comfort to the enemy would be the "worst kind of cowardice" and a disservice to one of the principal sources of democratic strength.[28]

The Cold War did present special problems for an editor who had to decide what subjects should be dealt with cautiously because of national security and what subjects needed full and open discussion. Allen wrote to Elmer Davis for "any wise counsel" he might have about the frustrating situation. He told Davis that the average citizen found himself in a fog, and editors forever faced a feeling of "You can't print that." "We feel we ought to make some contributions to the discussion of such overwhelming problems but also feel pretty much hog-tied."[29]

Whittaker Chambers, the former *Time* senior editor who both

213

terrified and enthralled Americans with his accounts of Communist espionage circles in the federal government, fascinated Allen. In an unpublished review of Chambers' autobiography, *Witness,* Allen acknowledged the book's absorbing qualities, especially in providing insights into the motivations of Communists.

But again and again before and during the Hiss case he [Chambers] harbored suspicions which were later proved unjustified. . . . Clearly Mr. Chambers has been a man of such distorted judgments that his over-all political, economic, and moral conclusions should be regarded with a more skeptical eye than his testimony as to Communist methods. One may accept his damning judgment of Hiss (as I do) and yet reject his interpretations of larger matters.[30]

Chambers seemed to Allen consistently to overrate Communist power in the United States, and he especially censured him for attributing to New Dealers and liberals sympathy toward Communism. The trouble with Chambers' judgment, Allen wrote, was that "he sees himself very big . . . and sees the C.P. [Communist party] very big too—whereas his own picture of its activities suggests no such widespread influence."[31]

In 1952 Allen found himself on a speaker's rostrum with Chambers at the *New York Herald-Tribune* Forum at the Waldorf-Astoria Hotel. Allen felt compelled to preface his own speech with an explanation lest the audience wonder whether he and Chambers were "running on the same team." He said he wholeheartedly disagreed with some of Chambers' conclusions, but he nevertheless deeply respected his courage and sincerity.[32]

Allen then directly countered Chambers' cries of alarm, saying the charge that the nation was "in danger of national subversion by the American Communists and their dupes" was "nonsense." He added that "the delusion we are being subverted is being fostered by ignorant people whose capacity for suspicion is greater than their capacity for observation; by desperately sincere people who, having once got caught in the Communist trap and then shaken themselves free of it, can see almost nothing else on the horizon."[33] Allen's comments gained top billing in the *New York Times'* account of the all-day forum, at which Walter Lippmann, James Roosevelt, and James Michener also spoke.

When he published *The Big Change* later, he lamented that inquisitions into the loyalty of suspected Americans had frightened many useful and productive people into a nervous conformity. "Never before have we been subjected to the sort of prolonged strain that we feel today, and our patience, humor, and courage are being sorely tested."[34]

John Chamberlain, the leftist-oriented writer who had been *Harper's* book reviewer from 1939 to 1947 and who had since undergone an ideological turnabout to the right, challenged Allen to cite cases of people who had been frightened into conformity. Allen responded that the fright could be seen in "many, many" manuscripts sent to *Harper's* and in many that were printed; it was reflected in conversations of writers and broadcasters after the Red Channels blacklisting broke; it was evidenced in the conversation of government employees after Senator Joseph McCarthy "smeared" Philip Jessup, the United States' representative to the United Nations General Assembly. "I have even felt it myself," Allen said, saying that a McCarthy could isolate his own past statements and make him appear to be a friend of the Communists.[35]

As Allen saw it, the basic disagreement between him and Chamberlain was in their conceptions of the size of the Communist menace. Allen agreed that in the international sphere the menace was "terrific," but he saw it as minimal on the domestic scene.

While Allen believed that the American Communists had infiltrated certain organizations, that persons such as Fuchs had done incalculable harm, and that party members should be kept under "rigorous surveillance" by the Federal Bureau of Investigation, he also felt it easy to overestimate the importance of Communist influence. As one who had encountered Communists in the Authors' League, Allen said he found their chief accomplishment was to "make life very distasteful" for the officers of the organization and to force them to expend their energy on internal warfare with them.[36]

Chamberlain had charged Allen with being so innocent he did not realize what was happening around him. Allen saw Chamberlain as an individual who had been so closely brushed by the conspiracy because of his former Marxist sympathies that he saw it bigger than it really was. Chamberlain's *Farewell to Reform* had been "very useful," Allen thought, except for Chamberlain's "special aberration [Marxism]."[37] Now, he wondered if Chamberlain's viewpoints did not represent an overcompensating reaction.[38]

Allen went on to say that he had changed his own credo very little in the past thirty to forty years; that at times he had been "a bit more radical than others" but at heart had remained what might be called a nineteenth century liberal. "I've been amused at how much more durable this sort of attitude seems to be than an adherence to some ideology or other," and one evidence seemed to be that he could read *Only Yesterday* "and feel I wasn't too far off in my judgment."

Chamberlain had told Allen he was writing to him in "sorrow rather than anger." Allen concluded by saying he was writing to Chamberlain in the same spirit.[39]

Chamberlain responded finally by saying he had firsthand knowledge of how the Communists intimidated and blacklisted certain people, because they had done it to his own friends. He challenged Allen to verify it with Morrie Ryskind or Adolphe Menjou. With that, their correspondence over the nature of the Communist threat in America apparently ended.[40]

Allen's convictions, agreed upon by the magazine staff, found expression through a series of anti-McCarthy articles as well as crusades by DeVoto in his "Easy Chair." The August 1950 issue, for example, rapped McCarthy's knuckles in two separate articles, which prompted expected charges that *Harper's* favored Communism.

A DeVoto "Easy Chair" column written in September 1949, which was highly critical of the Federal Bureau of Investigation's inquiries into the lives of suspected individuals, caught the eye of McCarthy himself and ultimately led to economic pressures against the magazine from prospective advertisers.[41] After cataloguing the dangers of

216

governmental investigations into personal lives, DeVoto recommended that citizens henceforth cease giving the FBI private information about individuals. J. Edgar Hoover responded with a furious letter to the editor, directed not so much at DeVoto as at the "Personal & Otherwise" column's note praising DeVoto for "single-handedly taking on the FBI—a job, by the way, which no one is better equipped to do. And a job which needed doing."[42] Senator McCarthy enlarged upon DeVoto's statement by quoting him as saying no one should give the FBI information on Communists in government.[43] Subsequently, the Chicago office of the joint *Harper's* and *Atlantic* advertising enterprise advised the main sales office in Boston that McCarthy's charge was "getting in our hair out here." Allen was informed that the Chicago advertising crowd was putting *Harper's* salesmen in a difficult position by asking pointblank whether DeVoto did or did not make the alleged statement.[44] Asked for a mollifying comment to assuage the ire, Allen answered that he could not refute the statement because DeVoto's own words were close enough to the McCarthy charge to make denial impossible.

While he disagreed with DeVoto's position, he said he had printed the piece "because I thought such an outburst from an undeniably patriotic citizen ought to get into the public discussion."[45] By 1952, however, the magazine had printed so much on the Senator that the staff, said Allen, was "inclined to let him alone for the time being lest we seem to be obsessed."[46]

Allen rejected an article on investigating Communists which was proposed by the California senator who had gained headlines through his perseverance in the Alger Hiss case, Richard M. Nixon. Despite the message from Nixon's literary agent, Lurton Blassingame, that Nixon wanted to take the matter out of politics (he was now presidential candidate Dwight D. Eisenhower's running mate), Allen declined: publication before the November 1952 elections would put it *into* politics. One editor, Catherine Meyer, scribbled a note that perhaps the article could be considered on its merits *after* November. A notation followed in Allen's own handwriting, "After Nov. who'll want to hear from Nixon?"[47]

Allen involved himself more directly the following spring in the anti-McCarthy movement by aligning publicly with the National Committee for an Effective Congress. The group had been founded in 1948 by Maurice Rosenblatt, a Washington lobbyist, to support liberal political candidates. Though nonpartisan, its liberal stance soon placed it squarely in the debate over McCarthyism. Its leaders viewed McCarthyism not merely as anticommunist but as a movement aimed at destroying the foundations of the democratic society. The organization turned its attention to combating this threat by establishing an informed opposition in the Congress itself.[48]

Robert E. Sherwood extended Allen an invitation to become a member of the Committee's Board of Sponsors in February 1952. He said that good men of Allen's ilk were especially needed to help elect enlightened Congressmen, "since the proponents of anti-Democratic policies *have* succeeded in dominating Congress through a well-run minority bloc led by men of the McCarthy-Hickenlooper-McCarren stripe." The issue was simple in Sherwood's mind: "Predatory and prejudiced interests are now pin-pointing vast resources on key election contests, with a view to enlarging their bloc of servile Senators." Allen readily agreed to join the organization, although he said he would be unable right away to contribute anything more than his name.[49]

In May 1953, in behalf of the Committee, Allen and Oscar Hammerstein II, evidently chosen because of their national reputations, jointly issued the first of at least two fund-raising letters. They announced that for the first time the Committee would operate fully between campaigns. Money raised would not only support candidates, it would also finance such projects as helping to get a hearing for individuals "unjustly accused before Congressional committees" and establishing a research branch to gather and evaluate information about plans and activities of the "nationalist-isolationist element" in America. Such data would go to Congressmen, the press, clergymen, educators, and other public leaders engaged in the fight to combat McCarthyism. "This strategically vital area is unfilled today," the letter pointed out, "whereas the McCormick-McCarthy-Velde axis is amply financed and furiously active in preparation for 1954."

Enlightened candidates were said to face uphill battles, and they needed funds, accurate information, unified strategies and public support—"more than just denunciatory letters to the editor, or idle gossip about McCarthy." The letter closed with a plea for donations of any size, explaining that "our sources do not include General [Robert] Wood [the arch-conservative chairman of Sears, Roebuck] and his friends, who raised $75,000 for one nationwide TV broadcast by McCarthy."[50]

Five thousand persons received the plea for support, and five weeks later 425 persons had contributed a total of about $7,250.[51] A second letter repeated the stop-McCarthy theme, labeling his forays as "depredations." Through these funds and others, the NCEC's Clearing House accumulated extensive information about the Senator for use as a weapon against him, and the collection remains today the greatest single source of material concerning McCarthy.[52]

To a certain degree McCarthy was responsible for causing Allen to vote in 1952 for Adlai Stevenson rather than for Dwight Eisenhower. Allen liked both men, but John Fischer remembers that Eisenhower's failure to repudiate McCarthy for his attack on General George C. Marshall was the deciding factor that led to his vote for Stevenson. Agnes Rogers Allen agrees that Eisenhower's inaction infuriated her husband.[53]

When Allen's name was announced in the *New York Times* in October as one of several prominent people who had changed his support from Eisenhower to Stevenson, a *Harper's* reader from Iowa wrote to ask if it really were true.[54] Allen acknowledged the switch, saying that he was by custom a habitual but independent Democrat and that he had planned in the spring to vote for Eisenhower because he admired him and felt the country needed a change. But the Eisenhower vote was tentative—"unless conceivably the Democrats should nominate Stevenson." To Allen's surprise, they did.

I found Stevenson a refreshingly honest and intelligent and liberal man who I thought would bring considerable change in the Washington atmosphere anyhow. And so after a period of trying to hold my balance on the fence, I dropped over into his camp.[55]

He explained to one friend that he voted for Stevenson because he demonstrated the statesmanship of a mind that was "very rare anywhere."[56] So close did he come to voting for Eisenhower, however, that as late as August, Allen edited and rewrote a speech for the General which had been composed by Charles R. Hook, Jr. of the Chesapeake and Ohio Railway Company. But he reminded Hook that if the election were held on that day, he would vote for Stevenson.[57]

During the 1952 campaign Allen often annoyed his Stevenson friends by saying he thought the nation certainly was lucky to have two first-class candidates. After Eisenhower's victory he even guessed that he would find himself defending the Eisenhower administration more often than most of those who had voted for him. "I'm afraid it's a peculiarity of mine that I tend to identify myself with the people who have a problem to solve rather than with their critics." Eisenhower's supporters soon would be criticizing their own choice, too, Allen felt, because Americans seemed to have formed the habit over the past twenty years of crabbing at Washington.[58]

A month after Eisenhower's victory, Allen issued Stevenson an open invitation to write about anything he wished for *Harper's*. A year later Stevenson, to whom Allen's friends often compared him in looks and thought, accepted the offer.[59]

19

NEW CHALLENGES FOR *HARPER'S*

The postwar years promised an uncertain challenge to *Harper's* and to Allen as editor. The war had promoted an unusual interest in public affairs, creating a boom in demand for magazines and all sources of news, and *Harper's* had thrived with the rest of the magazine industry. Now, the problem was how to transfer reader interest to peacetime topics. Newsstands sagged from the weight of new mass-oriented periodicals. From January to June in 1946 more than two hundred new titles were offered, most of them ephemeral and of dubious merit; the market became flooded, and many publications died about as quickly as they appeared.[1] Although no great harm had come to the established magazines, there was general concern over the future of all magazines in light of competition from such diversions as the movies, the automobile, the radio, and, soon, television.[2] Readers alone did not pay enough of the costs to publish any general circulation magazine, and many speculated whether *Harper's* and the *Atlantic* could survive for long in a neon-lighted world.

While the constant knowledge of a precarious battle between

profit and loss concerned Allen during these years, he focused his own efforts toward producing the best possible publication. The product had changed. The war had confirmed that Harper's now clearly was a magazine of public affairs first and a literary medium second. If there had been any doubt before, there was no longer.

Near the close of the war, Allen found opportunity to assess in his own mind just what a magazine like Harper's should do in American society. The nation's oldest school of journalism (at the University of Missouri) offered Allen its Honor Award for Distinguished Service in Journalism and asked him to make a speech about his profession. He combined the occasion with a trip to San Francisco to cover the United Nations' founding conference; he hoped to return to New York leisurely via train with a stopover at the university to speak and accept the award.

Allen could not shake the fever which had confined him to his hotel room in San Francisco. When he arrived at the university in Columbia, doctors hospitalized him in the school's infirmary and diagnosed the illness as lobar pneumonia. He canceled his lengthy speech, but bravely entertained from his hospital bed those few professors and students who dared enter. Eventually, the school published his undelivered speech, "The Function of a Magazine in America."[3]

Despite the broad title, Allen centered his observations on Harper's own function. He categorized five basic prerequisites for the magazine: to be interesting, to provide news in the widest sense, to provide interpretation and discussion of the important issues before the public, to provide a platform for original and inventive thinkers, and to provide a vehicle for "artists in literature."

Harper's deliberately sought an audience of opinion-makers: the segment of educated, intelligent, and responsible people who were the real leaders of America. Discussion of important issues for these readers needed to be honest, searching, and independent. There should be "no special pleading, no pressure-group stuff, no axe-grinding, no kowtowing to any private interest or power, no evasion of the uncomfortable fact."[4]

The world had become so full of powerfully organized institutions promoting their own special interests that Allen felt a special need to provide a forum for the solitary, unorganized individual. What Allen wanted was

the seminal idea, the objective judgment on the trend of things, the air-clearing outburst of indignation, the long-awaited satirical indictment, the shout of profane laughter, which will suddenly throw everything about us into a new perspective—and which is as likely as not to come from some individual who sits all by himself, unorganized, unrecognized, unorthodox, and unterrified.[5]

In its literary goals, Allen said the magazine did not seek to offer shelter for "the finicky products of the ivory tower." It aimed to print only "the excitingly creative, the lustily energetic, the freshly amusing, the newly beautiful, the illuminating, the profound."[6]

The practical difficulties in attaining these high goals seemed immense, especially if one relied heavily, as did *Harper's*, on unsolicited manuscripts. Some fifty proposed articles and stories then were arriving every day, and the editors spent at least half of their time reading these manuscripts. If one contained a valuable idea or ingredient, the editors might return it to the author for suggested revisions, or they might rewrite it themselves to make it suitable for publication (gaining the author's permission for changes). To ensure that the magazine dealt with issues the editors deemed of critical importance, the staff proposed ideas for articles to trusted authors.

Allen thoughtfully outlined the subtle threats to editorial integrity which an editor invariably felt. Although commercial pressure at *Harper's* had never been direct, such pressure often lay in an editor's own mind through his knowledge that the magazine, after all, was a commercial venture.

The editor will say to himself, "You want the magazine to make money, don't you? Well, don't go round insulting the people whose favor you need. Flatter them. Eliminate anything disrespectful to them. Play ball with them." That's how the pressure works.[7]

Many magazines yielded so cheerfully to this pressure that they hardly felt it, Allen said. Others overcompensated through one-sided attacks against business.

A second danger to independent magazines, Allen felt, was government pressure. Wartime censorship had been basically fair, he said, though he noted the navy's overzealous censorship. The bigger danger, again, seemed more subtle than that. When travel permits and credentials were issued by the War and Navy Departments with the writer's knowledge that these same agencies would be reviewing his work, then he could refrain only with difficulty from allowing these factors to temper his writings.

Finally, Allen saw pressure from readers as endangering a magazine's integrity: pressure to make the magazine's contents less serious and more lively, to be an entertainment medium, or to provide escapist fare. On the other hand, pressure to push a certain ideological line was a constant factor with which *Harper's* contended.

Sometimes the thought occurs to us that we are really idiots not to recognize that a magazine is just a commodity, and that we could probably sell more copies if we made everything short, easy, inoffensive, and trivial; or else just adopted a party line of some sort and made everything comfortably one-sided.[8]

Difficult though it all might be, it was a task that the *Harper's* editors believed worth trying, Allen concluded, for the proper functioning of American society demanded a well-informed, clear-headed, thoughtful, and civilized populace.

Two years later, Allen again assessed the magazine scene in America, this time more pessimistically. The occasion arose when the National Publishers Association asked him to participate in a discussion of the magazine industry's responsibilities to society at their 1947 conference at the Waldorf-Astoria Hotel. His remarks, carefully prepared, came to be known as his "closed mind" speech.[9] Although no more than fifteen minutes long, the talk created a minor sensation because Allen told the publishers that the free marketplace of ideas so cherished in American journalism seemed to be drying up within the magazine industry. The result was an undue hardening of the nation's intellectual arteries, he told the seven hundred fifty editors and publishers.

New or unorthodox ideas, he lamented, had far better chance for publication in books than in magazines. He saw several reasons for this, none of them commendable. Too many magazines were willing to cater to the reader who simply wanted to be amused, and too many magazines also hesitated to risk alienating their advertisers or subscribers by presenting an idea that would run counter to their preconceptions. Furthermore, editors too often held their magazines to a particular line of persuasion to give their publications unique personality and influence. Allen criticized here the rise of staff-written magazines which inevitably tended toward rigid content. "The policy chosen may be wholly sound, wholly reasonable; but when every contribution to the magazine is processed to fit it, inevitably a great deal of diversity will get sandpapered out." Allen did not name the Luce publications, but clearly he had them in mind.

The journalists themselves received the other side of Allen's blame, and the liberal writers who *claimed* to be open to new thoughts but really were not earned particular scorn. Somehow the notion had risen, Allen told the magazine executives, that an inevitable war of ideas existed between right and left, or conservatives and progressives, and that the function of the journalist was to decide which army to join. "The liberal journalist is the fellow who chooses the Army of the Left. He isn't interested in the interplay of ideas; he is a soldier in a holy cause; all who side with him are great and good, and all who oppose him are scoundrels." These journalists, confronted with a particular topic, invariably chose facts which reinforced their own particular viewpoints. The result too frequently was "a pitched battle of propagandas between two sets of determined bigots."

A "certain amount" of such partisanship might be valuable for discussion, Allen acknowledged. He was urging variety, not tepidity. "What I am arguing is that there is another function even more valuable than partisanship—the function of facilitating the free play of ideas."[10]

Allen left the noon luncheon feeling that his speech had fallen

225

"quite flat." Next morning he was astonished to see "such a play" in the newspapers.[11]

What he had said soon would be backed up by the report of the Commission on Freedom of the Press, a panel of scholars, philosophers, writers, and public figures headed by Robert M. Hutchins. The Commission declared that the day of the classical free marketplace of ideas now had disappeared, and asserted that as a result the mass media now had the responsibility for presenting all sides of public issues and events. Otherwise, all viewpoints could not be heard.[12]

When Allen talked about *Harper's* more immediate needs, Russell Lynes recalls, he often referred to a need for a table of contents that would be a promising menu permitting the intelligent reader to select from a varied assortment of important articles and stories to fit his particular taste. Allen told C. Hartley Grattan that he would be happy if every reader could find at least one article in each issue that especially appealed to him. The August 1948 issue seemed to him to have an ideal mix: it included an article with suggestions for a peacetime army, a description on a tragic slum housing fire, a piece on Palm Springs, two foreign affairs analyses, a community improvement story, and two good short stories.[13]

Allen acknowledged that his basic philosophy for editing came from Ellery Sedgwick. "The principal thing I got from Sedgwick," he said, "was the idea that you don't basically imagine the reading public and try to give them what they want." That would be impossible. What Allen did, following Sedgwick and other outstanding editors, was to edit to please *himself*—"then you are likely to interest other people." Allen followed this policy not as a dominant tyrant but as a referee who combined his own interests with those of his editors. "Once in a while I go against the lot of them but this happens very seldom," he said. Generally, he strove for "plenty of human interest" and "authoritative discussion of the kind of general current issues that don't get adequately covered in the press."[14]

It was important to Allen to refrain from imposing his own outlook or anyone else's on the magazine. When a reader picked up an issue of *Harper's*, he could not predict the essence of the articles, other than that they would be broadly humanitarian and liberal in a nonideological sense. Allen was eager to use any sort of talent— so long as the talent was there. Above all, the magazine was a haven for individuals, and by 1953 some five hundred to six hundred writers or would-be writers were submitting manuscripts each week to *Harper's*.

Although reading manuscripts required more of the editors' time than any other duty, as late as 1950 the staff employed no readers or researchers. The six editors divided the manuscripts on the basis of arrival dates. Those which showed promise were circulated from editor to editor, each of whom succinctly posted his opinion on the manuscript's envelope. Manuscripts surviving this process went to Allen for a final decision.[15]

The editors sometimes joked that the newest staff member automatically received the designation "poetry editor." Few relished the task. When one aspiring poet demanded an explanation as to why her poem had been rejected, Allen replied with all the critical power he could muster in a brief letter:

If I were to try to put into words why we aren't wholly keen about it, I could only say that it seems to me a little strained—I was almost going to say overblown. But the real difficulty may be that I don't fully understand or am half impervious to the mystical intent of it. These things are very hard to phrase, and I know I am not succeeding, but that is the best I can do now. If there is anything harder to do than judge poetry, it is to write intelligibly why one feels as one does about it.[16]

There were few qualms in the office, however, about improving submitted poems to meet publication requirements if the contributor consented.

The editors hammered out basic editorial decisions at a weekly Tuesday morning meeting at which Allen presided. It functioned as a sort of "group democracy" in which there was only one final vote—Allen's. Sometimes he would permit the staff's wishes to override his own; occasionally he would make a decision of his own with which the staff disagreed. Eric Larrabee recalls in particular one submitted article which the staff found delightful. It was entitled "How to Wash a Venetian Blind." Allen adamantly refused to print it, despite pleas, and the staff acquiesced good-naturedly. "We decided later that he had never washed a venetian blind," Larrabee said.[17]

Those who worked with Allen seemed to agree universally that the genial New Englander was a quiet inspiration. His easy-going personality and his tweed jacket with elbow patches belied his aggressiveness in seeking out the provocative article that struck nerve centers. "He felt controversial journalism was box-office journalism," recalled John Fischer, Allen's successor as editor. Fischer remembers also that Allen taught "clarity and organization and consistency of ideas to a lot of journalists who had been mediocre until he came along."[18]

Allen's relations with *Harper's* contributors were normally tranquil, but not always. James Jones, three years away from the fame that came with *From Here to Eternity*, was incensed when Allen sought in 1948 to edit two accepted stories, "The Way It Is," and "Just Like the Girl." Jones wanted to spell "don't" without the apostrophe (a spelling which soon came to be a Jones stylistic trademark) and he fought desperately to preserve his punctuation against changes that Allen felt to be minimal and essential.

"The Way It Is" had been retyped routinely in the *Harper's* office with what Allen considered to be a normal number of stylistic and editorial corrections. Allen also changed "hot-assed bitch" to "low bitch." Merle Miller, an assistant editor from 1947 to 1949, returned the manuscript to Jones in Illinois for approval.

Jones' response to the editing was not appreciative. "I cannot attempt to express how goddam mad it makes me for some literary-cocktail-party stenographer to take my stories and attempt to rewrite them for me." He agreed to accept, for the sake of *Harper's* family readers, the substitution of another phrase for "hot-assed bitch," but certainly not the suggested "low bitch."[19]

Now, Jones wrote, he could see why Hemingway had a clause written into his contract saying that not a single comma could be changed without his knowledge. "While I'm admittedly very slipshod sometimes about my personal life (and some days do not even take a bath), I am not slipshod at all about my writing. . . . No comma, no period or set of dots, no leftout apostrophe, is an oversight or a typographical mistake."[20]

Miller handed the twelve-page letter to Allen, who responded to Jones immediately:

May I answer your letter to Merle Miller as I am the "self-styled intellectual who works as a third rate editor," not to say "literary-cocktail-party stenographer," who is responsible for the revisions in your article.

I have been puzzled by your letter because in a great many years of editorial experience I have never got one quite like it. Fiction writers as well as article writers practically always accept without question minor changes of spelling and punctuation which are made to bring a manuscript into conformity with the rules of style employed by a given publication.[21]

For instance, John Dos Passos had made no objection, Allen said, to the separation of some words that ran together in his manuscript. "We didn't do this in all cases because the running together of words had become a sort of trademark of his style, but we worked out a kind of compromise between his preferences and our usual practices and he made no issue of the matter whatever." Allen said he was puzzled as to what possible difference in "inflection, rhythm, or anything else" existed between the correctly spelled "don't" and "dont," and he did not understand the necessity of omitting periods after Mr. and Lt.[22]

Perhaps the real difficulty, Allen reasoned, had been one of communication; Merle Miller had not sufficiently explained that the stories were accepted on the assumption that a few textual changes for the sake of propriety were essential, and, further, that such changes were merely tentative and subject to revision by Jones himself. Allen explained that he had sought to inject a clarification of the setting early in "The Way It Is" because it was distracting not to know whether the episode was taking place before or during the war or at Pearl Harbor, North Africa, or Italy. But that, too, was subject to Jones' own approval.

Allen said he was writing Jones "to make it plain that we don't make a practice of taking liberties with manuscripts beyond those which are the virtually universal publishing practices as to matters of style.". He apologized if the magazine had given the impression of being "high-handed."[23]

If he thought, as he surely did, that the matter was settled, he reckoned wrongly about Jones. Jones replied vehemently, again to Miller rather than to Allen. "I had thought that style was the author's, not the publication's; and that the publication served the purpose of publishing the author, not the author the purpose of elaborating the publication." In Jones' dealings with the *Atlantic*, Edward Weeks had permitted his only published story to date to appear as written—"(excepting, of course, the word 'pisspot.')." It was common knowledge, argued Jones, that Maxwell Perkins did not change a writer's style to fit a publication.[24]

Besides, he pointed out, a "story" was different from an article and "Mr Allen" (Jones followed the same punctuation style in his letters as he did in his fiction) apparently did not know that, since he had referred to his short story as an "article."

I'll bet on articles Mr Allen is a top notch man. I like your articles in *Harpers* [sic]. That one on Einstein and the Universe is a beaut.

But my *story* is not an *article,* and you didn't commission me to write it. . . .

And whether Mr Allen sees any difference between "don't" and "dont" or not, I do. Maybe I'm a nut. But, I do. There it is. Now, that being the case, the only question is: do we print it the author's way or do we print it *Harpers* [sic] way? A whole philosophy of publishing might hang on that very simple question. Because dont forget Max Perkins's basic principle of editing.[25]

Allen again responded quickly. "Well, I hardly know what to say," he began. "I'm quite bewildered over your making an issue over such matters as the use of an apostrophe in the word don't." He believed that Jones misunderstood the meaning of "style" in the sense that he had intended. There are two definitions of style, Allen pointed out: an author's way of writing, his choice of words, constructions, rhythm, and so on; and the rules of spelling, punctuation,

230

and capitalization followed by a given publication. He was referring only to the second sense, he assured Jones:

For instance, if in a story you were to spell the name of our magazine *Harpers*, as you do in your letter, we'd change it to *Harper's*, which is our style. That Max Perkins would have done this if he had been in our shoes I can't of course prove; but it seems likely in view of the fact that he so far interfered with Thomas Wolfe's writing as to cut several hundred thousand words out of a manuscript. I can assure you that in the second sense, style changes are the universal or all-but universal custom among magazines.[26]

Allen said he would go over the manuscript of "The Way It Is" one more time, making only such changes as seemed necessary, send it to Jones for his approval, and then they would try to adjust the differences.

Jones, at last, relented and accepted the new version. "The truth is, Mr Allen, the money you people paid me is already spent. I bought a much needed pair of slacks and jacket and paid off some bills and went on one good drunk."[27]

A few weeks later Jones amiably requested Allen to return his manuscript after the magazine was through with it. "(I'm making a collections [*sic*] of my own originals. Maybe my grandchildren will need them to live off of someday.)"[28]

When "The Way It Is" finally appeared in *Harper's* in June 1949, "don't" was spelled with the apostrophe. A note identified Jones as a twenty-seven-year-old former enlisted man in the army "now at work on a novel about the peacetime Regular Army in Hawaii before Pearl Harbor."[29]

The second Jones story which the magazine had accepted lay dormant for two years until Allen reread it and decided that he did not care to publish it after all. He returned it to Jones even though payment long since had been made.[30]

If Jones perhaps was Allen's least favorite fiction contributor in the postwar years, his favorite probably was Wallace Stegner, director of Stanford University's creative writing program. He confided to Stegner in 1952 about the genuine enthusiasm in the *Harper's* office for his fiction. "All in all, I think it is about the best we get from anybody. And that's a rather strong statement." One of Stegner's *Harper's* stories, "The Blue-Winged Teal," won first place in the annual O. Henry awards competition for 1950.[31]

Allen did not accept Stegner's fiction without seeking to improve it, however. When Stegner's agent submitted "Maiden in a Tower," Allen felt that the story's macabre aspects were so severe as to detract from the overall effect. He made rather extensive changes to de-emphasize this tone. Katherine Gauss Jackson, who specialized more than the other *Harper's* editors in fiction, felt compelled to justify to Stegner's agent Allen's changes. She said that for fifteen years she had "watched the operation of Fred's sixth sense of the fitness of things, have seen him make better stories out of good ones, and always had to admit he was right."[32] She assured the agent that the changes Allen had made were beneficial.

The magazine declined to publish a chapter from the galley proofs of Ralph Ellison's *Invisible Man*, a novel which would be adjudged by some as the most important novel of the postwar era. Assistant editor Anne L. Goodman explained, "I am extremely impressed by the book . . . and I only regret that we could not find a section in it that we felt we could use."[33] But the list of fiction writers who did appear under Allen's editorship in the postwar years was formidable. It included William Faulkner, J. D. Salinger, Truman Capote, Joyce Cary, Nelson Algren, Katherine Anne Porter, Shirley Jackson, John Cheever, Arthur Miller, Sloan Wilson, Peter DeVries, Max Steele, Niccolò Tucci, Kay Boyle, Roald Dahl, V. S. Prichett, and Mary McCarthy.

The magazine continued generally to publish two fiction pieces per issue in these years, and the short stories, distinctive in quality though they were, remained secondary to articles.[34] Concentration in nonfiction was on political, economic, and sociological matters, although areas such as the arts, science, and education were not neglected. Regular nonfiction contributors to the magazine included Grattan, John Bartlow Martin, Wolfgang Langwiesche, Peter Drucker, Richard Neuberger, and C. Lester Walker.

One of the most important articles ever published by *Harper's*, and certainly one of the most publicized, was Henry L. Stimson's inside story about the decision to drop the atomic bomb.[35] *Harper's* acquired the article in an unusual but not altogether rare fashion. Stimson, former secretary of war and the man who recommended to President Truman that the bomb be used, was composing his memoirs for publication by Harper & Brothers, and found himself besieged by friends urging him not to delay his story about the bomb any further.[36] Critics were contending that the bomb need not have been dropped for military reasons and should not have been dropped for moral reasons. Stimson called Cass Canfield in December 1946 to ask his advice about early publication of that portion of his manuscript. Canfield brought Allen with him to discuss the matter at Stimson's apartment.[37]

Stimson explained to them the pressures he was under to release the information. He wondered if early publication would in any way interfere with the book, and he had prepared a tentative article to read to Allen and Canfield. "Whereupon," Allen later recounted, "sitting on the sofa before the fire, he read the whole thing aloud to us—with the result that we were with him for nearly two and a half hours."[38]

When his listeners expressed great admiration for the article and agreed that they "should be proud and happy" to publish it in *Harper's*, Stimson became uncertain. He was eager to reach as broad an audience as possible, and others recommended magazines of larger circulation. Allen and Canfield guaranteed to Stimson that if *Harper's* were permitted to publish the article, they would make every effort to ensure the widest possible audience.

Allen went back to the office and optimistically drew up a detailed plan for wide distribution of Stimson's article to newspapers, magazines, and broadcasting stations all over the country. *Harper's* would agree to reprinting in full by all the various media, asking only a credit for the magazine. Allen sent the plan to Stimson, and two or three days later McGeorge Bundy (whom Allen identified as "Mr. Stimson's young assistant in his writing work") called to say that the article would be ready soon. On Saturday, December 21, a messenger delivered it to Allen's house.

Stimson's revelation made front-page headlines throughout the nation and world. Some newspapers reprinted in full the eight thousand-word article, and the American Broadcasting System, in a special broadcast, dramatized an edited version with sound effects.

No other article in the postwar years aroused so much emotion, furor, and controversy as Eric Larrabee's summary of Immanuel Velikovsky's *Worlds in Collision*.[39] The article brought to a head rumblings that had been reverberating quietly in the scientific community over the as-yet-unpublished suppositions of Velikovsky, a Russian-born physician and psychoanalyst. His theories concerned the manner in which the earth gained its physical characteristics, and they created debate in scientific circles reminiscent of that over Charles Darwin's theories on evolution. Depending on one's viewpoint, *Harper's* record in presenting the issues stands as a model of calm courage and detachment despite highly influential opposition or as a sensationalized and irresponsible blasphemy upon years of work by careful scientists.

Velikovsky sought to prove that the earth had undergone repeated catastrophes which had folded its crust, displaced the seas, decimated life, and even reversed the magnetic poles; that several of these catastrophic events had occurred within historical times as verified independently by legends and the ancient writings of different peoples from all over the world (and cited by Velikovsky as part of his evidence); and that the most recent events occurred as a result of the newborn planet Venus (sprung from Jupiter) swinging wildly near the earth's path before settling into orbit. If true, Velikovsky's sweeping theories would revolutionize and even negate scientific doctrines built up over years of research.

After Velikovsky's long search for a publisher, the Macmillan Company accepted the manuscript after much agonizing. Allen, ever alert to the possibility of printing excerpts from important books, obtained galley proofs and asked Eric Larrabee to prepare a condensation.

234

Larrabee at first was reluctant, and nearly a year passed before he completed the complicated task of summing up the far-ranging book.[40] When the article, "The Day the Earth Stood Still," finally appeared in January 1950, it created an immediate sensation. Within days the issue sold out.[41] In the popular mind the article seemed to be a heartening scientific substantiation of many Old Testament miracles such as Moses and the Israelites crossing the Red Sea.

Upon publication in April in book form, Velikovsky's *Worlds in Collision* quickly headed the nation's bestselling nonfiction list. The scientific community, led by Harlow Shapley, director of the Harvard College Observatory, launched a vigorous attack against Velikovsky and those who deigned to publish him. Macmillan, threatened by a boycott of its books, turned over the rights to Doubleday, and fired James Putnam, the editor who had been chiefly instrumental in causing the firm to publish the book. Gordon A. Atwater, curator of the Hayden Planetarium and director of the Astronomy Department of the American Museum of Natural History, resigned both of these posts under pressure because he had favorably acknowledged *Worlds in Collision.*

Readers claimed that *Harper's* had been "had," that it suffered from an "atrocious lack of good judgment," that the editors had insulted "every sound scientist in this country," that the article constituted a "serious disservice to the cause of science, history, and religion," that the old warfare between science and theology had been reopened, and that it cast suspicion on all articles appearing in the magazine.[42] Other magazines—the *New Yorker, Time,* and *Newsweek*—took varying positions on judging *Harper's* for its treatment of *Worlds in Collision.*

Allen decided to tie the dispute still closer to the magazine by having a scientist debate Velikovsky via printed page. Shapley, as well as others, declined Allen's offer, but John Q. Stewart, a Princeton astronomical physicist, accepted the challenge. In June 1951, the debate between Velikovsky and Stewart appeared under the title "Velikovsky and His Critics." An introductory editors' note criticized the scientists' attack on Velikovsky. "A theory so revolutionary ought to be met by careful appraisal rather than by denunciation and boycott."[43]

The October 1950 edition of *Harper's* celebrated the magazine's one hundredth anniversary with a three-hundred-page issue.[44] It was more than three years in the making. In the spring of 1947, Allen proposed a special anniversary issue of 144 or 160 pages instead of the usual 96. John Kouwenhoven began planning, and as 1950 drew nearer, the size of the issue grew larger. Illustrated throughout, it recounted the colorful past of *Harper's* and the American nation as well. All the authors most familiar to the magazine's readers were represented: Allen, DeVoto, Lynes, Kouwenhoven, Grattan, Elmer Davis, Langwiesche, Rebecca West, Gerald W. Johnson, and Richard Rovere. Philip Hamburger, Thomas Mann, and Roger Burlingame also contributed nonfiction. William Faulkner, long absent from *Harper's* pages, returned with a short story, "A Name for the City," and Katherine Anne Porter also contributed fiction. Poetry came from W. H. Auden and Peter Viereck. A congratulatory letter from President Harry S. Truman occupied a full page, and the State Department purchased, sight unseen, 10,000 copies of the issue for distribution to its overseas embassies and consulates.[45]

Many articles over the years introduced elements into American life and thought, or defined them for the first time. Walter Prescott Webb's frontier boom thesis was first expanded in *Harper's*. The initial explanation of "Technocracy" in *Harper's* in 1933 helped that subject become one of the fads of the day. In June 1940, the discovery of atomic power was delineated for the first time in any magazine; despite the weeks of preparation required for the publication of a monthly magazine, the *Harper's* article had trailed newspaper stories only by a few days. Before the Kinsey Report had been released in full, *Harper's* already had published a thorough account of its findings.[46]

There could be little doubt that the magazine's influence on public opinion was significant through its "opinion-maker" readers. Measuring that influence precisely was more difficult. Dave Frederick, general manager of the magazine's business operations, aptly called the publication "an ignition system in the engine of American public opinion."[47]

One justification for such a self-flattering comment was the *Harper's* audience. A survey in the early 1950s showed 71 percent of the readers to be college graduates. *Harper's* findings indicated that an extraordinary number of these readers were persons who wrote, spoke, taught, preached, edited, managed, or governed. While the magazine's circulation (159,000 in 1951) was minuscule compared to that of, say, *Reader's Digest*, its particular audience made its influence disproportionate to its circulation.[48]

The magazine never earned large profits for Harper & Brothers. Cass Canfield has said that over a period of twenty-five years the magazine's profits totaled just about zero.[49] After World War II, which had been a prosperous era, the magazine's economic situation declined. Large circulation gains in 1947 were accompanied by financial losses rather than profits.[50] Allen cited climbing printing costs and reduced advertising as the culprits, and although the magazine's economics were basically outside his responsibility, he told Hildegarde, "This weighs on me heavily."[51] While Harper & Brothers could afford the magazine's red ink, Allen realized that the financial showing needed to improve because "it would be most unhealthy if the magazine were to operate at a deficit year after year." The *Atlantic* apparently was in worse shape, in danger of folding, Allen believed. He confided to Hildegarde that a merger of *Harper's* and the *Atlantic* had been suggested, but Harper & Brothers had said no "in sympathetic tones." *Harper's* could not afford the *Atlantic's* mounting debts.

And if the Atlantic should fold up, the position of *Harper's* will be pretty lonely, as the one remaining magazine of an old group; uniqueness has its advantages, but not in getting advertising. So there's a lot to be thought out.[52]

Despite what might have been assumed to be a natural rivalry, the editors of the two magazines were very close. Allen and Edward Weeks often exchanged notes about their progress, and occasionally they forwarded manuscripts to each other. So friendly were the two that Allen even wrote two articles for the *Atlantic* during his long association with *Harper's*.[53]

Not only were the two magazines similar in intent, content, and appearance, but both were published by the same printer, Rumford Press of Concord, New Hampshire. With the July 1948 issue, however, *Harper's* switched to the Williams Press in Albany, New York. The move cut about $35,000 a year in printing costs, and it was accompanied by other changes: a larger page, larger typefaces, and broader margins.[54]

Shortly after acquiring a new printer, the magazine made another move to improve its shaky financial situation. The 30 percent gain in circulation since the last full war year had strained *Harper's* distributing techniques, and beginning in August 1948, the Curtis Publishing Company agreed to distribute the magazine. Curtis had its own distribution network, and it easily could accommodate the modest circulation of *Harper's*. *Harper's* was eager to increase its newsstand sales, which had been averaging 25,000 per issue, and Allen was disappointed when sales did not double within three months under the Curtis arrangement.[55]

In 1952 *Harper's* and the *Atlantic*, long plagued with the burden of competing against gigantic, mass-appeal publications for advertising revenue, merged advertising forces in an organization called Harper-Atlantic Sales. Harper-Atlantic salesmen could sell advertising for both magazines. Surveys had shown surprisingly that only a few persons read both publications, and thus the advertiser who bought space in both magazines was not repeating his message to the same audience. Advertising volume in both magazines increased significantly in future years as a result of the merger.[56]

But by the time the advertising sales were united, *Harper's* already had begun its climb back to solvency. By mid-1950, the magazine was losing less money than before, and Allen hoped that by year's end it would be breaking even.[57] A year later he told contributor Louis Cassels, who was complaining because of the meager two hundred fifty dollars he had been paid for an article, that the magazine now was running "narrowly and precariously in the black." He consoled Cassels about the small payment by offering solace that publication in *Harper's* often turned out to be "indirectly pretty remunerative" because of its prestige.[58]

In addition to the alliances with the Curtis Publishing Company and the *Atlantic, Harper's* and Allen always had a close working relationship with DeWitt Wallace and the *Reader's Digest,* where Agnes had started working after the war. Soon after Allen joined *Harper's* in 1923, Wallace had come into the office to seek permission to reprint *Harper's* articles in his new digest, and Allen had looked on the project dubiously. "If you had told me Wallace was headed for a huge success, I'd have said you were crazy. Who would want to read warmed-over material a month late?"[59]

Eventually a contract between the two magazines afforded the *Reader's Digest* the privilege of condensing any *Harper's* articles it pleased. Besides the flat fee for condensation rights, the *Digest* also made separate payment to the author, invariably much larger than *Harper's* payment for the original article.

In 1941 a reader submitted to Allen his own reply to a *Harper's* article condensed in the latest *Digest.* Allen responded: "We should consider publishing it in some form were it not for one odd fact. That article originally appeared in *Harper's* in the 1920's!" He explained that the *Digest* sometimes picked up old articles without indicating their antiquity. "If it contains any reference to President Coolidge or the booming stock market, they just cut that out."[60]

By the time Allen resigned as editor in 1953, the magazine had been converted gradually to something akin to its present modern appearance. None of the changes had come overnight—the most immediately obvious one had been the bigger page format. The pen and ink illustrations that had crept into the magazine during World War II as maps and charts blossomed afterwards to become integral to many articles and stories. In 1952 a subdued illustration was placed on the cover for the first time; it took a decided secondary role to the article headings, but the cover sketches soon grew to predominate. Internally, more white space and larger typefaces, com-

239

bined with the sketches, gave the pages an appearance far removed from the dull pages of the 1930s. As for content, Allen made no startling changes. After the war, however, articles began to emphasize as they never had done before issues confronting the United States with a concurrent decline in attention to European affairs. International articles invariably included the United States' involvement and responsibilities. The magazine's historical emphasis on literary matters continued to play a secondary role to current events; still, some of the nation's most distinguished short fiction appeared as a matter of course in *Harper's*.

20

RESUMING A WRITING CAREER

One night several weeks after Japan surrendered, Allen and Agnes
were chatting about the epochal events and outstanding personalities
of the past few years. Suddenly, it occurred to Allen that he should
write a biography of Franklin D. Roosevelt. The more he talked,
the more logical it seemed. He knew well the general history of
the period; he was acquainted with many of the persons whom a
biographer would have to approach for personal data. Furthermore,
he knew intimately the Groton-Harvard background from which
both Roosevelt and he had sprung. The next day at the office, Allen
casually mentioned the idea to Cass Canfield and Edward Aswell,
editor in chief of books for the Harper firm. Allen was delighted
when they "ignited furiously: said it was a natural."[1]

He had not attempted a book since the completion in 1939 of
Since Yesterday. Both the war and his new duties as editor in chief
had demanded his full attention. Except for his contributions to
Harper's on war-related topics, he had given up free-lance writing.
Now the time seemed appropriate to resume a dual role: editor by
day and writer by night.

Encouraged by the enthusiastic office response to the proposed biography, Allen began laying plans. He had a good idea of the formidable task before him. "Lord, what a raft of material, what hornet's nests of conflicting interpretations! And maybe ten other people will be going at Roosevelt biographies. Yet I kind of think it's my meat."[2]

As was his custom, Allen purchased a ledger book and drew up in it his tentative schedule of background reading and an outline of the planned work. From January 1, 1946 to April 1, he would read both secondary works and memoirs of persons who had been close to Roosevelt. The next three months would involve detailed research and personal interviews. For nine months beginning July 1, he planned to write a chapter a month, taking perhaps one week a month away from the office. The book would open with a chapter entitled "The End of a Career," built around the attack of poliomyelitis. Flashbacks would illuminate Roosevelt's background and his prior achievements. Specific incidents would dramatize each of the nine chapters. Allen noted that "reading & study should disclose what are the best scenes to pivot the chapters on. They should be, so far as possible, both characteristic scenes and real turning points, as a dramatist might see them."

One notation summed up the central theme as well as Allen's final assessment of Franklin D. Roosevelt. Despite FDR's "frequent glib departures from the truth, his incapacity to understand economic policies, his shortcomings in administration," he was great because of his "contagious ability as a cheerer and persuader," his "sympathy for people: a genuinely friendly feeling," and his "judgment of forces—forces of public opinion and, subsequently, military forces, too." Allen added that Hitler had possessed a judgment of forces and lost it, while the Japanese "utterly lacked" it.[3]

Allen obtained Roosevelt's school record at Groton and the medical reports of his hospitalization after the polio attack, but he proceeded no further. Perhaps the preparatory work had acted as a catharsis; he had analyzed the former President to his satisfaction in his own preliminary outline, and there seemed to be little need to plow over the ground that had occupied him continuously as an editor and writer since 1932. Later, when he learned that John Gunther was doing research for a biography of Roosevelt, he lent the medical records to him.[4]

Another project had captured Allen's attention—once again, a picture book with Agnes as co-author. Work on it began in the summer of 1946 and was completed before the year's end for fall 1947 publication. Agnes again "assembled" the book and Allen provided the running commentary in captions accompanying the photographs. The book was called *I Remember Distinctly: A Family Album of the American People, 1918–1941*.[5] As the Allens described it, it was "a panorama of American life during the years of peace from 1918 to 1941, ranging from politics and business to fashions, sports, famous crimes, entertainments, and popular fads."[6] Without apology the book was a frothy recapitulation of the twenties and thirties, stressing the picturesque rather than the significant. Almost every important and colorful personality of the period was portrayed, and the Allens earned more than twenty-five thousand dollars for their best-seller.[7]

After *I Remember Distinctly*, Allen's interest was renewed in a biographical subject: J. Pierpont Morgan. In *The Lords of Creation*, he had made Morgan the central figure, and Allen said this gave him the idea for the Morgan biography.

Believing that the extant biographies of Morgan were inadequate, Allen went to work to provide a detached study of the Wall Street financier. He dated the customary ledger book April 26, 1947. For a while he felt the study might result in a magazine series rather than a book, and not until February 1948, did he inform Canfield that it definitely would be book-length.[8]

Allen contacted top officials of the Morgan firm to obtain reminiscences and company records. He wrote to Thomas W. Lamont in Maine, and, with apologies, asked if he might visit him to probe his memory. He told Lamont that he hoped to convey a sense of Morgan's background, the traditions he represented in his way of life, the way in which his great collections of art objects and his philanthropy fitted into the social and cultural pattern of the time, and the manner in which he exercised authority. "I should like to show as vividly as possible the whole pattern of his life as representing the power and splendor of finance capital at its apogee." Whether it might be considered favorable to Morgan or unfavorable he did not know; "all I can say is that I would try to make it as true an interpretation as possible and that I regard him as a fascinating and impressive figure."[9]

Lamont replied to "Dear Freddie" that he would be happy to have him visit, and soon he sought to correct what he considered to be one of the most flagrant distortions of Morgan the man: the impression that he was a tyrant.[10] The reputation had stemmed from such descriptions as Lincoln Steffens' statement that even partners in the firm did not go near Morgan, and when called by him they "looked alarmed and darted in like office-boys."[11]

After visiting with Lamont, Allen notified Morgan's grandson, Junius S. Morgan, about his intentions to write his grandfather's life story.[12] Morgan, R. Gordon Wasson, and Leonhard A. Keyes, all House of Morgan officials, agreed to cooperate, and they permitted Allen to study for the first time many of the firm's records and papers.

In September 1948, Allen took a one-month leave to complete and polish the manuscript, and by late October he had finished. His own suggested title, *The Great Pierpont Morgan*, prevailed over the Harper & Brothers choice, "The Great J. P.," which Allen complained sounded "a little too breezy, too flip . . . as if it were one of the slick Hearsty books that are put out from time to time." Besides, he argued, to most people under forty a reference merely to J. P. Morgan really meant J. P. Morgan, Jr., "the man with the midget."[13] A stern-looking portrait of Morgan taken by photographer Edward Steichen adorned the cover. After being excerpted by both *Harper's* and *Life,* the book went on sale in the spring.[14] It was soon on best-seller lists, yet Allen was disappointed; sales totaled just 20,000. "I suppose my point of view on him was not sufficiently pro or con to make the book a football for discussion."[15]

Critics generally praised Allen's even-handed assessment of Morgan and his personality. He emphasized the character, integrity, and good intentions of the man, believing that whatever the faults of the economic system which Morgan helped to fashion, he had acted upon high intentions. As Allen stated in the book's Preface:

Pierpont Morgan was a man with whom I would have disagreed strongly on most political and economic issues if I had been his contemporary. To me he represented a trend in the direction of economic affairs which had to be altered for the good of the country. But I am also convinced that he was a man great in character and force, whose immense influence was in many respects salutary.[16]

He sought to show Morgan as a product of the privileged background and traditions to which he belonged. Some readers, Allen predicted correctly, would believe he had naïvely followed the testimony of Morgan's admirers, while others would insist he followed too closely the reasoning of his detractors.

Even though Allen did more primary research for Morgan's biography than for his other works, he included, as was his custom, only chapter notes on sources and obligations, omitting footnotes. Publisher Alfred A. Knopf, while paying his compliments on a "fine job," complained to Allen about being "gun shy" of footnotes. Trying to tie the sources at the back of the book with the text, he said, "is exasperating to the nth degree." Knopf also asked Allen what disease caused Morgan's death.

I can understand reticence in the case of a certain celebrated actress and other ladies [a reference probably to actress Maxine Elliott, who accompanied Morgan on his yacht], but I don't see why a biographer should presume a reader's knowledge of his subject's passing from this happy world comparable to his knowledge of how the subject came to enter it.[17]

Allen confessed that he really did not know what caused Morgan's death, that he had simply thought of it as a "general collapse." "This makes me feel like an extremely amateur biographer." As for the lack of footnotes, Allen said he believed that placing them at the bottom of pages was "cumbersome and rather forbidding to most readers."[18]

The book's most important achievement was the study of Morgan's personality; yet Allen also unveiled new information as a result of his being allowed access to many important records of the House of Morgan. Most significantly, he provided substantial new information about Morgan's role in stemming the depletion of U.S. gold in the financial crisis of 1895, settling finally the wide-ranging speculations about the firm's exact profits in the controversial bond issue made through agreement with the federal government.[19]

Morgan officials were pleased with the generally favorable biography. Leonhard Keyes complained only about a passage in which Allen said Morgan had winked at a graft payment, and he suggested to Allen before publication that the incident be changed. Allen penciled in his own terse reminder on the letter, "no change." Despite the one complaint, Keyes said he felt a "deep sense of gratitude" to Allen for writing so well about "my late beloved chief, John Pierpont Morgan."[20]

The Morgan biography echoed Allen's father's penchant that "the other hand" be shown. Charges of prejudice in his book indicated to Allen that he had succeeded in being objective, for the criticism ranged from accusations that he was too sympathetic to Morgan to comments that he was not kind enough.

Hollywood, now in an age of movie biographies, approached Allen about a film based on his book. Allen expressed a willingness to discuss the matter, but he remained lukewarm because he doubted a film could be made that would not distort Morgan unduly, and the movie never materialized.[21]

Because of his enormous success at recapitulating the twenties and thirties, Allen was expected to duplicate the feat for the forties. But he balked at repeating himself as a "sort of ten year locust."[22] He had in mind at the conclusion of the forties a more ambitious project, an assessment of the meaning for Americans of the changes that had taken place since 1900.

The many critics of American society, both right and left, who despaired of recent developments for different reasons, irritated Allen, and he wanted to answer them. Some of the critics were well-heeled conservative friends who complained of Washington politics; others were intellectual friends who deprecated the dominance of the "mass mind." Allen admitted that, because of his own nature, if he had been surrounded by optimists instead of critics he probably would emphasize the dangers and difficulties facing the nation rather than accomplishments and possibilities. "My bias was that of the judicial-minded man who thinks that the time has come to say, 'Yes, but on the other hand. . . .' "[23]

Allen had another didactic purpose in writing his next book: to show that when Russian leaders berated the United States government as a pawn of Wall Street financiers, they were describing the America of 1900 instead of 1950. Many basic alterations in American society since 1900 had not been fully grasped by most Americans, either, Allen believed.[24]

He began planning the book in late 1950, and he wrote it during 1951 and early 1952 with the culminating push coming during a month's leave from the office in January 1952. As had been the case with *Only Yesterday,* the book sprang from a magazine article, "The Big Change," written especially for *Harper's* centennial edition.[25]

He divided the text into three sections. The first, "The Old Order," described the wide gulf at the beginning of the century between rich and poor, the power of Wall Street, and the weakness of the federal government, the elite living patterns of prosperous families, the unique role held by women, and the distinctively lower status of the masses.

The second part, "The Momentum of Change," explained what altered the old order: the rise of the muckrakers and Progressivism, the women's rights and suffrage movement, mass production, the automobile, changes in manners and morals, the Depression and the New Deal, the professionalization of business, World War II, advances in diet and medicine, and growing rights and opportunities for Negroes.

Part three, "The New America," described the nation at mid-century: the remarkable narrowing of economic and social gaps between upper and lower classes, wider distribution of necessities and luxuries through mass production, and broader cultural opportunities for everyone through movies, magazines, books, and broadcasting.

What had happened in the half century, Allen concluded, was a democratization of the economic system, an adjustment of capitalism toward democratic ends. The expansion of industry and business had combined with a series of political, social, and economic forces to alter not only the standard of living but also the average American's way of thinking and his status as a citizen. The expansion of purchasing power among the poor had opened a new economic frontier which augured well. "If you thus bring advantages to a great lot of previously underprivileged people, they will rise to their opportunities and, by and large, will become responsible citizens."[26] This was the foundation on which Allen based his liberal optimism on the perfectibility of man. His review of the half century convinced him that economic, educational, and cultural opportunities had been greatly expanded; thus, the very nature of man was reaching a higher level. In simple economic terms, the United States was not evolving *toward* socialism, as so many believed, but was moving *past* it to something better. The economic changes undergirded all cultural and social change, he was convinced.

The Big Change: America Transforms Itself, 1900–1950 achieved instant popular success when it appeared in 1952. *Saturday Review* highlighted it with a lengthy review and a cover portrait of Allen. For the second time the Book-of-the-Month Club chose an Allen book as its monthly selection.[27] Book-club sales alone totaled 170,000, and the regular Harper & Brothers edition sold 122,600 copies.[28]

Its optimistic tone attracted the attention of State Department officials as a good explanation of the American way of life. When the centennial edition article had appeared, the State Department had obtained Allen's permission to reprint it in the Russian language magazine *Amerika* and in its India edition of *Free World*.[29] Now, the department's Information Service was inspired to interpret the book's message to its entire overseas audience, and a kit of articles, pictures, and posters illustrating the Allen theme was prepared for distribution to sixty-five U.S. Information posts abroad.[30]

Reviews generally were laudatory, and Allen learned proudly that both corporate and labor officers found reason to advise their associates to read the book. Frequent commentary about *The Big Change* echoed Bernard DeVoto's belief that it should be required reading for despairing intellectuals.[31]

Of all Allen's works, this final, most inclusive effort is less enduring in retrospect than his earlier books. Allen's optimism about the progress and future of American society today seems excessive. Economic and social discrepancies continued between classes and races of people in the next decade, leading to great urban disorders that indicated a long-term malaise unnoticed by Allen. Allen's unduly optimistic outlook may be seen in his chapter "Old Ark A'Moverin,' " describing what he felt to be rapidly improving race relations through broader civil rights, integration of higher education in the South, significantly reduced illiteracy, and economic uplift arising from World War II. Allen saw no overnight miracles, but he was satisfied that the "battleground of opinion" was moving slowly to a location less disadvantageous to the Negro. What Allen and others understandably failed to consider was the theory of revolution of rising expectations, although he did note "little prospect" that discrimination would "move toward a solution without further friction and mutual antagonism."[32] His mild note of warning, however, was all but lost in a chapter filled with notations of accomplishments made in race relations.

Before publication, Allen had sent his chapter on race relations to Walter White, long-time secretary of the National Association for the Advancement of Colored People, for criticism. White responded optimistically, "It is an excellent—even a remarkable summary." White even thought Allen had underplayed improvement in the media in their portrayals of the Negro. He criticized the chapter in two respects. He disagreed with Allen's view that the decline in lynching was the result of a moral regeneration; White credited it to persistent agitation for federal anti-lynching legislation. (Allen

jotted down the word "no" next to the statement in White's letter.)
White also felt Allen was too gradualist concerning the proper pace
of integration, and Allen promised to think "long and hard" about
this.[33]

Upon publication, Allen's second cousin, Alfred Baker Lewis,
criticized him for failing even to mention the NAACP. "It shows
a serious lack of understanding of how the social changes you mention in this chapter were actually brought about." Allen chastised
himself for the omission as well, noting on Lewis' letter, "And I
showed it to White."[34] It was an embarrassing oversight.

Allen's outlook as a man who held "enlightened" views on race relations and who was committed to racial equality offers an interesting
insight into the liberal mind as it existed prior to the 1954 Supreme
Court's Brown vs. Topeka decision. He appears to be somewhat
typical of the reformist, New Deal-oriented mind that did not isolate
the problem of Negro inequality as an immediate priority. As an
editor, Allen could point to a number of bold articles which attacked
discrimination. The *Harper's* stance on racial equality was widely
understood, and articles sympathetic to the Negro cause invariably
prompted segregationist attacks. Still, Allen generally followed an
attitude of not wishing to agitate unnecessarily the racial situation for
fear of disturbing progress already being made.

When Virginius Dabney of the *Richmond Times-Dispatch* offered
an explicit manuscript about growing bitterness among Southern
Negroes and the possibility of some sort of outbreak during World
War II, Allen wanted to print it but declined after much discussion
for fear the article might create trouble. He admired Dabney's spirit,
his willingness to face the abuse which surely would come his way
as a white Southerner, and he did not deny that the situation was
acute and must not be ignored. Yet, he preferred to follow the advice
of experts on racial problems (one was George Havell of the Council
for Democracy) who told him that the best way the tense situation
could be handled was "for responsible Negroes to work among their
own people, and particularly with the press."[35]

About a year later W. E. B. Du Bois submitted a manuscript about race relations. Allen indicated to Du Bois that such matters ought to be postponed until after the war.

I must confess that I personally am somewhat uneasy about your most interesting and sober and thoughtful discussion of segregation and inter-marriage toward the close of the manuscript. This topic does not often get this sort of discussion and ought to have it, and yet I am uneasy about provoking the discussion just now. . . . In view of the present tension in many places I have been wondering whether this discussion had not better be adjourned for the time being while we concentrate on those matters on which men of good will of both races can work together with the least sense that they are playing with dynamite. Maybe this is a timid attitude, especially for a journalist, but I have had so strong a feeling that the need of the moment is to concentrate upon the things on which we can agree and to defer wrangles on other points that I am inclined to take this attitude even as an editor.[36]

Allen still remained cautious, however, after the war's end. Barry Bingham of the *Courier-Journal* in Louisville proposed an article about successful undergraduate integration at the University of Louisville, which he said was the first institution in the South to admit Negroes on the same basis as whites. All the predictions of student resentment, incidents, and other misfortunes had proved unjustified. "It seems that the college generation in this part of the South are far ahead of their parents and grandparents on the race issue, as many of us suspected," Bingham said. Allen declined the proposal. It should be delayed, he thought, at least until the con-clusion of the first full year because publicity about integration in a magazine which Southerners surely would consider "Northern" might arouse some "sleeping dogs" who would cause trouble.[37]

Allen unquestionably had the best intentions in his belief that undue publicity of racial situations would stir up racists and create tension which could only harm the advances already being made by Negroes. Editors throughout the mass media seldom matched even *Harper's* attempts to explore critically racial discrimination, though, and the effect ultimately was a virtual exclusion of material on minorities.[38]

251

On one occasion Allen directly used his personal influence to combat an instance of discrimination against a Jew at the Harvard Club in New York City. Harold Solomon, a Jewish classmate of Oliver's at Harvard, was denied membership in the club without explanation in 1948. The exclusion distressed Oliver, and Allen sent a letter to the club saying he could not resist concluding that Solomon had been rejected by the admissions committee on racial grounds; he threatened his own resignation in protest. "Generally speaking, a club has a right to reject for membership whom it pleases," he wrote. "If a club bears the name of Harvard, however, its membership policy can hardly help being subject to a different principle."[39]

Allen thought such a protest from a Harvard overseer, a long-time member of the club, and a well-known editor and author would carry some weight. Resignation by such a member because of alleged discrimination would have received considerable publicity, and Allen preferred not to resign as long as there was a chance the committee might reverse itself. He hesitated, too, to take steps to draw Solomon into the publicity. So Allen confined his actions to the letter. No resignation occurred, and several years later the club admitted Solomon to membership.[40]

Allen continued, as always, to write magazine articles. Usually they were for *Harper's,* but not exclusively. In "This Time and Last Time," he contrasted the immediate postwar events of both conflagrations, hoping history might teach some lessons. He likened the Red scare of 1919 and 1920 to the House Un-American Activities Committee's probings into radicalism; he saw evidence that a literary renaissance similar to that of the twenties might be on the horizon; and he ended the article with a curt reminder that one important difference distinguished the two eras: there had been no atomic bomb after the First World War.[41]

Several pieces derived from *The Big Change.* For *Life* magazine in January 1953, Allen restated with added vigor his hopes and admiration of the new American system of life. "A major factor in our new prosperity," he wrote, "is that we are constantly redistributing the national income into the pockets of the less prosperous."[42] For those who were not sharing in the general prosperity, Allen pointed to "all manner of relief measures and free services which simply did not exist a generation ago." The nation had experienced a bloodless social revolution which had expanded the purchasing power of the formerly poor. Moreover, the new technology had released many people from formerly exhausting and dreary jobs. The good news about America, Allen concluded, was that the problems for which socialism and Communism were devised already had been surmounted in the United States. It was a system which not only helped the underdog but which maintained free enterprise "without the stultification that bureaucratic management might cause, or the threat of tyranny that government control might bring."[43]

In a paper presented at about the same time, Allen offered a revision of his earlier expressed theories on the broad scope of history and also continued with the theme of economic plenty. In 1938 he had cited the period of World War I as the pivotal point in American history. Now, speaking before the Columbia University-sponsored American Assembly, he contrasted his own judgment with that of Henry Steele Commager (who believed the 1890s to be the watershed of modern American life and thought) and chose the early 1930s as the time of transition. Those critical years, he thought, brought forth a lasting change in American attitudes toward economic and political institutions. He cited the widespread acceptance of Social Security and other schemes to insure individual security from the vagaries of economic caprice; a new conviction that the federal government held a responsibility for the welfare of its citizens; a realization that the fortunes of all Americans, rich and poor, were inextricably interlocked; and the reliance by individuals to an increasing degree on governmental or private institutions.[44]

There remained a significant number of Americans, Allen acknowledged, who were not protected by the new security measures, and the problem of caring for this large group represented the nation's most acute and pressing problem.[45] His expressed concern for the underprivileged was reminiscent of his often stated conviction that unemployment must be conquered fully before the Depression could be considered over. His description of poverty, though, as a sort of bouncing ball that struck one and then another person, ran counter to later theories of an endless chain that seemed to tie generation after generation of certain families to poverty. Although Allen still had a deep concern for those outside the growing circles of abundance, his economic thought now contrasted significantly with his beliefs of the 1930s. But, then, so did that of most Americans.

21

HARVARD OVERSEER

In addition to his other interests, Allen spent many days and hours on a job which, judging by the fullness of his correspondence, amounted almost to a full-time occupation: his role as a Harvard overseer. Time-consuming though it was, he participated in it with genuine interest and enthusiasm. He served a six-year term from 1942 to 1948 and was elected in 1950 to a second term. He became closely involved in a number of Harvard activities, especially as chairman of the committee charged with overseeing the Harvard University Press. His latter years as an overseer encompassed a critical and tense period for the university as a whole because Senator Joseph R. McCarthy chose Harvard as a special target of investigation for harboring Communists.

Allen intimately viewed Harvard from several different perspectives over the years. Having participated in Harvard life as a student, he next saw it from another point of view as an English instructor. Then, after World War I, he was part of the Harvard community as the secretary to the Corporation who organized the school's first publicity office.

The double project of democratizing the student body and stressing intellectual achievement, which Lowell had begun to push during Allen's undergraduate days, had come a long way even since Allen's return to Harvard as secretary from 1919 to 1923. Edward S. Harkness' ten-million-dollar donation in 1928 enabled Harvard to adopt a system of "houses" in which undergraduates of varied backgrounds and interests lived and studied together with resident tutors and masters.[1] Harvard also now was much closer to being a truly national university. By 1945 only 49 percent of incoming freshmen were from New England.[2]

In the great debate as to the proper direction of higher education—toward the specialization which science seemed to indicate or to a return to the classical values expressed in the "great books"—Harvard sought to achieve a balance. The widely read 1945 report by a faculty committee, *General Education in a Free Society*, urged a reconciliation between the heritage of the past and the new directions deriving from the sciences.[3] Yet, the report offered no firm blueprint, and as the postwar jump in college enrollment came Harvard had no firm answers itself on how best to answer the educational needs of the day.

The Board of Overseers was one of the two central governing bodies of Harvard. The other, the more dominant Corporation composed of the President and Fellows, maintained immediate control of finances and executive management, but many of its policy decisions and appointments were subject to the overseers' consent. The overseers participated more intimately in school affairs through so-called visiting committees charged with scrutinizing the various faculties and departments and making broad recommendations. Overseers served as chairmen of the several committees, whose membership included alumni, and at least once a year they made oral reports to the full Board of Overseers. Every three years they rendered written reports.[4]

At various times Allen served as chairman of committees for the history department, department of social relations, department of English, and the Harvard University Press. The frequent visits to

Cambridge to fulfill his duties were enjoyable occasions. Usually he stayed with his sister, Hildegarde, giving Allen opportunity to visit relatives and old friends. President James B. Conant, a long-time friend, often extended Allen an invitation to stay at his home while in Cambridge.

Allen participated most in Harvard affairs through his chairmanship of the Committee to Visit the Harvard University Press. The Harvard University Press, despite its prestige and apparent success, faced difficult problems after the war. President Conant was dubious about its very existence; the problem of defining a university press's role had not been solved to anyone's satisfaction; the director was retiring after considerable irritation over relationships with the administration; and there was constant concern about sufficient funds.

University presses in America had been late in developing, not appearing until the late nineteenth century. The first press was established at Cornell in 1869, and by the time Harvard founded its own press in 1913, only nine others existed.[5] At Harvard and elsewhere the economics of scholarly publishing—high costs and limited audiences—dictated a dependence on subsidies. By 1946, when Allen became chairman of the University Press Committee, the Harvard University Press was issuing some sixty new titles each year.

"Staggered" by the appointment but willing to assume the position because of his interest, Allen went to Cambridge on a Sunday night in October to learn about the Press's problems. Roger L. Scaife, director of the Press, told Allen that his staff was depleted; the faculty's goodwill had been lost and only partially recovered; printing was done off-campus by commercial firms; the printing office and press were operated separately when they should be under one administrative head; there was no endowment; and Scaife himself was due to retire, although no successor was in sight. The only good news seemed to be that the press was operating in the black—at the moment.[6]

The next day, President Conant startled Allen by telling him that he had always been dubious about the Harvard University Press because he felt it inappropriate for a department of the university to be engaged in business. Furthermore, he thought the press needlessly diverted its energies by publishing much unworthy scholarly material merely because of academic departmental pressure and by printing material which should be reserved for commercial publishers. Conant also expressed concern that the Board of Syndics, the faculty governing body for the Press, was not sufficiently knowledgeable about the financial matters involved. He admitted to Allen his own lack of knowledge about publishing, and he hoped Allen could provide some guidance. A final damper on Allen's enthusiasm was that Conant was not pleased with the fund-raising drive initiated by Roy Larsen, past chairman of the University Press Committee.[7]

The drive, called "The Friends of the Harvard University Press," was an effort to obtain financial backing from individuals to subsidize specific books. Members of the "Friends" could contribute in units of one hundred dollars for publishing specific books on the pending list, or could simply donate for unspecified books. Such subsidies, prospective donors were informed, would make possible the issuing of books which were "of the utmost importance from a scholarly viewpoint but which cannot be expected to produce a monetary gain."[8]

Conant felt that the fund-raising project should be delayed until Scaife's successor had an opportunity to formulate his own policies and an overall fund-raiser for the university could be hired. "Neither I nor the Corporation are willing to bless this particular undertaking at this time," Conant wrote to Allen.[9]

Allen deferred to Conant's wishes, but Scaife expressed great dissatisfaction. He implored Allen in vain to seek a reversal of the decision. Scaife had not long to complain, for a new director replaced him on July 1, 1947. He was Thomas J. Wilson, director of the University of North Carolina Press and formerly associated with Henry Holt & Co.

In May, after discussions and one lengthy committee meeting attended by the Board of Syndics and both Scaife and Wilson, Allen reported to the Board of Overseers a number of committee conclusions about the Press. It should continue to function as a department of the university, but with its business operations supervised by a newly appointed business board of directors. The Board of Syndics should continue to advise in editorial matters. Despite some doubts about the legitimacy of a press operation as a university function, as expressed by Conant, the committee believed "selling knowledge" to be legitimate: after all, teaching departments also "sold knowledge" through tuition fees. Possible competition with commercial houses was not to be a consideration, following the enunciation years earlier by Professor Ralph Barton Perry that the Press's only limitations should be scholarly validity and the ability to do an effective job of bringing the book before its public. The committee believed that because of the expensive nature of book publishing, the Press was to be commended for studying other possibilities for reproducing scholarly documents. Furthermore, committee members hoped to be able to resume their own fund-raising drives.[10]

Soon the embargo on "The Friends of the Harvard University Press" was lifted as requested, and before Allen's first term as overseer expired, letters of invitation to a carefully chosen list of one hundred persons had been mailed and a number of affirmative responses received.[11] In his 1948 oral report to the overseers, Allen announced that the Press's confused financial relationship to the university had been cleared, a successful transition had been made under the new director, and the "Friends" fund-raising project had begun with high hopes.[12]

Before his six-year term ended in 1948, Allen had chaired two other committees that were concerned with aspects of academic life. His first significant attempt to shape Harvard's educational programs came in his capacity as chairman of the Visiting Committee on the Summer School and University Extension, a responsibility rendered more significant by the massive return of war veterans to civilian life. He became convinced that Harvard had a responsibility to educate not just young students who had had no professional experience, but adults who needed a revitalization of their intellects by returning to an academic setting removed from the restricting ties of daily work. What he envisioned was a program similar to that of the Nieman

Fellows, which allowed experienced journalists to spend a year at Harvard at mid-career. With this thought, Allen wrote to the deans of the law, business, and medical schools to inquire into their postwar plans for adult education. After much correspondence, meetings with various deans and faculty members, and sessions of the committee, Allen submitted in behalf of the committee a special seven-page report in the spring of 1945. The report recommended expansion of continuing education programs on a small, quality scale so as to benefit "special groups of mature men and women of unusual ability and importance to the community" rather than broader programs of lesser quality. Aside from the standard arguments in favor of refresher training, he pointed out his belief that Harvard needed to get involved in the community at large because it often was accused of holding itself aloof.[13] By the time President Conant resigned in 1953, emphasis on such programs had been noted as a special achievement of his administration.

As chairman of the Committee to Visit the Department of History, Allen expressed strong misgivings about "publish or perish" requirements: "too much emphasis is generally placed upon research, narrowly interpreted in terms of 'publication,' and too little upon teaching ability." The committee reported that those members of the history department with whom they had talked agreed with them. The present emphasis on scholarly publication, though noble in intent, "has also brought about a preposterous state of affairs in which a teacher's success in his career may be determined, not by his product, but by his by-product (the books he writes on the side.)" The committee also noted the extreme wartime hardship placed on the history department because nine of its permanent members had been on leave of absence.[14] Now, the great flood of new students after the war prolonged the manpower problem.

When his six-year term as overseer ended, Allen did not cease working for Harvard. He served as a member of committees, including those for the English department and the Press, until he was reelected as an overseer in 1950. He then resumed duties as chairman of the Committee to Visit the Harvard University Press.

The Press was in better condition than ever. The bequest of the late Waldron Phoenix Belknap, Jr., class of 1920, granted five-sixths of his large estate to the Harvard University Press upon the death of his wife. The bequest eventually would result in a distinct publishing branch, the Belknap Press of Harvard University Press.[15] The Press now trailed only the Chicago and Columbia university presses in volume of business. In 1950, 103 titles were published, the Press had a generous profit, and the Press Committee reaffirmed its support of the statement of policy devised four years earlier in the meeting chaired by Allen.[16]

Allen, early in 1953, dashed the enthusiasm of a persistent committee member, William L. White, who thought the Harvard University Press should enter the paperback field with scholarly offerings. An explosion in paperback book sales had followed the war, but the multitude of racks which had sprung up in drugstores, newsstands, and supermarkets had offered largely paperbacks which were less than "respectable." Suggestions just now were being made for higher quality material in paperback, but certainly no university press yet considered the paperback market.[17]

White thought offerings such as the Penguin paperbacks in England would be of great service to undergraduates. "We have nothing like this in America and I wish we did. As you know, our pocketbooks sold in drug stores are devoted largely to rape, a field in which I do not suggest we compete," White wrote to Allen. If the scholarship were kept reasonably high, White joked, the Press "would avoid the danger of ever going dangerously into the black on such a venture."[18]

Evidently, Allen's reply was cool, for White wrote again to him:

Actually, my plan is far more subtle than you seem to think. I would make certain that the operation as a whole doggedly lost a stipulated sum of money each year. Under no such circumstances would I permit it to lurch perilously into the black. Were there any threat of this, before the close of the tax year I should rush into print with a 300-page booklet on Egyptology, just to make certain that we lost money.[19]

When White presented his proposal to the full committee at

its March meeting, it got nowhere. Harvard thus missed an opportunity to be the first university press to take advantage of the cheaper production costs, greater sales, and boon to education that paperbacks represented. Not until two and a half years later did a university press, Cornell, condescend to enter the paperback field.[20]

During his second term as overseer, Allen also chaired the history committee. The history department, he wrote to fellow committee member Dexter Perkins, "has the devil of a time getting its work done with so heavy a load upon it" because of its excellent reputation. To Professor Crane Brinton, Allen expressed his concern that undergraduate education might be suffering because professors were becoming more and more specialized. He felt it necessary to remind the department of the enormous importance of good undergraduate instruction; yet he hated to make the committee appear allergic to graduate work and research.[21]

At one time Allen served simultaneously as chairman of three visiting committees: history, Press, and the department of social relations. He also acted as a member during his second term on the committees for English, classics, summer school of arts and sciences and of education, and as a director of the *Harvard Alumni Bulletin*.

Senator Joseph R. McCarthy posed a perplexing problem for the Harvard Overseers. He continually attacked the university as a harbor for crypto-Communist faculty members who quietly were indoctrinating students. Before Conant departed in early 1953 for an ambassadorial post in West Germany, he told the overseers that he did not believe any Communists were on the Harvard faculty, and even if there were, the damage done to the academic community by an investigation would cause far greater harm than any such person could.[22] A month later, McCarthy found an opportunity to taunt the school which he did not pass up. Granville Hicks and historian Daniel Boorstin, while they were no longer at Harvard, admitted at a House Un-American Activities Committee hearing that they had belonged to a small Communist cell with other Harvard faculty members in the 1930s. A third witness, Associate Professor of Physics Wendell H. Furry, still on the Harvard faculty, refused to answer the committee's questions, pleading the Fifth Amendment to avoid self-incrimination. Afterwards, he told the press he was not then a Communist and had not been one at any time over the past two years.[23]

Some prominent alumni, incensed at the apparent presence of a former Communist on the faculty, began to apply pressure to the overseers and other Harvard officials to punish Furry. Allen resisted the move. Furry was scheduled to appear again before HUAC on April 16, and Allen expressed considerable sympathy for him if he would answer questions up to the point of refusing to identify former associates who could lose their jobs and whom he did not regard as a menace to national security. If Furry followed that course, Allen favored only a reprimand, not a dismissal.[24]

In April, Furry declined to do more than acknowledge that he had been a Party member but no longer was. A month later the Harvard Corporation declared Furry guilty of "grave misconduct" and placed him on probation for three years. Two other faculty members were declared guilty of "misconduct," a lesser penalty, for refusal to testify before the committee.[25]

Allen advised David W. Bailey, secretary to the overseers, to explain Harvard's position on Furry with this wording:

Against the advice of the Law School professors who tried to aid him, and with what we consider to have been bad legal advice, Professor Furry, when called to testify, declined to answer certain questions and sought the refuge of the Fifth Amendment. This was damaging to his reputation, and to the University. But, as we have already stated, we do not believe that refusal to testify constitutes in itself grounds for dismissal.

Professor Furry informs us that he has not been connected with the Communist Part[y] since 1947. We believe him, and the evidence that we have collected does not dispute his assertion. Since he has seen the error of his former ways, and since we believe that there would have been even fewer Communists in this country today than there actually are if ex-Communists were not penalized after liberating themselves from the Party, we see no grounds for taking action. No further action will be taken in the case of Professor Furry.[26]

The news that Furry, as well as the other two less-publicized faculty members, would be retained greatly disgusted Senator McCarthy, who launched a tirade against Harvard's new president, Nathan Pusey. McCarthy claimed that a "smelly mess" pervaded the school. "I cannot conceive of anyone sending their children anywhere where they might be open to indoctrination by Communist professors." In January 1954 McCarthy went to Boston to launch his own Senate investigation into Communism at Harvard. Again Furry was grilled; this time he gave more details about his past, but he still refused to name his Communist associates. McCarthy threatened to have him jailed for contempt, saying it might be the only way of dealing with "Pusey's Fifth Amendment Communists." He added sarcastically that he would "hate to decimate" Harvard's faculty by this method.[27]

Following McCarthy's demands that Harvard should fire rather than merely reprimand Furry, more pressure arose for the overseers to go beyond the Corporation's own action. Robert Cutler, a Harvard overseer who had become Eisenhower's special assistant for national security affairs, proposed a unilateral declaration by the overseers to define the terms of disqualification for ex-Communists.

Allen campaigned by letter against the proposal because it would look as if the overseers were reprimanding the Corporation and Faculties, "which would be in my opinion unwarranted and would in any case be unfortunate." He suggested instead that President Pusey merely reaffirm the university's stated policy that it would neither appoint nor retain known members of the Communist party, nor would a past member be retained "if in the University's most scrupulous judgment he has not shaken himself free from the bonds of communism."[28]

The investigation into the U.S. Army soon diverted McCarthy's attention. Harvard was ignored as the Senator from Wisconsin pursued another course that ended his spectacular career.

22

NEW AVENUES OPEN—AND CLOSE

When Allen reached the age of sixty he began to consider shifting priorities by writing full-time and editing as a sideline. He notified Cass Canfield in 1950 that he had no intention of remaining as editor of *Harper's* until the age of sixty-five. After occasional reminders to Canfield during the next two years, he wrote to the publisher on December 8, 1952 that he would resign as editor on September 30, 1953. It would not mean, he hoped, the end of his relationship with Harper & Brothers. He proposed to take off at least three months upon his resignation to give his successor a free hand, then return as a part-time consulting editor. Furthermore, he was a vice president of Harper & Brothers, and he hoped to maintain that position.

Aside from the desire to free himself for full-time writing, Allen preferred not to run the risk of becoming outdated as an editor. "This is always a danger as people grow older," he told Canfield in the memo.

I had my apprenticeship long ago; and while I think I have retained a lively interest in changes and adjustments to the new conditions of new times, I realize that I am not the best judge of whether I am able to keep up with the needs of the day. I am proud of the job we have done at *Harper's*; but by the time I have sat in the driver's seat for twelve years (which, we must remember, is equal to three presidential terms) I'd rather climb down to a subordinate perch and let somebody who is younger take the wheel, long (I trust) before it occurs to anybody to wish that the old dodo would go somewhere else.[1]

Allen did not mention that *The Big Change*, just published, clearly would sell many copies, freeing him from the need to continue editorial work. He confessed to George Pfeiffer III that the book's success gave him the necessary confidence to go ahead with his long-contemplated decision to resign.[2]

As a successor Allen recommended to Canfield, who held the ultimate responsibility of naming a new editor, that John Fischer be named. Fischer, now head of Harper & Brothers' literary department, seemed particularly qualified to guide the magazine in the areas in which Allen believed it should make its main contributions: politics, economics, and foreign affairs. Russell Lynes, who held short seniority over Fischer, had special interests in cultural fields that would make him an admirable complement to Fischer, and Eric Larrabee, a man of "extraordinary and varied promise," should play a full part, too, Allen recommended.[3] Both Lynes and Larrabee could have been considered candidates for the job, but Fischer combined maturity with broader experience. Canfield, who agreed with Allen's recommendation, had admired Fischer since he had suggested to Allen in World War II that he hire him as a staff member.

Allen, presumably for his own records (the two-page memorandum was not addressed to anyone), described his feelings of guilt about attempting to write and edit simultaneously. When an editor is writing a book, he observed,

his subconscious will be occupied mostly with his book rather than with his magazine. . . . He'll be looking for ideas for his book rather than for ideas for articles. As he walks up the street, his mind will be composing a new conclusion for Chapter V rather than a new title for the leading

266

article for the May number. As a result, if the editor's conscience is in good repair, he will write books infrequently, lest he shirk his editorial assignment.[4]

When public announcement of Allen's impending resignation was made late in January, the news release also named Fischer as his successor. Notes of praise for Allen's editorial career began arriving soon. Robert L. Heilbroner told Allen he was "far and away the first editor in the business," and he thanked him for being the one who three years earlier had urged him to write full-time. "It was you who put me off to a running start by carpentering my first efforts until they were good enough for your Magazine—and what was good enough for *Harper's* was good enough for anybody." C. Hartley Grattan said he could not imagine what it would be like without Allen. "Of all the magazine editors with whom I have worked intimately over the last thirty years—first H. L. Mencken, then Alfred Dashiell, then Fred Allen—none has meant so much to me personally or has contributed so much to my instruction professionally as Fred Allen."[5]

Edward Weeks told Allen that by holding up *Harper's* standards he had stimulated the *Atlantic* to maintain its own standards. He lamented the retirement because Allen had been friend, adviser, and competitor in the literary scene as long as Weeks had known it.[6]

Walter Lippmann probably assessed the situation closest to Allen's thoughts when he wrote:

I see that you are arranging to work harder after September 30th, and I want to send you my affectionate greetings. Don't think that I am joking when I say that. Writing books is much harder than any kind of administrative or editorial job, as you well know.[7]

As Allen's last months as editor in chief passed, many new opportunities arose. He told Oliver and Deborah that it was unbelievable how many people wanted him to serve on boards or committees of impressive organizations. He would have to choose the one which he could do best and consent to just that one because he held a cordial dislike for famous men who sat on all sorts of boards without having the time really to contribute. "Don't ever volunteer to do anything that you can't do to the best of your ability, but when you've decided what to do, then really go at it," he advised Oliver. On the last day of April, the "one" offer that stood out above the others came: Henry Ford II personally asked him to become a trustee of the Ford Foundation.[8]

He was thrilled at the compliment, but he told Ford he had best ponder the offer overnight. The next day he penned a brief note: "Contemplation overnight has failed to produce any solid reason why I should not accept your invitation. . . . It's a very heavy and difficult responsibility, but it's also a challenge; and so I say yes."[9]

The Ford Foundation's objectives, as Robert Heilbroner had written in a *Harper's* article in 1951, were "as wide as the sky"—to strengthen peace, aid democracy, advance education, support economic well-being, and extend man's knowledge of human behavior.[10] And to help attain these goals the Foundation, which owned 90 percent of the Ford Motor Company stock, had half a billion dollars. "The biggest blank check in history," said its director, Paul Hoffman.[11]

Allen was uncertain what being a trustee entailed. When he told Agnes about the prestigious invitation, she, although elated as he was, had the presence to ask what the position paid. Allen felt sure that there was no pay.[12] But the position, to their delight, provided an honorarium of $1,250 for every three months of service.[13]

To avoid possible conflicts of interest, Allen resigned from two organizations which were seeking Ford Foundation funds.[14] To provide more time for his new assignment, he also gave up his chairmanship of the social relations committee at Harvard, but he retained chairmanship of the history and Press committees.

Shortly after he became a trustee, Allen began questioning the Foundation's implied assumption that it should give short-term grants for specific projects but not endowments. What happened, he asked, when money was granted for fellowships in a field for which there were no endowed professorships? If foundations represented modern counterparts to yesteryear's rich benefactors, then should not the

Foundation give endowments just as did the rich benefactors? He also wondered if foundations, admittedly bold in forward planning, were not too timid in effecting implementations of this planning. Finally, he wanted the trustees to ponder whether or not they often were not overly generous with academic research in the behavioral sciences, "where the ratio of academic mumbo-jumbo is high," and too niggardly in supporting nonacademics who possessed the native wit to ask the right questions and look for the vital answers even though they operated "half by hunch and very little by academically respectable statistical analysis."[15]

Another new dimension to the careers of the Allens as a team opened in 1952. They were commissioned to prepare the script outline for the Ford Motor Company's two-hour television production commemorating fifty years of the company's existence.[16]

The couple had participated in radio broadcasts since they had begun publishing books and were asked to appear as guests for radio interviews. Allen's credits included "Information Please," the Jinx and Tex McCrary show, "Luncheon at Sardi's," Mary Margaret McBride's talk show, a television show called "Who Said That?," the Dwight Cooke program, and the "Cliché Club." Agnes had been a regular panelist on the "Cliché Club," as well as a guest on other shows.

Broadcasting became an increasingly important medium of communication just as the Allens' own careers blossomed, and they found themselves more and more attracted to it. Frequently their opinions were sought by persons involved in broadcasting, and they were especially solicited for advice on how to present history via the airwaves.

Leland Hayward, producer for the Ford show, approached the Allens in late 1952 to see if they would prepare a script outline for the extravaganza. As a former literary agent, Hayward frequently had submitted his clients' work to Allen for consideration. Now, for five thousand dollars, the Allens agreed to deliver by January 15, 1953, a "complete outline for a television script . . . suitable for use on the proposed two-hour television program to be sponsored by the Ford Motor Company." The contract specified that the Allens would agree to modify the script as instructed by Hayward on or before February 26, and Hayward would be under no obligation to use the material. When they signed the contract on December 30, 1952, the Allens already were hard at work.[17]

The couple, hoping to create a memorable two hours of television entertainment, plunged into the project fearlessly. Their sixty-page script outline was based on a series of five flashbacks to former times, beginning with 1903 (the year of Ford's founding) and illustrating the everyday life of a middle-class family of four. Each episode would picture the family in the costumes of the time. A bare minimum of plot would be used, and intervening periods or bridges would be filled with film clips of notable events accompanied by a narrator's comments, musical and dance numbers of the periods, a few acted segments unrelated to the unifying family of four, and occasional graphs and cartoons to illustrate important points.

The Allens proposed Carl Sandburg as narrator, Mary Martin and James Stewart as the "typical couple," child actor Brandon de Wilde as one of their two children, Fred Astaire as the dancer to illustrate the transition from waltz to ragtime, and Irving Berlin to talk about the early ragtime music days.[18]

Hayward was "very pleased" with the outline.[19] But as the show's live performance in June came near and revisions were constantly made, the Allens felt that less and less of their own work was visible. Nevertheless, the final presentation closely followed the Allen format. It was based on the fifty-year flashback theme, showing changes in wearing apparel, dancing, singing, and other aspects of American life. Mary Martin was one of the stars of the show. She not only sang duets with Ethel Merman but portrayed Emily in a sketch from *Our Town* with Oscar Hammerstein II as Stage Manager. Filmstrips of early newsmakers enlivened the two-hour production as the Allens had suggested.

The show cost half a million dollars to produce, and it was carried live by both the Columbia Broadcasting System and the National Broadcasting Company. A two-hour performance of such diversity and dimension carried with it enormous problems of timing. During the broadcast Hayward was informed that the show was running nineteen minutes beyond schedule. In desperation, he began cutting out segments to regain the lost time, but he was so energetic that he eliminated too much and the program suddenly was running short. There was considerable ad libbing, Marian Anderson sang an unscheduled performance of "The Battle Hymn of the Republic," and the closing credits were shown at a glacial pace.[20]

Hardly any critics noticed the desperate padding, for they widely declared the show to be a great landmark in television entertainment. The Allens shared in the widespread congratulations, but they felt self-conscious about it—they were not certain that they could be credited with the show's success. "As time went on," Allen explained, "our suggestions got thrown out in favor of new acts and ideas to such an extent that it was difficult to say, when we saw the show, what we had contributed, if anything."[21] Two months later, however, they hesitantly agreed to accept a Christopher Award for their part in producing the Ford show.[22]

Even before the Ford production was broadcast, Samuel Goldwyn, Jr. approached the Allens for their ideas about a proposed retrospective television series. After deliberation with her husband, Agnes responded that they believed a great range of subjects would be worthy. One was a favorite Allen theme: the contrasting of yesterday's customs and social conditions with modern ones. Other shows in the series could deal with such persons as Woodrow Wilson and Babe Ruth, or with exciting events. Together the Allens had conjured possible topics: the great houses of the old-time rich, the "dashing youth" of the automobile, the evolution of ballroom dancing, the evolution of the cowboy, the shrinking of distances, the coming of the weekend, the rise of aviation, the domestic servant, and changes in etiquette.[23] It would have been an admirable attempt to relate on television social history in an entertaining fashion. Television, however, was more intent on situation comedies and westerns.

No matter, the Allens were willing to make a gesture toward the market for westerns. In May they devised a plan for a show or series of shows examining the cowboy, an unusual subject for the urban-minded Allens. The general theme would be that the cowboy represented a vanishing breed. "All the cowboys are truck drivers now," was one observation, and another note said, "Now, cowboys tie *radio* to saddlehorn." The proposed approaches included examining the factors that ended the cowboy's heyday (barbed wire, railroads, new and improved breeds of cattle, fatter cattle, farmers, improved grasses, pickup trucks, and mechanization in general) and a look at the actual old-time cowboy legend as portrayed in books, movies, and songs and on radio and television. Dude ranches and ranch-style homes were to be taken into account also.[24]

Further demands on Allen's anticipated free time came from the U.S. Department of State, which was making such good use of *The Big Change*. The Department's Educational Exchange Service tempted Allen with a proposed sojourn to India to talk formally and informally with university groups and others, but he decided finally not to go.[25] When he declined writing an article for the Department of State's International Information Administration, the agency prepared a ghost-written article for his signature. Outraged, he refused to permit his signature to be used for something which he had not written himself.[26]

That same summer Allen turned down the offer of an honorary doctorate from Bates College in Lewiston, Maine. He thought it inappropriate since he had accepted one in 1951 from Dartmouth and had been awarded his first honorary doctorate from Northeastern University at Boston in 1946.[27]

The year of 1953 moved toward September and the long-anticipated easier schedule. Meanwhile, relaxing weekends filled with tennis and watercolor painting were being spent four hours away in Tyringham; Leland Hayward was after the couple again to do more television writing; Oliver and Deborah, with their toddling son Stephen and a new baby, Frederick, were frequent visitors; Allen was at the New York Public Library several evenings a week as usual; unexpected pleasure had been found in the new television set ("We confess to being more or less addicts"); and reservations already had been made for a trip to England two days after the resignation. There had been one alarming note. One night Allen experienced a "sort of hop-skip-and-jump heart action," but the doctor attributed it to a chemical imbalance and suggested only that he confine his tennis to morning or late afternoon instead of the heat of the day.[28]

On September 30 Allen said his temporary good-byes at the office, and on October 2 he and Agnes departed for England aboard the *Liberté*. With them they carried the happy memory of a *Harper's* testimonial dinner, which had included a glittering guest list and appreciative talks by Edward Weeks and Bernard DeVoto. The Allens made London their headquarters and enjoyed a trip to Scotland, automobile drives into the countryside, a weekend with the Michael Huxleys, and attending as special guests a cocktail party given by the London office of *Reader's Digest*.[29]

Six weeks later they returned, and Allen began writing about a topic that had interested him since he had moved to Scarsdale in the 1920s—the suburbs and their impact on people.[30] Scarsdale, where he once had enjoyed bird-watching in fields and woods, had been converted into a developer's paradise. Allen urged as a "first order of business" that every suburban governmental body and citizens' association begin considering "ways and means for preserving open land for the benefit of succeeding generations," residents in general, and nature-lovers. It was too late to stop the engulfing trends; now it was incumbent upon citizens to channel and direct those changes. "And we cannot even do that, unless we act in good season. For it's later than you think."[31]

While he was preparing the article, which turned into a two-part series, Allen even went to Scarsdale personally to warn Westchester County residents that they needed "immediate planning on an exceptionally big basis." Suburan life was "strikingly out of balance," he said, pointing to the isolation in the suburbs of people of like incomes and interests.[32] Allen was again demonstrating the manner in which the nineteenth-century liberal heritage of pastoral virtue and minimal government had been reversed. Now, big government was *necessary* if pastoral virtue was to be preserved.

The Allens also began catching up on their entertaining upon returning from England. In mid-January they held a black-tie party for some twenty-five guests.[33] January also marked the end of Allen's planned three-month absence from the office, and he now began part-time consulting work for the magazine.

Allen agreed that month to a request from Yale that he visit the campus and give a series of talks over a five-day period to various classes and groups. He was to be a Chubb Fellow, a participant in a program at the university's Timothy Dwight College which occasionally brought in outsiders for discussions with students. When the proposed schedule arrived, Allen was horrified to see that within a five-day period he was scheduled for eleven classes in history, English, and American studies, and other groups as well.

"That is an altogether impossible program," Allen wrote to the program's planner. He explained that he never had been apt at spontaneous speech-making and that his public speaking required careful advance preparation. "The best I can say is that I shall try to meet all the assignments provided it is understood that on some occasions I shall be talking with rather than to the various groups and provided that I may to some extent repeat myself." The engagement was just four days away, and Allen promised to arrive on time, laden with notes, prepared to do his best, and "praying that I can survive those five days without laryngitis or total exhaustion!"[34]

The letter was the last that Allen wrote. On the same day he went to the office and spent his time reading a book-length manuscript by Russell Lynes, *The Tastemakers*.[35] The book had been inspired by the article "The Age of Taste," which Allen had encouraged Lynes to do for the October 1950 centennial issue.[36] That evening Allen and Agnes attended a *Harper's* party. At home, after they had retired, Agnes heard a noise in the bathroom. She found her husband unconscious on the floor. Physicians at New York Hospital determined that Allen had suffered a cerebral hemorrhage, and for two weeks he lingered unconscious and in critical condition. On February 13, 1954, just before midnight, he died at the age of sixty-three.

While Allen had had minor illnesses, nothing in recent years had suggested any serious dimming of his physical or mental capabilities. Complete retirement from work was unthinkable to him—after all, his father had lived a hearty life to the age of eighty-four. Allen certainly anticipated devoting more time than ever to writing, and his last project, the *Harper's* articles on suburbia, indicated his growing concern for contemporary problems in society.

His death was given front-page coverage in the next morning's Sunday *New York Times*; he was termed a "tweedy Bostonian" favorably know as the "Herodotus of the Jazz Age." The lengthy news story emphasized his contributions as a historian, but noted that he regarded himself more as an editor than writer.[37] The next day the *Times* editorially paid him high tribute:

His personal successes with books showed that he could write for a mass audience when he wished to. He totally lacked that species of snobbery which looks down on the "crowd." He liked and respected his fellow citizens of all walks and occupations—as his writing showed—and was also often amused by them. But he chose to edit a publication of comparatively small circulation, keeping alive within those limits humane and cultural values. A rare and engaging personality, he died too soon and will be sorely missed.[38]

The *Saturday Review* lamented that the publishing world had lost "one of its most loved and respected editors and American letters a distinguished popular historian."[39]

Allen's schoolboy friend at Groton, John Suter, officiated at services held at the Church of Epiphany on February 17. Ushers were Allen's associates at Harper & Brothers: John Fischer, Russell Lynes, Eric Larrabee, John A. Kouwenhoven, Cass Canfield, and Frank S. MacGregor. Some 350 mourners attended the services, including Edward Weeks, Walter Lippmann, Bernard DeVoto, Bruce Barton, John Gunther, DeWitt Wallace, Cleveland Amory, and Amy Loveman. In London the previous fall, Agnes had noted a poem on the tombstone of musician and music historian Charles Burney in Westminster Abbey which seemed to describe her husband, and Allen was so flattered that he had copied it down. It was read aloud at his funeral services:

> High principles and pure
> benevolence,
> Goodness with gaiety, talents
> with taste,
> Were of his gifted mind the
> blended attributes;
> While the genial hilarity of
> his airy spirits
> Animated, or softened, his
> very earthly toil;
> And a conscience without
> reproach
> Prepared,
> In the whole tenour of his
> mortal life
> Through the mediation of our
> Lord Jesus Christ
> His soul for heaven. Amen.[40]

The burial was at Forest Hills Cemetery in Boston.

The Ford Foundation remembered Allen's brief service there with a $25,000 grant to the New York Public Library to establish a special room for writers at work, the "Frederick Lewis Allen Memorial Room." Allen had used the library for most of the research on his books, and now the room was established to afford better working conditions for selected scholars and authors. Since Allen had lamented that no smoking was allowed in the library, the Allen Room specifically permitted smoking.[41]

Harper's eulogized Allen in a two-page memorial, written anonymously by Eric Larrabee. "His absence from this office is as unexpected as it is irredeemable." He was "the leading practitioner—in many respects, an inventor—of the contemporary style of writing informal social history." Larrabee continued:

His associates wish to record their gratitude for a number of his less public accomplishments—for putting up with them, individually and collectively, for more than a dozen years; for arbitrating their differences, smoothing their ruffled egos, and maintaining order in their crises; for being able to do their jobs better than they could, though not admitting it; for copy-reading their spelling, correcting their grammar, and bringing clarity to their snarled sentences; for holding the reins on disparate temperaments with a hand that was always sure but never in evidence; for bowing to their majority opinions when he thought he ought to and for not, when he didn't; for causing drudgery to disappear by doing more than his share of it, for holding fast to his own opinions but allowing always for a contrary view; for editing more manuscripts than the rest of his editors together, yet giving them the credit; for writing all the hard letters and leaving them the easy ones; for being interested in everything and for enlivening other imaginations with the vigor of his own; for wit in the presence of embarrassment, for calm in the face of the unexpected, and for durability in the endless exercise of judgment; for being the best editor in the United States and finding the time, without burden to his subordinates, to be the author whose name, whose works, and whose lasting reputation will be their pride.[42]

It was a fine tribute, but the message that his family loved best came from a friend, David Yellin, who said, "Everybody who knew him knew the same man."[43]

Sources Consulted

This biography is based largely on Allen's own papers, which are found in three primary collections. Most important are the Frederick Lewis Allen Papers, held by the Manuscript Division, Reference Department, Library of Congress. This collection of twenty-six containers consists of more than 9,000 items:

Container 1—Diaries of Allen's trips to London in 1943 and to San Francisco in 1945 for the founding conference of the United Nations; twenty-five datebooks listing Allen's appointment schedules and routine activities during the 1930s, 1940s, and 1950s; and a folder of biographical material.

Containers 2 through 6—Correspondence dating from 1913 to 1954, arranged chronologically.

Container 7—Files on Allen's relationships with Harvard and the Foreign Policy Association, and a correspondence file related to the "closed mind" speech in 1947 before the National Publishers Association in New York City.

Container 8—Manuscript for *Only Yesterday*.

Container 9—Manuscripts for *Only Yesterday* and *Since Yesterday*.

Containers 10 through 15—Manuscript for *Since Yesterday*.

Containers 16 through 18—Manuscript for *The Great Pierpont Morgan*.

Container 19—Manuscript for *I Remember Distinctly.*

Container 20—Manuscript for *The Big Change.*

Container 21—Manuscripts for *The Lords of Creation, Metropolis,* the "Golden Twenties" film, magazine articles, and notes for an uncompleted biography of Franklin D. Roosevelt.

Containers 22 through 23—Speeches and shorter works.

Container 24—Articles, speeches, and *Harper's* magazine data.

Container 25—Television scripts and shorter miscellaneous works.

Container 26—Material on Allen's childhood, including a baby book kept by his mother, childhood correspondence (notably from Groton), and biographical material.

The Oliver Allen Collection (as I have named it for my purposes) consists of some two hundred personal letters written by Frederick Lewis Allen to his parents and sister, Hildegarde. Dated from 1916 to 1954, Allen details in these letters his thoughts and his personal life, his career, and his views on current events. The collection is particularly full concerning Allen's activities in Washington, D.C. during World War I, and it also provides a detailed picture of his thoughts concerning the Depression and World War II. The materials came into the possession of Oliver Allen of Pelham, New York, after the death of his aunt, Hildegarde Allen, and he kindly forwarded them to me before depositing them in the Library of Congress, where they will become a part of the Frederick Lewis Allen Papers.

The third primary source consists of the *Harper's Magazine* Editorial Correspondence files, also in the Manuscript Division, Reference Department, Library of Congress. These papers contain correspondence regarding editorial decisions made by the editors of the magazine. Many of the letters were written by Frederick Lewis Allen. In this collection are 400 containers of materials, almost all of which concern correspondence to and from writers concerning contributions to the magazine. Although the file ostensibly includes materials dated from 1869 to 1965, virtually nothing exists prior to 1940, and for the years most pertinent to this study an unfortunate gap exists between 1944 and 1950. When Harper & Brothers moved in 1933 from their historic offices on Franklin Square to the East Thirty-third Street location in New York City, great masses of materials were thrown away because no one realized their importance. Not until 1943 was it suggested that the magazine's records should be given to the Library of Congress.

The manuscript by Frederick Lewis Allen entitled "The Council of Defense System: A History Submitted to the Director of the Council of National Defense," May 5, 1919, provides the best information on the Council's functions. It is located in Record Group No. 62 (Council of National Defense) Files and Records Division (Post War) 17-B1 Administrative File, Box 1053, U.S. National Archives, Washington, D.C.

Records concerning Allen's classes at Harvard were obtained from the Office of the Registrar and the University Archives at Harvard.

In the acknowledgments I have listed the people who granted me interviews, talked with me over the telephone, or corresponded with me about my subject.

Of course, the voluminous published writings of Allen in books and magazine articles contain invaluable material about his work and his personal life as well. The "Personal & Otherwise" columns in *Harper's* proved to be a very useful supplement.

For historical background on the period I have relied on many secondary sources, which are cited extensively in the footnotes. My dissertation, *Yesterday's Historian: Frederick Lewis Allen of Harper's Magazine*, is a lengthier treatment of Allen from which the present book was adapted. It is available on microfilm from University Microfilms, Ann Arbor, Michigan 48106. An unpublished master's thesis by Norman Kolin, "Frederick Lewis Allen and *Harper's Magazine*" (University of Missouri, 1950), was especially helpful because of the author's interviews with Allen.

Notes to Chapters

1: THE BEGINNINGS

1. Roger Butterfield in the introduction to the 1957 edition of *Only Yesterday: An Informal History of the Nineteen-Twenties* (New York: Harper & Brothers).

2. They were by name John Alden, Isaac Allerton, James Chilton, Priscilla Mullens, Richard Warren, and Francis and Esther Cooke. The means by which the ancestry was traced is unknown, but the claim is attributed by Frederick Lewis Allen to his father, the Reverend Frederick Baylies Allen, in the privately printed book, *Frederick Baylies Allen: A Memoir* (Cambridge: Riverside Press, 1929), p. 4. Except where otherwise indicated, details about the Allen ancestry that follow are from this work.

3. Francis Richmond Allen (1843–?) studied at Massachusetts Institute of Technology and École des Beaux Arts in Paris after graduating from Amherst in 1865. An architect, he designed buildings at Williams College and Vassar College, as well as residences, hospitals, and office buildings.

4. Telephone interview with Agnes Rogers Allen, January 30, 1972.

5. Allen, *Frederick Baylies Allen*, pp. 28–32. Frederick Lewis Allen recalled that as a boy he greeted this information with skepticism. It

reminded him of a small classmate whose father was governor of Massachusetts. The teacher asked the boy who the governor was, and the youngster did not know. Instructed to go home and ask his father, the boy returned the next day and responded, "He says *he* is Governor, but of course you can't believe anything he says." (The anecdote is related in *Frederick Baylies Allen*, pp. 28–29).

6. Josephine Francis, born February 1, 1868, eventually married Preston Clark, a prominent businessman. Rebecca Gorham, born October 12, 1869, never married. Louisa Ripley, born November 22, 1871, married Malcolm Taylor, an Episcopal minister.

7. Josephine, or "Auntie," who never married, is much-remembered by the Allen family today. An ardent lover of royalty, she once bullied a retired British officer into writing a history of the Medicis. The result was the definitive history of the royal family, *The Medici*, by Colonel G. F. Young, published in 1910, and since reissued many times. Colonel Young dedicated the work "To Miss Mary Josephine Allen of Boston, U.S.A., to whose enthusiasm for the remarkable family whose history is here told this book owes its origin."

8. Seven of his pencil sketches of the outdoors illustrate *Guide-boat Days and Ways,* ed. Kenneth Durant, and published in 1963 by the Adirondack Museum in Blue Mountain Lake, N.Y. The finely detailed sketches are remarkably similar in technique to those rendered by Frederick Lewis Allen many years later.

9. Johann Lewis' grandson, George Albert Lewis, eventually traced the history of the Lewis family in Philadelphia through a series of vivid watercolors showing the many family residences through the years. Some of them are reproduced in *American Heritage,* 14 (December 1962), 65–80. The commentary, from which much of the above Lewis family history was obtained, is by Oliver Ellsworth Allen, son of Frederick Lewis Allen and great-great-great-grandson of the German officer who elected to stay in America.

10. Walter Muir Whitehill, *Boston: A Topographical History* (Cambridge: The Belknap Press of Harvard University Press, 1968, 2d ed.), p. 235.

11. Bainbridge Bunting, *Houses of Boston's Back Bay: An Architectural History, 1840–1917* (Cambridge: The Belknap Press of Harvard University Press, 1967), pp. 414, 420.

12. *The American Scene* (Bloomington: Indiana University Press, 1968), p. 248.

13. The journal is in Box 26, Allen Papers, Library of Congress (hereinafter identified as Allen Papers). It is identified mistakenly as a journal maintained by Allen's father. Unless otherwise indicated, all details of Allen as an infant come from the journal.

14. Agnes Rogers Allen to the writer, February 23, 1973; the sketchbook is in the possession of Oliver E. Allen.

15. Allen to his father, January 4, 1903, Box 26, Allen Papers.

16. Volkmann to Frederick Baylies Allen, May 26, 1903, ibid.

2: GROTON AND HARVARD

1. *New York Times*, June 3, 1934, p. 5. col. 1.

2. Interview with Agnes Rogers Allen, September 25, 1971.

3. Cass Canfield, *Up and Down and Around: A Publisher Recollects the Time of His Life* (New York: Harper's Magazine Press, 1971), p. 19.

4. George Biddle, "As I Remember Groton School," *Harper's*, 179 (August 1939), 293–94.

5. Allen to his mother, September 26, 1903, Box 26, Allen Papers.

6. Allen to Hildegarde Allen, November 16, 1903; Allen to father, May 29, 1904; ibid.

7. Allen to father, April 30, 1905, ibid.

8. Allen to mother, February 24, 1907, ibid.

9. Allen to father, November 25, 1906; Allen to mother, December 9, 1906; ibid.

10. Norman Kolin, "Frederick Lewis Allen and *Harper's Magazine*" (unpublished master's thesis, University of Missouri, 1950), pp. 5–6.

11. Hodges dedicated the book "To my neighbor, The Reverend Frederick Baylies Allen, to whom I owe my first acquaintance with Holderness." The Houghton Mifflin Company published the book in Boston in 1907.

12. Allen to mother, April 19, 1907, Box 26, Allen Papers.

13. March 11, 1908, ibid.

14. Allen to father, January 14, 1906, ibid.

15. Endicott Peabody to Frederick Baylies Allen, January 25, 1906, ibid.

16. Allen to Hildegarde Allen, March 1, 1905; Allen to father [May 1906]; ibid.

17. Allen to Hildegarde Allen, September 1, 1904, ibid.

18. Allen to mother, January 7, 1906, ibid.

19. January 25, 1906, ibid.

20. Allen to father, February 26, 1906; Allen to mother, March 18, 1906; Frederick Baylies Allen to Frederick Lewis Allen, September 21, 1905; ibid.

21. Allen to mother, May 8, 1904; Allen to father, February 18, 1906; ibid.

22. Allen to mother, May [n.d.], 1906, ibid.

23. January 8, 1907, ibid.

24. *Franklin D. Roosevelt: The Apprenticeship* (Boston: Little, Brown and Company, 1952), p. 41.

25. Allen to mother, February 4, 1908, Box 26, Allen Papers.

26. Samuel Eliot Morison, *Three Centuries of Harvard* (Cambridge: Harvard University Press, 1946), p. 389.

27. Ibid., p. 342.

28. Samuel Eliot Morison, ed., *The Development of Harvard University Since the Inauguration of President Eliot, 1869–1929* (Cambridge: Harvard University Press, 1930), pp. xlv–xlvi.

29. Quoted by Henry Aaron Yeomans in *Abbott Lawrence Lowell, 1856–1943* (Cambridge: Harvard University Press, 1948), p. 106.

30. Ibid., pp. 165–75.

31. John Reed, "Almost Thirty," *New Republic*, 86 (April 29, 1936), 332–33.

32. Allen to mother, March 2, 1919, Oliver Allen Collection, Harold Stearns, evidently suffering from disillusionment even as a Harvard undergraduate just as he did in the twenties, took a contrary reading of the college temper from Reed. Stearns complained that the environment was not conducive to gaining knowledge. He contended that the college failed to be intellectually stimulating, encouraged bad work habits, and had a shallow, crass student body. See "The Confessions of a Harvard Man," *Forum*, 50 (December 1913), 819–26; 51 (January 1914), 69–81.

33. Morison, *Three Centuries of Harvard*, pp. 434–38.

34. Charles M. Storey to writer, December 27, 1972.

35. Ibid.

36. Ibid.

37. Benchley (1889–1945) was born in Worcester, Mass., the son of a minor city official. He attended the Philips Exeter Academy before entering Harvard, and after graduation he attained a national reputation as a humorist via the printed page, stage, and screen.

38. Years later, in an unusal parallel, Allen's son Oliver became ibis of the *Lampoon*, second to Robert Benchley, Jr. Oliver eventually succeeded Benchley as president.

39. Kolin, "Frederick Lewis Allen and *Harper's Magazine*," p. 6.

40. Oliver E. Allen to writer, February 6, 1973.

41. Ibid.

42. Kolin, "Frederick Lewis Allen and *Harper's Magazine*," pp. 143–44.

43. Record of Frederick Lewis Allen, Class of 1912, Harvard College, Office of the Registrar, Marion C. Belliveau.

44. Morison, *Three Centuries of Harvard*, p. 402; Harvard class rolls, Harvard University Archives.

45. Storey to writer, December 27, 1972.

46. Biographical information sheet filled out by Allen, Box 4, Allen Papers; Record of Frederick Lewis Allen, Graduate School of Arts and Sciences, Harvard University, Office of Registrar, Marion C. Belliveau.

47. The poem was printed in the November 6, 1912 issue of the *Harvard Bulletin*.

48. Storey to writer, January 17, 1973.

49. *The Proper Bostonians* (New York: E.P. Dutton & Co., Inc., 1947), p. 298.

50. Stephen M. Foster to Allen, October 8, 1941, Box 2; undated Harvard grade reports, Box 26; Allen Papers.

3: THE MAGAZINE APPENTICESHIP

1. Frank Luther Mott, *A History of American Magazines, 1885–1905* (Cambridge: The Belknap Press of Harvard University Press, 1957), p. 2.

2. Merle Curti, *The Growth of American Thought* (New York: Harper & Brothers, 1943), pp. 593–604.

3. Kolin, "Frederick Lewis Allen and *Harper's Magazine*," p. 6.

4. Crowninshield to Allen, November 26, 1912, Box 26, Allen Papers.

5. Masson to Crowninshield, December 13, 1912, ibid.

6. Crowninshield to Allen, December 16, 1912, ibid.

7. For personality sketches of Crowninshield, see the profile by Frederic Bradlee in *Vanity Fair: Selections from America's Most Memorable,* ed. Bradlee and Cleveland Amory (New York: The Viking Press,

1960), pp. 11–12; Geoffrey T. Hellman, "That Was New York: Crowninshield," *New Yorker*, 24 (February 14, 1948), 68, 71–73; and Robert C. Benchley, "Mr. Vanity Fair," *Bookman*, 50 (January 1920), 429–433.

8. Hellman, "That Was New York: Crowninshield," p. 68.

9. Crowninshield to Allen, December 16, 1912, Box 26, Allen Papers.

10. "Forced Cards," 144 (March 5, 1913), 186; "The Optimist," 144 (May 7, 1913), 369; and "The Creative Gift," 145 (July 9, 1913), 42.

11. *Century*, 86 (August 1913), 632–34.

12. Crowninshield to Allen, June 3, 1913, June 5, 1913, August 28, 1913, Box 26, Allen Papers.

13. "Sleeping Outdoors," *Century*, 87 (November 1913), 153–56; "A Night of the Bath," *Century*, 87 (January 1914), 483–86; Crowninshield to Allen, September 24, 1913, Box 26, Allen Papers.

14. Vol. 92 (October 27, 1911), 35–37.

15. Crowninshield to Allen, June 24, 1913, Box 26, Allen Papers.

16. Sedgwick (1872–1906) was to play a pivotal role in Allen's magazine career. An 1894 Harvard graduate, he taught at Groton from 1895 to 1896. He was assistant editor of *Youth's Companion*, 1896–1900; editor of *Leslie's Magazine*, 1900–1905; and editor of *American Magazine*, 1906–1907, before beginning in 1908 his thirty-year editorship of the *Atlantic Monthly*.

17. *Atlantic Monthly*, 112 (October 1913), 516–19.

18. Virginia Holbrook Dick to Allen, October 3, 1913; Sedgwick to Allen, October 16, 1913; Box 26, Allen Papers.

19. Sedgwick to Allen, December 3, 1913, ibid.

20. Crowninshield to Allen, December 5, 1913, ibid.

21. Theodore Peterson, *Magazines in the Twentieth Century* (Urbana, Ill.: University of Illinois Press, 1964), p. 270.

22. Crowninshield to Allen, December [n.d.], 1913, January 12, 1914, Box 26, Allen Papers. Crowninshield had asked Allen if there were any more like him at Harvard. Allen had said yes, and he called his attention to Benchley and Gluyas Williams. Allen believed this "got them started on their careers to some extent." (Kolin, "Frederick Lewis Allen and *Harper's Magazine*," p. 6.) From 1919 to 1920 Benchley served as Crowninshield's managing editor of *Vanity Fair*.

23. Sedgwick to Allen, February 25, 1914, Box 26, Allen Papers.

24. Crowninshield to Allen [1914], ibid.

25. Crowninshield to Allen, March 30, 1914, ibid.

26. Doty to Allen, April 27, 1914, February 27, 1915, ibid.

27. Ellery Sedgwick, *The Happy Profession* (Boston: Little, Brown and Company, 1946), p. 156.

28. Frederick Lewis Allen, "Sedgwick of the *Atlantic*," *Saturday Review of Literature,* 29 (September 28, 1946), 8.

29. Kolin, "Frederick Lewis Allen and *Harper's Magazine*," p. 124.

30. Ibid., p. 125.

31. Douglas Graham, M.D., *Writers Cramp and Allied Affections: Their Treatment by Massage and Kinestherapy* (Detroit: E. G. Swift [n.d.], passim.

32. Crowninshield to Allen, January 16, 1915; Allen to Crowninshield, January 25, 1915; Box 26, Allen Papers.

33. Vol. 4, pp. 47–48.

34. Doty to Allen, December 21, 1915, Box 26, Allen Papers.

35. Peterson, *Magazines in the Twentieth Century*, p. 150.

36. Allen to father, January 20, 1916, Oliver Allen Collection.

37. Doty to Allen, December 21, 1915, Box 26, Allen Papers.

38. Allen to father, January 20, 1916, Oliver Allen Collection.

39. Telephone interview with Agnes Rogers Allen, January 30, 1972. This episode was related to Mrs. Allen by Allen.

40. Allen to father, January 20, 1916, Oliver Allen Collection.

41. Allen to father, June 6, 1916, ibid.

42. Telephone interview with the former Marion Cleveland, Mrs. John Harlan Amen, April 25, 1972. Mrs. Amen recalled Allen as having a "wonderful brain and a wonderful sense of humor." Mrs. Amen also knew, independently of Allen, Dorothy Cobb, the woman who was to become Allen's first wife.

43. "Small Talk," Vol. 93 (February 1917), 636–39; "Ode to Professor James Harvey Robinson," Vol. 93 (January 1917), 480.

44. *New Republic*, 10 (March 31, 1917), 264–65.

45. Sedgwick to Allen, April 17, 1917, Box 26, Allen Papers.

46. Vol. 104 (April 26, 1917), 484–85.

47. Ibid.

4: WARTIME PUBLICIST

1. *Boston Evening Transcript*, May 28, 1917, clipping in Oliver Allen Collection.

2. Telegram from Sedgwick to Allen, May 10, [1917]; W. Morgan Shuster to Allen, May 15, 1917; Box 26, Allen Papers.

3. Vol. 105 (November 22, 1917), 559.

4. For the beginnings of public relations see Alan R. Raucher, *Public Relations and Business, 1900–1929* (Baltimore: Johns Hopkins Press, 1968); Eric F. Goldman, *Two-Way Street: The Emergence of the Public Relations Counsel* (Boston: Bellman Publishing Co., Inc., 1948); and Scott M. Cutlip and Allen H. Center, *Effective Public Relations: Pathways to Public Favor* (New York: Prentice-Hall, Inc., 1952), pp. 34–60.

5. Letter from Writers' War Committee to Professor George A. Reisner, Cambridge, Mass., June 27, 1917, Box 26, Allen Papers.

6. Personal report from Frederick Lewis Allen to the Writers' War Committee, July 12, 1917, ibid.

7. Writers' War Committee news release, Oliver Allen Collection.

8. Allen to the Writers' War Committee, July 12, 1917, Box 26, Allen Papers.

9. See newspaper clippings from *Boston Record,* July [13 or 14], 1917; *Boston Globe,* July [13 or 14], 1917; *Boston Evening Transcript,* July 13, 1917; and *Boston Traveler,* July [13 or 14], 1917; Box 26, Allen Papers.

10. Allen to the Writers' War Committee, July 12, 1917, ibid.

11. William J. Breen, "The Council of National Defense: Industrial and Social Mobilization in the United States, 1916–1920" (unpublished doctoral dissertation, Duke University, 1968), p. 145.

12. Sedgwick's letter is an enclosure in an Allen letter to his mother, September 27, 1917, Oliver Allen Collection.

13. *Information Circular No. 11, Council of National Defense: Section on Cooperation with States,* September 19, 1917, enclosure in letter from Allen to his mother, September 21, 1917, Oliver Allen Collection.

14. Memorandum to George F. Porter, August 31, 1917, Oliver Allen Collection.

15. Typewritten summary of publicity work accomplished between August 28, 1917 and November 23, 1917, Allen to Buehl, ibid.

16. Allen to mother, August 28, 1917, September 26, 1917, ibid.

17. Ibid., September 10, 1917.

18. Ibid.

19. James R. Mock and Cedric Larson, *Words That Won the War: The Story of the Committee on Public Information, 1917–1919* (Princeton: Princeton University Press, 1939), p. 12.

20. Allen to mother, September 20, 1917, Oliver Allen Collection.

21. Ibid., December 2, 1917, September 20, 1917, September 2, 1917.

22. Ibid., September 26, 1917, September 2, 1917.

23. Ibid., September 10, 1917.

24. Ibid., September 26, 1917.

25. Typewritten summary of publicity work done August 28, 1917 to November 23, 1917, to Mr. Buehl, Oliver Allen Collection.

26. "The Forty-Eight Defenders: A Study of the Work of the State Councils of Defense," *Century*, 95 (December 1917), 261–66; "Building the Bridge to France: Why the Government Is Calling for the United States Shipyard Volunteers," *Outlook*, 118 (February 20, 1918), 284–86.

27. Allen to mother, November 24, 1917, Oliver Allen Collection.

28. See the poster, "Spies and Lies," reproduced opposite page 64 in Mock and Larson, *Words That Won the War.*

29. Allen, "The Forty-Eight Defenders," p. 265.

30. Allen to mother, July 14, 1918, Oliver Allen Collection; the bulletin was entitled "Loyalty and Sedition: Supplementary to Bulletin No. 99," July 18, 1918, and it was issued by the Council of National Defense under the signature of Arthur H. Fleming.

31. Allen to mother, June 28, 1918, Oliver Allen Collection.

32. Ibid., July 27, 1918.

33. "Philadelphia and the Liberty Sing," *Outlook*, 120 (September 4, 1918), 13–14.

34. Bulletin No. 103, July 15, 1918, Council of National Defense, State Councils Section. Enclosure in letter from Allen to his mother, July 19, 1918, Oliver Allen Collection.

35. Allen to mother, August 16, 1918, ibid.

36. Ibid.

37. Allen, "Confidential Report on Mr. Allen's Trip to the Florida State Council Meetings," August 15, 1918, Oliver Allen Collection.

38. Allen to mother, December 2, 1917, ibid.

39. *New York Times*, June 25, 1918, p. 1. Scherer later wrote a book about his Council of National Defense duties, *The Nation at War* (New York: George H. Doran Co., 1918).

40. Allen to mother, June 28, 1918, Oliver Allen Collection.

41. Woodrow Wilson to Newton D. Baker, July 30, 1918. A copy of the letter is enclosed in Allen's letter to his mother, August 3, 1918, ibid.

42. Arthur H. Fleming, chief of State Councils Section, to the state councils, August 3, 1918; copy enclosed in a letter from Allen to his mother, August 3, 1918, Oliver Allen Collection.

43. Woodrow Wilson to Franklin K. Lane, October 26, 1918, copy in Oliver Allen Collection.

44. Allen to Hildegarde Allen, July 4, 1918, Box 1, Allen Papers.

45. Ibid.

5: NEW HORIZONS

1. Allen to mother, September 26, 1917, Oliver Allen Collection.

2. Emily Cobb Holmes to writer, December 27, 1971.

3. Allen to father, July 25, 1918, Oliver Allen Collection.

4. Allen to mother, August 8, 1918, ibid.

5. The Rev. Mr. Cobb (1863–1943) was born in Hopewell, N.Y., and received his A.B. from Rutgers in 1884 and his doctor of divinity degree in 1901 from New York University. He served as a minister in West Troy, N.Y., from 1888 to 1902 before assuming the pastorate at West End Collegiate Church in 1903, a position he held until 1931. From 1915 to 1933 he was president of the board of foreign missions for the Dutch Reformed Church in America.

6. Allen to father, September 17, 1918, Oliver Allen Collection.

7. Allen to mother, September 4, 1918, September 14, 1918, ibid.

8. Clarkson (1882–1937), a native of Des Moines, Iowa, had been a New York newspaper reporter, an investigator for the U.S. Interior Department, and employed in advertising before associating with the Council of National Defense. As a result of his war work he wrote *Industrial America in the World War—The Strategy Behind the Lines* (Boston: Houghton Mifflin Co., 1923).

9. News release from Franklin K. Lane, October 1, 1918, Oliver Allen Collection. The remaining sections were federal agencies, organization and information, field staff, Americanization, and child conservation.

10. Dorothy Cobb to Mrs. Frederick B. Allen, October 5, 1918; Allen to mother, October 5, 1918; Oliver Allen Collection.

11. Allen to mother, October 13, 1918, October 5, 1918, ibid.

12. Allen to father, October 15, 1918; Allen to mother, October 13, 1918; ibid.

13. Allen to mother, October 20, 1918, ibid.

14. Ibid.

15. Ibid., October 24, 1918.

16. Ibid.

17. Ibid.

18. Ibid., October 31, 1918.

19. Ibid., November 10, 1918.

20. Ibid.

21. Allen to father, January 15, 1919; Allen to mother, November 19, 1918; ibid.

22. Allen to mother, November 22, 1918, ibid.

23. Ibid., November 19, 1918.

24. Letters from Allen and Dorothy to Allen's mother, December 4, 5, 9, and 12, 1918, ibid.

25. Allen to mother, December 12, 1918, ibid.

26. Allen to father, January 15, 1919, ibid.

27. Ibid.

28. Allen to mother, February 25, 1919, ibid.

29. Walter Davenport, *Power and Glory: The Life of Boies Penrose* (New York: G. P. Putnam's Sons, 1931), p. v.

30. Dorothy Cobb Allen to Mrs. Frederick B. Allen, May 16, 1919, Oliver Allen Collection.

31. Allen to mother, March 2, 1919, ibid.

32. Ibid., February 21, 1919.

33. Ibid., December 12, 1918, March 2, 1919.

34. Dorothy Cobb Allen to Mrs. Frederick B. Allen, April 2, 1919, ibid.

35. The magazine's masthead does not list Benchley until the August 1919 issue.

36. "Opening of the Presidential Candidate Season," *Vanity Fair*, 12 (August 1919), 43.

37. "Personnel, Politics, and Red Tape," 119 (June 19, 1918), 310–13; "Does the Administration Need a War Cabinet?" 119 (June 26, 1918), 344–46.

38. All the quoted profiles are on page 311, "Personnel, Politics, and Red Tape."

39. Vol. 121, pp. 693–96.

40. Ibid.

41. Ibid., p. 693.

42. Allen to mother, April 13, 1919, Oliver Allen Collection.

1. Scott M. Cutlip, "The Nation's First Public Relations Firm," *Journalism Quarterly*, 43 (Summer 1966), 269–80.

2. Center and Cutlip, *Effective Public Relations*, pp. 54, 57–58.

3. Sedgwick to Allen, March 25, 1919, a copy of which is enclosed in a letter from Allen to his mother, April 14, 1919, Oliver Allen Collection.

4. Sedgwick to Allen, March 27, 1919, a copy of which is enclosed in a letter from Allen to his mother, April 14, 1919, ibid.

5. Dorothy Allen to Mrs. Frederick B. Allen, April 2, 1919; Allen to mother, April 14, 1919, April 13, 1919; ibid.

6. Allen to parents, April 30, 1919, ibid.

7. Ibid.

8. Allen to mother, April 13, 1919, March 2, 1919, ibid.

9. Allen's wife of many years, Agnes Rogers Allen, and his son, Oliver, learned of the manuscript only in 1971 when an Australian scholar, William J. Breen, unearthed it in the National Archives. The manuscript is in Record Group No. 62 (Council of National Defense) Files and Records Division (Post War) 17–B1 Administrative File, Box No. 1053. It is entitled "The Council of Defense System: A History Submitted to the Director of the Council of National Defense."

10. Morison, *Three Centuries of Harvard*, pp. 439–49.

11. Ibid., pp. 453–60.

12. "Harvard Men in the Boston Police Strike," *School and Society*, 10 (October 11, 1919), 425–26.

13. Yeomans, *Abbott Lawrence Lowell*, pp. 316–17; Morison, *Three Centuries of Harvard*, p. 466.

14. *New York Times*, August 28, 1921, p. 23.

15. Yeomans, *Abbott Lawrence Lowell*, pp. 317–27.

16. Ibid., pp. 209–13.

17. Born in Elizabeth, N.J., in 1898, Weeks received an A.B. from Harvard in 1922. He started in the publishing business as a manuscript reader and book salesman for Horace Liveright, Inc. in 1923. In 1924 he was named associate editor of the *Atlantic Monthly*. He became editor of the Atlantic Monthly Press in 1928 and did not relinquish that position

until 1938 when he returned to the magazine as editor. He retired as editor in 1966.

18. Copy of speech sent to Allen by Weeks on February 15, 1950, Box 4, Allen Papers.

19. Allen to Weeks, February 21, 1950, ibid.

20. Ibid.

21. "University and College Publicity," 15 (May 6, 1922), 485–89.

22. Yeomans, *Abbott Lawrence Lowell*, p. 199.

23. *Harper's*, 139 (July 1919), 277.

24. Ibid., 145 (June 1922), 124.

25. Ibid., 144 (December 1921), 121–23.

26. *Atlantic Monthly*, 129 (January 1922), 44–54.

27. *Century*, 100 (May 1920), 142–44.

28. Undated newspaper clipping, Box 23, Allen Papers.

29. *Twenty-fifth Anniversary Report*, Harvard Class of 1912, p. 9.

30. Frank (1887–1940) was born in Queen City, Mo., and received B.A., M.A., and LL.D. degrees from Northwestern University. Upon leaving the *Century* in 1925, he assumed the presidency of the University of Wisconsin, remaining there until 1937. Also in 1925, Frank began writing a daily syndicated column for American newspapers.

31. Peterson, *Magazines in the Twentieth Century*, p. 150.

32. Allen to father, March 30, 1922, Oliver Allen Collection.

33. Ibid.

34. *New York Times*, May 28, 1922, Section II, p. 5.

35. Kolin, "Frederick Lewis Allen and *Harper's Magazine*, p. 7.

7: A CAREER AT HARPER'S

1. Charles A. Beard, "New York, the Metropolis of To-day," *The American Review of Reviews*, 69 (June 1924), 608–24.

2. Eugene Exman, *The House of Harper: One Hundred and Fifty Years of Publishing* (New York: Harper & Row, Publishers, 1967), pp. 215–19.

3. Canfield (1897–   ), a native of New York City, was, like Allen, a Groton-Harvard product, receiving his A.B. in 1919. He did graduate work at Oxford in England and began an association in 1924 with Harper & Brothers which continues to the present through the firm's successor, Harper & Row. He served Harper & Brothers as president from 1931 to

1945, as chairman of the board from 1945 to 1955, and as chairman of the executive committee and editorial board, 1955 to 1962. From 1962 to 1967 he also held the latter position with Harper & Row.

4. J. Henry Harper, *The House of Harper* (New York, 1912), p. 84, as quoted by Peterson, *Magazines in the Twentieth Century*, p. 409.

5. "One Hundred Years of *Harper's*," *Harper's*, 201 (October 1950), 32.

6. Mott, *A History of American Magazines, 1885–1905*, pp. 729–31.

7. Allen to father, August 19, 1923, Oliver Allen Collection.

8. Ibid.

9. Wells (1875–1941) was a native of Painesville, Ohio, who graduated from Yale in 1896 with an A.B. degree. He became editor of the magazine in 1919 upon the death of Henry Alden Mills.

10. Allen to father, August 19, 1923, Oliver Allen Collection.

11. See letter to mother, May 23, 1924, and to father, February 2, 1924, both in Oliver Allen Collection. Bradford's *Bare Souls* and Ritchie's book on Thackeray were published in 1924. Allen named the Wilson volumes *The Public Papers of Woodrow Wilson*. Ray Stannard Baker and William E. Dodd edited the volumes, published in 1925 and 1927.

12. *Harper's*, 150 (March 1925), 512.

13. Allen to father, August 27, 1924, Oliver Allen Collection.

14. *Harper's*, Vol. 151, p. 382.

15. Allen, "One Hundred Years of *Harper's*," p. 32.

16. Allen to mother, November 29, 1925, November 15, 1925, May 23, 1926, Oliver Allen Collection.

17. Hartman (1879–1941) was born in Fort Wayne, Ind., and earned an A.B. degree from Wesleyan College in 1901. After brief sojourns with the *New York Journal* and Associated Sunday Magazines, he joined Harper & Brothers in 1904, switching to the magazine staff in 1908. He became associate editor in 1918 and editor in 1931, serving until his death in 1941.

18. Allen to mother, August 26, 1927, Oliver Allen Collection.

19. Ibid., December 4, 1927.

20. Ibid., September 5, 1924.

21. *Harper's*, 153 (October 1926), 647–50.

22. Allen to mother, May 23, 1926, Oliver Allen Collection.

23. Ibid., January 12, 1924.

24. Allen to father, June 29, 1924, ibid.

25. "The Model Son," *Harper's*, 147 (November 1923), 850–52.

26. Ibid., 149 (October 1924), 668–70.

27. "Spring and the Poets," *Forum*, 77 (April 1927), 483.

28. *Harper's*, 148 (March 1924), 545–47.

29. Ibid., 152 (December 1925), 122–24.

30. *Independent*, 118 (April 9, 1927), 378–79.

31. Allen to mother, March 27, 1927, Oliver Allen Collection.

32. *Independent*, 118 (June 4, 1927), 587–88; *Harper's*, 156 (December 1927), 122–24.

33. *Independent*, 115 (November 14, 1925), 547–49.

34. Quoted by Allen in letter to mother, November 29, 1925, Oliver Allen Collection.

35. *Independent*, 116 (April 10, 1926), 411–12, 430–31.

36. Ibid., 114 (June 13, 1925), 670–71.

37. *Forum*, 74 (December 1925), 894–96.

38. *Independent*, 115 (October 31, 1925), 498, 512.

39. *Paul Revere Reynolds: A Biographical Sketch* [New York, 1944].

40. Allen, *Frederick Baylies Allen*, pp. 91, 92, 94.

41. Martin to Peabody, November 24, 1925, reprinted in Frank D. Ashburn, *Peabody of Groton: A Portrait* (New York: Coward McCann, Inc., 1944), pp. 279–80.

42. Allen to father, June 29, 1924, Oliver Allen Collection.

43. Allen to mother, August 26, 1927, ibid.

44. Ibid.

8: TRAGEDY—AND TRIUMPH

1. Entries in Emily Cobb Holmes' diaries, November 5 and 7, 1928.

2. Emily Cobb Holmes to writer, August 28, 1972.

3. Ibid.

4. Ibid., January 19, 1971, August 17, 1972.

5. Allen to Hildegarde Allen, March 31, 1929, Oliver Allen Collection.

6. Kolin, "Frederick Lewis Allen and *Harper's Magazine*," p. 5.

7. Vol. 154, pp. 208–209, 239–40. The magazines merged in October 1928.

8. Kolin, "Frederick Lewis Allen and *Harper's Magazine*," p. 34.

9. Allen to mother, May 3, 1930, Oliver Allen Collection.

10. Interview with Agnes Rogers Allen, September 23, 1971.

11. This calendar may be found in Box 28, Allen Papers.

12. Emily Cobb Holmes to writer, August 17, 1972.

13. Ibid., September 12, 1972.

14. Ibid., March 17, 1972.

15. Allen to mother, October 26, 1930, Oliver Allen Collection.

16. Allen to Geoffrey Parsons, September 8, 1943, Box 3, Allen Papers.

17. Allen to mother, October 26, 1930, Oliver Allen Collection.

18. Ibid.

19. Emily Cobb Holmes to writer, March 20, 1973. The great-aunt was Dr. Cobb's sister, Eliza P. Cobb.

20. Allen to mother, April 5, 1931, Oliver Allen Collection.

21. Ibid., April 5, 1931, March 30, 1931.

22. Ibid., March 22, 1931, June 6, 1931.

23. Ibid., May 23, 1931.

24. Figures from *N. W. Ayer & Sons Directory of Newspapers and Periodicals* (Philadelphia: N. W. Ayer & Son, Inc., 1931).

25. Allen to mother, November 29, 1931, Oliver Allen Collection.

26. Ibid., October 12, 1931.

27. *Book-of-the-Month Club News* (New York: Book-of-the-Month Club, Inc., 1931).

28. Allen to mother, October 21, 1931, Oliver Allen Collection.

29. Ibid., November 29, 1931.

30. Ibid.

31. Ibid., December 13, 1931.

32. Ibid., November 22, 1931.

33. The 1931 edition sold 67,300 copies; a one-dollar text edition in 1932, 4,760; Blue Ribbon edition, 1933, 40,290; Bantam paperback, 1946, 283,100; Bantam paper reissue, 1963–64, 76,000; 1957 regular edition reissue, 36,500; Harpercrest edition, 1961, 14,100; and Perennial paper edition, 1964, 589,211. Figures provided by Beulah Hagen, Harper & Row, in letter to writer, June 17, 1971.

34. Undated typewritten notes prepared by Allen for publicity on *The Big Change* in 1952.

35. Ibid.

36. *Only Yesterday*, 1931 edition, p, xiv.

37. Burl Noggle, "The Twenties: A Historiographical Frontier," *The Journal of American History*, 53 (September 1966), 300.

38. *Only Yesterday*, p. xiv. This citation and those that follow are from the original 1931 edition.

39. Ibid., pp. 19, 62, 69.

40. Ibid., pp. 48, 167.

41. For revisions of this belief, see Robert K. Murray, *The Harding Era: Warren G. Harding and His Administration* (Minneapolis: University of Minnesota Press, 1969), pp. 25–42, and Andrew Sinclair, *The Available Man: The Life Behind the Masks of Warren G. Harding* (Chicago: Quadrangle Books, 1969), pp. 136–54.

42. Allen, *Only Yesterday*, p. 154.

43. Ibid., p. 94.

44. "The American Tradition and the War," *Nation*, 104 (April 26, 1917), 484–85.

45. Allen, *Only Yesterday*, pp. 220–22.

46. Ibid., p. 319.

47. Ibid., pp. 338, 347–48.

48. Ibid., pp. 355–56.

49. Bantam edition, 1946, p. viii.

50. *Middletown: A Study in American Culture* (New York: Harcourt, Brace and Company, 1929).

51. *The Twenties*, Vol. VI of *Our Times: The United States, 1900–1925* (New York: Charles Scribner's Sons, 1935), p. vi.

52. Clipping from *New York World-Telegram* dated November 25, 1939, in Box 15, Allen Papers.

53. Andrew Sarris, *The American Cinema: Directors and Directions, 1929–1968* (New York: E. P. Dutton & Co., Inc., 1968), pp. 139–40.

54. *News-Week*, 2 (November 18, 1933), 35.

55. The script for *The Golden Twenties* is in Box 21, Allen Papers.

56. Interviews with Canfield, September 22, 1971; Lynes, September 22, 1971; and Allen, September 25, 1971.

57. Lewis to Allen, July 31, 1936, Box 2, Allen Papers.

9: A SENSE OF MISSION

1. Allen to mother, July 22, 1932, Oliver Allen Collection.

2. Ibid., August 7, 1932.

3. Ibid., July 10, 1932, and July 18, 1932.

4. Ibid., August 7, 1932, July 18, 1932.

5. Ibid., September 3, 1932; Agnes Rogers Allen to writer, February 23, 1973.

6. Quoted by the President's secretary, Theodore G. Joslin, in *Hoover Off the Record* (Garden City: Doubleday, Doran & Company, Inc., 1934), p. 366.

7. Frederick Lewis Allen, *The Lords of Creation* (Chicago: Quadrangle Books, 1966, c. 1935), p. ix.

8. Allen to mother, March 26, 1933, Box 1, Allen Papers; Allen to mother, October 1, 1933, Oliver Allen Collection.

9. Ibid., September 3, 1933, Box 1, Allen Papers.

10. "Theme for Wall Street," handwritten notes, Box 21, ibid.

11. Allen to mother, January 22, 1933, Box 1, ibid.

12. Allen to Hildegarde Allen, October 28, 1934, Box 2, ibid.

13. Allen to mother, March 26, 1933, Box 1, ibid.

14. Ibid., April 2, 1933.

15. Ibid.

16. Ibid., April 16, 1933.

17. Undated memo to Lee Hartman, Box 21; Allen to Hildegarde Allen, June 17, 1935, Box 2; Allen Papers.

18. Allen to father, March 3, 1907, February 16, 1908, Box 26, Allen Papers.

19. Allen to mother, May 3, 1934, Box 2, ibid.

20. Allen to Hildegarde Allen, May 3, 1934, June 17, 1935, Box 2, Allen Papers.

21. Ibid., July 16, 1935.

22. "Books of the Times," undated review, *New York Times*, clipping in Box 21, ibid.

23. Allen, *The Lords of Creation*, pp. 96–97.

24. Ibid., pp. 381–82.

25. Ibid., p. 442.

26. Allen to Hildegarde Allen, October 27, 1935, November 9, 1935, Box 2, Allen Papers.

27. A Quadrangle paperback, issued in December 1966, had sold 4,540 copies through mid-1971. Beulah Hagen to writer, June 17, 1971.

28. Allen to Hildegarde Allen, January 26, 1936, Box 2, Allen Papers.

29. Ibid., April 21, 1935.

30. Ibid., January 26, 1936.

31. More than twelve million had been unemployed in 1932 and 1933, the worst years of the Depression in this respect. In 1934 the figure was more than eleven million, and the figure for 1935, the year in which Allen spoke, was ten and a half million. The figures are from the U.S. Department of Commerce's *Historical Statistics of the United States* (1960), p. 70, as quoted by Lester Chandler, *America's Greatest Depression, 1929–1941* (New York: Harper & Row, 1970), p. 5.

32. Handwritten notes for speech given at Greenville Church [April, 1935], Box 12, Allen Papers.

33. Allen to Hildegarde Allen, April 7, 1935, Box 2, ibid.

34. Ibid.

35. Allen to Hildegarde Allen, April 21, 1935, Box 2, Allen Papers.

36. Ibid., November 3, 1936.

37. Allen to Rebecca Allen, November 3, 1936, Oliver Allen Collection.

38. Allen to Hildegarde Allen, February 22, 1937, Box 2, Allen Papers.

39. Ibid., December 21, 1937.

40. Charles C. Alexander, *Nationalism in American Thought, 1930–1945* (Chicago: Rand McNally & Co., 1969), p. 166.

41. Allen to Hildegarde Allen, April 8, 1935, Oliver Allen Collection.

10: PIONEERING THE PICTURE BOOKS

1. Kolin, "Frederick Lewis Allen and *Harper's Magazine*," p. 62.

2. Allen to mother, March 26, 1933, April 2, 1933, Box 1, Allen Papers.

3. Ibid., May [n.d.], 1933, Oliver Allen Collection.

4. New York: Simon and Schuster, 1933.

5. Of the photographs, 111 came from Brown Brothers, 72 from Culver Service, 23 from the Harold Seton Collection, 19 from the U.S. Signal Corps (including some taken by Mathew Brady), and the remainder from nine other sources.

6. *The American Procession*, p. ii.

7. Roderick Nash, *The Nervous Generation: American Thought, 1917–1930* (Chicago: Rand McNally Co., 1970), p. 19.

8. New York: Harper & Brothers.

9. Kolin, "Frederick Lewis Allen and *Harper's Magazine*," p. 63.

10. *Saturday Review*, 10 (October 28, 1933), 215; Arthur C. Cole, *Mississippi Valley Historical Review*, 21 (September 1934), 287.

11. Allen to mother, October 1, 1933, Oliver Allen Collection.

12. Beulah Hagen to writer, June 17, 1971.

13. Allen to mother, April 22, 1934, Box 2, Allen Papers.

14. New York: Harper & Brothers, 1934.

15. Lynes (1910–), a native of Massachusetts, received a B.A. degree from Yale in 1932 and first worked at *Harper's* from 1932 to 1936. From 1936 to 1940 he was assistant principal and then principal of Shipley School at Bryn Mawr, Pennsylvania, before becoming assistant chief of the civilian training branch of the Army Service Forces. In 1944 he returned to *Harper's*. He is the author of *Highbrow, Lowbrow, Middlebrow* (1949), *Tastemakers* (1954), *Art-Makers of 19th Century America* (1970), and *Good Old Modern* (1973).

16. Allen may be seen on the right in photograph 49 and also in photograph 50. Agnes is in photos 71, 88, 89, and 91.

17. Allen to Hildegarde Allen, November 5, 1934, November 11, 1934, Box 2, Allen Papers.

18. Allen to Hildegarde Allen, September 28, 1935, Oliver Allen Collection.

19. Allen to mother, May 1, 1933, ibid.

20. Ibid., May 9, 1933.

21. Ibid., October 15, 1933.

22. Agnes Rogers Allen to writer, February 13, 1973.

23. Allen to mother, May 1, 1933, Oliver Allen Collection. Allen had considered sending Oliver to Groton despite his own misgivings about the school, but decided against it, partly because of Endicott Peabody's advanced age.

24. Allen to mother, October 15, 1933, Oliver Allen Collection.

25. Allen to Hildegarde Allen, August 8, 1935, ibid.

26. Ibid., April 8, 1935.

27. Allen to mother, June 27, 1934, ibid.

28. Agnes Rogers Allen to writer, March 3, 1973.

29. Allen to mother, May 21, 1933, Box 1, Allen Papers.

30. Ibid., May 13, 1934, Oliver Allen Collection.

31. Ibid., April 2, 1933, Box 1; Allen to Hildegarde Allen, February 1, 1935, Box 2; Allen Papers.

32. Interview with Agnes Rogers Allen, September 22, 1971; letter from Mrs. Allen to writer, February 6, 1973.

33. Allen to Hildegarde Allen, July [n.d.], 1936, and August 3, 1936, Oliver Allen Collection.

34. Ibid., October 1, 1936.

35. Ibid., November 23, 1936.

36. Ibid., January 22, 1937, Box 2, Allen Papers.

37. Ibid. Allen's earnings included: salary at *Harper's*, $6,750; payments for articles and lectures, $1,150; royalties on books, $2,600; income from securities, $4,550; profits on stock sales, $4,700. Agnes income amounted to $3,500. The couple gave to charities and other causes nearly $2,000.

38. Agnes Rogers Allen to writer, February 13, 1973.

39. Allen to Hildegarde Allen, January 12, 1938, Box 2, Allen Papers.

40. Allen to Philip Allan Friedman, April 27, 1953, Box 6, ibid.

11: IMPROVING THE MAGAZINE

1. Allen to Hildegarde Allen, April 8, 1935, Oliver Allen Collection.

2. Conant (1893–   ), was born in Dorchester, Mass., and received his A.B. degree from Harvard in 1913, one year after Allen. He earned a Ph.D. from Harvard in 1916, and in 1919 he began a long career there as a chemistry professor that culminated in his 1933 election to the presidency. In 1953 he resigned that position to accept an appointment from President Eisenhower as High Commissioner (later ambassador) to West Germany, where he served until 1957. Since that time Conant has been involved in various studies of higher education and has published more than a dozen books concerning science education and education in general.

3. Allen to mother, May 9, 1933, Oliver Allen Collection.

4. Ibid., May 3, 1934, Box 2, Allen Papers.

5. Circulation figures (rounded off here) are from the annual volumes of *N. W. Ayer & Sons Directory of Newspapers and Periodicals*.

6. Leighton was born in 1902 in Methol, N.Y., and attended Harvard College from 1922 to 1926. He quit *Harper's* in 1944, then worked for the Republican Senate Policy Committee and as a consultant to the Interstate Commerce Committee. He wrote *Five Cities* (1939) and was co-author with Anita Brenner of *Winds That Swept Mexico, 1910–1942* (1943). He died in the late 1950s.

7. Allen to Hildegarde Allen, July 16, 1935, Box 2, Allen Papers.

8. DeVoto (1897–1955) was born in Ogden, Utah, and educated

at Harvard, where he received an A.B. degree in 1920. Early in his career he taught English at Northwestern University (1922–1927), and then moved to Cambridge, Mass., and combined a free-lance writing career with part-time teaching at Harvard. He won the Pulitzer and Bancroft prizes for *The Course of Empire* (1952), and his *Mark Twain's America* (1932) rebutted assertions that Twain's literary genius was limited by America's hostile environment. From 1935 until his death in 1955 DeVoto wrote "The Easy Chair" column for *Harper's*. His life is portrayed by Wallace Stegner in *The Uneasy Chair: A Biography of Bernard DeVoto* (Garden City: Doubleday & Company, Inc., 1974).

9. Allen to Hildegarde Allen, August 8, 1935, Oliver Allen Collection.

10. Davis (1890–1958) was born in Aurora, Ind., and received his A.B. and A.M. degrees from Franklin College in 1910 and 1911 respectively. He gained fame as a commentator on public affairs as a *New York Times* reporter, as a free-lance writer, and as a CBS radio news analyst from 1939 to 1942. From 1942 to 1945 he directed the Office of War Information.

11. Allen to Hildegarde Allen, November 9, 1935, Box 2, Allen Papers.

12. Vol. 179, pp. 337–51.

13. Grattan (1902–   ) began writing extensively for *Harper's* in the mid-1930s and continued to write for it frequently through the mid-1950s, concentrating on economics, foreign affairs, and literary criticism. Born in Wakefield, Mass., Grattan received an A.B. degree from Clark College in 1923. His books, in addition to *Why We Fought*, include *Bitter Bierce: A Mystery of American Letters* (1929), *The Three Jameses: A Family of Minds* (1932), *Introducing Australia* (1942, rev. ed., 1947), and *The Southwest Pacific: A Modern History*, 2 vols. (1963).

14. Vol. 178 (April, 1939), 457–65.

15. Gunther tells how he came to write the book in *Fragments of an Autobiography: The Fun of Writing the Inside Books* (New York: Harper & Row, 1961), pp. 3–12.

16. Allen to Hildegarde Allen, March 8, 1935, June 14, 1936, Oliver Allen Collection. Childs' article appeared in Vol. 172 (May 1936), 634–42.

17. The article was entitled "The Kingfish of Massachusetts" and it appeared in Vol. 173 (September 1936), 343–57. Sales jumped from

the normal 500 to 2,000 copies. (Allen to Hildegarde Allen, August 29, 1936, Box 2, Allen Papers.)

18. Allen to Hildegarde Allen, August 29, 1936, Box 2, Allen Papers.

19. A three-page typewritten memorandum entitled "Proposed Program for Harper's Magazine," dated September 1937. The memo is in Box 24, Allen Papers.

20. *Harper's* could hardly afford rates that were much higher; at the end of 1937, the magazine had shown profits of nearly $5,000. (Allen to Hildegarde Allen, December 31, 1937, Oliver Allen Collection.)

21. "Proposed Program for Harper's Magazine," September 1937, Box 24, Allen Papers.

22. "Private Memo of FLA on status of mag. staff, April, 1938, before discussions with LFH," ibid.

23. Elwyn Brooks White (1899–   ) was born in Mount Vernon, N.Y., and was graduated from Cornell University. He wrote "One Man's Meat" for *Harper's* from 1938 to 1943, and he has continued writing for the *New Yorker*.

24. The poem is in Box 24, Allen Papers.

12: FREE-LANCING IN THE THIRTIES

1. "Breaking World's Records," *Harper's*, 173 (August 1936), 302–10.

2. *Saturday Review of Literature*, 13 (December 7, 1935), 3–4, 20, 24, 26.

3. Ibid., 22 (June 29, 1940), 16.

4. "Memorandum to Messrs. Canfield and Hartman, October 6, 1938," Box 11, Allen Papers.

5. Ibid.

6. Robert Van Gelder, "Writing Contemporary History," *New York Times*, February 18, 1940. Clipping in Box 15, Allen Papers.

7. New York: Harcourt, Brace, 1937.

8. New York: Macmillan Co., 1939.

9. "Note on Mss of *Since Yesterday*," April 16, 1944, Box 9, Allen Papers.

10. *New York World-Telegram*, clipping dated November 25, 1939, Box 15, ibid.

11. William James Fadiman to Allen, October 12, 1939, Box 10, ibid.

12. Vol. 8 (February 26, 1940), 67–79.
13. *Since Yesterday* (New York: Bantam Books, 1965), pp. 266, 271.
14. Ibid., p. 267.
15. Allen cited E. D. Kennedy, *Dividends to Pay* (New York: Reynal & Hitchcock, 1939).
16. Allen, *Since Yesterday*, pp. 107–110.
17. Ibid., pp. 118–24.
18. Ibid., p. 276.
19. Allen to Hildegarde Allen, March 1, 1940, Box 2, Allen Papers.
20. Ibid., April 13, 1940.
21. Published in booklet form under the same title in 1938. No publishing details are listed. A copy is in Box 24, Allen Papers.
22. Ibid., p. 3.
23. Ibid., p. 6.
24. Ibid., pp. 8, 10.
25. Ibid., p. 11.
26. Ibid., pp. 14–15.

13: THE EDITORSHIP

1. Allen to Hildegarde Allen, April 13, 1940, Box 2, Allen Papers; May 19, 1940, Oliver Allen Collection.
2. James J. Martin, *American Liberalism and World Politics: Liberalism's Press and Spokesmen on the Road Back to War Between Mukden and Pearl Harbor*, II (New York: The Devin-Adair Co., 1964). See Chapter 30 for a full discussion of the intellectual battle raging during 1940 and 1941 over isolationism, pp. 1139–1188.
3. Allen to William T. Pheiffer, January 23, 1941, Box 11, *Harper's* Correspondence Files, Library of Congress (hereinafter referred to as *Harper's* Files).
4. Allen to Hildegarde Allen, April 10, 1941, May 4, 1941, Box 2, Allen Papers.
5. Editor's note preceding Ellsworth Barnard's "War and the Verities," 180 (January 1940), 114.
6. Grattan, "The Struggle for Peace," pp. 297–304; Flynn, "Can Hitler Beat American Business?" 180 (February 1940), 321–28.
7. "The Lesson of 1917," 181 (September 1940), 344–53.
8. "Personal & Otherwise," *Harper's*, 183 (September 1941), back unnumbered pages.

9. "Introduction to America," March 5, 1941. Handwritten notes in Box 25, Allen Papers.

10. Note dated June 8, 1941, ibid.

11. Allen to Hildegarde Allen, January 22, 1940, Oliver Allen Collection.

12. The 1939 figure was 101,260. The lowest circulation in the 1930s was in 1934 when readers numbered 100,105. Figures from yearly volumes of N. W. Ayer & Sons Directory of Newspapers and Periodicals.

13. Harper's, 182 (April 1941), 493–502.

14. Allen to Hildegarde Allen, May 4, 1941, Box 2, Allen Papers.

15. Ibid., May 19, 1940, Oliver Allen Collection.

16. Dewey to Allen, March 11, 1941, and Allen to Dewey, March 5, 1941, Box 3, Harper's Files; Allen to Hildegarde Allen, January 11, 1942, Box 3, Allen Papers.

17. Farrell to Allen, October 1, 1940, Box 2, Harper's Files.

18. Leighton memorandum, Box 2, Harper's Files.

19. Allen to Farrell, October 9, 1940, ibid.

20. "James T. Farrell: Moralist," Harper's, 209 (October 1954), 93–98.

21. Allen to Hildegarde Allen, September 28, 1941, Box 2, Allen Papers.

22. "Personal & Otherwise," Harper's, 183 (November 1941), unnumbered back pages.

23. Bernard DeVoto, "The Easy Chair," Harper's, 184 (December 1941), 110.

24. Allen to Hildegarde Allen, September 28, 1941, Box 2, Allen Papers.

25. DeVoto to Allen, September 24, 1941, Box 3, Harper's Files.

26. Kouwenhoven (1909–   ) had joined the magazine in 1941, beginning what was to be a relationship that continued until 1954. Born in Yonkers, N.Y., he received an A.B. from Wesleyan University in 1931, an M.A. from Columbia in 1933, and a Ph.D. from Columbia in 1948. Allen had come to know Kouwenhoven when the latter taught English at Harvey School from 1932 to 1936, where Oliver was a student, and then as a faculty member at Bennington College, where Allen was a trustee. Beginning in 1946 Kouwenhoven began a part-time association with Harper's and resumed his teaching career at Barnard College. He is the author of Made in America: The Arts in Modern Civilization (1948), and other books.

27. Telephone interview with John Kouwenhoven, September 25, 1971; Cass Canfield to writer, December 19, 1972.

28. Allen to Dr. Robert D. Leigh, October 31, 1941, Box 2, Allen Papers.

29. Allen to Hildegarde Allen, October 13, 1941, Oliver Allen Collection.

30. Ibid.

31. Ibid.

32. "Harper's Sixth," *Time*, 38 (October 20, 1941), 62–64.

33. *New York Times*, October 9, 1941, clipping in Box 1, Allen Papers.

34. Sedgwick to Allen, October 10, 1941; Allen to Sedgwick, October 21, 1941; Box 1, Allen Papers.

35. DeVoto to Allen, October 7, 1941; Emily Cobb Holmes to Allen [n.d.]; ibid.

36. "Looking Ahead," *Harper's*, 184 (December 1941), unnumbered front pages.

37. Allen to Hildegarde Allen, November 16, 1941, Oliver Allen Collection.

38. Ibid.

39. "Advertising Trend," *Business Week*, No. 623 (August 9, 1941), p. 36.

40. Peterson, *Magazines in the Twentieth Century*, p. 124.

14: WAR COMES TO THE NATION AND TO *Harper's*

1. Allen to Hildegarde Allen, December 12, 1941, Box 2, Allen Papers.

2. Ibid.

3. Ibid.

4. Ibid.

5. Ibid.

6. Ibid.

7. Ibid.

8. DeVoto to Allen, December 9, 1941, Box 3, *Harper's* Files.

9. Allen to DeVoto, December 22, 1941, ibid.

10. "The Easy Chair," *Harper's*, Vol. 179, p. 671.

11. DeVoto to Allen, December 9, 1941, Box 3, *Harper's* Files.

12. Allen to DeVoto, May 5, 1941; DeVoto to Allen, May 6, 1941; Allen to DeVoto, May 13, 1941; ibid.

13. "Personal & Otherwise," *Harper's*, 184 (February 1942), unnumbered back pages.

14. Allen to Wallace Stegner, February 6, 1942, Box 12, *Harper's* Files.

15. "The Magazine Market in Wartime," *The Writer*, 55 (February 1942), 44.

16. Allen to Gunther, April 15, 1942, Box 9, *Harper's* Files.

17. Allen to Elmer Davis, October 14, 1942, Box 5, ibid.

18. "Censorship Ground Rules," *Time*, 39 (January 26, 1942), 56.

19. "Memorandum on the Adventures of Fletcher Pratt's First Article," September 21, 1942, Box 5, *Harper's* Files; Allen to Hildegarde Allen, September 27, 1942, Oliver Allen Collection.

20. Allen to Elmer Davis, October 14, 1942, Box 5, *Harper's* Files.

21. "Marshall, Arnold, King: Three Snapshots," *Harper's*, 190 (February 1945), 286.

22. Ibid., p. 288.

23. Fleet Admiral E. J. King to Allen, February 21, 1945, Box 3, Allen Papers.

24. Allen to Dos Passos, July 7, 1942, Box 7, *Harper's* Files.

25. Ibid., January 14, 1942.

26. Ibid.

27. Allen to Cass Canfield, December 14, 1942, Box 7, *Harper's* Files.

28. Allen to Chamberlin, May 26, 1942, ibid.

29. Ibid.

30. *Harper's* editorially expressed concern over the questions involved in the massive roundup of Japanese-Americans and favored a quick disposition on an individual rather than group basis, releasing those whose loyalty to the United States could be determined. See editors' note preceding "The Japanese in America," *Harper's*, 185 (October 1942), 489–90.

31. "Up to Now: The First Year and a Half," *Harper's*, 187 (July 1943), 99.

32. Ibid., pp. 105–106.

33. Ibid., pp. 106–107.

34. London diary, entry for November 7, 1943, Box 1, Allen Papers.

35. Ibid.

1. Dorothy Ducas to Allen, October 14, 1942, Box 19, *Harper's* File.

2. Allen to Dorothy Ducas, November 27, 1942, ibid.

3. Two-page undated memorandum from Magazine Section, Office of War Information, Box 19, *Harper's* Files.

4. Allen to Early, August 18, 1942; Early to Allen, August 21, 1942; Box 7, ibid.

5. "Flags on the Stands," *Newsweek*, 20 (July 6, 1942), 58–59.

6. Interview with C. Hartley Grattan, February 7, 1973.

7. Allen to LeRoy Adams Crumbine, July 17, 1942, Box 9, *Harper's* Files.

8. Allen to Walker, December 23, 1941, Box 13, ibid.

9. Allen to DeVoto, January 6, 1943, Box 15, ibid. DeVoto's column appeared in the February 1943 issue.

10. The correspondence may be found in a *Buffalo Courier Express* newspaper clipping, probably July 25 or 26, 1942, in Box 13, *Harper's* Files, and in the "Personal & Otherwise" column, *Harper's*, 185 (October 1942), unnumbered back pages.

11. Allen to C. Lester Walker, August 5, 1942, Box 13, *Harper's* Files.

12. "Harper's Fury," *Newsweek*, 23 (May 15, 1944), 102; "MacArthur and the Censorship," *Harper's*, 188 (May 1944), 537.

13. "MacArthur and the Censorship," p. 537.

14. "Harper's Fury," p. 103.

15. Quoted by John Gunther, *The Riddle of MacArthur: Japan, Korea and the Far East* (New York: Harper & Brothers, 1950), p. 61.

16. Allen to Hildegarde Allen, June 18, 1942, Oliver Allen Collection.

17. Allen to Bernard DeVoto, December 16, 1942, Box 7, *Harper's* Files.

18. "Personal & Otherwise," *Harper's*, 187 (September 1943), unnumbered back pages.

19. Allen to Robert Cheney, March 3, 1943, Box 20, *Harper's* Files.

20. "New Newsprint Cuts," *Newsweek*, 23 (January 3, 1944), 58.

21. "Advertising Holds," *Business Week*, No. 700, January 30, 1943, p. 44; "New Top for Ads," *Business Week*, No. 803, January 20, 1945, p. 84.

22. Allen to Hildegarde Allen, April 3, 1943, Box 3, Allen Papers.

23. Allen to E. B. White, August 30, 1943, Box 21; Allen to DeVoto, June 14, 1944, Box 44; *Harper's* Files.

24. Allen to Oliver Allen, March 31, 1945, Box 3, Allen Papers.

25. Allen to Fadiman, August 13, 1942, Box 9, *Harper's* Files.

26. Allen to Cass Canfield, November 2, 1942, Box 7, ibid.

27. Allen to Andrew Stewart, July 24, 1942, Box 12, ibid.

28. Allen to Wallace Stegner, September 25, 1942, Box 12; Allen to Genevieve Taggard, July 20, 1942, Box 13; Allen to Earl P. Hanson, August 12, 1942, Box 9; Allen to Oscar Ogg, September 11, 1942, Box 11; *Harper's* Files.

29. "Personal & Otherwise," *Harper's*, 182 (February 1941), unnumbered back pages.

30. Allen to Kate McNeal, July 3, 1942, Box 10, *Harper's* Files.

31. Interview with C. Hartley Grattan, October 11, 1972.

32. Allen to Hildegarde Allen, May 28, 1944, Box 3, Allen Papers; Allen to Bernard DeVoto, May 22, 1944, *Harper's* Files.

33. Fischer (1910–   ), was born in Texhoma, Okla., and was educated at the University of Oklahoma (1928–1932) before becoming a Rhodes scholar at Oxford. He worked as a United Press reporter in England and Germany from 1933 to 1935 and was with the Associated Press in Washington from 1935 to 1937. Upon leaving the Associated Press, he joined the U.S. Department of Agriculture, staying there until 1942 when he served briefly with the Board of Economic Warfare before becoming a *Harper's* staff member in 1944. Upon Allen's resignation as editor in 1953, Fischer was named to succeed him, and he continued as editor until 1967.

34. Hunter Bell to Allen, November 1, 1943, Box 14, *Harper's* Files.

35. George Leighton to Hunter Bell, November 13, 1943, ibid.

16: DEALING WITH CONTRIBUTORS

1. "On the Horizon," *Harper's*, 184 (April 1942), front advertising pages.

2. Allen to A. Annikov, August 26, 1943, Box 14, *Harper's* Files.

3. Allen, "The Magazine Market in Wartime," *The Writer*, 55 (February 1942), 45.

4. Allen to Wallace Stegner, September 14, 1942, Box 12, *Harper's* Files.

5. Speech given at Allentown, November 20, 1942. The script is in Box 22, Allen Papers.

6. Interview with Agnes Rogers Allen, September 22, 1971.

7. Ibid., September 24, 1971.

8. Telephone interview with John Kouwenhoven, September 25, 1971.

9. Allen to Harold Ober, February 17, 1942, July 23, 1942, August 26, 1942, and September 21, 1942, Box 11, *Harper's* Files.

10. Katherine Gauss Jackson to Malcolm Cowley, July 24, 1944, Box 23, ibid. See also Malcolm Cowley to William Faulkner, July 22, 1944, on page 9 of Cowley's *The Faulkner-Cowley File: Letters and Memories, 1944–1962* (New York: The Viking Press, 1966).

11. Allen to Oliver Allen, March 31, 1945, Box 3, Allen Papers. Marquand arranged for the U.S. Navy to sponsor his Pacific trip, according to Stephen Birmingham, *The Late John Marquand* (Philadelphia: J. B. Lippincott Co., 1972), p. 190.

12. Allen to Wescott, July 29, 1942, July 20, 1942, Box 13, *Harper's* Files.

13. Allen to Kazin, July 26, 1943, Box 17, ibid.

14. Allen to Nabokov, November 12, 1941, Box 11, ibid.

15. Allen to Edna Ferber, October 2, 1944, Box 23, ibid.

16. Agnes Rogers Allen to writer, March 8, 1973.

17. Allen to Stegner, May 20, 1943, Box 20, *Harper's* Files.

18. Allen to Spock, May 3, 1943, ibid.

19. Allen to Mencken, February 19, 1943, Box 18, ibid.

20. Mencken to Allen, March 12, 1943, ibid.

21. Allen to Mencken, May 31, 1944, Box 25, ibid.

22. White to Allen, March 13, 1943, Box 21, ibid.

23. Allen to White, March 16, 1943, ibid.

24. White to Allen, March 20, 1943, ibid.

25. Allen to White, August 30, 1943, ibid.

26. Allen to Franklin P. Adams, August 7, 1944, Box 22, ibid.

27. "The Easy Chair," *Harper's*, 189 (November 1944), 554–57. As for DeVoto's legal maneuver, the ban was upheld against the book, but the eventual result was a new law which made the district attorney rather than the police department responsible for initiating formal censorship action, and changed violation of the law from a criminal to a

civil matter. See Hellmut Lehman-Haupt, *The Book in America: A History of the Making and Selling of Books in the United States* (New York: R. R. Bowker Co., 1951), p. 401.

28. Grattan's article, "Salute to the Litterateurs," appeared in Vol. 190 (December 1944), 34–37.

29. Allen to Willkie, March 24, 1943, Box 21, *Harper's* Files.

30. "Washington Evening," *Harper's*, 187 (October 1943), 419.

31. Earl Brown, "The Truth About the Detroit Riot," *Harper's*, 187 (November 1943), 488–98.

32. Thomas Sanction, "Race Clash," *Harper's*, 188 (January 1944), 135–40.

33. Earl Brown, "The Negro Vote, 1944: A Forecast," *Harper's*, 189 (July 1944), 152–54; Henry Pratt Fairchild, "The Truth About Race," *Harper's*, 189 (October 1944), 418–25; and Will W. Alexander, "Our Conflicting Racial Policies," *Harper's*, 190 (January 1945), 172–79.

34. "The Man in the Blue Serge Suit," *Harper's*, 188 (May 1944), 481–90.

35. Ibid., p. 481.

36. Interview with Grattan, October 18, 1972.

37. Hoover to Allen, June 26, 1944, Box 26, *Harper's* Files.

38. Johnson to Allen, May 24, 1944, Box 24; Allen to Walter R. Suppes, June 21, 1944, Box 26; Memorandum by Allen, October 6, 1944, Box 26; *Harper's* Files.

39. *Harper's*, 189 (June 1944), pp. 1–10.

40. Ibid., 181 (September 1940), 350.

17: ALLEN ON THE HOME FRONT

1. Allen to Hildegarde Allen, July 1, 1942, Oliver Allen Collection.

2. Interview with Agnes Rogers Allen, September 24, 1971.

3. Robert E. Spiller to Allen, August 28, 1943; Allen to Spiller, August 31, 1943, Box 20, *Harper's* Files. *The Literary History of the United States* was published in 1946 by the Macmillan Company under the editorship of Spiller, et al.

4. Allen to Hildegarde Allen, June 18, 1942, Oliver Allen Collection.

5. Allen to Ferril, June 23, 1942, Box 7, *Harper's* Files.

6. New York: Farrar & Rinehart, Inc., 1942, pp. 114–122.

7. Allen to Hildegarde Allen, September 2, 1943, Oliver Allen Collection.

8. That election year Agnes Rogers Allen had supposed that her husband went to the polls to vote for Roosevelt; Allen thought his wife would vote for Willkie. At the end of the day they compared notes to learn that just the opposite had occurred. (Oliver Allen to writer, March 3, 1973.)

9. Typewritten manuscript entitled "Pre-election Speech given at Bennington College, October 27, 1944, by Mr. Frederick Lewis Allen," Box 22, Allen Papers.

10. Ibid.

11. Ibid.

12. The Board had been created just two days after Pearl Harbor as a liaison with various government agencies. It served as a propaganda arm of the government, undertaking such chores as assisting the Treasury Department in the sale of war bonds and supplying speakers for various causes. A summary of its activities may be found in *Publisher's Weekly* in an article entitled "Writers' War Board Decides to Continue in Response to Many Requests," 148 (July 28, 1945), 308–311.

13. Agencies represented were the U.S. Army, the United Nations Relief and Rehabilitation Administration (UNRRA), the Office of Price Administration, Department of Agriculture, War Food Administration, Foreign Economic Administration, Department of State, and the International Food Committee. The British Embassy also was represented.

14. "Memo from AG [Allan Green] to WWB," September 4, 1944; "Memorandum on Food Dinner, August 31, 1944"; Box 3, Allen Papers.

15. "Memorandum on Food Dinner, August 31, 1944," ibid.

16. San Francisco Diary, 1945, Box 1, ibid.

17. Allen to Oliver Allen, March 31, 1945, Box 3, ibid.

18. Ibid.

19. Allen to Hildegarde Allen, August 4, 1945, Oliver Allen Collection.

20. *Harper's*, 191 (October 1945), 327.

18: POSTWAR TENSIONS

1. Allen to Hildegarde Allen, December 25, 1945, Oliver Allen Collection.

2. Vol. 46 (December 24, 1945), 19.

3. Allen to W. G. Constable, April 12, 1950, Box 4, Allen Papers.

4. Larrabee (1922–   ) came to know Allen through his friendship at

Harvard with Oliver Allen. Born in Melrose, Mass., he received his A.B. in 1943 from Harvard. In 1946 he became associate editor of *Harper's*, a position he held until 1958. From 1958 to 1960 he was executive editor of *American Heritage* and he was managing editor from 1960 to 1962. In 1970 he became associated with the New York State Council on Arts.

5. Notes made by Oliver Allen for *Time* and adapted for *Book-of-the-Month Club News,* August 11, 1952, Box 1, Allen Papers.

6. "Speaking of Pictures," *Life,* 33 (December 29, 1952), 2–3.

7. Allen to Hildegarde Allen, April 23, 1950, Box 4, Allen Papers. See also "After Hours," *Harper's,* 201 (September 1950), 101–103, for a description of the game.

8. Interview with Agnes Rogers Allen, September 22, 1971.

9. Interview with Eric Larrabee, September 24, 1971.

10. Allen to Hildegarde Allen, October 23, 1948, Oliver Allen Collection.

11. Oliver Allen to writer, March 11, 1973.

12. Allen to William Benton, September 24, 1945, Box 3, Allen Papers.

13. "Must We Tell the World?" *Harper's,* 191 (December 1945), 553–59.

14. John W. Henderson, *The United States Information Agency* (New York: Frederick A. Praeger, 1969), pp. 35–41.

15. Allen to Senator James M. Mead, March 22, 1946, Box 3, Allen Papers.

16. John T. Flynn to Allen, April 1, 1946, ibid.

17. Ibid.

18. Allen to Stout, April 3, 1946, ibid.

19. Three years later Stout urged Allen to join the Writers' World Government Board to further the cause of world government. Allen declined, as he did again in 1953 when Stout again asked him.

20. *Fifty Years: The Story of the Foreign Policy Association, 1918–1968,* a pamphlet published by the Foreign Policy Association, New York, 1968.

21. "Report on Publications, Etc.," February 20, 1946, Box 7, Allen Papers.

22. "This Time and Last Time," *Harper's,* 194 (March 1947), 193–203.

23. Allen to S. K. Ratcliffe, September 6, 1946, Box 3, Allen Papers.

24. Allen repeated this belief as late as 1950 in a letter to William Henry Chamberlin [February 6, 1950, Box 43, *Harper's* Files], saying that one effect of this preoccupation might be finding German guns turned against the United States on the Soviet side.

25. Allen to S. K. Ratcliffe, September 6, 1946, Box 3, Allen Papers.

26. Quoted by Herbert Feis in *From Trust to Terror: The Onset of the Cold War, 1945–50* (New York: W. W. Norton & Co., 1970), pp. 161, 149.

27. Allen to Olin Downes, August 26, 1948, Box 4, Allen Papers.

28. Allen to Mrs. Stanley E. Tabor, February 28, 1951, Box 61, *Harper's* Files.

29. Allen to Davis, February 16, 1950, Box 44, ibid.

30. "My Own Review of *Witness*" (undated), Box 25, Allen Papers.

31. Ibid.

32. Undated notes for speech, Box 22, ibid.

33. *New York Times,* October 22, 1952, p. 25.

34. *The Big Change: America Transforms Itself, 1900–1950* (New York: Harper & Brothers, 1952), p. 283.

35. Allen to Chamberlain, October 29, 1952, Box 5, Allen Papers.

36. Ibid.

37. Subtitled *The Rise, Life and Decay of the Progressive Mind in America* (New York: The John Day Co., 1932), Chamberlain's book, as the title indicates, described what he believed to be the failure and futility of recent reformism.

38. Allen to Chamberlain, October 29, 1952, Box 5, Allen Papers.

39. Ibid.

40. Chamberlain to Allen, November 6, 1952, ibid.

41. Vol. 199, pp. 65–68.

42. "Personal & Otherwise," *Harper's,* 199 (October 1949), 10.

43. Allen to Miss Sidney Moore, Harper-Atlantic Sales, November 14, 1952, Box 62, *Harper's* Files.

44. Miss Sidney Moore to Allen, November 12, 1952; Allen to Miss Sidney Moore, November 14, 1952; ibid.

45. Miss Sidney Moore to Allen, November 12, 1952; Allen to Miss Sidney Moore, November 14, 1952; ibid.

46. Allen to Henry W. Bragdon, April 18, 1952, Box 5, Allen Papers.

47. Allen to Lurton Blassingame, August 21, 1952, Box 64, *Harper's* Files.

48. Robert Griffith, *The Politics of Fear: Joseph R. McCarthy and the Senate* (Lexington: The University Press of Kentucky, 1970), pp. 224–29.

49. Sherwood to Allen, March 3, 1952; Allen to Sherwood, March 3, 1952; Box 5, Allen Papers.

50. Circular letter by Allen and Oscar Hammerstein II, May 13, 1953, Box 26, ibid.

51. Three or four checks a day still were coming in, but the Committee's executive secretary, George E. Agree, reported that the peak was well past by then. (Agree to Allen, June 19, 1953, Box 6, Allen Papers.)

52. Griffith, *The Politics of Fear*, p. 321.

53. Telephone interview with John Fischer, September 23, 1971; interview with Agnes Rogers Allen, September 25, 1971.

54. G. F. Welch to Allen, October 17, 1952, Box 5, Allen Papers.

55. Allen to G. F. Welch, October 22, 1952, ibid.

56. Allen to S. K. Ratcliffe, December 29, 1952, Box 69, *Harper's* Files.

57. Allen to Hook, August 28, 1952, Box 5, Allen Papers.

58. Allen to Mrs. B. Preston Clark, November 10, 1952, ibid.

59. "The Reputation of the Government," *Harper's*, 208 (April 1954), 25–28.

19: NEW CHALLENGES FOR *Harper's*

1. "Magazine Flood," *Newsweek*, 27 (June 3, 1946), 61–62.

2. "Circulation Bust," *Business Week*, No. 871, May 11, 1946, pp. 71–72, 75.

3. *The University of Missouri Bulletin*, Journalism Series, No. 101, 46 (August 10, 1945).

4. Ibid., p. 4.

5. Ibid.

6. Ibid., pp. 4–5.

7. Ibid., p. 7.

8. Ibid., p. 11.

9. A copy of the speech is in Box 23, Allen Papers.

10. "Closed Mind Speech," ibid.

11. Allen to Clifford Strock, January 22, 1947, Box 7, ibid; *New York Times*, January 17, 1947, p. 21; and *Time*, "Closed-Mind Journalism," 44 (January 27, 1947), 49.

12. The report is presented in *A Free and Responsible Press: A General Report on Mass Communication, Newspapers, Radio, Motion Pictures, Magazines, and Books* (Chicago: University of Chicago Press, 1947).

13. Interview with Russell Lynes, September 23, 1971; interview with C. Hartley Grattan, October 18, 1972; unaddressed memorandum dated June 17, 1948, Box 48, *Harper's* Files.

14. Kolin, "Frederick Lewis Allen and *Harper's Magazine*," p. 125.

15. John A. Kouwenhoven to Michael Fishman, March 20, 1953, Box 77; Eric Larrabee to Kenneth M. Baker, July 11, 1950, Box 42; *Harper's* Files.

16. Allen to Mrs. Nancy Bickel, November 4, 1952, Box 2, ibid.

17. Interview with Eric Larrabee, September 24, 1971.

18. Telephone interview with John Fischer, September 23, 1971.

19. Eventually Jones decided upon "hot-legged bitch." See James Jones to Allen, May 18, 1948, Box 56, *Harper's* Files.

20. Jones to Merle Miller, April 22, 1948, ibid.

21. Allen to Jones, April 28, 1948, ibid.

22. Ibid.

23. Ibid.

24. Jones to Merle Miller, May 3, 1948, ibid.

25. Ibid. The article on Einstein to which Jones referred was a much heralded three-part series entitled "The Universe and Dr. Einstein" by Lincoln Barnett. It appeared in the April, May, and June 1948 (Vol. 196) issues.

26. Allen to Jones, May 14, 1948.

27. Jones to Allen, May 18, 1948, ibid.

28. Jones to Allen, June [n.d.] 1948, ibid.

29. Vol. 198 (June 1949), 13. The short story appeared on pages 90–97.

30. Allen to Jones, December 28, 1950, Box 56, *Harper's* Files.

31. Allen to Stegner, February 20, 1952, Box 70, ibid. The story appeared in *Harper's*, 200 (April 1950), 41–49.

32. Katherine Gauss Jackson to Bernice Baumgarten of Brandt and Brandt, July 31, 1953, Box 76, *Harper's* Files. The story appeared in Vol. 208 (January 1954), 78–84.

33. Anne L. Goodman to Albert Erskine, January 3, 1952, Box 65, *Harper's* Files.

34. The May 1946 issue (Vol. 192) contained four short stories, a rarity.

35. "The Decision to Use the Atomic Bomb," *Harper's,* 194 (February 1947), 97–107.

36. Published in 1947 as *On Active Service in Peace and War,* and listing MacGeorge Bundy as well as Stimson as author.

37. Notes made by Allen of events surrounding publication of the article, February 10, 1947, Box 49, *Harper's* Files.

38. Ibid.

39. Larrabee's article was entitled "The Day the Earth Stood Still," 200 (January 1950), 19–26. *Worlds in Collision* was published originally by Macmillan in 1950.

40. Interview with Eric Larrabee, September 24, 1971.

41. Ralph E. Juergens, "Minds in Chaos," *The Velikovsky Affair: The Warfare of Science and Scientism* (New Hyde Park, N. Y.: University Books, 1966), p. 19.

42. "Letters," *Harper's,* 200 (March 1950), 18–19.

43. *Harper's,* Vol. 202, pp. 51–66.

44. The centennial issue was Vol. 201.

45. Peterson, *Magazines in the Twentieth Century,* p. 408.

46. John J. O'Neill, "Enter Atomic Power," 181 (June 1940), 1–10; Albert Deutsch, "The Sex Habits of American Men," 195 (December 1947), 490–97. In a discussion that Allen had with Kinsey, the noted researcher told him that his chapter in *Only Yesterday* on the loosening morals of the twenties was wrong; his own data indicated an insignificant amount of change in sexual conduct from decade to decade. (Allen to Milton Crane, November 27, 1950, Box 4, Allen Papers.)

47. Quoted by Allen in speech to the Curtis Publishing Association, December 1, 1949, Box 22, Allen Papers.

48. Speeches by Allen to the Curtis Publishing Association, December 1, 1949, and undated, ibid.

49. Interview with Cass Canfield, September 22, 1971.

50. In 1944 circulation had been 105,276; in 1945, 115,033; and in 1947 it climbed to 137,742.

51. Allen to Hildegarde Allen, February 7, 1948, Oliver Allen Collection.

52. Ibid., December 4, 1948.

53. The articles in the *Atlantic* were "The American Magazine Grows

Up," 180 (November 1947), 77–82, and "An Editor's Creed," 192 (December 1953), 46–47.

54. Allen to Hildegarde Allen, February 7, 1948, Oliver Allen Collection; memorandums dated January 27, 1948, and August 27, 1948, Box 48, *Harper's* Files.

55. Speech by Allen to the Curtis Publishing Association, December 1, 1948, Box 22, Allen Papers.

56. Peterson, *Magazines in the Twentieth Century*, p. 408.

57. Allen to Hildegarde Allen, July 15, 1950, Box 4, Allen Papers.

58. Allen to Cassels, August 14, 1951, Box 54, *Harper's* Files.

59. Speech by Allen to National Publishers Association, January 16, 1947, Box 23, Allen Papers.

60. Allen to Mrs. Hermann Marnet, November 11, 1941, Box 10, ibid.

20: RESUMING A WRITING CAREER

1. Allen to Hildegarde Allen, November 17, 1945, Box 3, Allen Papers.

2. Ibid.

3. Ledger book containing notes on FDR Project, Box 7, ibid.

4. Allen to George Draper, M.D., December 19, 1949, Box 4, ibid. The biography appeared in 1950 as *Roosevelt in Retrospect: A Profile in History*, published by Harper & Brothers.

5. New York: Harper & Brothers, 1947.

6. Ibid., p. iii.

7. Allen to Miss Luise Sillcox, Authors' Guild, February 9, 1948, Box 4, ibid.

8. Allen memorandum to Cass Canfield, February 3, 1948, Box 18, Allen Papers.

9. Allen to Lamont, July 1, 1947, ibid.

10. Lamont to Allen, July 8, 1947, July 14, 1947, ibid.

11. Lincoln Steffens, *The Autobiography of Lincoln Steffens* (New York: Grosset & Dunlap, Publishers [n.d., copyright 1931 by Harcourt, Brace and Company, Inc.]), p. 189.

12. Allen to Junius S. Morgan, August 25, 1947, Box 18, Allen Papers.

13. Allen memorandum to Cass Canfield, October 28, 1948. When the junior Morgan had testified before a session of the Senate Banking

Committee in 1933 a circus midget had been placed on his knee to the delight of the photographers.

14. The *Harper's* excerpts were in Vol. 197, December through February, 25–37, 67–71, and 53–62. *Life's* excerpt, "Morgan the Great," appeared in Vol. 26 (April 25, 1945), 123–41.

15. Allen to John Blum, October 7, 1952, Box 5, Allen Papers. Later, paperback editions passed the 100,000 mark in sales.

16. Allen, *The Great Pierpont Morgan* (New York: Harper & Row Perennial Library edition, 1965), pp. vii–viii.

17. Alfred A. Knopf to Allen, December 21, 1949, Box 4, Allen Papers.

18. Allen to Knopf, December 29, 1949, ibid.

19. The profits totaled far less than previously imagined, $248,773.50 on $31,157,000 in bonds. The Cleveland administration was subjected to widespread criticism because of this private arrangement with Morgan to halt the gold flow to Europe. (Allen, *The Great Pierpont Morgan*, p. 100.)

20. Leonhard Keyes to Gordon Wasson, August 16, 1948, Box 18, Allen Papers.

21. Allen to William Herndon, March 31, 1949, Box 18, ibid.

22. Allen to Byron M. Saurman, June 12, 1949, Box 4, ibid.

23. Manuscript of Allen's speech before the *New York Herald-Tribune* Book and Author Luncheon, March 10, 1953, Box 22, ibid.

24. Allen, *The Big Change*, p. x.

25. "The Big Change: The Coming—and Disciplining—of Industrialism, 1850–1950," 201 (October 1950), 145–60.

26. Allen, *The Big Change*, p. 286.

27. It was the November 1952 selection.

28. Nearly a decade later, Bantam Books issued *The Big Change* in paperback and sold 301,600 copies; in 1969 Harper & Row published its own Perennial paperback edition, and by the early 1970s nearly 50,000 copies had been sold. The book was second to *Only Yesterday* in sales among Allen's works.

29. Miss Royce Moch to Allen, October 8, 1951, Box 5, Allen Papers.

30. Elizabeth P. Heppner to Allen, May 6, 1953, Box 6, ibid.

31. DeVoto to John Fischer, June 13, 1952, ibid.

32. Allen, *The Big Change*, p. 186.

33. White to Allen, December 18, 1951, Box 26; Allen to White, December 26, 1951, Box 5; Allen Papers.

34. Lewis to Allen, January 20, 1953, Box 6, ibid.

35. Allen to Dabney, October 19, 1942, Box 3, *Harper's* Files.

36. Allen to Du Bois, August 16, 1943, Box 15, ibid.

37. Bingham to Allen, September 12, 1951; Allen to Bingham, September 18, 1951; Box 53, ibid.

38. *Report of the National Advisory Commission on Civil Disorders* (New York: Bantam Books, 1968), Chapter 15, passim.

39. Allen to Barrett W. Stevens, July 14, 1948, Box 4, Allen Papers.

40. Allen to Oliver Allen, July 16, 1948, ibid.; Agnes Rogers Allen to writer, December 2, 1972.

41. *Harper's,* 194 (March 1947), 193–203.

42. "What Have We Got Here?" *Life,* 34 (January 5, 1953), 47.

43. Ibid., p. 57.

44. "Economic Security: a look back and a look ahead," *Economic Security for Americans,* participant's edition of The American Assembly, Columbia University Graduate School of Business, 1953, pp. 9–18.

45. Ibid., p. 18.

21: HARVARD OVERSEER

1. Morison, *Three Centuries of Harvard,* pp. 476–77.

2. Report of the Harvard Committee, *General Education in a Free Society* (Cambridge: Harvard University Press, 1945), p. 183.

3. Ibid., p. 50.

4. Pamphlet entitled *Board of Overseers of Harvard College, March 1948* [Publishing details are omitted but presumably the pamphlet was issued by the Harvard University Press].

5. Cornell discontinued its press in 1884. (Gene R. Hawes, *To Advance Knowledge: A Handbook on American University Press Publishing* [New York: American University Press Service, Inc., 1967], p. 39.)

6. Allen to Maurice Smith, August 21, 1946; Scaife to Allen, July 23, 1946; handwritten summary by Allen of his conversation with Scaife, October 1946; Box 3, Allen Papers.

7. Allen to Roy E. Larsen, October 16, 1946.

8. Unaddressed form letter, November 13, 1946, signed by Allen, Roy Larsen, and Maurice Smith, ibid.

9. Conant to Allen, December 17, 1946, ibid.

10. Allen, "Report of the Committee to Visit the Harvard University Press," May 12, 1947, Box 5, ibid.

11. Allen to John Walker, May 14, 1948, Box 4, ibid.

12. Typewritten copy of report dated April 12, 1948, ibid.

13. "Report of the Visiting Committee on the Summer School and University Extension," [Spring 1945], Box 7, ibid.

14. "Report of the Committee to Visit the Department of History," June, 1947, ibid.

15. Undated typewritten copy of report to the Board of Overseers [1951], ibid.

16. Allen to Thomas J. Wilson, August 12, 1953, Box 6, ibid.

17. Meyer Levin, "The Paper-Back Revolution: Cheaper Books, More Readers," *The Reporter*, 9 (September 1, 1953), 37–41.

18. White to Allen, February 3, 1953, Box 6, Allen Papers.

19. Ibid., February 26, 1953.

20. Ibid., March 25, 1953.

21. Allen to Brinton, March 25, 1952, ibid.

22. Allen to Robert Cutler, March 4, 1953; Allen to Conant, February 6, 1953; ibid.

23. *New York Times,* January 21, 1953, p. 26; February 27, 1953, p. 1.

24. Allen to Joe Hamlen, March 30, 1953, Box 6, Allen Papers.

25. They were Helen Dean Markham, an assistant professor of anatomy in the medical school, and Leon J. Kamin, a teaching fellow in the department of social relations. (*New York Times,* May 20, 1953, p. 11.)

26. Notes for letter from Allen to David W. Bailey, May 16, 1953, Box 26, Allen Papers.

27. *New York Times,* November 6, 1953, p. 13; January 16, 1954, p. 1.

28. Allen to David Owen, January 19, 1954, ibid.

22: NEW AVENUES OPEN—AND CLOSE

1. Allen to Canfield, December 8, 1952, Box 26, Allen Papers.

2. Allen to Pfeiffer, February 25, 1953, Box 6, ibid.

3. Allen to Canfield, December 8, 1952, Box 26, ibid.

4. Untitled, undated memorandum, Box 24, ibid.

5. Heilbroner to Allen, January 27, 1953; Grattan to Allen, January 28, 1953; Box 6, ibid.

6. Weeks to Allen, January 30, 1953, ibid.

7. Lippmann to Allen, January 29, 1953, ibid.

8. Allen to James R. Reynolds, May 1, 1953; Allen to Hildegarde Allen, May 4, 1953; ibid.

9. Allen to Henry Ford II, [May 1], 1953, ibid.

10. "The Fabulous Ford Foundation," *Harper's,* 203 (December 1951), 25–32.

11. Ibid., pp. 26–27.

12. Interview with Agnes Rogers Allen, September 22, 1971.

13. Ernest J. Perry to Allen, September 23, 1953, Box 6, Allen Papers.

14. He quit positions as a council member of the Society of American Historians and as a director of the Foreign Policy Association.

15. Notes entitled, "Puzzlers for a Foundation Trustee," July 15, 1953, Box 23, Allen Papers.

16. The opportunity was not connected in any way with Allen's appointment as a Ford Foundation trustee; the offer to prepare the script outline came months before the Foundation position was mentioned.

17. A copy of the contract is in Box 25, Allen Papers.

18. Typewritten script entitled "General Plan for the Ford Television Show," February 23, 1953, ibid.

19. Miriam Howell to Mr. and Mrs. Allen, March 10, 1953, Box 6, ibid.

20. Allen to Henry Salomon, Jr., June 25, 1953, ibid.

21. Ibid.

22. Allen to the Reverend James T. Keller, August 3, 1953, Box 77, *Harper's* Files.

23. Agnes Rogers Allen to Sam Goldwyn, Jr., April 17, 1953, Box 25, Allen Papers.

24. General plan for "The Cowboy," May 30, 1953, ibid.

25. Harold E. Howland to Allen, April 17, 1953, Box 6, ibid.

26. Elizabeth P. Heppner to Allen, June 3, 1953; Allen to Heppner, June 5, 1953; ibid.

27. Allen to Charles F. Phillips, June 29, 1953, ibid.

28. Allen to Hildegarde Allen, July 29, 1953, Oliver Allen Collection.

29. Ibid., October 30, 1953.

30. The articles were published posthumously. They were "The Big

Change in Suburbia," *Harper's,* 208 (June 1954), 21–28; "Crisis in the Suburbs," 209 (July 1954), 47–53.

31. "Crisis in the Suburbs," p. 53.

32. *New York Times,* December 17, 1953, p. 55.

33. Allen to Hildegarde Allen, January 15, 1954, Oliver Allen Collection.

34. Allen to Donald E. Stokes, January 28, 1954, Box 6, Allen Papers.

35. New York: Harper & Brothers, 1954.

36. Vol. 201, pp. 60–73.

37. *New York Times,* February 14, 1954, p. 1.

38. Ibid., February 15, 1954, p. 22.

39. "Frederick Lewis Allen," 36 (March 13, 1954), 24.

40. Interview with Agnes Rogers Allen, September 25, 1971. Burney died in 1814. His tomb is found in the north aisle in Westminster Abbey.

41. The *Wall Street Journal* reported in a page-one article on July 28, 1972, that since its inception in 1958 some two hundred books had been written in the room. There are eleven cubicles available, and admission for a maximum period of nine months is by application only. The room is so popular that there is a considerable waiting list at all times.

42. "F.L.A. (1890–1954)," *Harper's,* 208 (April 1954), 74–75.

43. Interview with Agnes Rogers Allen, September 25, 1971.

Acknowledgments

A biography, especially a biography of a person who died as recently as Frederick Lewis Allen, necessarily involves many people. I have many to thank for their help. Foremost is Agnes Rogers Allen, Allen's widow and his partner in many writing projects. Mrs. Allen cheerfully submitted to an interminable round of interviews, correspondence, and telephone calls. She did more than answer questions; she suggested many fruitful avenues for further research. As a writer herself, Mrs. Allen refrained, despite certain temptation, from seeking to influence my interpretations.

To Oliver E. Allen, Frederick Lewis Allen's son, I owe similar thanks. Moreover, I am indebted especially to him for uncovering a wealth of letters which were essential for any full account of his father's life and career and for making them available to me. Emily Cobb Holmes, the sister of Frederick Lewis Allen's first wife, Dorothy, provided me with many details about Allen's courtship and his marriage to Dorothy. Mrs. Holmes and her husband, Leonard Holmes, helped me avoid many stylistic errors by their close reading of my manuscript.

This work originated as a doctoral dissertation at the University of Texas at Austin, and I am grateful to many there. William H. Goetzmann, director of the American Studies and American Civilization programs, encouraged my suggestion to attempt a biographical study of Allen for my dissertation. To Professor Goetzmann I owe thanks not only for serving as chairman of my dissertation committee, but for the inspiration and guidance he has given me and other students at Austin. It also was my happy fate at the University of Texas to encounter C. Hartley Grattan. Professor Grattan, a writer and former contributing editor to *Harper's*, knew Allen well. He guided me in the preparation of this study and proved to be a storehouse of specific and general information. Two other faculty members, Robert M. Crunden of the American Civilization program and Clarence Lasby, chairman of the History Department, read the manuscript and made invaluable suggestions.

It undoubtedly was my good fortune that Allen was such a well-liked individual, for his friends and associates agreed readily to be interviewed or to correspond with me about him. To all of them I owe thanks: Marion Cleveland Amen (Mrs. John Harlan Amen), Cass Canfield, John Fischer, Beulah Hagen, Alfred Kazin, John A. Kouwenhoven, Eric Larrabee, Ralph Lowell, Russell Lynes, Charles M. Storey, and Edward A. Weeks. Three members of this group became involved more closely in this project than they had anticipated. Cass Canfield and Beulah Hagen became my editors at Harper & Row, and Russell Lynes graciously consented to write the Introduction.

I am especially appreciative for permission to quote letters from the following individuals: Hunter Bell, Adolf A. Berle, Barry Bingham, John Chamberlain, Stuart Chase, James B. Conant, Bernard DeVoto, James T. Farrell, John Kenneth Galbraith, Robert Heilbroner, Herbert Hoover, Gerald W. Johnson, James Jones, Alfred A. Knopf, Sinclair Lewis, Walter Lippmann, Endicott Peabody, Ellery Sedgwick, Edward A. Weeks, E. B. White, and William L. White.

Although this biography was undertaken at the University of Texas at Austin, most of the work was done during my association with Southern Methodist University in Dallas. Fondren Library on the S.M.U. campus has been a special headquarters, and I was assisted materially by the many librarians there, particularly those in the periodicals division. A summer research grant from the American Civilization program at the University of Texas at Austin enabled me to travel to Washington, D.C. and New York City to conduct interviews and to study the Allen Papers and the *Harper's Magazine* files in the Manuscripts Division of the Reference Department, Library of Congress.

Mildred Owen deserves special commendation for helping to trim my unwieldly dissertation into a more reasonable book length. William J. Breen, an Australian scholar, mailed me the unpublished manuscript of Allen's history of the Council of National Defense and provided me with insights into Allen's work during World War I. Martha Ann Zivley of Austin performed as a typist in the highest manner.

Finally, the patience and support of my wife Pat and my sons, Mark and Scott, sustained me during the several years of this project.

INDEX

Atomic bomb, 204, 252
Atomic Energy Act, 210
Atwater, Gordon A., 235
Authors' League, 215

Bailey, David, 263
Baker, Newton D., 46, 52, 53, 60
Bankhead, Tallulah, 29
Barber, Red, 104
Baruch, Bernard, 44, 64
Basler Nachicten, 31
Bates College, 272
Beard, Charles A. and Mary, 142,
    150, 152, 153, 211
Belknap, Waldron Phoenix, Jr., 261
Bell, Hunter, 183–84
Benchley, Robert C., 23, 24, 45–46,
    61, 64, 84–85, 286n, 288n
Benét, William Rose, 123–24
Bennington College, 146, 189, 200
Benton, William B., 209
Berlin, Irving, 270
Bermuda, 13, 108, 141, 143, 197
"Best-Sellers: 1900–1935," 141
Biddle, George, 13–14
Big Change, The, ix, 215, 246–250,
    252, 266, 272, 321n
Bingham, Barry, 251
Blakeslee, Lt. Comdr. Victor, 167
Blanchard, Fessenden S., 84
Blassingame, Lurton, 217
Bliven, Bruce, 151
Bolling, Robert H., 22
Book-of-the-Month Club, 99, 114,
    248
Boorstin, Daniel, 262
Boston, 70–71, 177, 193–94
Bourke-White, Margaret, 125
Bowles, Admiral Francis T., 41, 43
Brainard, C. T., 80
Briggs, William H., 82
Brinton, Crane, 262
Brooks, Rev. Phillips, 6, 8, 12
Brown v. Topeka, 250
Brown, Earl, 195
Brown, Thornton, 113
Brownsville, Tex., incident, 18
Bruce, Roscoe Conkling, 72
Buck, Pearl, 111, 188
Buffalo, N.Y., civil defense, 178
Bull Market of 1920's, 101, 103
Bundy, McGeorge, 233
Burnet, Mary, 183

Burney, Charles, 275, 325n
Bushnell, Horace, 5–6
Butler, Andrew and Kate, 98

Caldwell, Erskine, 125
Canfield, Cass, 128, 130, 131,
    141–42, 171, 182, 241, 243, 275,
    295n–96n; at Groton, 13; joins
    Harper & Bros., 80; assesses FLA,
    105; suggests picture book, 121,
    122; and *Inside Europe*, 135;
    names FLA editor, 157; and John
    Fischer, 183, 266; and atomic
    bomb article, 233; and *Harper's*
    profits, 237; and FLA resignation,
    265–66
Cassells, Louis, 238–39
Catts, Sidney J., 51–52
Censorship, U.S. Office of, 167, 175,
    177–79; by Navy, 167–69; in
    Boston, 6–7, 193–94
Century Association, Club, 85
Century Magazine, 28–33 *passim*,
    35–37, 39, 41, 49, 63, 80, 81, 83,
    160
Chafee, Zechariah, 71–72
Chamberlain, John, 114, 136, 138,
    183, 215–16
Chamberlin, William H., 162,
    171–72
Chambers, Whittaker, 213–14
Chase, J. Frank, 7
Chase, Stuart, 114, 133, 134, 171
Chemical Warfare Service, 57
Chevy Chase Club, 48, 97
Chicago Tribune, 179, 210–11
Childs, Marquis, 135
Christian Science Monitor, 42,
    179
Christopher Award, 271
Chubb Fellow program, 274
Churchill, Winston, 151, 163
"Clark, George R.," 154
Clarke, Rev. Merrill F., 108
Clarkson, Grosvenor, 57, 58–59,
    292n
Cleveland, Marion (Mrs. John
    Harlan Amen), 38, 289n
Cliché Club, 207–208, 269
Clos-Nargassans, Anna and Jean,
    108, 126–27, 203, 205
Cobb, Dorothy Penrose, *see* Allen,
    Dorothy Penrose Cobb

335

337

Munsey, Frank A., 27
Münsterberg, Hugo, 24, 70

Nabokov, Vladimir, 156, 190
Nast, Condé, 32
Nation, 39–40, 41, 151, 189
National Association for the
Advancement of Colored People,
249–250
National Committee for Effective
Congress, 218–19
National Geographic, 177
National Publishers Association, 224
National Recovery Act, 118, 119–
120
Navy, U.S., 111, 167–69, 224
New Deal, 3, 110, 115, 116–19,
142, 144, 163, 195, 200, 247
New Republic, 38, 61, 63, 114,
151
"New Tories, The," 87
New York Evening Post, 63, 77
New York Herald-Tribune forum,
214–15
New York Public Library, 109, 272;
and "Frederick Lewis Allen
Memorial Room," 276, 325n
New York Times, 52, 63, 71, 77,
99, 114, 125, 128, 156, 158,
219, 275
New Yorker, 81, 86, 137, 159, 192,
235
"Newspapers and the Truth," 75–
76
Newsweek, 178, 209, 235
"Night of the Bath, A," 30–31, 33
Nixon, Richard M., 217
Non-Partisan League, North
Dakota, 63
Norris Dam, 129

O. Henry Fiction Awards, 133–34,
186, 187, 232
Ober, Harold, 187
Ochs, Adolph, 128
"Ode to April," 86
"Ode to Professor James Harvey
Robinson," 38
Ogg, Oscar, 182
"Old Army Athletes," 84
On Native Grounds, 189
"One Man's Meat," 137, 162–63,
192–93, 305n

One World, 194
Office of War Information, 167,
168, 175–76, 182, 198, 208
Only Yesterday, vii, 94–95, 98, 99–
105, 108, 109, 114, 128, 142, 143,
144, 145, 216, 247, 298n
"Optimist, The," 30
"Our Widening American Culture,"
141
Outlook, 49, 64–66, 94–95, 160

Paddle tennis, x, 84
Parmentier, Douglas, 80
Parrington, V. L., 153
"Pause that refreshes, The," 183–84
Peabody, Rev. Endicott, 12–13, 16,
17, 90–91
Peabody, Malcolm, 20
Pearl Harbor, attack on, 161–66
Peffer, Nathaniel, 133
P.E.N. Club, 95
Penrose, Boies, 56, 62–63
Penrose, Clement Biddle, 56
"People at War, The," 169–171
Perkins, Maxwell, 230, 231
Perry, Bliss, 24, 25
Perry, Ralph Barton, 24, 259
Pfeiffer, George III, 266
Pheiffer, William T., 151
"Politics Up to Date," 76
Porter, George F., 44, 45, 46, 48
Pratt, Fletcher, 166–68, 169
Prescott, Allen, 104–105
"President Wilson: A Political and
Personal Interpretation," 65–66
Price, Byron, 167
Prideaux, Tom, 207
Prohibition, 101, 102, 114
Public Health Service, 71
"Public Opinion," 89
Publicity Bureau, 67
Publicity in higher education, 67–68,
73–74
Pujo Committee, 109
Punch, 30
Pusey, Nathan, 264
Putnam, James, 235

Race relations, 3, 17–18, 72, 170,
173, 194, 195, 247, 249–252
Radio, television and FLA, 99, 108,
145–46, 154, 199, 207–208, 269–
272

339